The Abandoned Empress

7

INA

Original Story by
Yuna

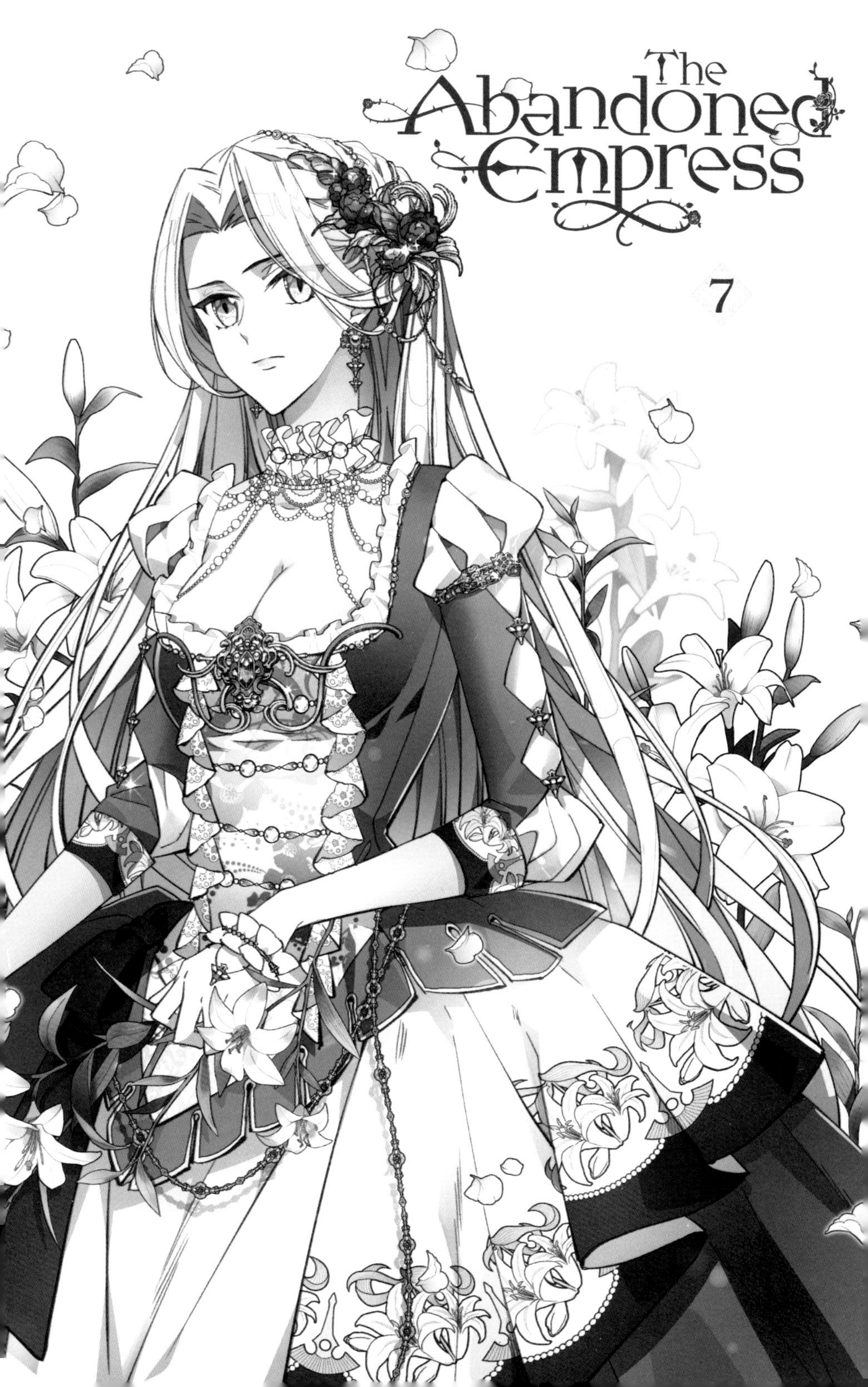
The Abandoned Empress
7

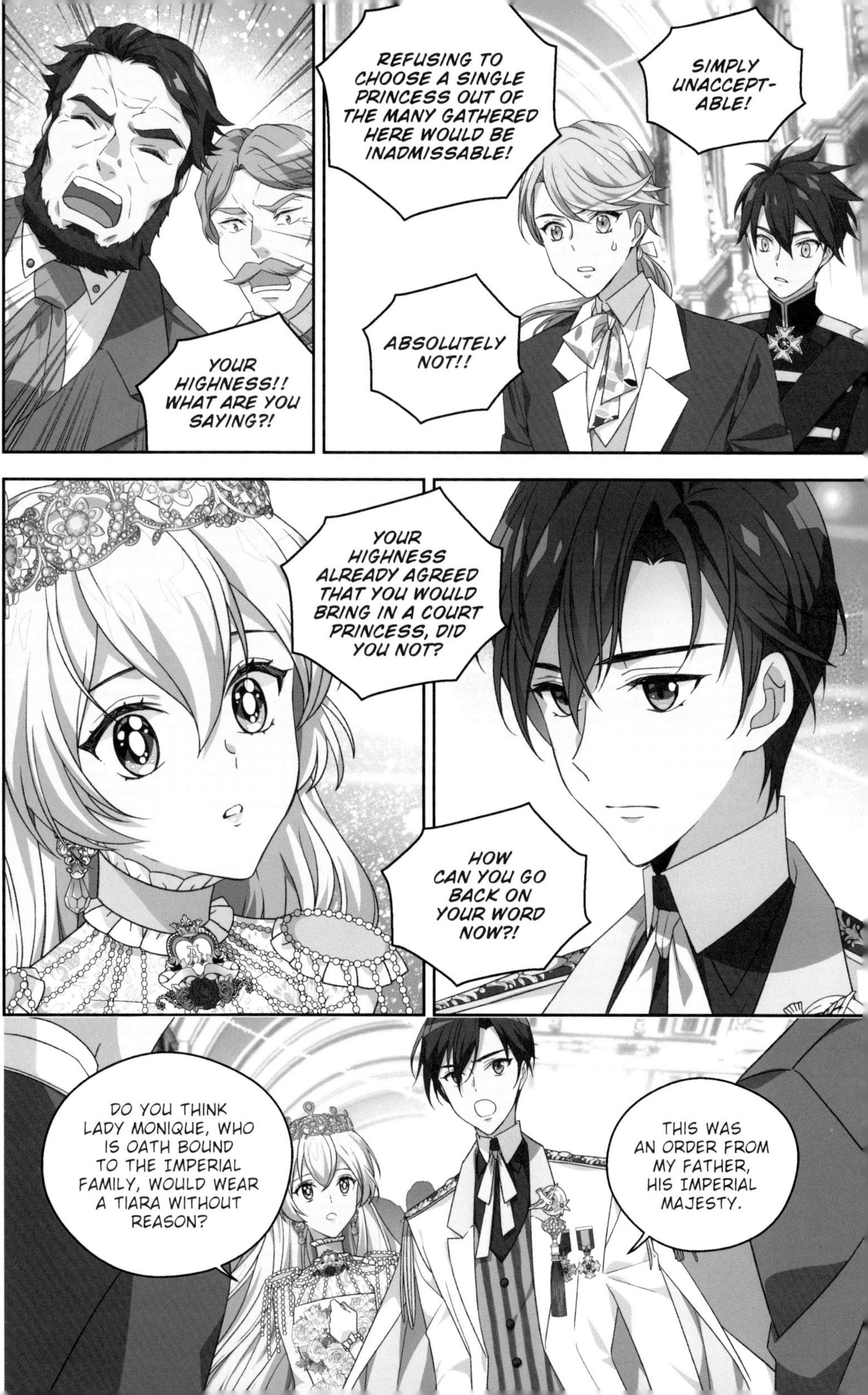
YOUR HIGHNESS!! WHAT ARE YOU SAYING?!
REFUSING TO CHOOSE A SINGLE PRINCESS OUT OF THE MANY GATHERED HERE WOULD BE INADMISSABLE!
SIMPLY UNACCEPT-ABLE!
ABSOLUTELY NOT!!
YOUR HIGHNESS ALREADY AGREED THAT YOU WOULD BRING IN A COURT PRINCESS, DID YOU NOT?
HOW CAN YOU GO BACK ON YOUR WORD NOW?!
DO YOU THINK LADY MONIQUE, WHO IS OATH BOUND TO THE IMPERIAL FAMILY, WOULD WEAR A TIARA WITHOUT REASON?
THIS WAS AN ORDER FROM MY FATHER, HIS IMPERIAL MAJESTY.

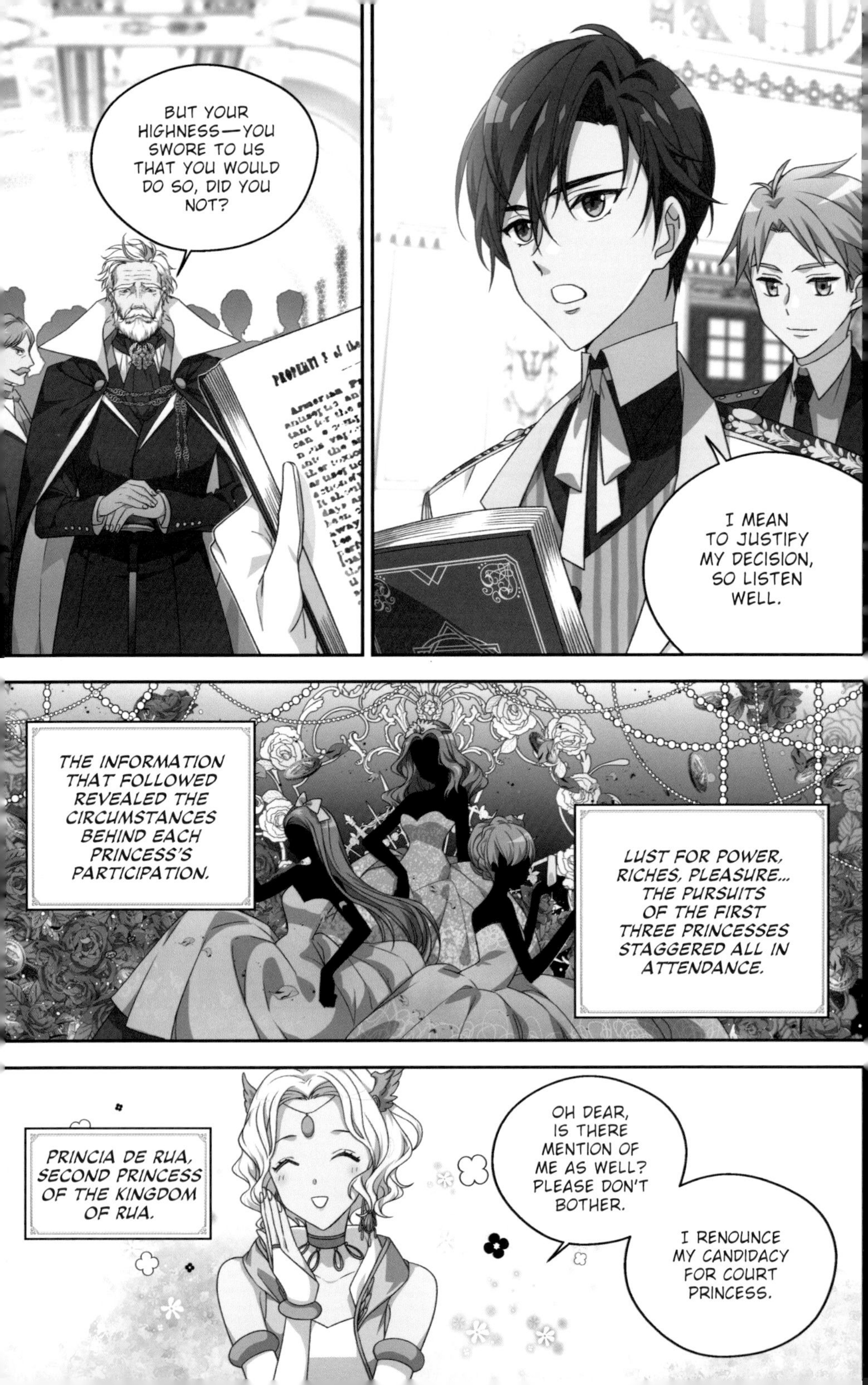
BUT YOUR HIGHNESS—YOU SWORE TO US THAT YOU WOULD DO SO, DID YOU NOT?
I MEAN TO JUSTIFY MY DECISION, SO LISTEN WELL.
THE INFORMATION THAT FOLLOWED REVEALED THE CIRCUMSTANCES BEHIND EACH PRINCESS'S PARTICIPATION.
LUST FOR POWER, RICHES, PLEASURE... THE PURSUITS OF THE FIRST THREE PRINCESSES STAGGERED ALL IN ATTENDANCE.
PRINCIA DE RUA, SECOND PRINCESS OF THE KINGDOM OF RUA.
OH DEAR, IS THERE MENTION OF ME AS WELL? PLEASE DON'T BOTHER.
I RENOUNCE MY CANDIDACY FOR COURT PRINCESS.

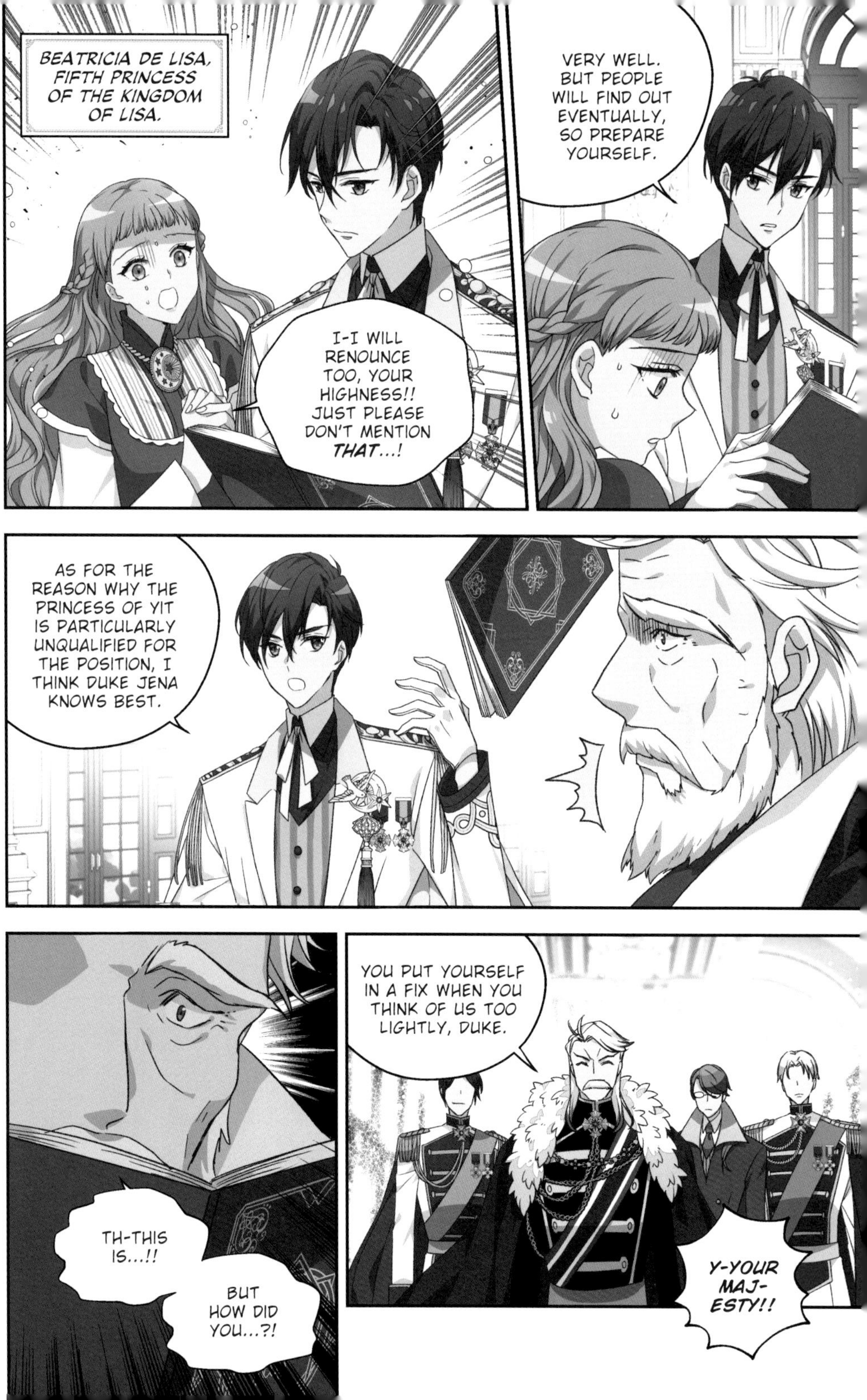
BEATRICIA DE LISA, FIFTH PRINCESS OF THE KINGDOM OF LISA.
I-I WILL RENOUNCE TOO, YOUR HIGHNESS!! JUST PLEASE DON'T MENTION *THAT*...!
VERY WELL. BUT PEOPLE WILL FIND OUT EVENTUALLY, SO PREPARE YOURSELF.
AS FOR THE REASON WHY THE PRINCESS OF YIT IS PARTICULARLY UNQUALIFIED FOR THE POSITION, I THINK DUKE JENA KNOWS BEST.
TH-THIS IS...!!
BUT HOW DID YOU...?!
YOU PUT YOURSELF IN A FIX WHEN YOU THINK OF US TOO LIGHTLY, DUKE.
Y-YOUR MAJ-ESTY!!

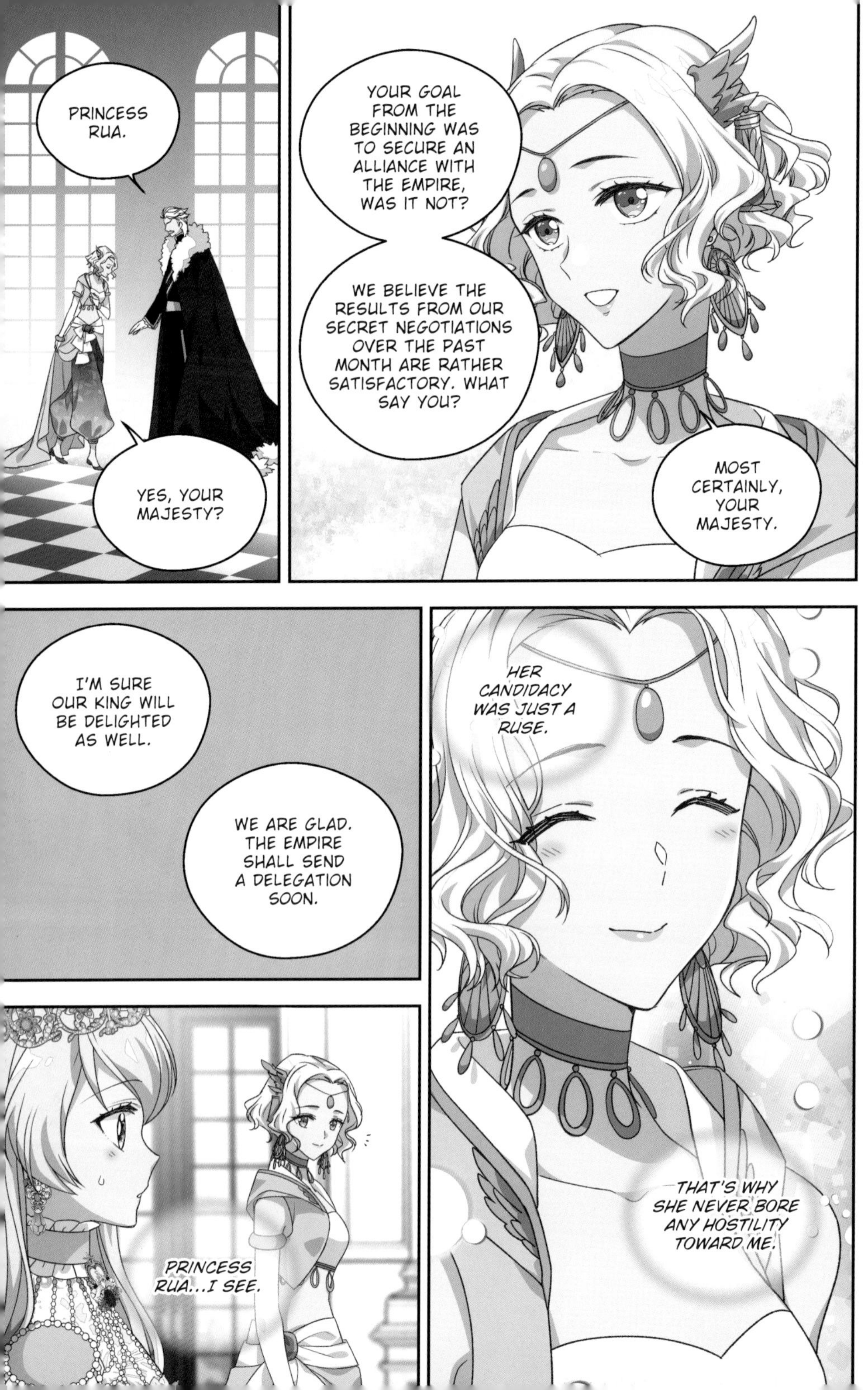
PRINCESS RUA.
YES, YOUR MAJESTY?
YOUR GOAL FROM THE BEGINNING WAS TO SECURE AN ALLIANCE WITH THE EMPIRE, WAS IT NOT?
WE BELIEVE THE RESULTS FROM OUR SECRET NEGOTIATIONS OVER THE PAST MONTH ARE RATHER SATISFACTORY. WHAT SAY YOU?
MOST CERTAINLY, YOUR MAJESTY.
I'M SURE OUR KING WILL BE DELIGHTED AS WELL.
WE ARE GLAD. THE EMPIRE SHALL SEND A DELEGATION SOON.
HER CANDIDACY WAS JUST A RUSE.
THAT'S WHY SHE NEVER BORE ANY HOSTILITY TOWARD ME.
PRINCESS RUA...I SEE.

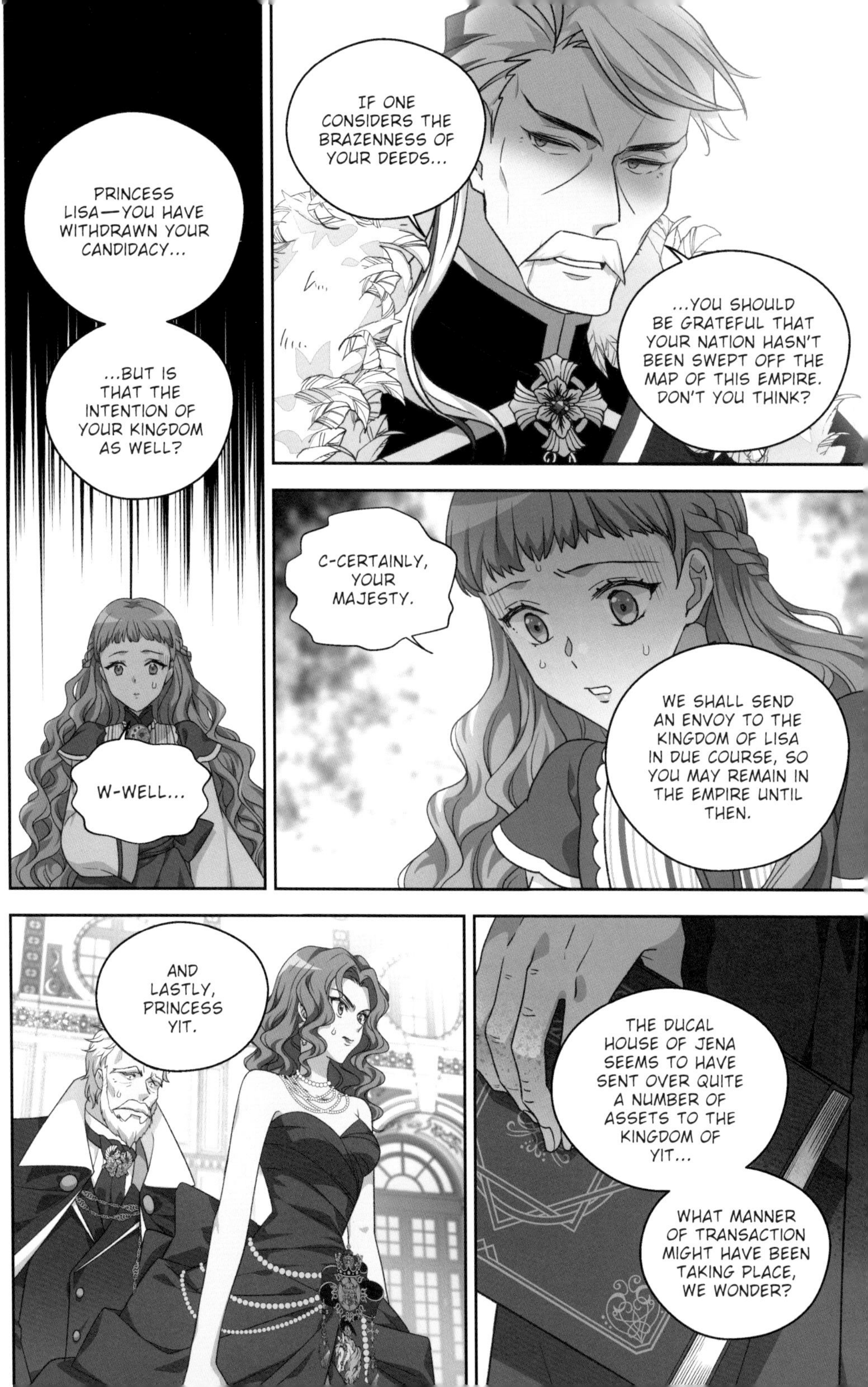
PRINCESS LISA—YOU HAVE WITHDRAWN YOUR CANDIDACY...
...BUT IS THAT THE INTENTION OF YOUR KINGDOM AS WELL?
IF ONE CONSIDERS THE BRAZENNESS OF YOUR DEEDS...
...YOU SHOULD BE GRATEFUL THAT YOUR NATION HASN'T BEEN SWEPT OFF THE MAP OF THIS EMPIRE. DON'T YOU THINK?
W-WELL...
C-CERTAINLY, YOUR MAJESTY.
WE SHALL SEND AN ENVOY TO THE KINGDOM OF LISA IN DUE COURSE, SO YOU MAY REMAIN IN THE EMPIRE UNTIL THEN.
AND LASTLY, PRINCESS YIT.
THE DUCAL HOUSE OF JENA SEEMS TO HAVE SENT OVER QUITE A NUMBER OF ASSETS TO THE KINGDOM OF YIT...
WHAT MANNER OF TRANSACTION MIGHT HAVE BEEN TAKING PLACE, WE WONDER?

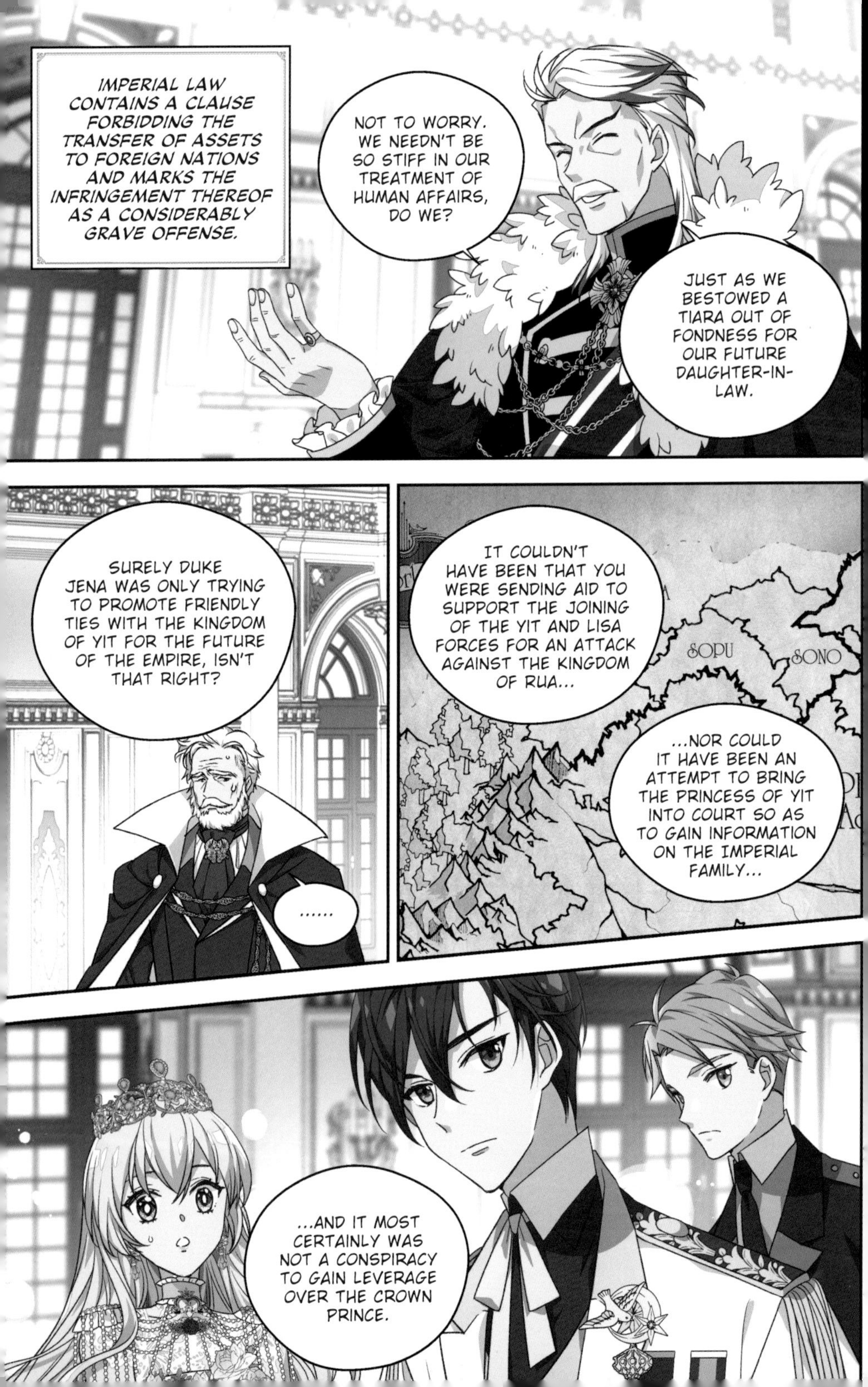
IMPERIAL LAW CONTAINS A CLAUSE FORBIDDING THE TRANSFER OF ASSETS TO FOREIGN NATIONS AND MARKS THE INFRINGEMENT THEREOF AS A CONSIDERABLY GRAVE OFFENSE.
NOT TO WORRY. WE NEEDN'T BE SO STIFF IN OUR TREATMENT OF HUMAN AFFAIRS, DO WE?
JUST AS WE BESTOWED A TIARA OUT OF FONDNESS FOR OUR FUTURE DAUGHTER-IN-LAW.
SURELY DUKE JENA WAS ONLY TRYING TO PROMOTE FRIENDLY TIES WITH THE KINGDOM OF YIT FOR THE FUTURE OF THE EMPIRE, ISN'T THAT RIGHT?
......
IT COULDN'T HAVE BEEN THAT YOU WERE SENDING AID TO SUPPORT THE JOINING OF THE YIT AND LISA FORCES FOR AN ATTACK AGAINST THE KINGDOM OF RUA...
SOPU
SONO
...NOR COULD IT HAVE BEEN AN ATTEMPT TO BRING THE PRINCESS OF YIT INTO COURT SO AS TO GAIN INFORMATION ON THE IMPERIAL FAMILY...
...AND IT MOST CERTAINLY WAS NOT A CONSPIRACY TO GAIN LEVERAGE OVER THE CROWN PRINCE.

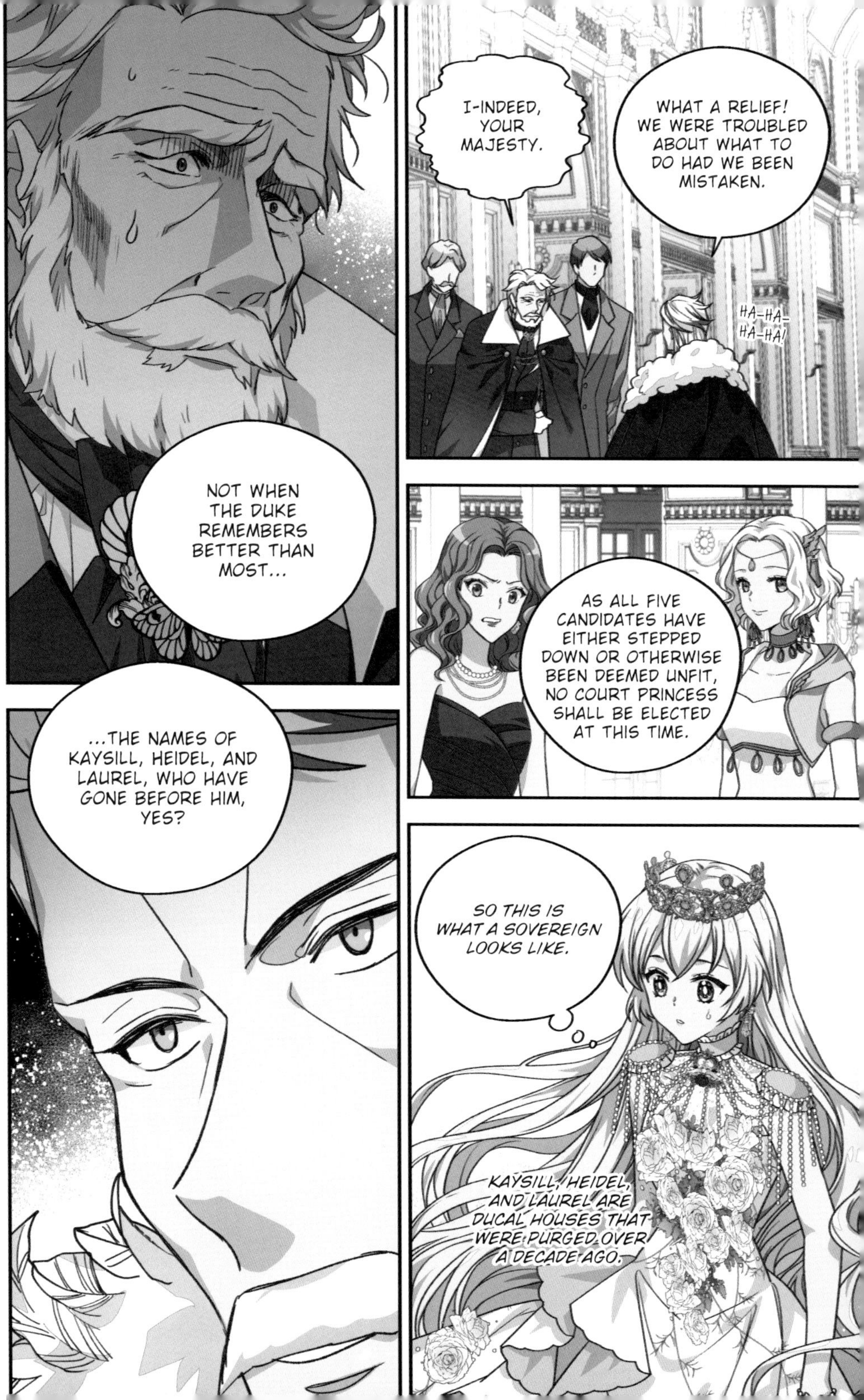
NOT WHEN THE DUKE REMEMBERS BETTER THAN MOST...
...THE NAMES OF KAYSILL, HEIDEL, AND LAUREL, WHO HAVE GONE BEFORE HIM, YES?
I-INDEED, YOUR MAJESTY.
WHAT A RELIEF! WE WERE TROUBLED ABOUT WHAT TO DO HAD WE BEEN MISTAKEN.
HA-HA-HA-HA!
AS ALL FIVE CANDIDATES HAVE EITHER STEPPED DOWN OR OTHERWISE BEEN DEEMED UNFIT, NO COURT PRINCESS SHALL BE ELECTED AT THIS TIME.
SO THIS IS WHAT A SOVEREIGN LOOKS LIKE.
KAYSILL, HEIDEL, AND LAUREL ARE DUCAL HOUSES THAT WERE PURGED OVER A DECADE AGO.

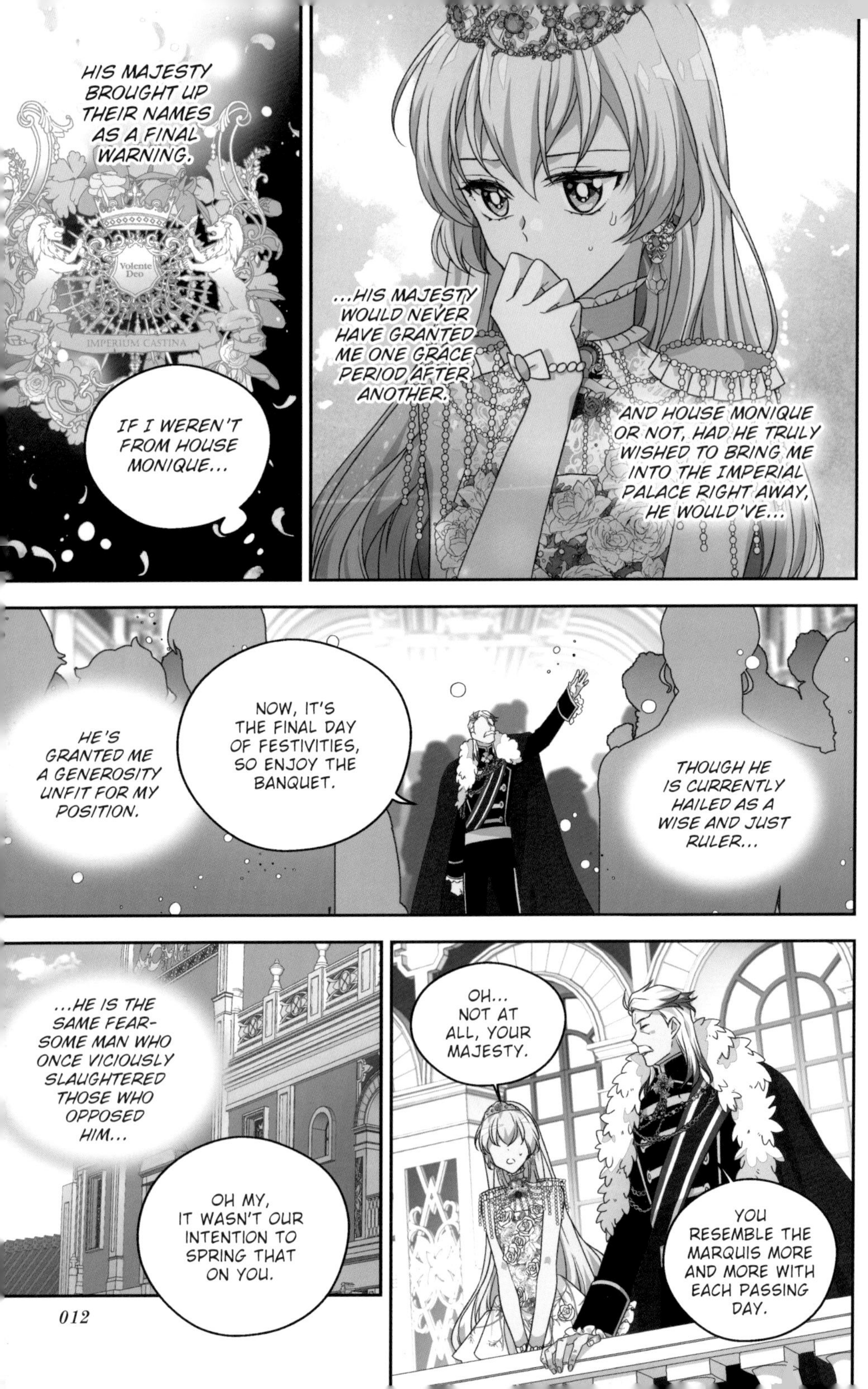
HIS MAJESTY BROUGHT UP THEIR NAMES AS A FINAL WARNING.
Volente Deo
IMPERIUM CASTINA
IF I WEREN'T FROM HOUSE MONIQUE...
...HIS MAJESTY WOULD NEVER HAVE GRANTED ME ONE GRACE PERIOD AFTER ANOTHER.
AND HOUSE MONIQUE OR NOT, HAD HE TRULY WISHED TO BRING ME INTO THE IMPERIAL PALACE RIGHT AWAY, HE WOULD'VE...
HE'S GRANTED ME A GENEROSITY UNFIT FOR MY POSITION.
NOW, IT'S THE FINAL DAY OF FESTIVITIES, SO ENJOY THE BANQUET.
THOUGH HE IS CURRENTLY HAILED AS A WISE AND JUST RULER...
...HE IS THE SAME FEAR-SOME MAN WHO ONCE VICIOUSLY SLAUGHTERED THOSE WHO OPPOSED HIM...
OH MY, IT WASN'T OUR INTENTION TO SPRING THAT ON YOU.
OH... NOT AT ALL, YOUR MAJESTY.
YOU RESEMBLE THE MARQUIS MORE AND MORE WITH EACH PASSING DAY.

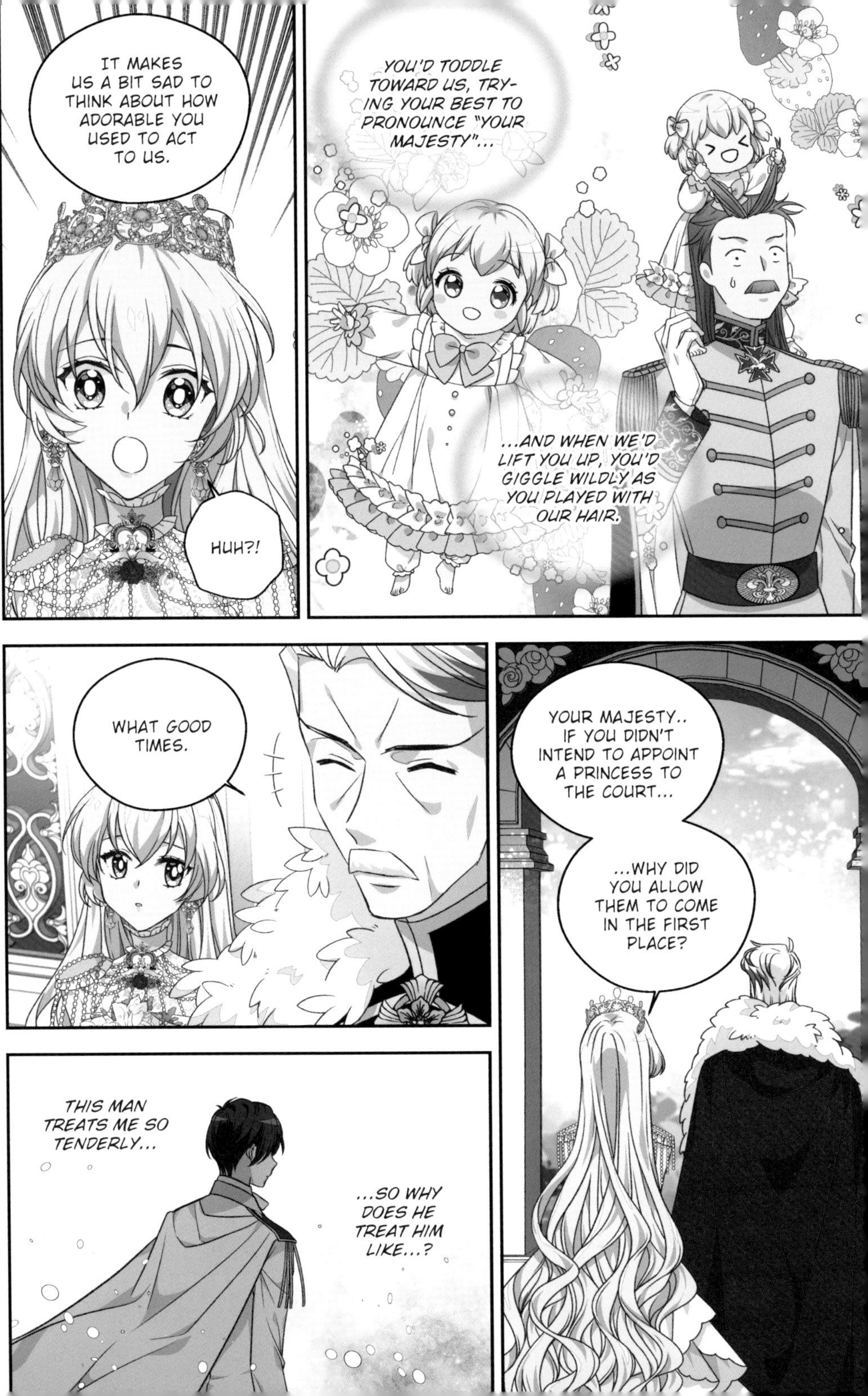
IT MAKES US A BIT SAD TO THINK ABOUT HOW ADORABLE YOU USED TO ACT TO US.
HUH?!
YOU'D TODDLE TOWARD US, TRY-ING YOUR BEST TO PRONOUNCE "YOUR MAJESTY"...
...AND WHEN WE'D LIFT YOU UP, YOU'D GIGGLE WILDLY AS YOU PLAYED WITH OUR HAIR.
WHAT GOOD TIMES.
YOUR MAJESTY.. IF YOU DIDN'T INTEND TO APPOINT A PRINCESS TO THE COURT...
...WHY DID YOU ALLOW THEM TO COME IN THE FIRST PLACE?
THIS MAN TREATS ME SO TENDERLY...
...SO WHY DOES HE TREAT HIM LIKE...?

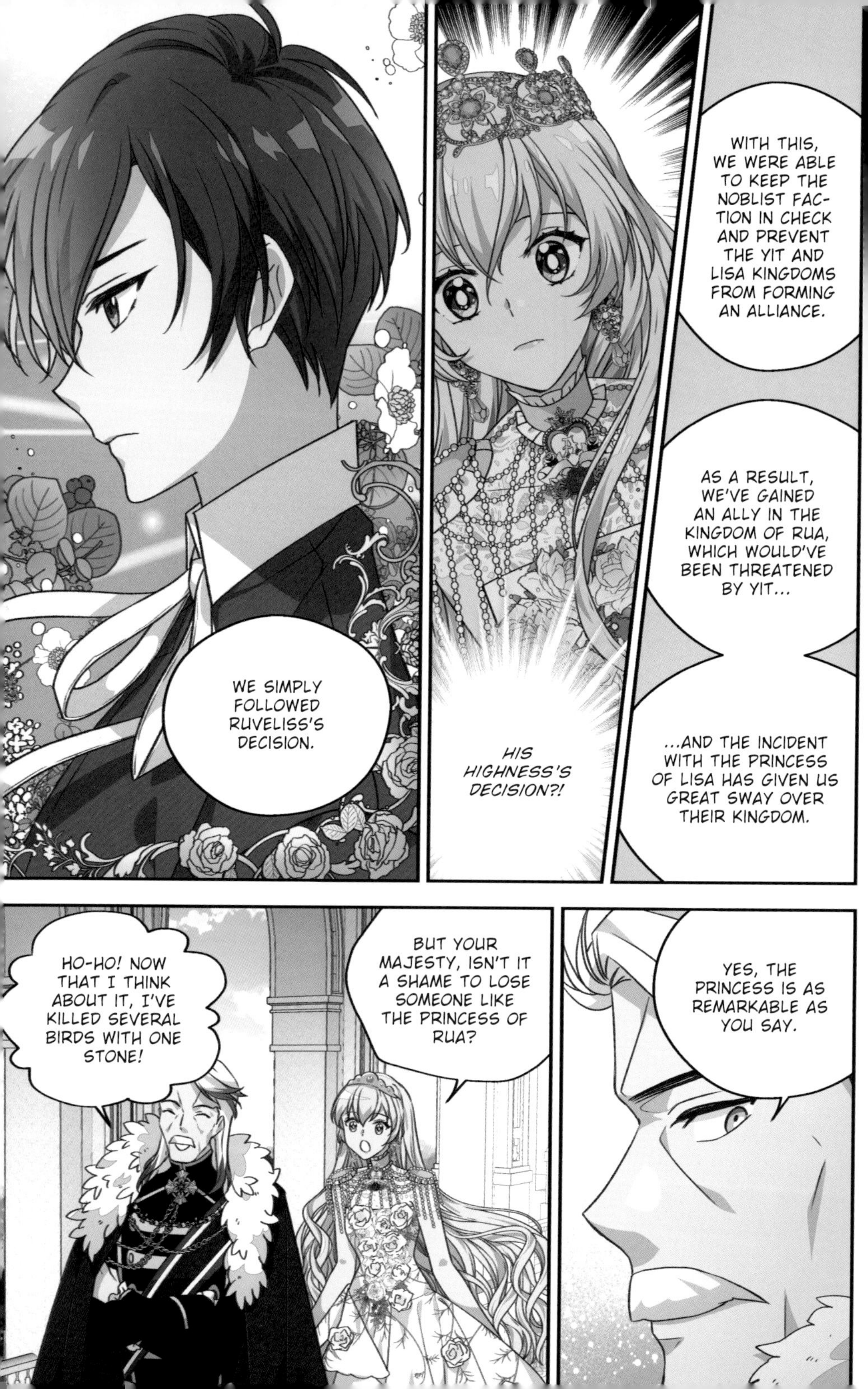

WE SIMPLY FOLLOWED RUVELISS'S DECISION.
HIS HIGHNESS'S DECISION?!
WITH THIS, WE WERE ABLE TO KEEP THE NOBLIST FAC-TION IN CHECK AND PREVENT THE YIT AND LISA KINGDOMS FROM FORMING AN ALLIANCE.
AS A RESULT, WE'VE GAINED AN ALLY IN THE KINGDOM OF RUA, WHICH WOULD'VE BEEN THREATENED BY YIT...
...AND THE INCIDENT WITH THE PRINCESS OF LISA HAS GIVEN US GREAT SWAY OVER THEIR KINGDOM.
HO-HO! NOW THAT I THINK ABOUT IT, I'VE KILLED SEVERAL BIRDS WITH ONE STONE!
BUT YOUR MAJESTY, ISN'T IT A SHAME TO LOSE SOMEONE LIKE THE PRINCESS OF RUA?
YES, THE PRINCESS IS AS REMARKABLE AS YOU SAY.

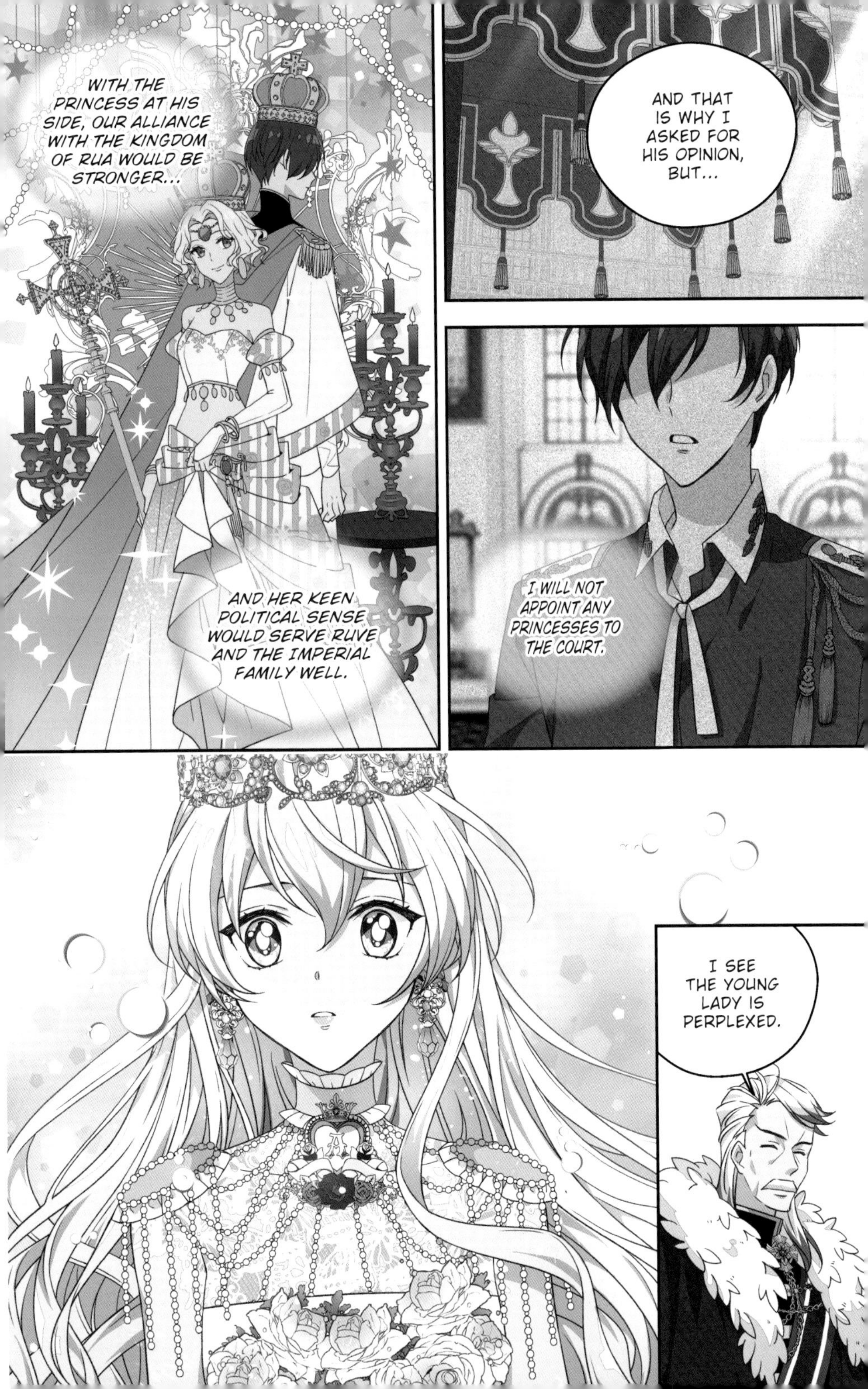
WITH THE PRINCESS AT HIS SIDE, OUR ALLIANCE WITH THE KINGDOM OF RUA WOULD BE STRONGER...
AND HER KEEN POLITICAL SENSE WOULD SERVE RUVE AND THE IMPERIAL FAMILY WELL.
AND THAT IS WHY I ASKED FOR HIS OPINION, BUT...
I WILL NOT APPOINT ANY PRINCESSES TO THE COURT.
I SEE THE YOUNG LADY IS PERPLEXED.

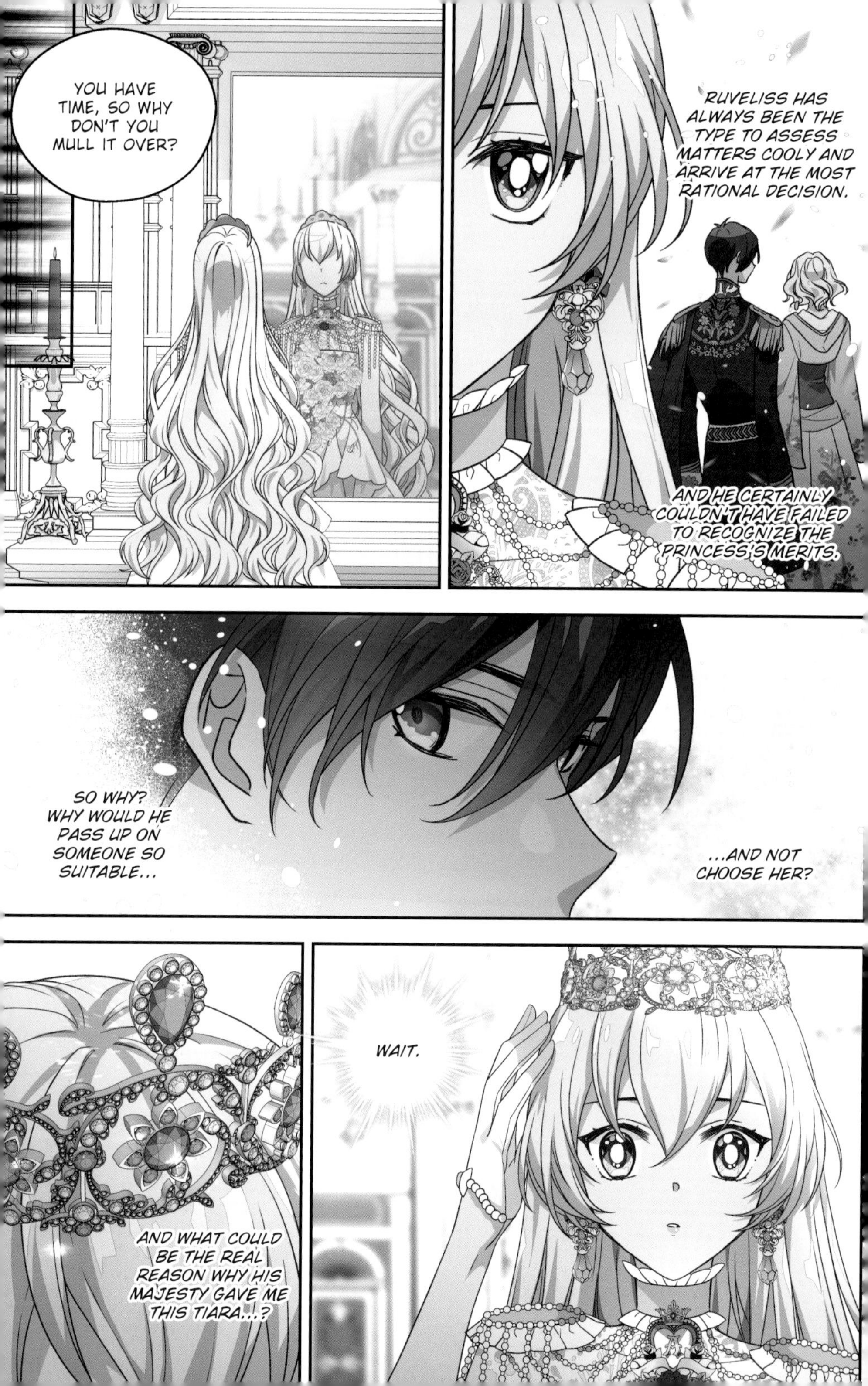
YOU HAVE TIME, SO WHY DON'T YOU MULL IT OVER?
RUVELISS HAS ALWAYS BEEN THE TYPE TO ASSESS MATTERS COOLY AND ARRIVE AT THE MOST RATIONAL DECISION.
AND HE CERTAINLY COULDN'T HAVE FAILED TO RECOGNIZE THE PRINCESS'S MERITS.
SO WHY? WHY WOULD HE PASS UP ON SOMEONE SO SUITABLE...
...AND NOT CHOOSE HER?
AND WHAT COULD BE THE REAL REASON WHY HIS MAJESTY GAVE ME THIS TIARA...?
WAIT.

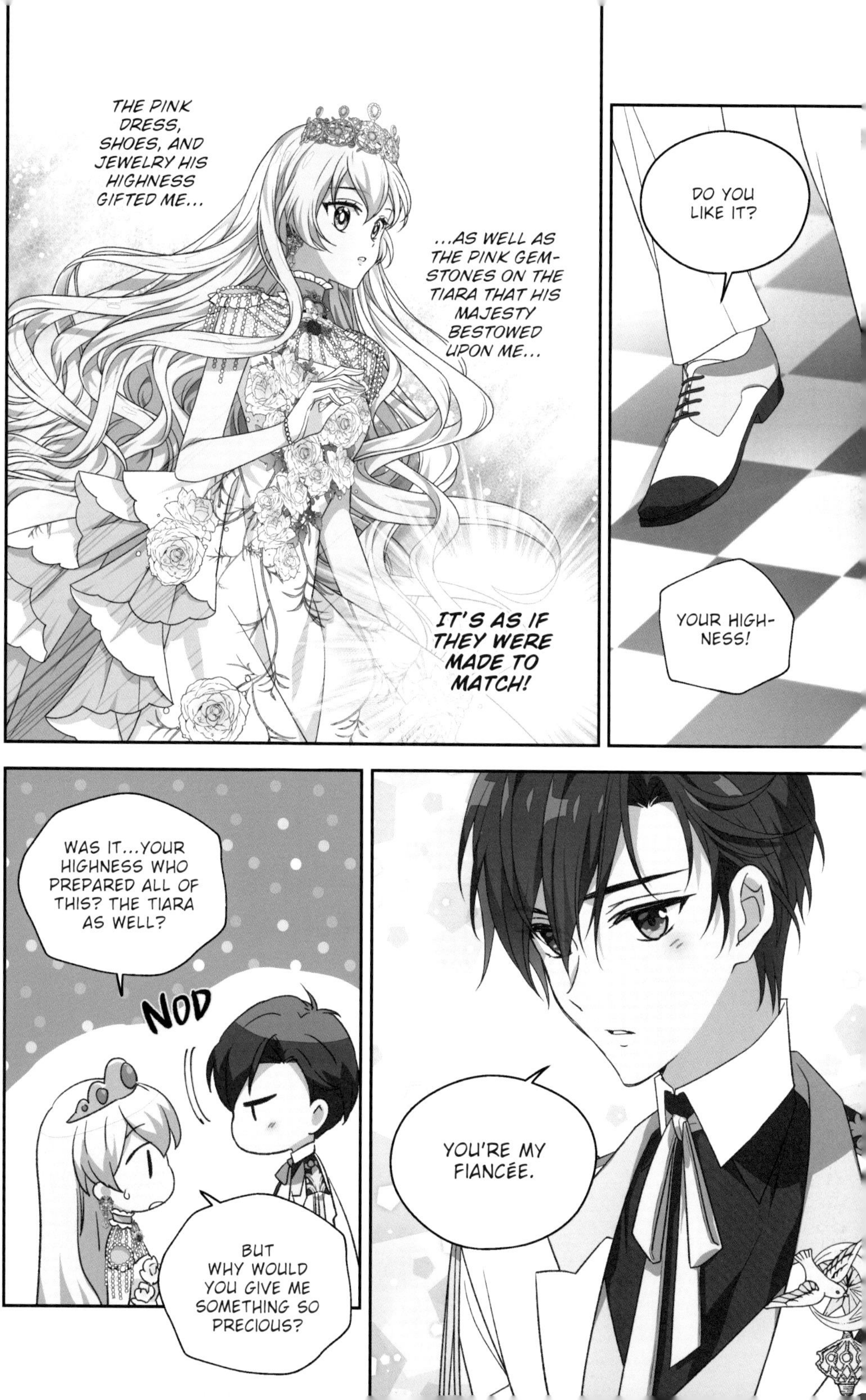
THE PINK DRESS, SHOES, AND JEWELRY HIS HIGHNESS GIFTED ME...
...AS WELL AS THE PINK GEM-STONES ON THE TIARA THAT HIS MAJESTY BESTOWED UPON ME...
IT'S AS IF THEY WERE MADE TO MATCH!
DO YOU LIKE IT?
YOUR HIGH-NESS!
WAS IT...YOUR HIGHNESS WHO PREPARED ALL OF THIS? THE TIARA AS WELL?
NOD
BUT WHY WOULD YOU GIVE ME SOMETHING SO PRECIOUS?
YOU'RE MY FIANCÉE.

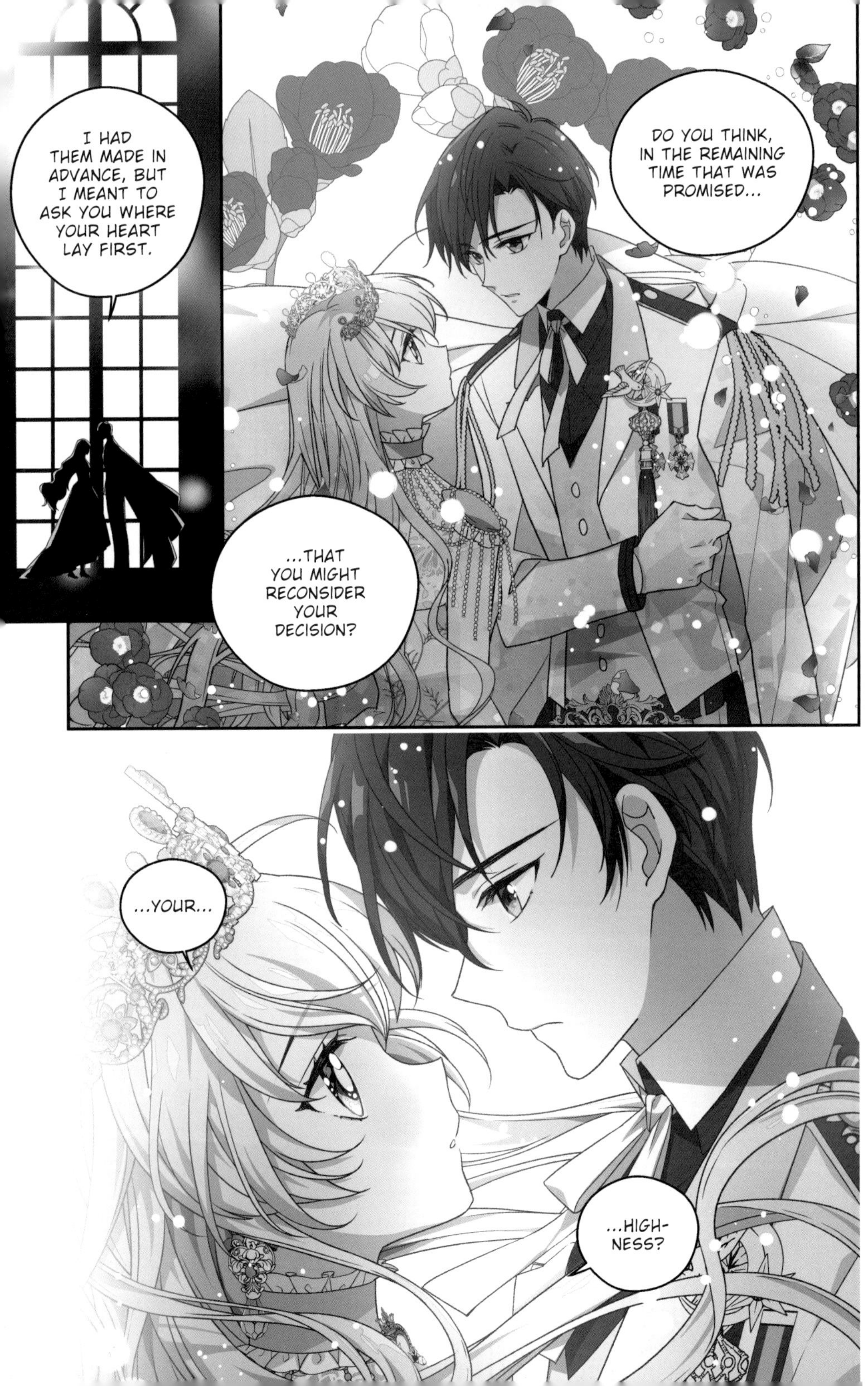

I HAD THEM MADE IN ADVANCE, BUT I MEANT TO ASK YOU WHERE YOUR HEART LAY FIRST.
DO YOU THINK, IN THE REMAINING TIME THAT WAS PROMISED...
...THAT YOU MIGHT RECONSIDER YOUR DECISION?
...YOUR...
...HIGH-NESS?

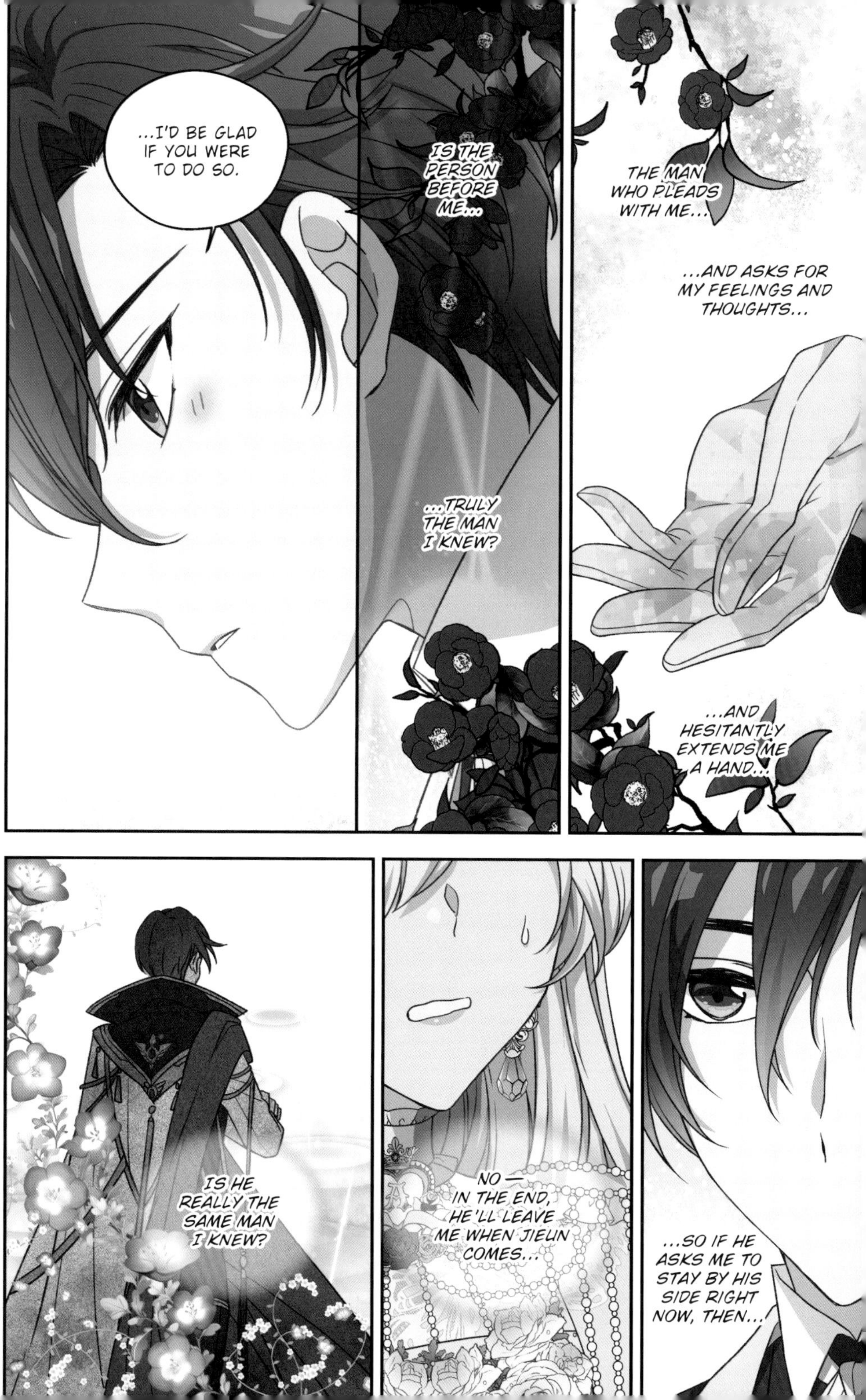
...I'D BE GLAD IF YOU WERE TO DO SO.
IS THE PERSON BEFORE ME...
...TRULY THE MAN I KNEW?
THE MAN WHO PLEADS WITH ME...
...AND ASKS FOR MY FEELINGS AND THOUGHTS...
...AND HESITANTLY EXTENDS ME A HAND...
IS HE REALLY THE SAME MAN I KNEW?
NO — IN THE END, HE'LL LEAVE ME WHEN JIEUN COMES...
...SO IF HE ASKS ME TO STAY BY HIS SIDE RIGHT NOW, THEN...

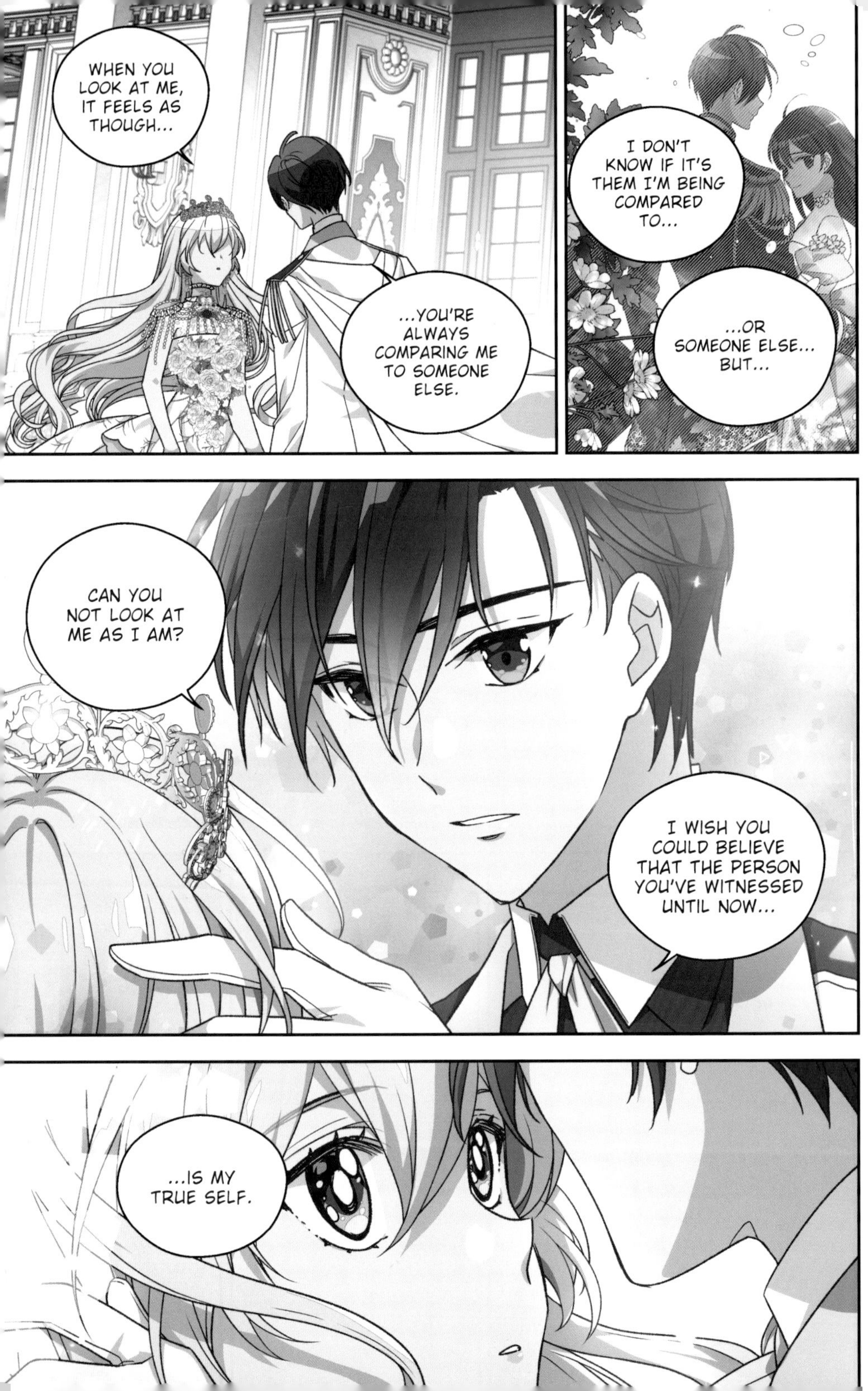
WHEN YOU LOOK AT ME, IT FEELS AS THOUGH...
...YOU'RE ALWAYS COMPARING ME TO SOMEONE ELSE.
I DON'T KNOW IF IT'S THEM I'M BEING COMPARED TO...
...OR SOMEONE ELSE... BUT...
CAN YOU NOT LOOK AT ME AS I AM?
I WISH YOU COULD BELIEVE THAT THE PERSON YOU'VE WITNESSED UNTIL NOW...
...IS MY TRUE SELF.

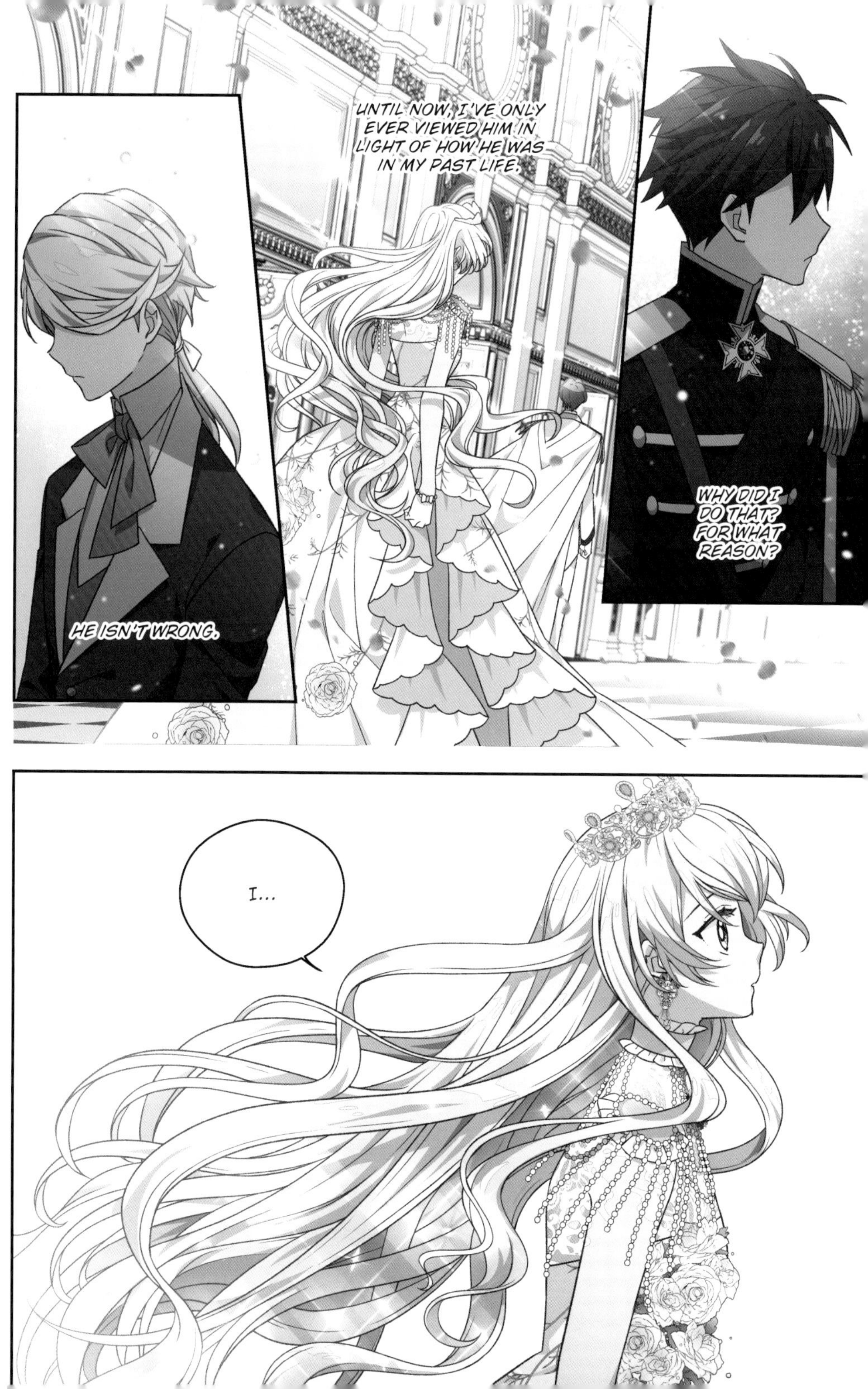
UNTIL NOW, I'VE ONLY EVER VIEWED HIM IN LIGHT OF HOW HE WAS IN MY PAST LIFE.
WHY DID I DO THAT? FOR WHAT REASON?
HE ISN'T WRONG.
I...

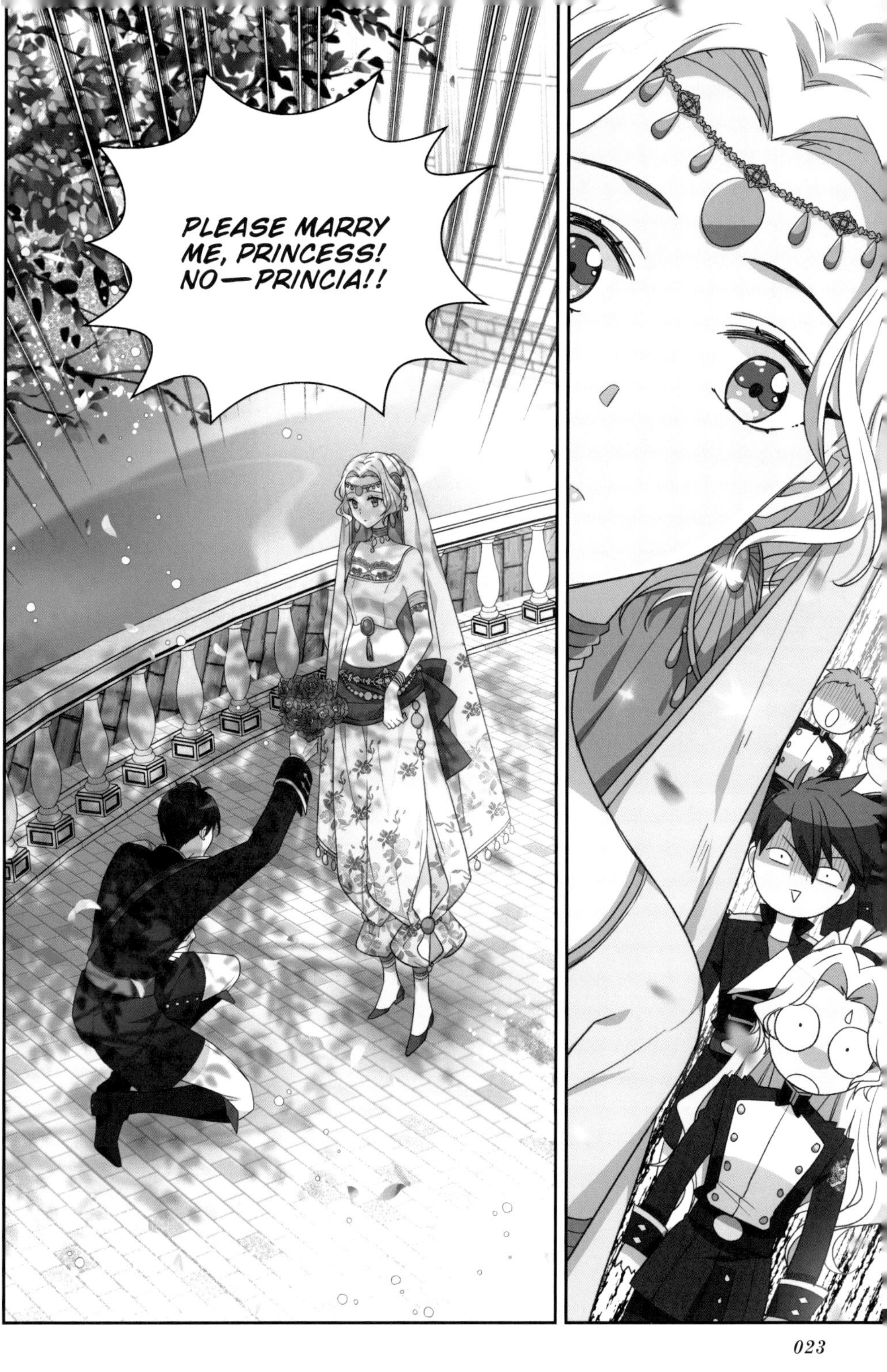
PLEASE MARRY ME, PRINCESS! NO—PRINCIA!!

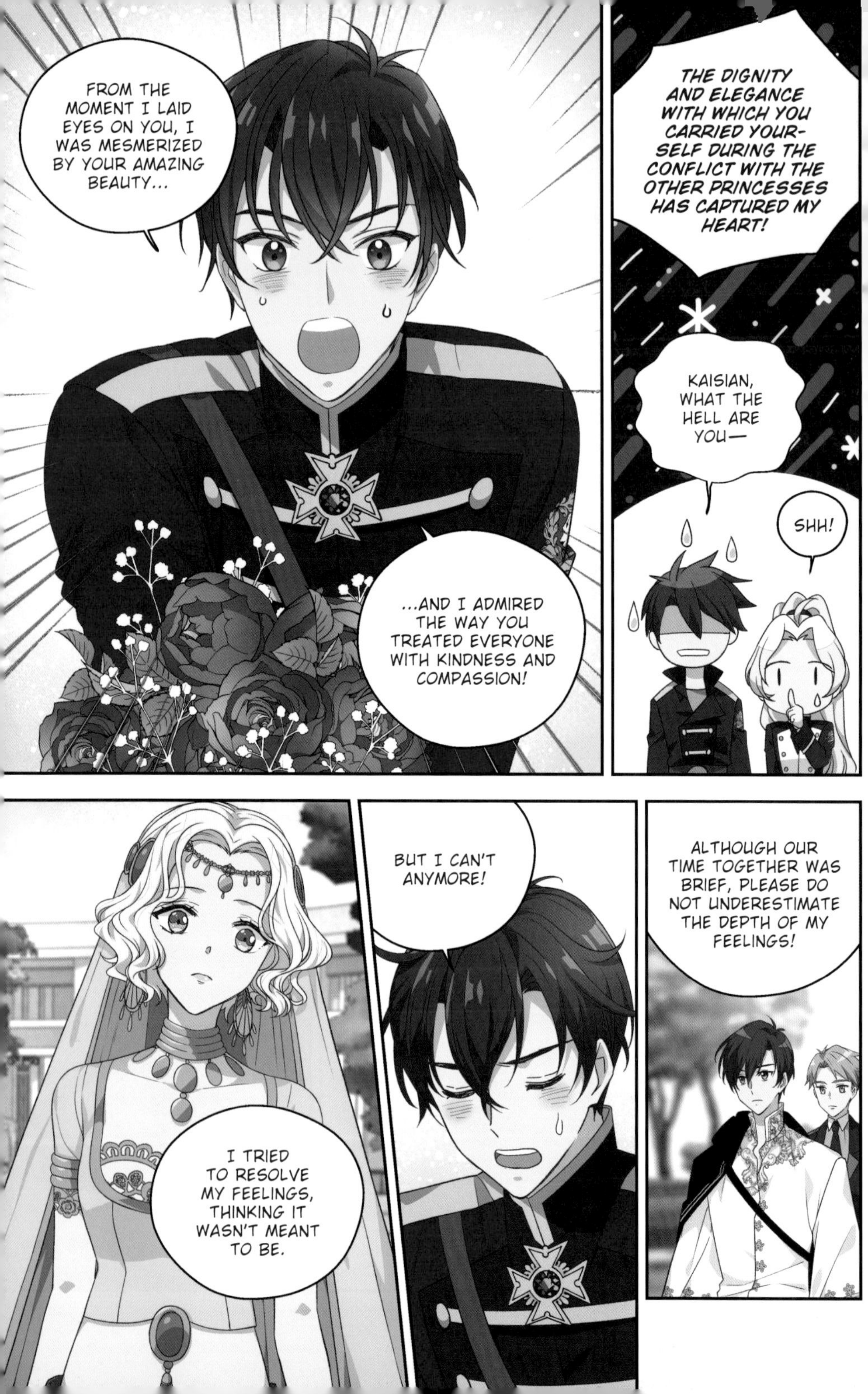
FROM THE MOMENT I LAID EYES ON YOU, I WAS MESMERIZED BY YOUR AMAZING BEAUTY...
...AND I ADMIRED THE WAY YOU TREATED EVERYONE WITH KINDNESS AND COMPASSION!
THE DIGNITY AND ELEGANCE WITH WHICH YOU CARRIED YOURSELF DURING THE CONFLICT WITH THE OTHER PRINCESSES HAS CAPTURED MY HEART!
KAISIAN, WHAT THE HELL ARE YOU—
SHH!
I TRIED TO RESOLVE MY FEELINGS, THINKING IT WASN'T MEANT TO BE.
BUT I CAN'T ANYMORE!
ALTHOUGH OUR TIME TOGETHER WAS BRIEF, PLEASE DO NOT UNDERESTIMATE THE DEPTH OF MY FEELINGS!

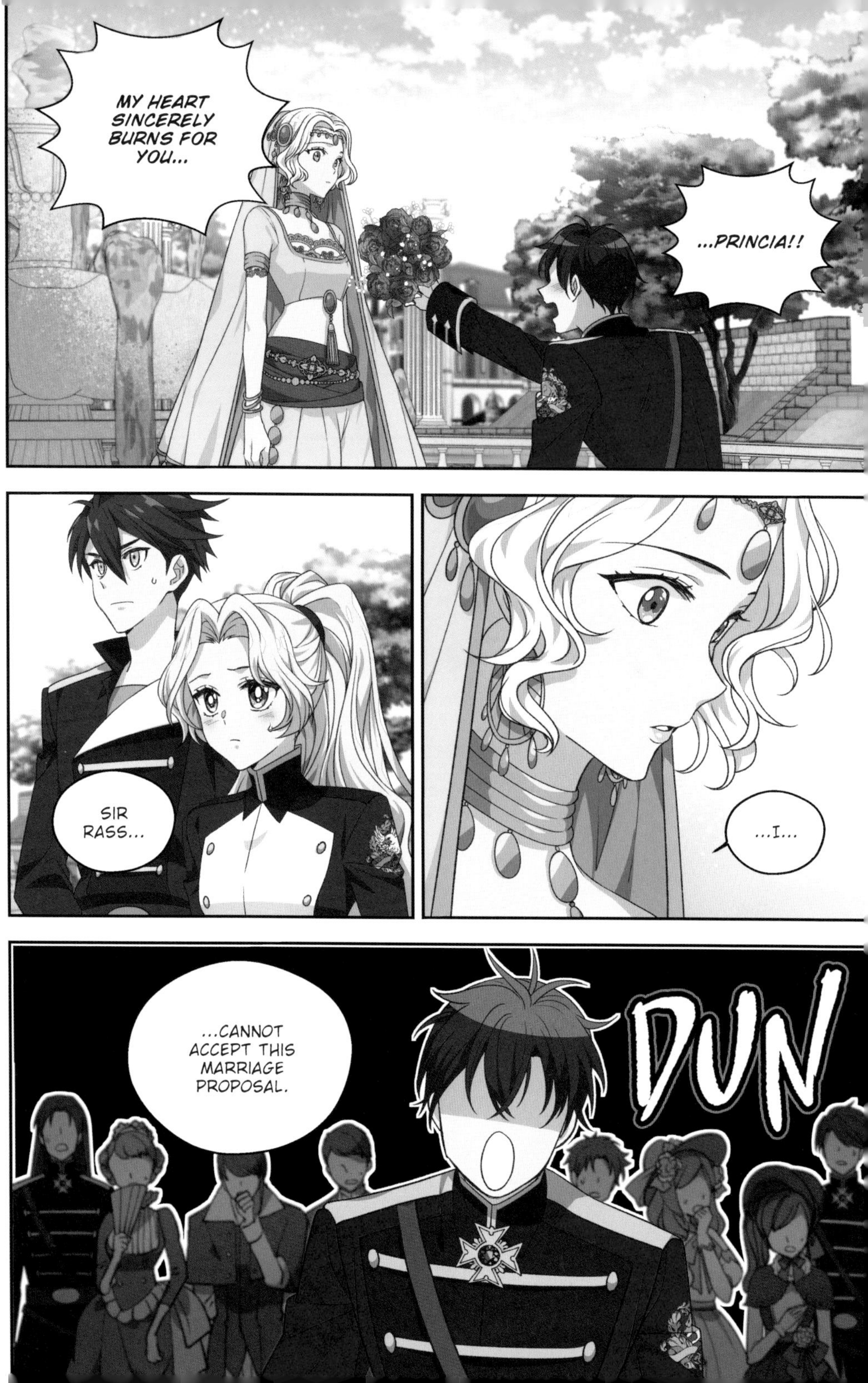
MY HEART SINCERELY BURNS FOR YOU...
...PRINCIA!!
...I...
SIR RASS...
...CANNOT ACCEPT THIS MARRIAGE PROPOSAL.
DUN

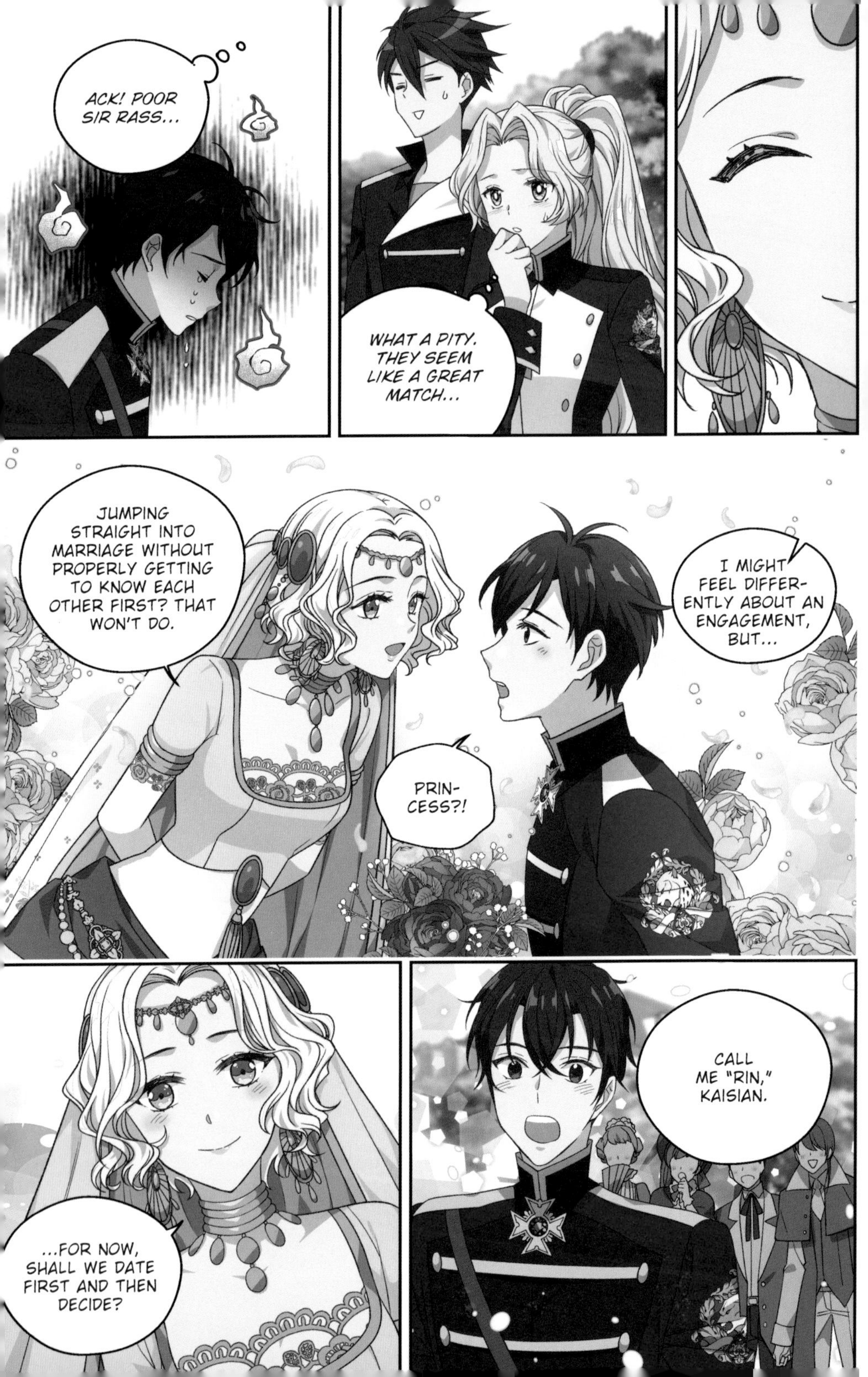
ACK! POOR SIR RASS...
WHAT A PITY. THEY SEEM LIKE A GREAT MATCH...
JUMPING STRAIGHT INTO MARRIAGE WITHOUT PROPERLY GETTING TO KNOW EACH OTHER FIRST? THAT WON'T DO.
I MIGHT FEEL DIFFER-ENTLY ABOUT AN ENGAGEMENT, BUT...
PRIN-CESS?!
...FOR NOW, SHALL WE DATE FIRST AND THEN DECIDE?
CALL ME "RIN," KAISIAN.

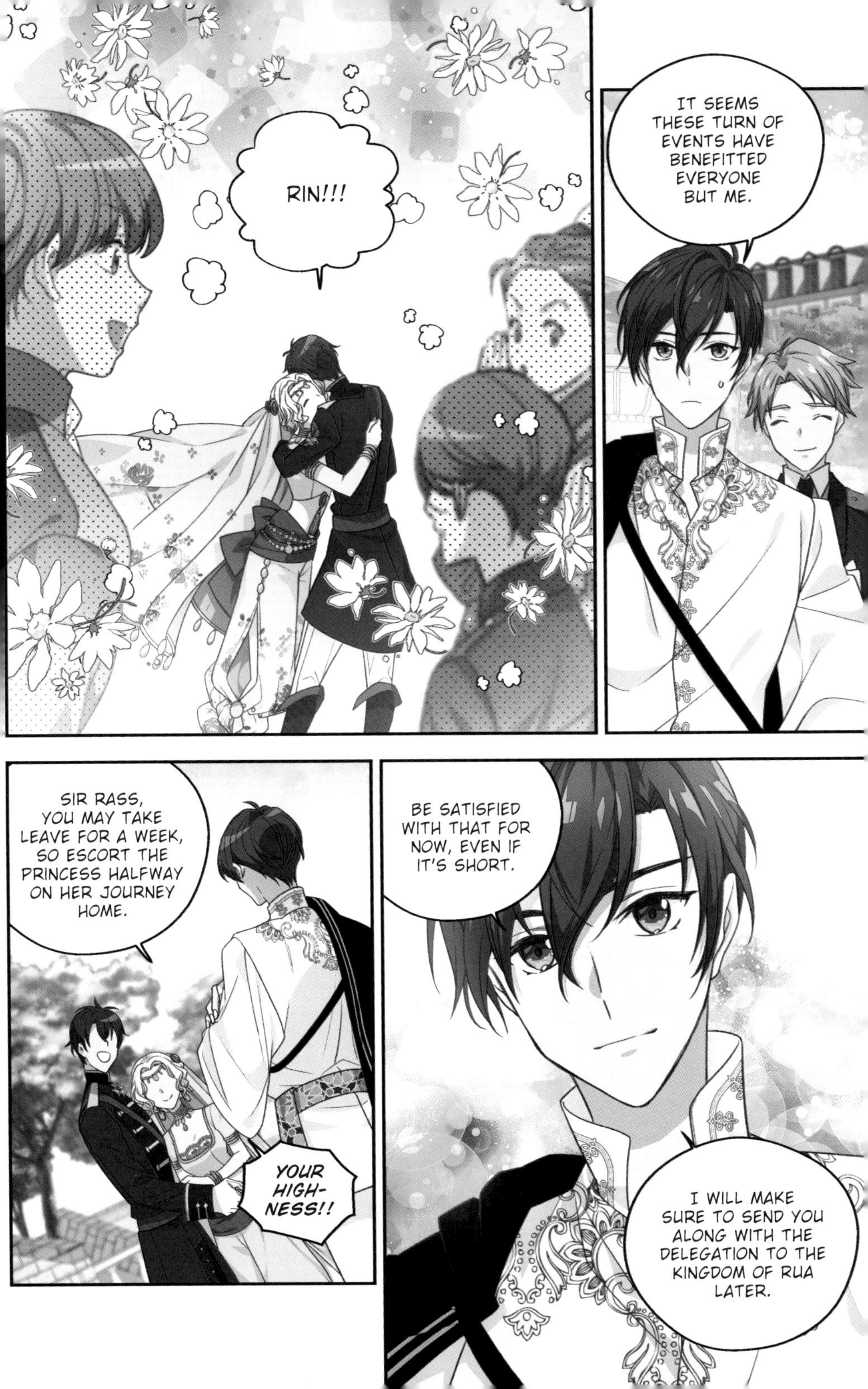
RIN!!!
IT SEEMS THESE TURN OF EVENTS HAVE BENEFITTED EVERYONE BUT ME.
SIR RASS, YOU MAY TAKE LEAVE FOR A WEEK, SO ESCORT THE PRINCESS HALFWAY ON HER JOURNEY HOME.
YOUR HIGH-NESS!!
BE SATISFIED WITH THAT FOR NOW, EVEN IF IT'S SHORT.
I WILL MAKE SURE TO SEND YOU ALONG WITH THE DELEGATION TO THE KINGDOM OF RUA LATER.

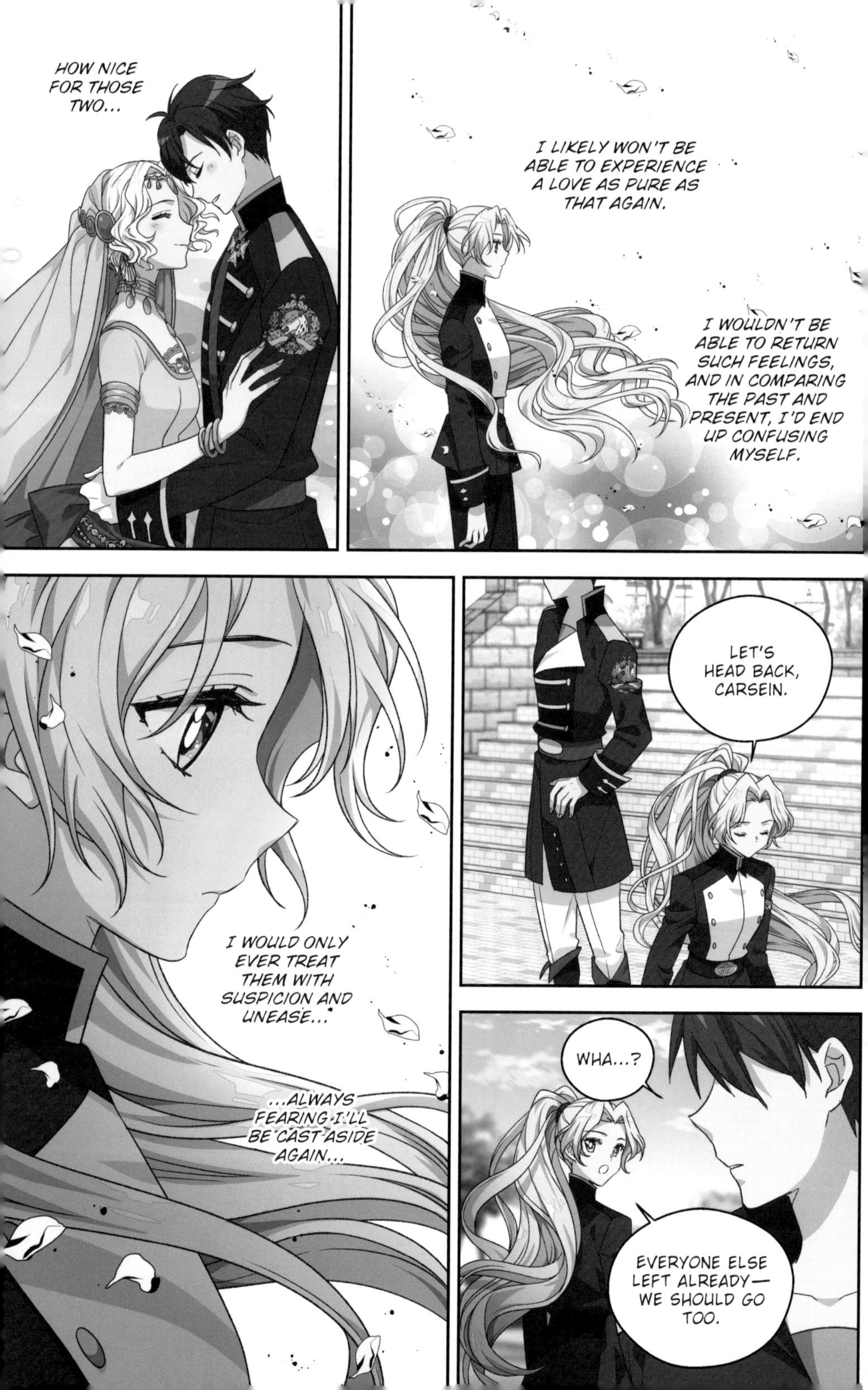
HOW NICE FOR THOSE TWO...
I LIKELY WON'T BE ABLE TO EXPERIENCE A LOVE AS PURE AS THAT AGAIN.
I WOULDN'T BE ABLE TO RETURN SUCH FEELINGS, AND IN COMPARING THE PAST AND PRESENT, I'D END UP CONFUSING MYSELF.
I WOULD ONLY EVER TREAT THEM WITH SUSPICION AND UNEASE...
...ALWAYS FEARING I'LL BE CAST ASIDE AGAIN...
LET'S HEAD BACK, CARSEIN.
WHA...?
EVERYONE ELSE LEFT ALREADY— WE SHOULD GO TOO.

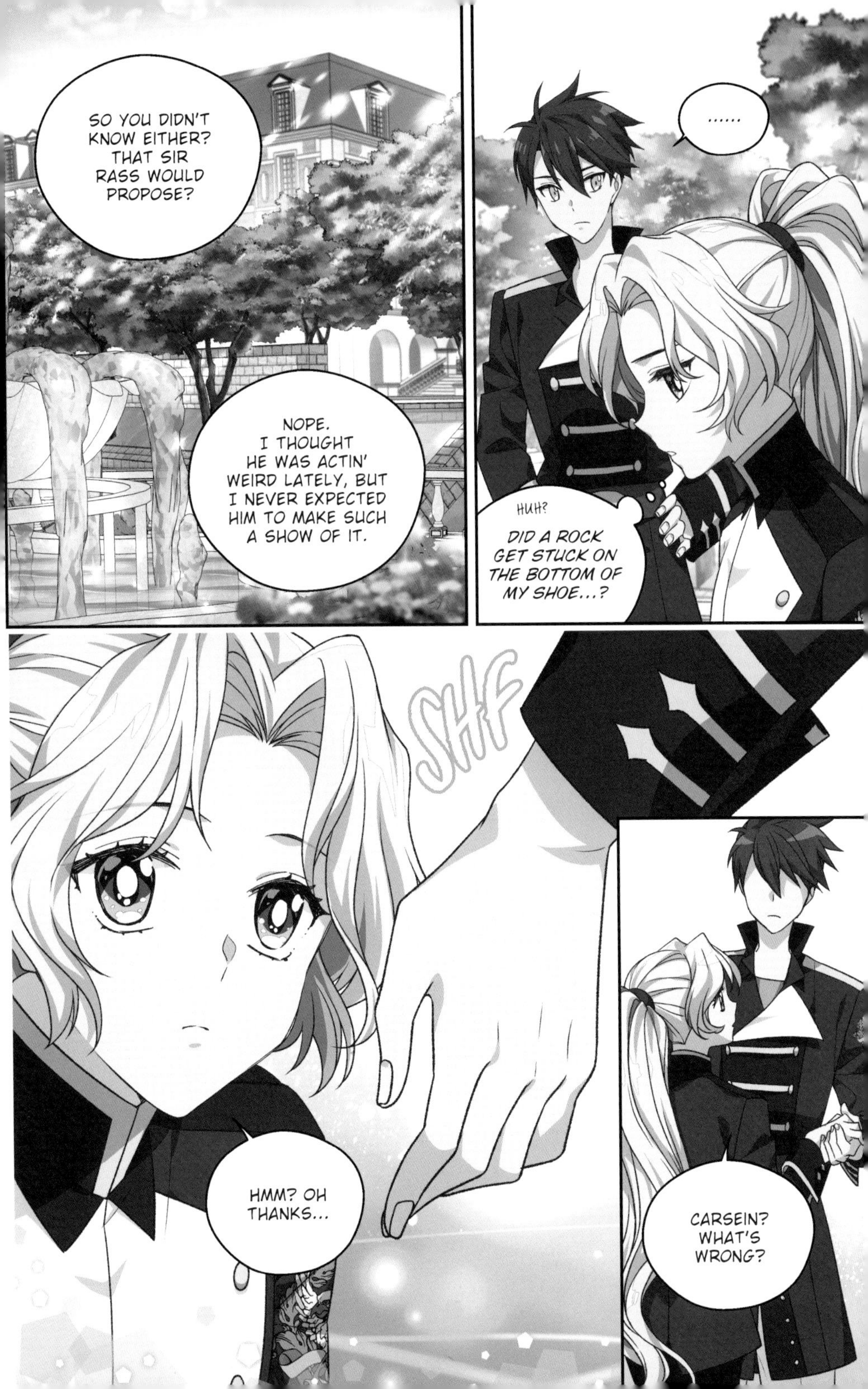
SO YOU DIDN'T KNOW EITHER? THAT SIR RASS WOULD PROPOSE?
NOPE. I THOUGHT HE WAS ACTIN' WEIRD LATELY, BUT I NEVER EXPECTED HIM TO MAKE SUCH A SHOW OF IT.
......
HUH?
DID A ROCK GET STUCK ON THE BOTTOM OF MY SHOE...?
SHF
HMM? OH THANKS...
CARSEIN? WHAT'S WRONG?

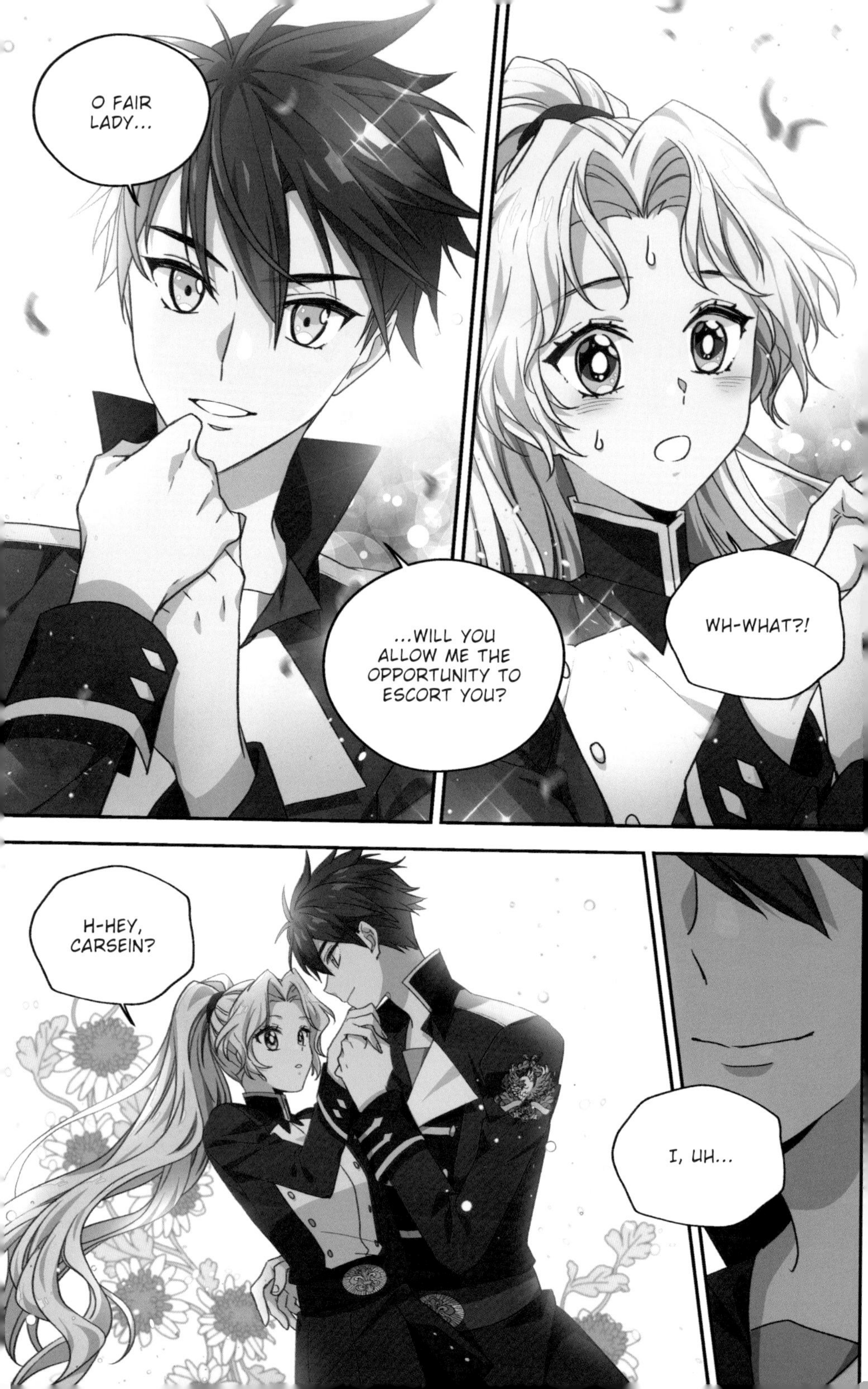
O FAIR LADY...
...WILL YOU ALLOW ME THE OPPORTUNITY TO ESCORT YOU?
WH-WHAT?!
H-HEY, CARSEIN?
I, UH...

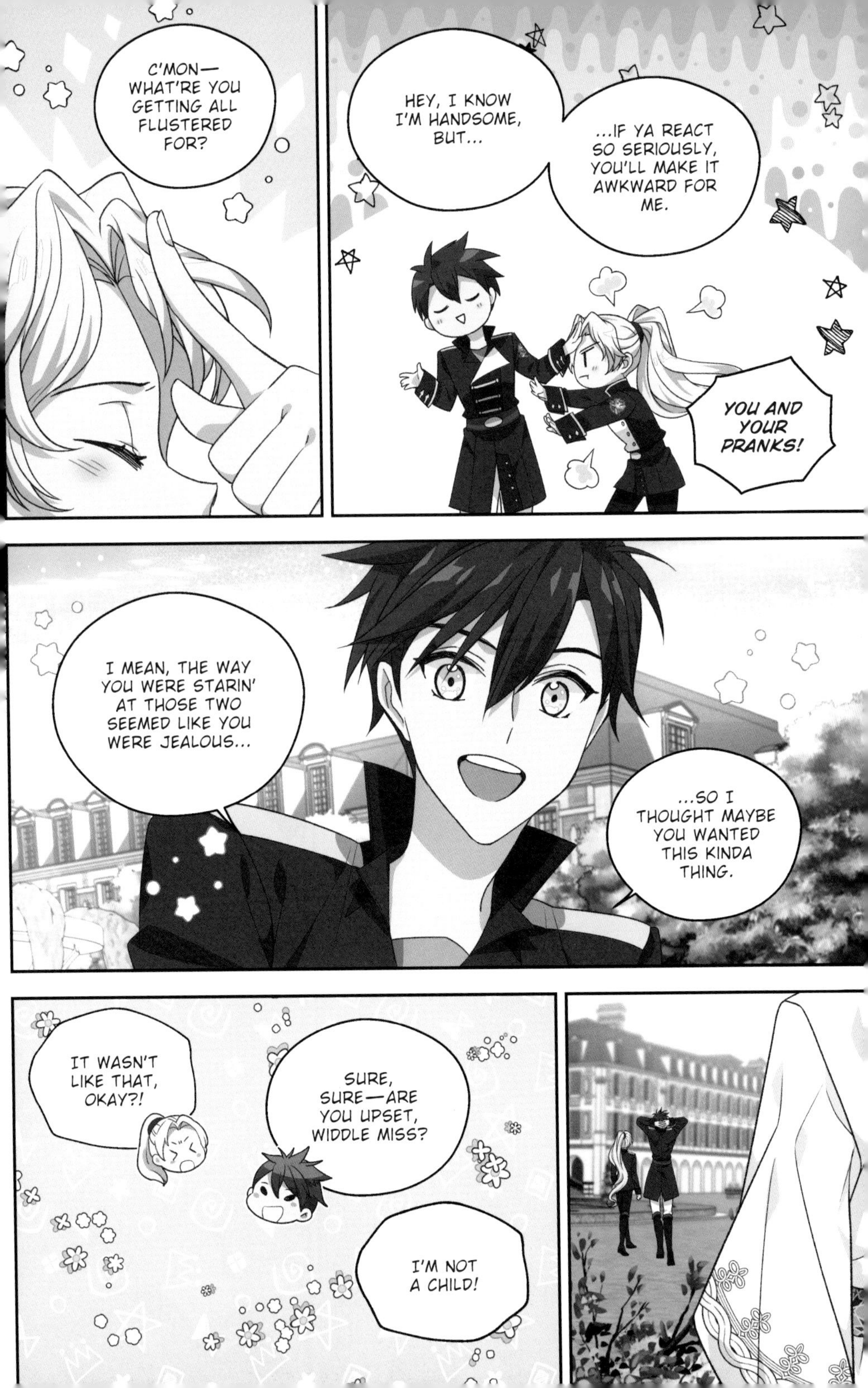
C'MON—WHAT'RE YOU GETTING ALL FLUSTERED FOR?
HEY, I KNOW I'M HANDSOME, BUT...
...IF YA REACT SO SERIOUSLY, YOU'LL MAKE IT AWKWARD FOR ME.
YOU AND YOUR PRANKS!
I MEAN, THE WAY YOU WERE STARIN' AT THOSE TWO SEEMED LIKE YOU WERE JEALOUS...
...SO I THOUGHT MAYBE YOU WANTED THIS KINDA THING.
IT WASN'T LIKE THAT, OKAY?!
SURE, SURE—ARE YOU UPSET, WIDDLE MISS?
I'M NOT A CHILD!

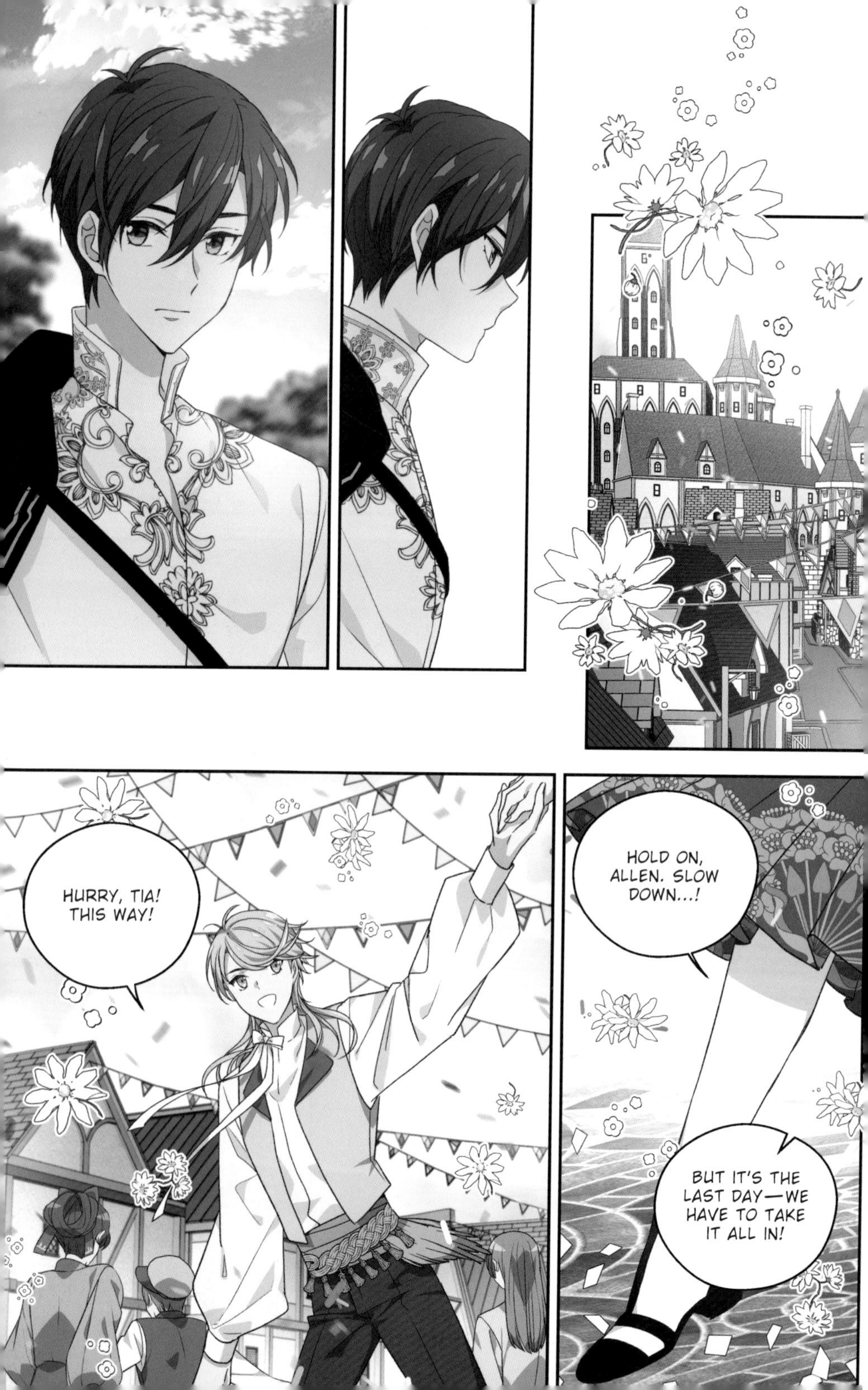
HURRY, TIA! THIS WAY!
HOLD ON, ALLEN. SLOW DOWN...!
BUT IT'S THE LAST DAY—WE HAVE TO TAKE IT ALL IN!

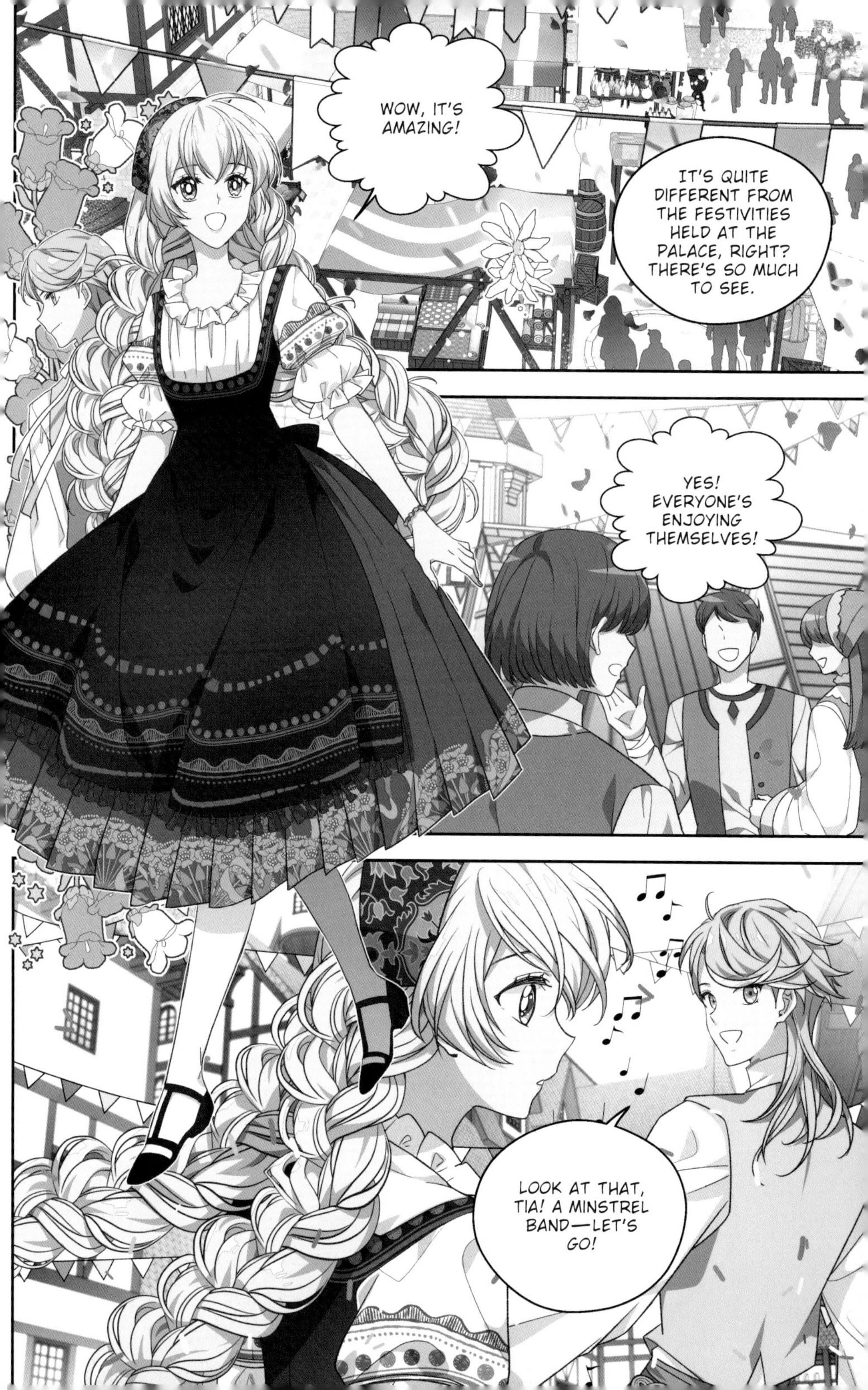
WOW, IT'S AMAZING!
IT'S QUITE DIFFERENT FROM THE FESTIVITIES HELD AT THE PALACE, RIGHT? THERE'S SO MUCH TO SEE.
YES! EVERYONE'S ENJOYING THEMSELVES!
LOOK AT THAT, TIA! A MINSTREL BAND—LET'S GO!

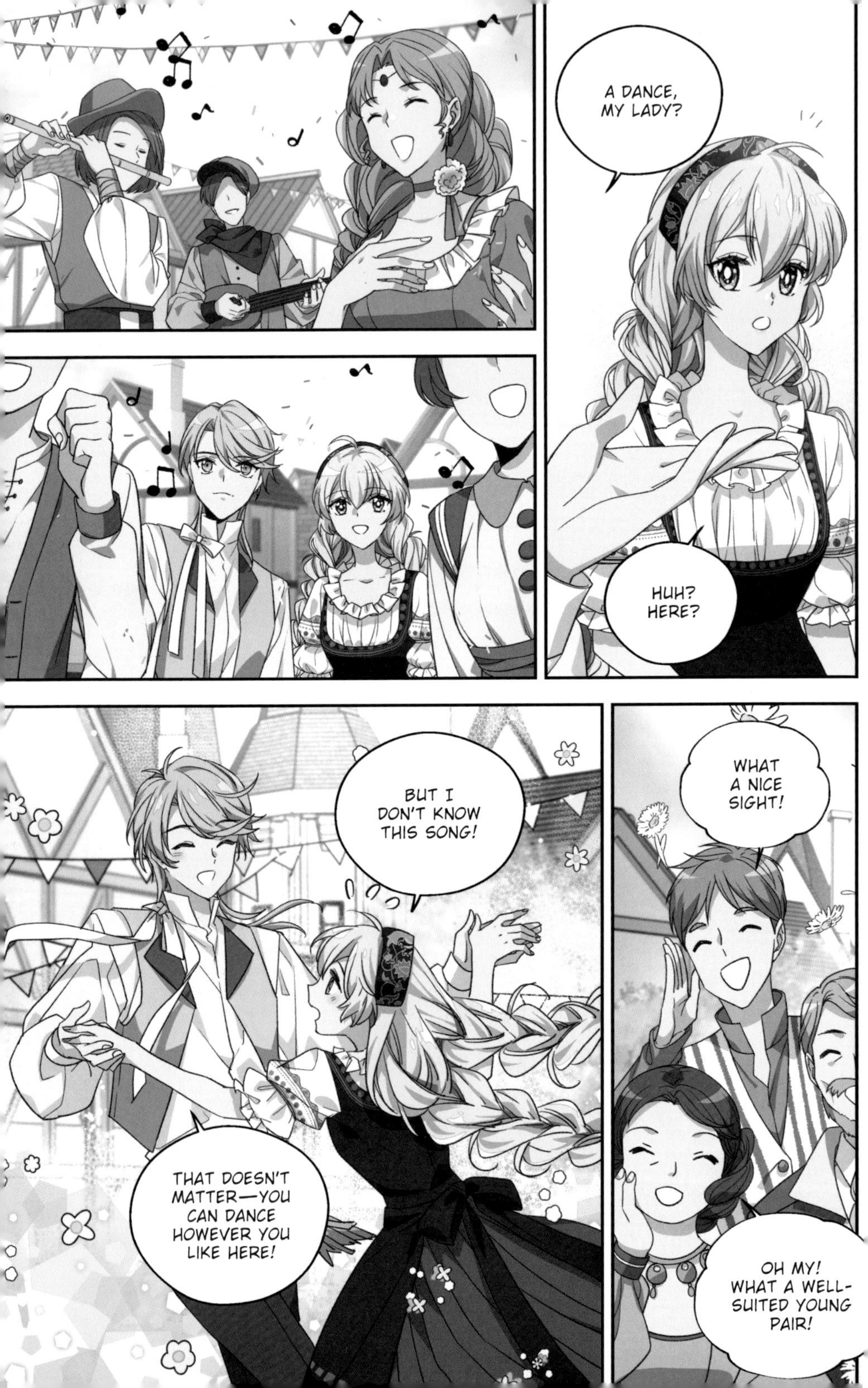
A DANCE, MY LADY?
HUH? HERE?
BUT I DON'T KNOW THIS SONG!
THAT DOESN'T MATTER—YOU CAN DANCE HOWEVER YOU LIKE HERE!
WHAT A NICE SIGHT!
OH MY! WHAT A WELL-SUITED YOUNG PAIR!

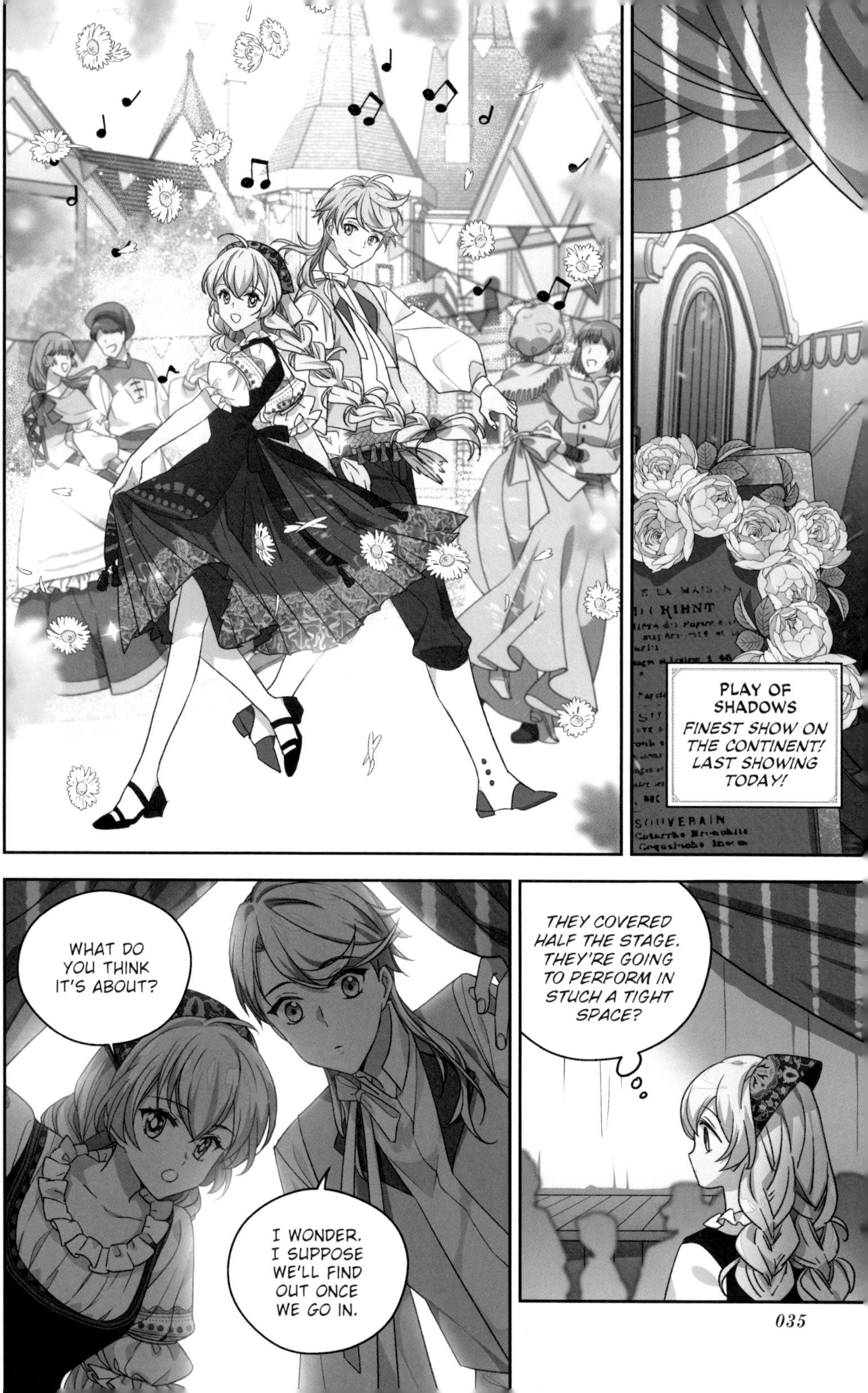
PLAY OF SHADOWS
FINEST SHOW ON THE CONTINENT! LAST SHOWING TODAY!
SOUVERAIN
WHAT DO YOU THINK IT'S ABOUT?
I WONDER. I SUPPOSE WE'LL FIND OUT ONCE WE GO IN.
THEY COVERED HALF THE STAGE. THEY'RE GOING TO PERFORM IN STUCH A TIGHT SPACE?

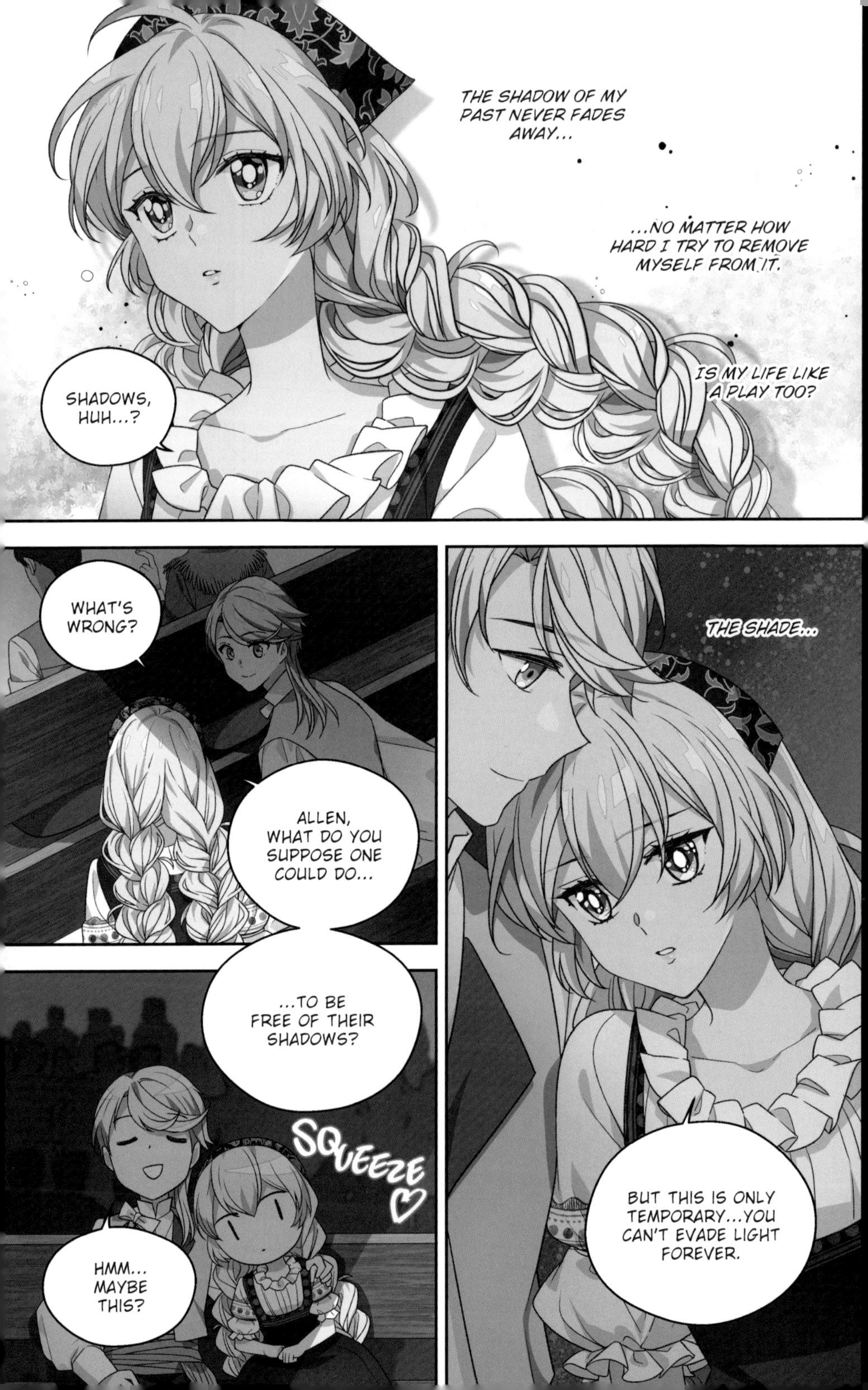
THE SHADOW OF MY PAST NEVER FADES AWAY...
...NO MATTER HOW HARD I TRY TO REMOVE MYSELF FROM IT.
IS MY LIFE LIKE A PLAY TOO?
SHADOWS, HUH...?
WHAT'S WRONG?
ALLEN, WHAT DO YOU SUPPOSE ONE COULD DO...
...TO BE FREE OF THEIR SHADOWS?
SQUEEZE
HMM... MAYBE THIS?
THE SHADE...
BUT THIS IS ONLY TEMPORARY...YOU CAN'T EVADE LIGHT FOREVER.

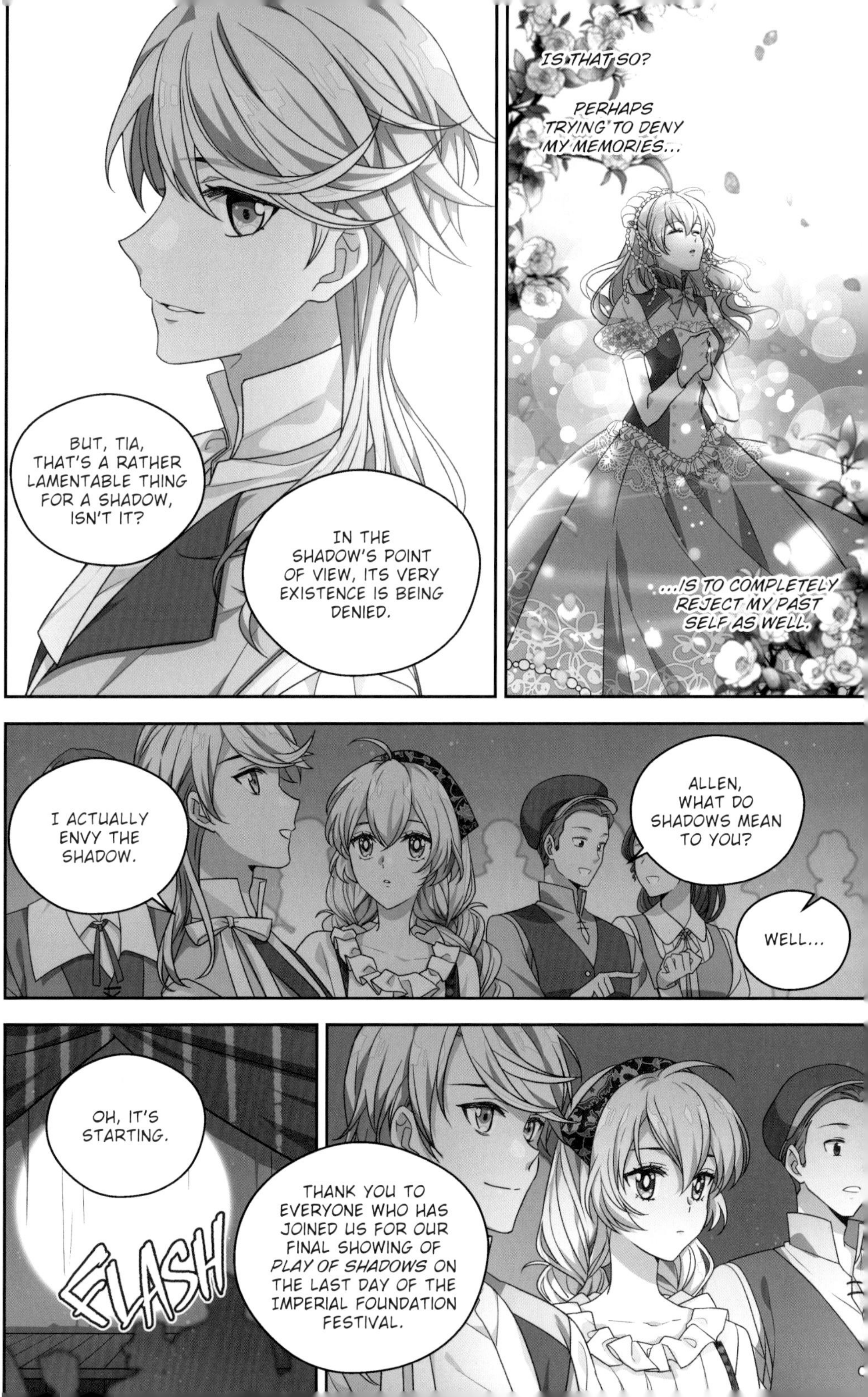
BUT, TIA, THAT'S A RATHER LAMENTABLE THING FOR A SHADOW, ISN'T IT?
IN THE SHADOW'S POINT OF VIEW, ITS VERY EXISTENCE IS BEING DENIED.
IS THAT SO?
PERHAPS TRYING TO DENY MY MEMORIES...
...IS TO COMPLETELY REJECT MY PAST SELF AS WELL.
ALLEN, WHAT DO SHADOWS MEAN TO YOU?
WELL...
I ACTUALLY ENVY THE SHADOW.
OH, IT'S STARTING.
FLASH
THANK YOU TO EVERYONE WHO HAS JOINED US FOR OUR FINAL SHOWING OF *PLAY OF SHADOWS* ON THE LAST DAY OF THE IMPERIAL FOUNDATION FESTIVAL.

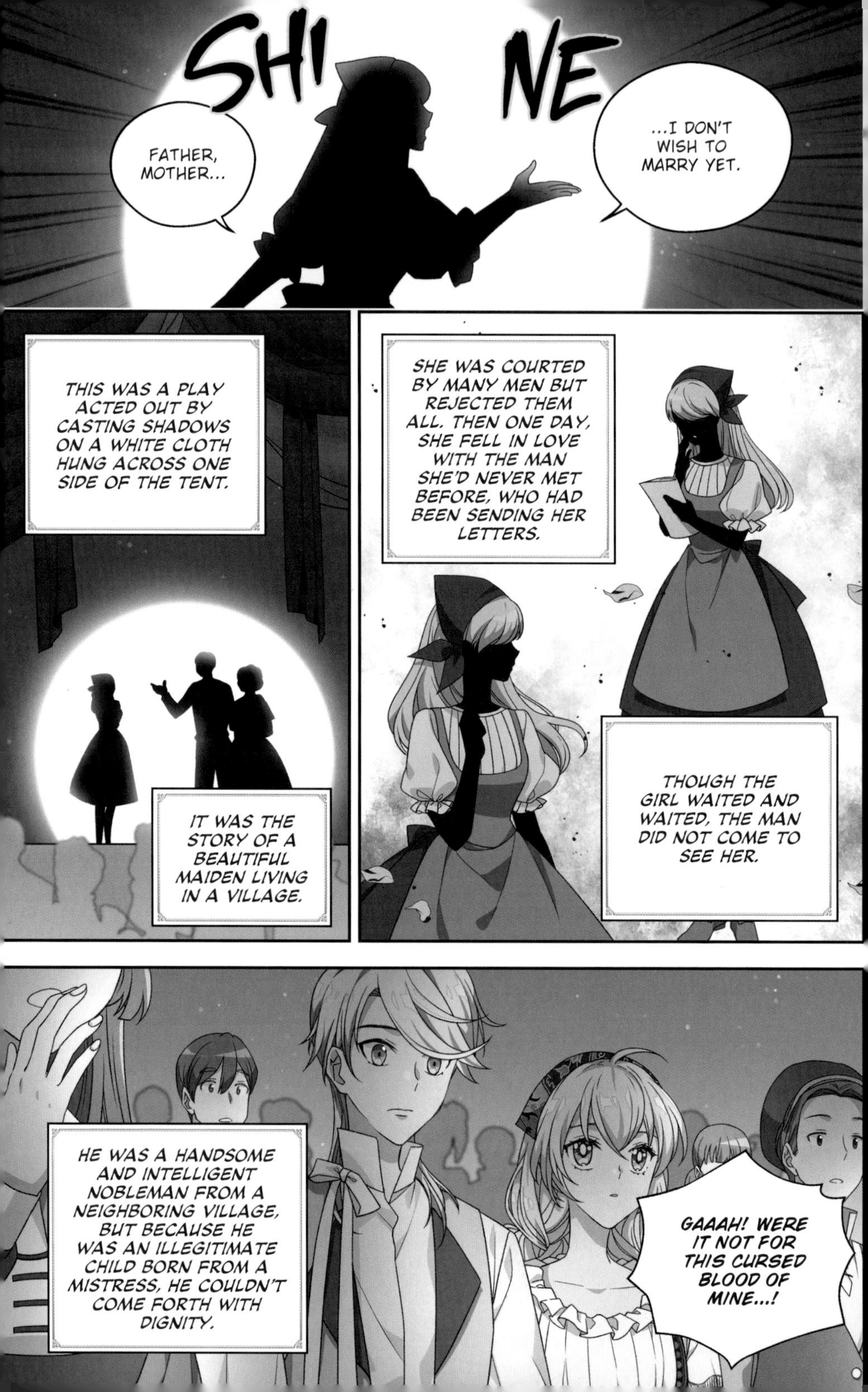
SHINE
FATHER, MOTHER...
...I DON'T WISH TO MARRY YET.
THIS WAS A PLAY ACTED OUT BY CASTING SHADOWS ON A WHITE CLOTH HUNG ACROSS ONE SIDE OF THE TENT.
IT WAS THE STORY OF A BEAUTIFUL MAIDEN LIVING IN A VILLAGE.
SHE WAS COURTED BY MANY MEN BUT REJECTED THEM ALL. THEN ONE DAY, SHE FELL IN LOVE WITH THE MAN SHE'D NEVER MET BEFORE, WHO HAD BEEN SENDING HER LETTERS.
THOUGH THE GIRL WAITED AND WAITED, THE MAN DID NOT COME TO SEE HER.
HE WAS A HANDSOME AND INTELLIGENT NOBLEMAN FROM A NEIGHBORING VILLAGE, BUT BECAUSE HE WAS AN ILLEGITIMATE CHILD BORN FROM A MISTRESS, HE COULDN'T COME FORTH WITH DIGNITY.
GAAAH! WERE IT NOT FOR THIS CURSED BLOOD OF MINE...!

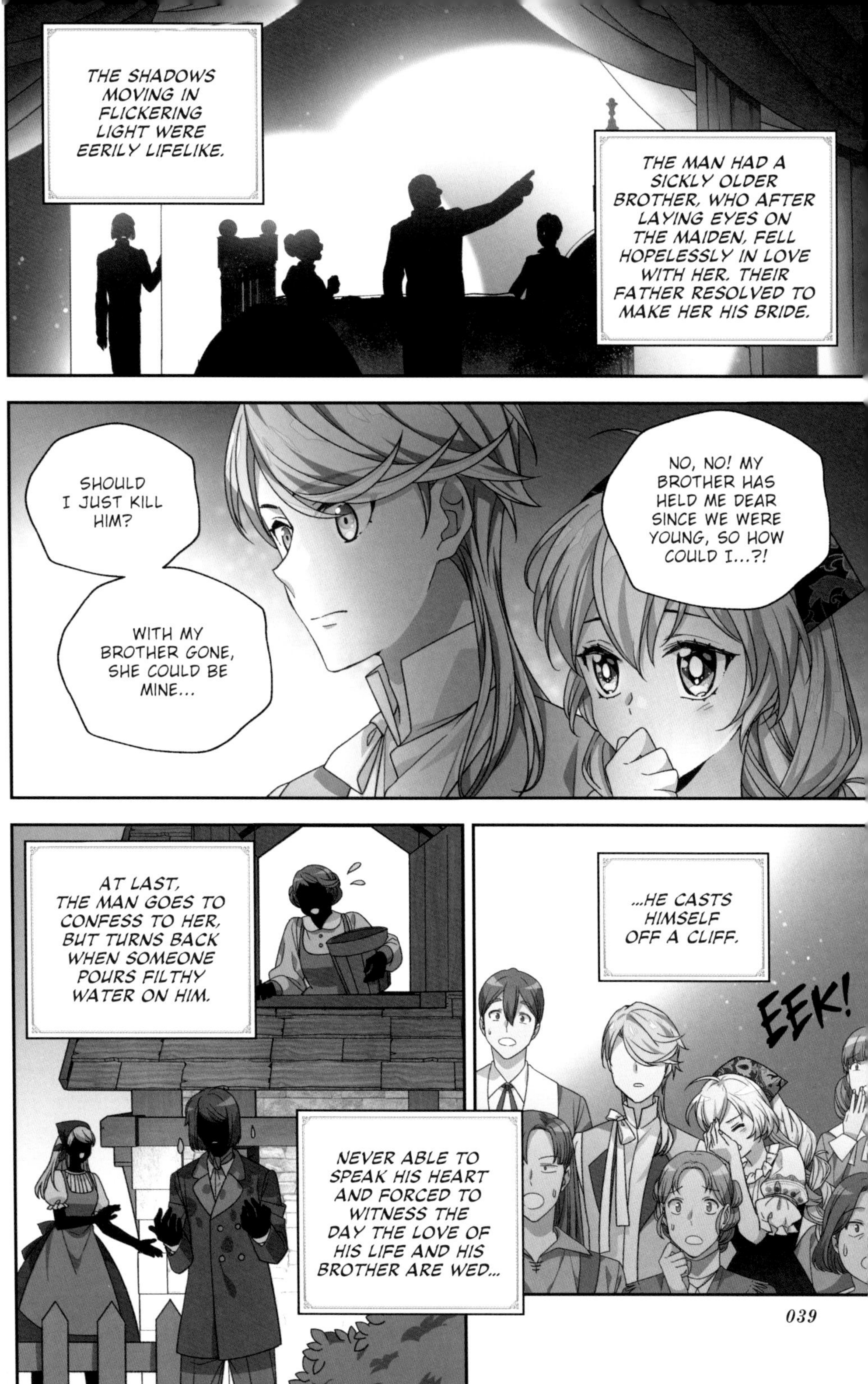
THE SHADOWS MOVING IN FLICKERING LIGHT WERE EERILY LIFELIKE.
THE MAN HAD A SICKLY OLDER BROTHER, WHO AFTER LAYING EYES ON THE MAIDEN, FELL HOPELESSLY IN LOVE WITH HER. THEIR FATHER RESOLVED TO MAKE HER HIS BRIDE.
SHOULD I JUST KILL HIM?
WITH MY BROTHER GONE, SHE COULD BE MINE...
NO, NO! MY BROTHER HAS HELD ME DEAR SINCE WE WERE YOUNG, SO HOW COULD I...?!
AT LAST, THE MAN GOES TO CONFESS TO HER, BUT TURNS BACK WHEN SOMEONE POURS FILTHY WATER ON HIM.
NEVER ABLE TO SPEAK HIS HEART AND FORCED TO WITNESS THE DAY THE LOVE OF HIS LIFE AND HIS BROTHER ARE WED...
...HE CASTS HIMSELF OFF A CLIFF.
EEK!

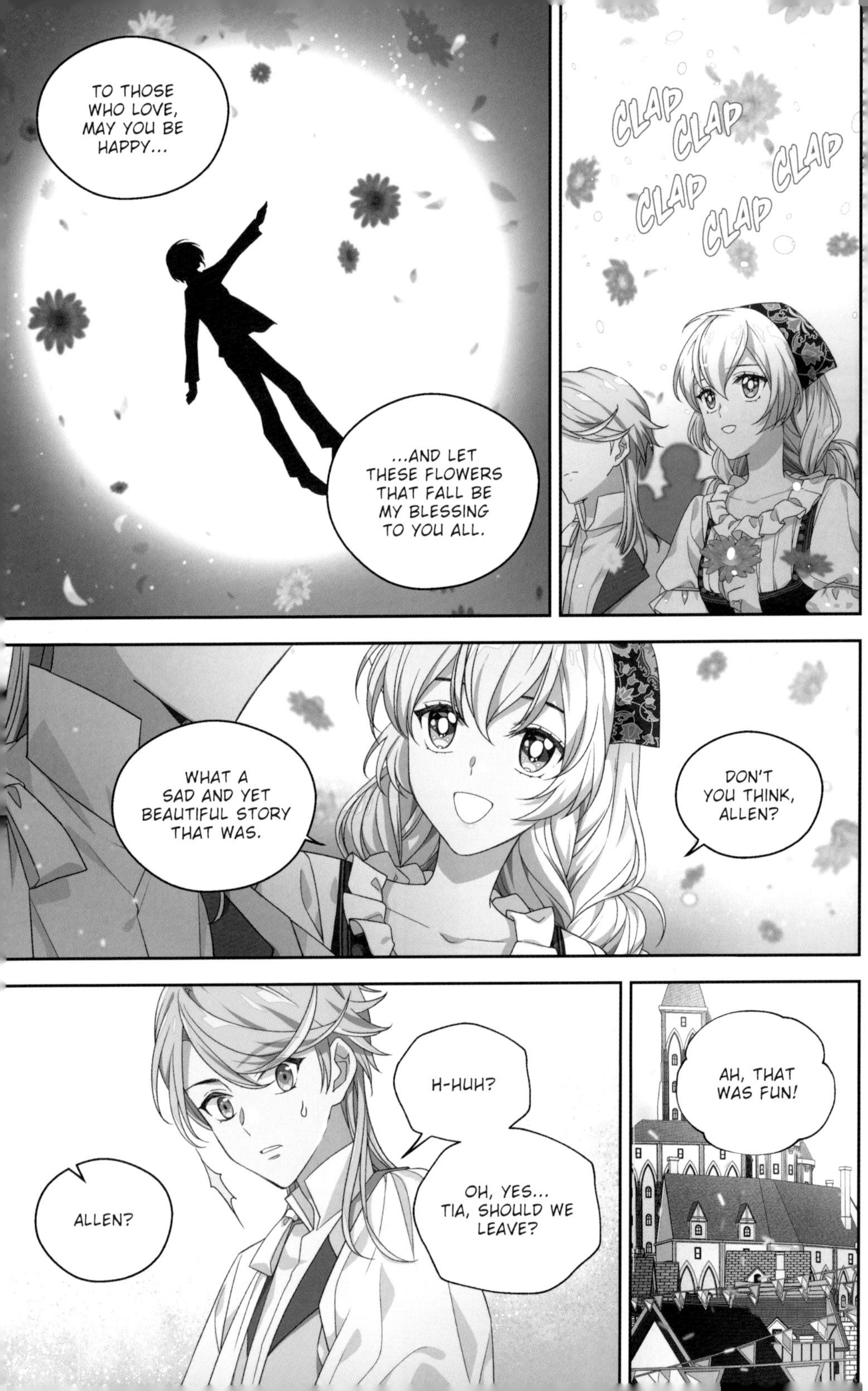
TO THOSE WHO LOVE, MAY YOU BE HAPPY...
...AND LET THESE FLOWERS THAT FALL BE MY BLESSING TO YOU ALL.
CLAP CLAP
CLAP CLAP
CLAP
WHAT A SAD AND YET BEAUTIFUL STORY THAT WAS.
DON'T YOU THINK, ALLEN?
ALLEN?
H-HUH?
OH, YES... TIA, SHOULD WE LEAVE?
AH, THAT WAS FUN!

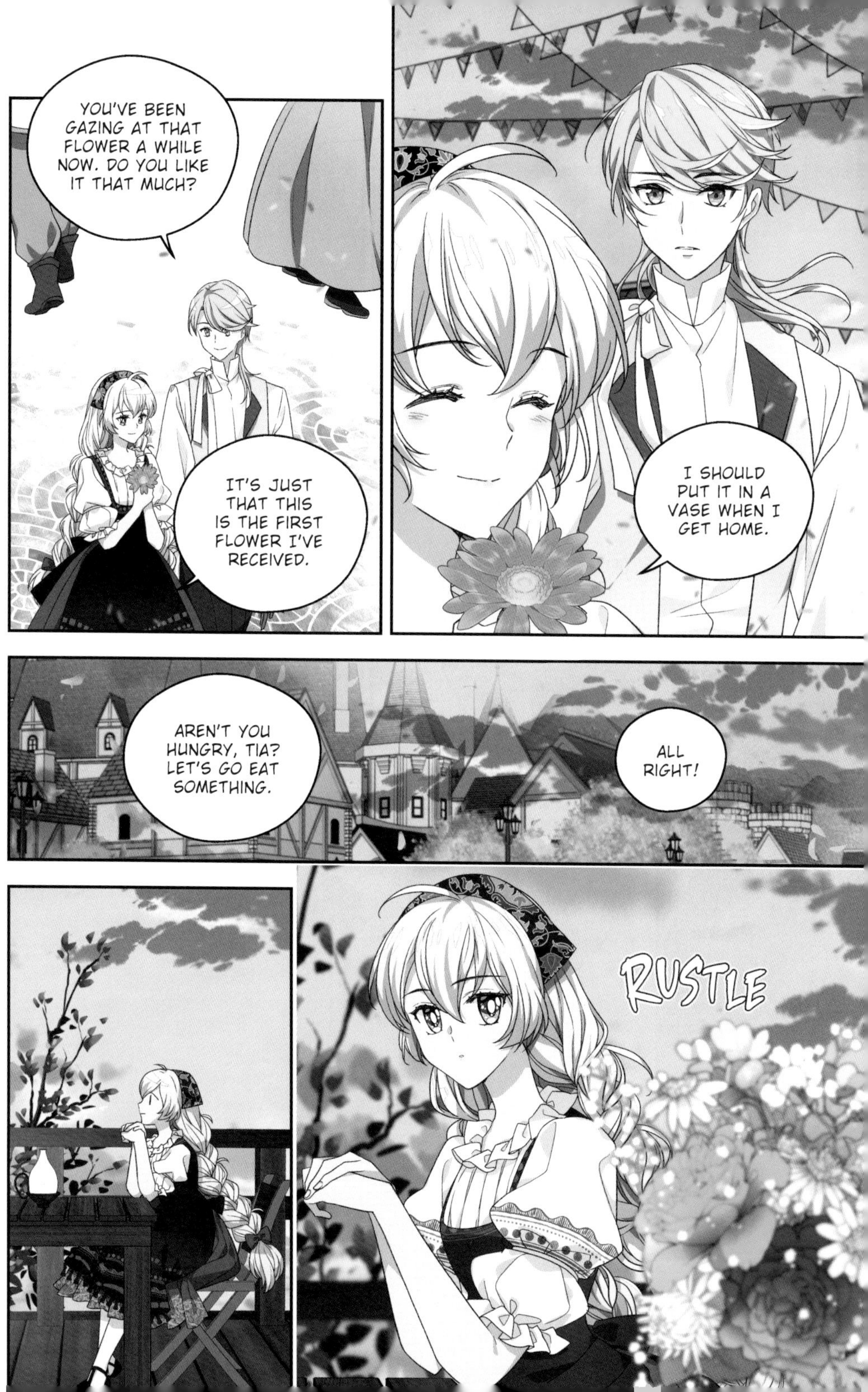
YOU'VE BEEN GAZING AT THAT FLOWER A WHILE NOW. DO YOU LIKE IT THAT MUCH?
IT'S JUST THAT THIS IS THE FIRST FLOWER I'VE RECEIVED.
I SHOULD PUT IT IN A VASE WHEN I GET HOME.
AREN'T YOU HUNGRY, TIA? LET'S GO EAT SOMETHING.
ALL RIGHT!
RUSTLE

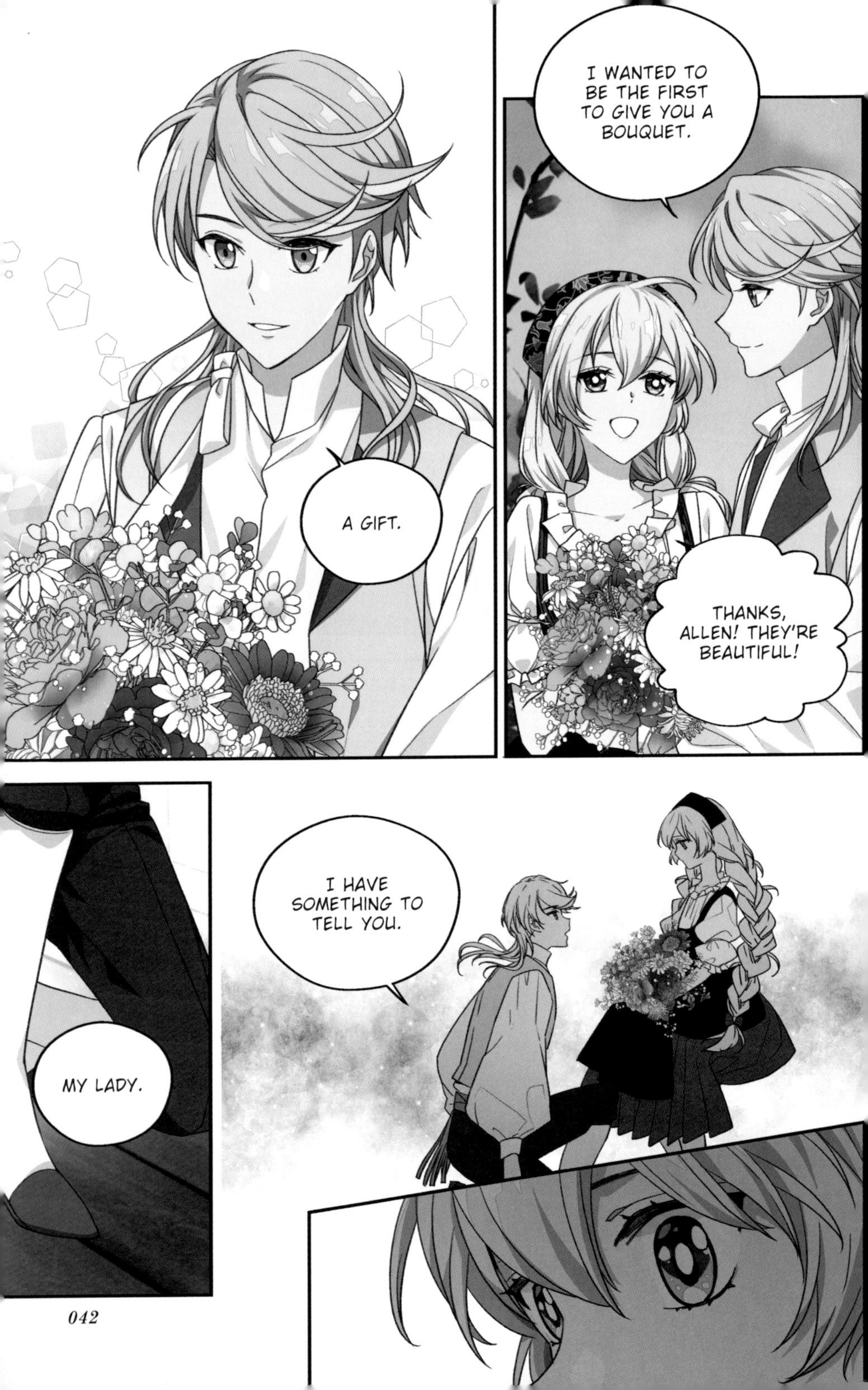
A GIFT.
I WANTED TO BE THE FIRST TO GIVE YOU A BOUQUET.
THANKS, ALLEN! THEY'RE BEAUTIFUL!
MY LADY.
I HAVE SOMETHING TO TELL YOU.

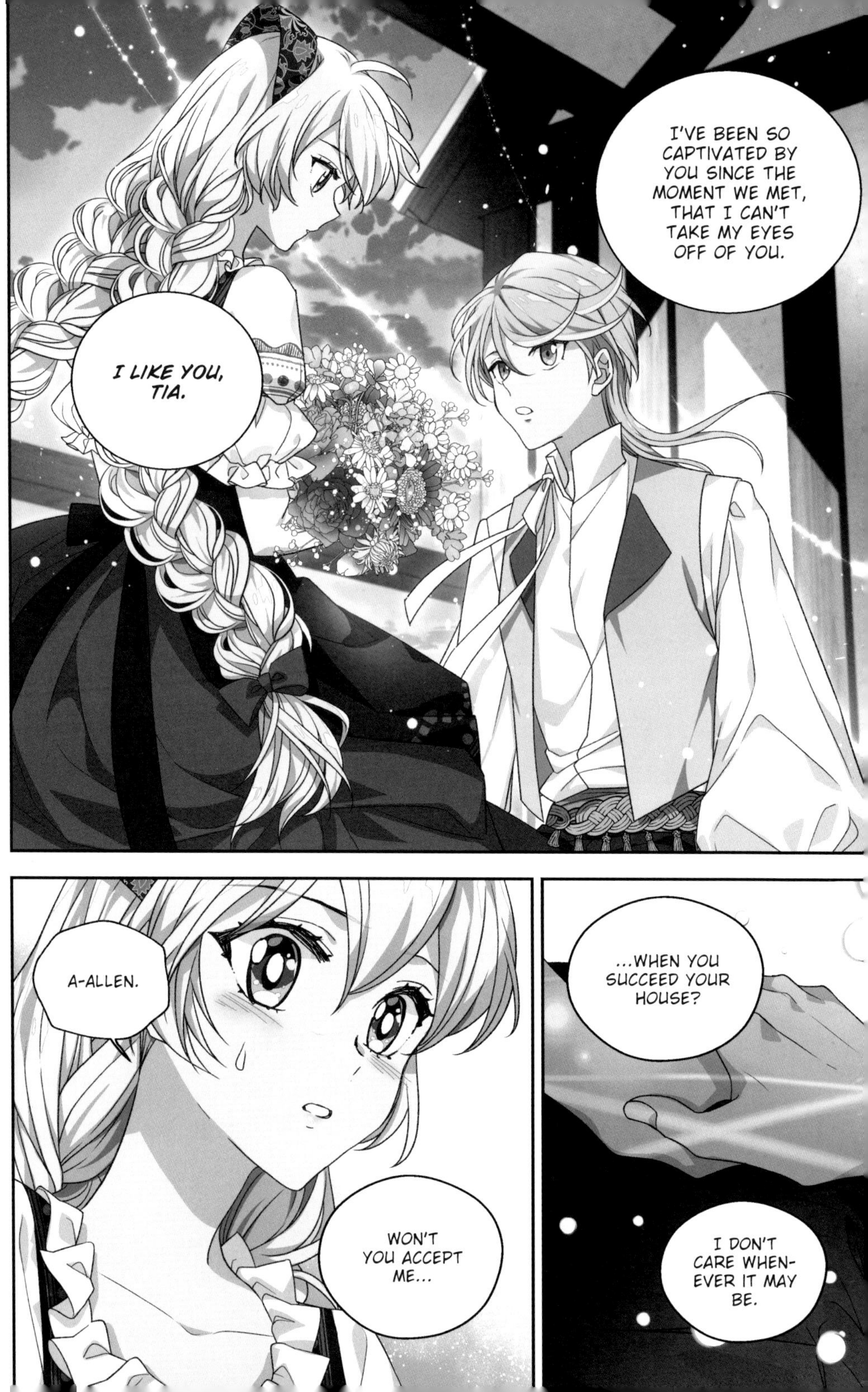
I'VE BEEN SO CAPTIVATED BY YOU SINCE THE MOMENT WE MET, THAT I CAN'T TAKE MY EYES OFF OF YOU.
I LIKE YOU, TIA.
A-ALLEN.
WON'T YOU ACCEPT ME...
...WHEN YOU SUCCEED YOUR HOUSE?
I DON'T CARE WHEN-EVER IT MAY BE.

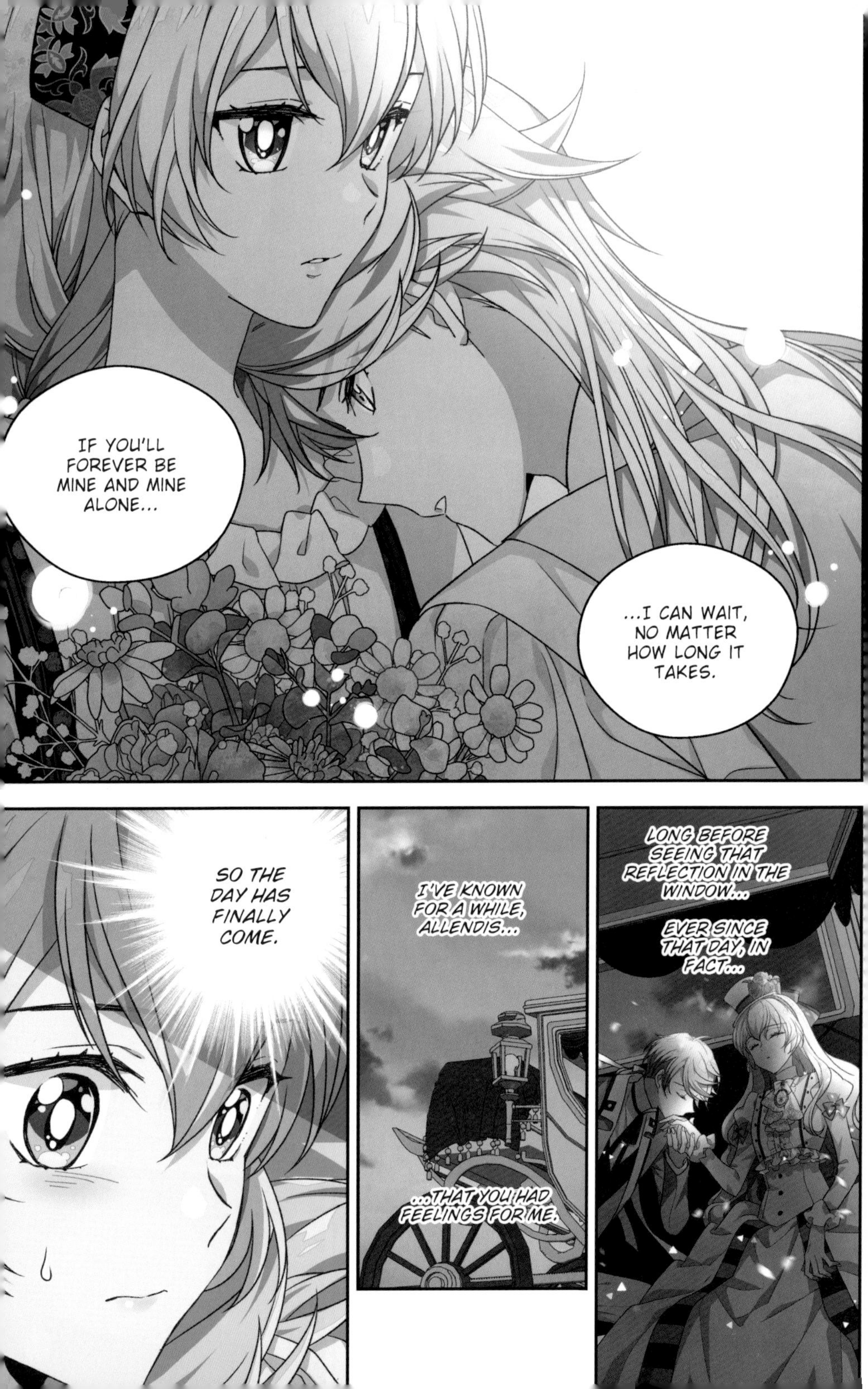
IF YOU'LL FOREVER BE MINE AND MINE ALONE...
...I CAN WAIT, NO MATTER HOW LONG IT TAKES.
SO THE DAY HAS FINALLY COME.
I'VE KNOWN FOR A WHILE, ALLENDIS...
...THAT YOU HAD FEELINGS FOR ME.
LONG BEFORE SEEING THAT REFLECTION IN THE WINDOW...
EVER SINCE THAT DAY, IN FACT...

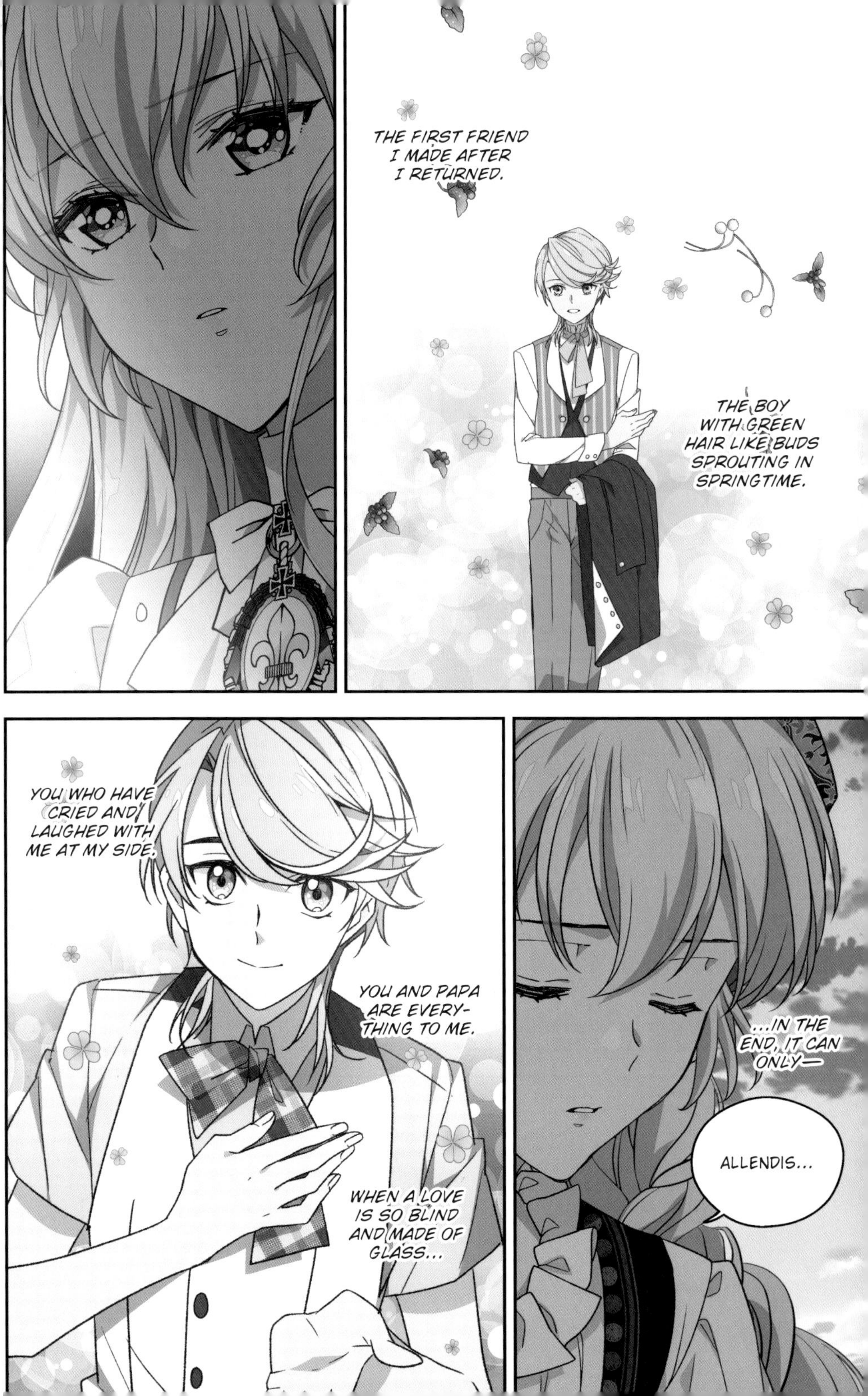
THE FIRST FRIEND I MADE AFTER I RETURNED.
THE BOY WITH GREEN HAIR LIKE BUDS SPROUTING IN SPRINGTIME.
YOU WHO HAVE CRIED AND LAUGHED WITH ME AT MY SIDE.
YOU AND PAPA ARE EVERY-THING TO ME.
WHEN A LOVE IS SO BLIND AND MADE OF GLASS...
...IN THE END, IT CAN ONLY—
ALLENDIS...

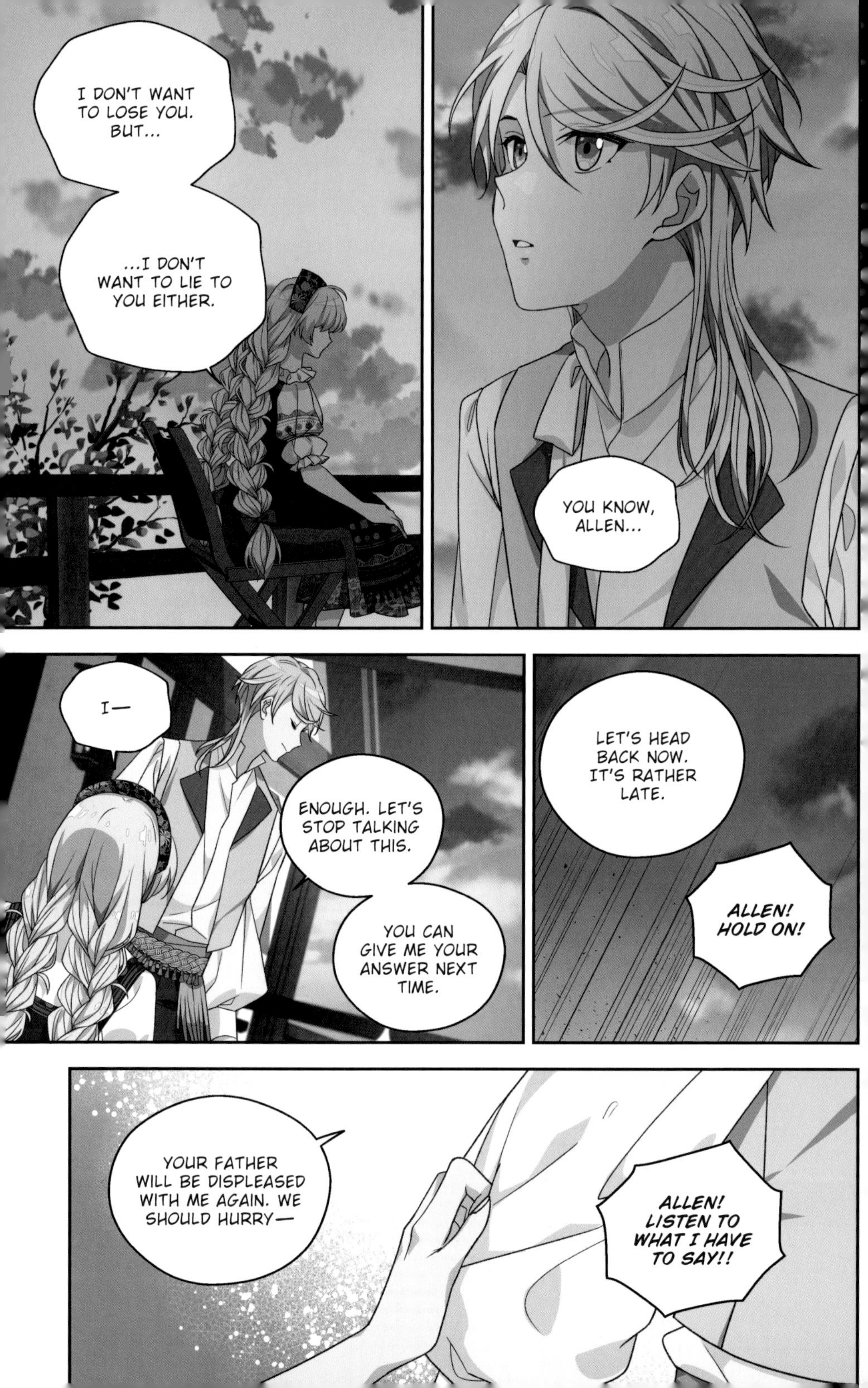
I DON'T WANT TO LOSE YOU. BUT...
...I DON'T WANT TO LIE TO YOU EITHER.
YOU KNOW, ALLEN...
I—
ENOUGH. LET'S STOP TALKING ABOUT THIS.
YOU CAN GIVE ME YOUR ANSWER NEXT TIME.
LET'S HEAD BACK NOW. IT'S RATHER LATE.
ALLEN! HOLD ON!
YOUR FATHER WILL BE DISPLEASED WITH ME AGAIN. WE SHOULD HURRY—
ALLEN! LISTEN TO WHAT I HAVE TO SAY!!

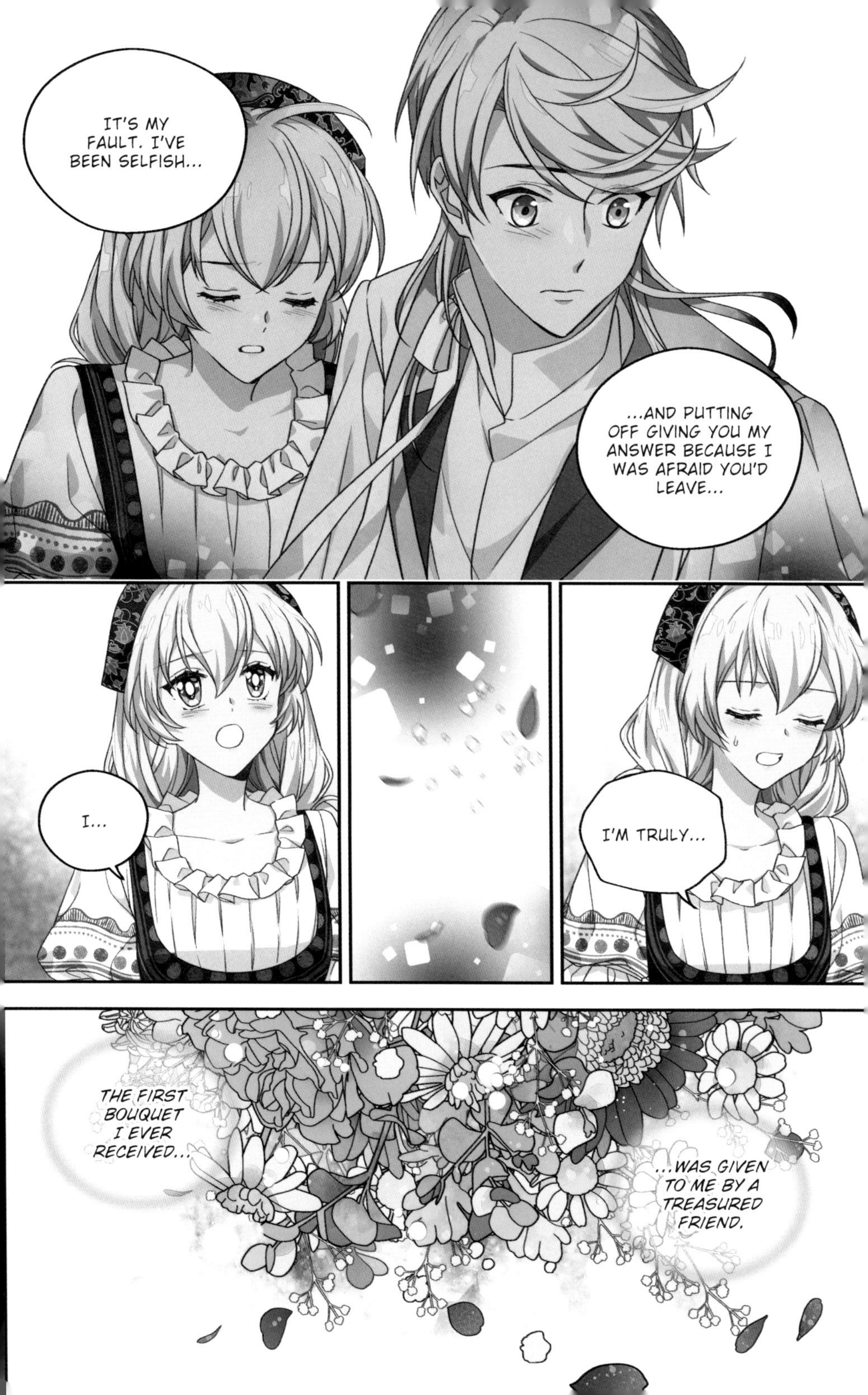
IT'S MY FAULT. I'VE BEEN SELFISH...
...AND PUTTING OFF GIVING YOU MY ANSWER BECAUSE I WAS AFRAID YOU'D LEAVE...
I...
I'M TRULY...
THE FIRST BOUQUET I EVER RECEIVED...
...WAS GIVEN TO ME BY A TREASURED FRIEND.

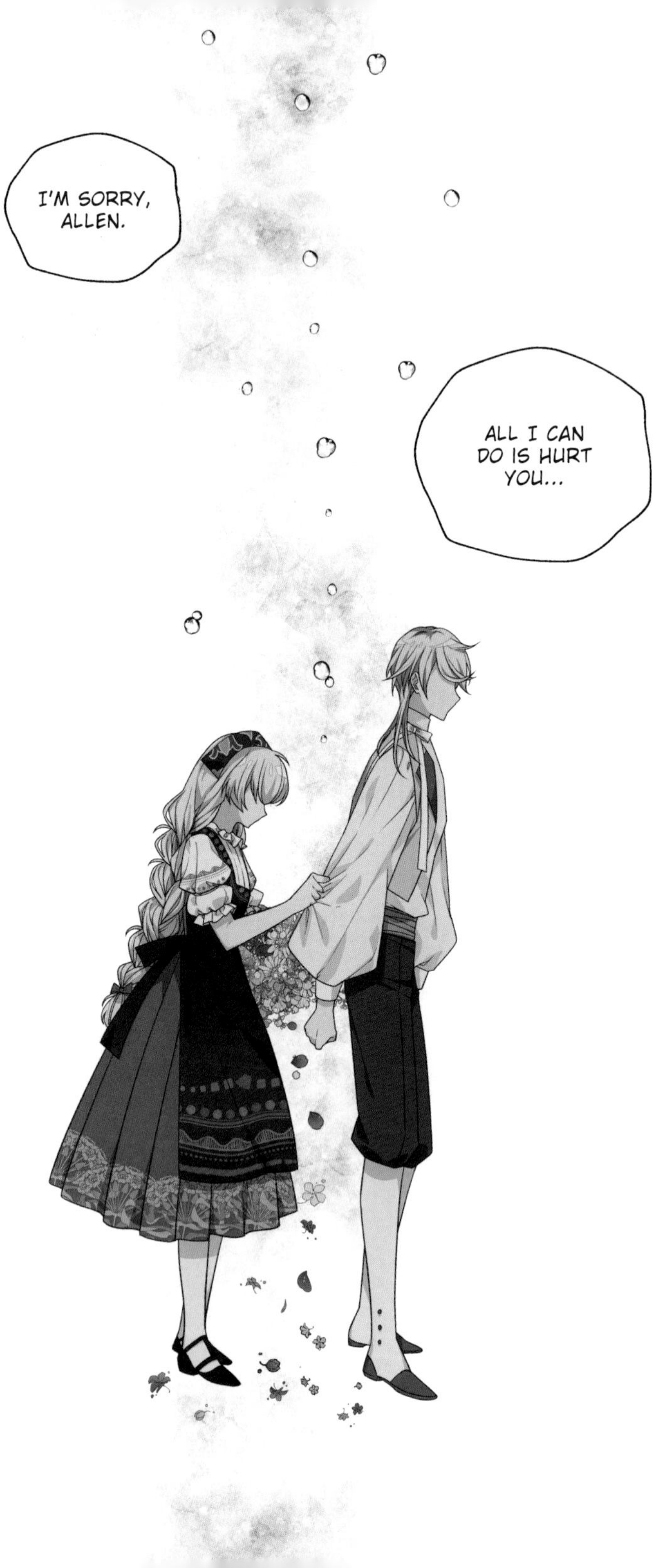
I'M SORRY, ALLEN.
ALL I CAN DO IS HURT YOU...

The Abandoned Empress

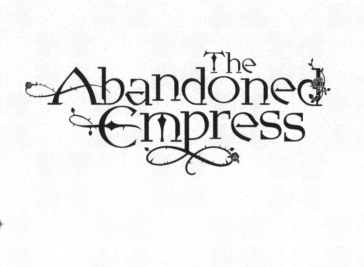

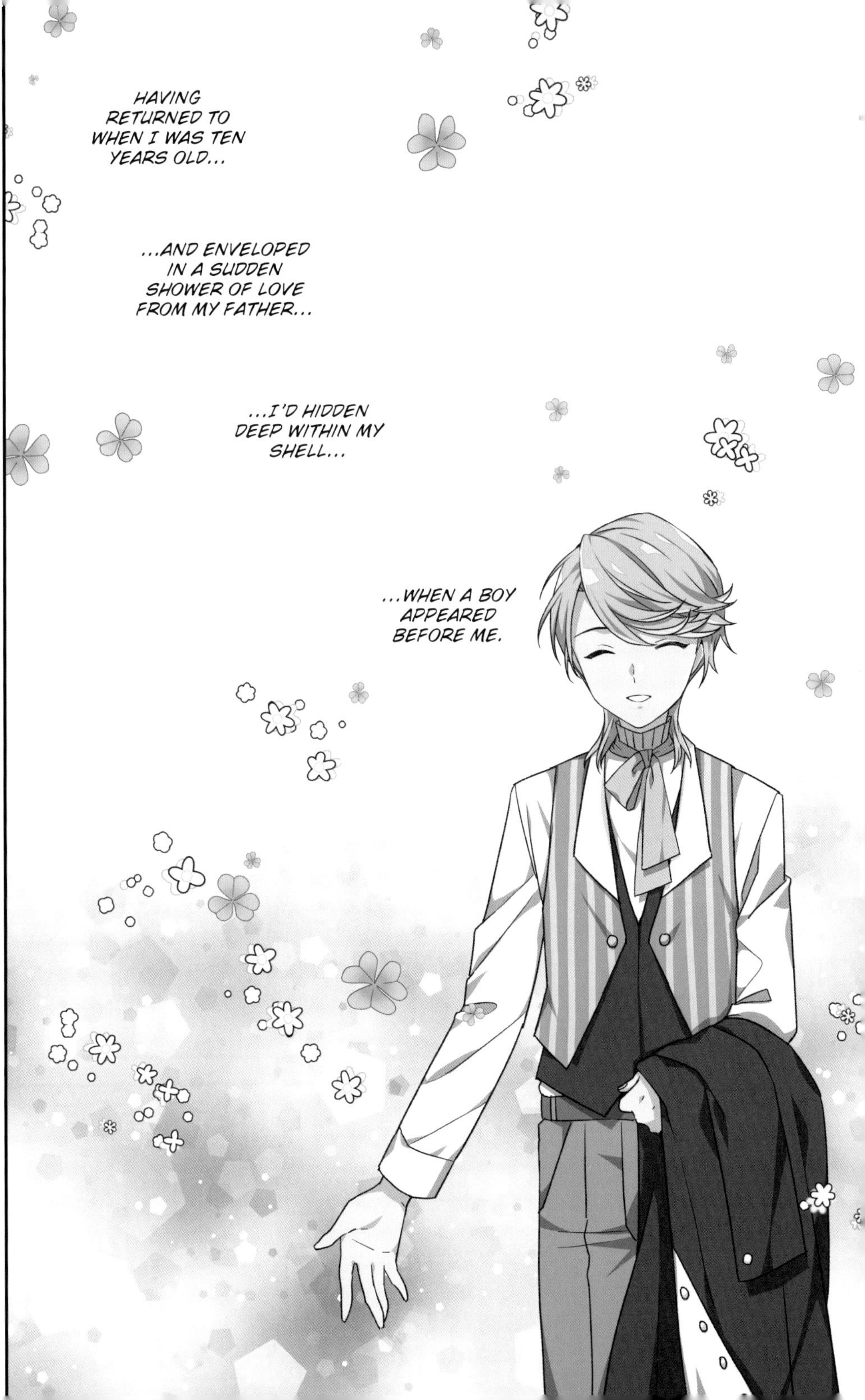
HAVING RETURNED TO WHEN I WAS TEN YEARS OLD...
...AND ENVELOPED IN A SUDDEN SHOWER OF LOVE FROM MY FATHER...
...I'D HIDDEN DEEP WITHIN MY SHELL...
...WHEN A BOY APPEARED BEFORE ME.

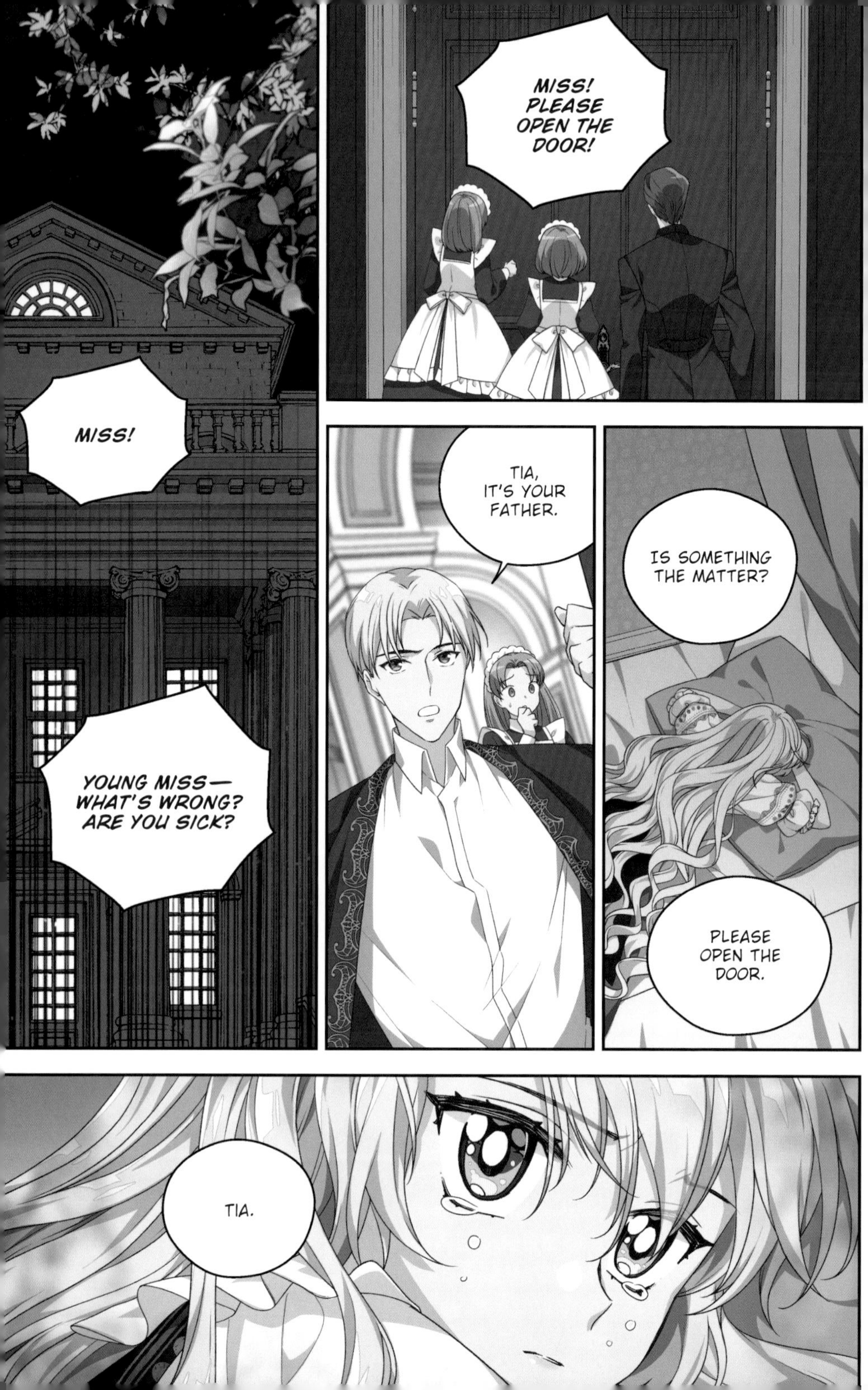
MISS!
MISS! PLEASE OPEN THE DOOR!
YOUNG MISS— WHAT'S WRONG? ARE YOU SICK?
TIA, IT'S YOUR FATHER.
IS SOMETHING THE MATTER?
PLEASE OPEN THE DOOR.
TIA.

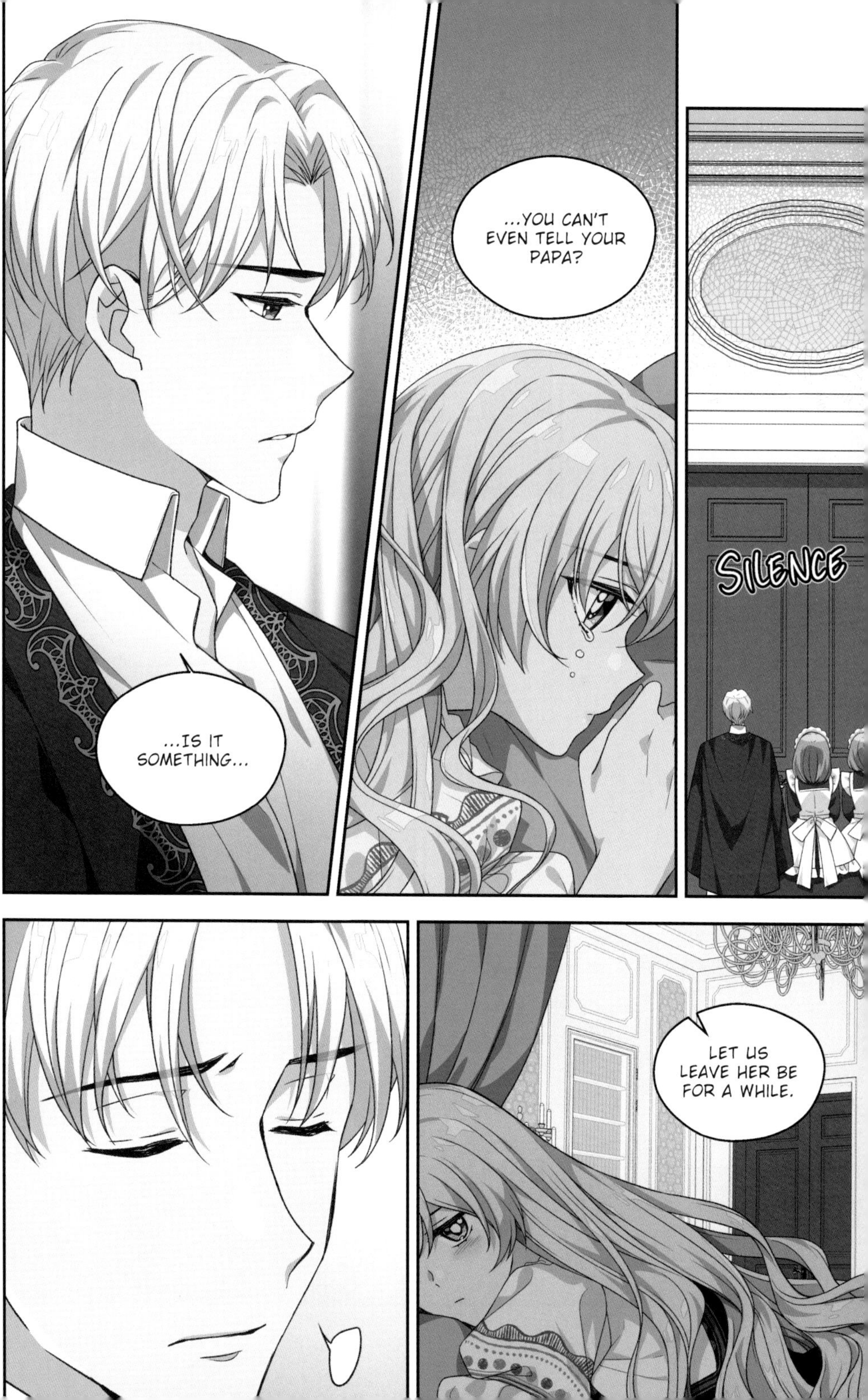
...IS IT SOMETHING...
...YOU CAN'T EVEN TELL YOUR PAPA?
SILENCE
LET US LEAVE HER BE FOR A WHILE.

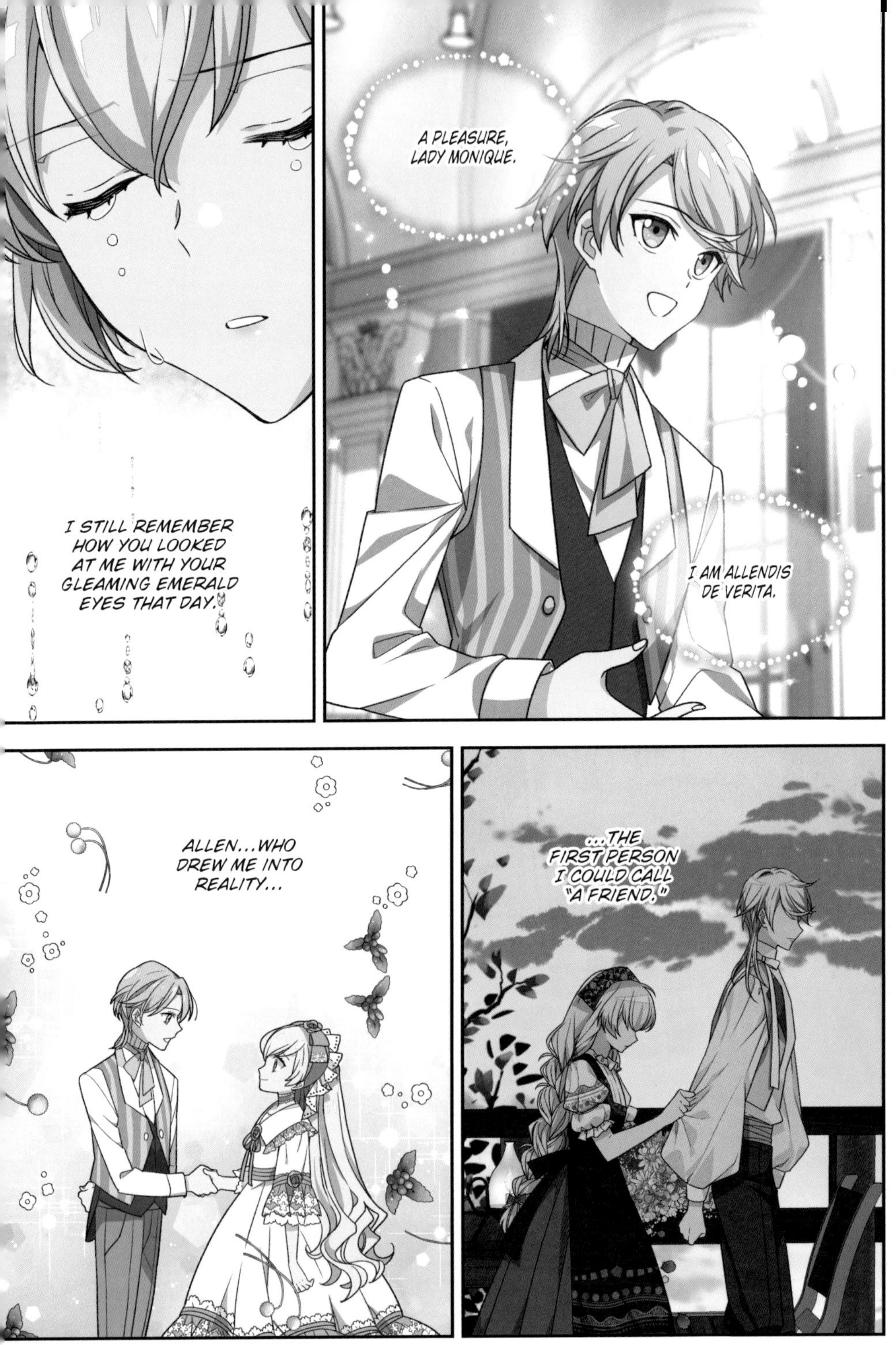
A PLEASURE, LADY MONIQUE.
I AM ALLENDIS DE VERITA.
I STILL REMEMBER HOW YOU LOOKED AT ME WITH YOUR GLEAMING EMERALD EYES THAT DAY.
...THE FIRST PERSON I COULD CALL "A FRIEND."
ALLEN...WHO DREW ME INTO REALITY...

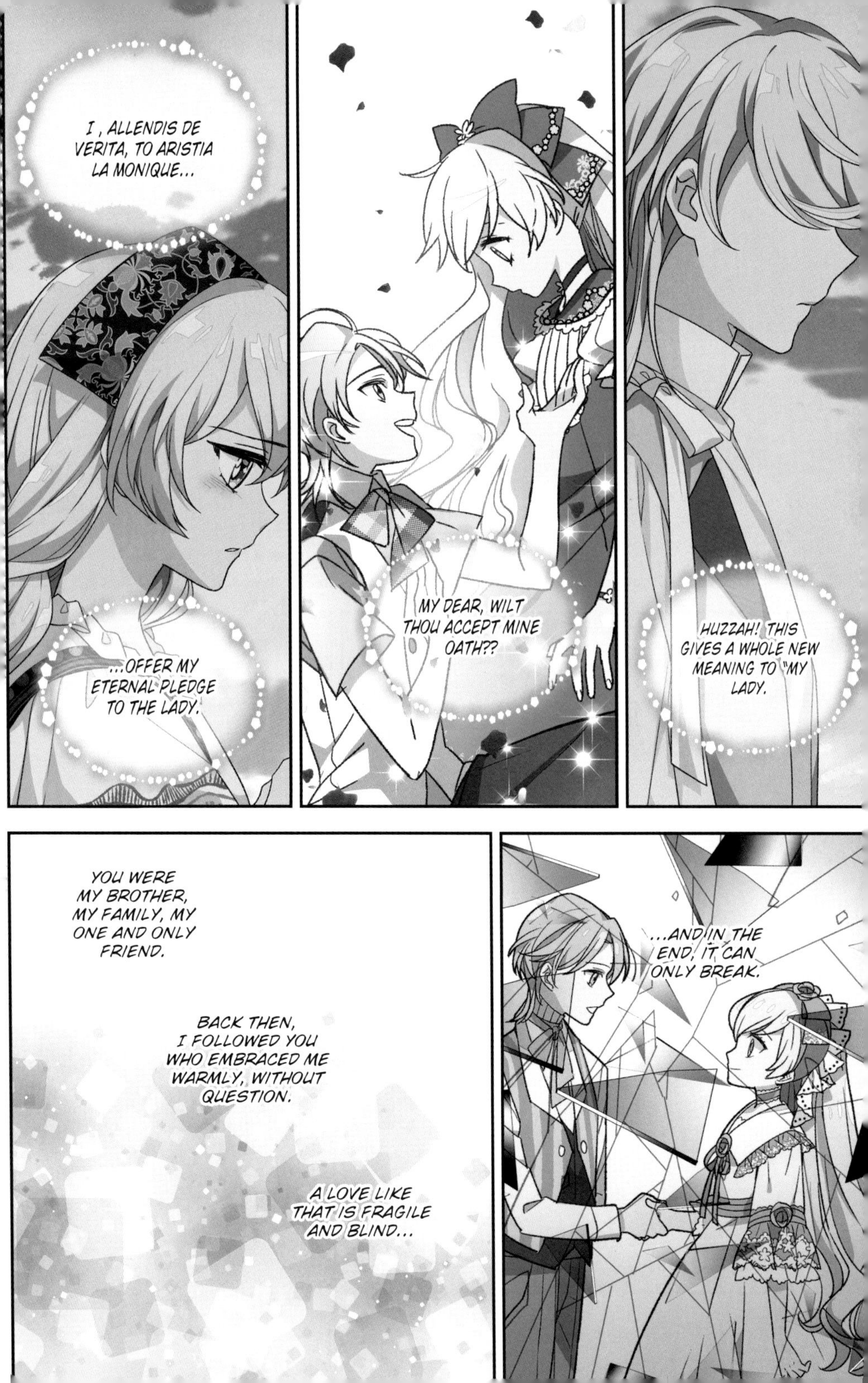
I, ALLENDIS DE VERITA, TO ARISTIA LA MONIQUE...
...OFFER MY ETERNAL PLEDGE TO THE LADY.
MY DEAR, WILT THOU ACCEPT MINE OATH??
HUZZAH! THIS GIVES A WHOLE NEW MEANING TO "MY LADY."
YOU WERE MY BROTHER, MY FAMILY, MY ONE AND ONLY FRIEND.
BACK THEN, I FOLLOWED YOU WHO EMBRACED ME WARMLY, WITHOUT QUESTION.
A LOVE LIKE THAT IS FRAGILE AND BLIND...
...AND IN THE END, IT CAN ONLY BREAK.

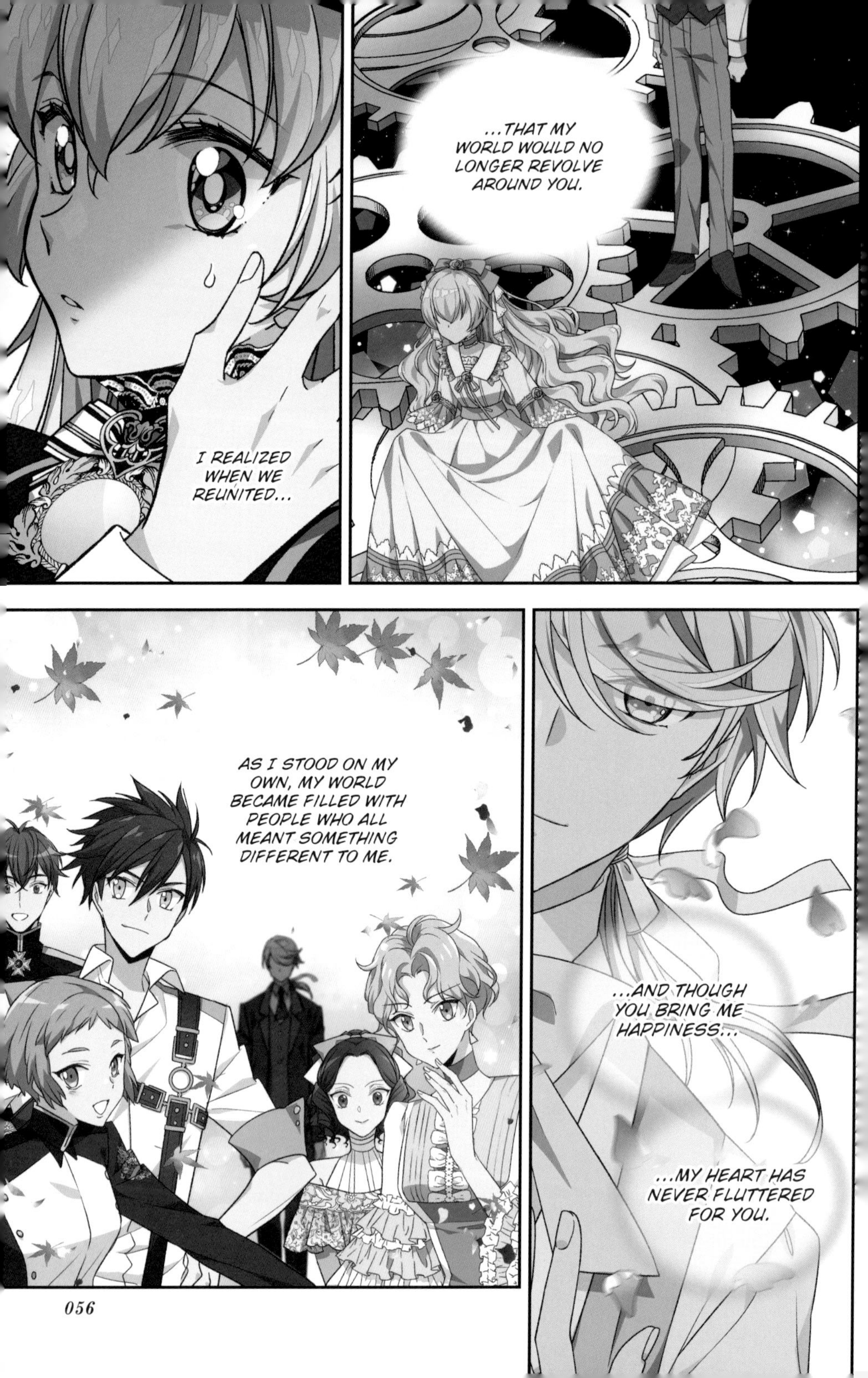
...THAT MY WORLD WOULD NO LONGER REVOLVE AROUND YOU.
I REALIZED WHEN WE REUNITED...
...AND THOUGH YOU BRING ME HAPPINESS...
...MY HEART HAS NEVER FLUTTERED FOR YOU.
AS I STOOD ON MY OWN, MY WORLD BECAME FILLED WITH PEOPLE WHO ALL MEANT SOMETHING DIFFERENT TO ME.

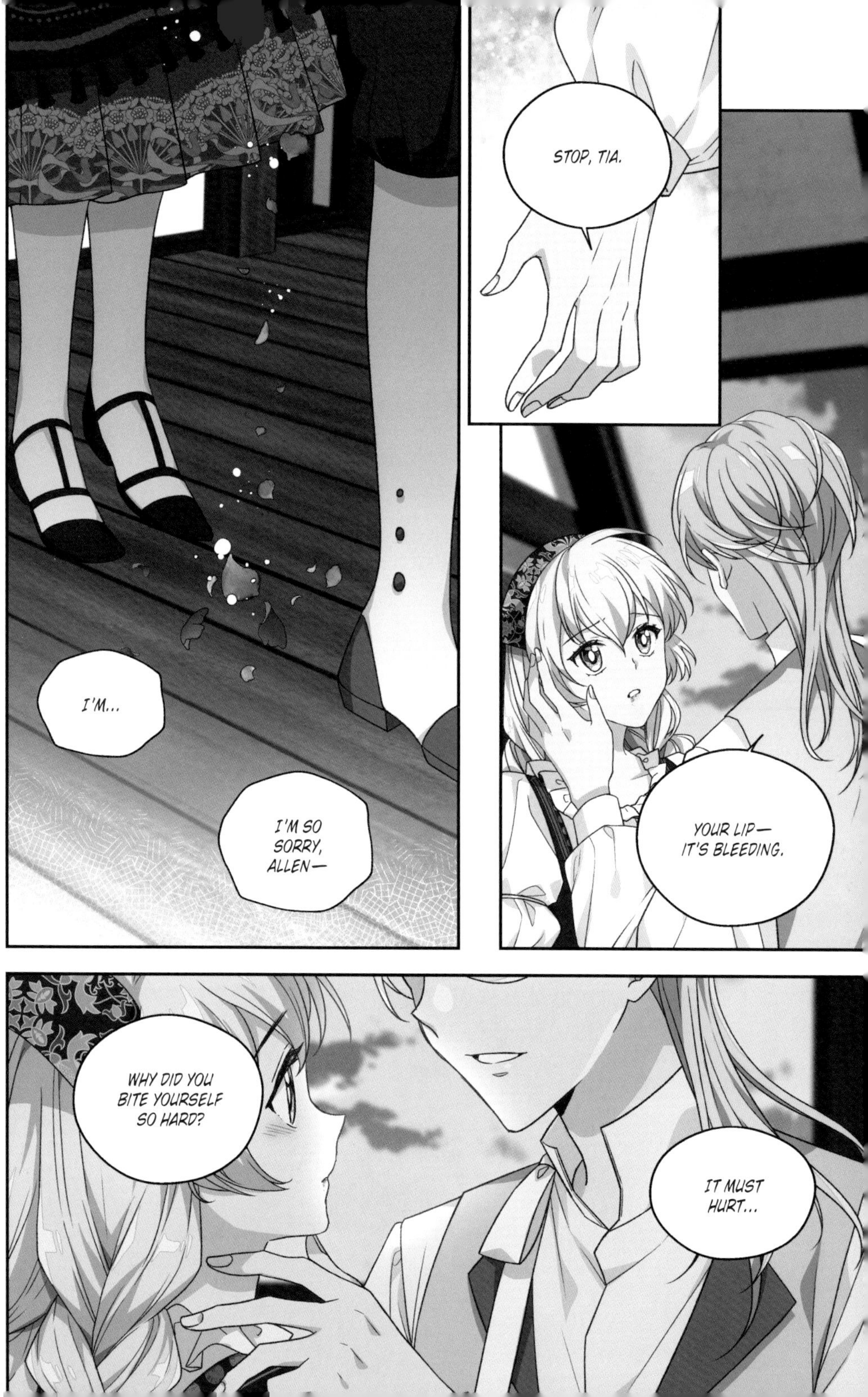
I'M...
I'M SO SORRY, ALLEN—
STOP, TIA.
YOUR LIP— IT'S BLEEDING.
WHY DID YOU BITE YOURSELF SO HARD?
IT MUST HURT...

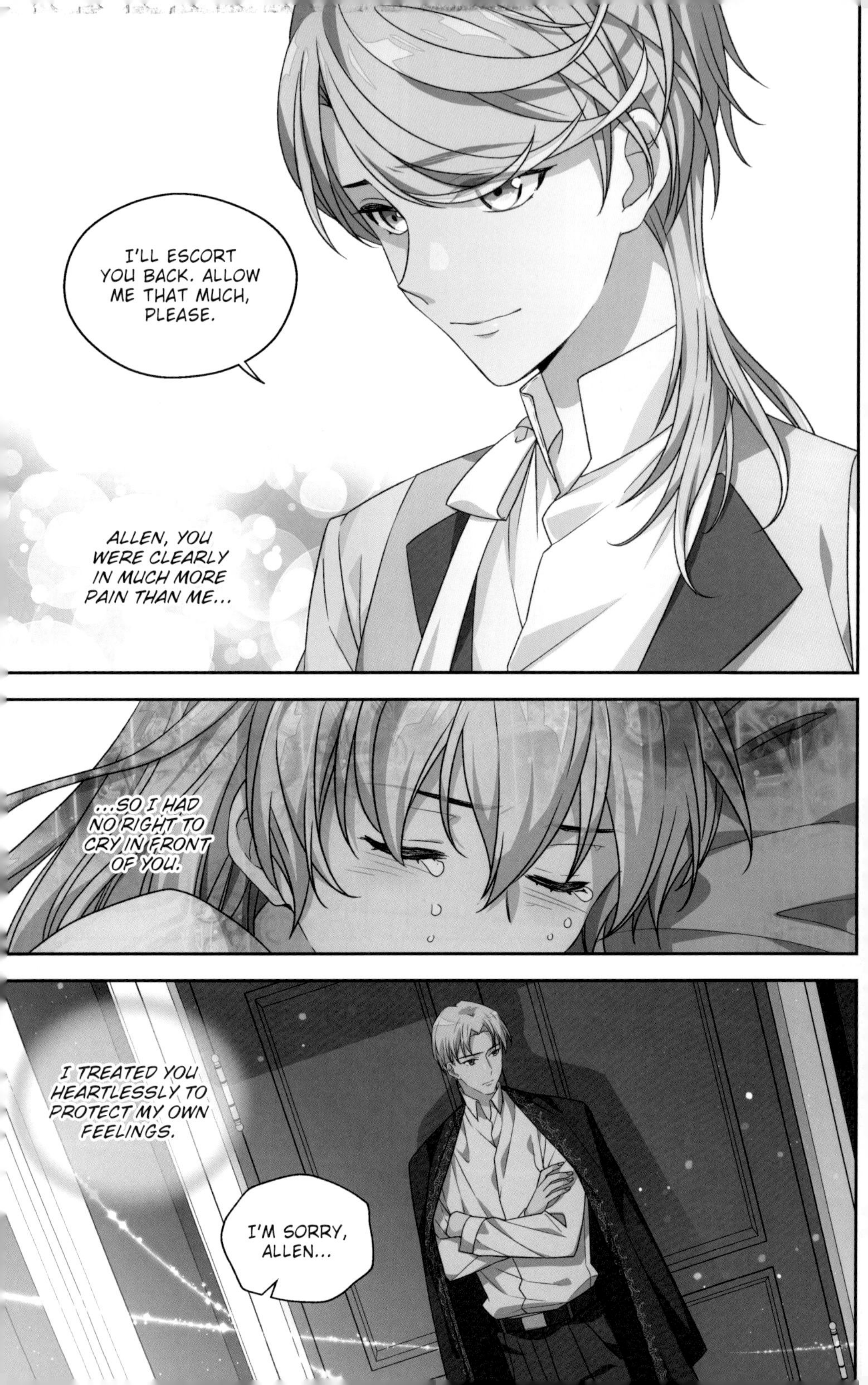
I'LL ESCORT YOU BACK. ALLOW ME THAT MUCH, PLEASE.
ALLEN, YOU WERE CLEARLY IN MUCH MORE PAIN THAN ME...
...SO I HAD NO RIGHT TO CRY IN FRONT OF YOU.
I TREATED YOU HEARTLESSLY TO PROTECT MY OWN FEELINGS.
I'M SORRY, ALLEN...

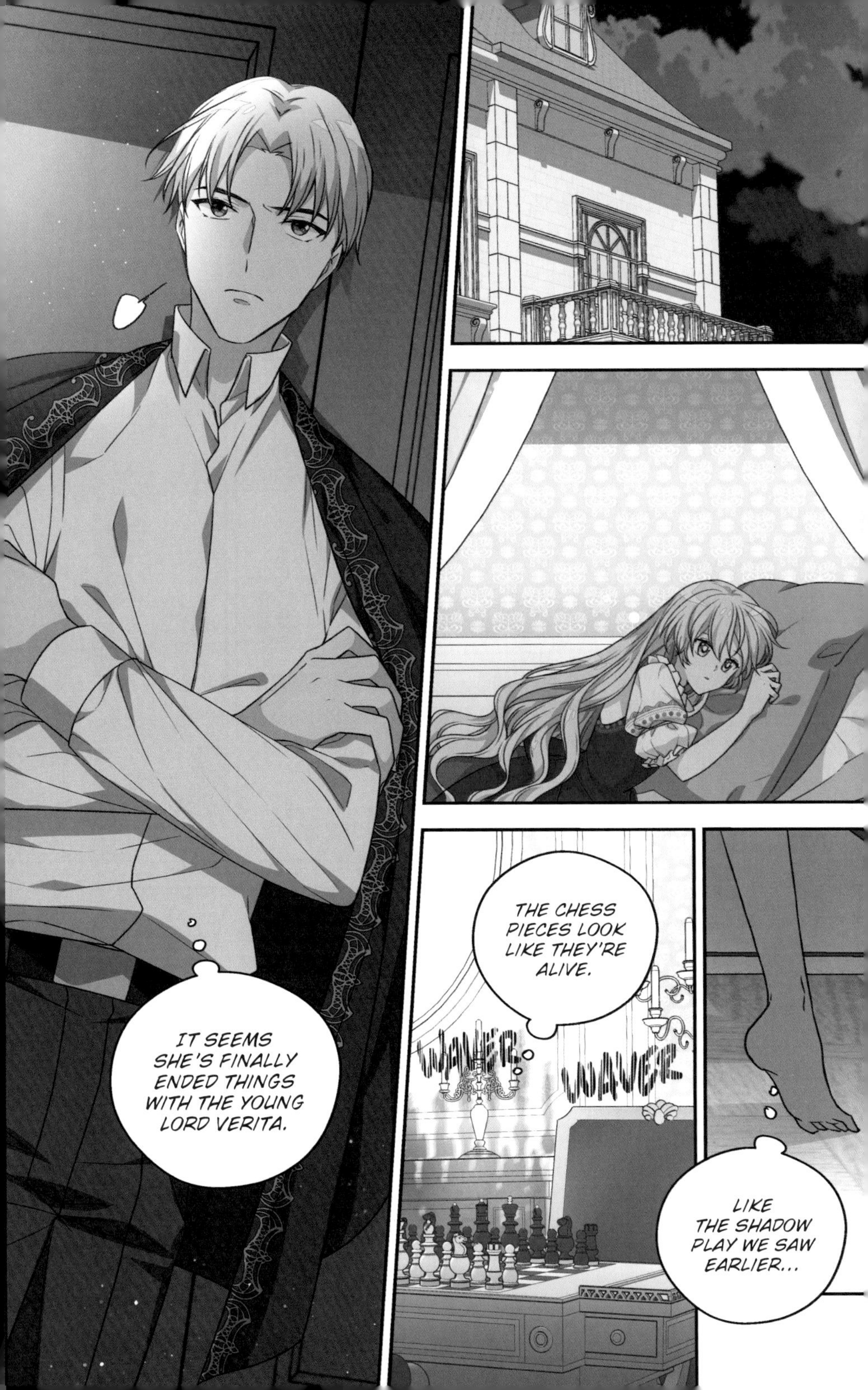
IT SEEMS SHE'S FINALLY ENDED THINGS WITH THE YOUNG LORD VERITA.
THE CHESS PIECES LOOK LIKE THEY'RE ALIVE.
WAVER
WAVER
LIKE THE SHADOW PLAY WE SAW EARLIER...

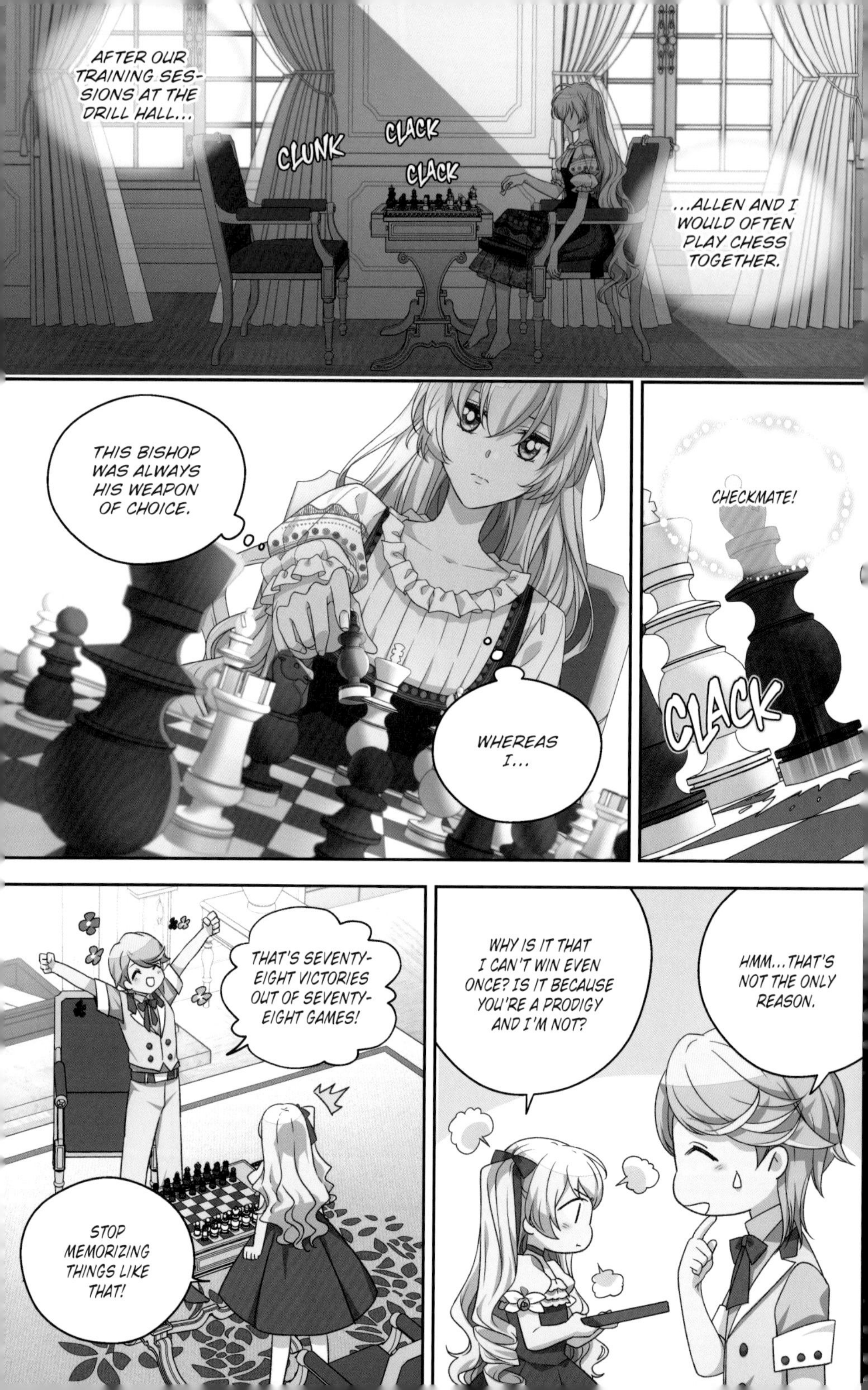
AFTER OUR TRAINING SESSIONS AT THE DRILL HALL...
CLUNK
CLACK
CLACK
...ALLEN AND I WOULD OFTEN PLAY CHESS TOGETHER.
THIS BISHOP WAS ALWAYS HIS WEAPON OF CHOICE.
WHEREAS I...
CHECKMATE!
CLACK
THAT'S SEVENTY-EIGHT VICTORIES OUT OF SEVENTY-EIGHT GAMES!
STOP MEMORIZING THINGS LIKE THAT!
WHY IS IT THAT I CAN'T WIN EVEN ONCE? IS IT BECAUSE YOU'RE A PRODIGY AND I'M NOT?
HMM...THAT'S NOT THE ONLY REASON.

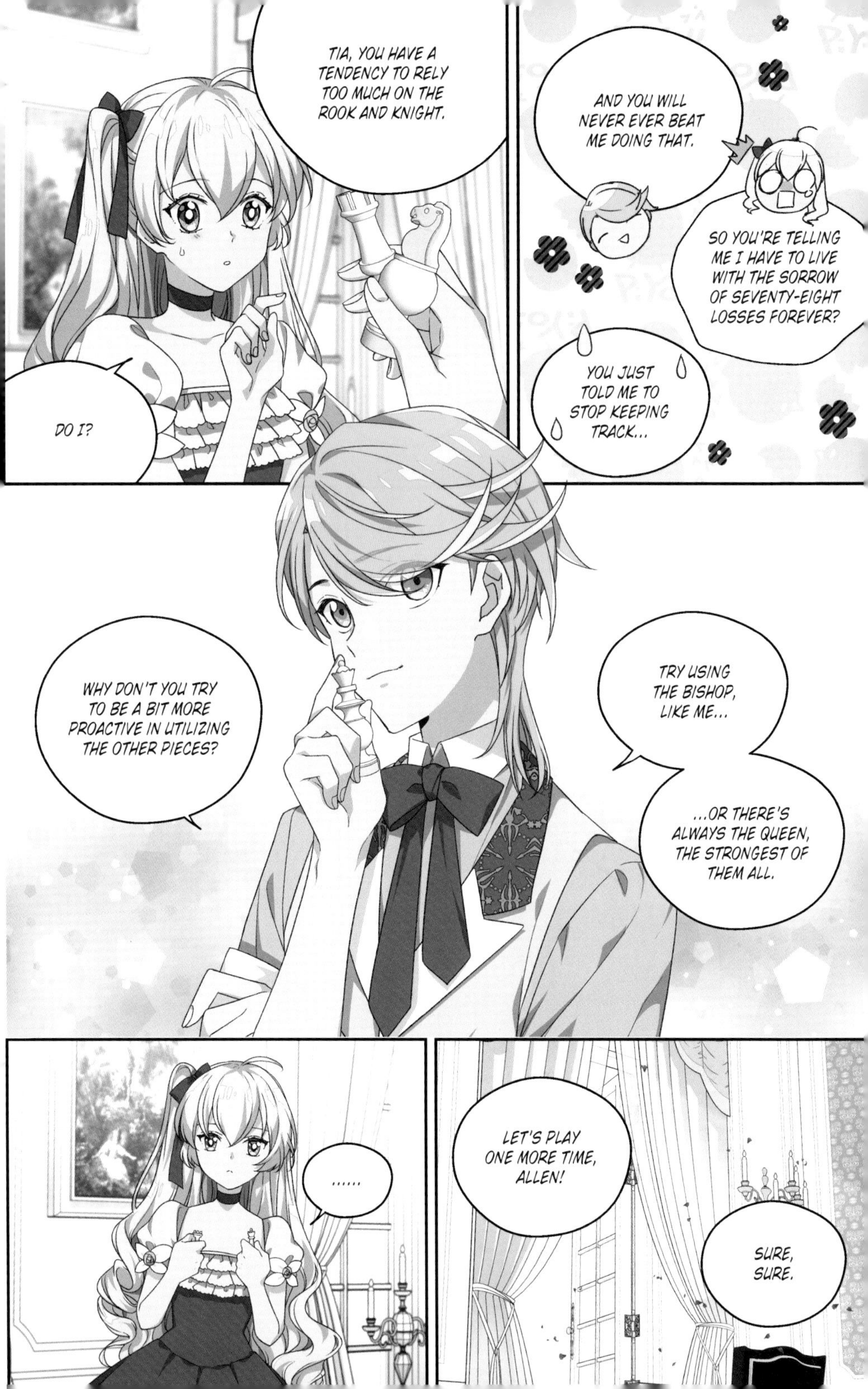
TIA, YOU HAVE A TENDENCY TO RELY TOO MUCH ON THE ROOK AND KNIGHT.
DO I?
AND YOU WILL NEVER EVER BEAT ME DOING THAT.
SO YOU'RE TELLING ME I HAVE TO LIVE WITH THE SORROW OF SEVENTY-EIGHT LOSSES FOREVER?
YOU JUST TOLD ME TO STOP KEEPING TRACK...
WHY DON'T YOU TRY TO BE A BIT MORE PROACTIVE IN UTILIZING THE OTHER PIECES?
TRY USING THE BISHOP, LIKE ME...
...OR THERE'S ALWAYS THE QUEEN, THE STRONGEST OF THEM ALL.
......
LET'S PLAY ONE MORE TIME, ALLEN!
SURE, SURE.

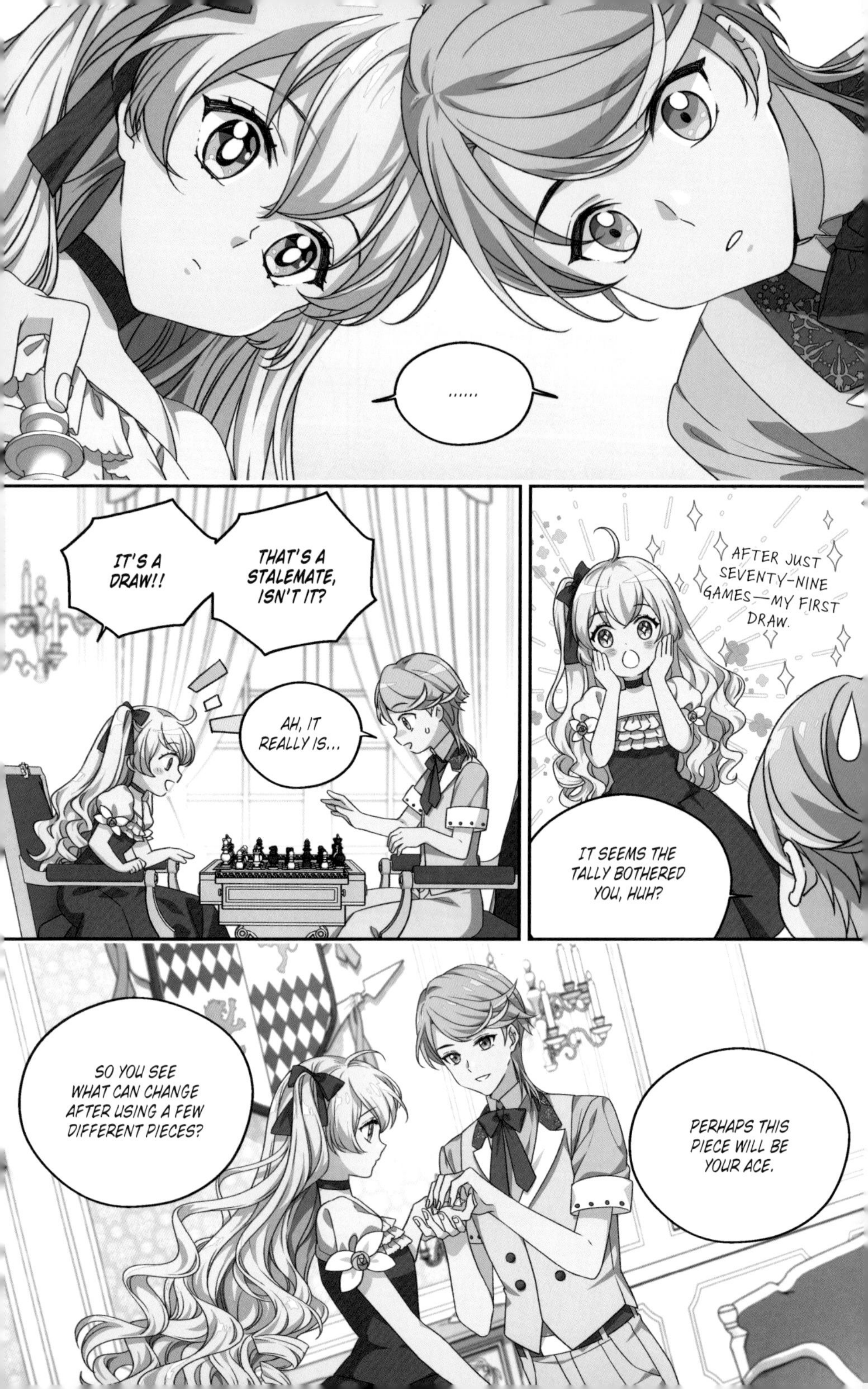
......
IT'S A DRAW!!
THAT'S A STALEMATE, ISN'T IT?
AH, IT REALLY IS...
AFTER JUST SEVENTY-NINE GAMES—MY FIRST DRAW.
IT SEEMS THE TALLY BOTHERED YOU, HUH?
SO YOU SEE WHAT CAN CHANGE AFTER USING A FEW DIFFERENT PIECES?
PERHAPS THIS PIECE WILL BE YOUR ACE.

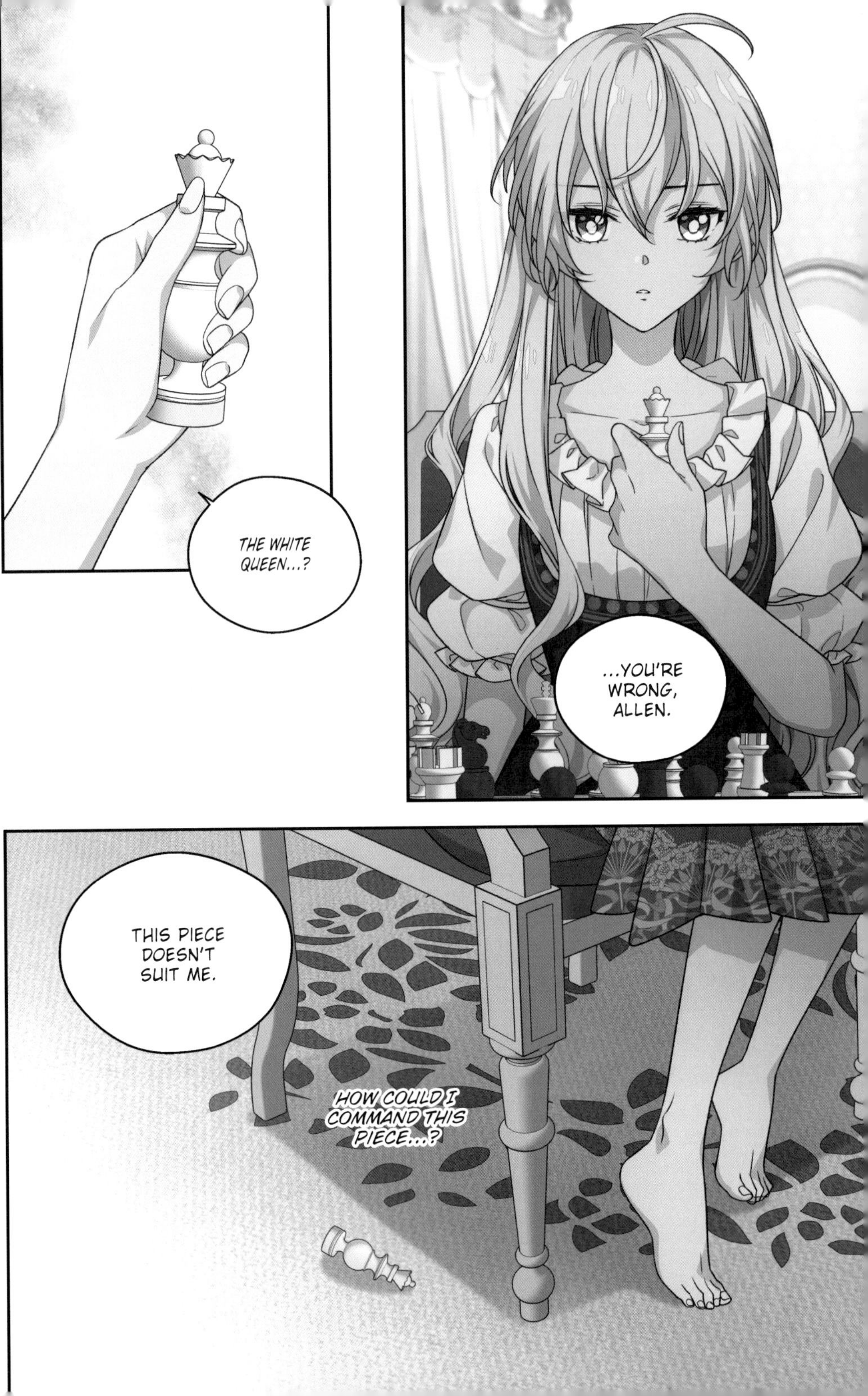
THE WHITE QUEEN...?
...YOU'RE WRONG, ALLEN.
THIS PIECE DOESN'T SUIT ME.
HOW COULD I COMMAND THIS PIECE...?

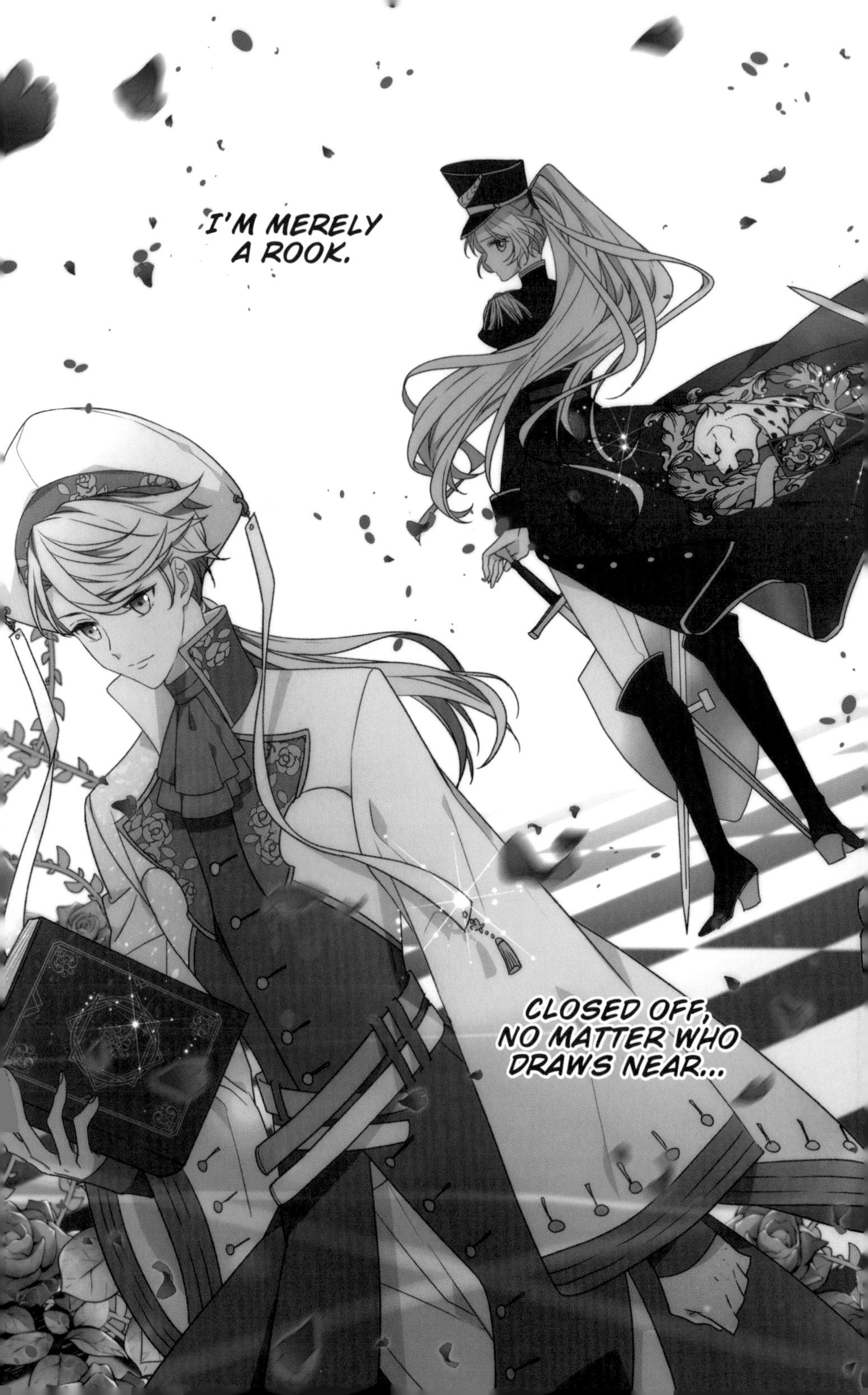
I'M MERELY A ROOK.
CLOSED OFF, NO MATTER WHO DRAWS NEAR...

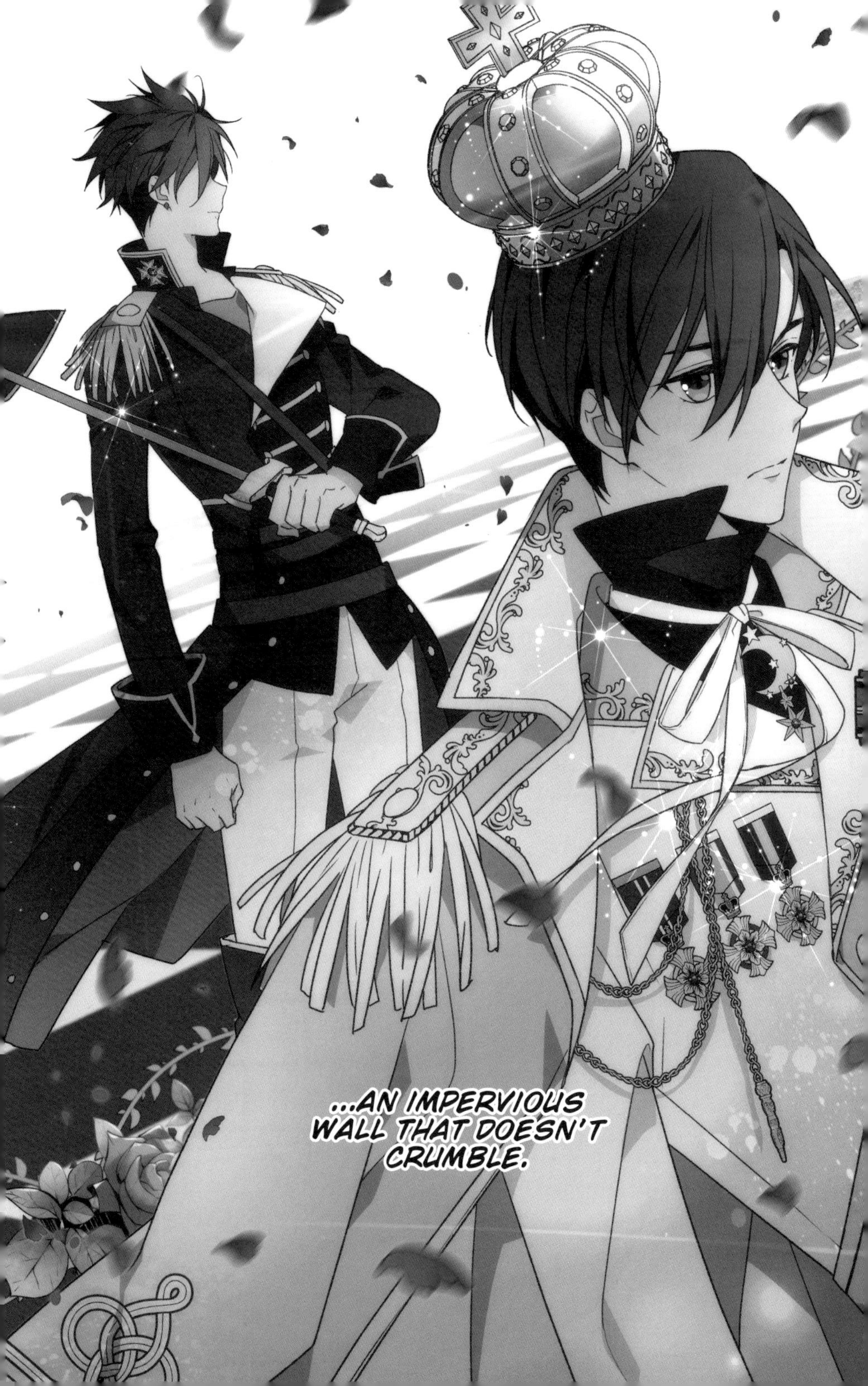
...AN IMPERVIOUS WALL THAT DOESN'T CRUMBLE.

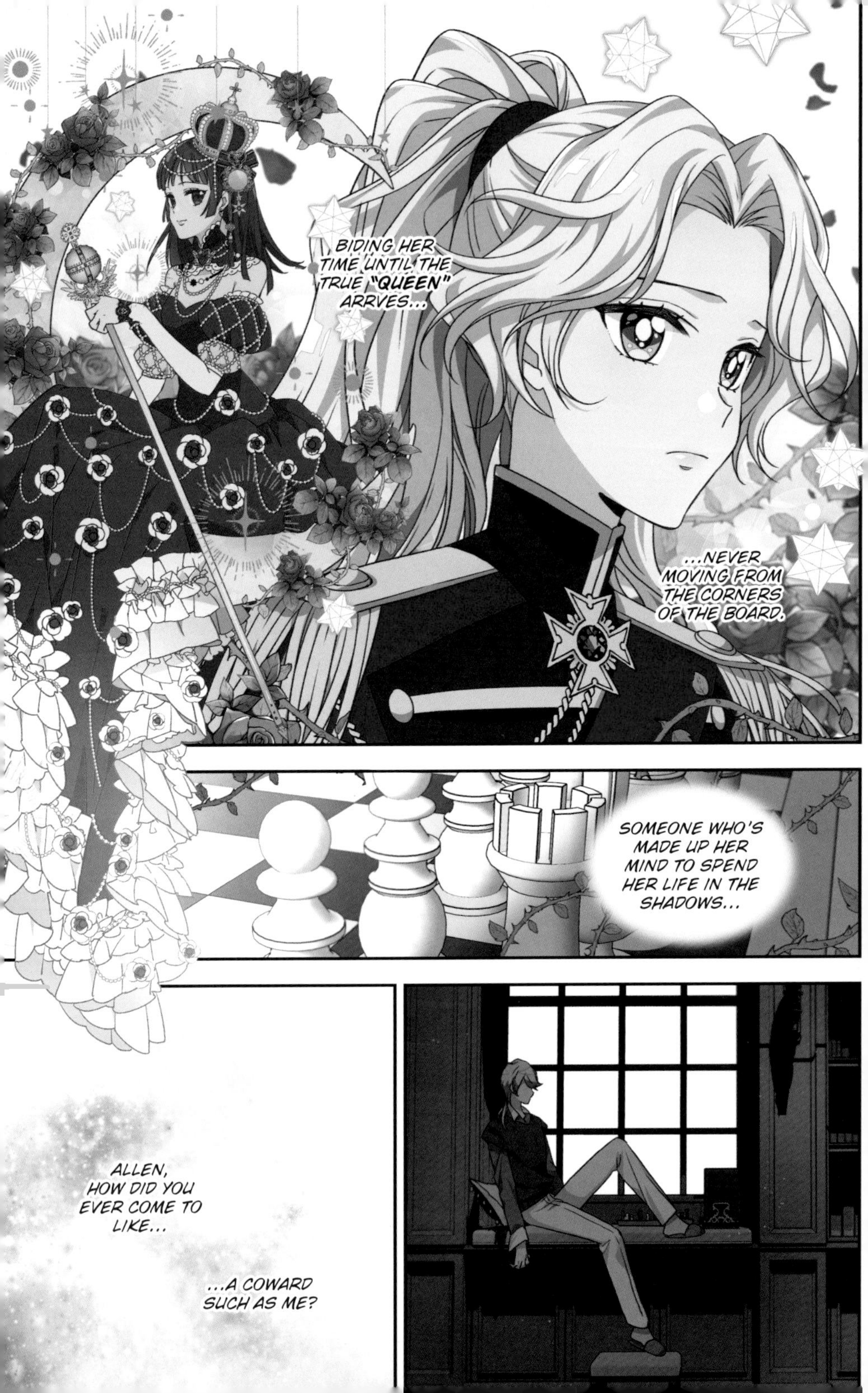
BIDING HER TIME UNTIL THE TRUE "QUEEN" ARRVES...
...NEVER MOVING FROM THE CORNERS OF THE BOARD.
SOMEONE WHO'S MADE UP HER MIND TO SPEND HER LIFE IN THE SHADOWS...
ALLEN, HOW DID YOU EVER COME TO LIKE...
...A COWARD SUCH AS ME?

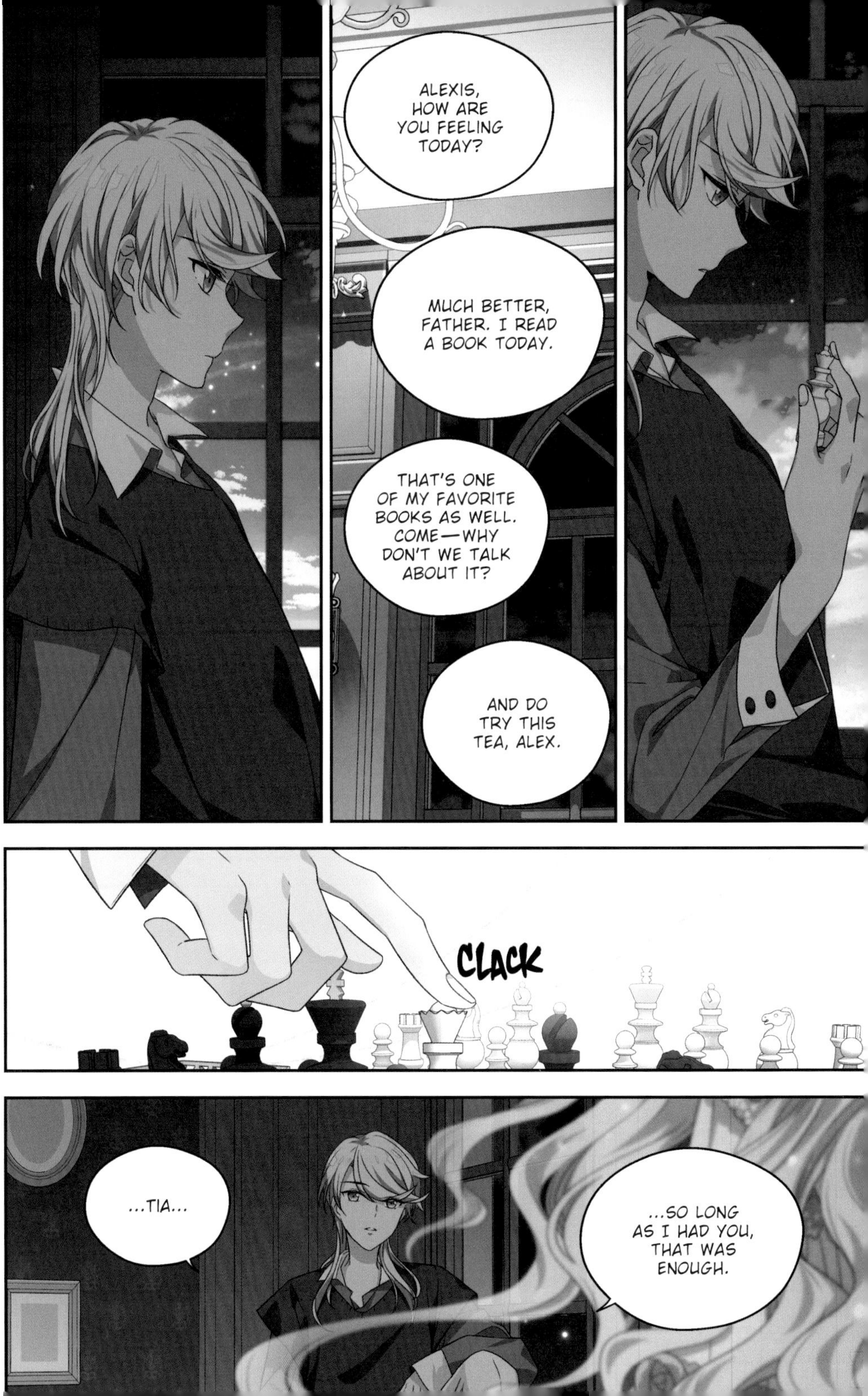
ALEXIS, HOW ARE YOU FEELING TODAY?
MUCH BETTER, FATHER. I READ A BOOK TODAY.
THAT'S ONE OF MY FAVORITE BOOKS AS WELL. COME—WHY DON'T WE TALK ABOUT IT?
AND DO TRY THIS TEA, ALEX.
CLACK
...TIA...
...SO LONG AS I HAD YOU, THAT WAS ENOUGH.

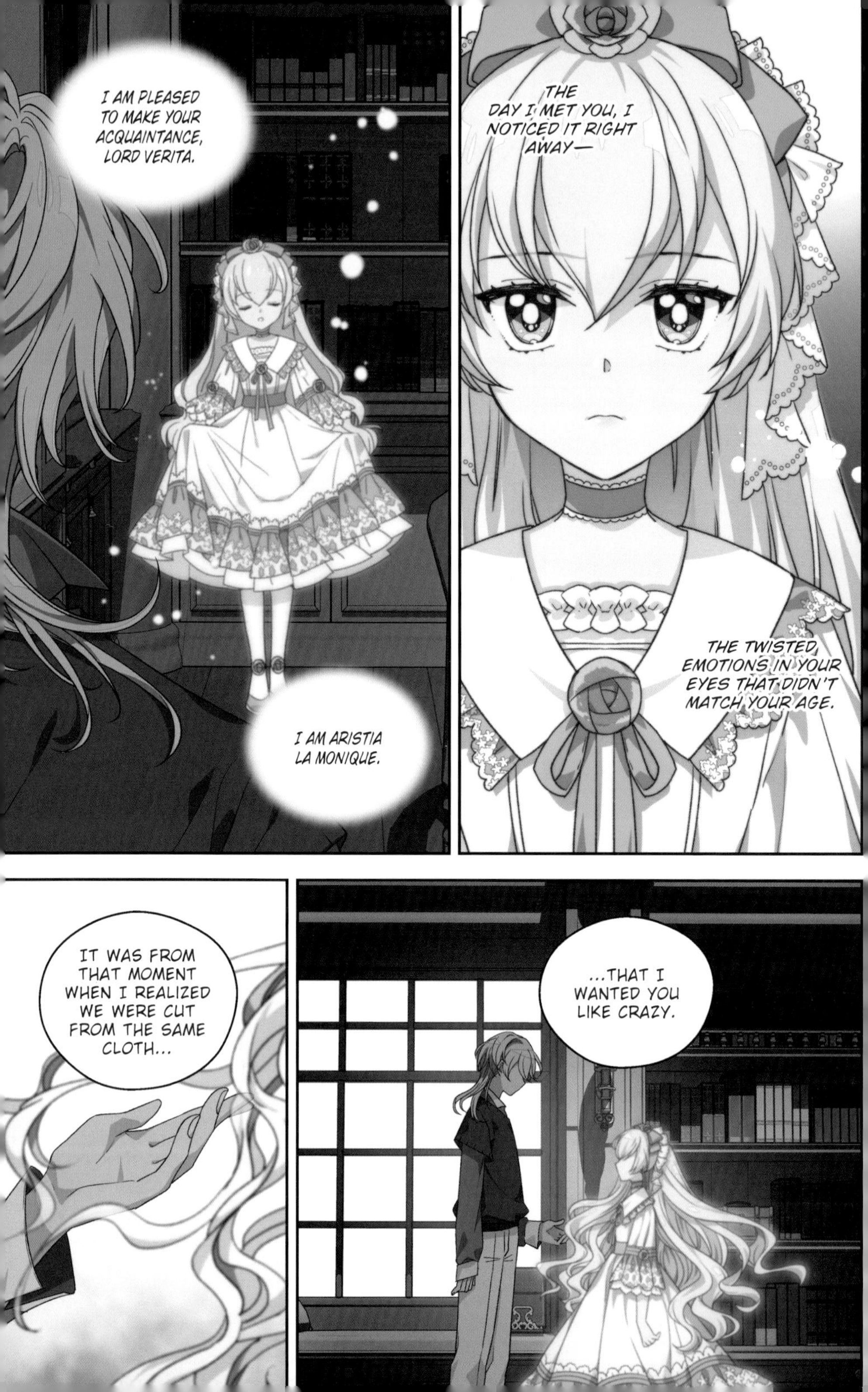
I AM PLEASED TO MAKE YOUR ACQUAINTANCE, LORD VERITA.
I AM ARISTIA LA MONIQUE.
THE DAY I MET YOU, I NOTICED IT RIGHT AWAY—
THE TWISTED EMOTIONS IN YOUR EYES THAT DIDN'T MATCH YOUR AGE.
IT WAS FROM THAT MOMENT WHEN I REALIZED WE WERE CUT FROM THE SAME CLOTH...
...THAT I WANTED YOU LIKE CRAZY.

The Abandoned Empress

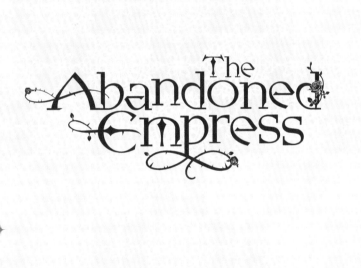

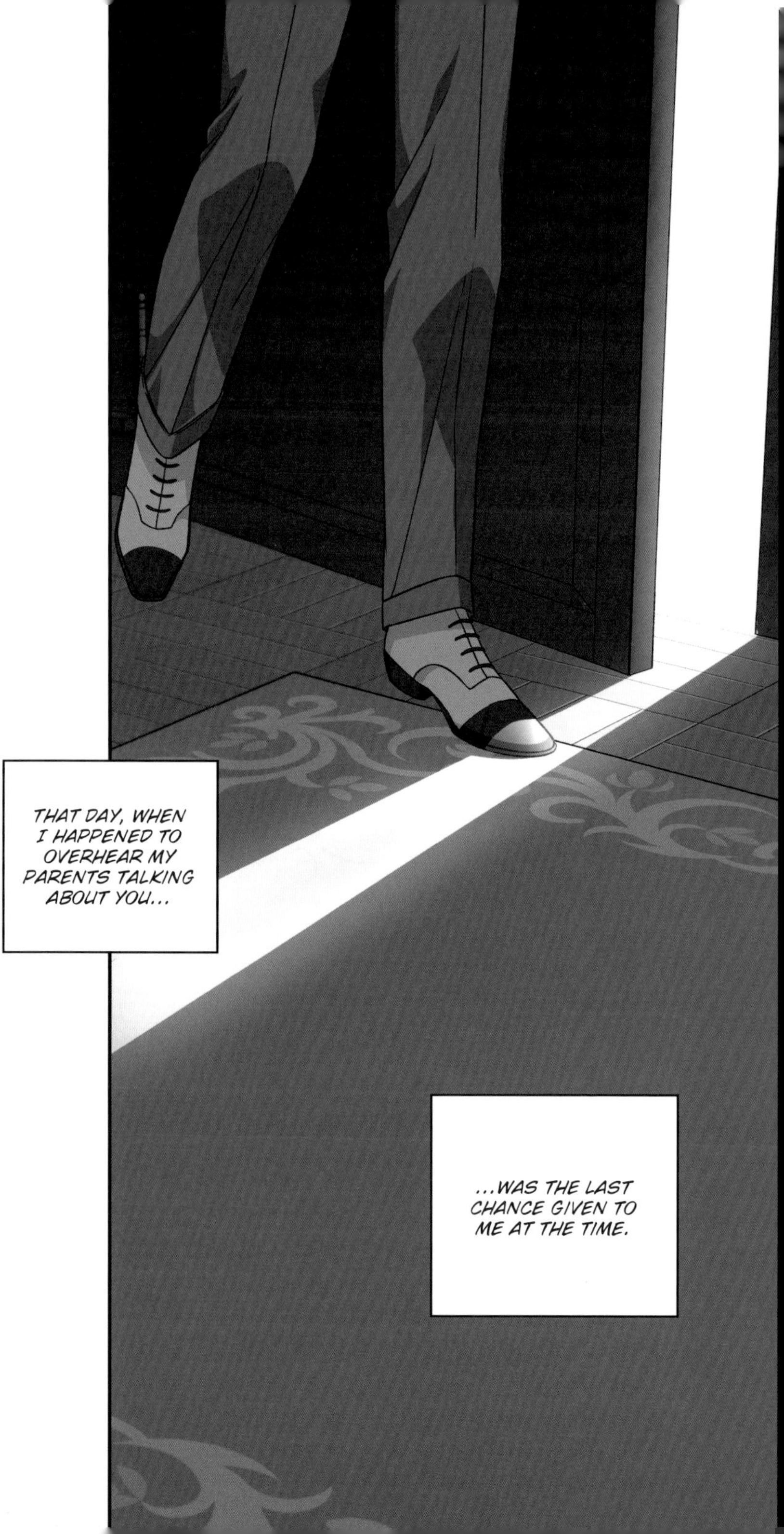
THAT DAY, WHEN I HAPPENED TO OVERHEAR MY PARENTS TALKING ABOUT YOU...
...WAS THE LAST CHANCE GIVEN TO ME AT THE TIME.

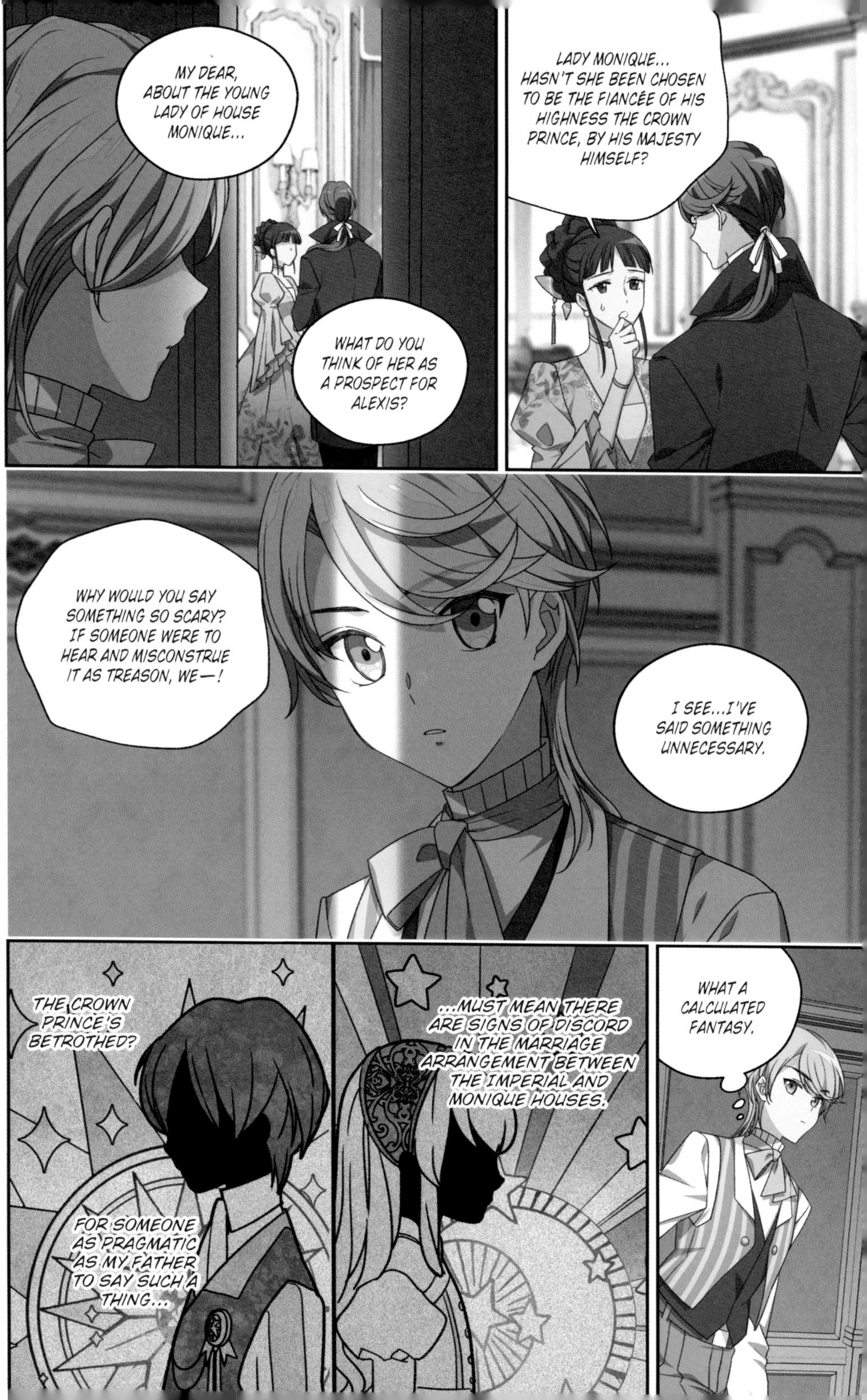
MY DEAR, ABOUT THE YOUNG LADY OF HOUSE MONIQUE...
WHAT DO YOU THINK OF HER AS A PROSPECT FOR ALEXIS?
LADY MONIQUE... HASN'T SHE BEEN CHOSEN TO BE THE FIANCÉE OF HIS HIGHNESS THE CROWN PRINCE, BY HIS MAJESTY HIMSELF?
WHY WOULD YOU SAY SOMETHING SO SCARY? IF SOMEONE WERE TO HEAR AND MISCONSTRUE IT AS TREASON, WE—!
I SEE...I'VE SAID SOMETHING UNNECESSARY.
THE CROWN PRINCE'S BETROTHED?
FOR SOMEONE AS PRAGMATIC AS MY FATHER TO SAY SUCH A THING...
...MUST MEAN THERE ARE SIGNS OF DISCORD IN THE MARRIAGE ARRANGEMENT BETWEEN THE IMPERIAL AND MONIQUE HOUSES.
WHAT A CALCULATED FANTASY.

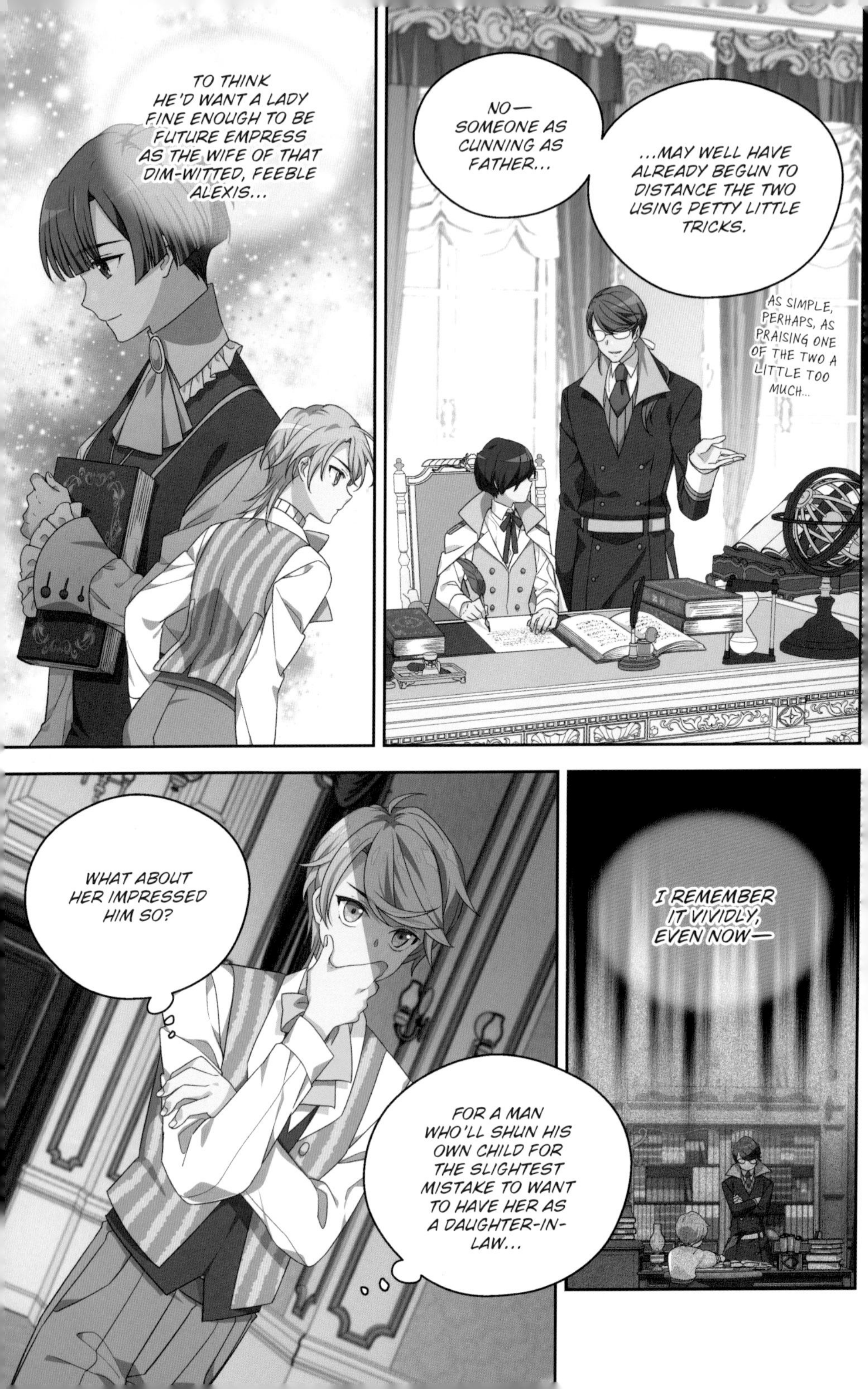
TO THINK HE'D WANT A LADY FINE ENOUGH TO BE FUTURE EMPRESS AS THE WIFE OF THAT DIM-WITTED, FEEBLE ALEXIS...
NO—SOMEONE AS CUNNING AS FATHER...
...MAY WELL HAVE ALREADY BEGUN TO DISTANCE THE TWO USING PETTY LITTLE TRICKS.
AS SIMPLE, PERHAPS, AS PRAISING ONE OF THE TWO A LITTLE TOO MUCH...
WHAT ABOUT HER IMPRESSED HIM SO?
FOR A MAN WHO'LL SHUN HIS OWN CHILD FOR THE SLIGHTEST MISTAKE TO WANT TO HAVE HER AS A DAUGHTER-IN-LAW...
I REMEMBER IT VIVIDLY, EVEN NOW—

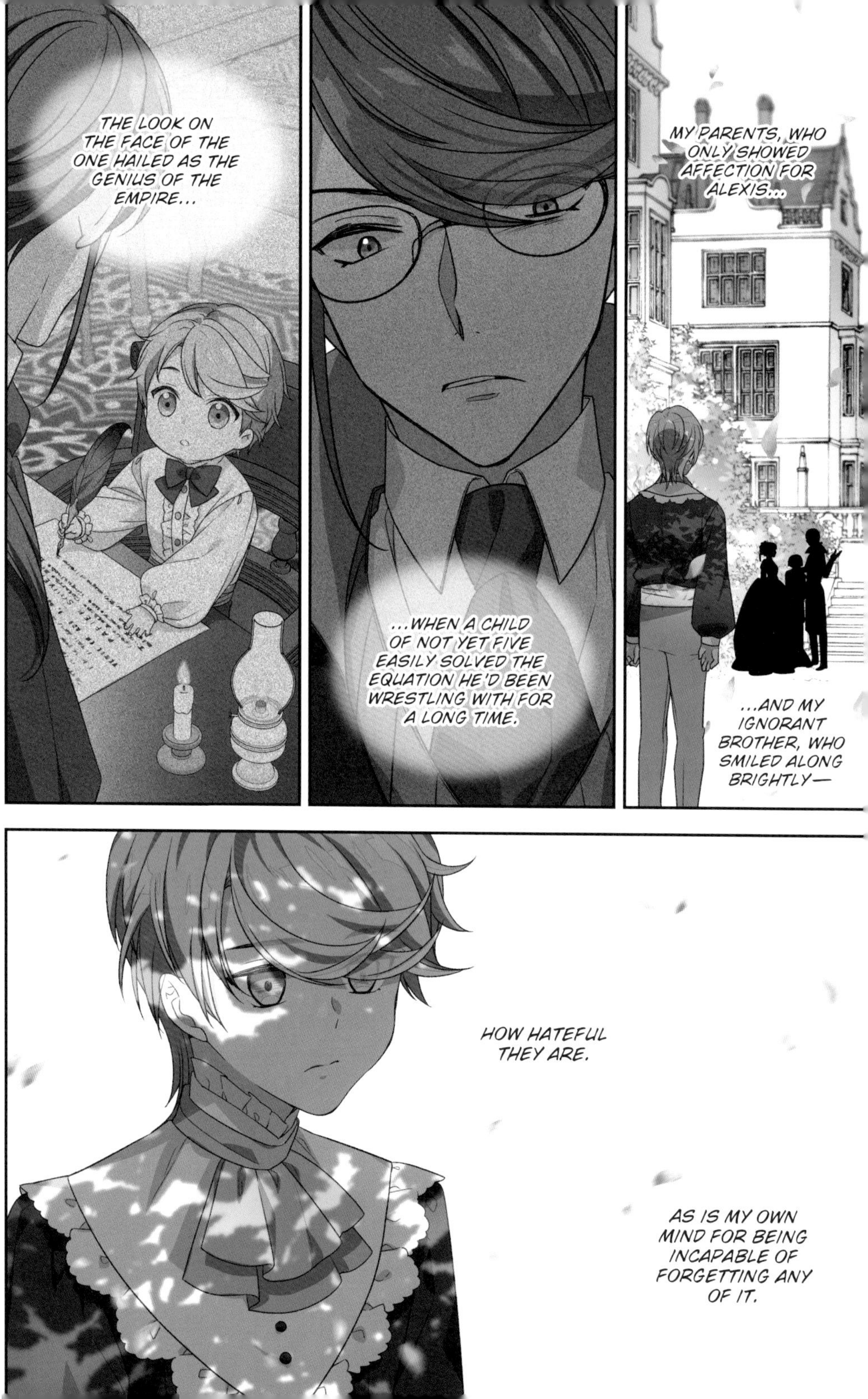
THE LOOK ON THE FACE OF THE ONE HAILED AS THE GENIUS OF THE EMPIRE...
...WHEN A CHILD OF NOT YET FIVE EASILY SOLVED THE EQUATION HE'D BEEN WRESTLING WITH FOR A LONG TIME.
MY PARENTS, WHO ONLY SHOWED AFFECTION FOR ALEXIS...
...AND MY IGNORANT BROTHER, WHO SMILED ALONG BRIGHTLY—
HOW HATEFUL THEY ARE.
AS IS MY OWN MIND FOR BEING INCAPABLE OF FORGETTING ANY OF IT.

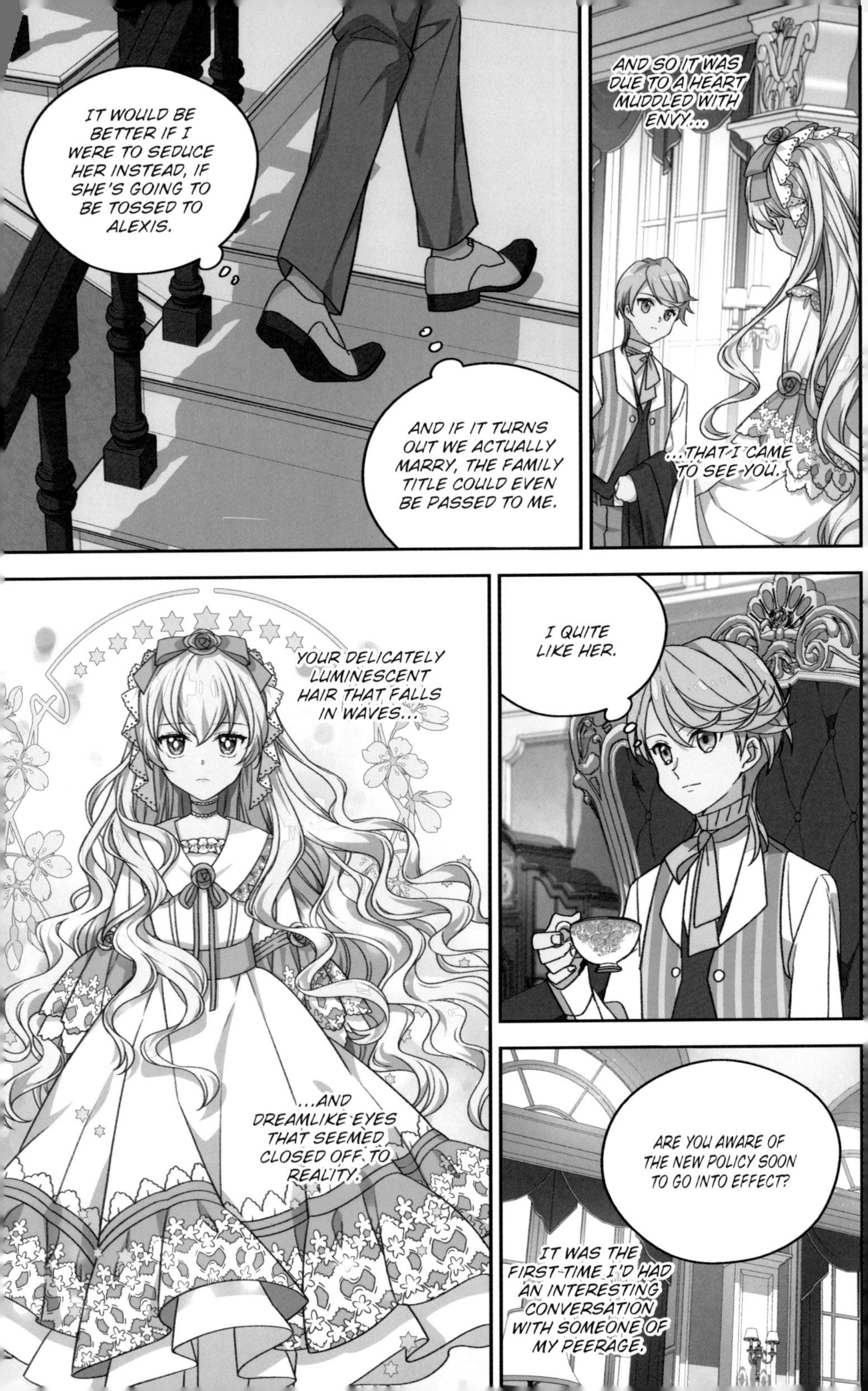
IT WOULD BE BETTER IF I WERE TO SEDUCE HER INSTEAD, IF SHE'S GOING TO BE TOSSED TO ALEXIS.
AND IF IT TURNS OUT WE ACTUALLY MARRY, THE FAMILY TITLE COULD EVEN BE PASSED TO ME.
AND SO IT WAS DUE TO A HEART MUDDLED WITH ENVY...
...THAT I CAME TO SEE YOU.
YOUR DELICATELY LUMINESCENT HAIR THAT FALLS IN WAVES...
...AND DREAMLIKE EYES THAT SEEMED CLOSED OFF TO REALITY.
I QUITE LIKE HER.
ARE YOU AWARE OF THE NEW POLICY SOON TO GO INTO EFFECT?
IT WAS THE FIRST TIME I'D HAD AN INTERESTING CONVERSATION WITH SOMEONE OF MY PEERAGE.

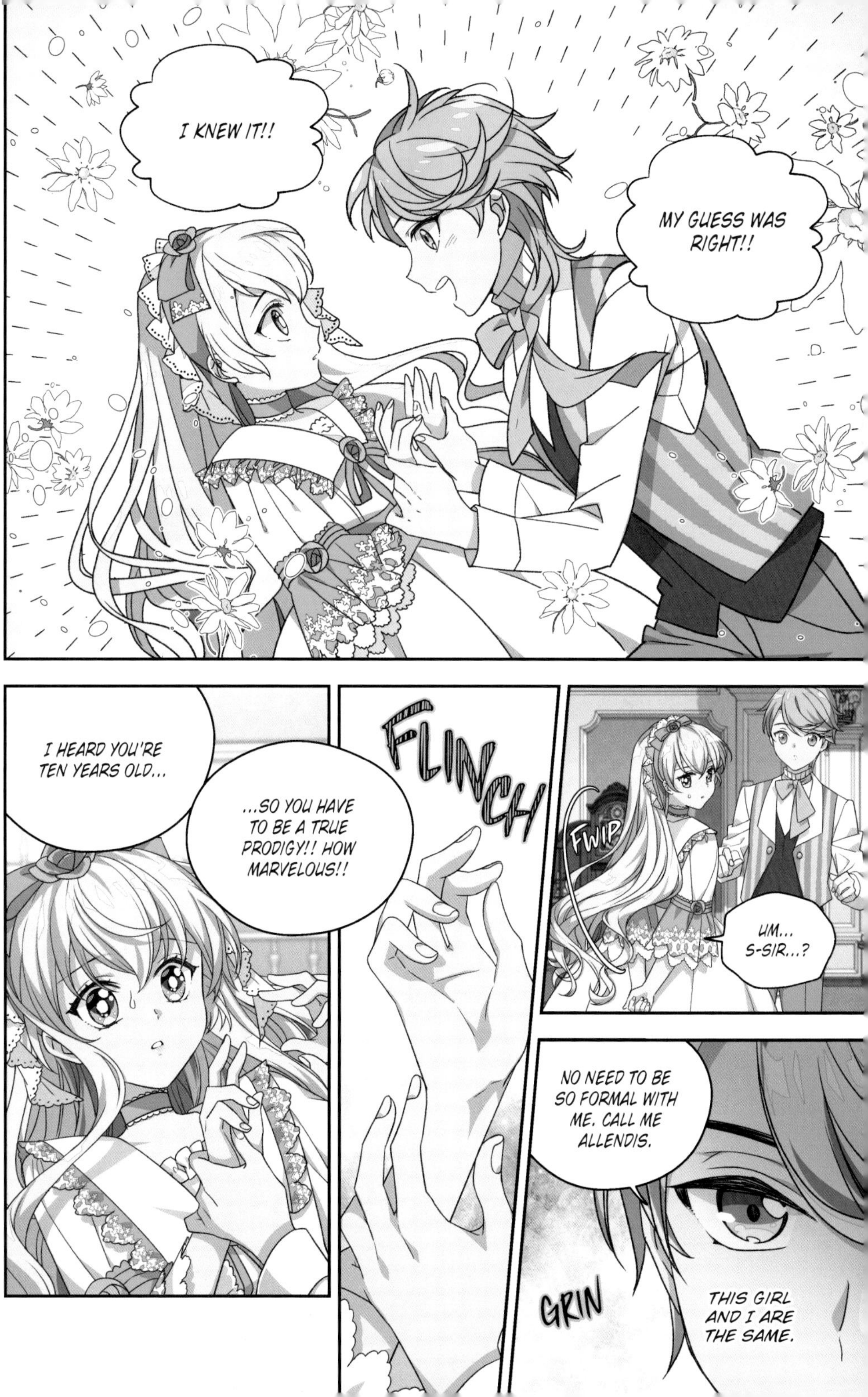
I KNEW IT!!
MY GUESS WAS RIGHT!!
I HEARD YOU'RE TEN YEARS OLD...
...SO YOU HAVE TO BE A TRUE PRODIGY!! HOW MARVELOUS!!
FLINCH
FWIP
UM... S-SIR...?
NO NEED TO BE SO FORMAL WITH ME. CALL ME ALLENDIS.
GRIN
THIS GIRL AND I ARE THE SAME.

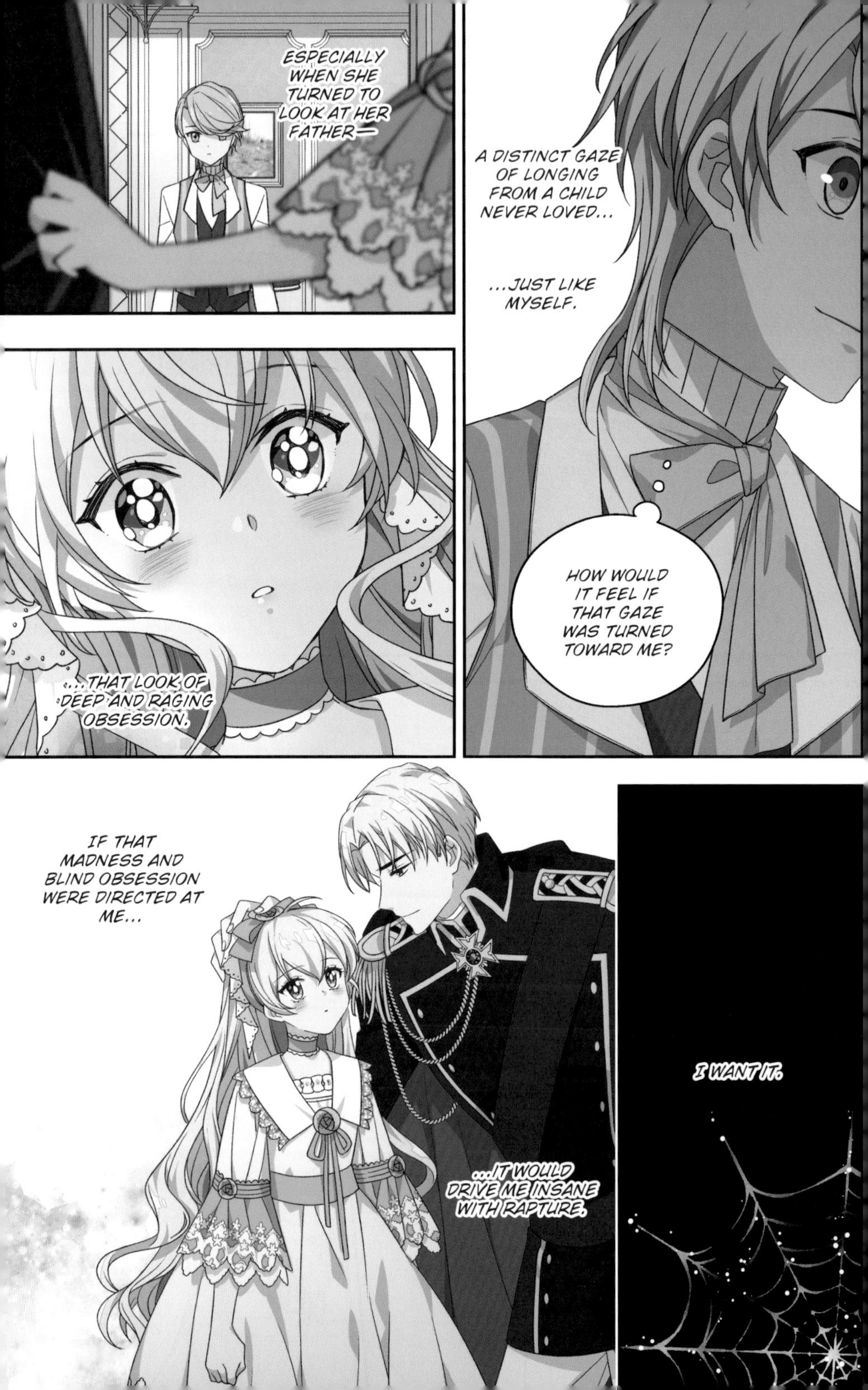
ESPECIALLY WHEN SHE TURNED TO LOOK AT HER FATHER—
A DISTINCT GAZE OF LONGING FROM A CHILD NEVER LOVED...
...JUST LIKE MYSELF.
...THAT LOOK OF DEEP AND RAGING OBSESSION.
HOW WOULD IT FEEL IF THAT GAZE WAS TURNED TOWARD ME?
IF THAT MADNESS AND BLIND OBSESSION WERE DIRECTED AT ME...
...IT WOULD DRIVE ME INSANE WITH RAPTURE.
I WANT IT.

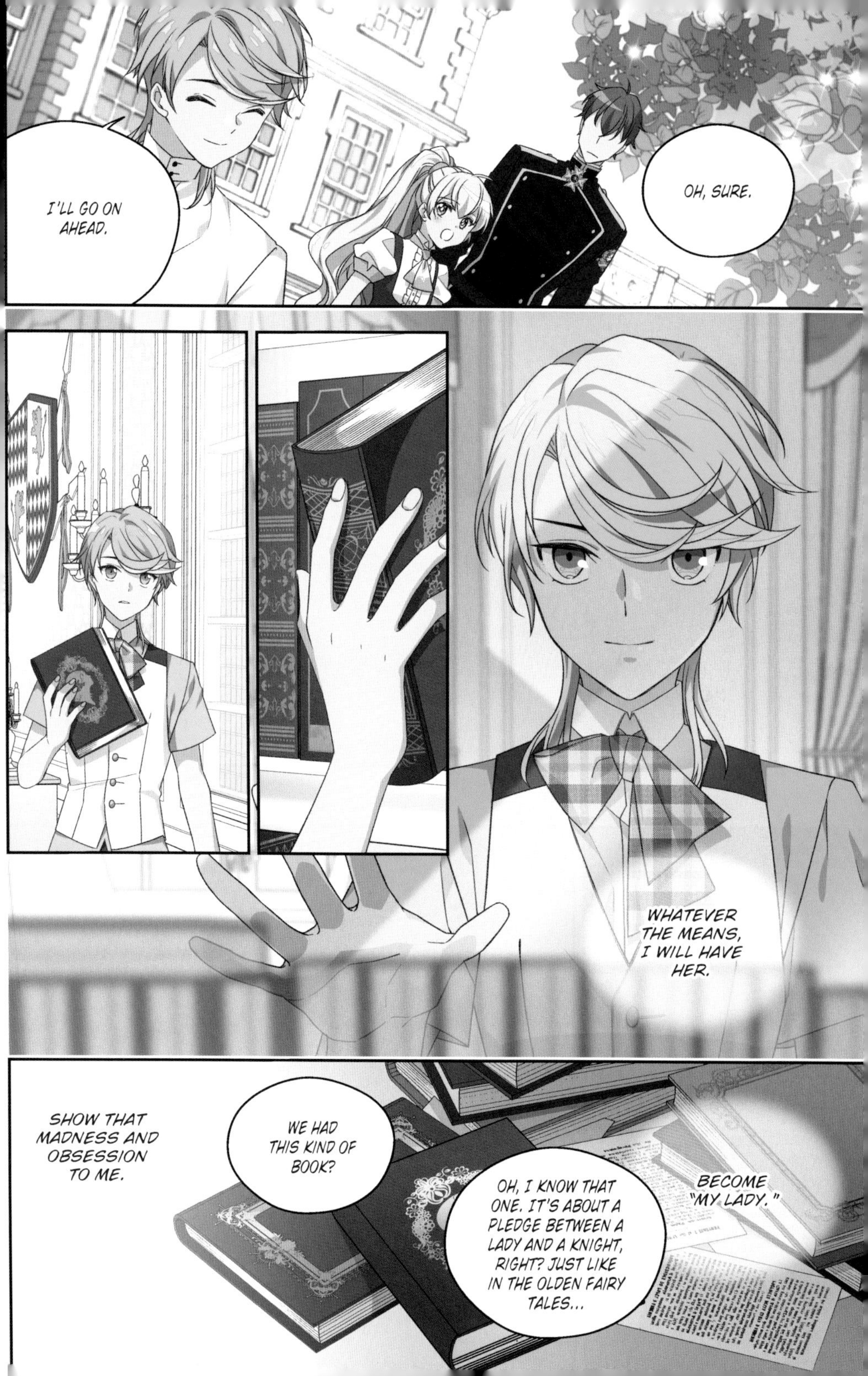
I'LL GO ON AHEAD.
OH, SURE.
WHATEVER THE MEANS, I WILL HAVE HER.
SHOW THAT MADNESS AND OBSESSION TO ME.
WE HAD THIS KIND OF BOOK?
OH, I KNOW THAT ONE. IT'S ABOUT A PLEDGE BETWEEN A LADY AND A KNIGHT, RIGHT? JUST LIKE IN THE OLDEN FAIRY TALES...
BECOME "MY LADY."

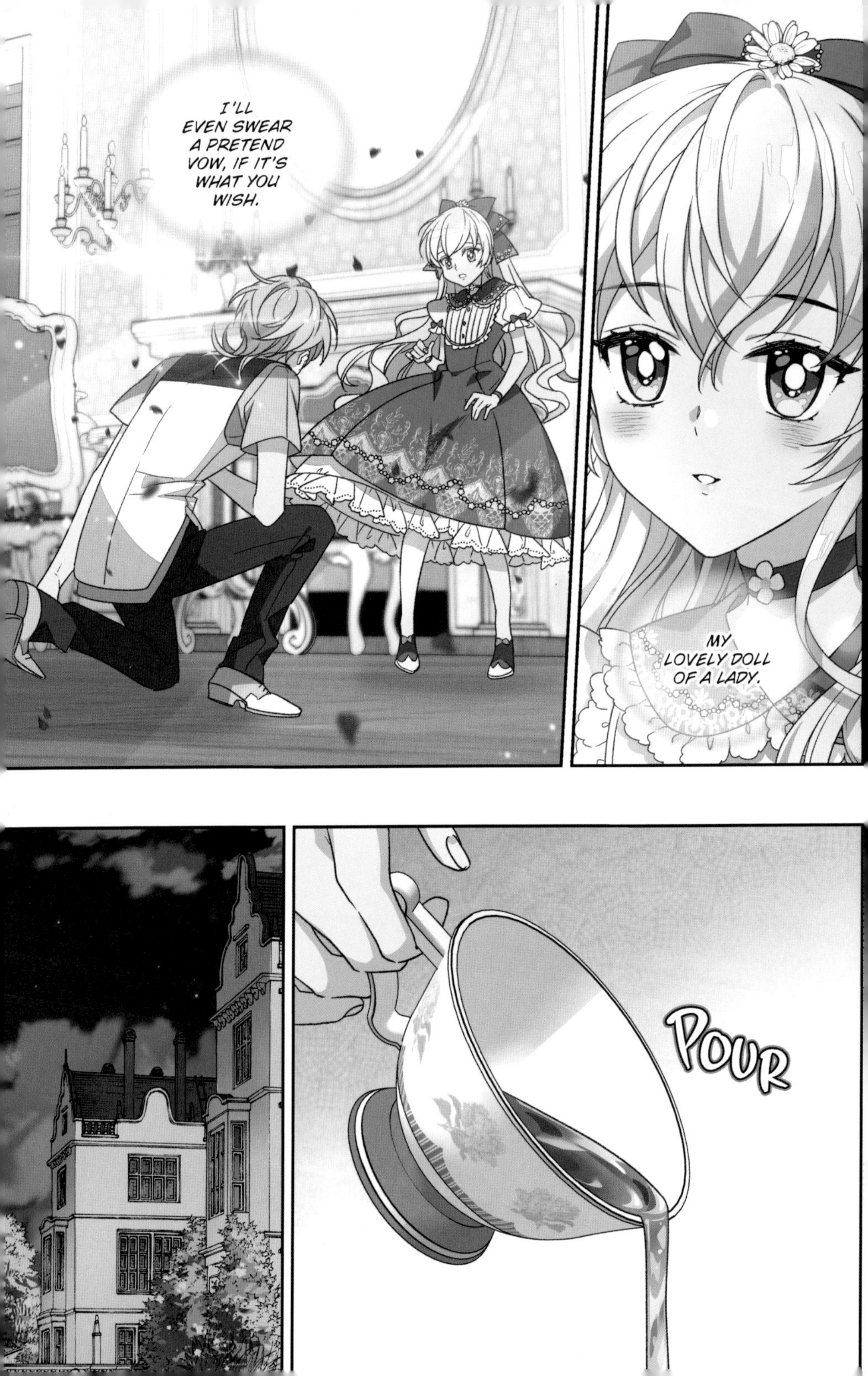
MY LOVELY DOLL OF A LADY.
I'LL EVEN SWEAR A PRETEND VOW, IF IT'S WHAT YOU WISH.
POUR

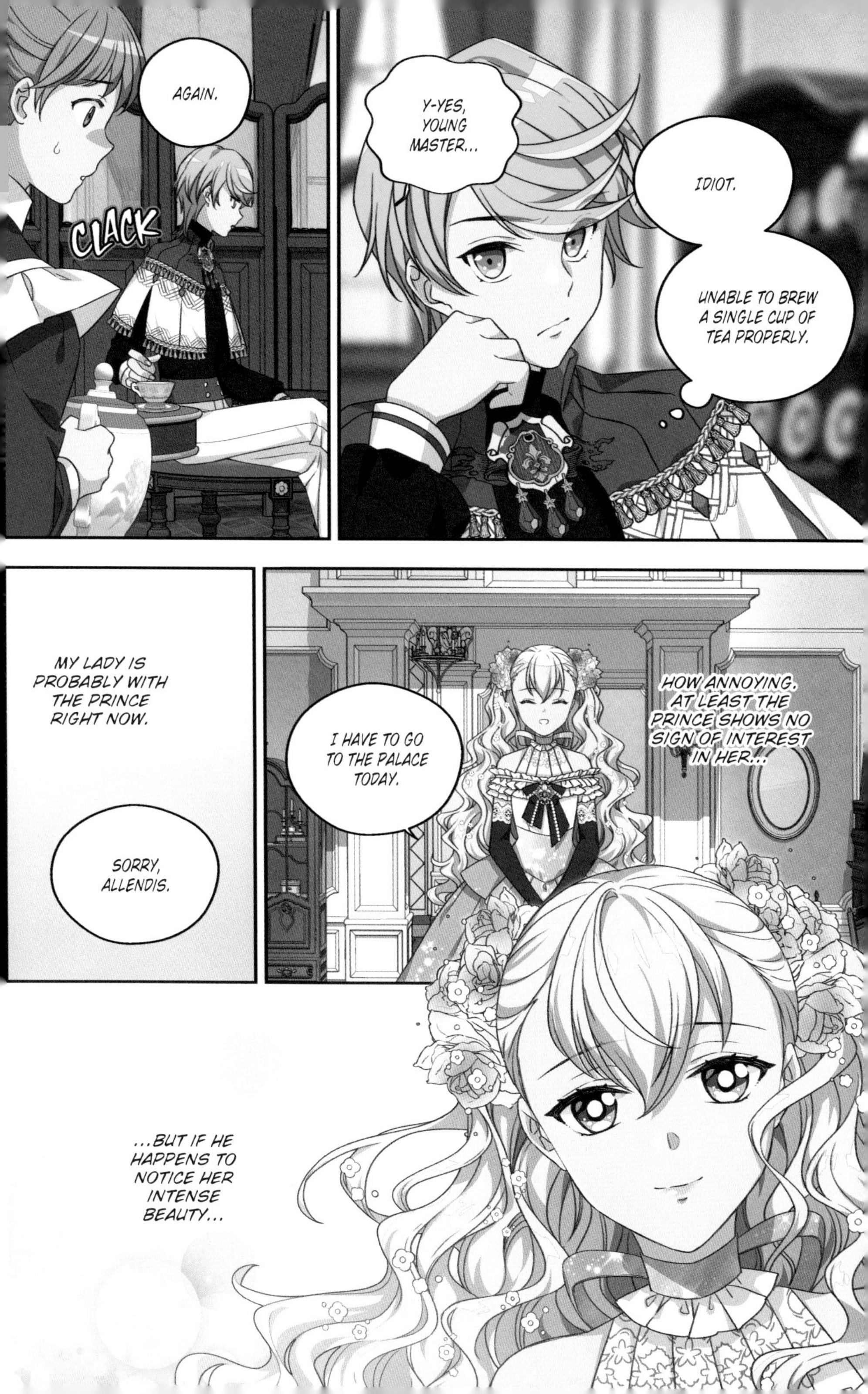
AGAIN.
CLACK
Y-YES, YOUNG MASTER...
IDIOT.
UNABLE TO BREW A SINGLE CUP OF TEA PROPERLY.
MY LADY IS PROBABLY WITH THE PRINCE RIGHT NOW.
I HAVE TO GO TO THE PALACE TODAY.
SORRY, ALLENDIS.
HOW ANNOYING. AT LEAST THE PRINCE SHOWS NO SIGN OF INTEREST IN HER...
...BUT IF HE HAPPENS TO NOTICE HER INTENSE BEAUTY...

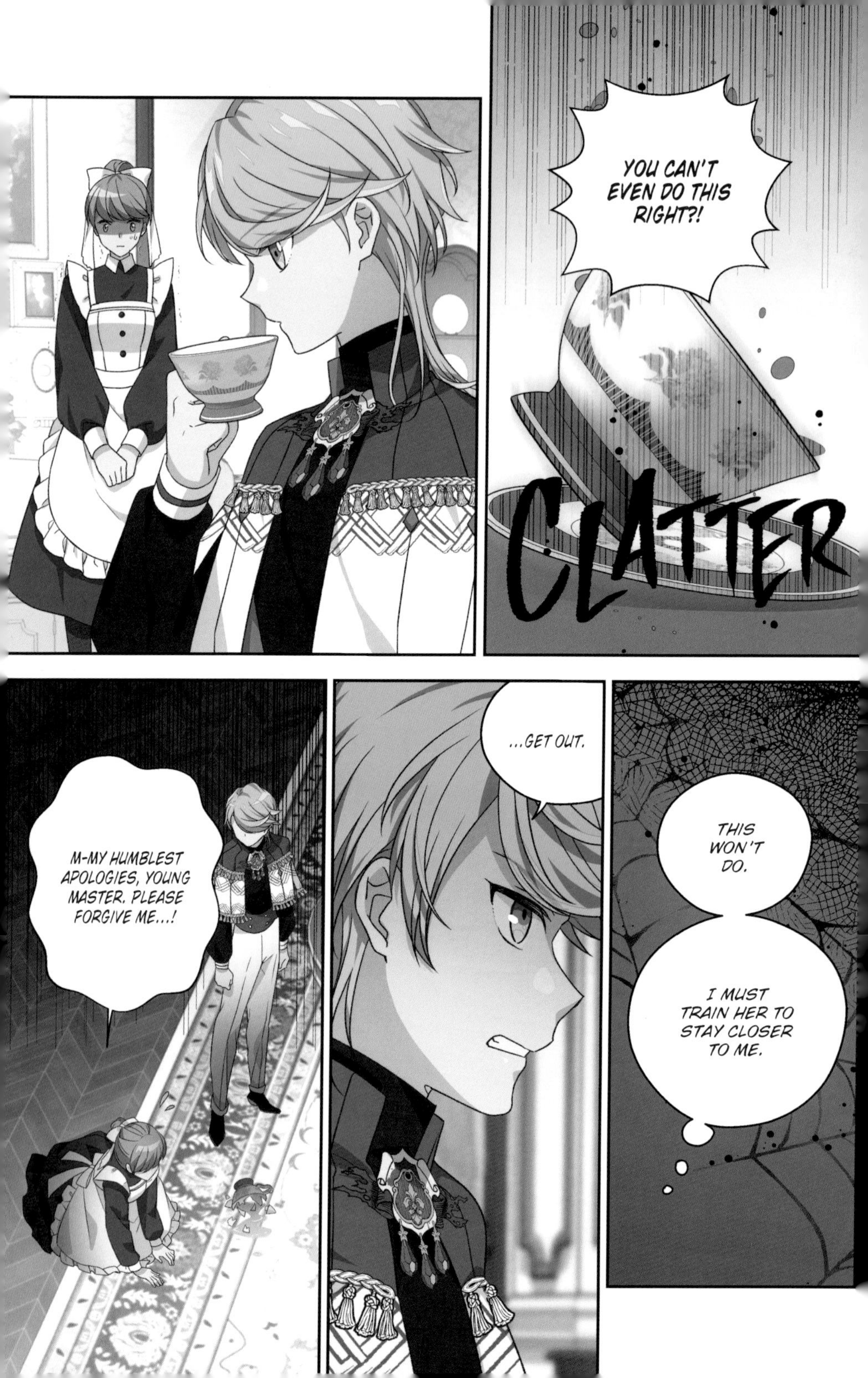
YOU CAN'T EVEN DO THIS RIGHT?!
CLATTER
M-MY HUMBLEST APOLOGIES, YOUNG MASTER. PLEASE FORGIVE ME...!
...GET OUT.
THIS WON'T DO.
I MUST TRAIN HER TO STAY CLOSER TO ME.

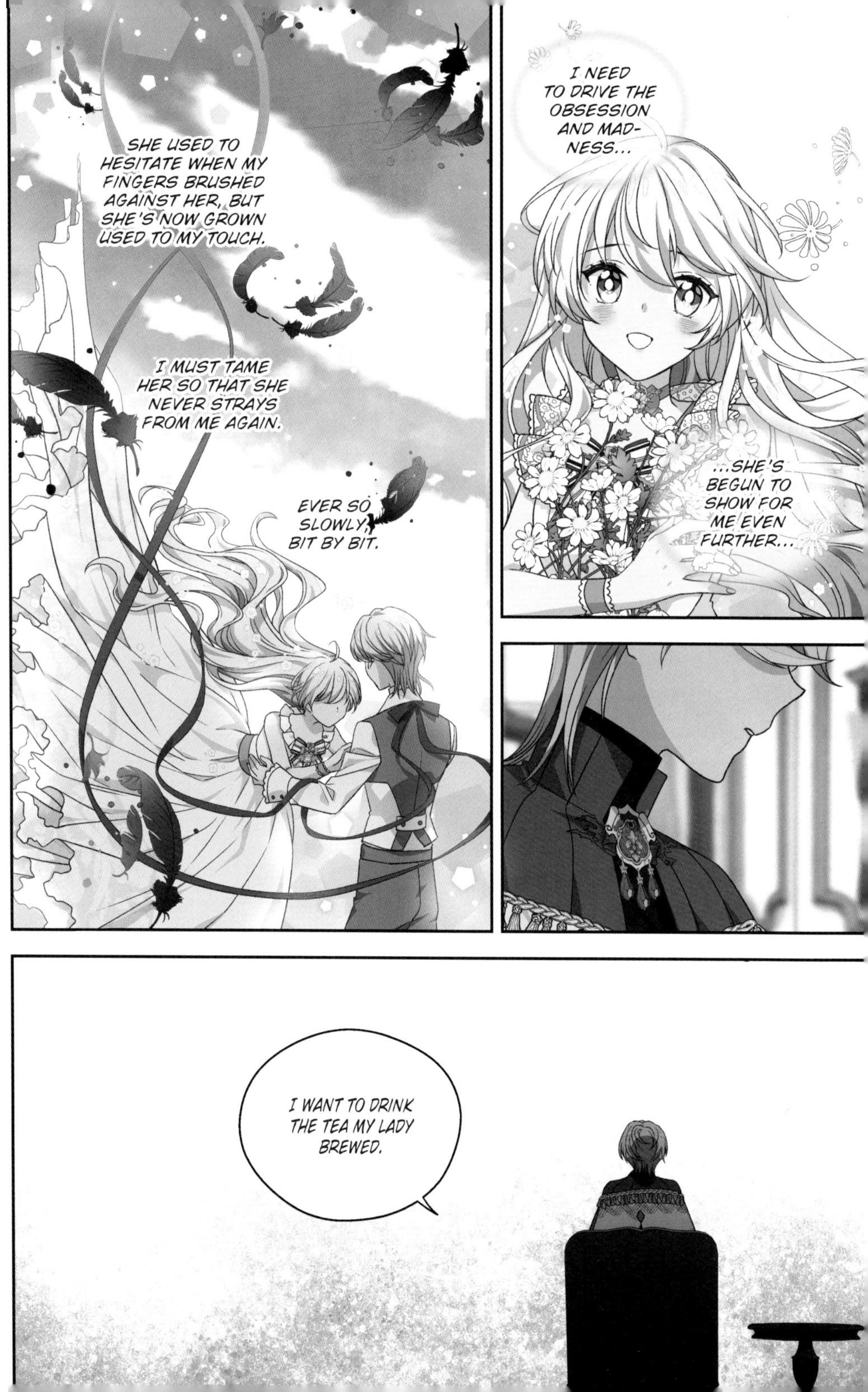
SHE USED TO HESITATE WHEN MY FINGERS BRUSHED AGAINST HER, BUT SHE'S NOW GROWN USED TO MY TOUCH.
I MUST TAME HER SO THAT SHE NEVER STRAYS FROM ME AGAIN.
EVER SO SLOWLY, BIT BY BIT.
I NEED TO DRIVE THE OBSESSION AND MAD-NESS...
...SHE'S BEGUN TO SHOW FOR ME EVEN FURTHER...
I WANT TO DRINK THE TEA MY LADY BREWED.

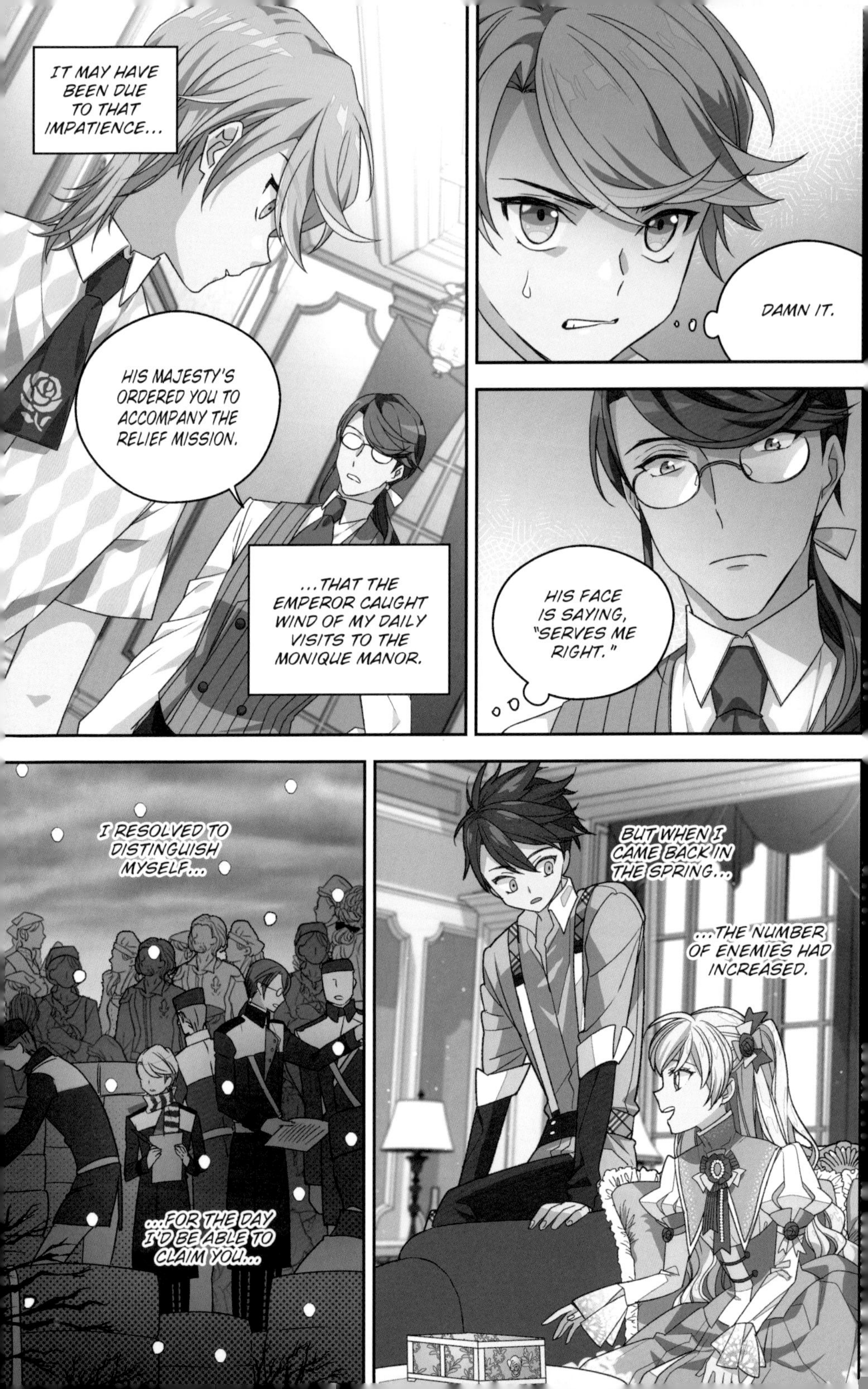
IT MAY HAVE BEEN DUE TO THAT IMPATIENCE...
DAMN IT.
HIS MAJESTY'S ORDERED YOU TO ACCOMPANY THE RELIEF MISSION.
...THAT THE EMPEROR CAUGHT WIND OF MY DAILY VISITS TO THE MONIQUE MANOR.
HIS FACE IS SAYING, "SERVES ME RIGHT."
I RESOLVED TO DISTINGUISH MYSELF...
...FOR THE DAY I'D BE ABLE TO CLAIM YOU...
BUT WHEN I CAME BACK IN THE SPRING...
...THE NUMBER OF ENEMIES HAD INCREASED.

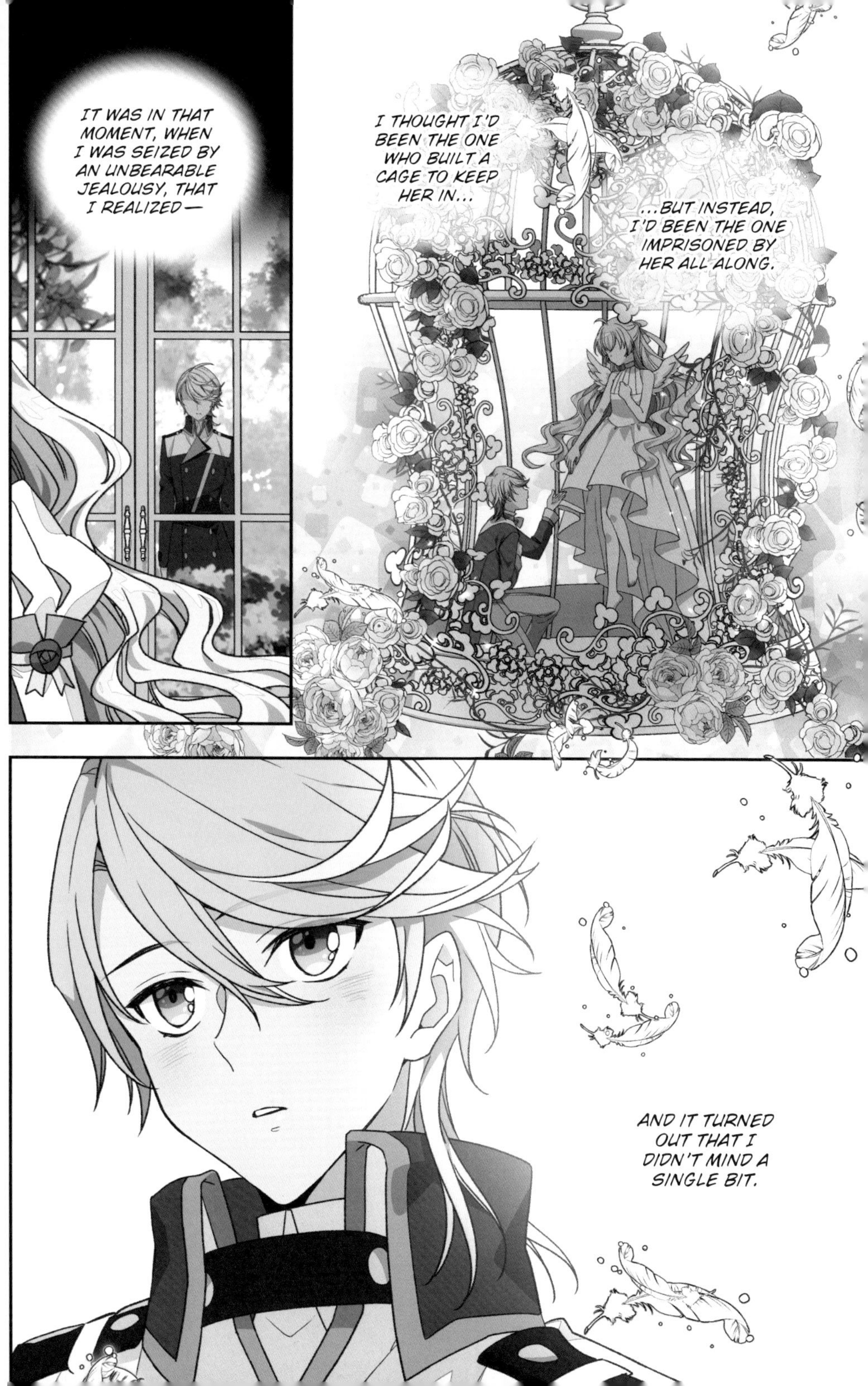
IT WAS IN THAT MOMENT, WHEN I WAS SEIZED BY AN UNBEARABLE JEALOUSY, THAT I REALIZED—
I THOUGHT I'D BEEN THE ONE WHO BUILT A CAGE TO KEEP HER IN...
...BUT INSTEAD, I'D BEEN THE ONE IMPRISONED BY HER ALL ALONG.
AND IT TURNED OUT THAT I DIDN'T MIND A SINGLE BIT.

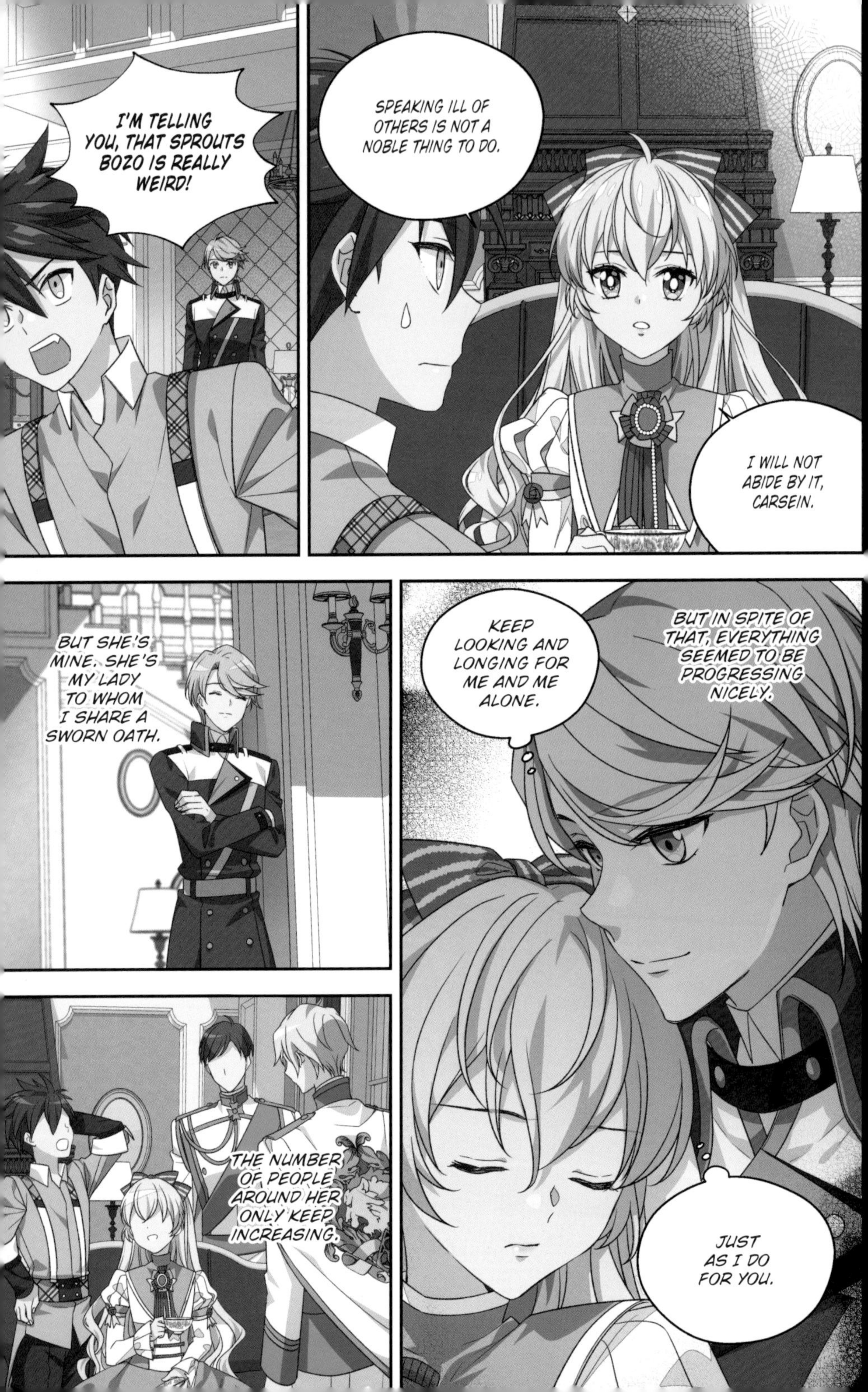
I'M TELLING YOU, THAT SPROUTS BOZO IS REALLY WEIRD!
SPEAKING ILL OF OTHERS IS NOT A NOBLE THING TO DO.
I WILL NOT ABIDE BY IT, CARSEIN.
BUT SHE'S MINE. SHE'S MY LADY TO WHOM I SHARE A SWORN OATH.
THE NUMBER OF PEOPLE AROUND HER ONLY KEEP INCREASING.
BUT IN SPITE OF THAT, EVERYTHING SEEMED TO BE PROGRESSING NICELY.
KEEP LOOKING AND LONGING FOR ME AND ME ALONE.
JUST AS I DO FOR YOU.

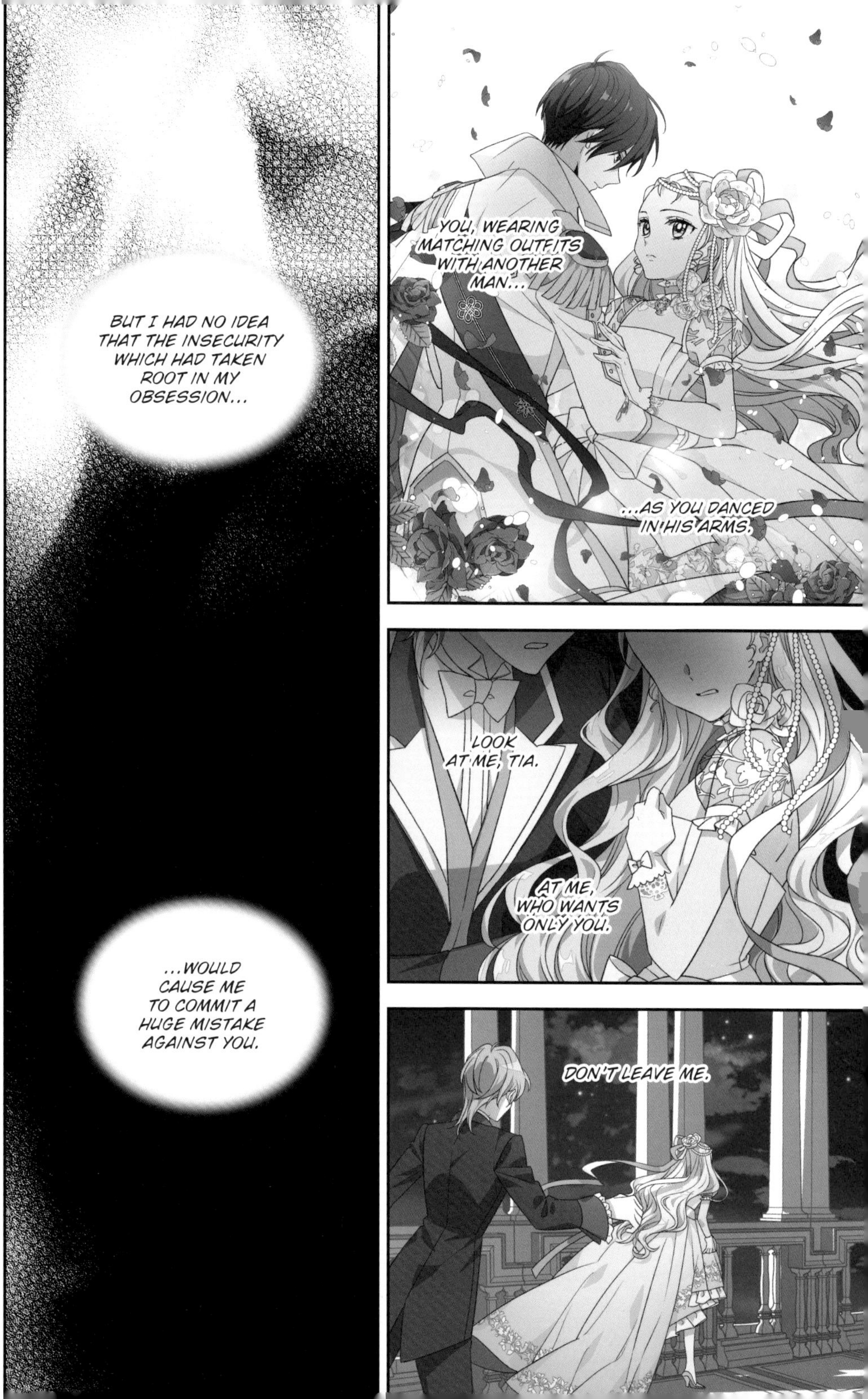
YOU, WEARING MATCHING OUTFITS WITH ANOTHER MAN...
...AS YOU DANCED IN HIS ARMS.
LOOK AT ME, TIA.
AT ME, WHO WANTS ONLY YOU.
DON'T LEAVE ME.
BUT I HAD NO IDEA THAT THE INSECURITY WHICH HAD TAKEN ROOT IN MY OBSESSION...
...WOULD CAUSE ME TO COMMIT A HUGE MISTAKE AGAINST YOU.

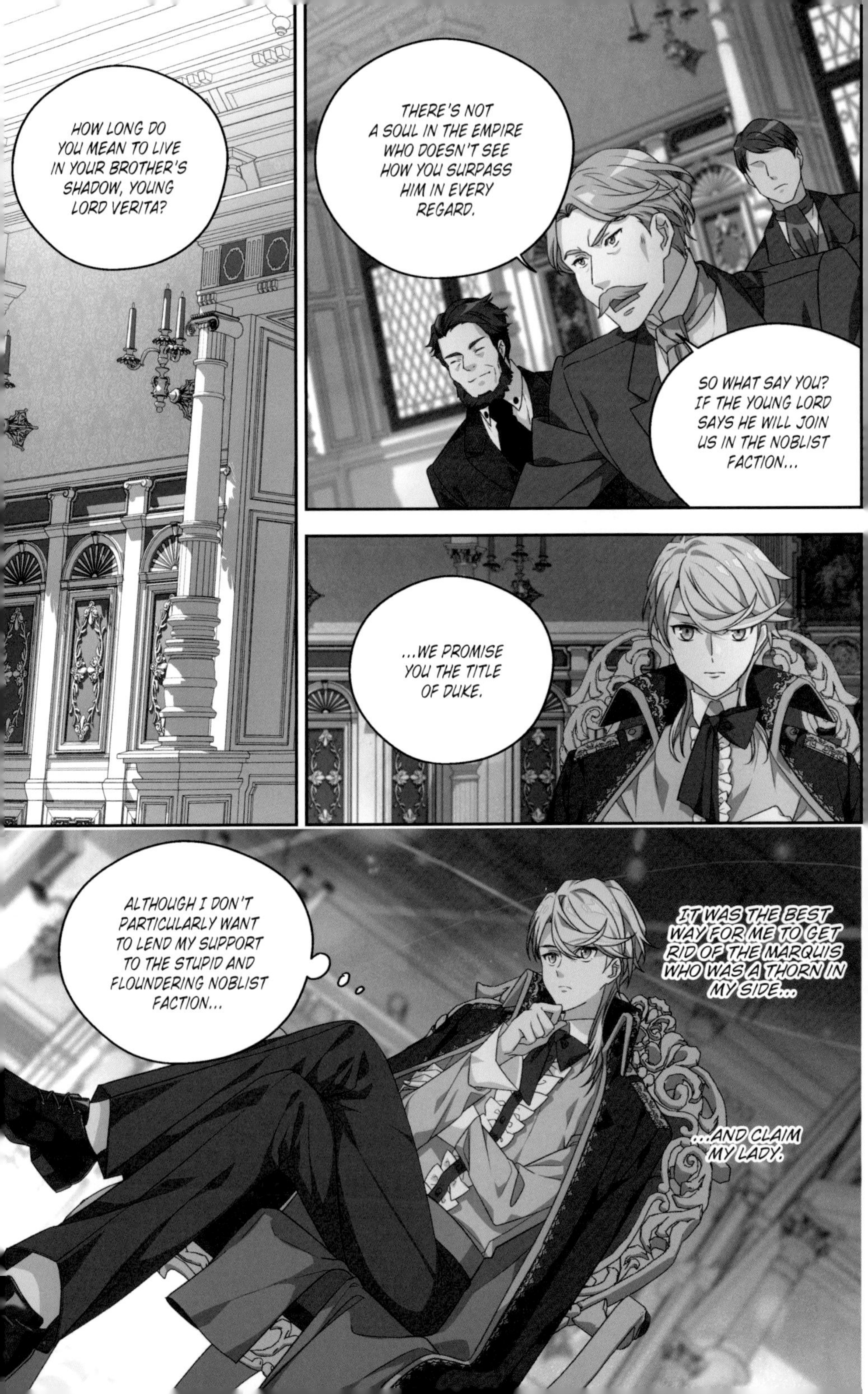
HOW LONG DO YOU MEAN TO LIVE IN YOUR BROTHER'S SHADOW, YOUNG LORD VERITA?
THERE'S NOT A SOUL IN THE EMPIRE WHO DOESN'T SEE HOW YOU SURPASS HIM IN EVERY REGARD.
SO WHAT SAY YOU? IF THE YOUNG LORD SAYS HE WILL JOIN US IN THE NOBLIST FACTION...
...WE PROMISE YOU THE TITLE OF DUKE.
ALTHOUGH I DON'T PARTICULARLY WANT TO LEND MY SUPPORT TO THE STUPID AND FLOUNDERING NOBLIST FACTION...
IT WAS THE BEST WAY FOR ME TO GET RID OF THE MARQUIS WHO WAS A THORN IN MY SIDE...
...AND CLAIM MY LADY.

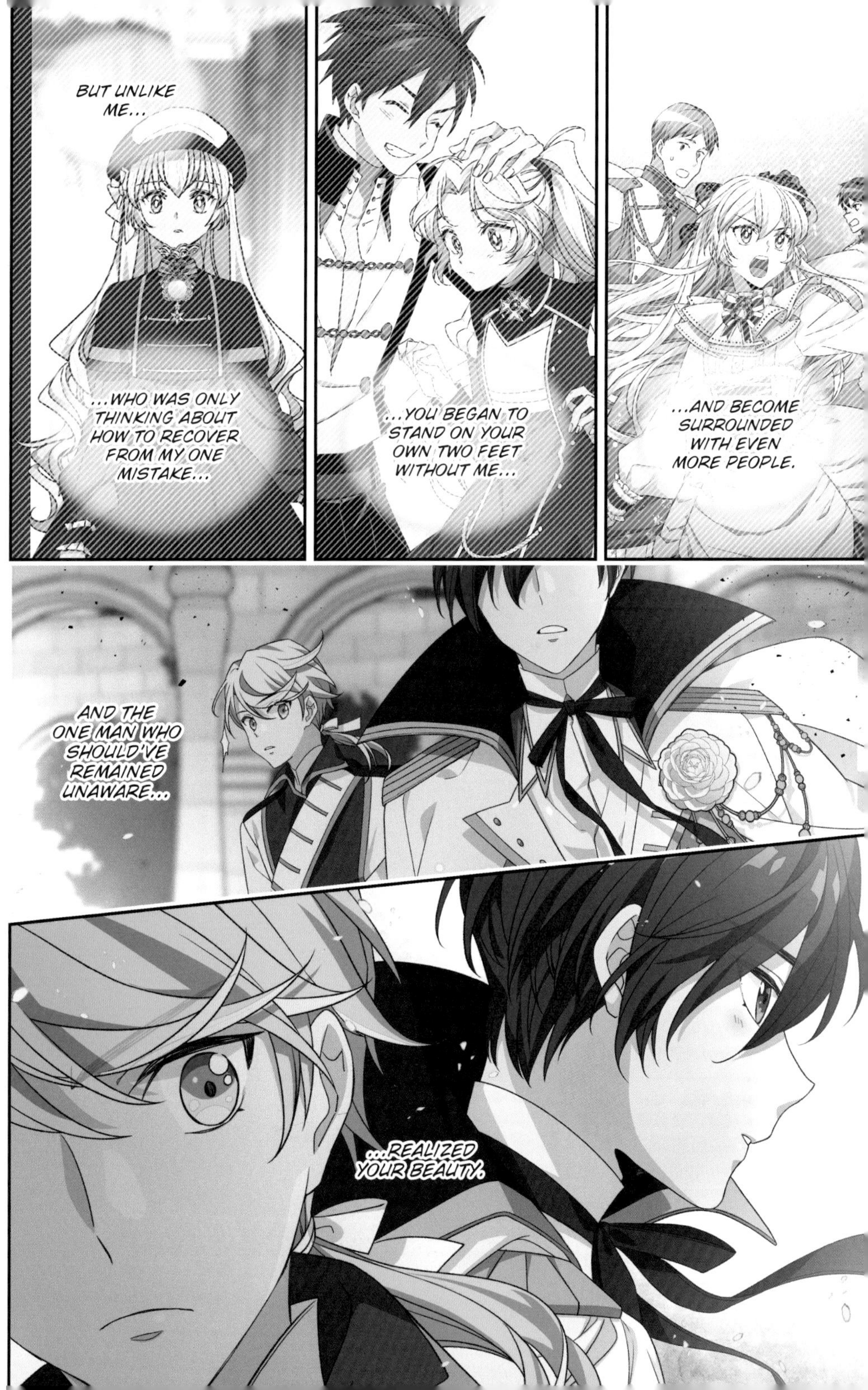
BUT UNLIKE ME...
...WHO WAS ONLY THINKING ABOUT HOW TO RECOVER FROM MY ONE MISTAKE...
...YOU BEGAN TO STAND ON YOUR OWN TWO FEET WITHOUT ME...
...AND BECOME SURROUNDED WITH EVEN MORE PEOPLE.
AND THE ONE MAN WHO SHOULD'VE REMAINED UNAWARE...
...REALIZED YOUR BEAUTY.

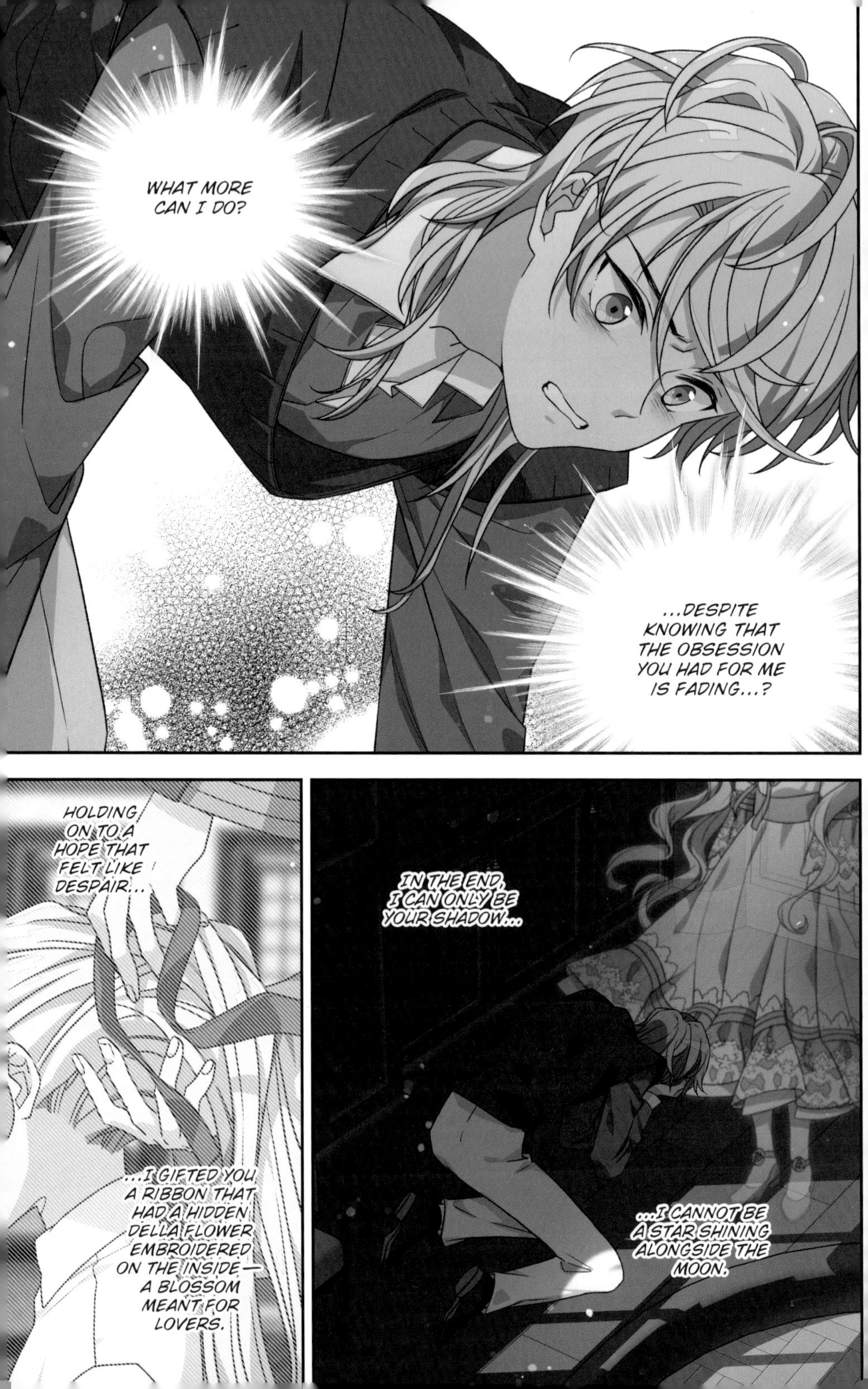
WHAT MORE CAN I DO?
...DESPITE KNOWING THAT THE OBSESSION YOU HAD FOR ME IS FADING...?
IN THE END, I CAN ONLY BE YOUR SHADOW...
...I CANNOT BE A STAR SHINING ALONGSIDE THE MOON.
HOLDING ON TO A HOPE THAT FELT LIKE DESPAIR...
...I GIFTED YOU A RIBBON THAT HAD A HIDDEN DELLA FLOWER EMBROIDERED ON THE INSIDE—A BLOSSOM MEANT FOR LOVERS.

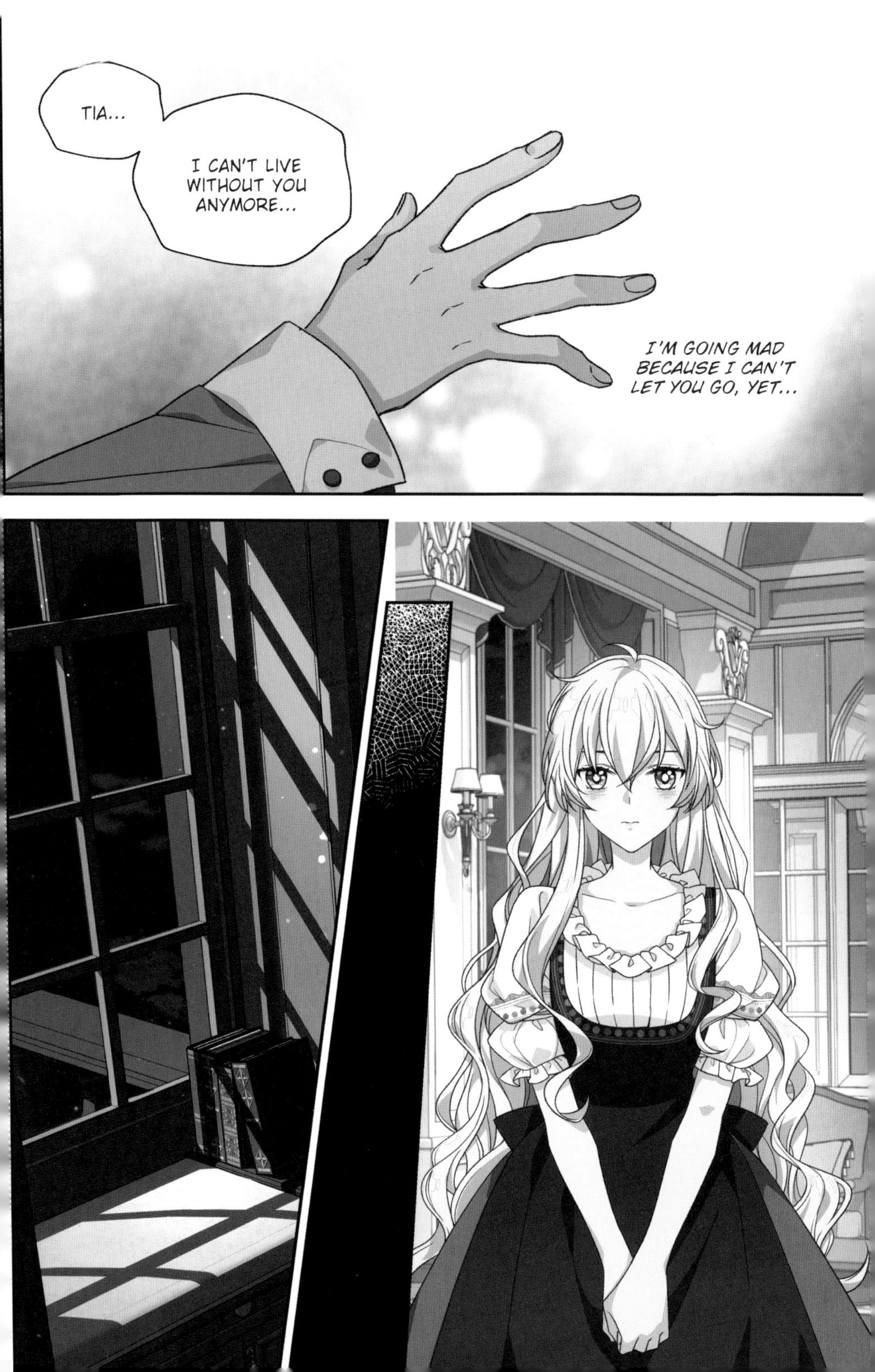
TIA...
I CAN'T LIVE WITHOUT YOU ANYMORE...
I'M GOING MAD BECAUSE I CAN'T LET YOU GO, YET...

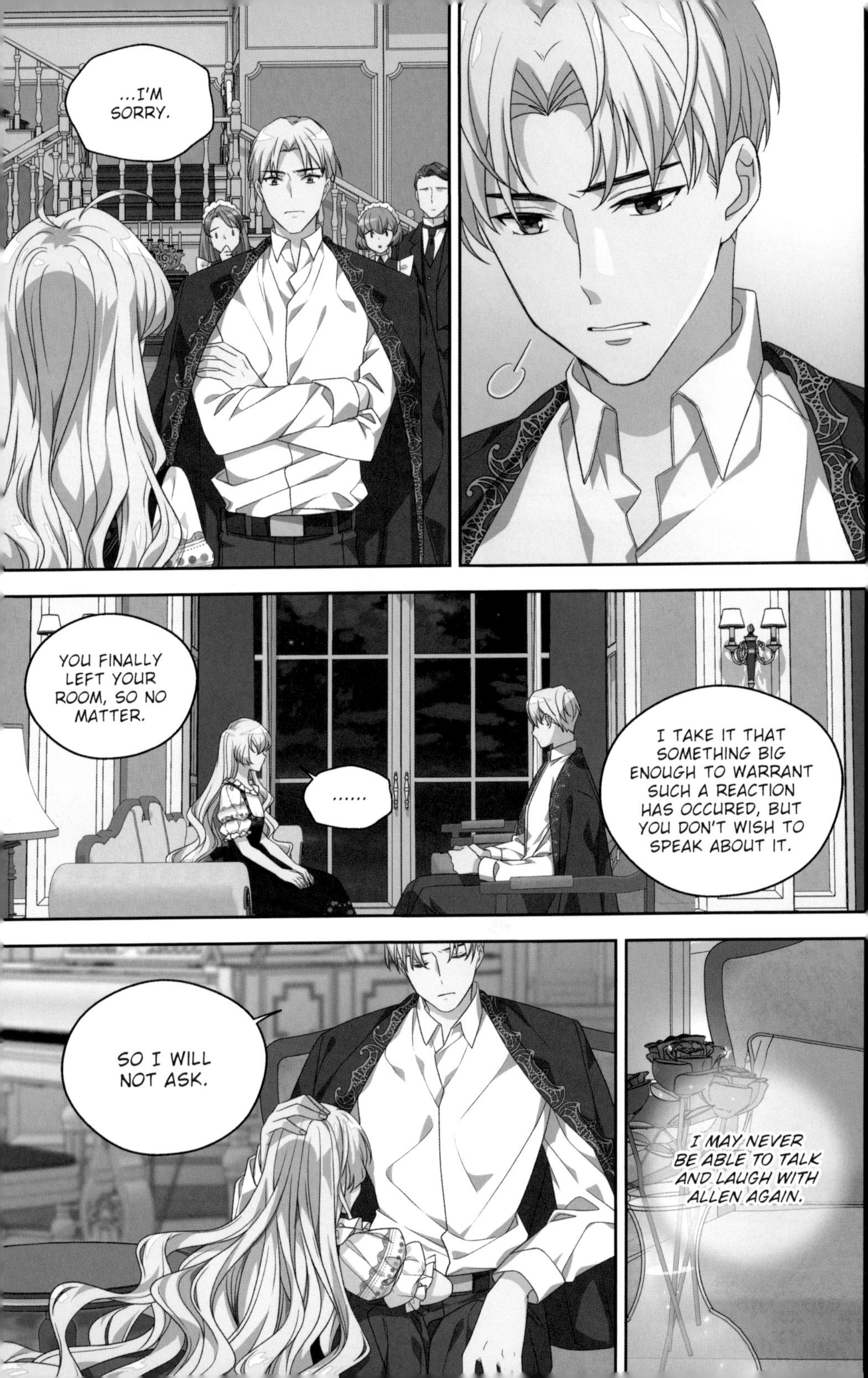
...I'M SORRY.
YOU FINALLY LEFT YOUR ROOM, SO NO MATTER.
......
I TAKE IT THAT SOMETHING BIG ENOUGH TO WARRANT SUCH A REACTION HAS OCCURED, BUT YOU DON'T WISH TO SPEAK ABOUT IT.
SO I WILL NOT ASK.
I MAY NEVER BE ABLE TO TALK AND LAUGH WITH ALLEN AGAIN.

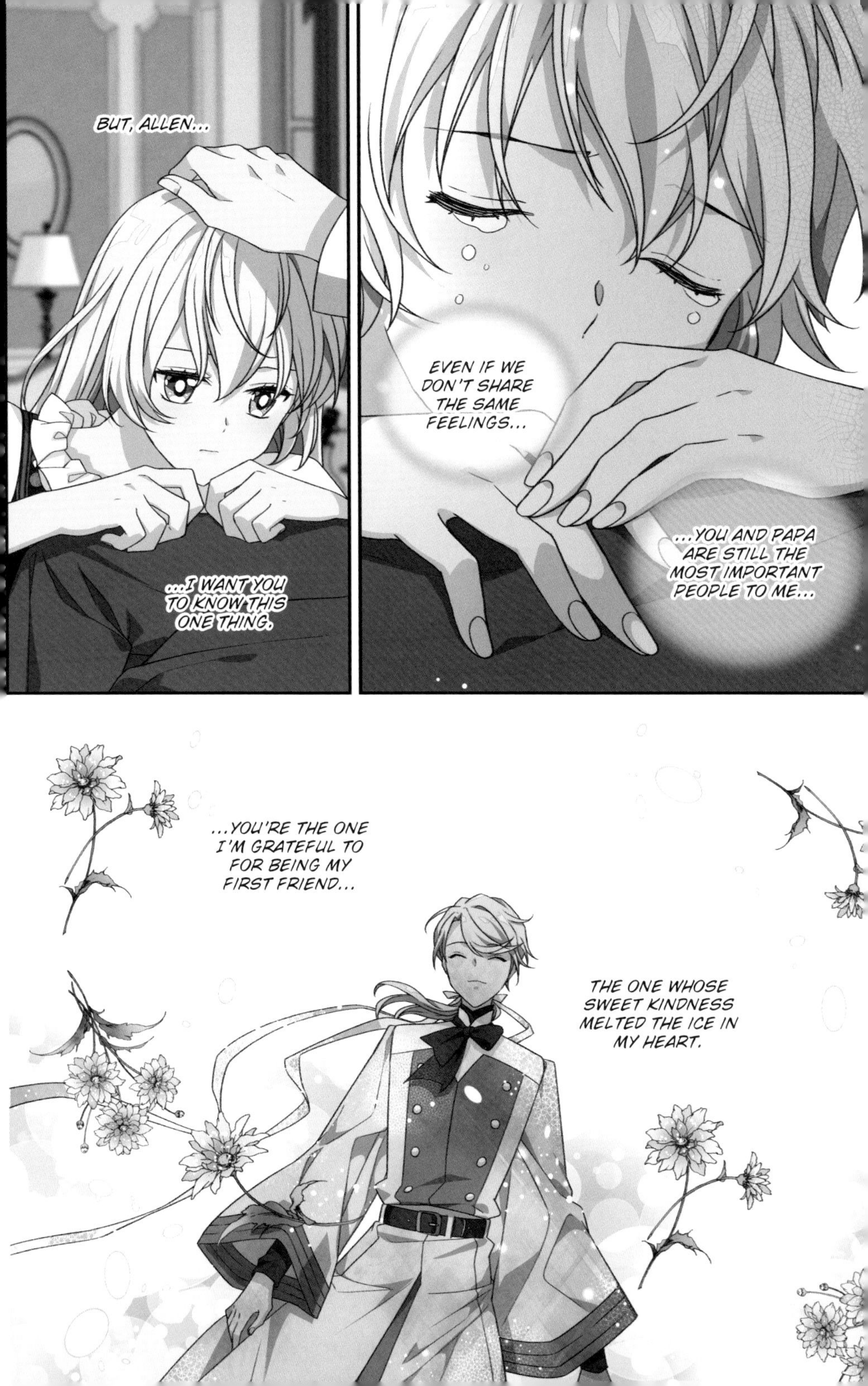
EVEN IF WE DON'T SHARE THE SAME FEELINGS...
...YOU AND PAPA ARE STILL THE MOST IMPORTANT PEOPLE TO ME...
BUT, ALLEN...
...I WANT YOU TO KNOW THIS ONE THING.
THE ONE WHOSE SWEET KINDNESS MELTED THE ICE IN MY HEART.
...YOU'RE THE ONE I'M GRATEFUL TO FOR BEING MY FIRST FRIEND...

The Abandoned Empress

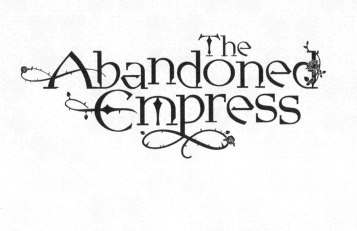

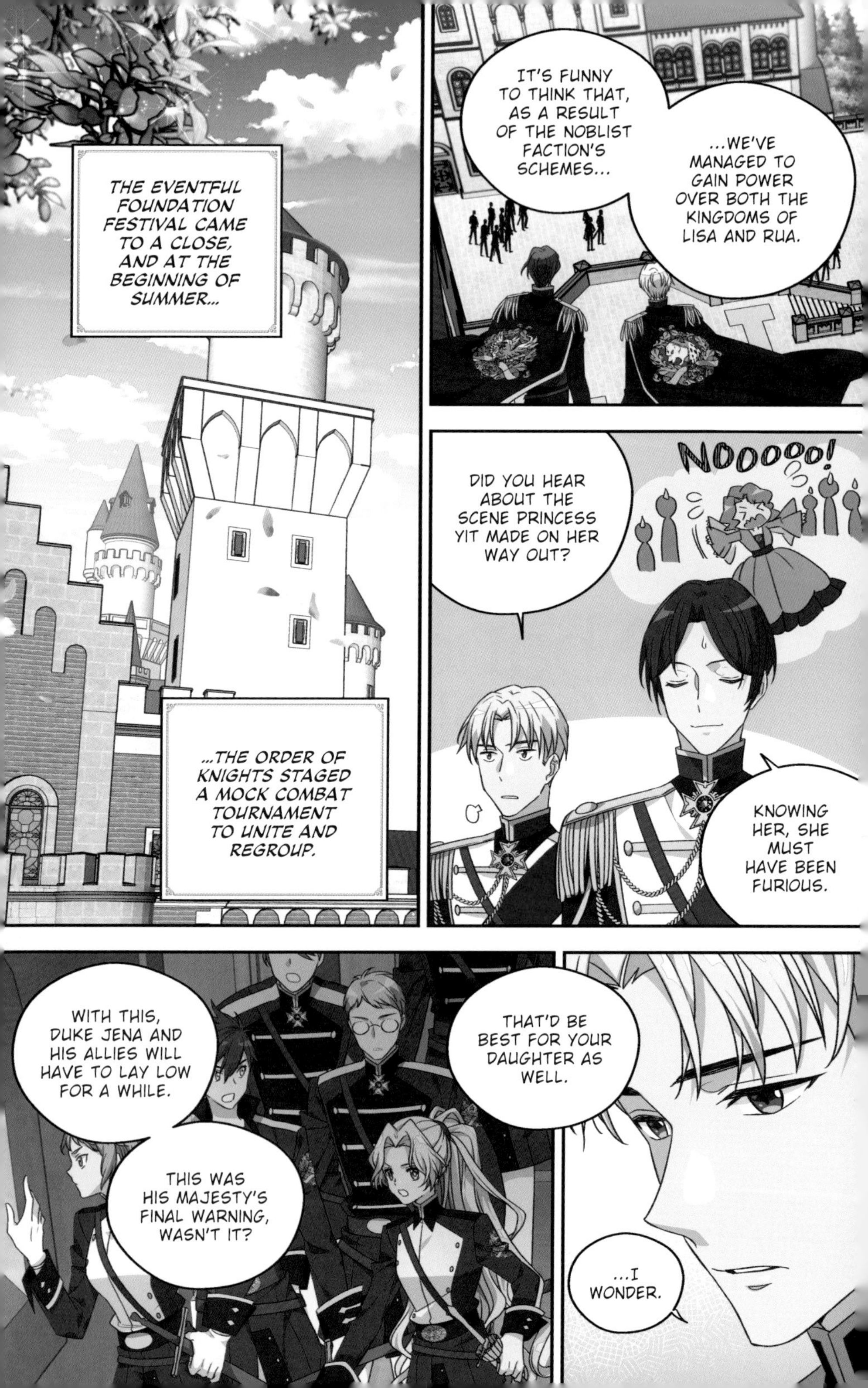
THE EVENTFUL FOUNDATION FESTIVAL CAME TO A CLOSE, AND AT THE BEGINNING OF SUMMER...
...THE ORDER OF KNIGHTS STAGED A MOCK COMBAT TOURNAMENT TO UNITE AND REGROUP.
IT'S FUNNY TO THINK THAT, AS A RESULT OF THE NOBLIST FACTION'S SCHEMES...
...WE'VE MANAGED TO GAIN POWER OVER BOTH THE KINGDOMS OF LISA AND RUA.
DID YOU HEAR ABOUT THE SCENE PRINCESS YIT MADE ON HER WAY OUT?
NOOOOO!
KNOWING HER, SHE MUST HAVE BEEN FURIOUS.
WITH THIS, DUKE JENA AND HIS ALLIES WILL HAVE TO LAY LOW FOR A WHILE.
THIS WAS HIS MAJESTY'S FINAL WARNING, WASN'T IT?
THAT'D BE BEST FOR YOUR DAUGHTER AS WELL.
...I WONDER.

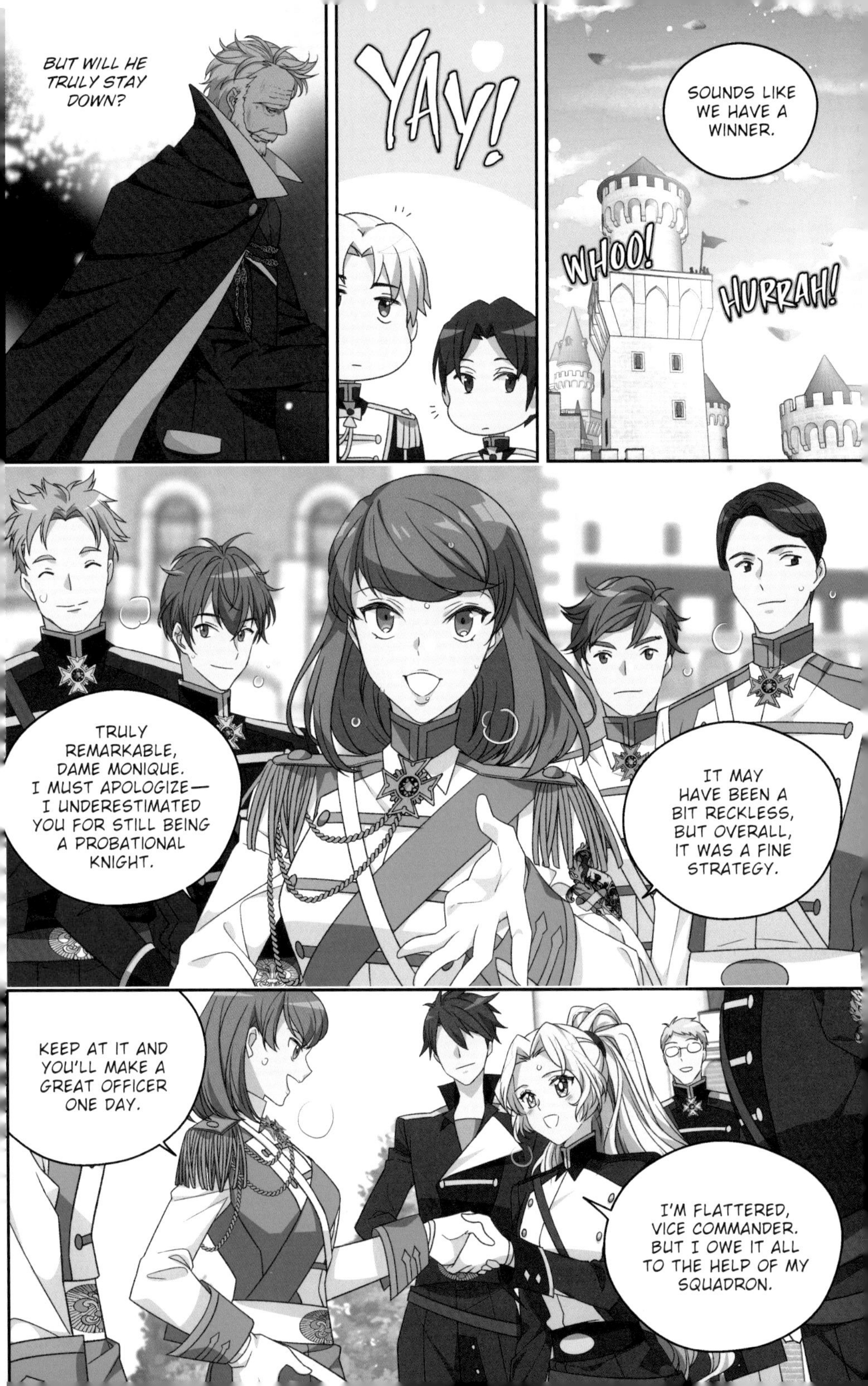
BUT WILL HE TRULY STAY DOWN?
YAY!
SOUNDS LIKE WE HAVE A WINNER.
WHOO!
HURRAH!
TRULY REMARKABLE, DAME MONIQUE. I MUST APOLOGIZE— I UNDERESTIMATED YOU FOR STILL BEING A PROBATIONAL KNIGHT.
IT MAY HAVE BEEN A BIT RECKLESS, BUT OVERALL, IT WAS A FINE STRATEGY.
KEEP AT IT AND YOU'LL MAKE A GREAT OFFICER ONE DAY.
I'M FLATTERED, VICE COMMANDER. BUT I OWE IT ALL TO THE HELP OF MY SQUADRON.

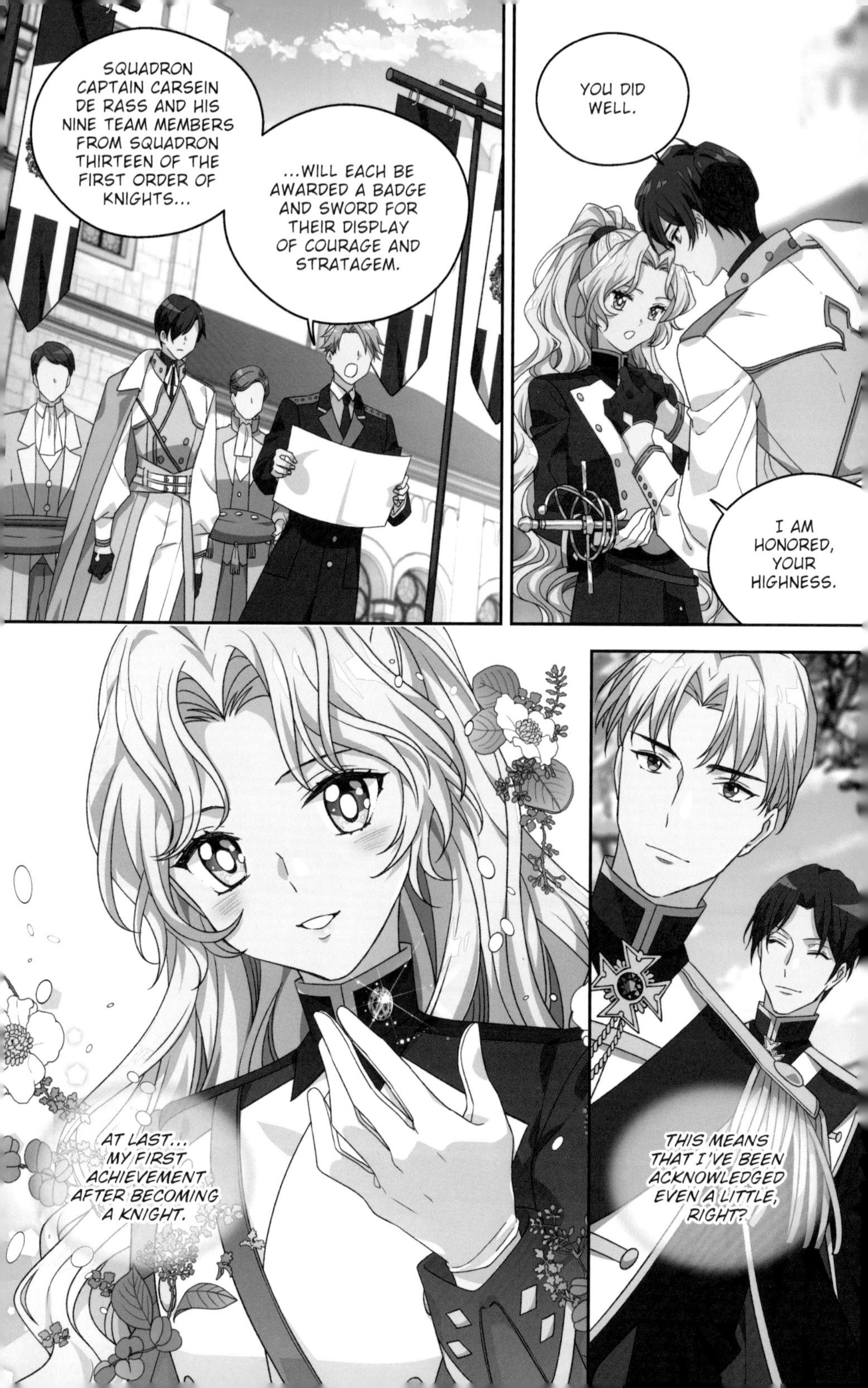
SQUADRON CAPTAIN CARSEIN DE RASS AND HIS NINE TEAM MEMBERS FROM SQUADRON THIRTEEN OF THE FIRST ORDER OF KNIGHTS...
...WILL EACH BE AWARDED A BADGE AND SWORD FOR THEIR DISPLAY OF COURAGE AND STRATAGEM.
YOU DID WELL.
I AM HONORED, YOUR HIGHNESS.
AT LAST... MY FIRST ACHIEVEMENT AFTER BECOMING A KNIGHT.
THIS MEANS THAT I'VE BEEN ACKNOWLEDGED EVEN A LITTLE, RIGHT?

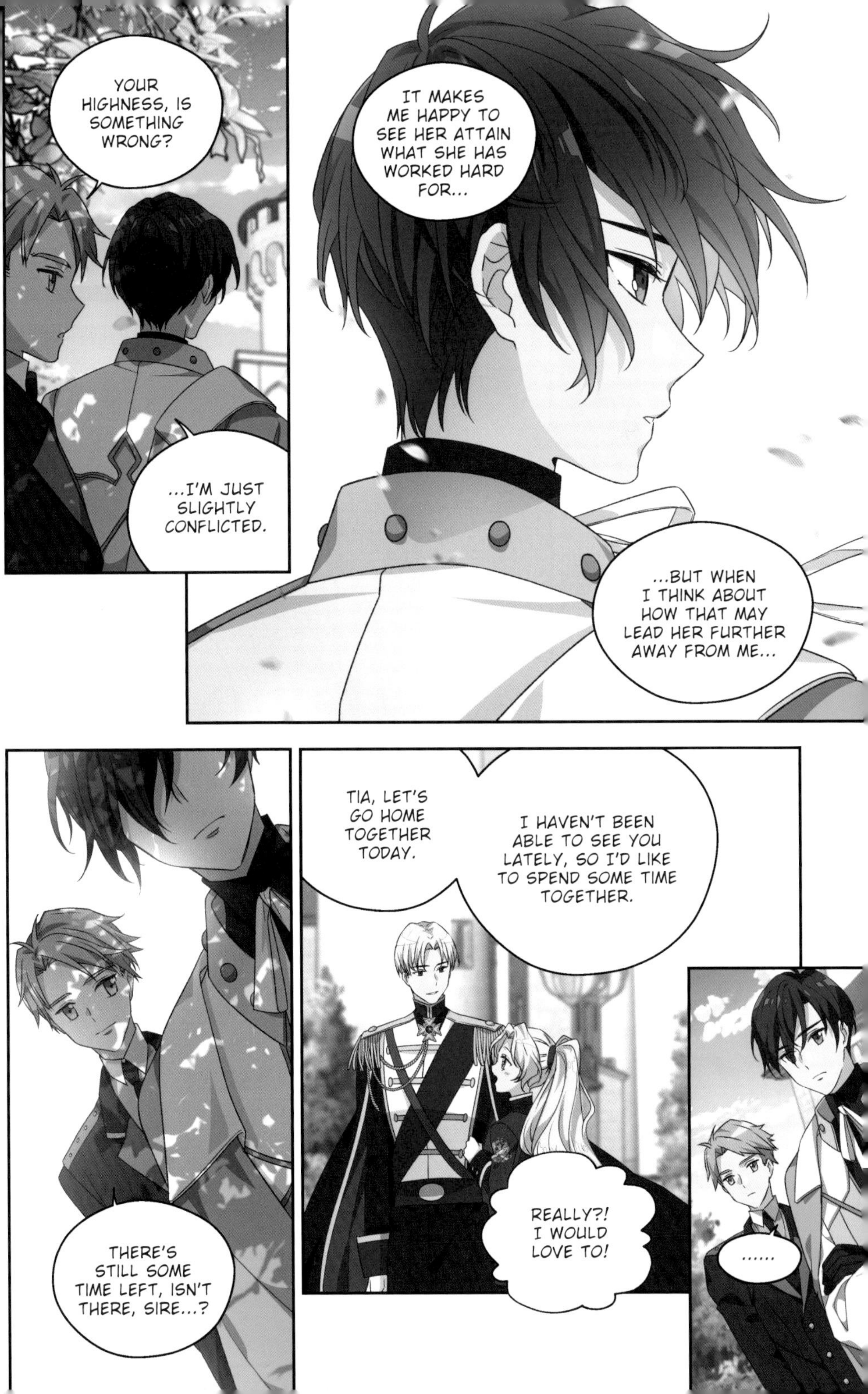
YOUR HIGHNESS, IS SOMETHING WRONG?
...I'M JUST SLIGHTLY CONFLICTED.
IT MAKES ME HAPPY TO SEE HER ATTAIN WHAT SHE HAS WORKED HARD FOR...
...BUT WHEN I THINK ABOUT HOW THAT MAY LEAD HER FURTHER AWAY FROM ME...
THERE'S STILL SOME TIME LEFT, ISN'T THERE, SIRE...?
TIA, LET'S GO HOME TOGETHER TODAY.
I HAVEN'T BEEN ABLE TO SEE YOU LATELY, SO I'D LIKE TO SPEND SOME TIME TOGETHER.
REALLY?! I WOULD LOVE TO!
......

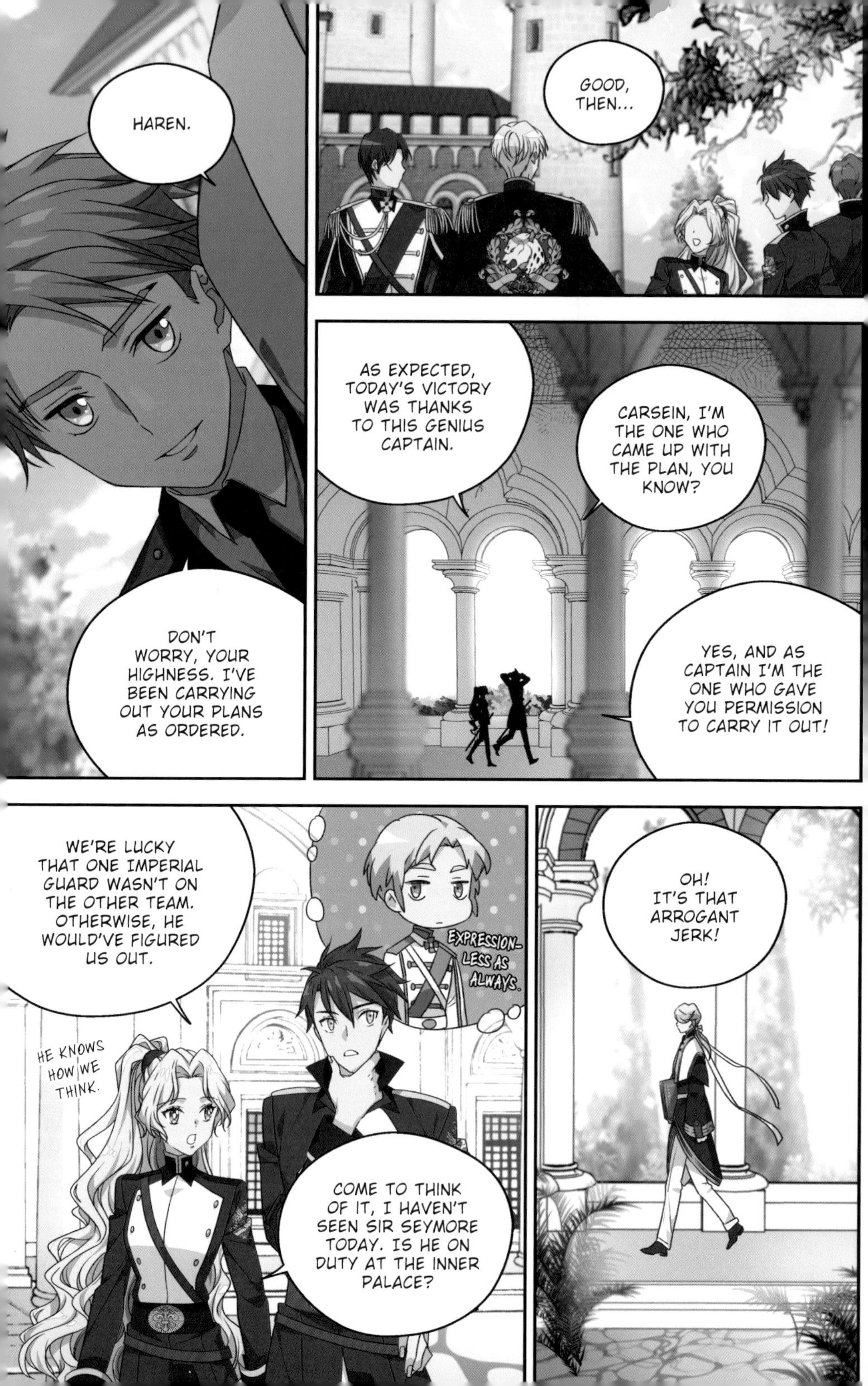
HAREN.
GOOD, THEN...
AS EXPECTED, TODAY'S VICTORY WAS THANKS TO THIS GENIUS CAPTAIN.
CARSEIN, I'M THE ONE WHO CAME UP WITH THE PLAN, YOU KNOW?
DON'T WORRY, YOUR HIGHNESS. I'VE BEEN CARRYING OUT YOUR PLANS AS ORDERED.
YES, AND AS CAPTAIN I'M THE ONE WHO GAVE YOU PERMISSION TO CARRY IT OUT!
WE'RE LUCKY THAT ONE IMPERIAL GUARD WASN'T ON THE OTHER TEAM. OTHERWISE, HE WOULD'VE FIGURED US OUT.
EXPRESSIONLESS AS ALWAYS.
HE KNOWS HOW WE THINK.
COME TO THINK OF IT, I HAVEN'T SEEN SIR SEYMORE TODAY. IS HE ON DUTY AT THE INNER PALACE?
OH! IT'S THAT ARROGANT JERK!

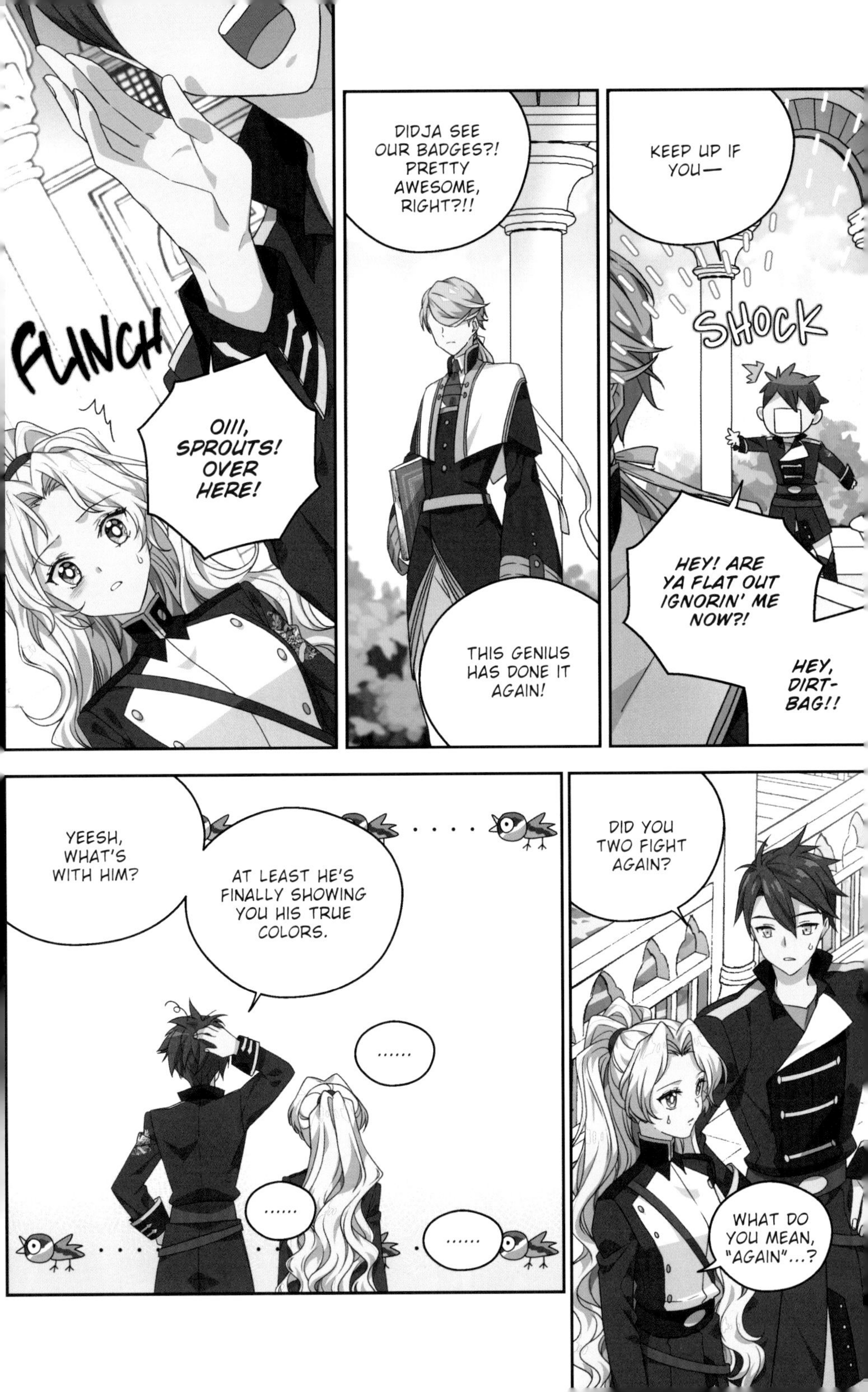
FLINCH
OIII, SPROUTS! OVER HERE!
DIDJA SEE OUR BADGES?! PRETTY AWESOME, RIGHT?!!
THIS GENIUS HAS DONE IT AGAIN!
KEEP UP IF YOU—
SHOCK
HEY! ARE YA FLAT OUT IGNORIN' ME NOW?!
HEY, DIRT-BAG!!
YEESH, WHAT'S WITH HIM?
AT LEAST HE'S FINALLY SHOWING YOU HIS TRUE COLORS.
......
......
......
DID YOU TWO FIGHT AGAIN?
WHAT DO YOU MEAN, "AGAIN"...?

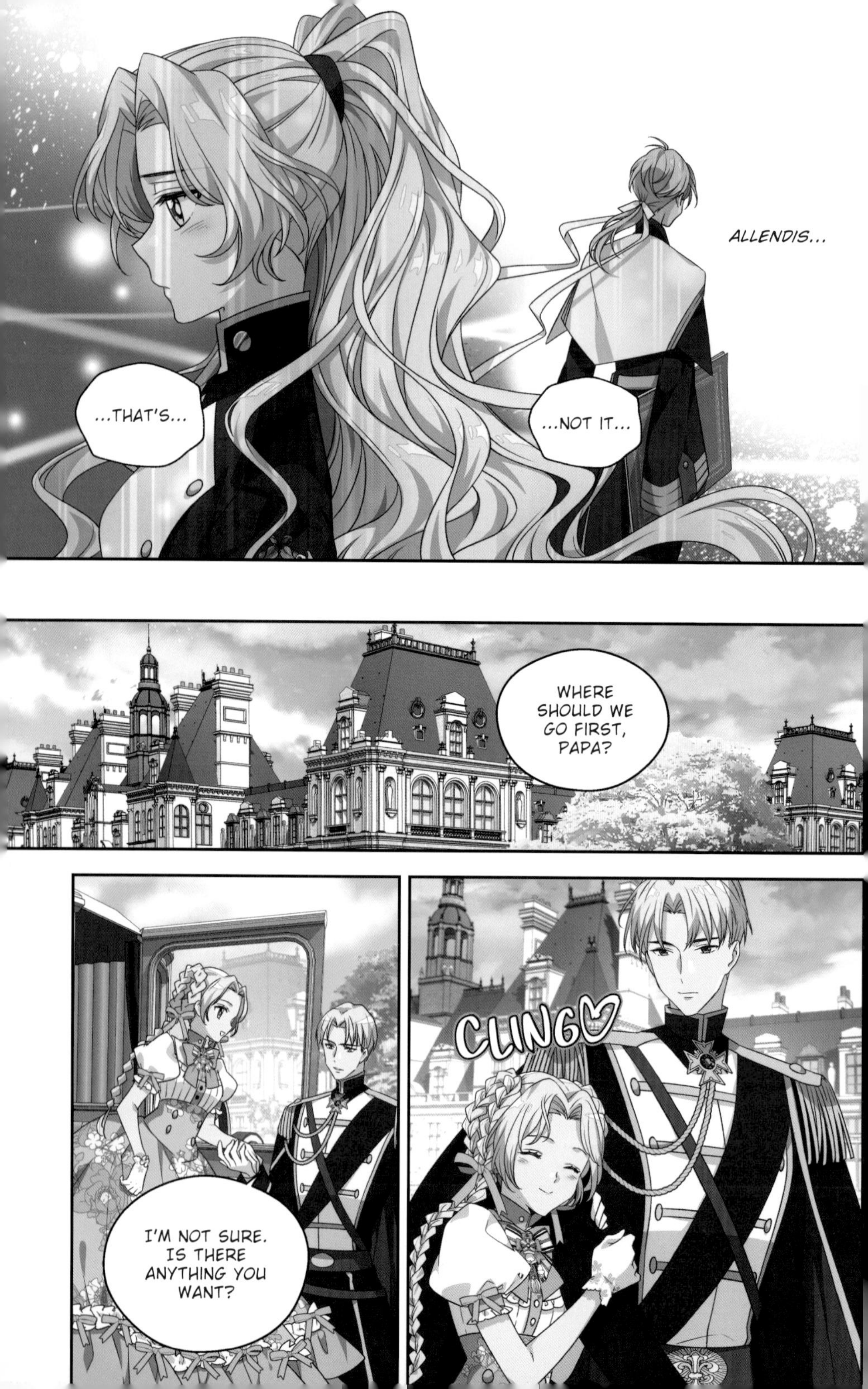
ALLENDIS...
...THAT'S...
...NOT IT...
WHERE SHOULD WE GO FIRST, PAPA?
I'M NOT SURE. IS THERE ANYTHING YOU WANT?
CLING♡

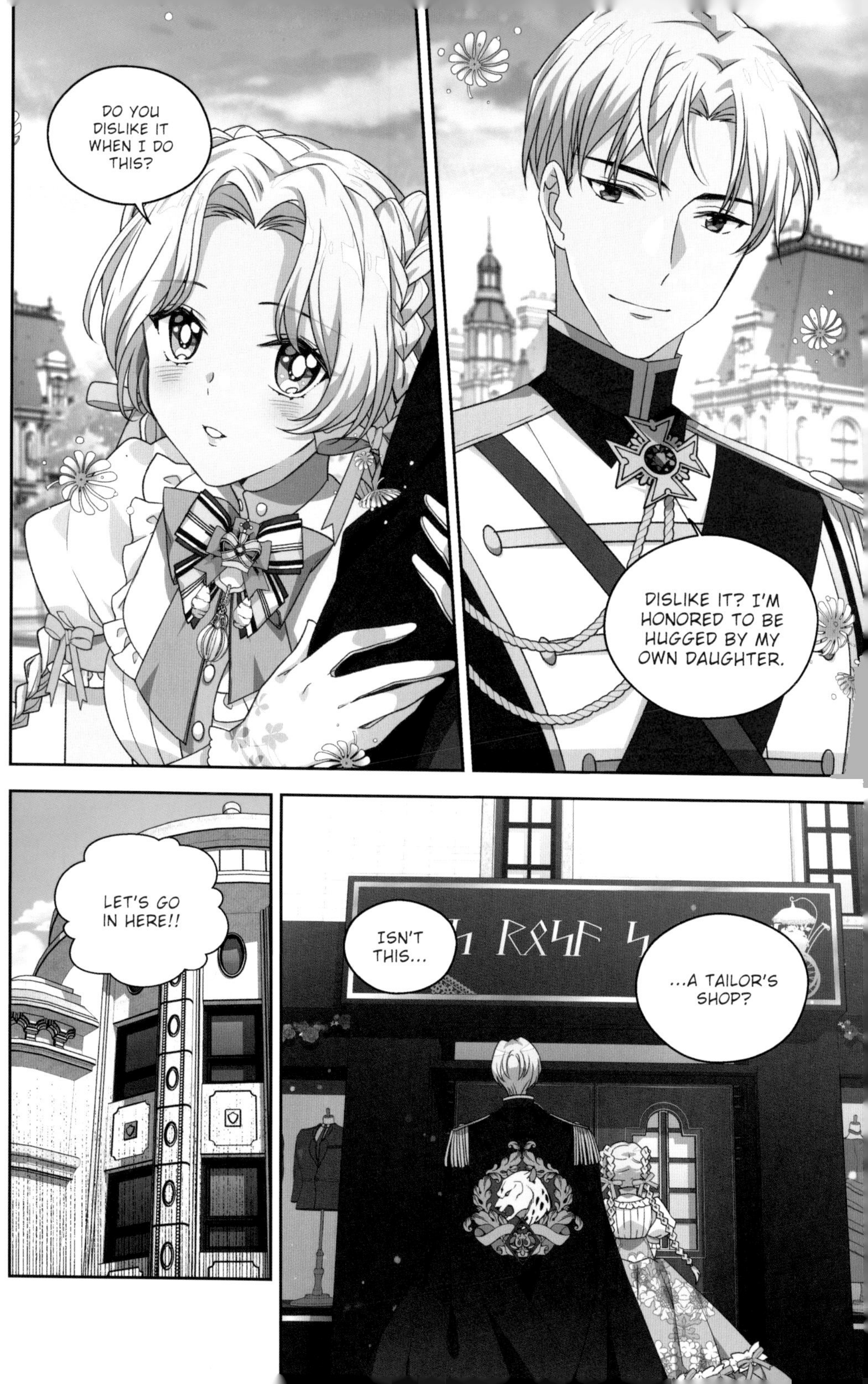
DO YOU DISLIKE IT WHEN I DO THIS?
DISLIKE IT? I'M HONORED TO BE HUGGED BY MY OWN DAUGHTER.
LET'S GO IN HERE!!
ISN'T THIS...
...A TAILOR'S SHOP?

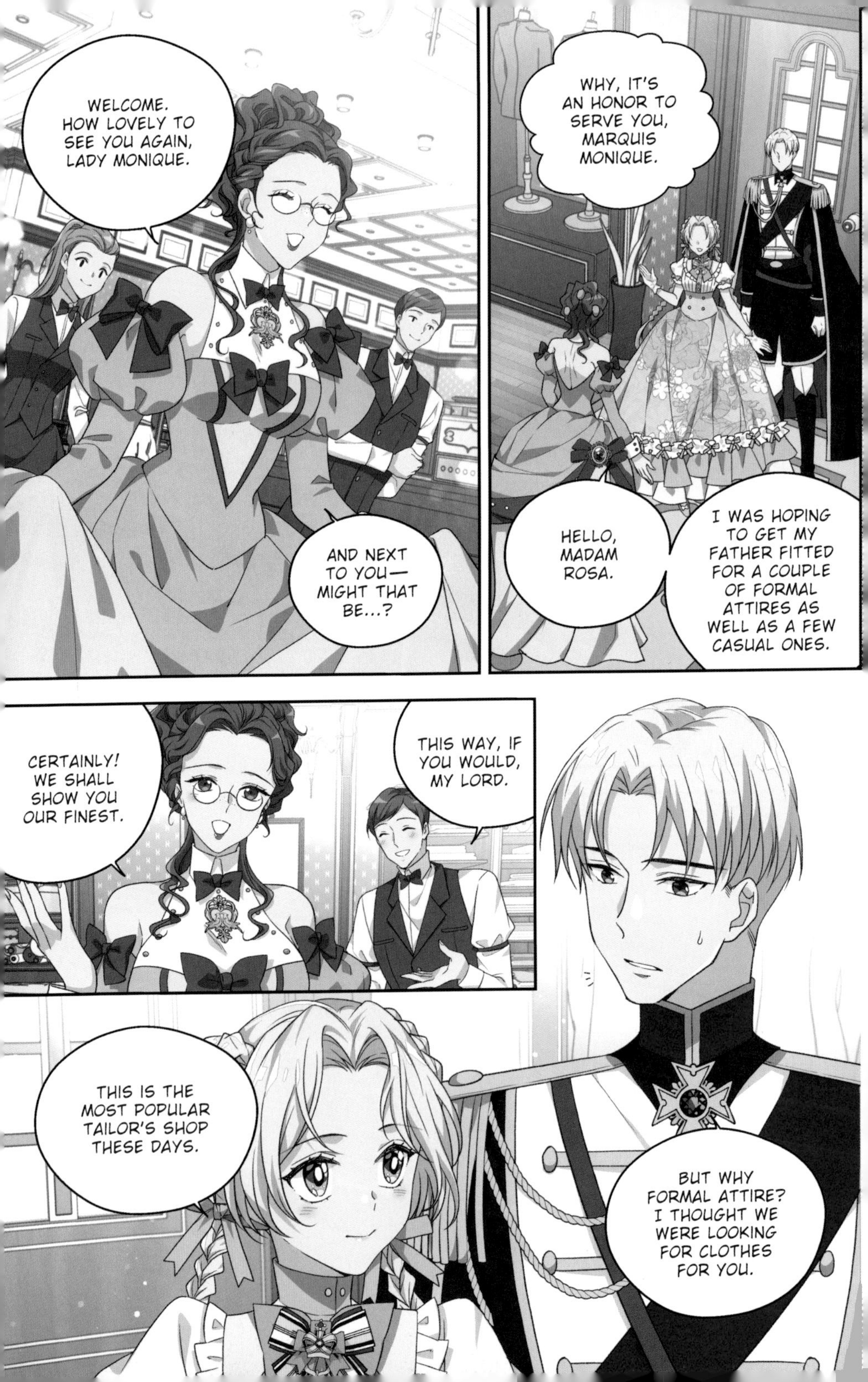
WELCOME. HOW LOVELY TO SEE YOU AGAIN, LADY MONIQUE.
AND NEXT TO YOU— MIGHT THAT BE...?
WHY, IT'S AN HONOR TO SERVE YOU, MARQUIS MONIQUE.
HELLO, MADAM ROSA.
I WAS HOPING TO GET MY FATHER FITTED FOR A COUPLE OF FORMAL ATTIRES AS WELL AS A FEW CASUAL ONES.
CERTAINLY! WE SHALL SHOW YOU OUR FINEST.
THIS WAY, IF YOU WOULD, MY LORD.
THIS IS THE MOST POPULAR TAILOR'S SHOP THESE DAYS.
BUT WHY FORMAL ATTIRE? I THOUGHT WE WERE LOOKING FOR CLOTHES FOR YOU.

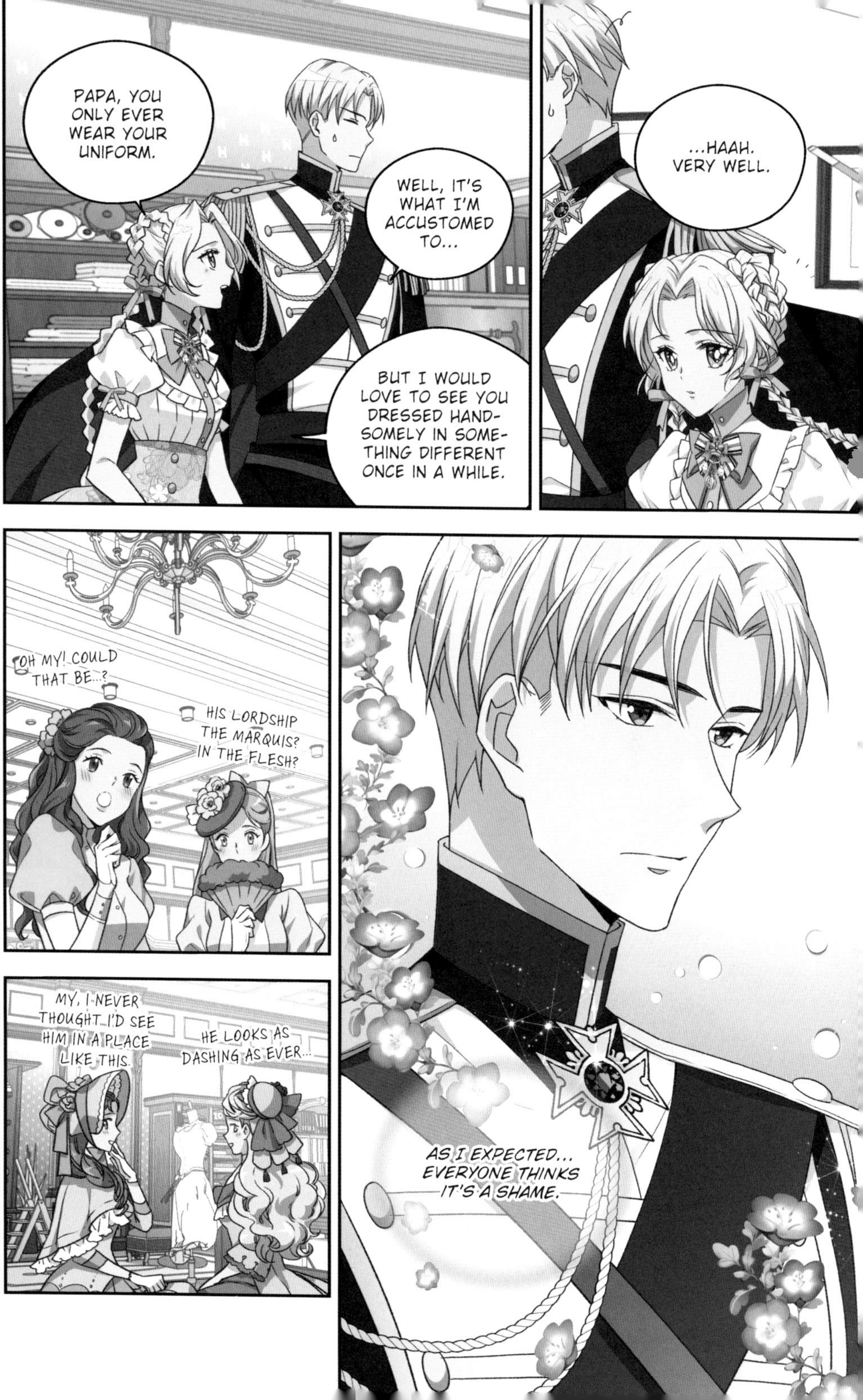
PAPA, YOU ONLY EVER WEAR YOUR UNIFORM.
WELL, IT'S WHAT I'M ACCUSTOMED TO...
BUT I WOULD LOVE TO SEE YOU DRESSED HAND-SOMELY IN SOME-THING DIFFERENT ONCE IN A WHILE.
...HAAH. VERY WELL.
OH MY! COULD THAT BE...?
HIS LORDSHIP THE MARQUIS? IN THE FLESH?
MY, I NEVER THOUGHT I'D SEE HIM IN A PLACE LIKE THIS.
HE LOOKS AS DASHING AS EVER...
AS I EXPECTED... EVERYONE THINKS IT'S A SHAME.

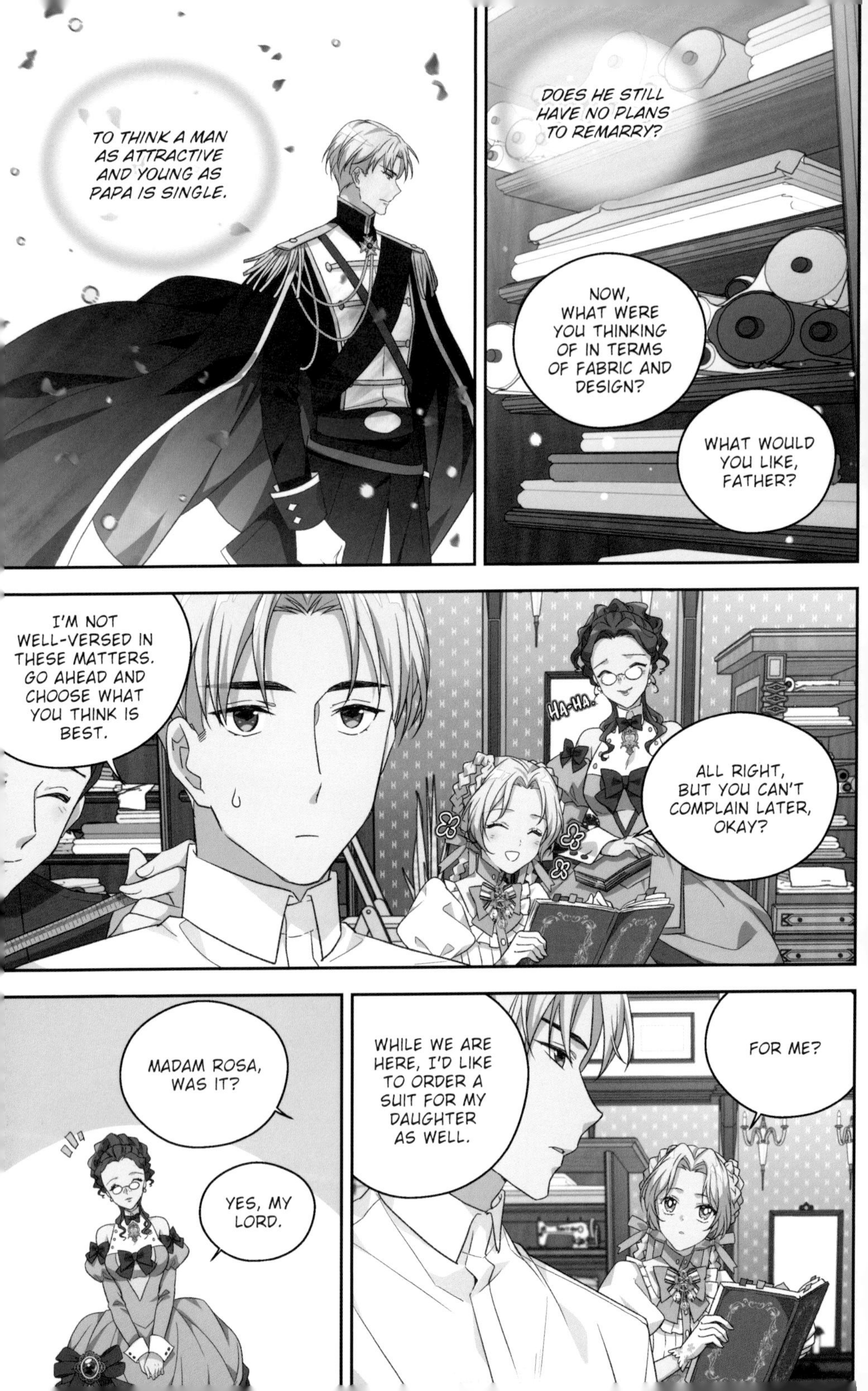
TO THINK A MAN AS ATTRACTIVE AND YOUNG AS PAPA IS SINGLE.
DOES HE STILL HAVE NO PLANS TO REMARRY?
NOW, WHAT WERE YOU THINKING OF IN TERMS OF FABRIC AND DESIGN?
WHAT WOULD YOU LIKE, FATHER?
I'M NOT WELL-VERSED IN THESE MATTERS. GO AHEAD AND CHOOSE WHAT YOU THINK IS BEST.
HA-HA.
ALL RIGHT, BUT YOU CAN'T COMPLAIN LATER, OKAY?
MADAM ROSA, WAS IT?
YES, MY LORD.
WHILE WE ARE HERE, I'D LIKE TO ORDER A SUIT FOR MY DAUGHTER AS WELL.
FOR ME?

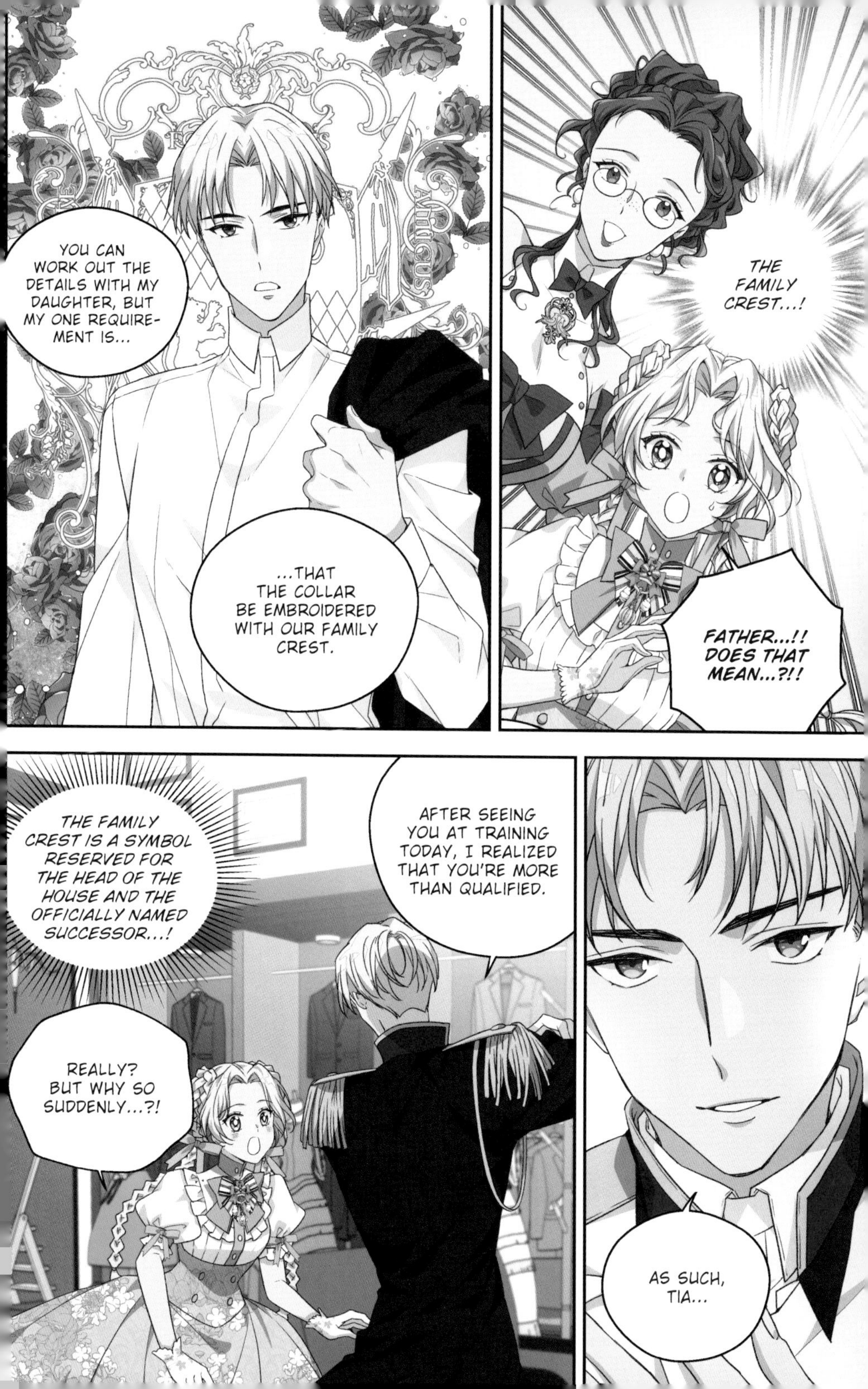
YOU CAN WORK OUT THE DETAILS WITH MY DAUGHTER, BUT MY ONE REQUIREMENT IS...
...THAT THE COLLAR BE EMBROIDERED WITH OUR FAMILY CREST.
THE FAMILY CREST...!
FATHER...!! DOES THAT MEAN...?!!
THE FAMILY CREST IS A SYMBOL RESERVED FOR THE HEAD OF THE HOUSE AND THE OFFICIALLY NAMED SUCCESSOR...!
AFTER SEEING YOU AT TRAINING TODAY, I REALIZED THAT YOU'RE MORE THAN QUALIFIED.
REALLY? BUT WHY SO SUDDENLY...?!
AS SUCH, TIA...

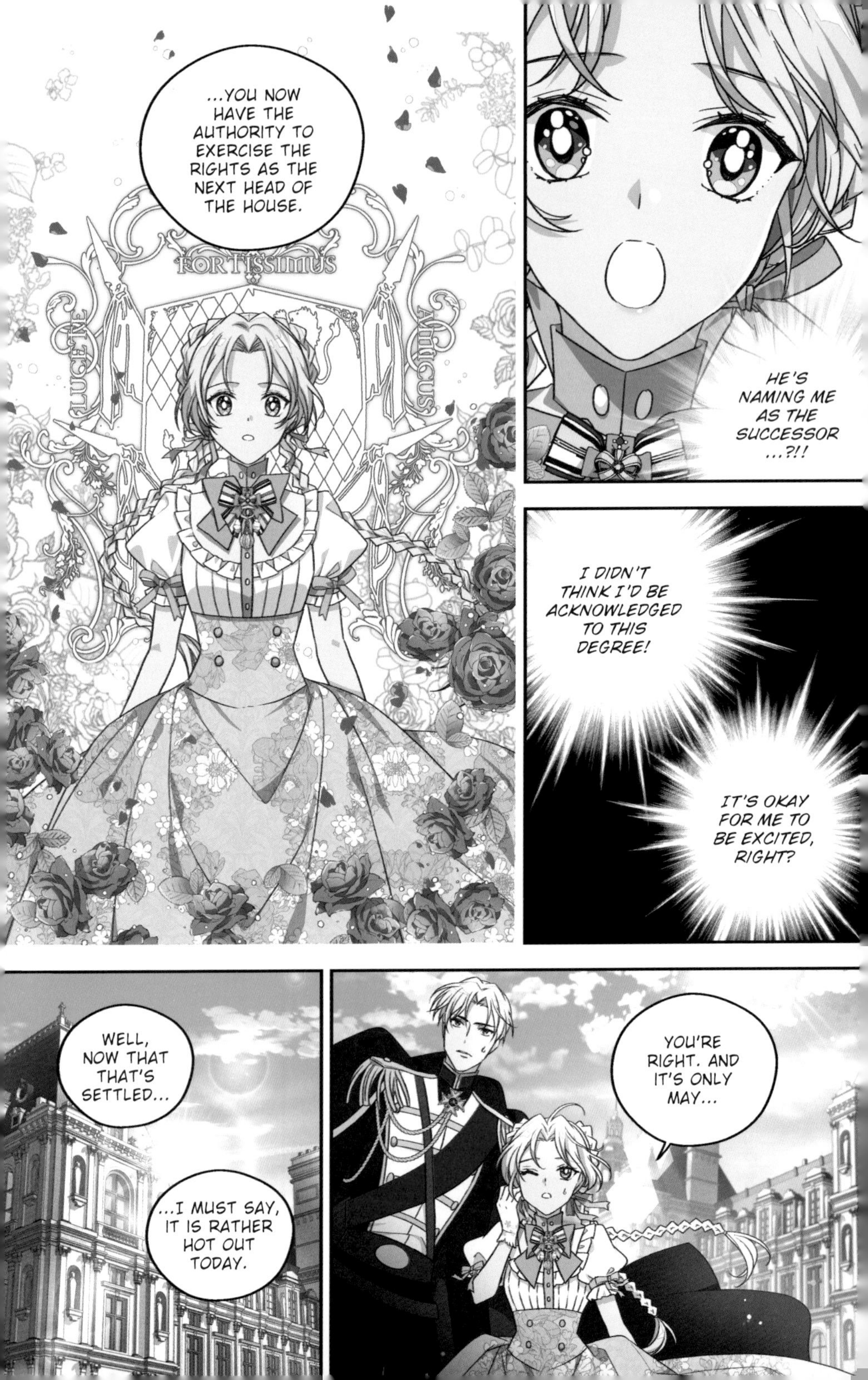
...YOU NOW HAVE THE AUTHORITY TO EXERCISE THE RIGHTS AS THE NEXT HEAD OF THE HOUSE.
FORTISSIMUS
LUCENTE
AMICUS
HE'S NAMING ME AS THE SUCCESSOR ...?!!
I DIDN'T THINK I'D BE ACKNOWLEDGED TO THIS DEGREE!
IT'S OKAY FOR ME TO BE EXCITED, RIGHT?
WELL, NOW THAT THAT'S SETTLED...
...I MUST SAY, IT IS RATHER HOT OUT TODAY.
YOU'RE RIGHT. AND IT'S ONLY MAY...

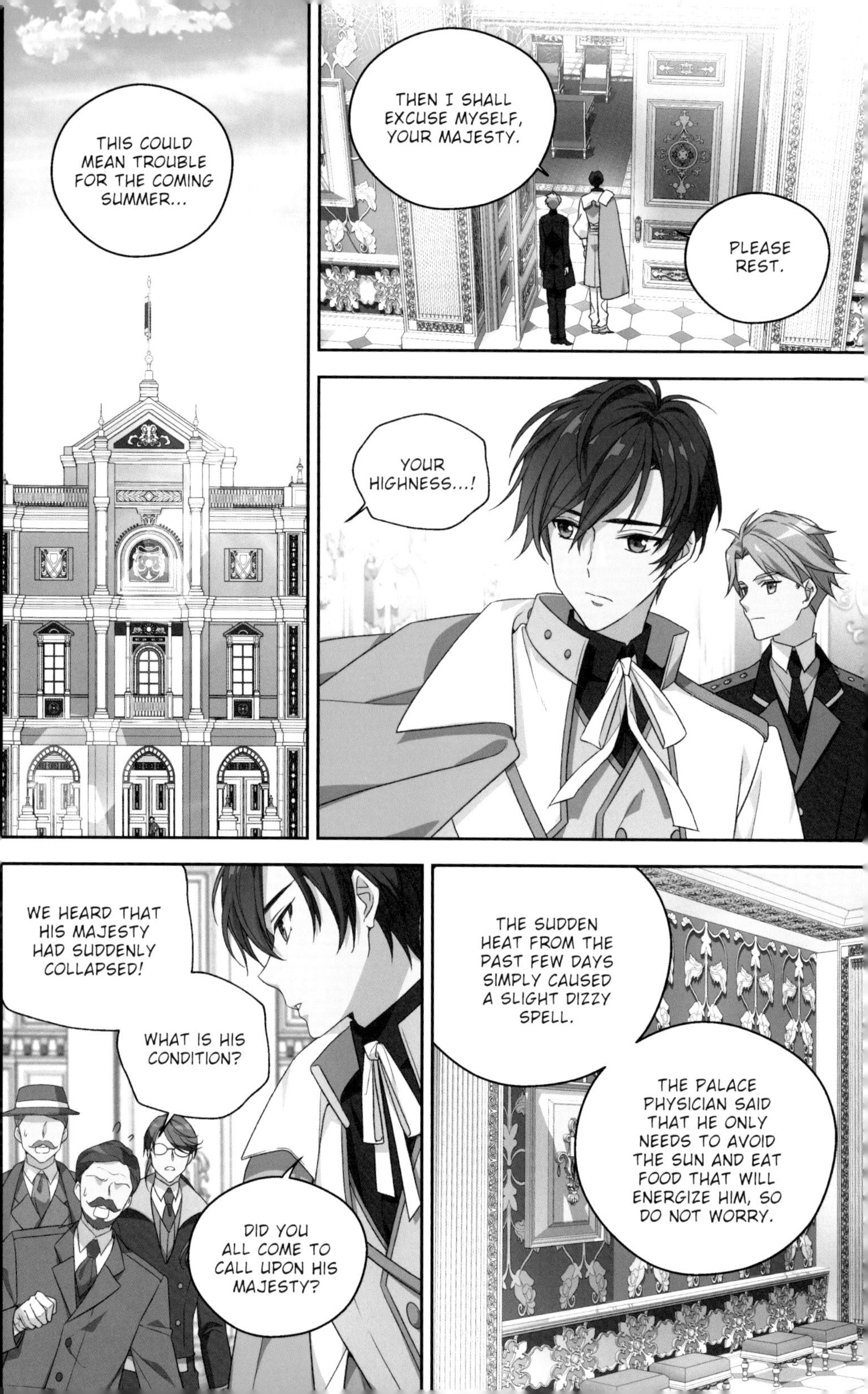
THIS COULD MEAN TROUBLE FOR THE COMING SUMMER...
THEN I SHALL EXCUSE MYSELF, YOUR MAJESTY.
PLEASE REST.
YOUR HIGHNESS...!
WE HEARD THAT HIS MAJESTY HAD SUDDENLY COLLAPSED!
WHAT IS HIS CONDITION?
DID YOU ALL COME TO CALL UPON HIS MAJESTY?
THE SUDDEN HEAT FROM THE PAST FEW DAYS SIMPLY CAUSED A SLIGHT DIZZY SPELL.
THE PALACE PHYSICIAN SAID THAT HE ONLY NEEDS TO AVOID THE SUN AND EAT FOOD THAT WILL ENERGIZE HIM, SO DO NOT WORRY.

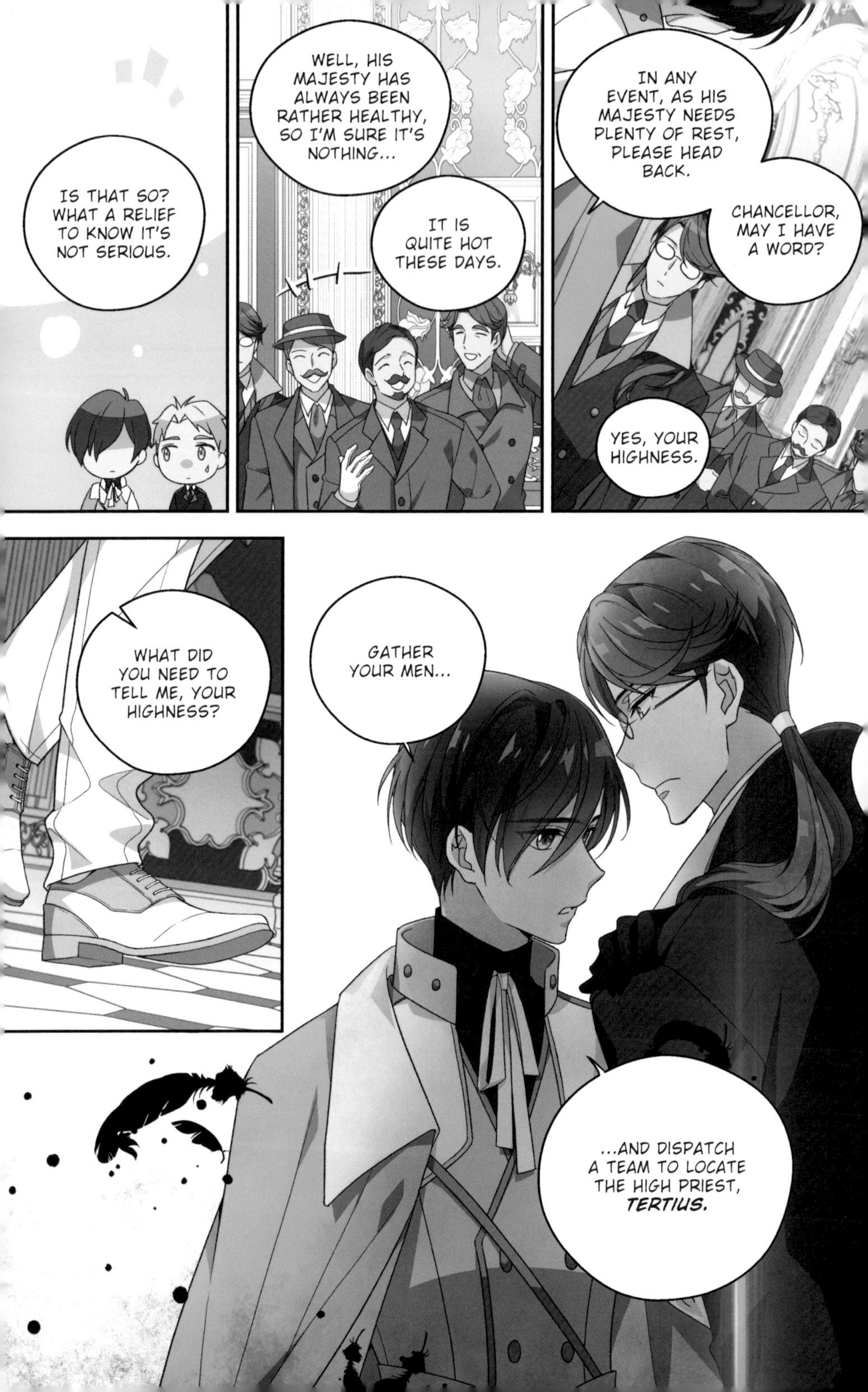
IS THAT SO? WHAT A RELIEF TO KNOW IT'S NOT SERIOUS.
WELL, HIS MAJESTY HAS ALWAYS BEEN RATHER HEALTHY, SO I'M SURE IT'S NOTHING...
IT IS QUITE HOT THESE DAYS.
IN ANY EVENT, AS HIS MAJESTY NEEDS PLENTY OF REST, PLEASE HEAD BACK.
CHANCELLOR, MAY I HAVE A WORD?
YES, YOUR HIGHNESS.
WHAT DID YOU NEED TO TELL ME, YOUR HIGHNESS?
GATHER YOUR MEN...
...AND DISPATCH A TEAM TO LOCATE THE HIGH PRIEST, TERTIUS.

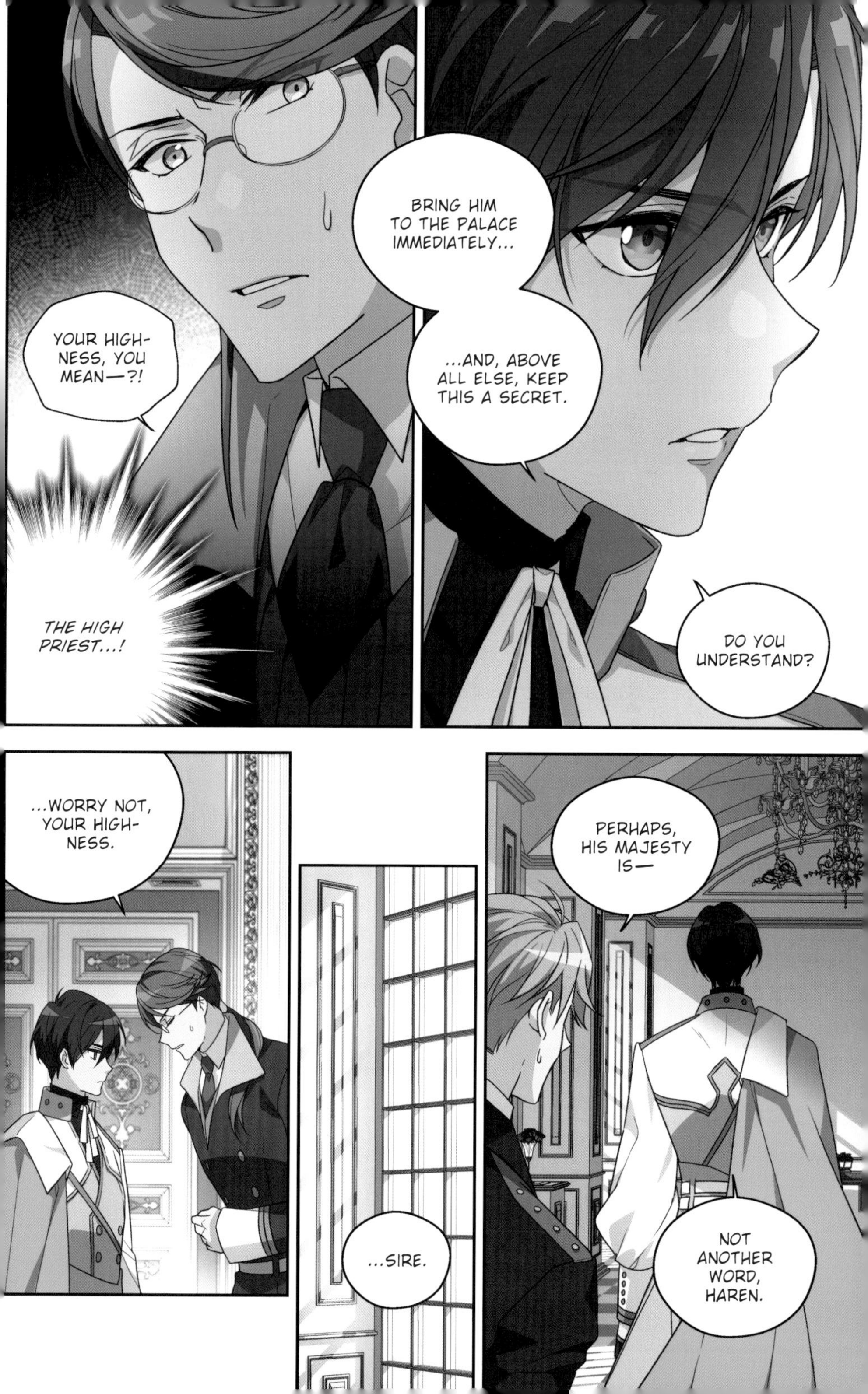
YOUR HIGH-NESS, YOU MEAN—?!
THE HIGH PRIEST...!
BRING HIM TO THE PALACE IMMEDIATELY...
...AND, ABOVE ALL ELSE, KEEP THIS A SECRET.
DO YOU UNDERSTAND?
...WORRY NOT, YOUR HIGH-NESS.
...SIRE.
PERHAPS, HIS MAJESTY IS—
NOT ANOTHER WORD, HAREN.

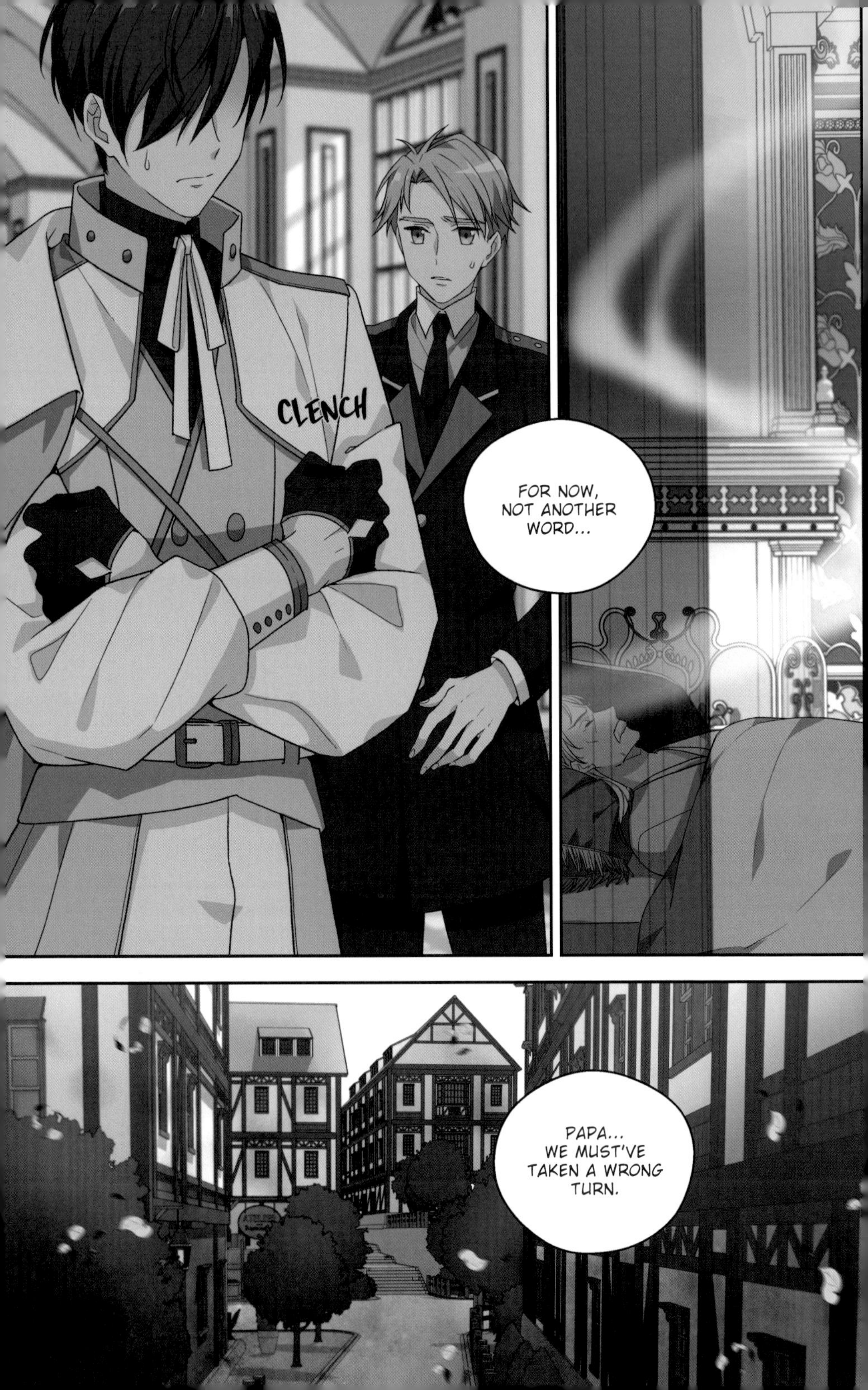
FOR NOW, NOT ANOTHER WORD...
CLENCH
PAPA... WE MUST'VE TAKEN A WRONG TURN.

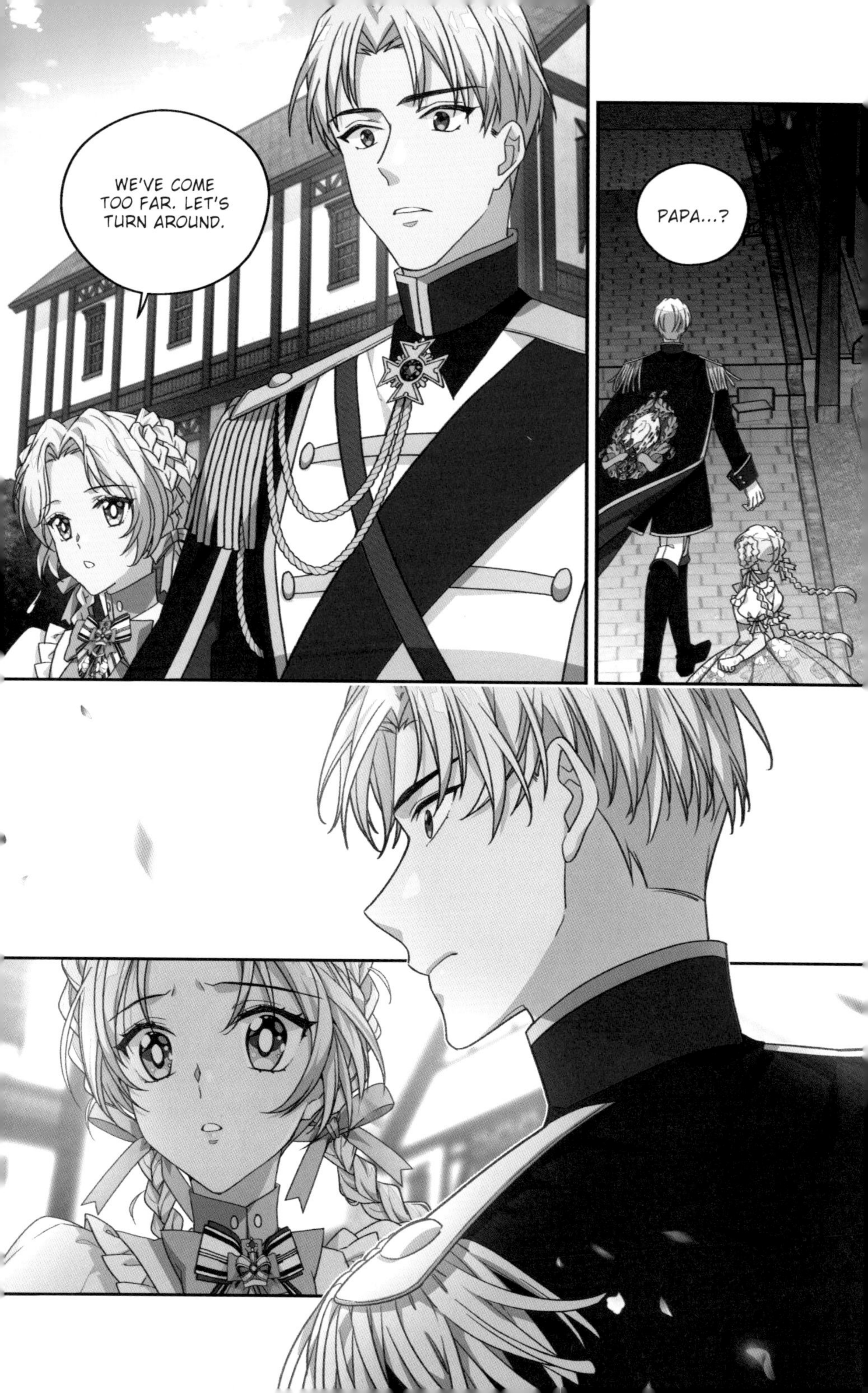
WE'VE COME TOO FAR. LET'S TURN AROUND.
PAPA...?

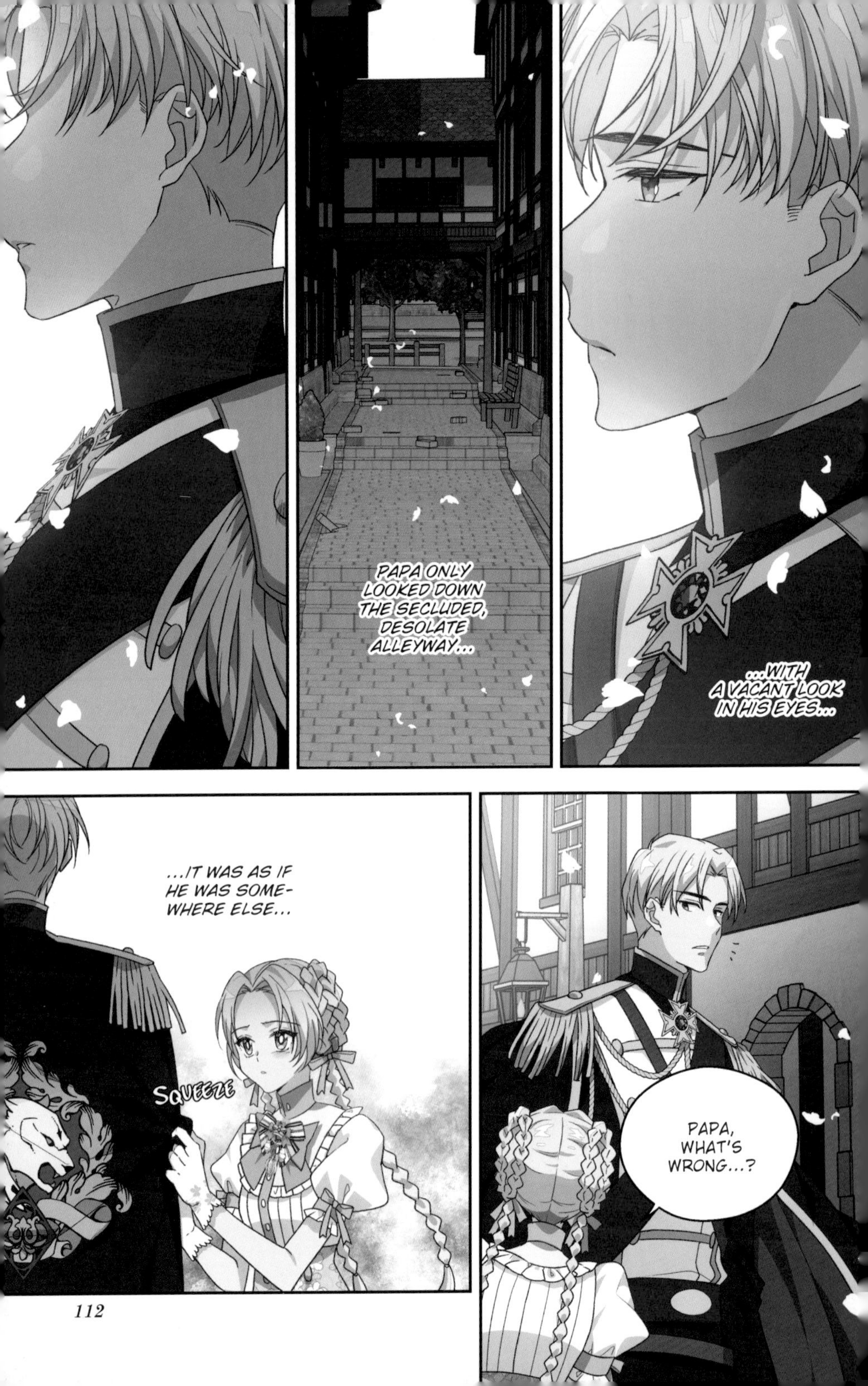

PAPA ONLY LOOKED DOWN THE SECLUDED, DESOLATE ALLEYWAY...
...WITH A VACANT LOOK IN HIS EYES...
...IT WAS AS IF HE WAS SOME-WHERE ELSE...
SQUEEZE
PAPA, WHAT'S WRONG...?

LET'S BE ON OUR WAY.

...IT'S NOTHING.

PAPA, HAVE YOU NO THOUGHTS OF REMARRYING?

...WHY DO YOU ASK OUT OF THE BLUE?

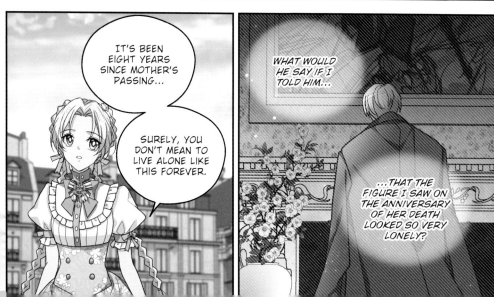

IT'S BEEN EIGHT YEARS SINCE MOTHER'S PASSING...

SURELY, YOU DON'T MEAN TO LIVE ALONE LIKE THIS FOREVER.

WHAT WOULD HE SAY IF I TOLD HIM...

...THAT THE FIGURE I SAW ON THE ANNIVERSARY OF HER DEATH LOOKED SO VERY LONELY?

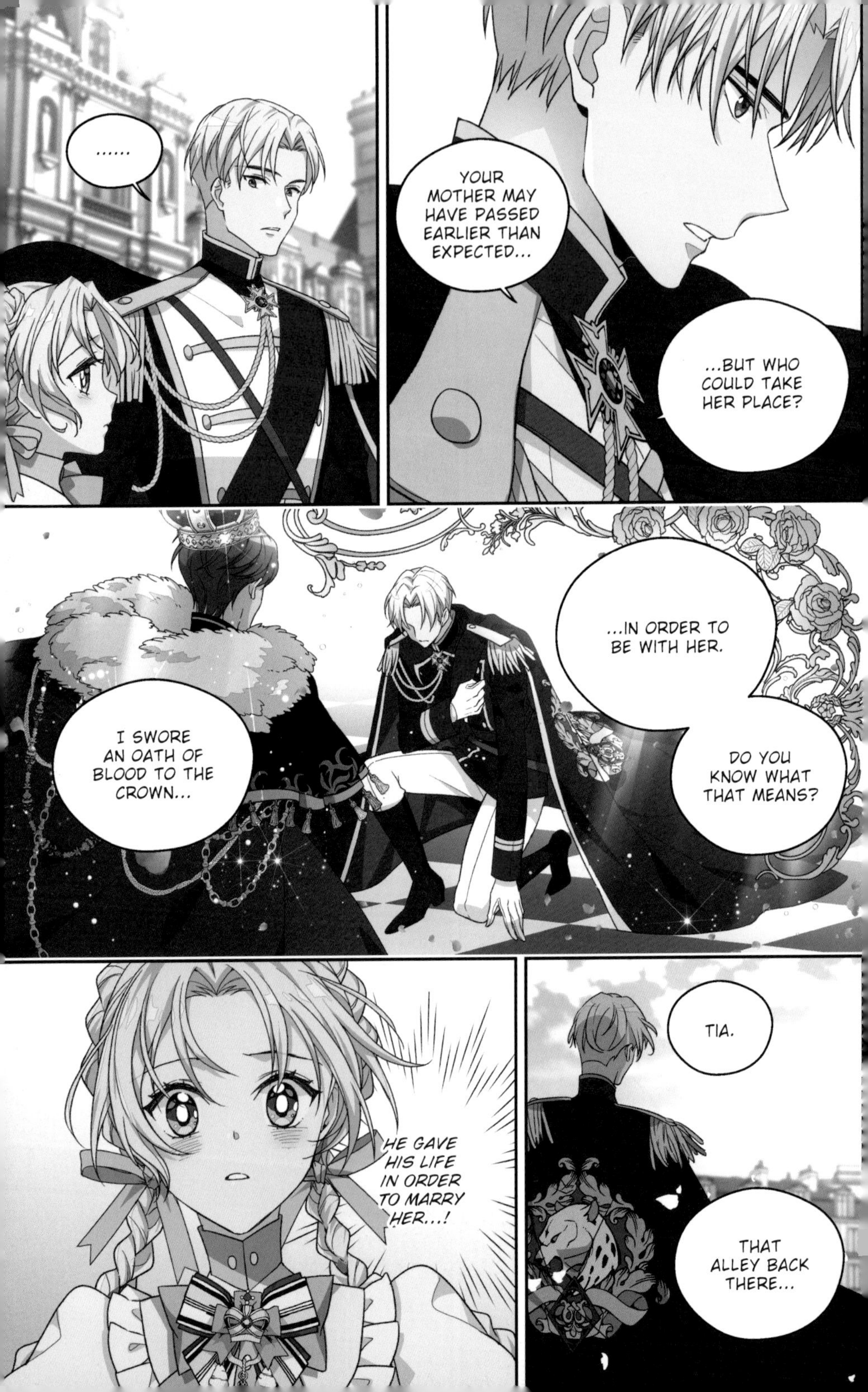
......
YOUR MOTHER MAY HAVE PASSED EARLIER THAN EXPECTED...
...BUT WHO COULD TAKE HER PLACE?
I SWORE AN OATH OF BLOOD TO THE CROWN...
...IN ORDER TO BE WITH HER.
DO YOU KNOW WHAT THAT MEANS?
HE GAVE HIS LIFE IN ORDER TO MARRY HER...!
TIA.
THAT ALLEY BACK THERE...

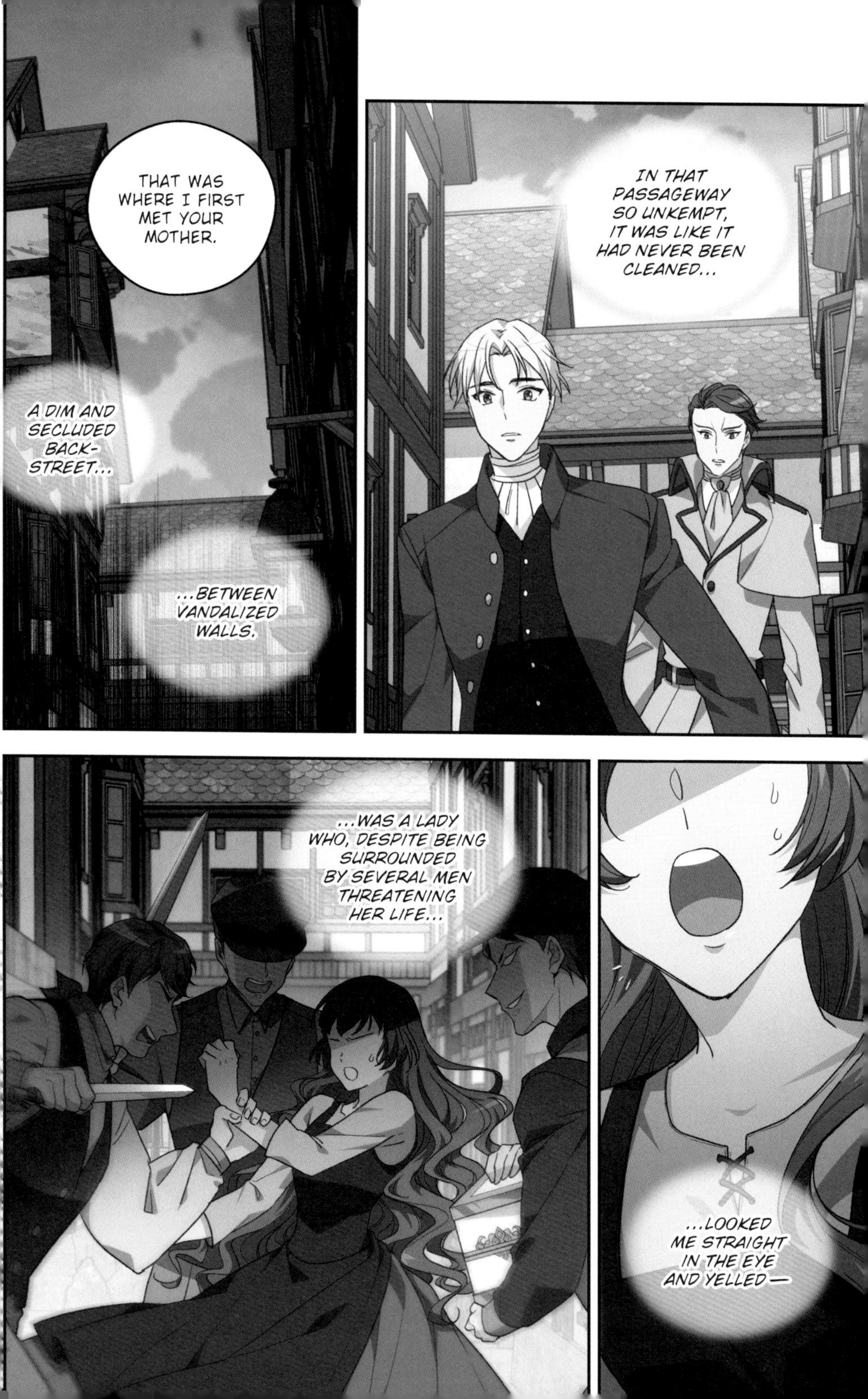
THAT WAS WHERE I FIRST MET YOUR MOTHER.
A DIM AND SECLUDED BACK-STREET...
...BETWEEN VANDALIZED WALLS.
IN THAT PASSAGEWAY SO UNKEMPT, IT WAS LIKE IT HAD NEVER BEEN CLEANED...
...WAS A LADY WHO, DESPITE BEING SURROUNDED BY SEVERAL MEN THREATENING HER LIFE...
...LOOKED ME STRAIGHT IN THE EYE AND YELLED—

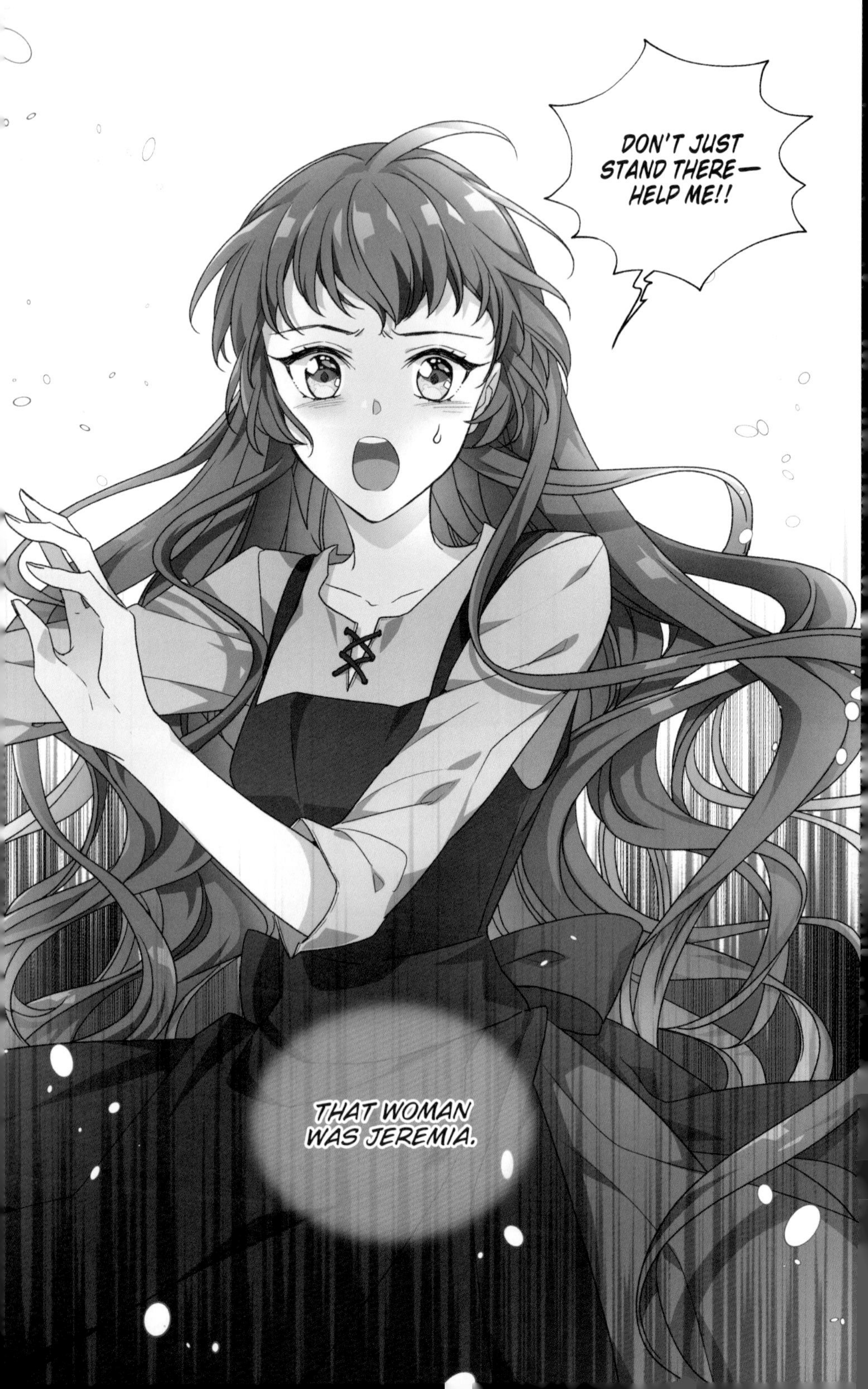
DON'T JUST STAND THERE—HELP ME!!
THAT WOMAN WAS JEREMIA.

The Abandoned Empress

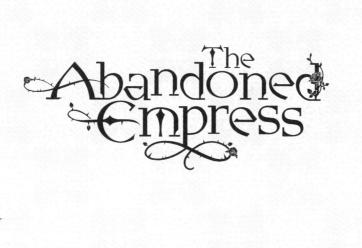

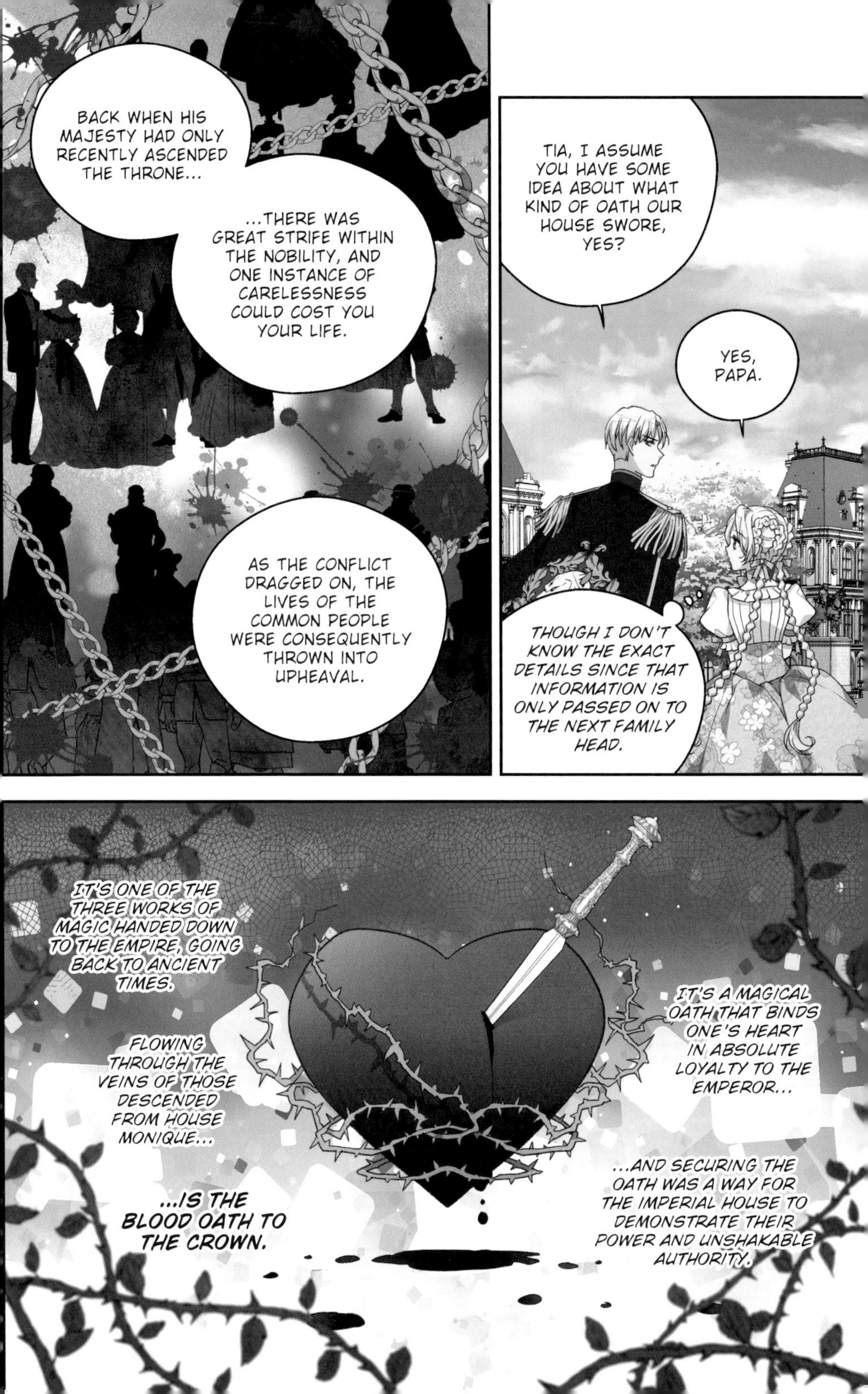
BACK WHEN HIS MAJESTY HAD ONLY RECENTLY ASCENDED THE THRONE...
...THERE WAS GREAT STRIFE WITHIN THE NOBILITY, AND ONE INSTANCE OF CARELESSNESS COULD COST YOU YOUR LIFE.
AS THE CONFLICT DRAGGED ON, THE LIVES OF THE COMMON PEOPLE WERE CONSEQUENTLY THROWN INTO UPHEAVAL.
TIA, I ASSUME YOU HAVE SOME IDEA ABOUT WHAT KIND OF OATH OUR HOUSE SWORE, YES?
YES, PAPA.
THOUGH I DON'T KNOW THE EXACT DETAILS SINCE THAT INFORMATION IS ONLY PASSED ON TO THE NEXT FAMILY HEAD.
IT'S ONE OF THE THREE WORKS OF MAGIC HANDED DOWN TO THE EMPIRE, GOING BACK TO ANCIENT TIMES.
FLOWING THROUGH THE VEINS OF THOSE DESCENDED FROM HOUSE MONIQUE...
...IS THE BLOOD OATH TO THE CROWN.
IT'S A MAGICAL OATH THAT BINDS ONE'S HEART IN ABSOLUTE LOYALTY TO THE EMPEROR...
...AND SECURING THE OATH WAS A WAY FOR THE IMPERIAL HOUSE TO DEMONSTRATE THEIR POWER AND UNSHAKABLE AUTHORITY.

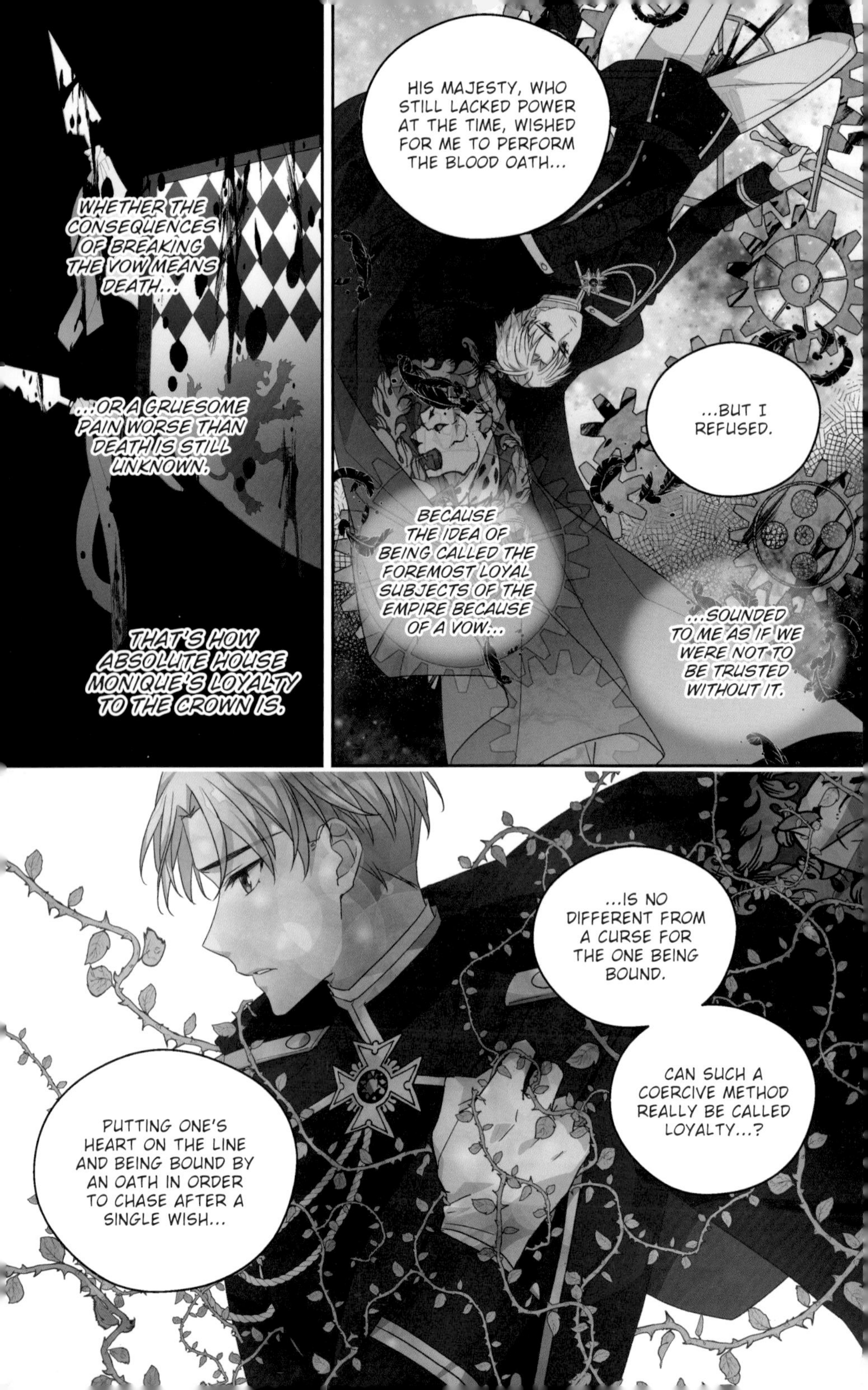
WHETHER THE CONSEQUENCES OF BREAKING THE VOW MEANS DEATH...
...OR A GRUESOME PAIN WORSE THAN DEATH IS STILL UNKNOWN.
THAT'S HOW ABSOLUTE HOUSE MONIQUE'S LOYALTY TO THE CROWN IS.
HIS MAJESTY, WHO STILL LACKED POWER AT THE TIME, WISHED FOR ME TO PERFORM THE BLOOD OATH...
...BUT I REFUSED.
BECAUSE THE IDEA OF BEING CALLED THE FOREMOST LOYAL SUBJECTS OF THE EMPIRE BECAUSE OF A VOW...
...SOUNDED TO ME AS IF WE WERE NOT TO BE TRUSTED WITHOUT IT.
PUTTING ONE'S HEART ON THE LINE AND BEING BOUND BY AN OATH IN ORDER TO CHASE AFTER A SINGLE WISH...
...IS NO DIFFERENT FROM A CURSE FOR THE ONE BEING BOUND.
CAN SUCH A COERCIVE METHOD REALLY BE CALLED LOYALTY...?

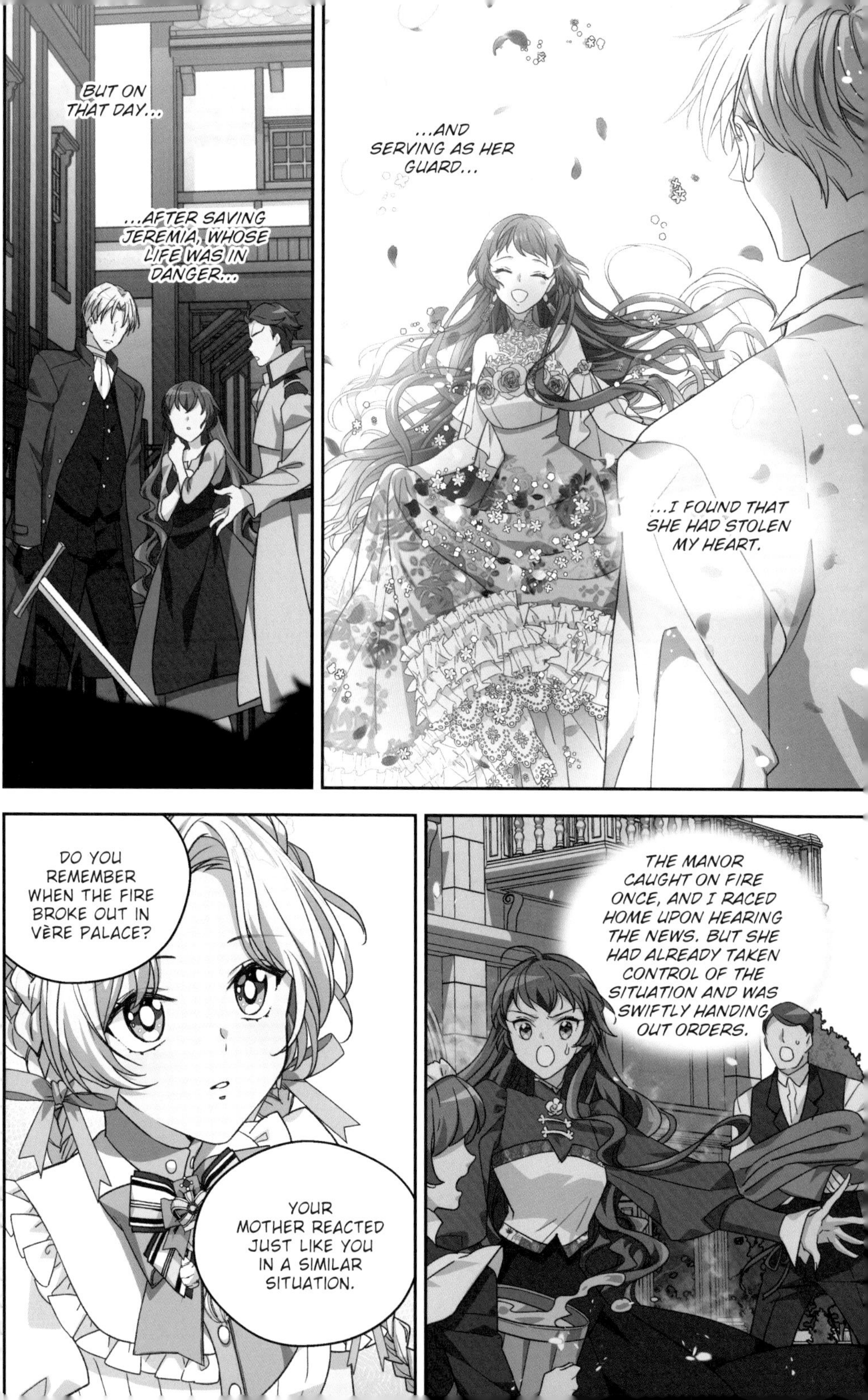
BUT ON THAT DAY...
...AFTER SAVING JEREMIA, WHOSE LIFE WAS IN DANGER...
...AND SERVING AS HER GUARD...
...I FOUND THAT SHE HAD STOLEN MY HEART.
DO YOU REMEMBER WHEN THE FIRE BROKE OUT IN VÈRE PALACE?
YOUR MOTHER REACTED JUST LIKE YOU IN A SIMILAR SITUATION.
THE MANOR CAUGHT ON FIRE ONCE, AND I RACED HOME UPON HEARING THE NEWS. BUT SHE HAD ALREADY TAKEN CONTROL OF THE SITUATION AND WAS SWIFTLY HANDING OUT ORDERS.

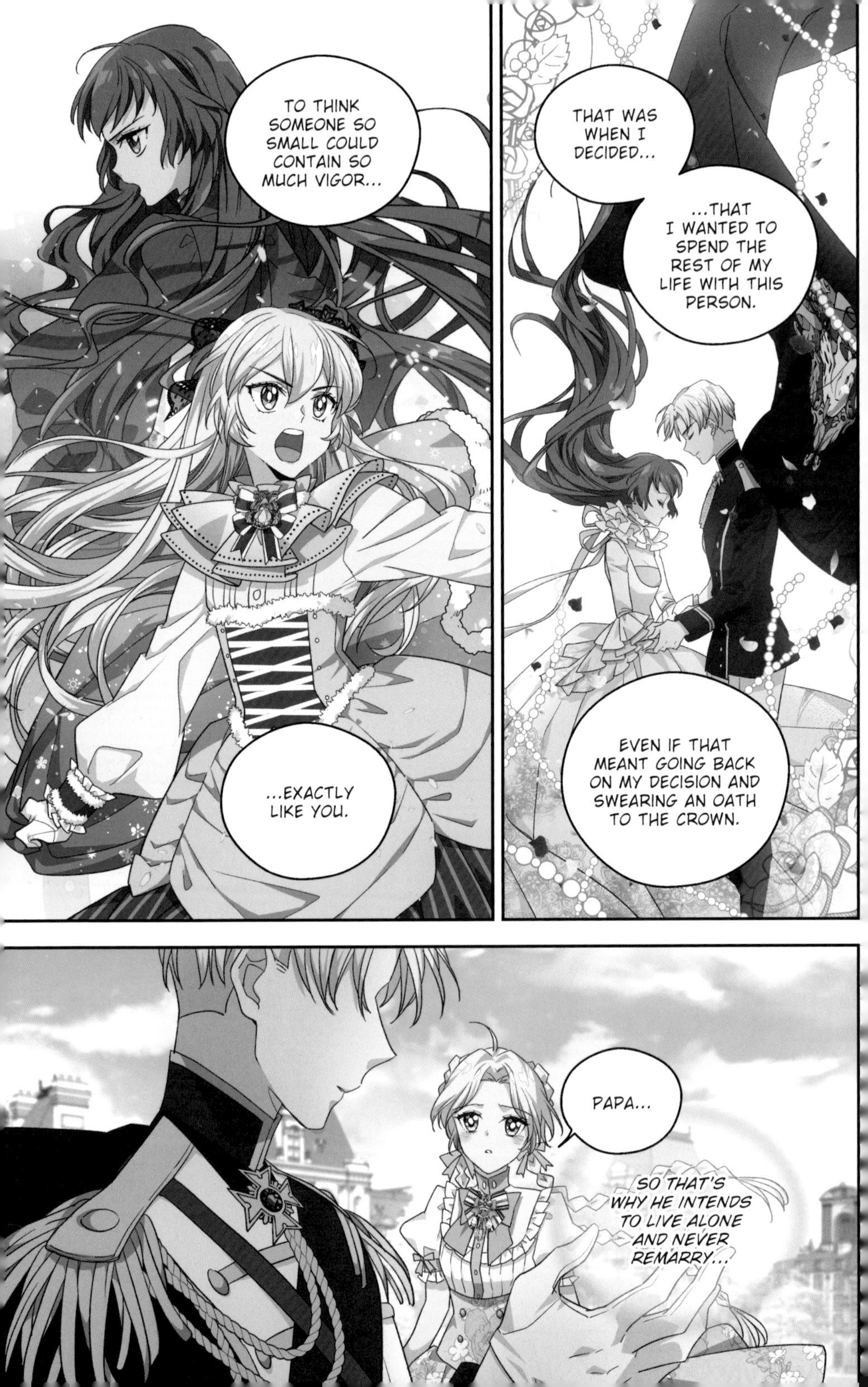
TO THINK SOMEONE SO SMALL COULD CONTAIN SO MUCH VIGOR...
...EXACTLY LIKE YOU.
THAT WAS WHEN I DECIDED...
...THAT I WANTED TO SPEND THE REST OF MY LIFE WITH THIS PERSON.
EVEN IF THAT MEANT GOING BACK ON MY DECISION AND SWEARING AN OATH TO THE CROWN.
PAPA...
SO THAT'S WHY HE INTENDS TO LIVE ALONE AND NEVER REMARRY...

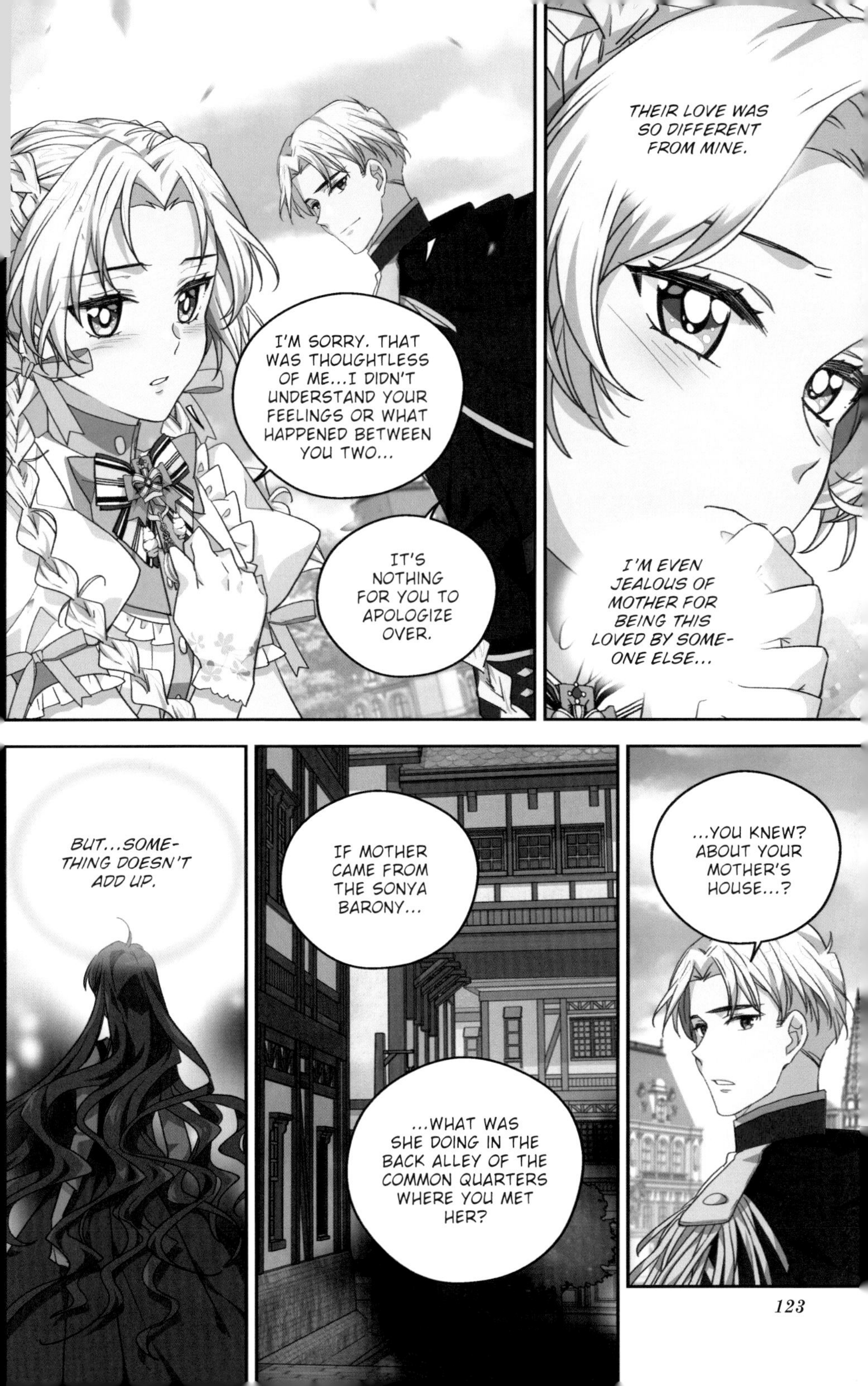
I'M SORRY. THAT WAS THOUGHTLESS OF ME...I DIDN'T UNDERSTAND YOUR FEELINGS OR WHAT HAPPENED BETWEEN YOU TWO...
IT'S NOTHING FOR YOU TO APOLOGIZE OVER.
THEIR LOVE WAS SO DIFFERENT FROM MINE.
I'M EVEN JEALOUS OF MOTHER FOR BEING THIS LOVED BY SOME-ONE ELSE...
BUT...SOME-THING DOESN'T ADD UP.
IF MOTHER CAME FROM THE SONYA BARONY...
...WHAT WAS SHE DOING IN THE BACK ALLEY OF THE COMMON QUARTERS WHERE YOU MET HER?
...YOU KNEW? ABOUT YOUR MOTHER'S HOUSE...?

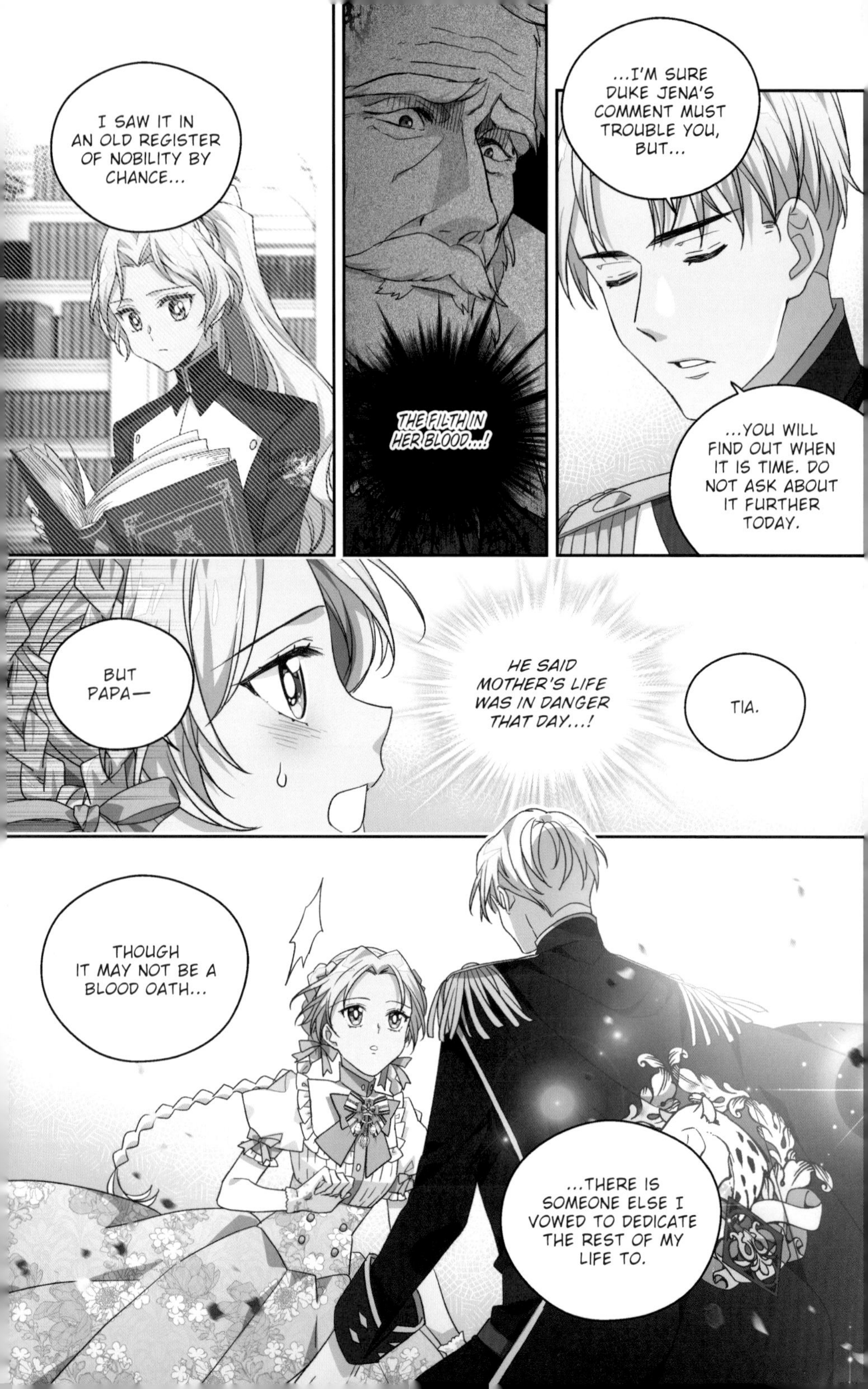
I SAW IT IN AN OLD REGISTER OF NOBILITY BY CHANCE...
THE FILTH IN HER BLOOD...!
...I'M SURE DUKE JENA'S COMMENT MUST TROUBLE YOU, BUT...
...YOU WILL FIND OUT WHEN IT IS TIME. DO NOT ASK ABOUT IT FURTHER TODAY.
BUT PAPA—
HE SAID MOTHER'S LIFE WAS IN DANGER THAT DAY...!
TIA.
THOUGH IT MAY NOT BE A BLOOD OATH...
...THERE IS SOMEONE ELSE I VOWED TO DEDICATE THE REST OF MY LIFE TO.

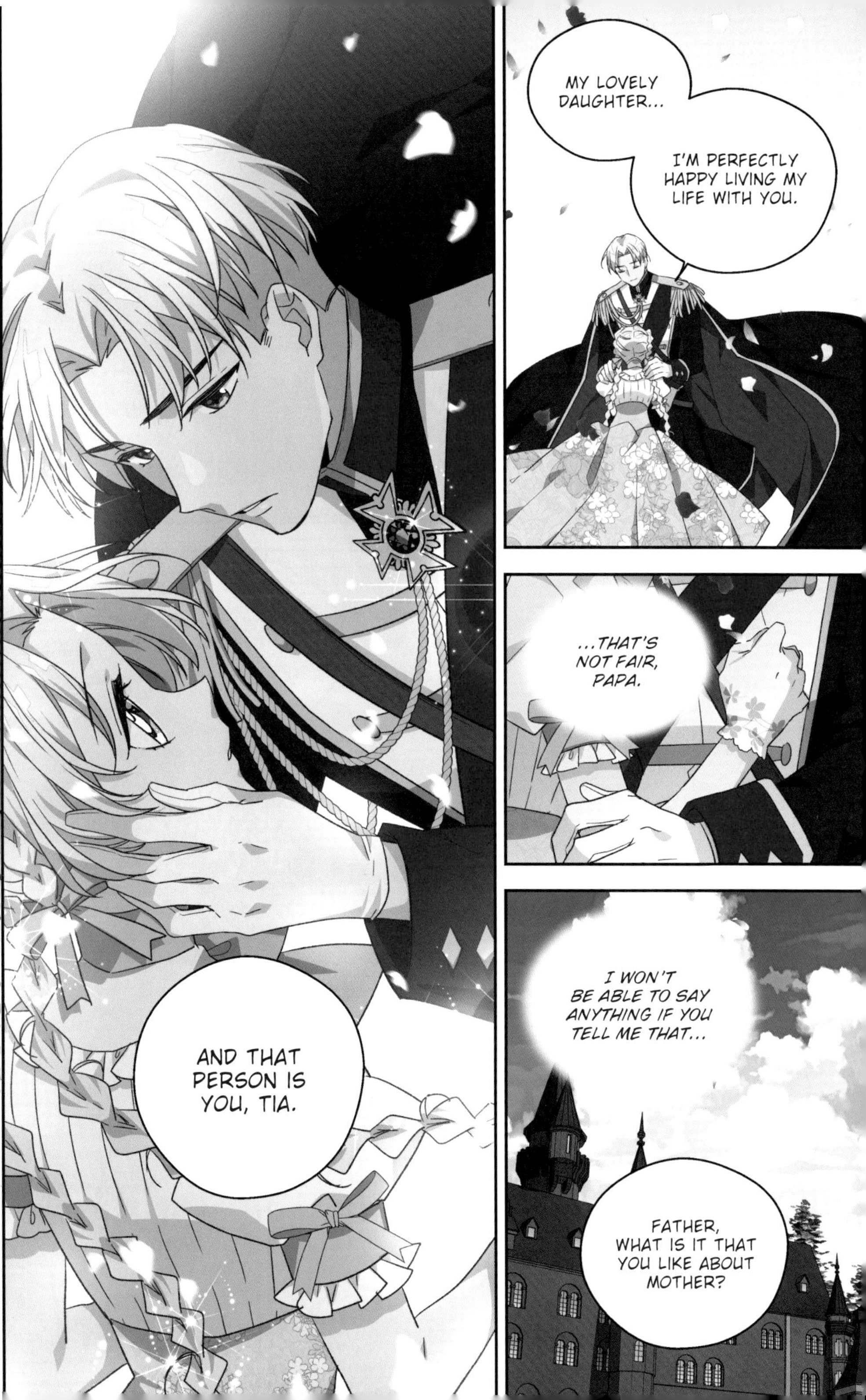
AND THAT PERSON IS YOU, TIA.
MY LOVELY DAUGHTER...
I'M PERFECTLY HAPPY LIVING MY LIFE WITH YOU.
...THAT'S NOT FAIR, PAPA.
I WON'T BE ABLE TO SAY ANYTHING IF YOU TELL ME THAT...
FATHER, WHAT IS IT THAT YOU LIKE ABOUT MOTHER?

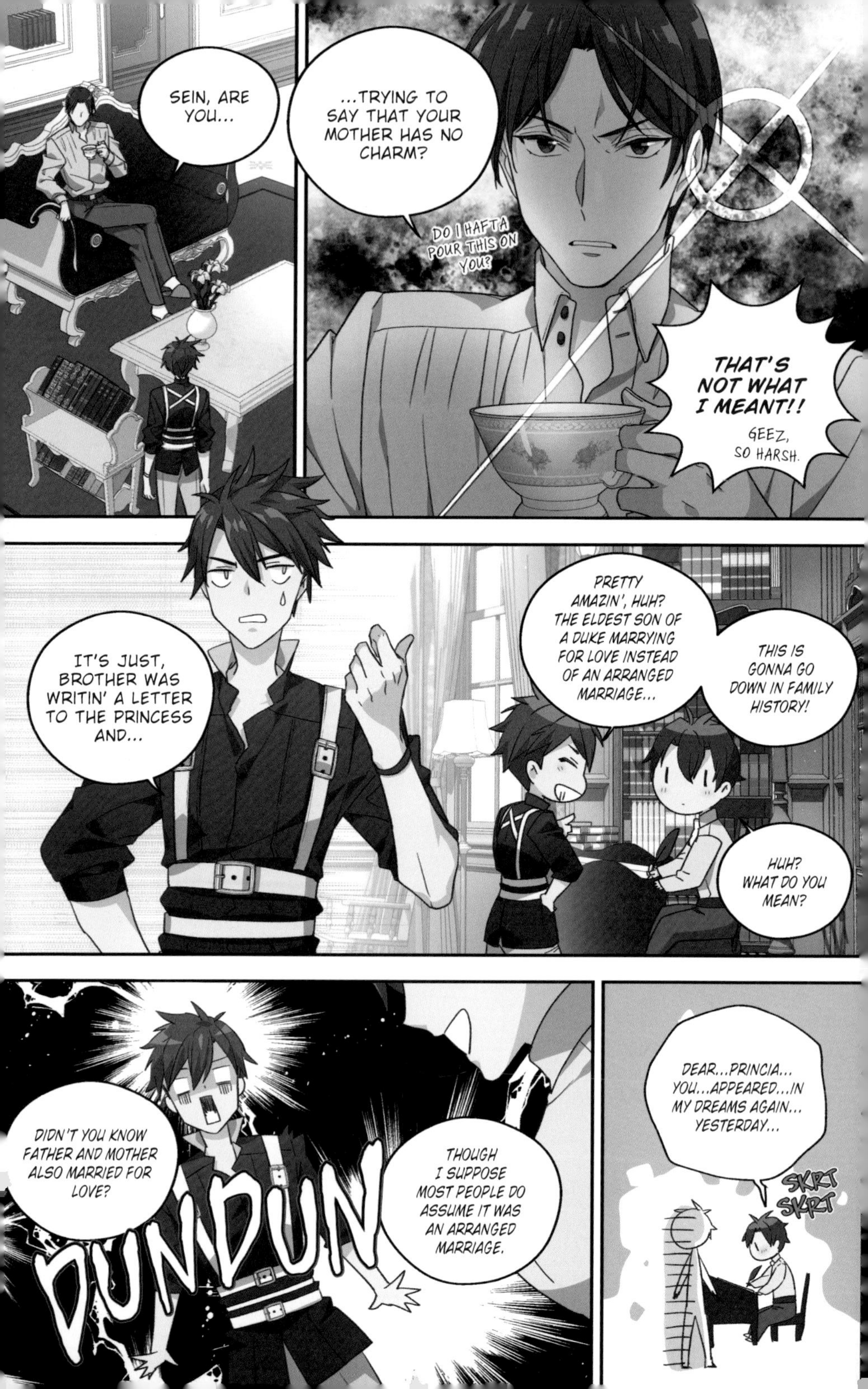
SEIN, ARE YOU...
...TRYING TO SAY THAT YOUR MOTHER HAS NO CHARM?
DO I HAFTA POUR THIS ON YOU?
THAT'S NOT WHAT I MEANT!!
GEEZ, SO HARSH.
IT'S JUST, BROTHER WAS WRITIN' A LETTER TO THE PRINCESS AND...
PRETTY AMAZIN', HUH? THE ELDEST SON OF A DUKE MARRYING FOR LOVE INSTEAD OF AN ARRANGED MARRIAGE...
THIS IS GONNA GO DOWN IN FAMILY HISTORY!
HUH? WHAT DO YOU MEAN?
DIDN'T YOU KNOW FATHER AND MOTHER ALSO MARRIED FOR LOVE?
DUN DUN
THOUGH I SUPPOSE MOST PEOPLE DO ASSUME IT WAS AN ARRANGED MARRIAGE.
DEAR...PRINCIA... YOU...APPEARED...IN MY DREAMS AGAIN... YESTERDAY...
SKRT SKRT

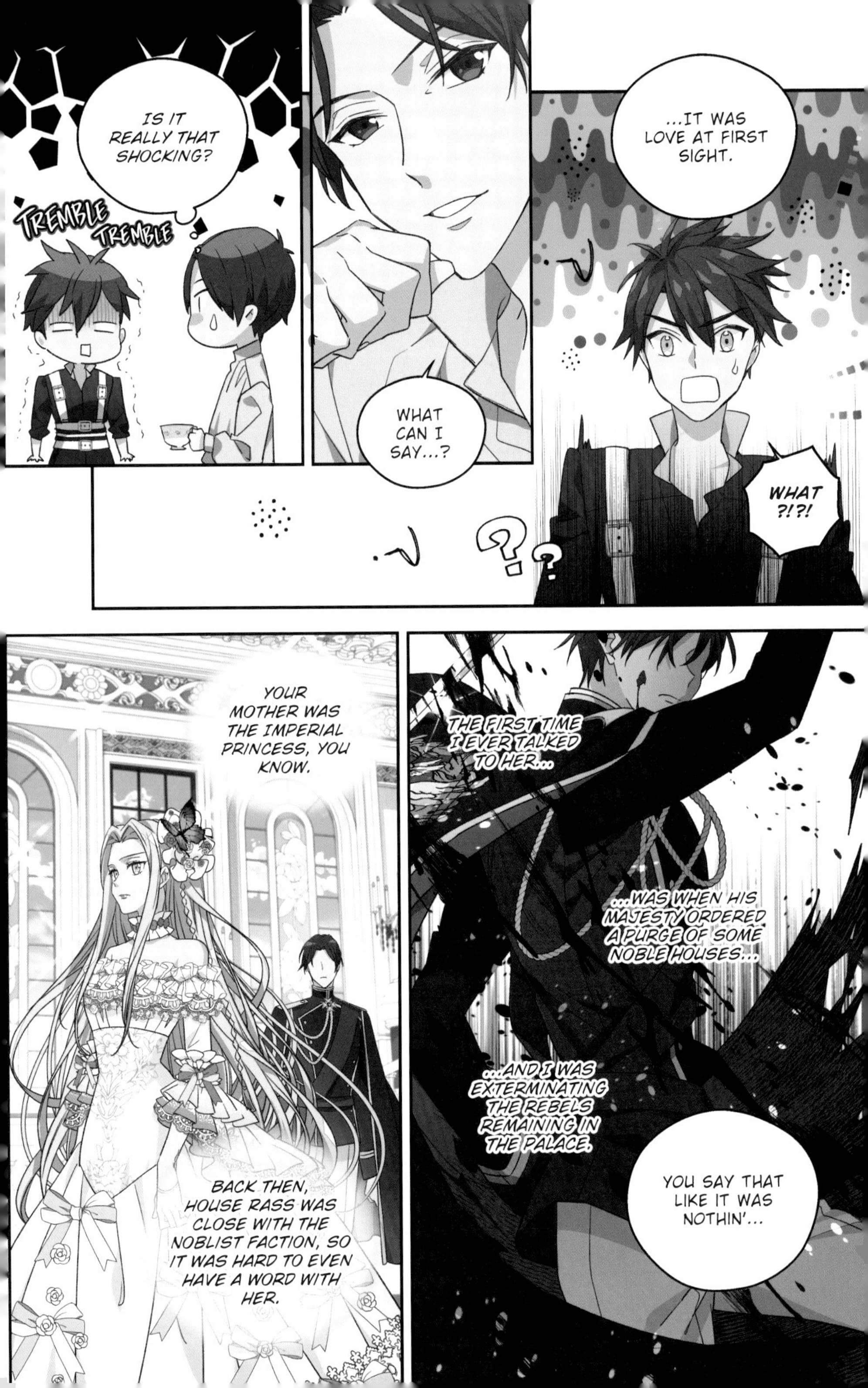
IS IT REALLY THAT SHOCKING?
TREMBLE TREMBLE
WHAT CAN I SAY...?
...IT WAS LOVE AT FIRST SIGHT.
WHAT ?!?!
YOUR MOTHER WAS THE IMPERIAL PRINCESS, YOU KNOW.
BACK THEN, HOUSE RASS WAS CLOSE WITH THE NOBLIST FACTION, SO IT WAS HARD TO EVEN HAVE A WORD WITH HER.
THE FIRST TIME I EVER TALKED TO HER...
...WAS WHEN HIS MAJESTY ORDERED A PURGE OF SOME NOBLE HOUSES...
...AND I WAS EXTERMINATING THE REBELS REMAINING IN THE PALACE.
YOU SAY THAT LIKE IT WAS NOTHIN'...

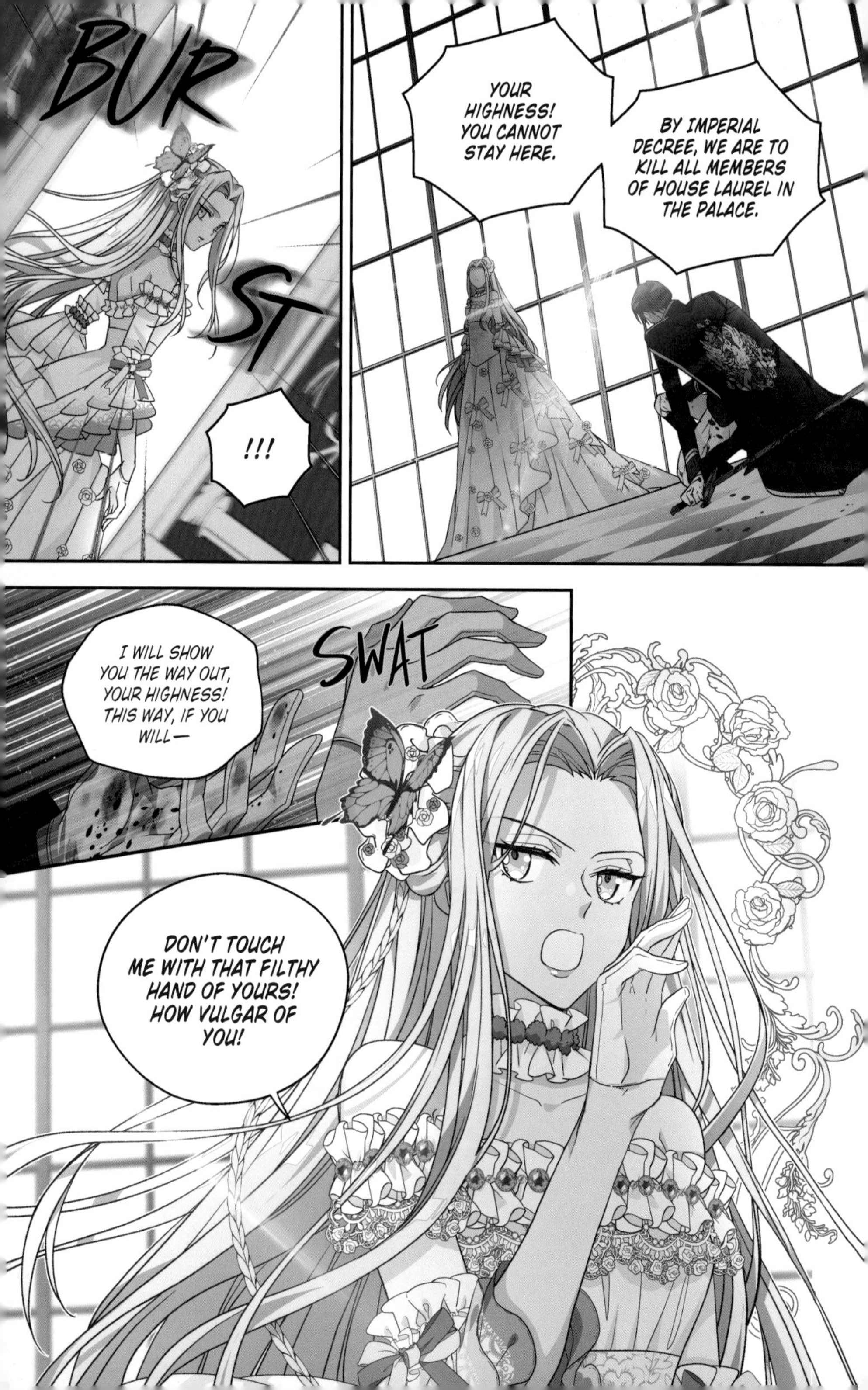
BURST
!!!
YOUR HIGHNESS! YOU CANNOT STAY HERE.
BY IMPERIAL DECREE, WE ARE TO KILL ALL MEMBERS OF HOUSE LAUREL IN THE PALACE.
I WILL SHOW YOU THE WAY OUT, YOUR HIGHNESS! THIS WAY, IF YOU WILL—
SWAT
DON'T TOUCH ME WITH THAT FILTHY HAND OF YOURS! HOW VULGAR OF YOU!

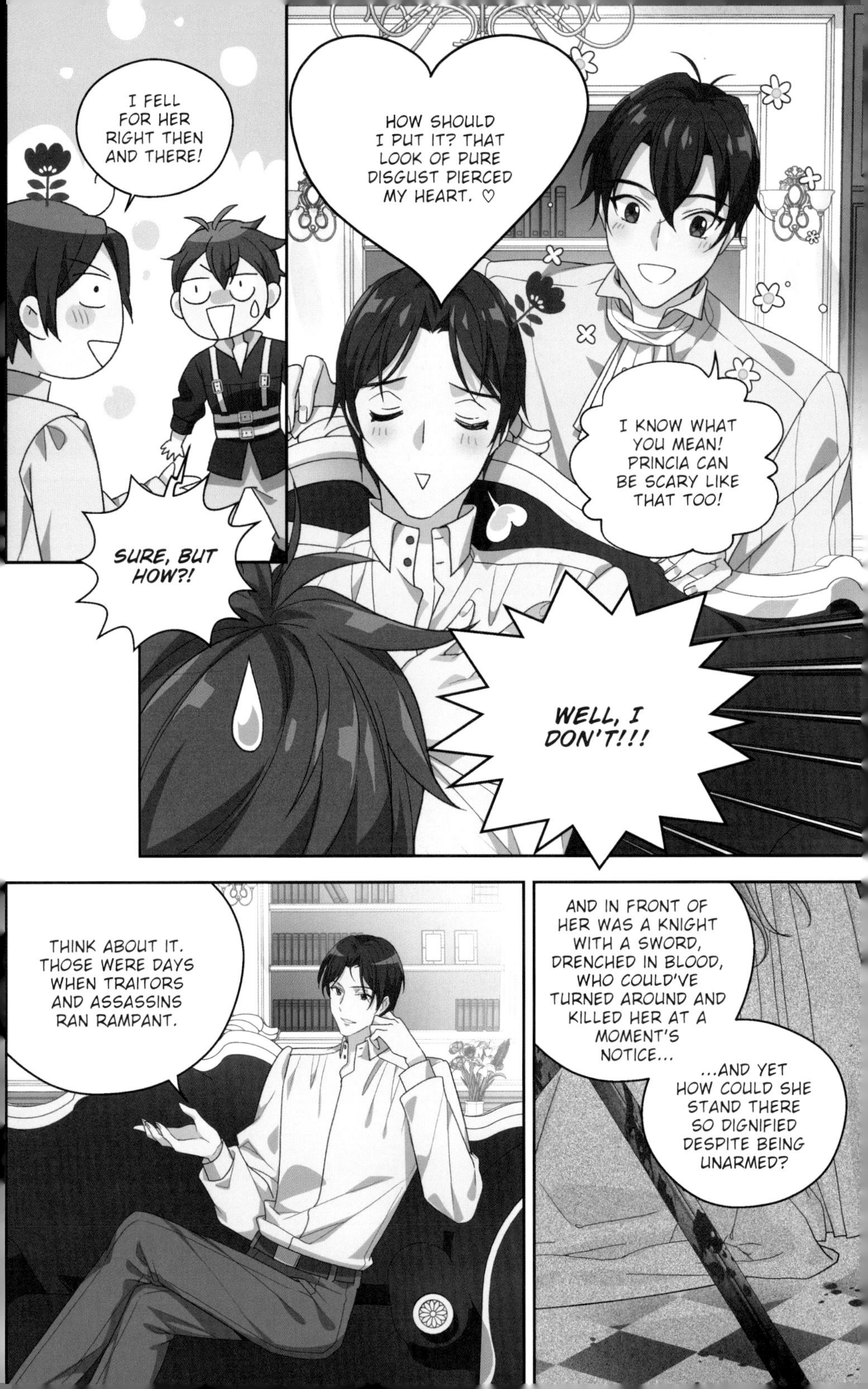
I FELL FOR HER RIGHT THEN AND THERE!
HOW SHOULD I PUT IT? THAT LOOK OF PURE DISGUST PIERCED MY HEART. ♡
I KNOW WHAT YOU MEAN! PRINCIA CAN BE SCARY LIKE THAT TOO!
SURE, BUT HOW?!
WELL, I DON'T!!!
THINK ABOUT IT. THOSE WERE DAYS WHEN TRAITORS AND ASSASSINS RAN RAMPANT.
AND IN FRONT OF HER WAS A KNIGHT WITH A SWORD, DRENCHED IN BLOOD, WHO COULD'VE TURNED AROUND AND KILLED HER AT A MOMENT'S NOTICE...
...AND YET HOW COULD SHE STAND THERE SO DIGNIFIED DESPITE BEING UNARMED?

THERE'S MORE TO KNIGHTHOOD THAN SWINGING A SWORD AROUND.

YOU TWO SHOULD BEAR THAT IN MIND.

WHEN YOU THINK ABOUT IT, THOSE DAYS BEING WHAT THEY WERE MADE THEM ALL THE STRONGER...

SHE WAS FAR MORE IMPRESSIVE THAN A KNIGHT LIKE ME.

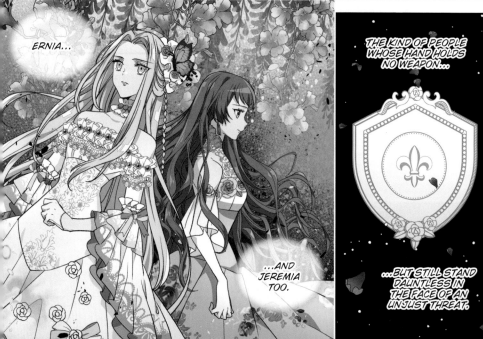

ERNIA...

...AND JEREMIA TOO.

THE KIND OF PEOPLE WHOSE HAND HOLDS NO WEAPON...

...BUT STILL STAND DAUNTLESS IN THE FACE OF AN UNJUST THREAT.

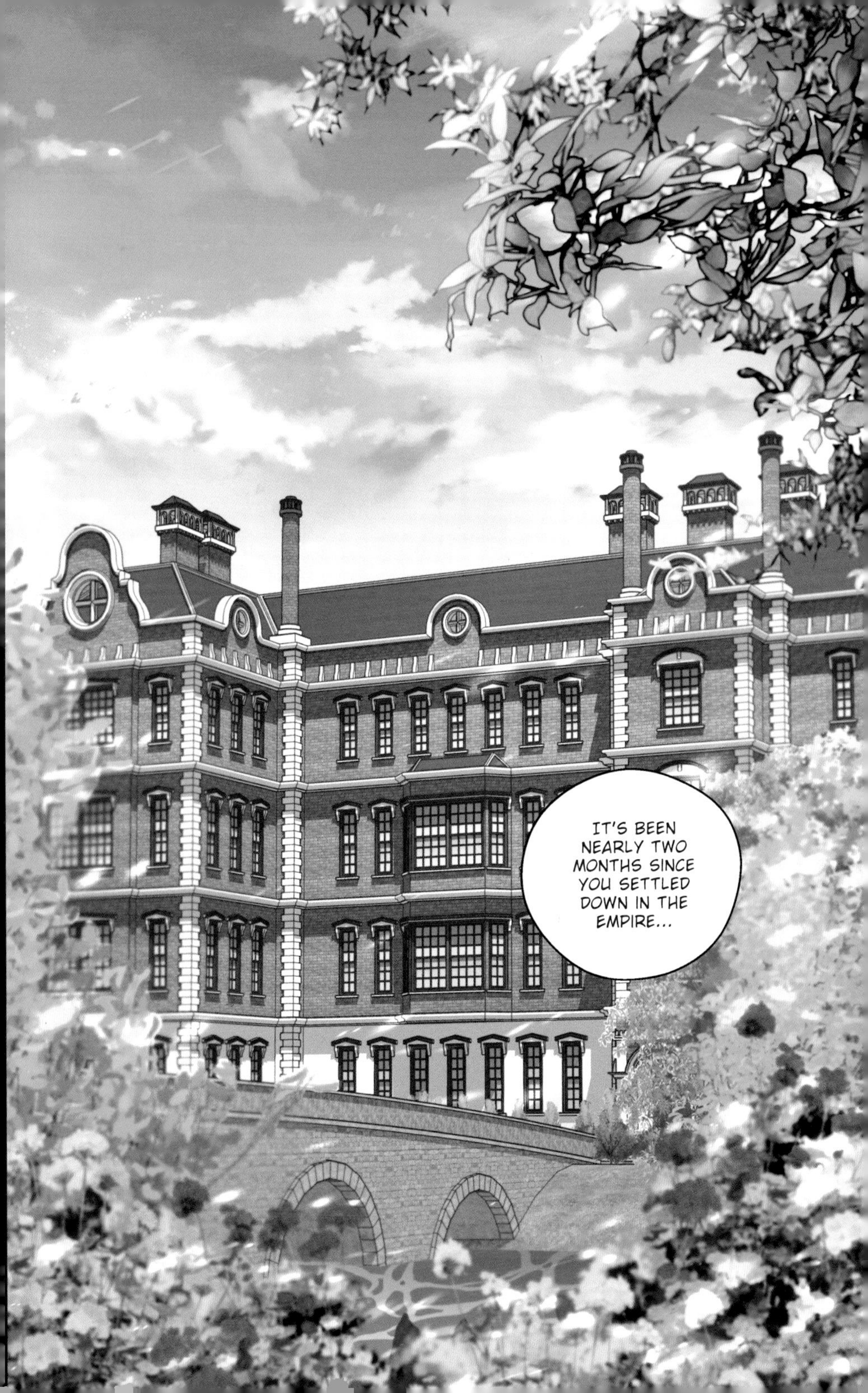
IT'S BEEN NEARLY TWO MONTHS SINCE YOU SETTLED DOWN IN THE EMPIRE...

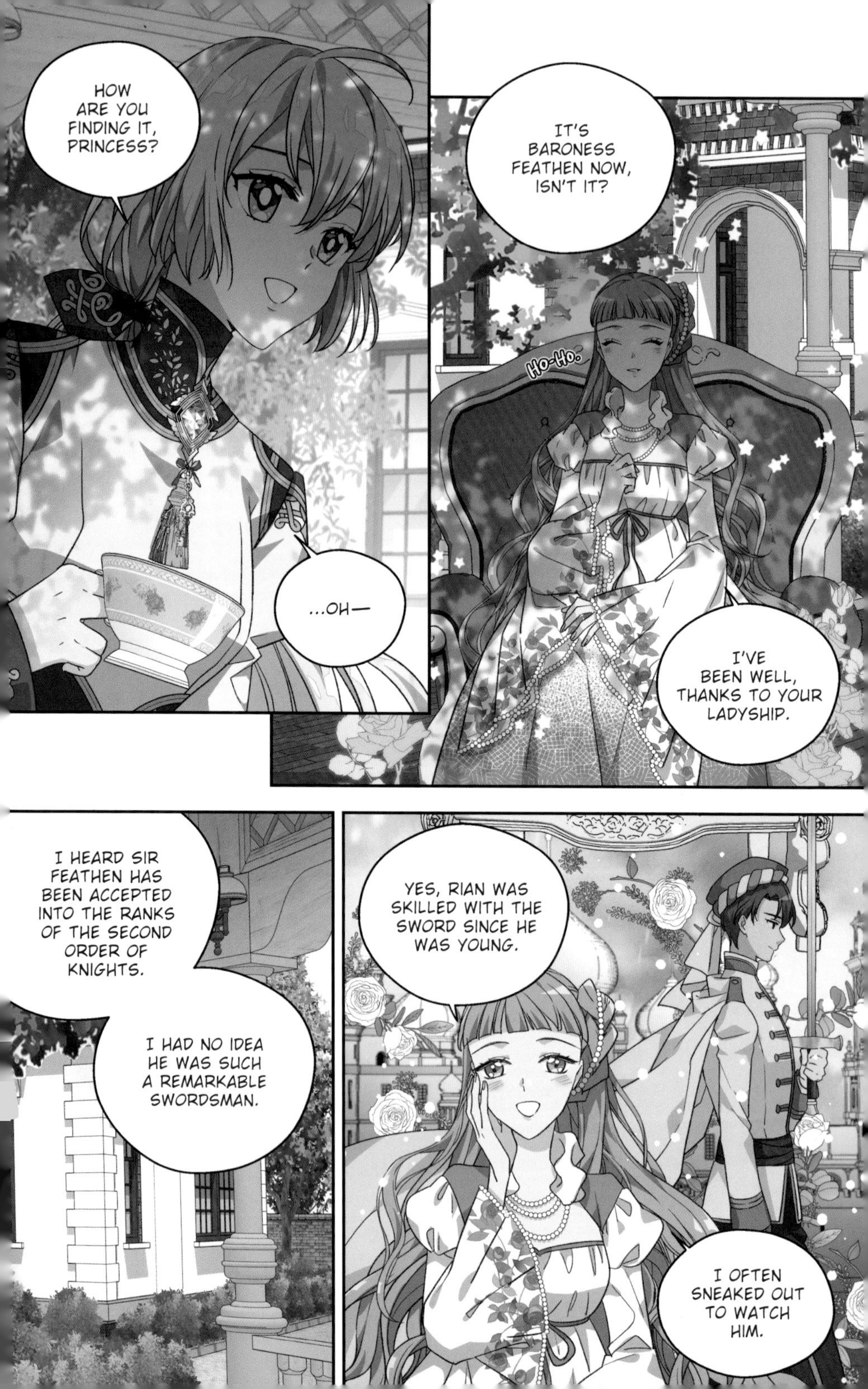
HOW ARE YOU FINDING IT, PRINCESS?
IT'S BARONESS FEATHEN NOW, ISN'T IT?
...OH—
HO-HO.
I'VE BEEN WELL, THANKS TO YOUR LADYSHIP.
I HEARD SIR FEATHEN HAS BEEN ACCEPTED INTO THE RANKS OF THE SECOND ORDER OF KNIGHTS.
I HAD NO IDEA HE WAS SUCH A REMARKABLE SWORDSMAN.
YES, RIAN WAS SKILLED WITH THE SWORD SINCE HE WAS YOUNG.
I OFTEN SNEAKED OUT TO WATCH HIM.

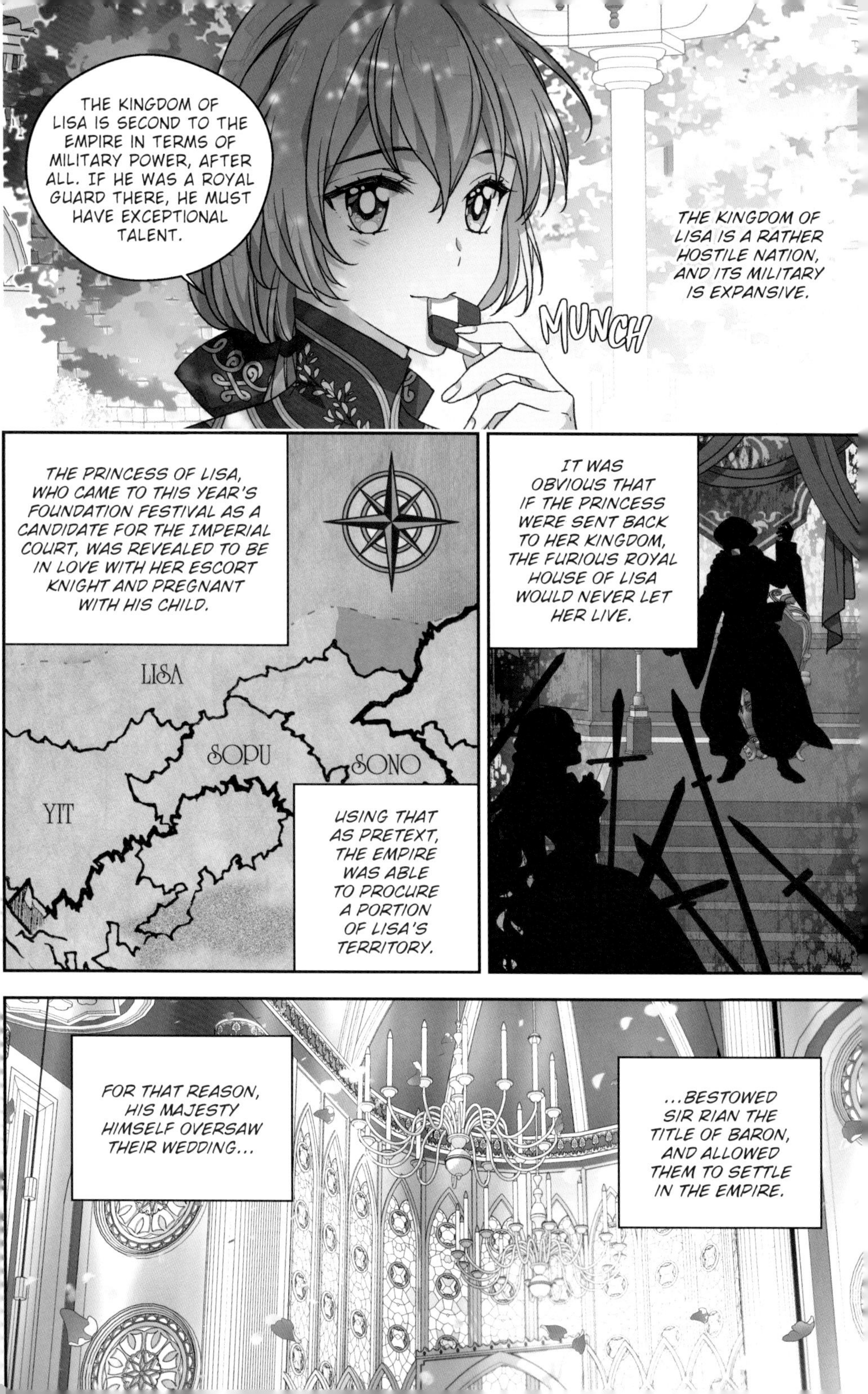
THE KINGDOM OF LISA IS SECOND TO THE EMPIRE IN TERMS OF MILITARY POWER, AFTER ALL. IF HE WAS A ROYAL GUARD THERE, HE MUST HAVE EXCEPTIONAL TALENT.
THE KINGDOM OF LISA IS A RATHER HOSTILE NATION, AND ITS MILITARY IS EXPANSIVE.
MUNCH
THE PRINCESS OF LISA, WHO CAME TO THIS YEAR'S FOUNDATION FESTIVAL AS A CANDIDATE FOR THE IMPERIAL COURT, WAS REVEALED TO BE IN LOVE WITH HER ESCORT KNIGHT AND PREGNANT WITH HIS CHILD.
LISA
SOPU
SONO
YIT
USING THAT AS PRETEXT, THE EMPIRE WAS ABLE TO PROCURE A PORTION OF LISA'S TERRITORY.
IT WAS OBVIOUS THAT IF THE PRINCESS WERE SENT BACK TO HER KINGDOM, THE FURIOUS ROYAL HOUSE OF LISA WOULD NEVER LET HER LIVE.
FOR THAT REASON, HIS MAJESTY HIMSELF OVERSAW THEIR WEDDING...
...BESTOWED SIR RIAN THE TITLE OF BARON, AND ALLOWED THEM TO SETTLE IN THE EMPIRE.

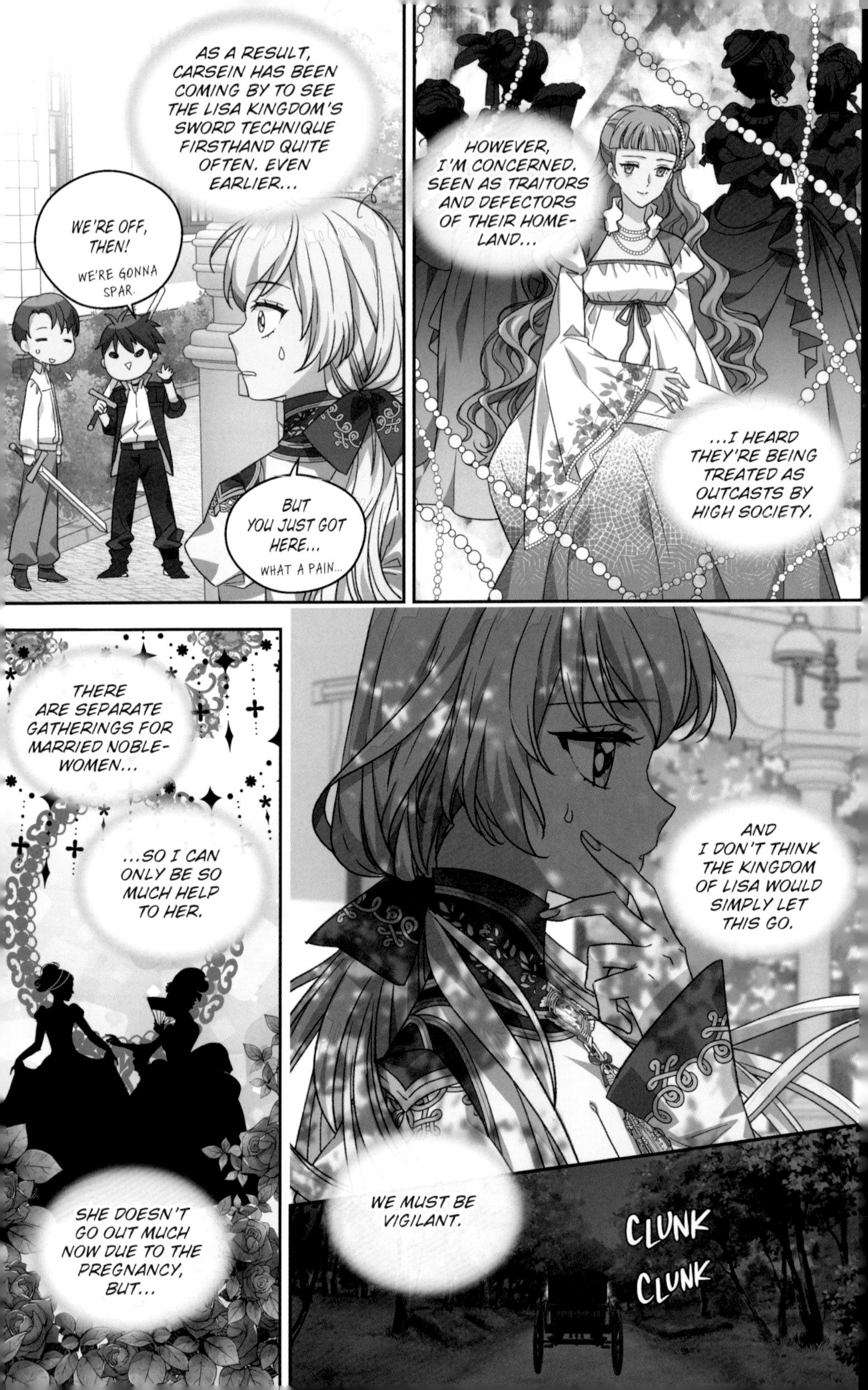

AS A RESULT, CARSEIN HAS BEEN COMING BY TO SEE THE LISA KINGDOM'S SWORD TECHNIQUE FIRSTHAND QUITE OFTEN. EVEN EARLIER...
WE'RE OFF, THEN!
WE'RE GONNA SPAR.
BUT YOU JUST GOT HERE...
WHAT A PAIN...
HOWEVER, I'M CONCERNED. SEEN AS TRAITORS AND DEFECTORS OF THEIR HOME-LAND...
...I HEARD THEY'RE BEING TREATED AS OUTCASTS BY HIGH SOCIETY.
THERE ARE SEPARATE GATHERINGS FOR MARRIED NOBLE-WOMEN...
...SO I CAN ONLY BE SO MUCH HELP TO HER.
SHE DOESN'T GO OUT MUCH NOW DUE TO THE PREGNANCY, BUT...
AND I DON'T THINK THE KINGDOM OF LISA WOULD SIMPLY LET THIS GO.
WE MUST BE VIGILANT.
CLUNK
CLUNK

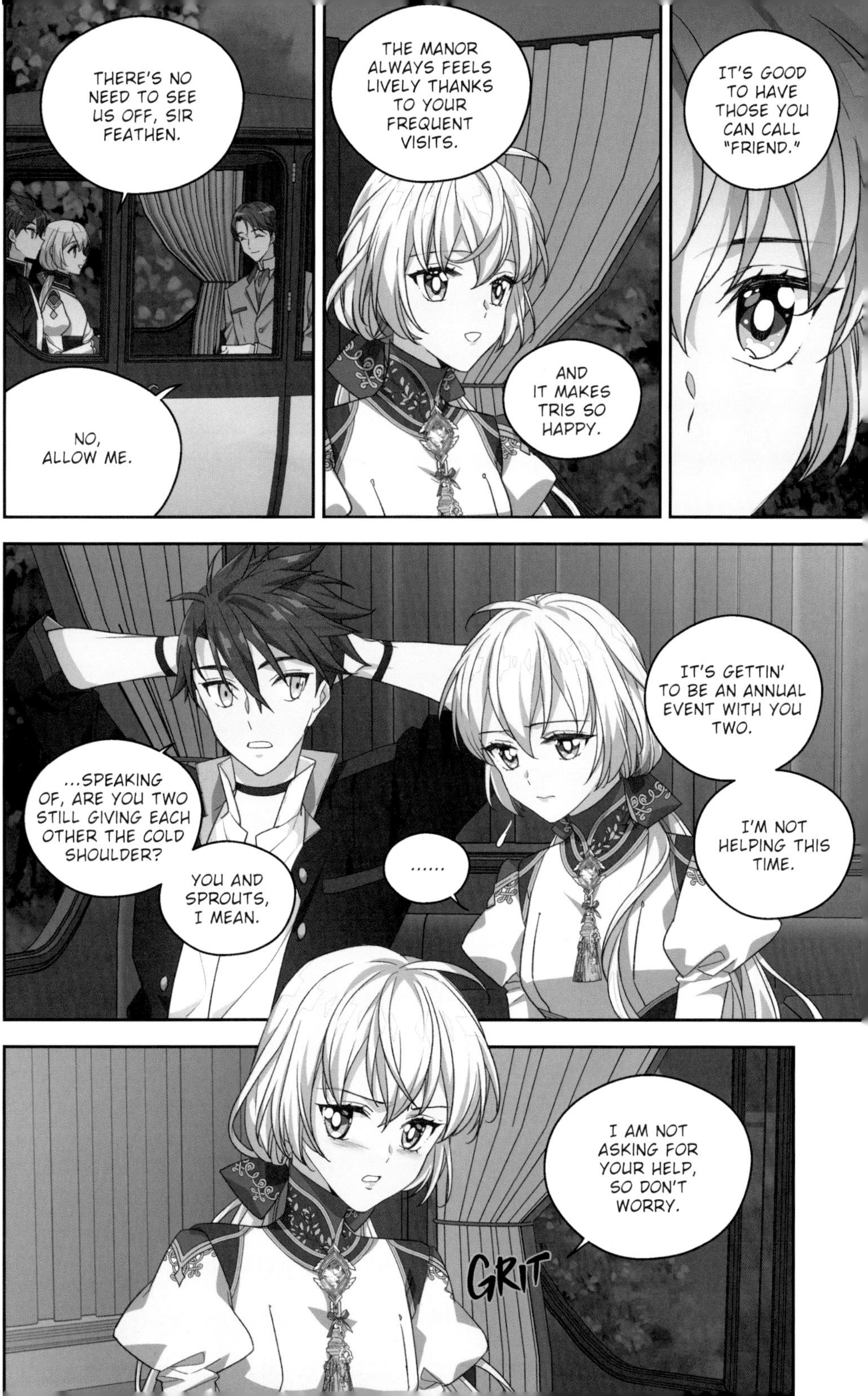

THERE'S NO NEED TO SEE US OFF, SIR FEATHEN.
NO, ALLOW ME.
THE MANOR ALWAYS FEELS LIVELY THANKS TO YOUR FREQUENT VISITS.
AND IT MAKES TRIS SO HAPPY.
IT'S GOOD TO HAVE THOSE YOU CAN CALL "FRIEND."
IT'S GETTIN' TO BE AN ANNUAL EVENT WITH YOU TWO.
I'M NOT HELPING THIS TIME.
...SPEAKING OF, ARE YOU TWO STILL GIVING EACH OTHER THE COLD SHOULDER?
YOU AND SPROUTS, I MEAN.
......
I AM NOT ASKING FOR YOUR HELP, SO DON'T WORRY.
GRIT

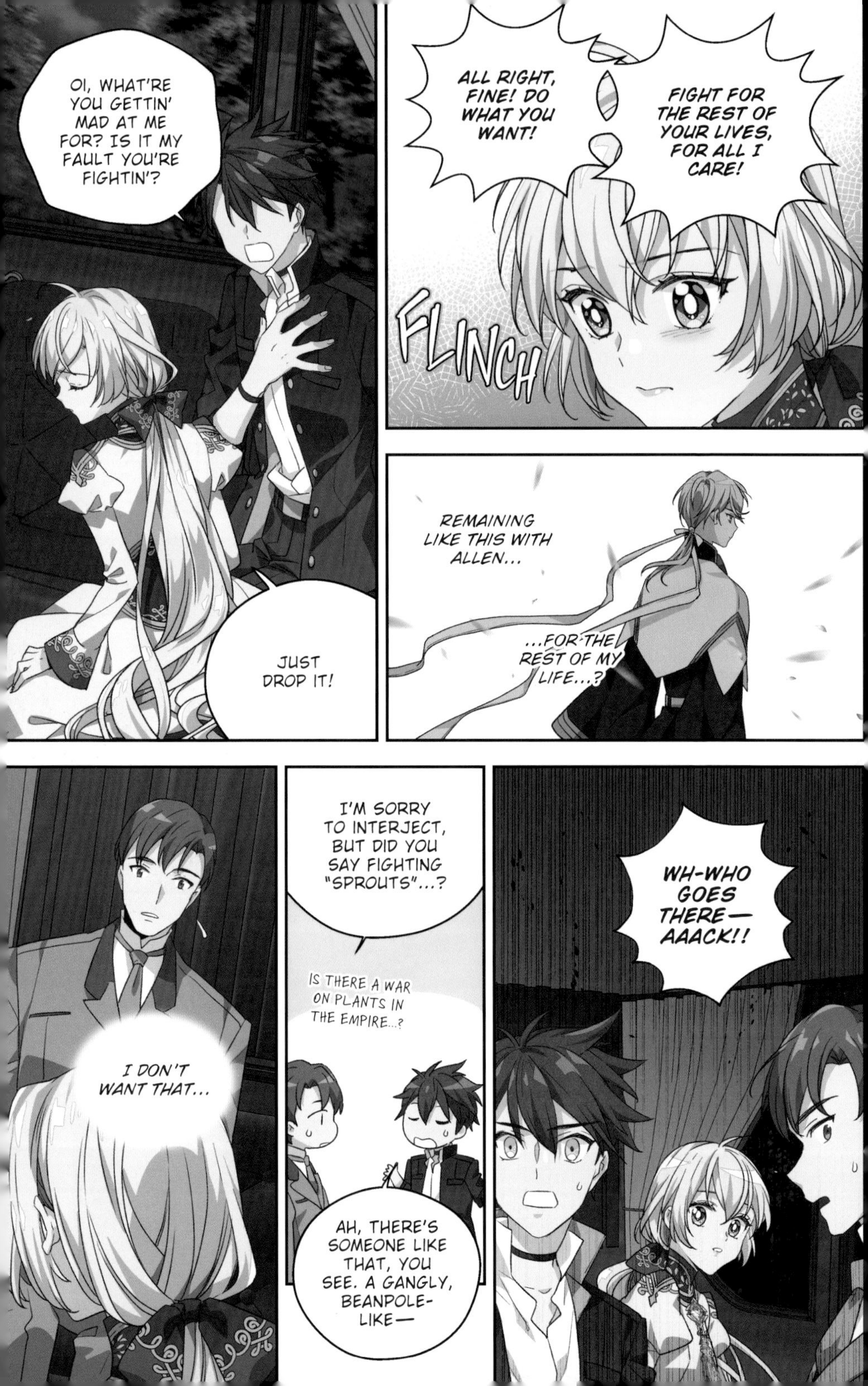
OI, WHAT'RE YOU GETTIN' MAD AT ME FOR? IS IT MY FAULT YOU'RE FIGHTIN'?
JUST DROP IT!
ALL RIGHT, FINE! DO WHAT YOU WANT!
FIGHT FOR THE REST OF YOUR LIVES, FOR ALL I CARE!
FLINCH
REMAINING LIKE THIS WITH ALLEN...
...FOR THE REST OF MY LIFE...?
I DON'T WANT THAT...
I'M SORRY TO INTERJECT, BUT DID YOU SAY FIGHTING "SPROUTS"...?
IS THERE A WAR ON PLANTS IN THE EMPIRE...?
AH, THERE'S SOMEONE LIKE THAT, YOU SEE. A GANGLY, BEANPOLE-LIKE—
WH-WHO GOES THERE—AAACK!!

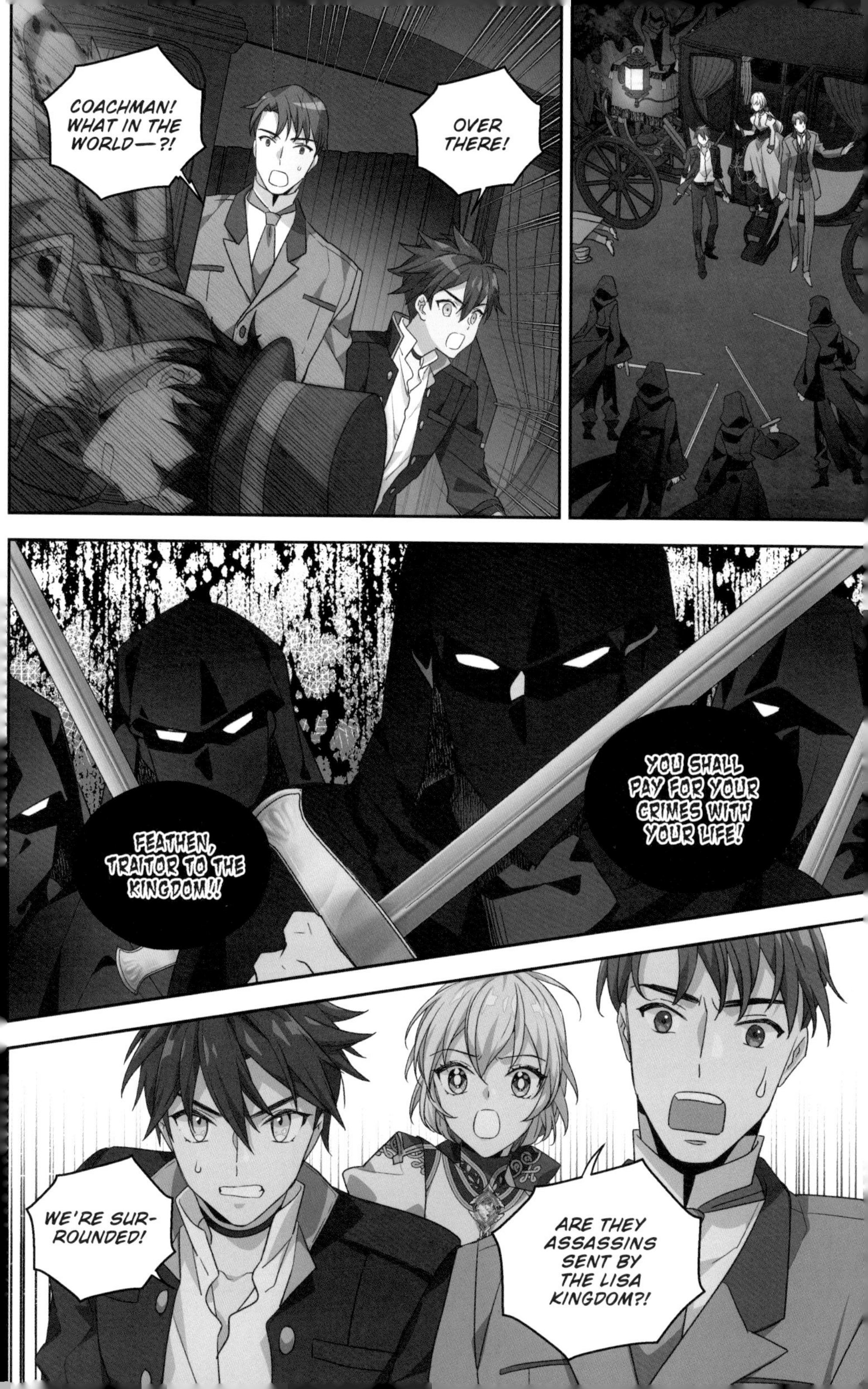
COACHMAN! WHAT IN THE WORLD—?!
OVER THERE!
FEATHEN, TRAITOR TO THE KINGDOM!!
YOU SHALL PAY FOR YOUR CRIMES WITH YOUR LIFE!
WE'RE SUR-ROUNDED!
ARE THEY ASSASSINS SENT BY THE LISA KINGDOM?!

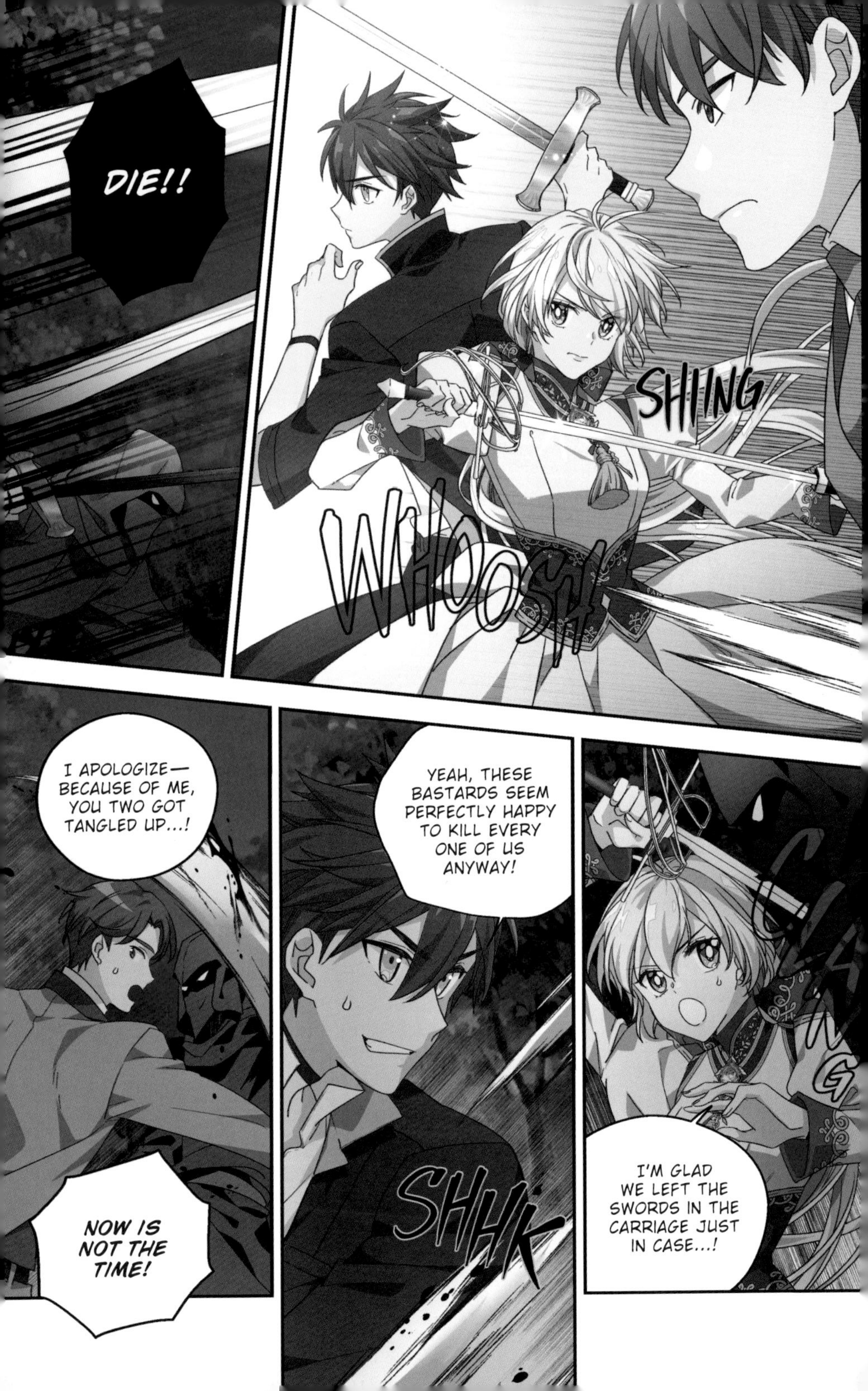

SHIING
WHOOSH
DIE!!
I'M GLAD WE LEFT THE SWORDS IN THE CARRIAGE JUST IN CASE...!
YEAH, THESE BASTARDS SEEM PERFECTLY HAPPY TO KILL EVERY ONE OF US ANYWAY!
SHHK
I APOLOGIZE— BECAUSE OF ME, YOU TWO GOT TANGLED UP...!
NOW IS NOT THE TIME!

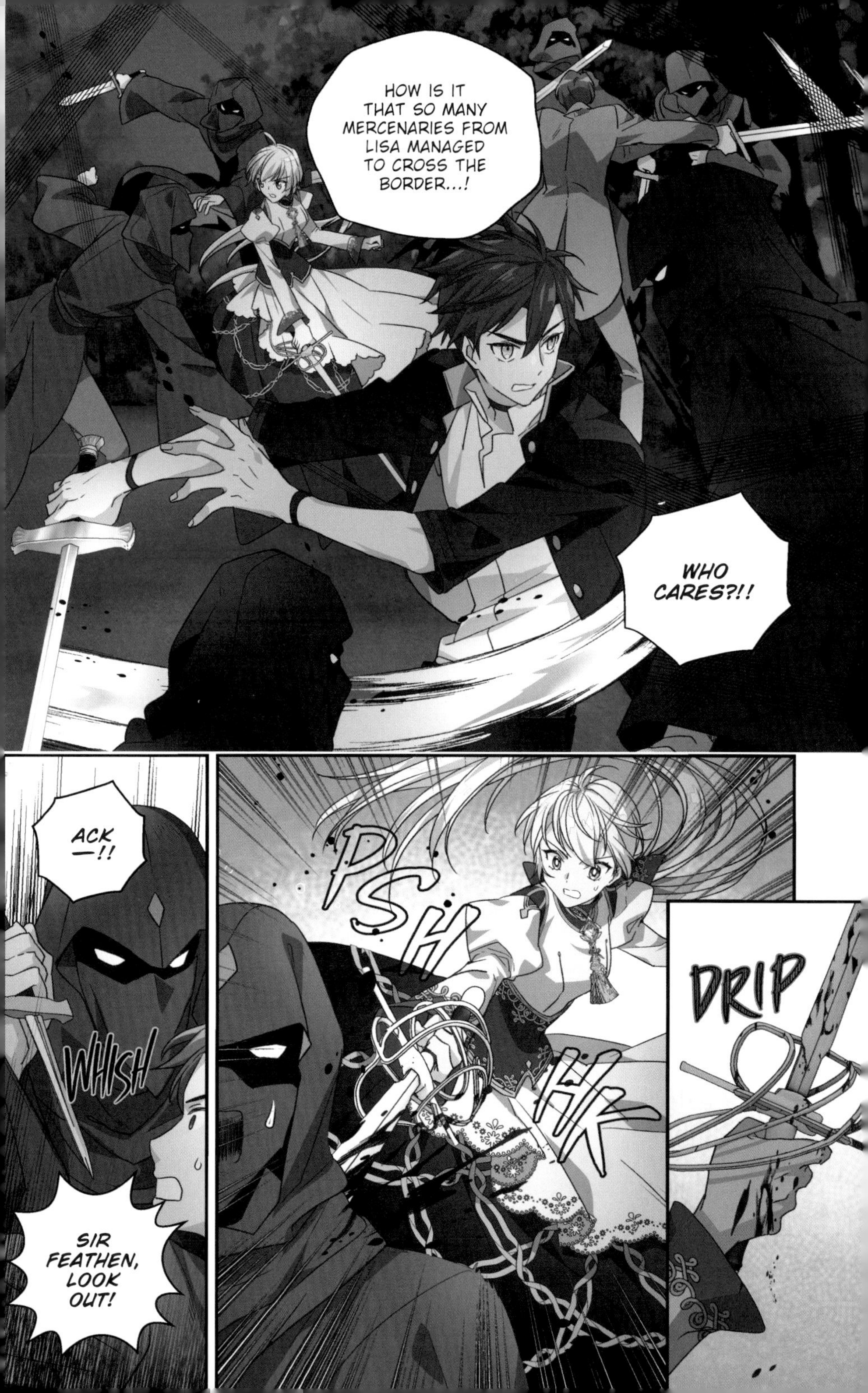
HOW IS IT THAT SO MANY MERCENARIES FROM LISA MANAGED TO CROSS THE BORDER...!
WHO CARES?!!
DRIP
PSHHK
ACK—!!
WHISH
SIR FEATHEN, LOOK OUT!

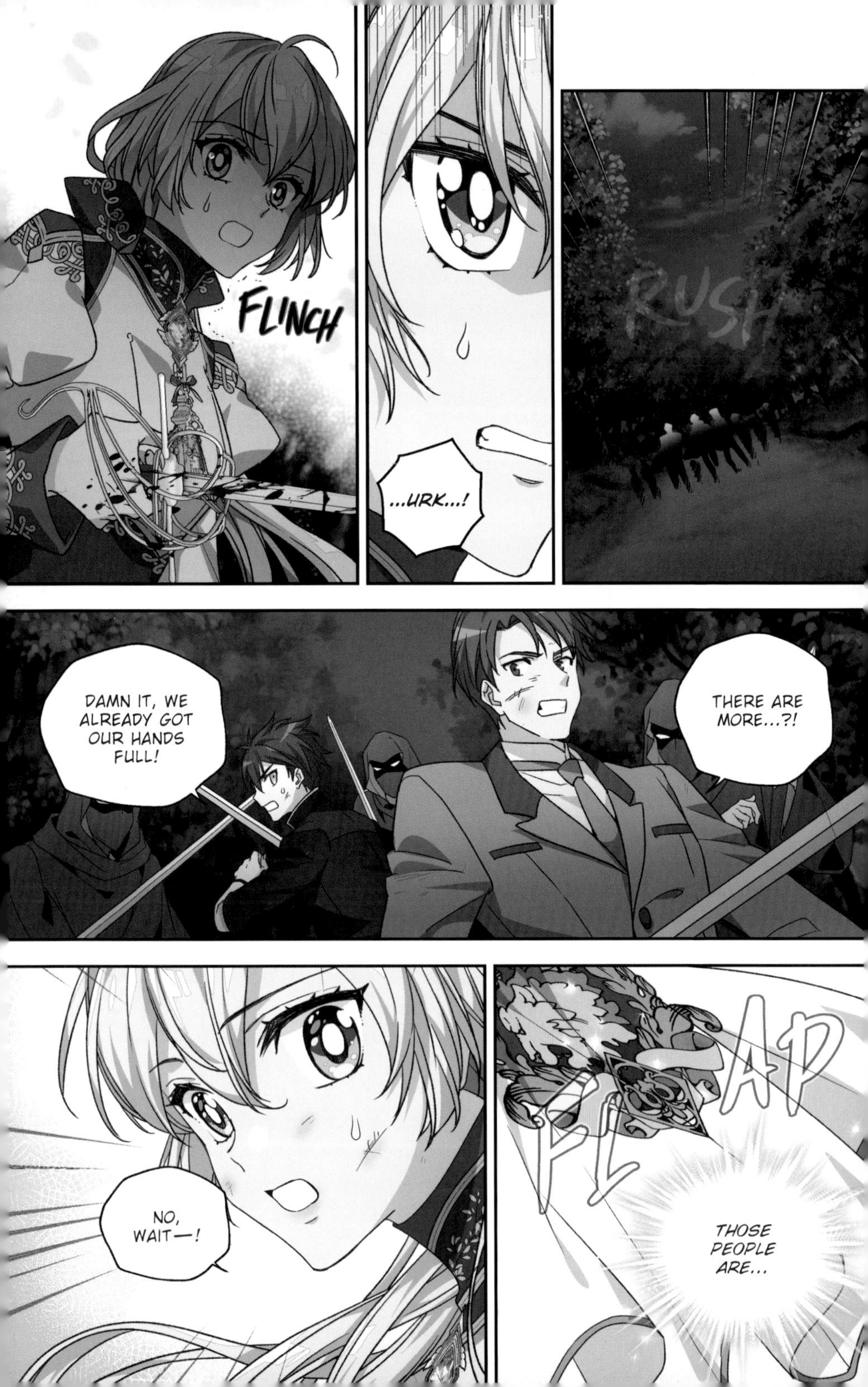
FLINCH
...URK...!
RUSH
DAMN IT, WE ALREADY GOT OUR HANDS FULL!
THERE ARE MORE...?!
NO, WAIT—!
FLAP
THOSE PEOPLE ARE...

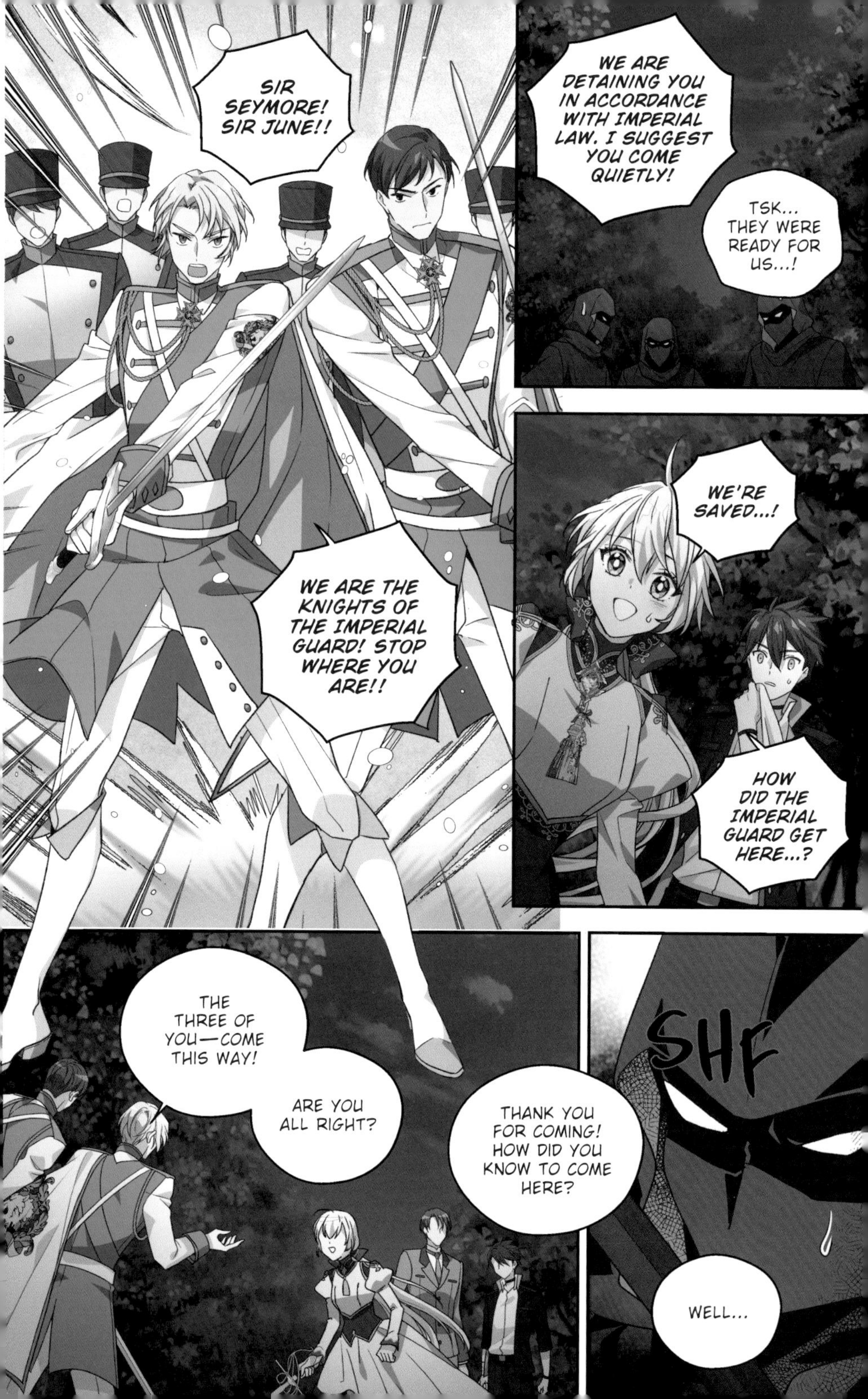
SIR SEYMORE! SIR JUNE!!
WE ARE DETAINING YOU IN ACCORDANCE WITH IMPERIAL LAW. I SUGGEST YOU COME QUIETLY!
TSK... THEY WERE READY FOR US...!
WE ARE THE KNIGHTS OF THE IMPERIAL GUARD! STOP WHERE YOU ARE!!
WE'RE SAVED...!
HOW DID THE IMPERIAL GUARD GET HERE...?
THE THREE OF YOU—COME THIS WAY!
ARE YOU ALL RIGHT?
THANK YOU FOR COMING! HOW DID YOU KNOW TO COME HERE?
SHF
WELL...

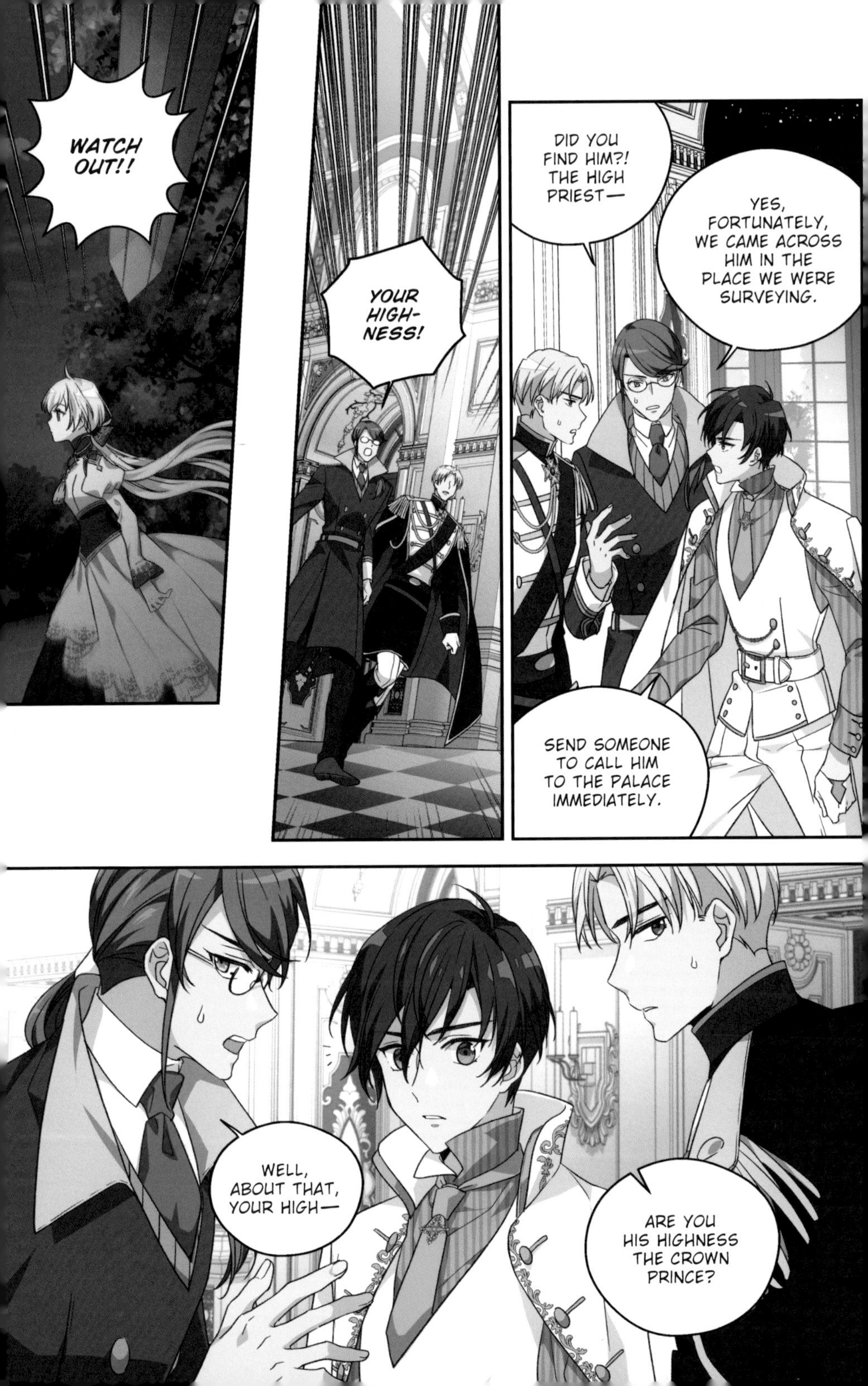
WATCH OUT!!
YOUR HIGH-NESS!
DID YOU FIND HIM?! THE HIGH PRIEST—
YES, FORTUNATELY, WE CAME ACROSS HIM IN THE PLACE WE WERE SURVEYING.
SEND SOMEONE TO CALL HIM TO THE PALACE IMMEDIATELY.
WELL, ABOUT THAT, YOUR HIGH—
ARE YOU HIS HIGHNESS THE CROWN PRINCE?

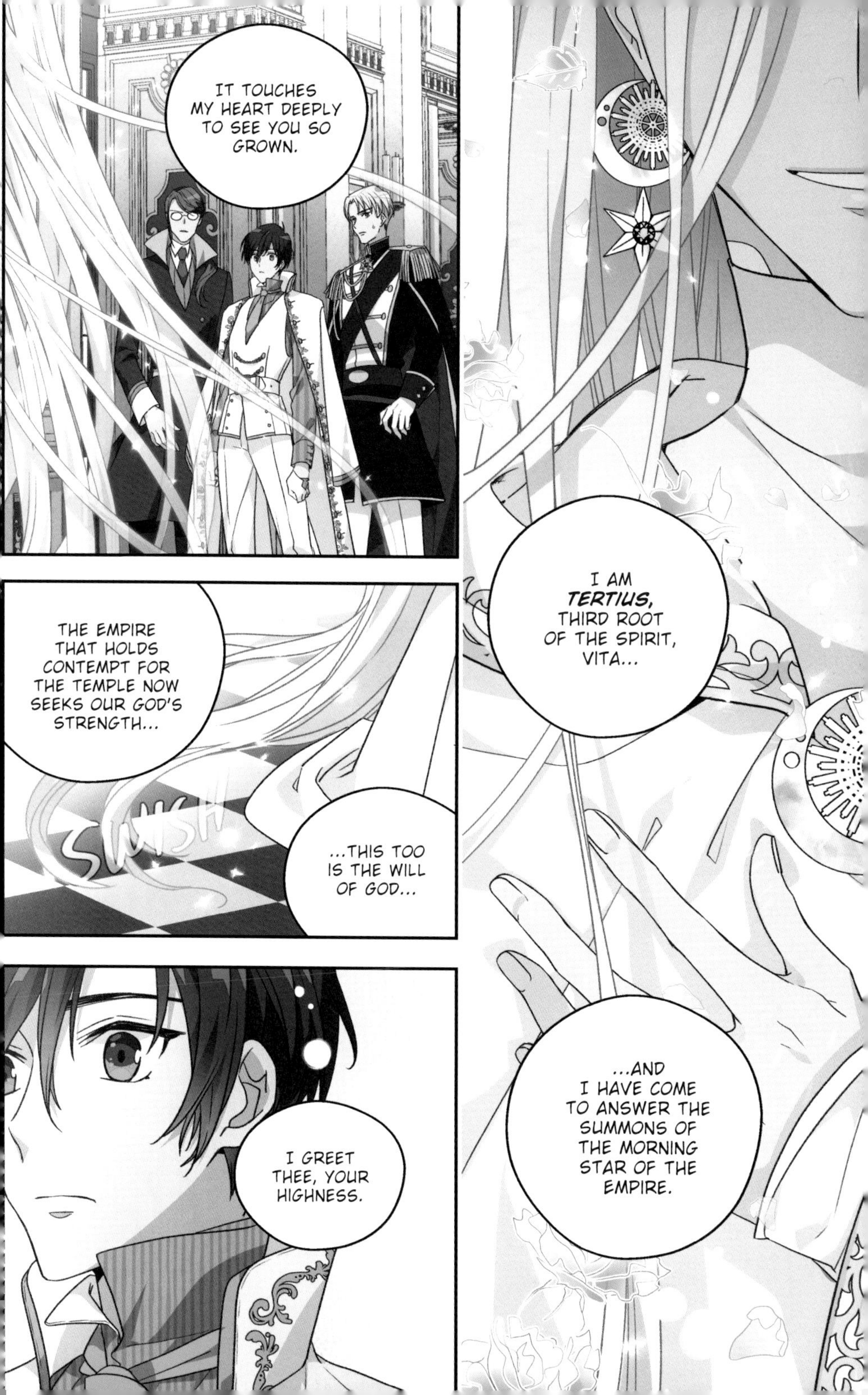
IT TOUCHES MY HEART DEEPLY TO SEE YOU SO GROWN.
THE EMPIRE THAT HOLDS CONTEMPT FOR THE TEMPLE NOW SEEKS OUR GOD'S STRENGTH...
SWISH
...THIS TOO IS THE WILL OF GOD...
I GREET THEE, YOUR HIGHNESS.
I AM **TERTIUS,** THIRD ROOT OF THE SPIRIT, VITA...
...AND I HAVE COME TO ANSWER THE SUMMONS OF THE MORNING STAR OF THE EMPIRE.

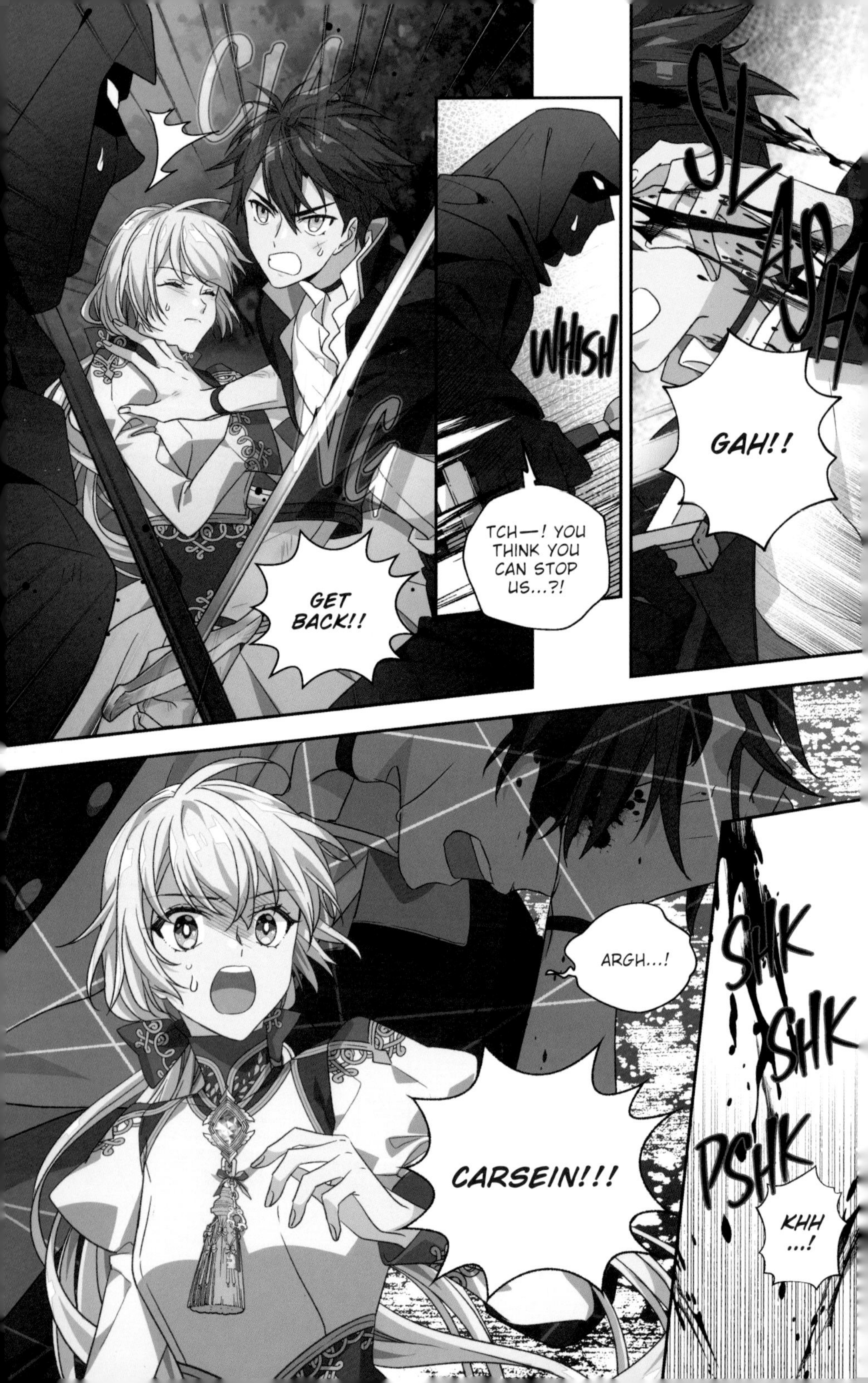
GET BACK!!
WHISH
TCH—! YOU THINK YOU CAN STOP US...?!
SLASH
GAH!!
ARGH...!
SHK
SHK
PSHK
CARSEIN!!!
KHH ...!

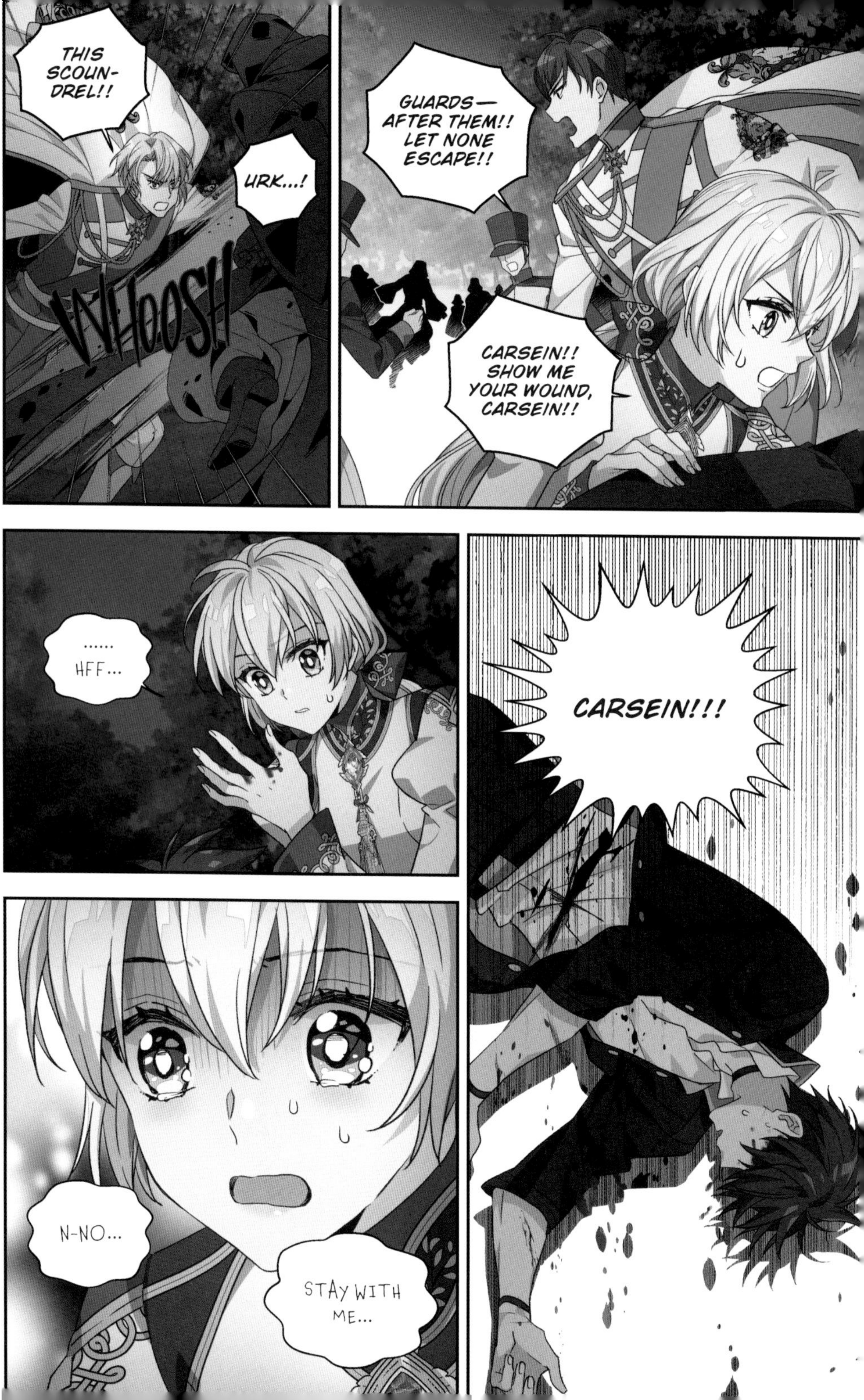
THIS SCOUNDREL!!
URK...!
WHOOSH
GUARDS— AFTER THEM!! LET NONE ESCAPE!!
CARSEIN!! SHOW ME YOUR WOUND, CARSEIN!!
...... HFF...
CARSEIN!!!
N-NO...
STAY WITH ME...

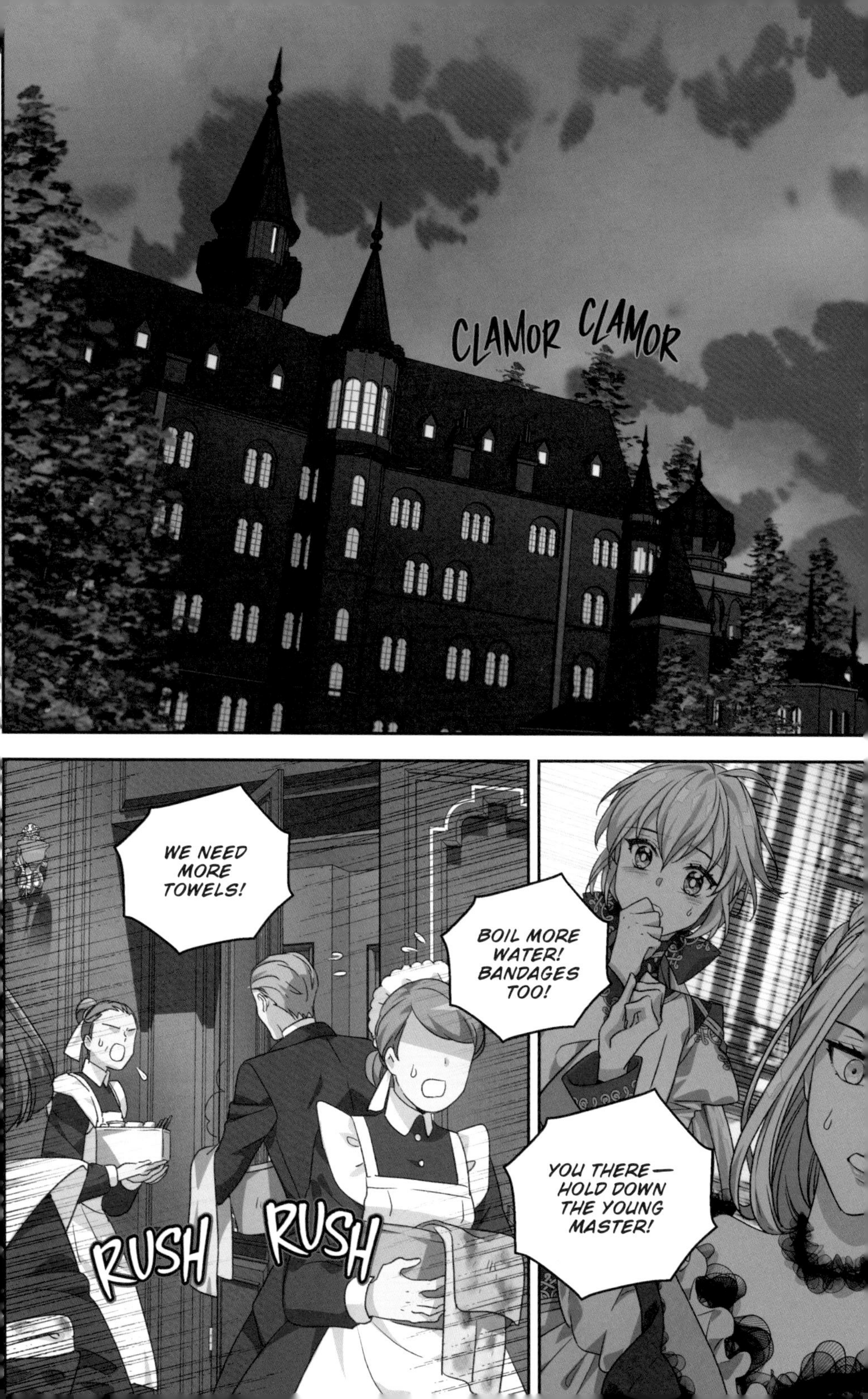
CLAMOR CLAMOR
WE NEED MORE TOWELS!
BOIL MORE WATER! BANDAGES TOO!
RUSH RUSH
YOU THERE—HOLD DOWN THE YOUNG MASTER!

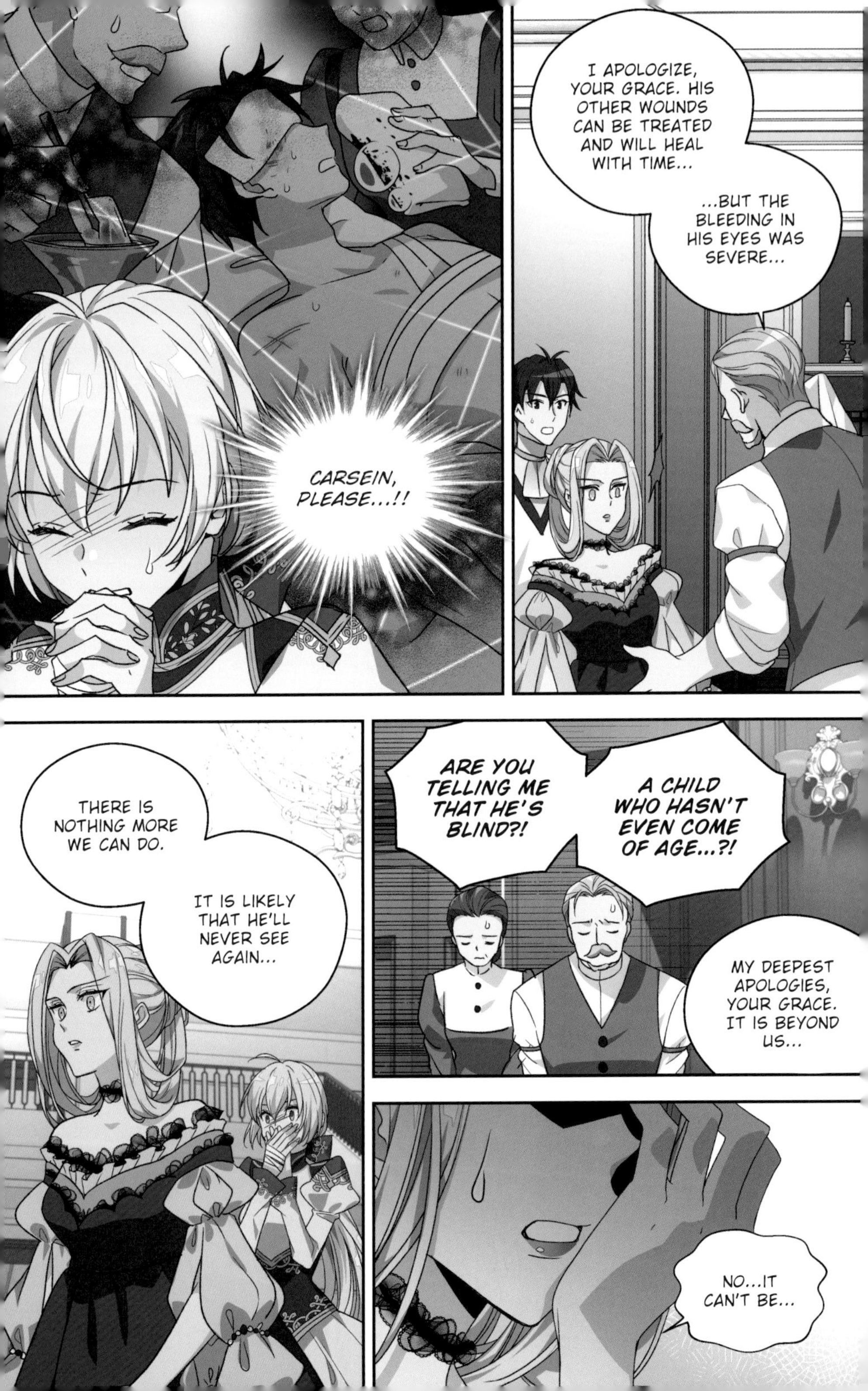

CARSEIN, PLEASE...!!
I APOLOGIZE, YOUR GRACE. HIS OTHER WOUNDS CAN BE TREATED AND WILL HEAL WITH TIME...
...BUT THE BLEEDING IN HIS EYES WAS SEVERE...
THERE IS NOTHING MORE WE CAN DO.
IT IS LIKELY THAT HE'LL NEVER SEE AGAIN...
ARE YOU TELLING ME THAT HE'S BLIND?!
A CHILD WHO HASN'T EVEN COME OF AGE...?!
MY DEEPEST APOLOGIES, YOUR GRACE. IT IS BEYOND US...
NO...IT CAN'T BE...

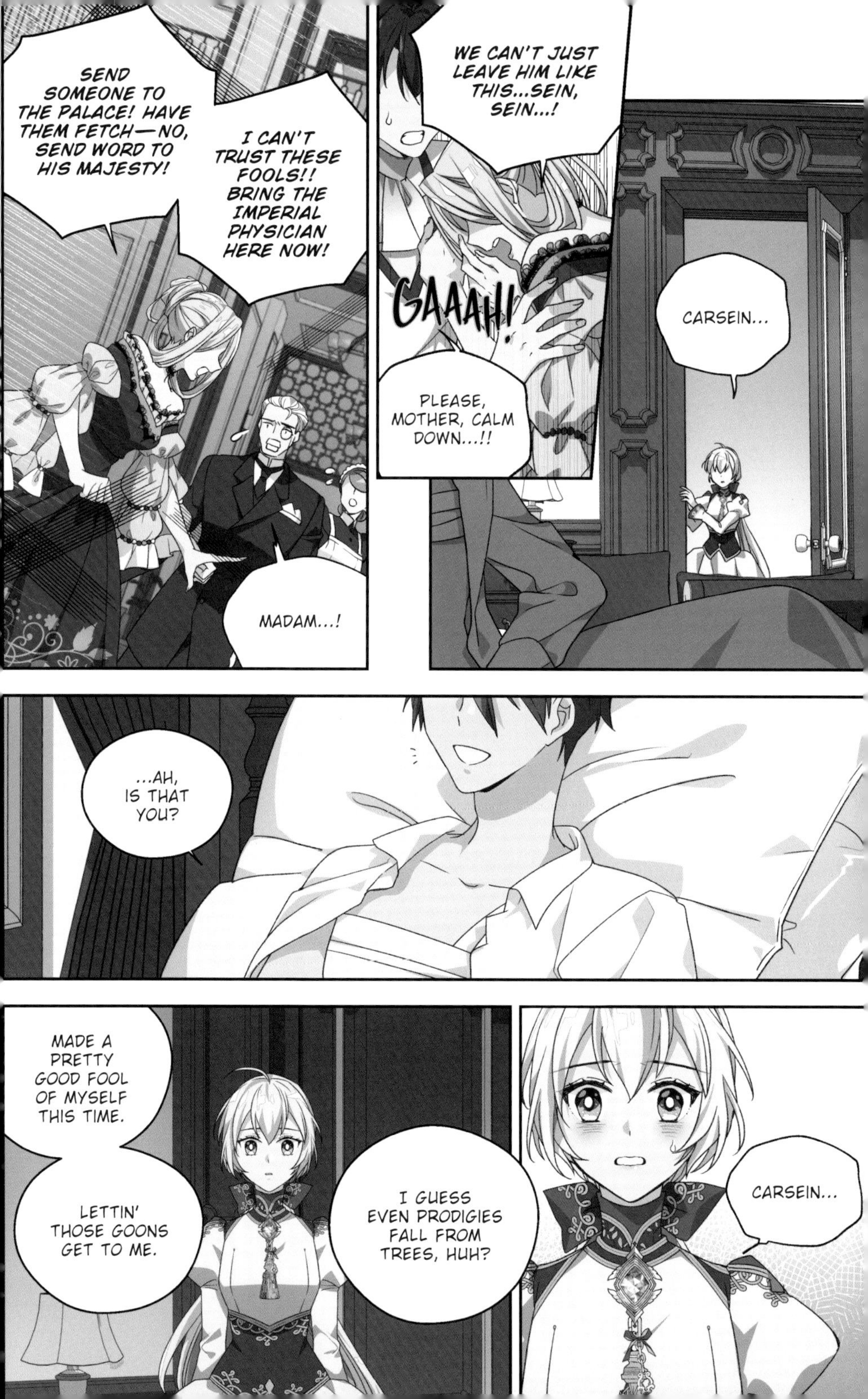
SEND SOMEONE TO THE PALACE! HAVE THEM FETCH—NO, SEND WORD TO HIS MAJESTY!
I CAN'T TRUST THESE FOOLS!! BRING THE IMPERIAL PHYSICIAN HERE NOW!
MADAM...!
WE CAN'T JUST LEAVE HIM LIKE THIS...SEIN, SEIN...!
GAAAH!
PLEASE, MOTHER, CALM DOWN...!!
CARSEIN...
...AH, IS THAT YOU?
MADE A PRETTY GOOD FOOL OF MYSELF THIS TIME.
LETTIN' THOSE GOONS GET TO ME.
I GUESS EVEN PRODIGIES FALL FROM TREES, HUH?
CARSEIN...

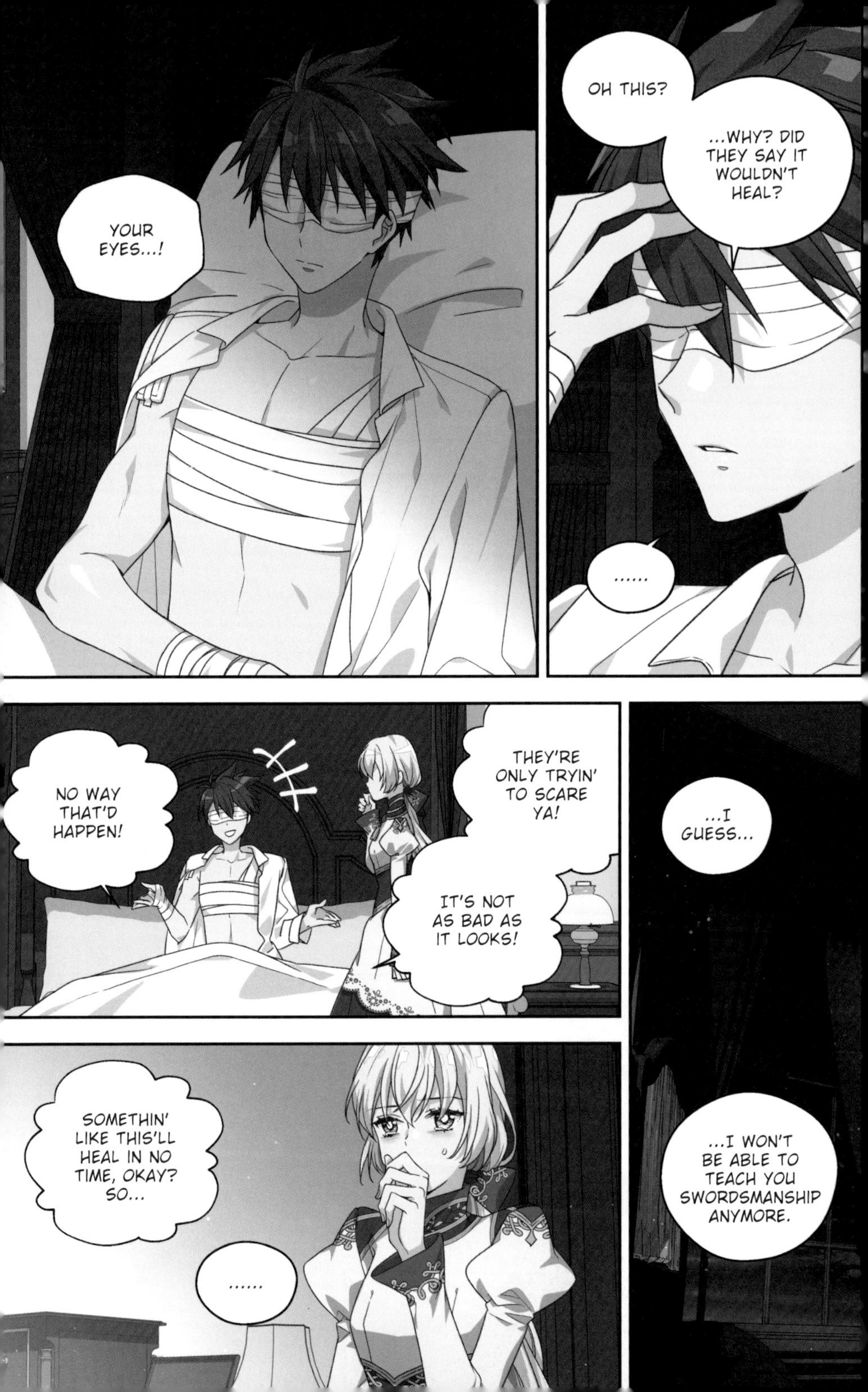
YOUR EYES...!
OH THIS?
...WHY? DID THEY SAY IT WOULDN'T HEAL?
......
NO WAY THAT'D HAPPEN!
THEY'RE ONLY TRYIN' TO SCARE YA!
IT'S NOT AS BAD AS IT LOOKS!
...I GUESS...
SOMETHIN' LIKE THIS'LL HEAL IN NO TIME, OKAY? SO...
......
...I WON'T BE ABLE TO TEACH YOU SWORDSMANSHIP ANYMORE.

......I'D LIKE TO REST.

...OKAY.

I'LL GO...

ARISTIA.

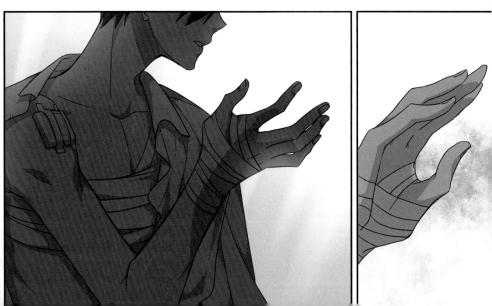

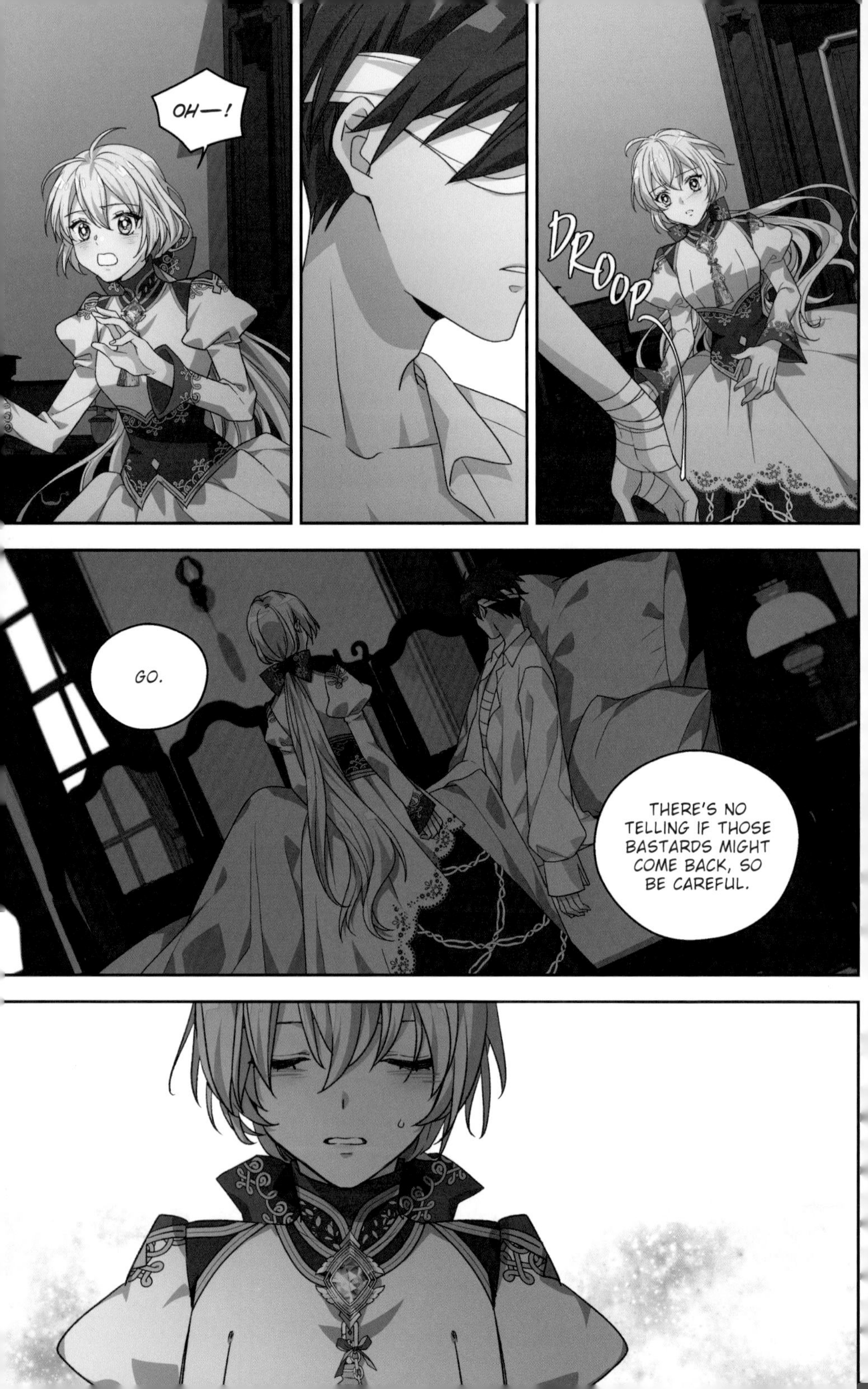
OH—!
DROOP
GO.
THERE'S NO TELLING IF THOSE BASTARDS MIGHT COME BACK, SO BE CAREFUL.

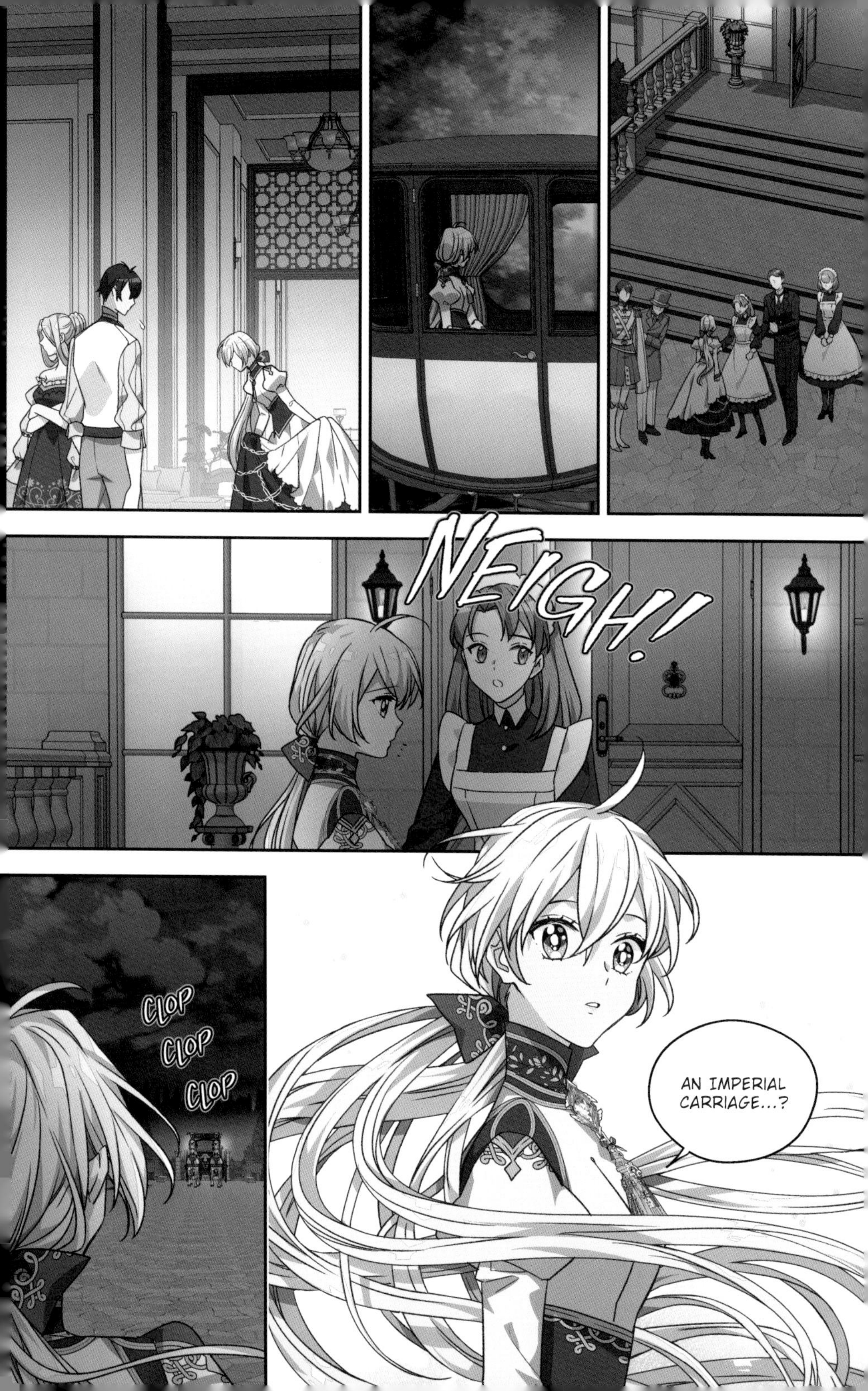
NEIGH!
CLOP
CLOP
CLOP
AN IMPERIAL CARRIAGE...?

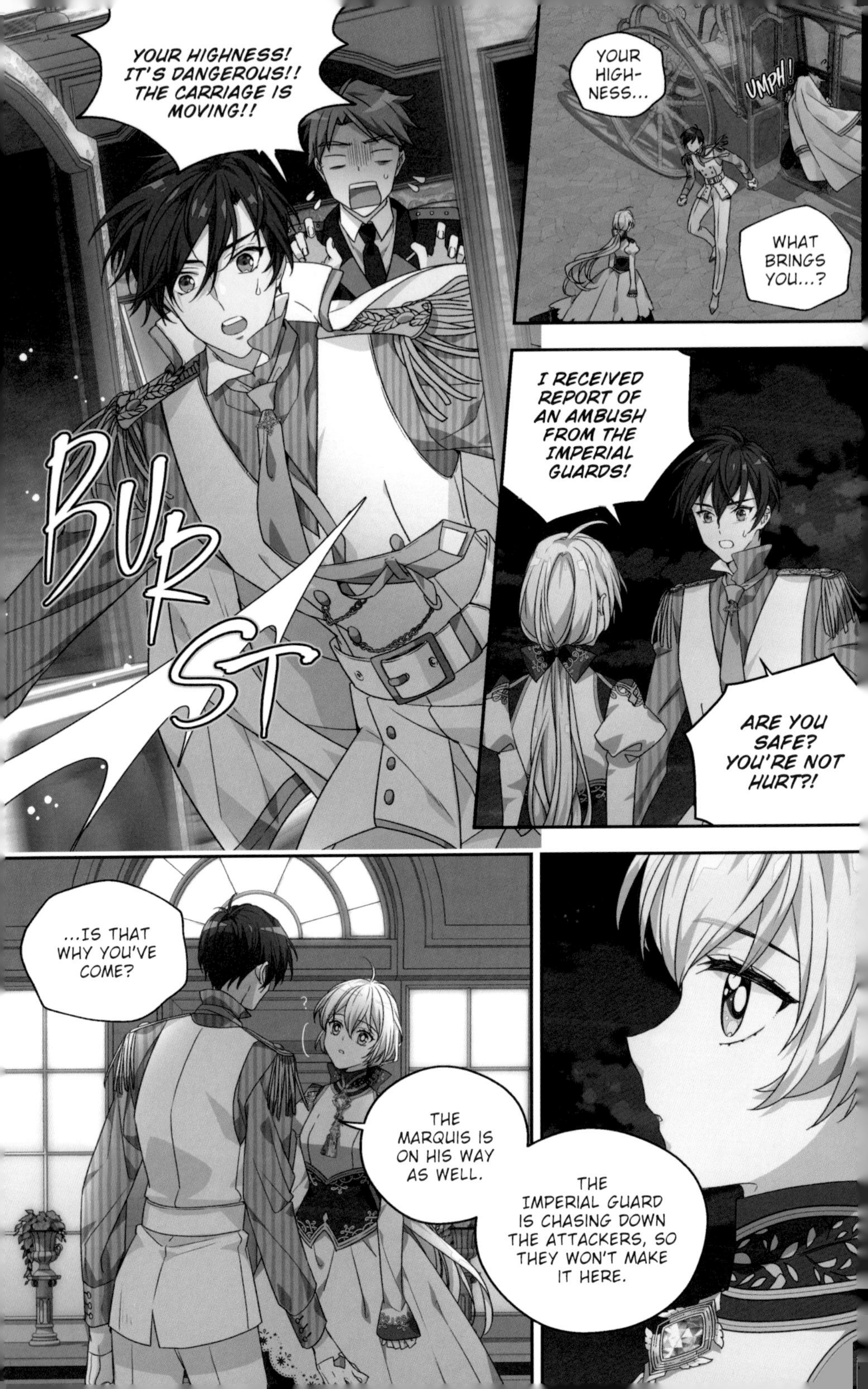
YOUR HIGHNESS! IT'S DANGEROUS!! THE CARRIAGE IS MOVING!!
BURST
YOUR HIGH-NESS...
UMPH!
WHAT BRINGS YOU...?
I RECEIVED REPORT OF AN AMBUSH FROM THE IMPERIAL GUARDS!
ARE YOU SAFE? YOU'RE NOT HURT?!
...IS THAT WHY YOU'VE COME?
?
THE MARQUIS IS ON HIS WAY AS WELL.
THE IMPERIAL GUARD IS CHASING DOWN THE ATTACKERS, SO THEY WON'T MAKE IT HERE.

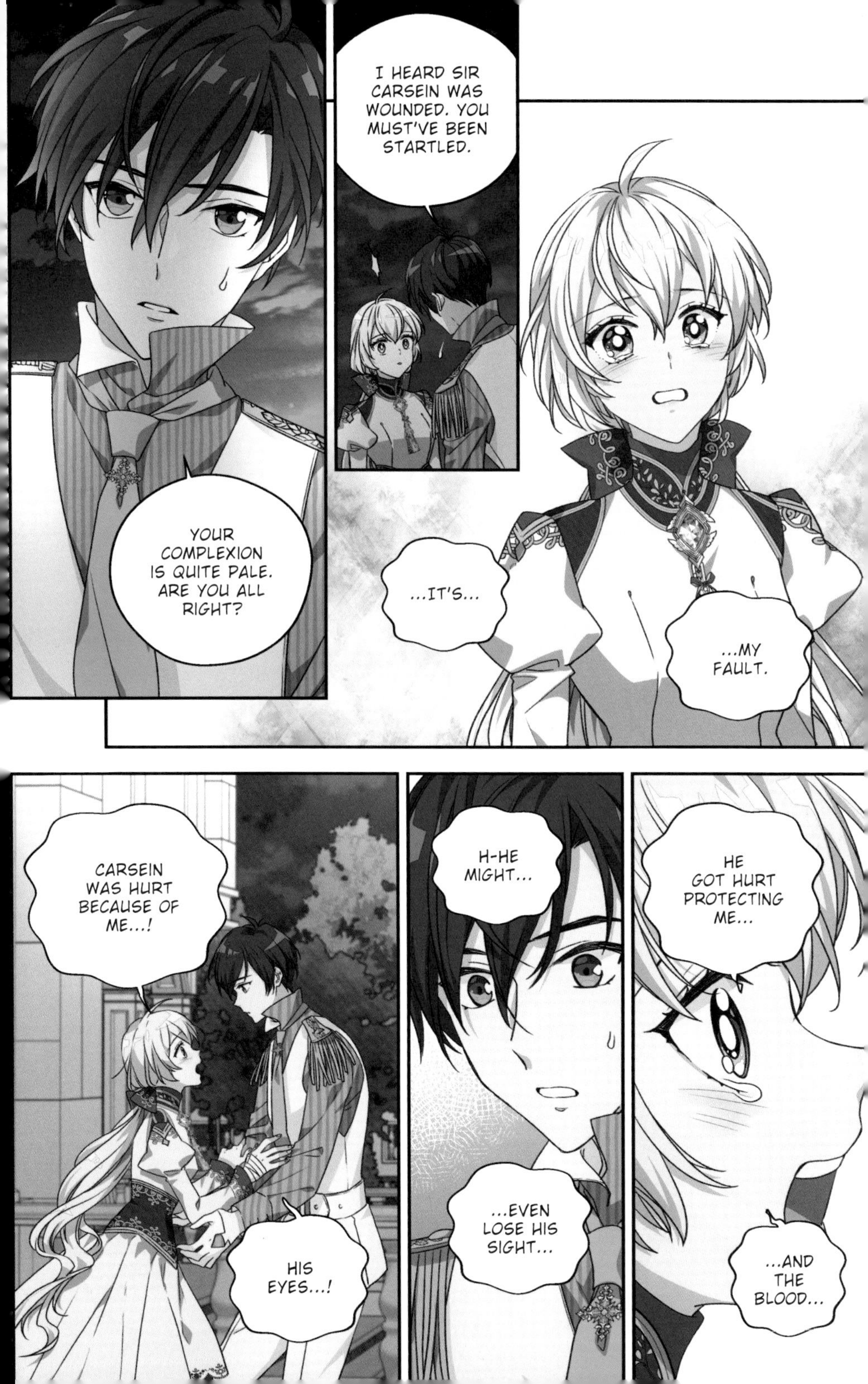
I HEARD SIR CARSEIN WAS WOUNDED. YOU MUST'VE BEEN STARTLED.
YOUR COMPLEXION IS QUITE PALE. ARE YOU ALL RIGHT?
...IT'S...
...MY FAULT.
CARSEIN WAS HURT BECAUSE OF ME...!
HIS EYES...!
H-HE MIGHT...
...EVEN LOSE HIS SIGHT...
HE GOT HURT PROTECTING ME...
...AND THE BLOOD...

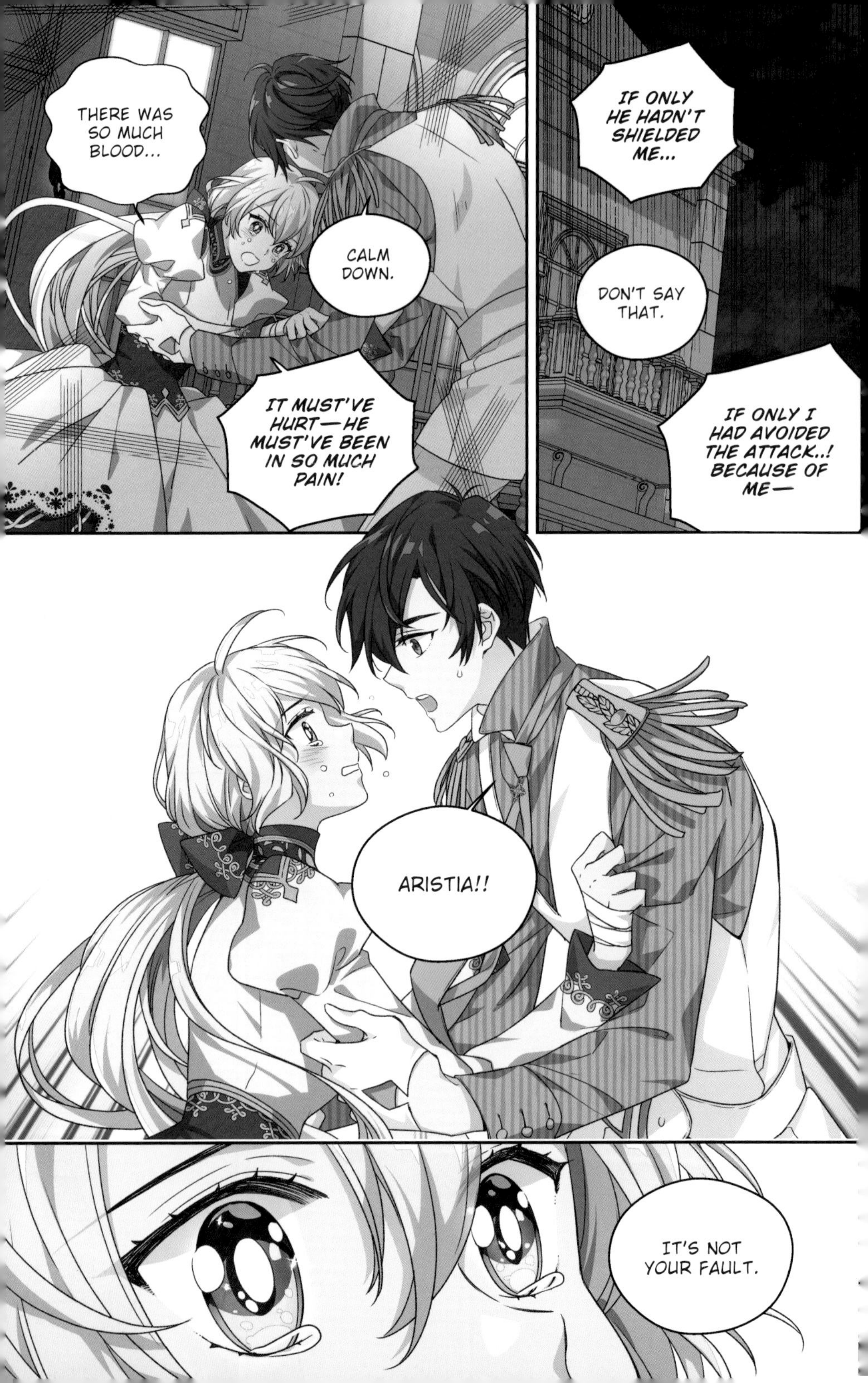
THERE WAS SO MUCH BLOOD...
CALM DOWN.
IT MUST'VE HURT—HE MUST'VE BEEN IN SO MUCH PAIN!
IF ONLY HE HADN'T SHIELDED ME...
DON'T SAY THAT.
IF ONLY I HAD AVOIDED THE ATTACK..! BECAUSE OF ME—
ARISTIA!!
IT'S NOT YOUR FAULT.

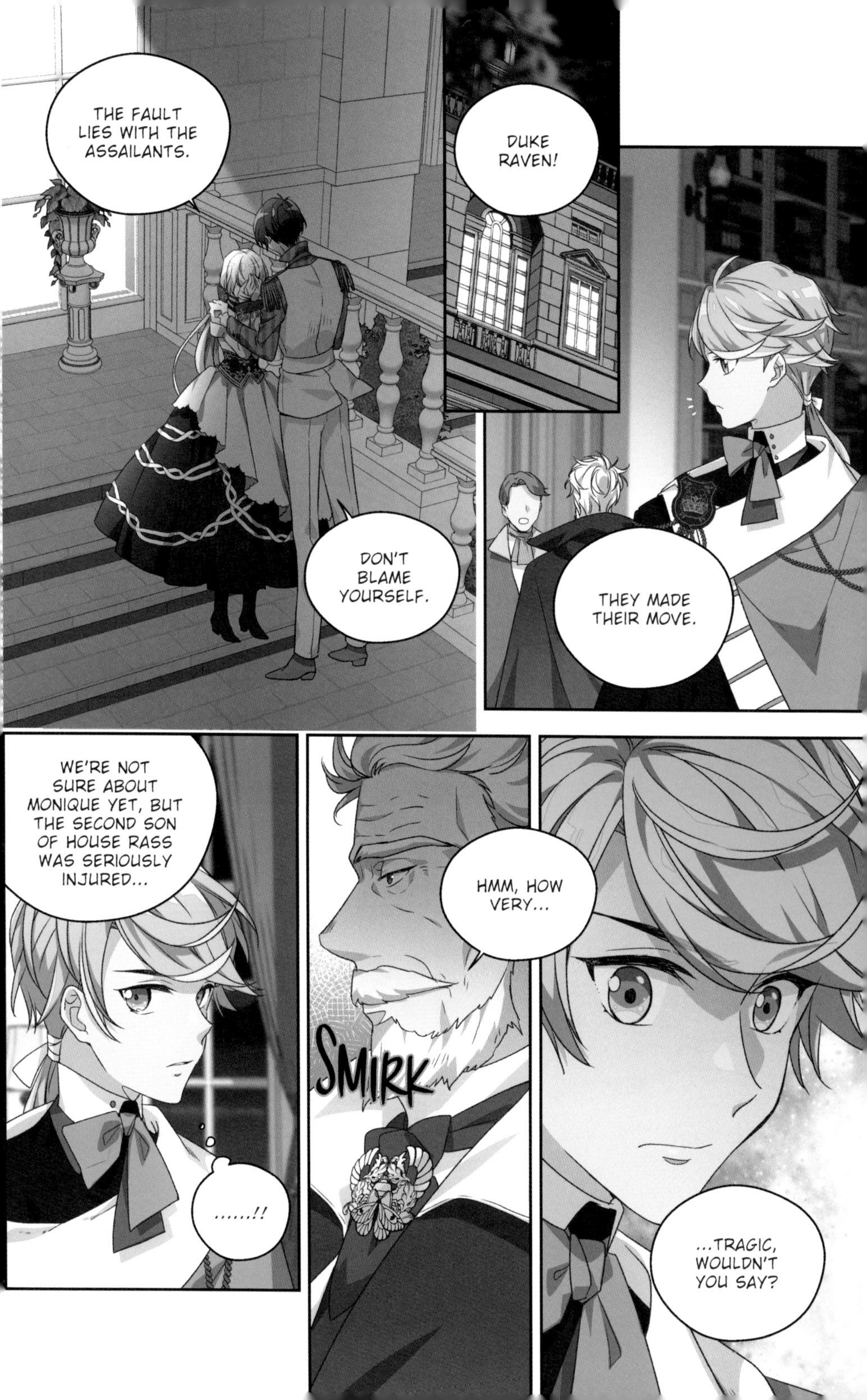
THE FAULT LIES WITH THE ASSAILANTS.
DON'T BLAME YOURSELF.
DUKE RAVEN!
THEY MADE THEIR MOVE.
WE'RE NOT SURE ABOUT MONIQUE YET, BUT THE SECOND SON OF HOUSE RASS WAS SERIOUSLY INJURED...
......!!
HMM, HOW VERY...
SMIRK
...TRAGIC, WOULDN'T YOU SAY?

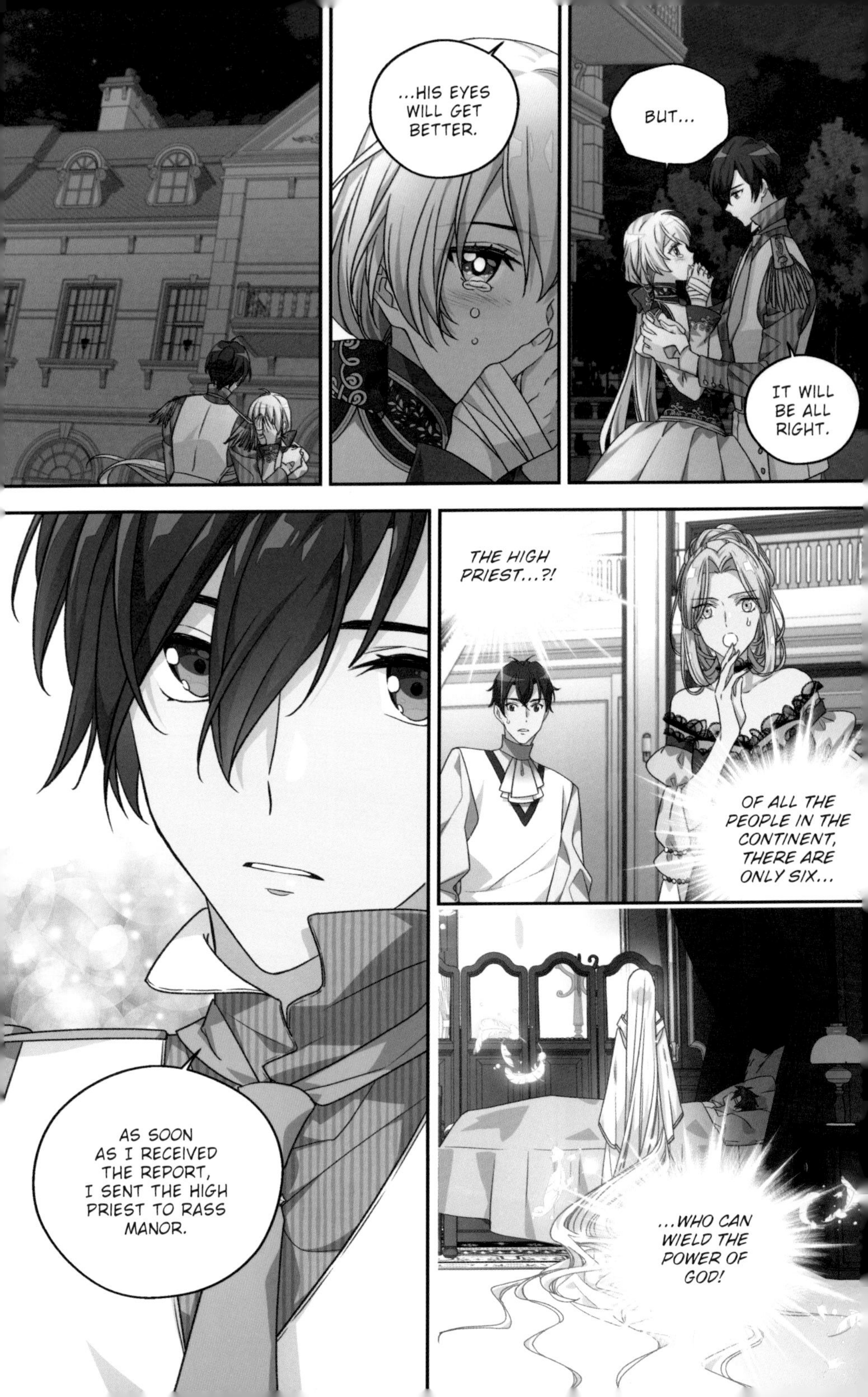
...HIS EYES WILL GET BETTER.
BUT...
IT WILL BE ALL RIGHT.
AS SOON AS I RECEIVED THE REPORT, I SENT THE HIGH PRIEST TO RASS MANOR.
THE HIGH PRIEST...?!
OF ALL THE PEOPLE IN THE CONTINENT, THERE ARE ONLY SIX...
...WHO CAN WIELD THE POWER OF GOD!

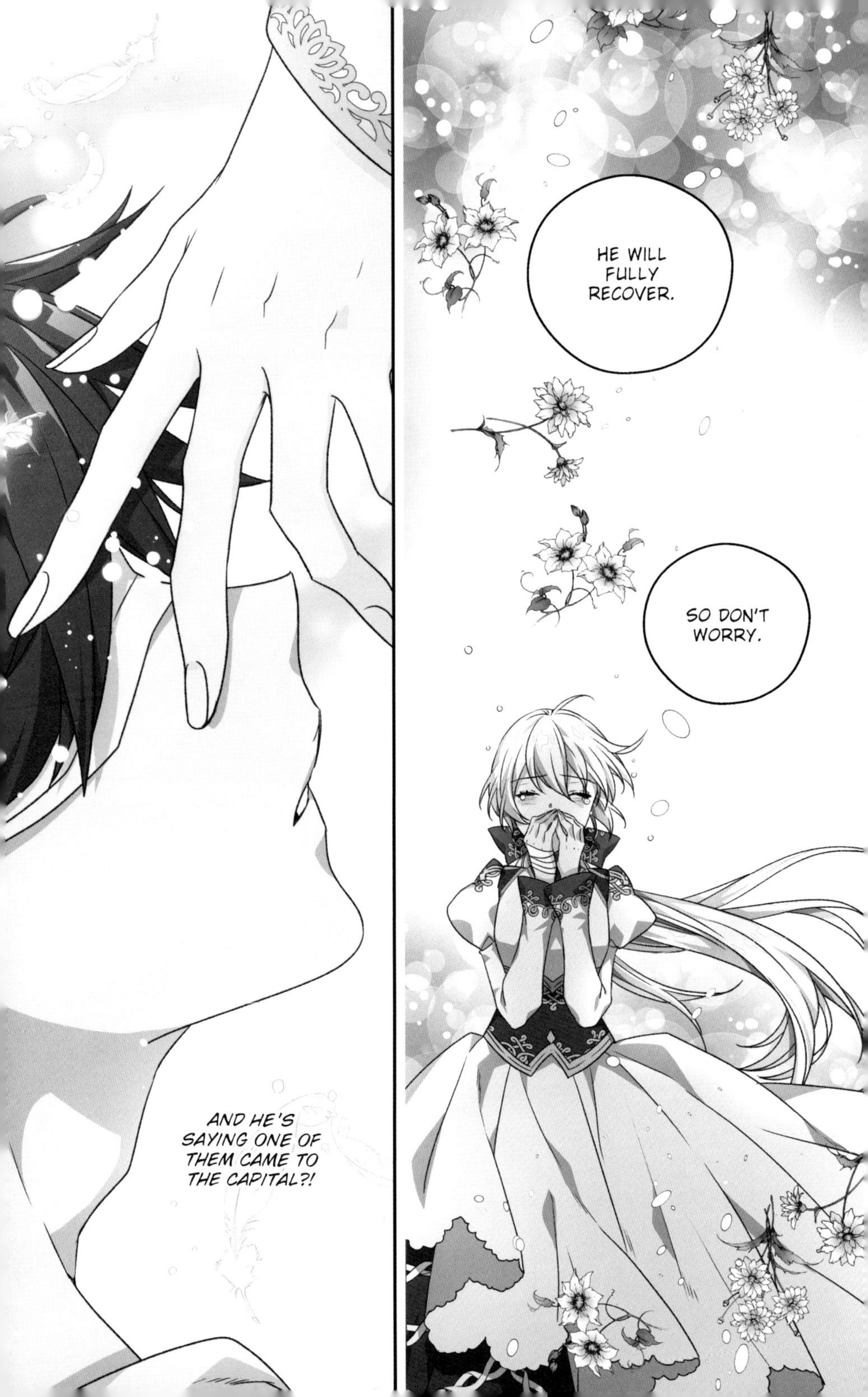
HE WILL FULLY RECOVER.
SO DON'T WORRY.
AND HE'S SAYING ONE OF THEM CAME TO THE CAPITAL?!

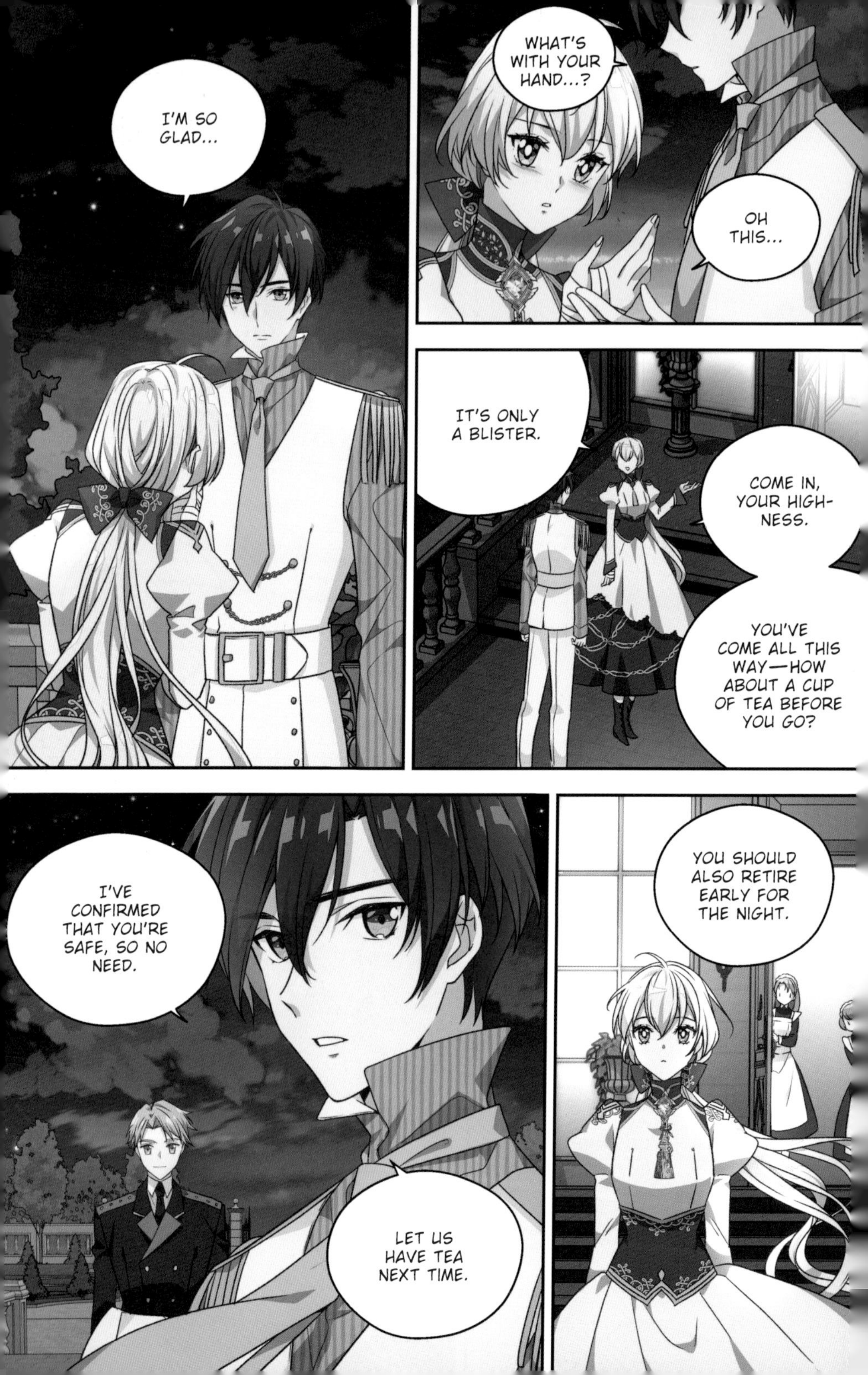
I'M SO GLAD...
WHAT'S WITH YOUR HAND...?
OH THIS...
IT'S ONLY A BLISTER.
COME IN, YOUR HIGH-NESS.
YOU'VE COME ALL THIS WAY—HOW ABOUT A CUP OF TEA BEFORE YOU GO?
I'VE CONFIRMED THAT YOU'RE SAFE, SO NO NEED.
LET US HAVE TEA NEXT TIME.
YOU SHOULD ALSO RETIRE EARLY FOR THE NIGHT.

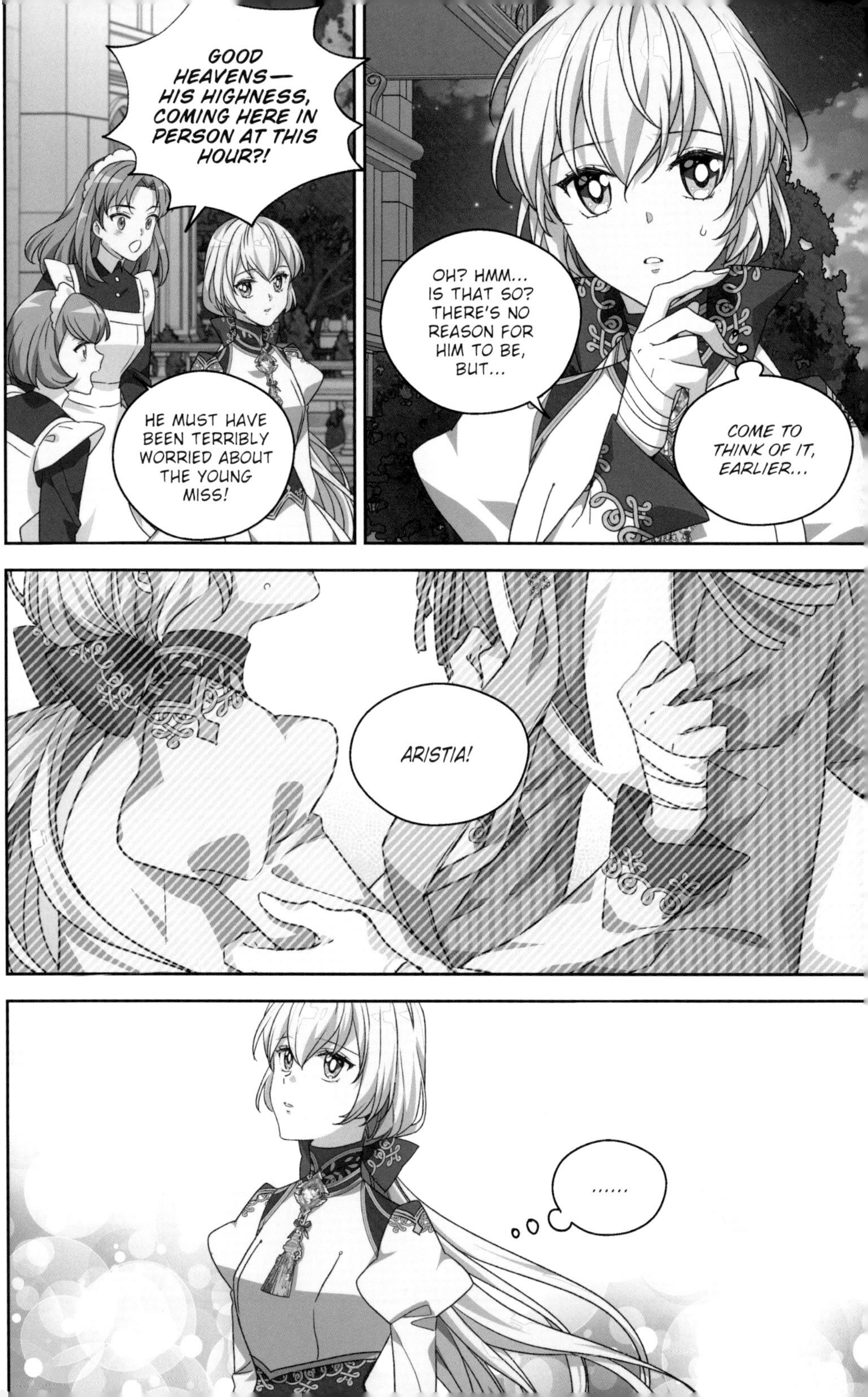
GOOD HEAVENS— HIS HIGHNESS, COMING HERE IN PERSON AT THIS HOUR?!
HE MUST HAVE BEEN TERRIBLY WORRIED ABOUT THE YOUNG MISS!
OH? HMM... IS THAT SO? THERE'S NO REASON FOR HIM TO BE, BUT...
COME TO THINK OF IT, EARLIER...
ARISTIA!
......

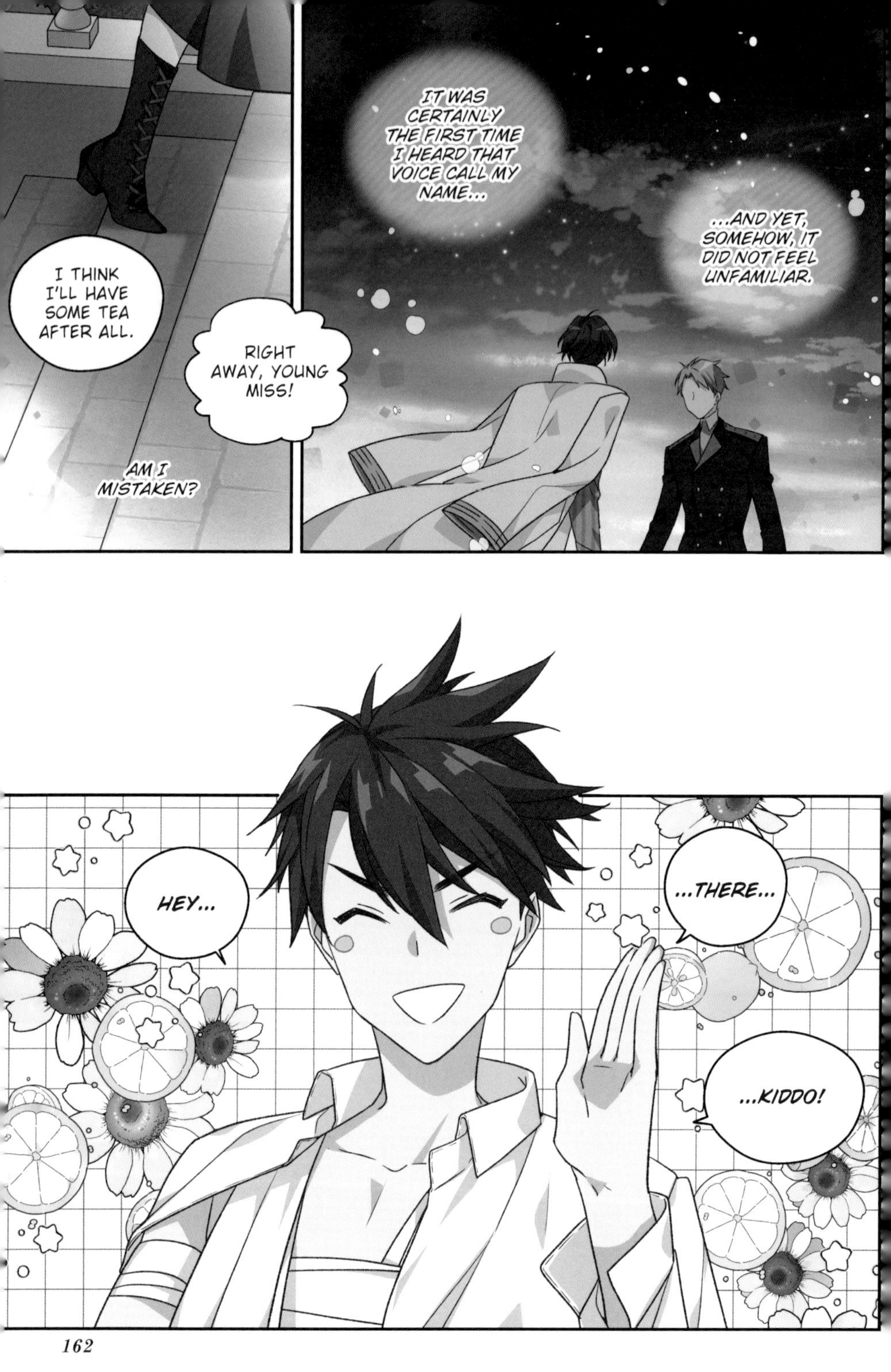
I THINK I'LL HAVE SOME TEA AFTER ALL.
RIGHT AWAY, YOUNG MISS!
AM I MISTAKEN?
IT WAS CERTAINLY THE FIRST TIME I HEARD THAT VOICE CALL MY NAME...
...AND YET, SOMEHOW, IT DID NOT FEEL UNFAMILIAR.
HEY...
...THERE...
...KIDDO!

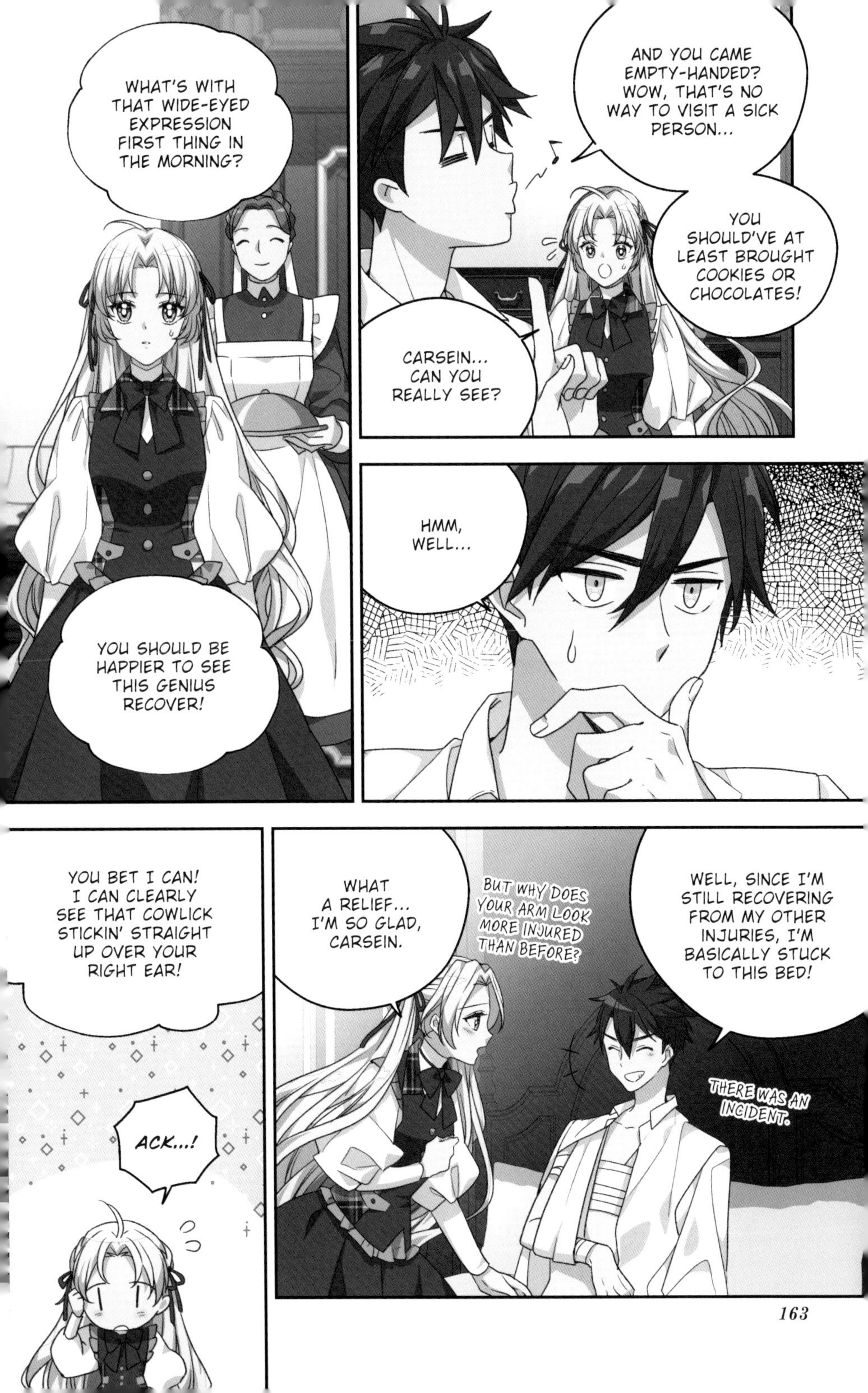

WHAT'S WITH THAT WIDE-EYED EXPRESSION FIRST THING IN THE MORNING?
YOU SHOULD BE HAPPIER TO SEE THIS GENIUS RECOVER!
AND YOU CAME EMPTY-HANDED? WOW, THAT'S NO WAY TO VISIT A SICK PERSON...
YOU SHOULD'VE AT LEAST BROUGHT COOKIES OR CHOCOLATES!
CARSEIN... CAN YOU REALLY SEE?
HMM, WELL...
YOU BET I CAN! I CAN CLEARLY SEE THAT COWLICK STICKIN' STRAIGHT UP OVER YOUR RIGHT EAR!
ACK...!
WHAT A RELIEF... I'M SO GLAD, CARSEIN.
BUT WHY DOES YOUR ARM LOOK MORE INJURED THAN BEFORE?
WELL, SINCE I'M STILL RECOVERING FROM MY OTHER INJURIES, I'M BASICALLY STUCK TO THIS BED!
THERE WAS AN INCIDENT.

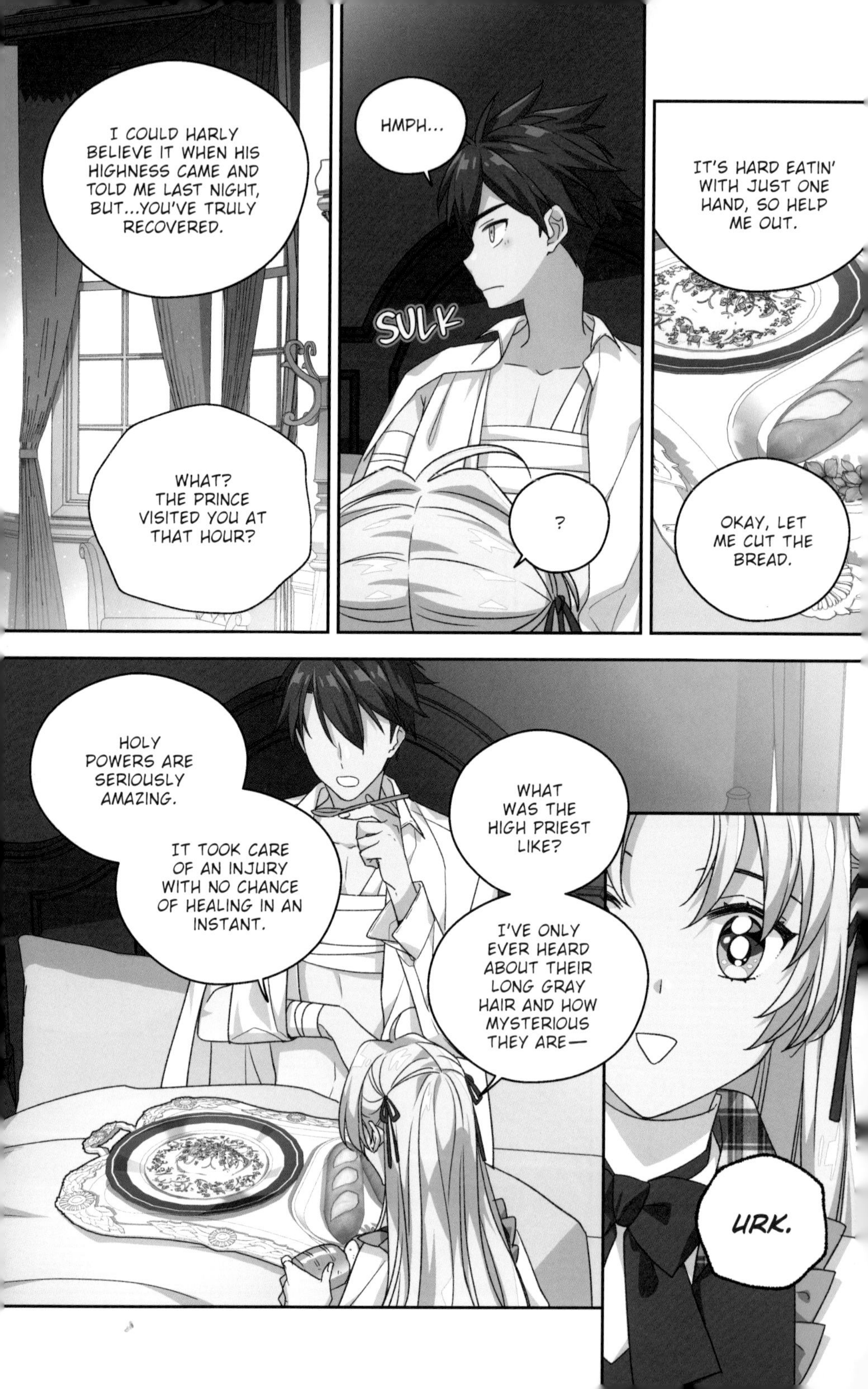
I COULD HARLY BELIEVE IT WHEN HIS HIGHNESS CAME AND TOLD ME LAST NIGHT, BUT...YOU'VE TRULY RECOVERED.
WHAT? THE PRINCE VISITED YOU AT THAT HOUR?
HMPH...
SULK
?
IT'S HARD EATIN' WITH JUST ONE HAND, SO HELP ME OUT.
OKAY, LET ME CUT THE BREAD.
HOLY POWERS ARE SERIOUSLY AMAZING.
IT TOOK CARE OF AN INJURY WITH NO CHANCE OF HEALING IN AN INSTANT.
WHAT WAS THE HIGH PRIEST LIKE?
I'VE ONLY EVER HEARD ABOUT THEIR LONG GRAY HAIR AND HOW MYSTERIOUS THEY ARE—
URK.

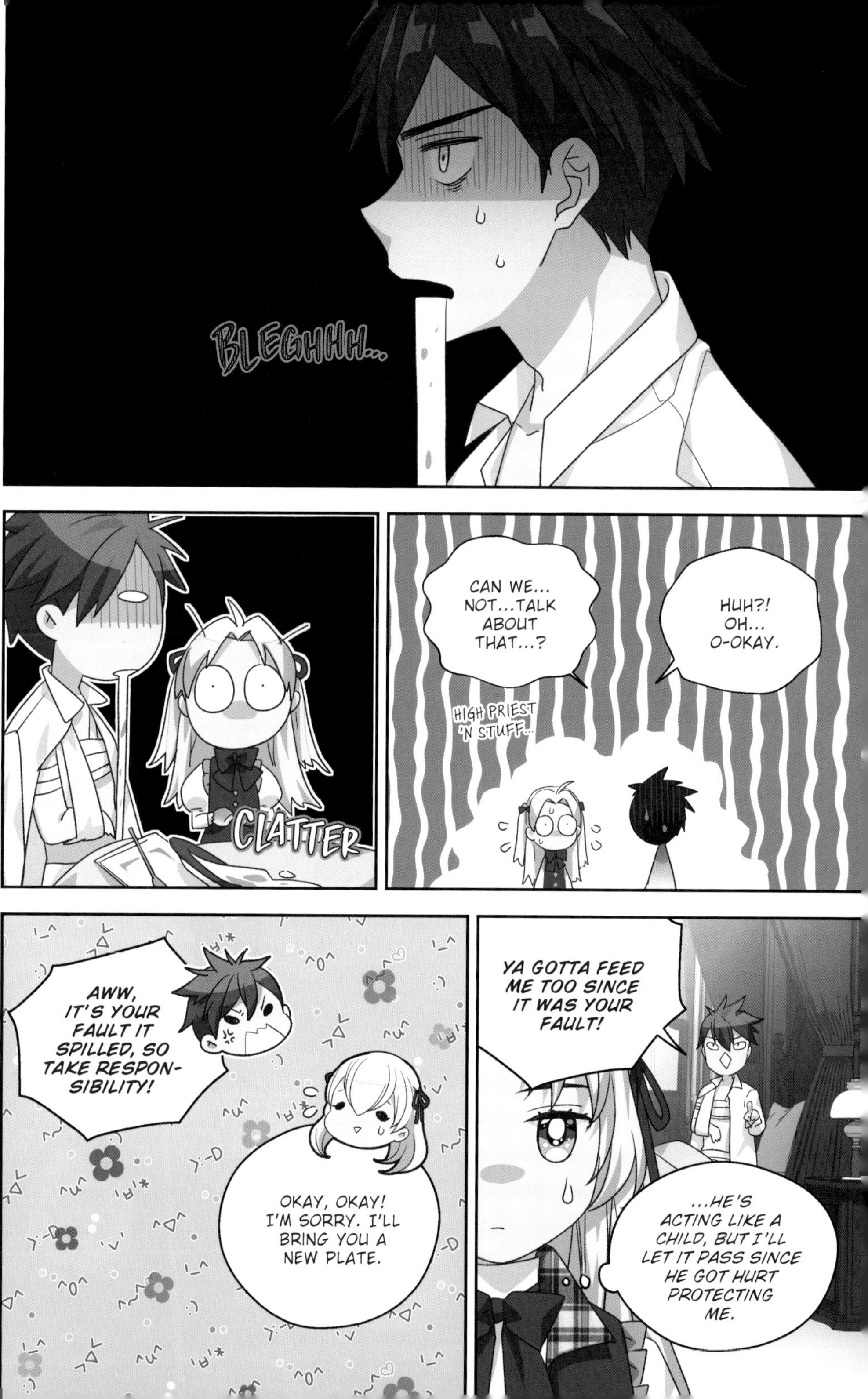
BLEGHHH...
CLATTER
CAN WE... NOT...TALK ABOUT THAT...?
HUH?! OH... O-OKAY.
HIGH PRIEST 'N STUFF...
AWW, IT'S YOUR FAULT IT SPILLED, SO TAKE RESPON-SIBILITY!
OKAY, OKAY! I'M SORRY. I'LL BRING YOU A NEW PLATE.
YA GOTTA FEED ME TOO SINCE IT WAS YOUR FAULT!
...HE'S ACTING LIKE A CHILD, BUT I'LL LET IT PASS SINCE HE GOT HURT PROTECTING ME.

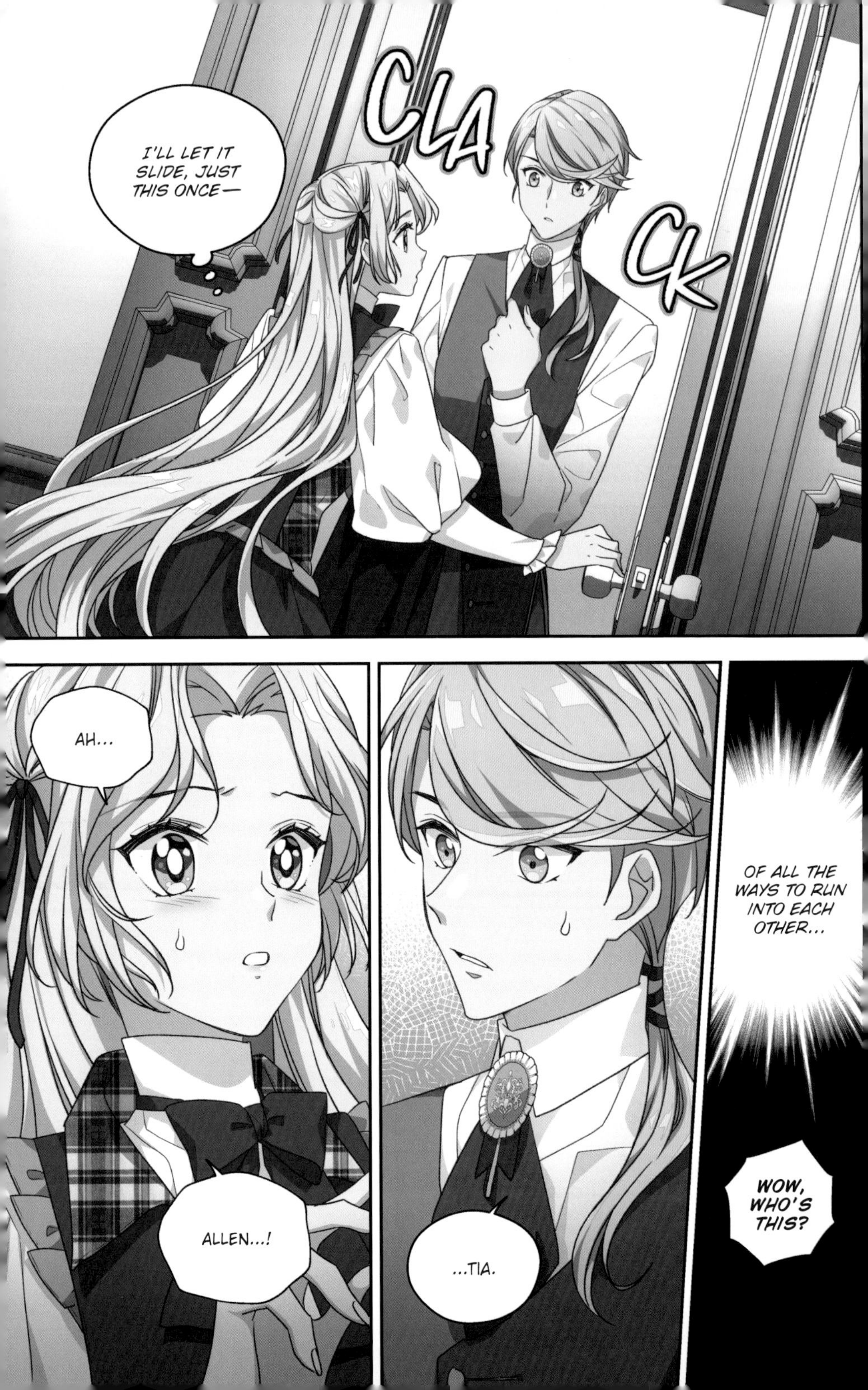
CLACK
I'LL LET IT SLIDE, JUST THIS ONCE—
OF ALL THE WAYS TO RUN INTO EACH OTHER...
WOW, WHO'S THIS?
...TIA.
AH...
ALLEN...!

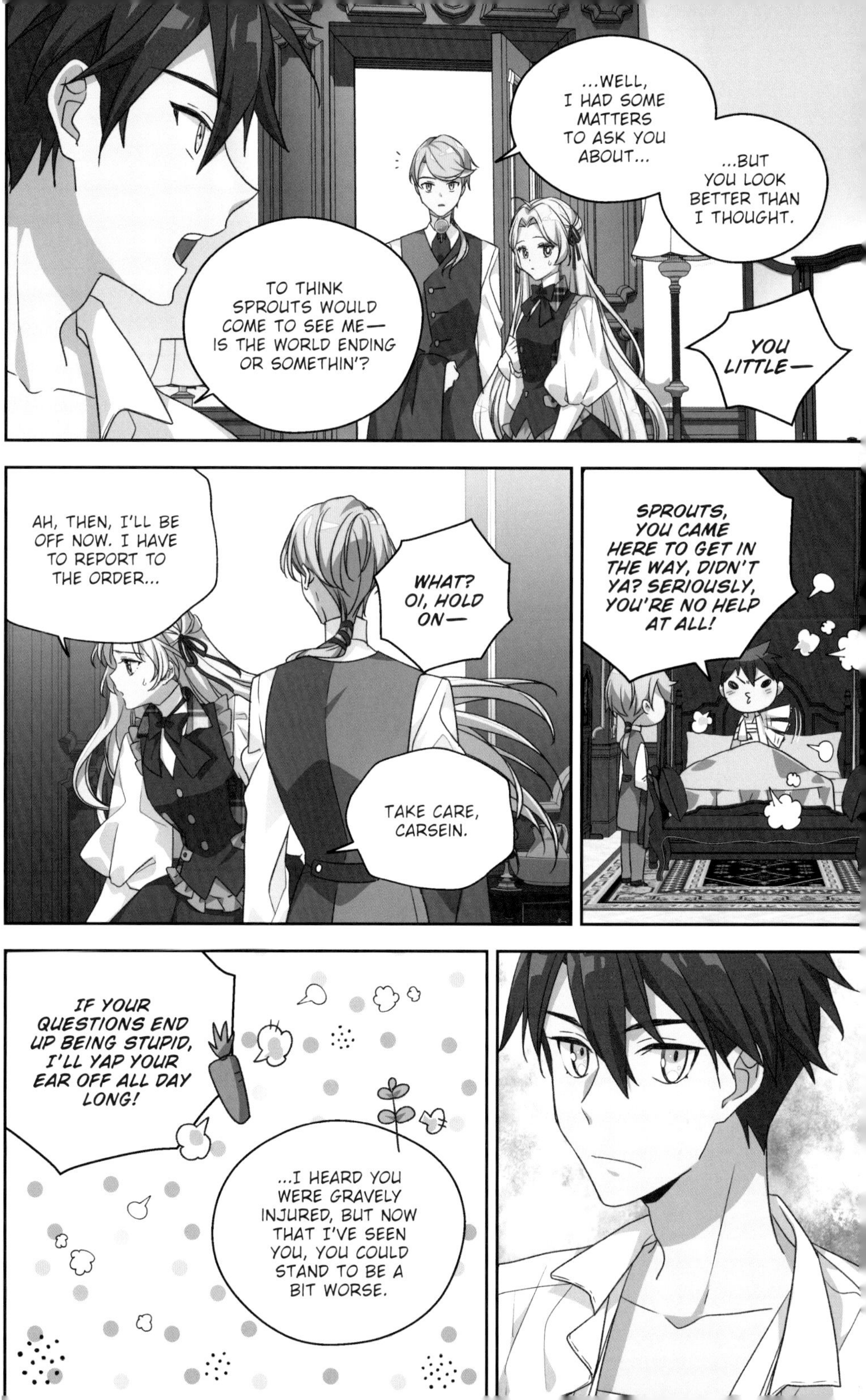
TO THINK SPROUTS WOULD COME TO SEE ME— IS THE WORLD ENDING OR SOMETHIN'?
...WELL, I HAD SOME MATTERS TO ASK YOU ABOUT...
...BUT YOU LOOK BETTER THAN I THOUGHT.
YOU LITTLE—
AH, THEN, I'LL BE OFF NOW. I HAVE TO REPORT TO THE ORDER...
WHAT? OI, HOLD ON—
TAKE CARE, CARSEIN.
SPROUTS, YOU CAME HERE TO GET IN THE WAY, DIDN'T YA? SERIOUSLY, YOU'RE NO HELP AT ALL!
IF YOUR QUESTIONS END UP BEING STUPID, I'LL YAP YOUR EAR OFF ALL DAY LONG!
...I HEARD YOU WERE GRAVELY INJURED, BUT NOW THAT I'VE SEEN YOU, YOU COULD STAND TO BE A BIT WORSE.

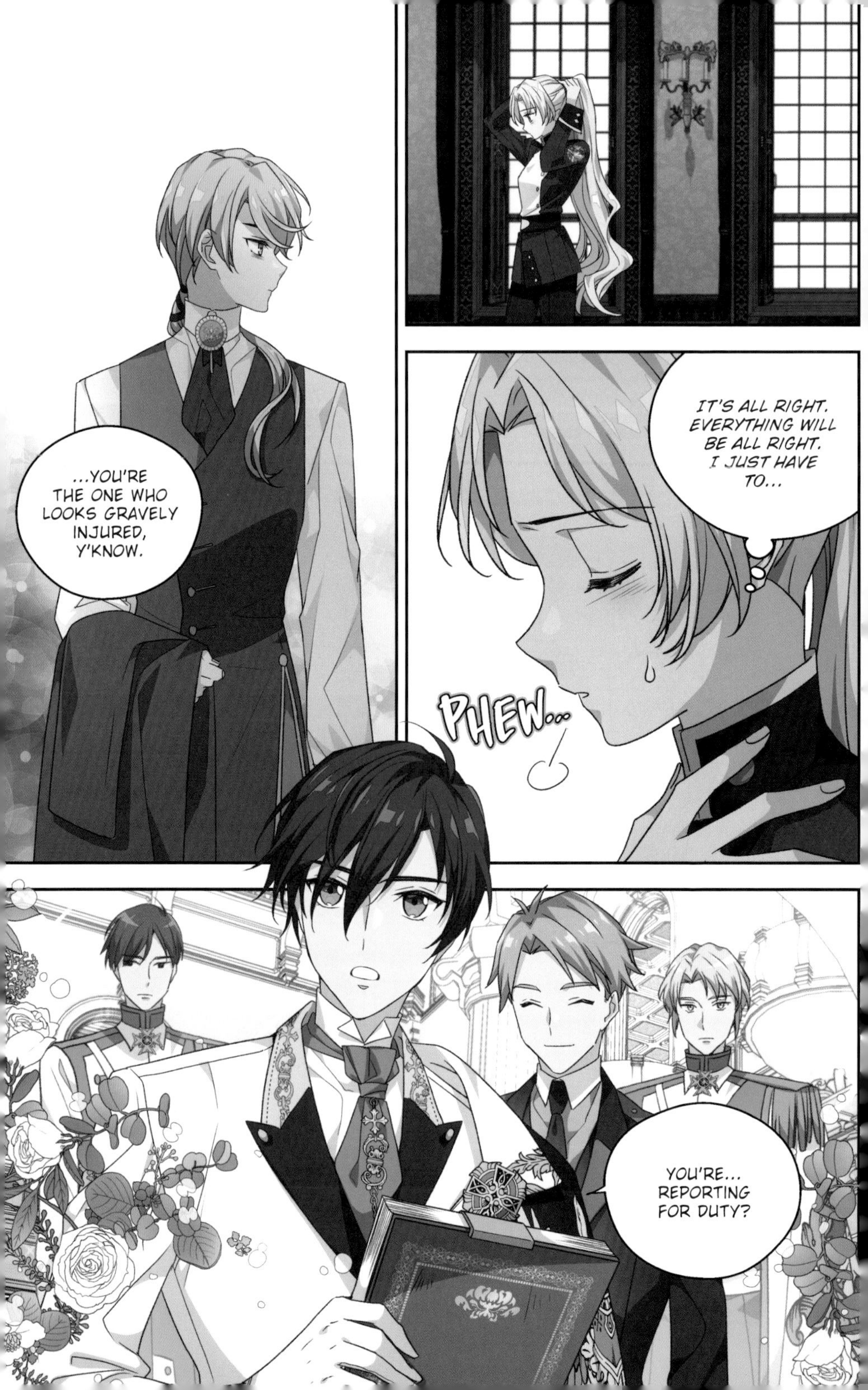

...YOU'RE THE ONE WHO LOOKS GRAVELY INJURED, Y'KNOW.
IT'S ALL RIGHT. EVERYTHING WILL BE ALL RIGHT. I JUST HAVE TO...
PHEW...
YOU'RE... REPORTING FOR DUTY?

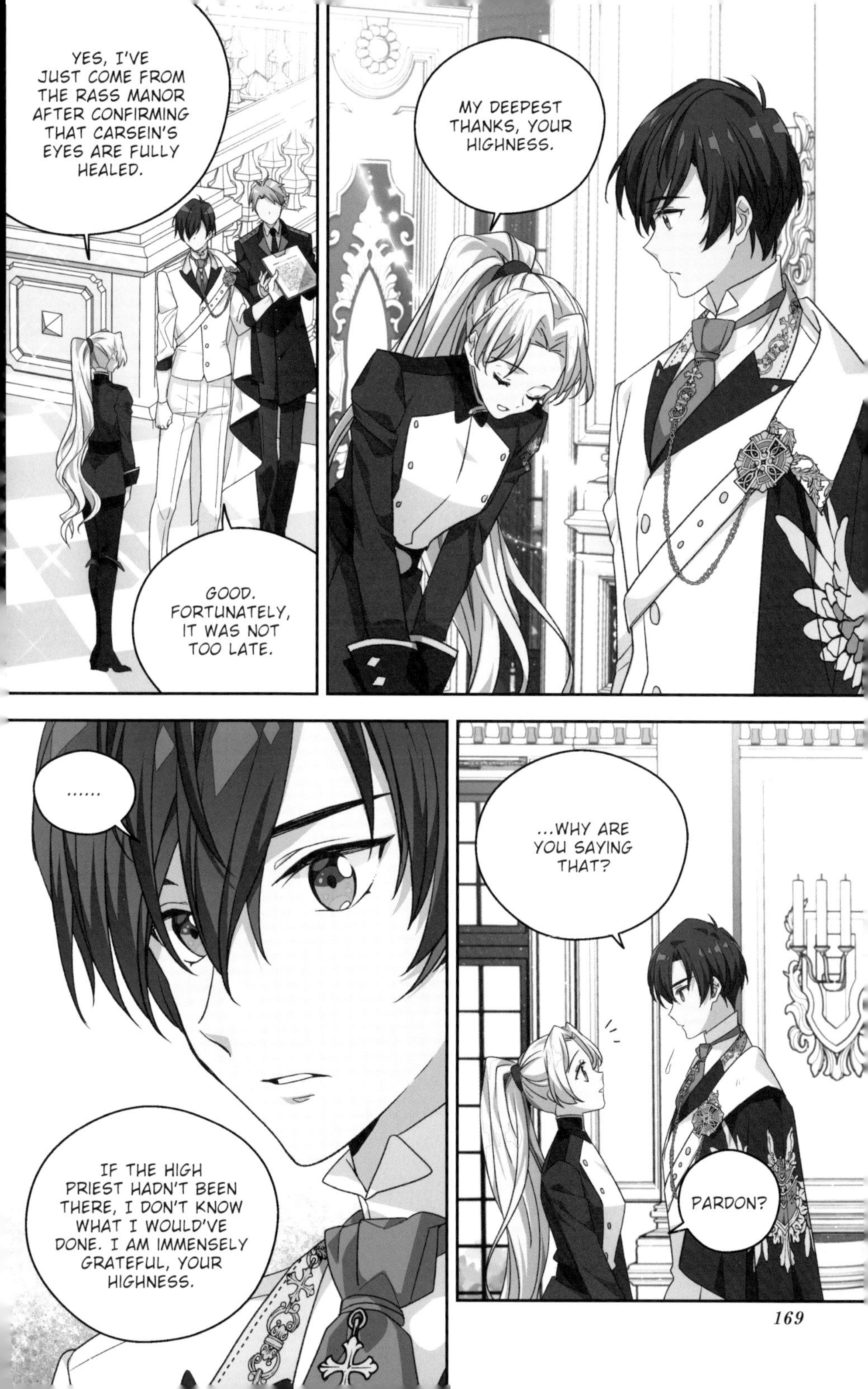
YES, I'VE JUST COME FROM THE RASS MANOR AFTER CONFIRMING THAT CARSEIN'S EYES ARE FULLY HEALED.
GOOD. FORTUNATELY, IT WAS NOT TOO LATE.
MY DEEPEST THANKS, YOUR HIGHNESS.
......
IF THE HIGH PRIEST HADN'T BEEN THERE, I DON'T KNOW WHAT I WOULD'VE DONE. I AM IMMENSELY GRATEFUL, YOUR HIGHNESS.
...WHY ARE YOU SAYING THAT?
PARDON?

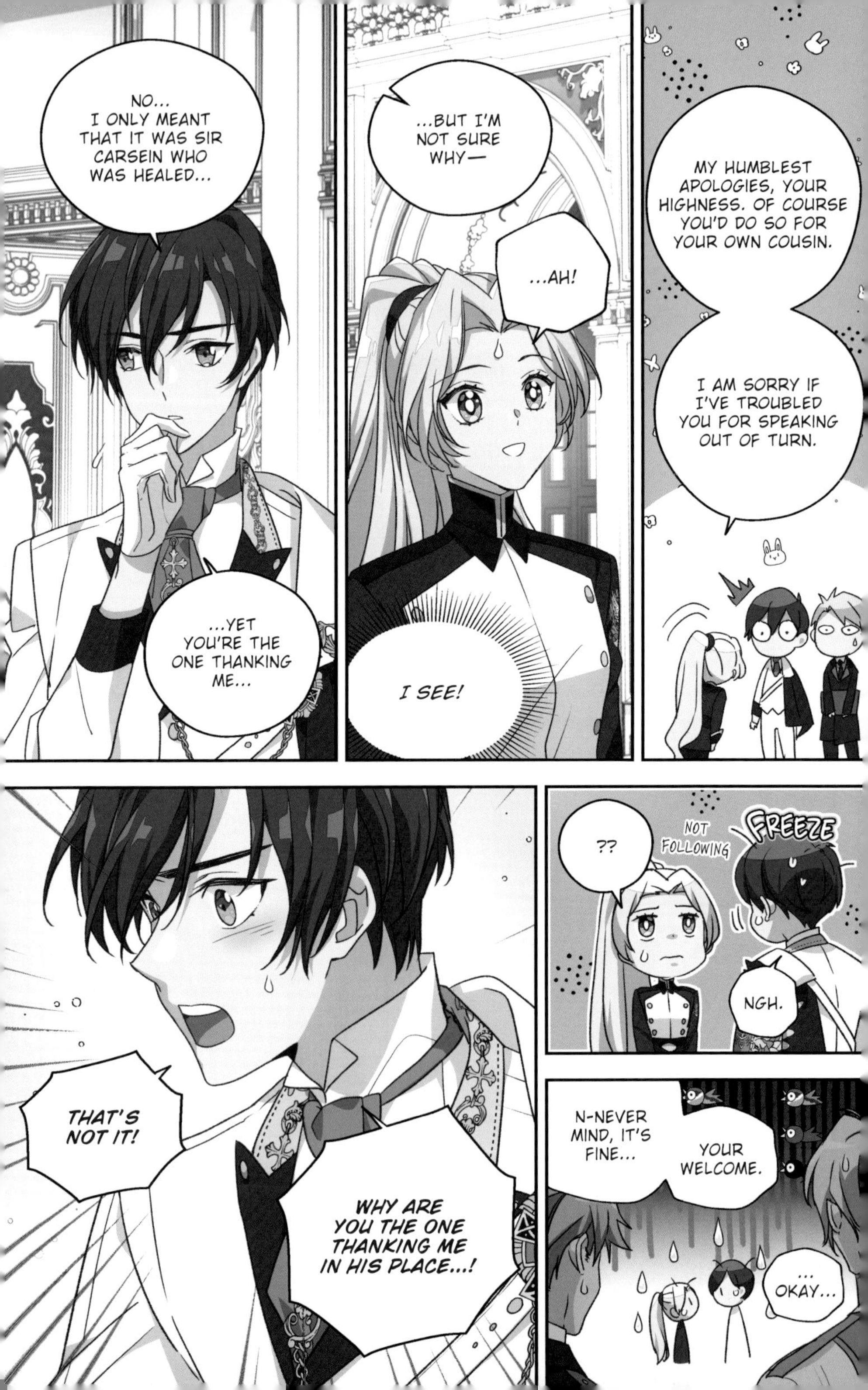
NO... I ONLY MEANT THAT IT WAS SIR CARSEIN WHO WAS HEALED...
...YET YOU'RE THE ONE THANKING ME...
...BUT I'M NOT SURE WHY—
...AH!
I SEE!
MY HUMBLEST APOLOGIES, YOUR HIGHNESS. OF COURSE YOU'D DO SO FOR YOUR OWN COUSIN.
I AM SORRY IF I'VE TROUBLED YOU FOR SPEAKING OUT OF TURN.
THAT'S NOT IT!
WHY ARE YOU THE ONE THANKING ME IN HIS PLACE...!
??
NOT FOLLOWING
FREEZE
NGH.
N-NEVER MIND, IT'S FINE...
YOUR WELCOME.
...OKAY...

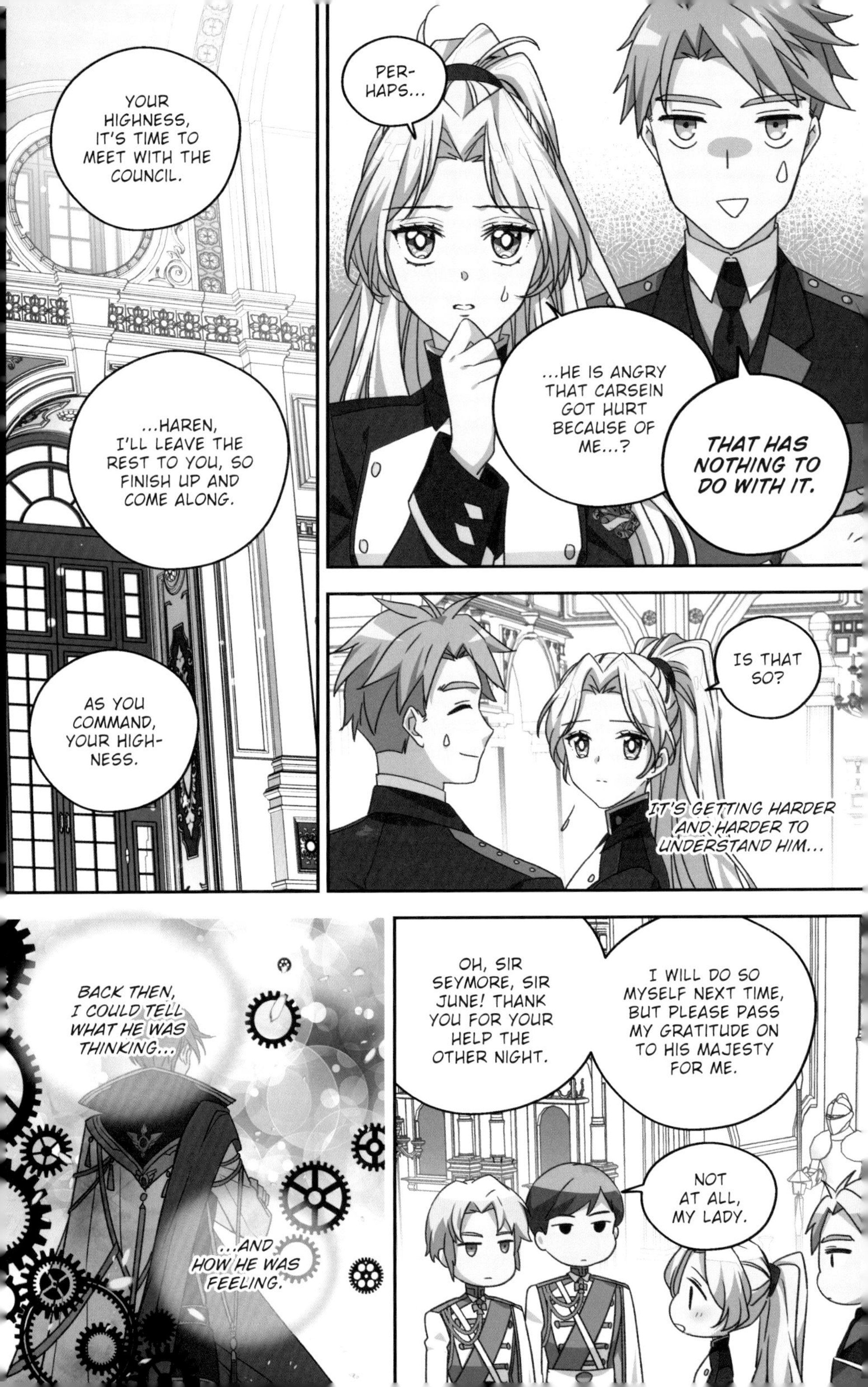
YOUR HIGHNESS, IT'S TIME TO MEET WITH THE COUNCIL.
...HAREN, I'LL LEAVE THE REST TO YOU, SO FINISH UP AND COME ALONG.
AS YOU COMMAND, YOUR HIGH-NESS.
PER-HAPS...
...HE IS ANGRY THAT CARSEIN GOT HURT BECAUSE OF ME...?
THAT HAS NOTHING TO DO WITH IT.
IS THAT SO?
IT'S GETTING HARDER AND HARDER TO UNDERSTAND HIM...
BACK THEN, I COULD TELL WHAT HE WAS THINKING...
...AND HOW HE WAS FEELING.
OH, SIR SEYMORE, SIR JUNE! THANK YOU FOR YOUR HELP THE OTHER NIGHT.
I WILL DO SO MYSELF NEXT TIME, BUT PLEASE PASS MY GRATITUDE ON TO HIS MAJESTY FOR ME.
NOT AT ALL, MY LADY.

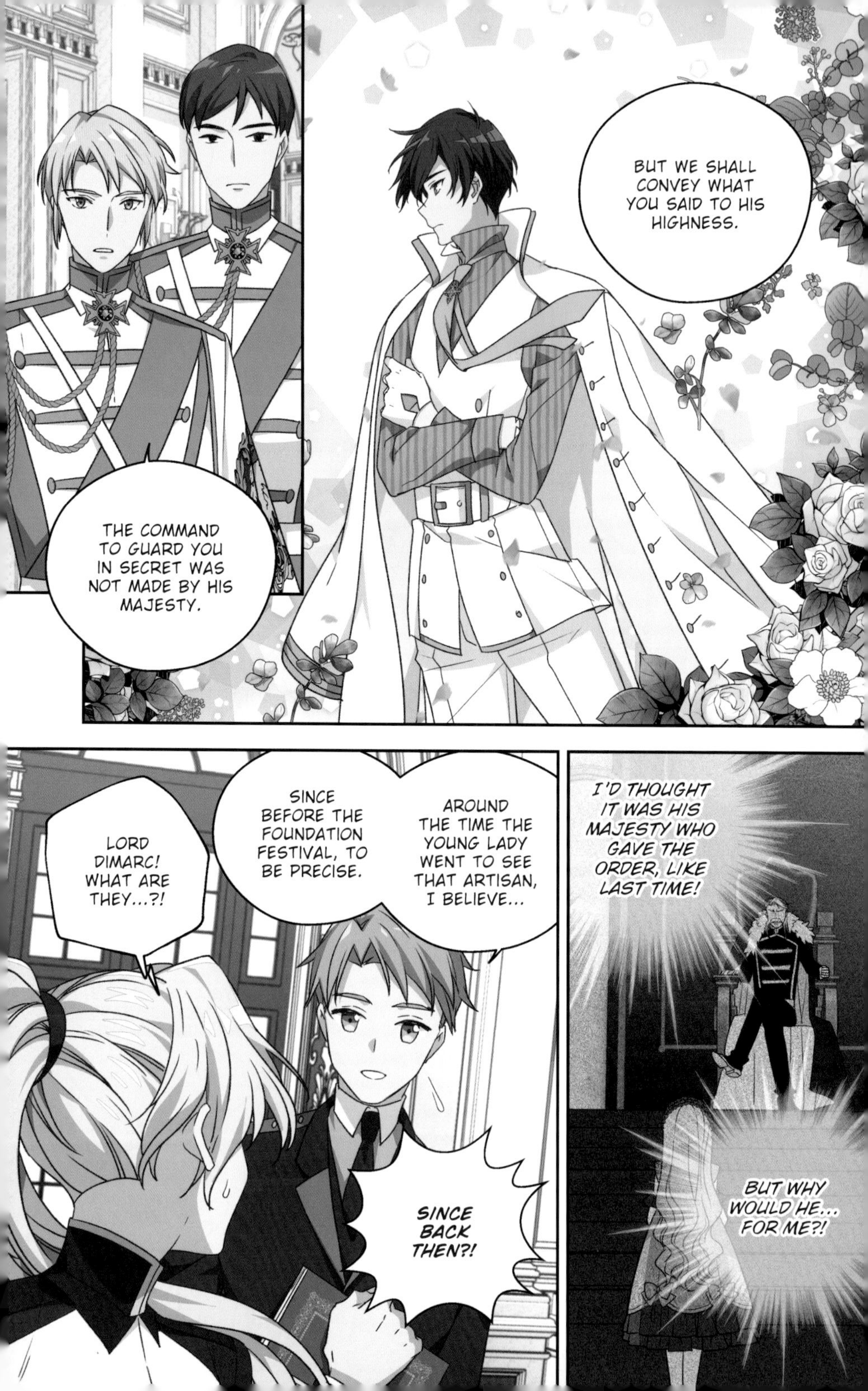
BUT WE SHALL CONVEY WHAT YOU SAID TO HIS HIGHNESS.
THE COMMAND TO GUARD YOU IN SECRET WAS NOT MADE BY HIS MAJESTY.
LORD DIMARC! WHAT ARE THEY...?!
SINCE BEFORE THE FOUNDATION FESTIVAL, TO BE PRECISE.
AROUND THE TIME THE YOUNG LADY WENT TO SEE THAT ARTISAN, I BELIEVE...
SINCE BACK THEN?!
I'D THOUGHT IT WAS HIS MAJESTY WHO GAVE THE ORDER, LIKE LAST TIME!
BUT WHY WOULD HE... FOR ME?!

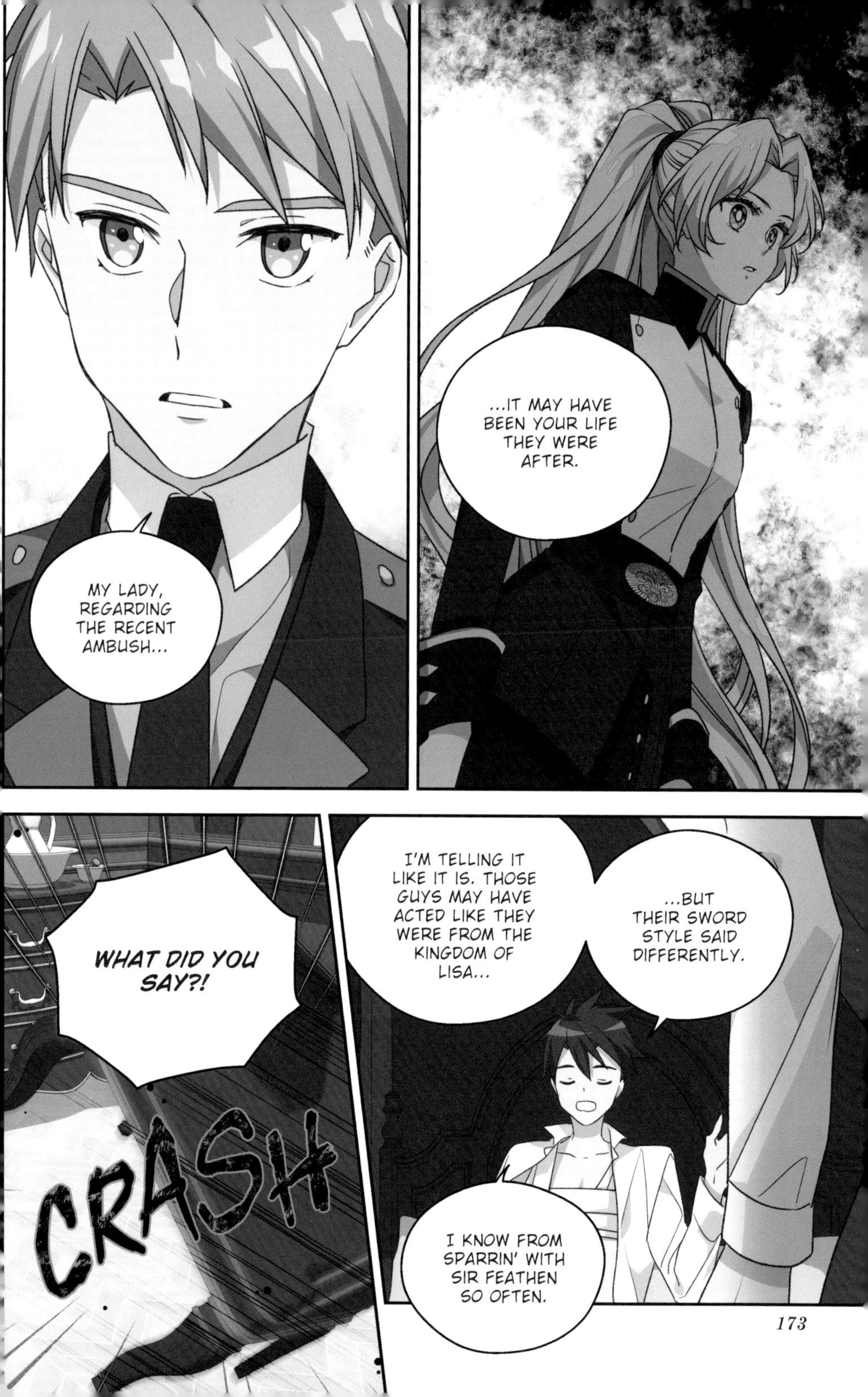

MY LADY, REGARDING THE RECENT AMBUSH...
...IT MAY HAVE BEEN YOUR LIFE THEY WERE AFTER.
WHAT DID YOU SAY?!
CRASH
I'M TELLING IT LIKE IT IS. THOSE GUYS MAY HAVE ACTED LIKE THEY WERE FROM THE KINGDOM OF LISA...
...BUT THEIR SWORD STYLE SAID DIFFERENTLY.
I KNOW FROM SPARRIN' WITH SIR FEATHEN SO OFTEN.

ALSO, THAT LAST GUY...

...SAID THAT I WAS IN THE WAY.

THEY WERE SUPPOSED TO BE AFTER FEATHEN FOR BETRAYING THE KINGDOM OF LISA...

...BUT AT THE END, THEY AIMED FOR TIA...!

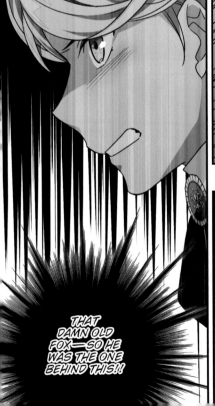

THAT DAMN OLD FOX—SO HE WAS THE ONE BEHIND THIS!!

DO YOU HAVE SOME KIND OF HUNCH—

SLAM

OI!! SPROUTS!!

DUKE JENA! DID YOU DO SOMETHING TO LADY MONIQUE?

TO CARELESSLY LAY A HAND ON A CHILD OF PROPHECY—!

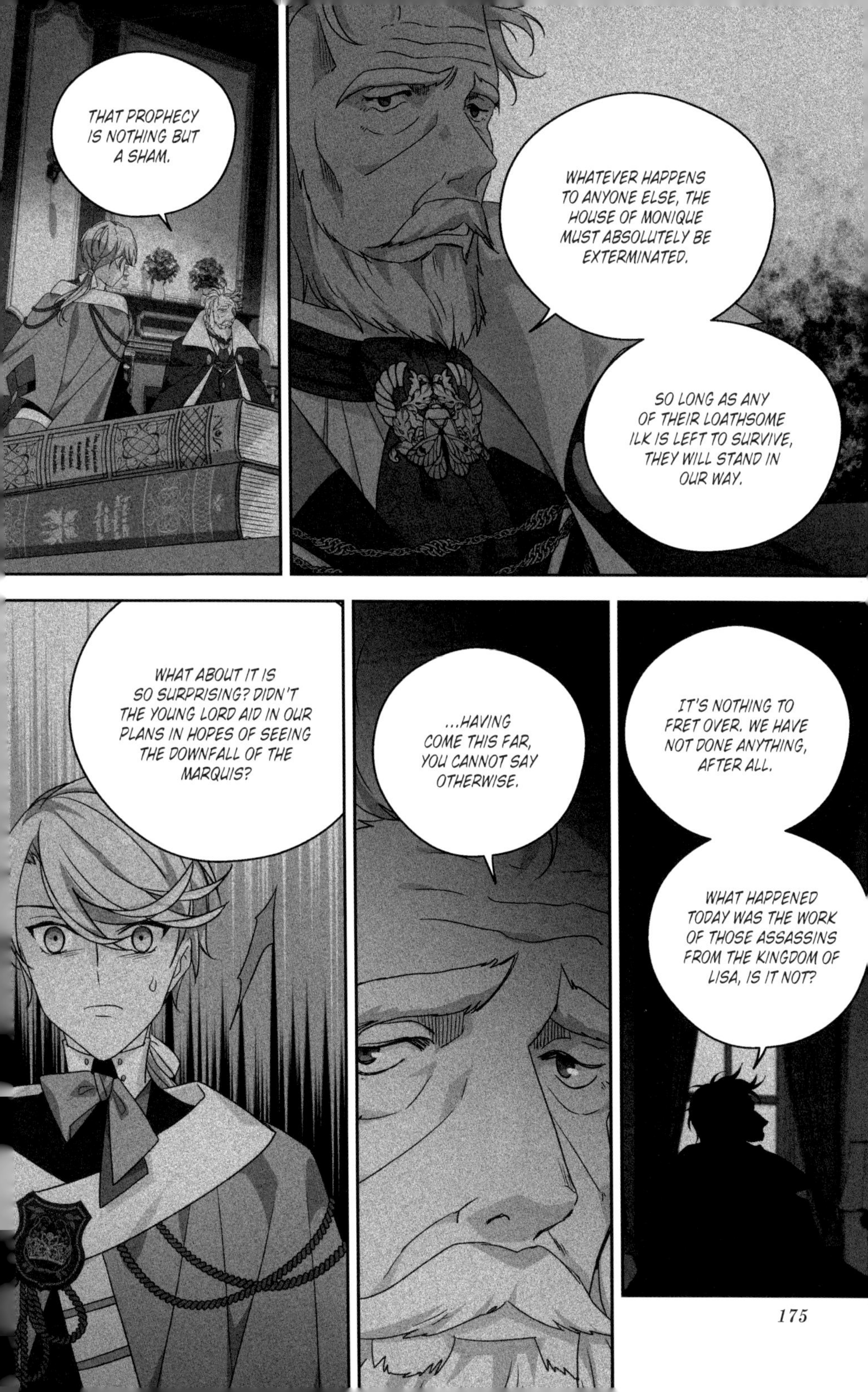
THAT PROPHECY IS NOTHING BUT A SHAM.
WHATEVER HAPPENS TO ANYONE ELSE, THE HOUSE OF MONIQUE MUST ABSOLUTELY BE EXTERMINATED.
SO LONG AS ANY OF THEIR LOATHSOME ILK IS LEFT TO SURVIVE, THEY WILL STAND IN OUR WAY.
WHAT ABOUT IT IS SO SURPRISING? DIDN'T THE YOUNG LORD AID IN OUR PLANS IN HOPES OF SEEING THE DOWNFALL OF THE MARQUIS?
...HAVING COME THIS FAR, YOU CANNOT SAY OTHERWISE.
IT'S NOTHING TO FRET OVER. WE HAVE NOT DONE ANYTHING, AFTER ALL.
WHAT HAPPENED TODAY WAS THE WORK OF THOSE ASSASSINS FROM THE KINGDOM OF LISA, IS IT NOT?

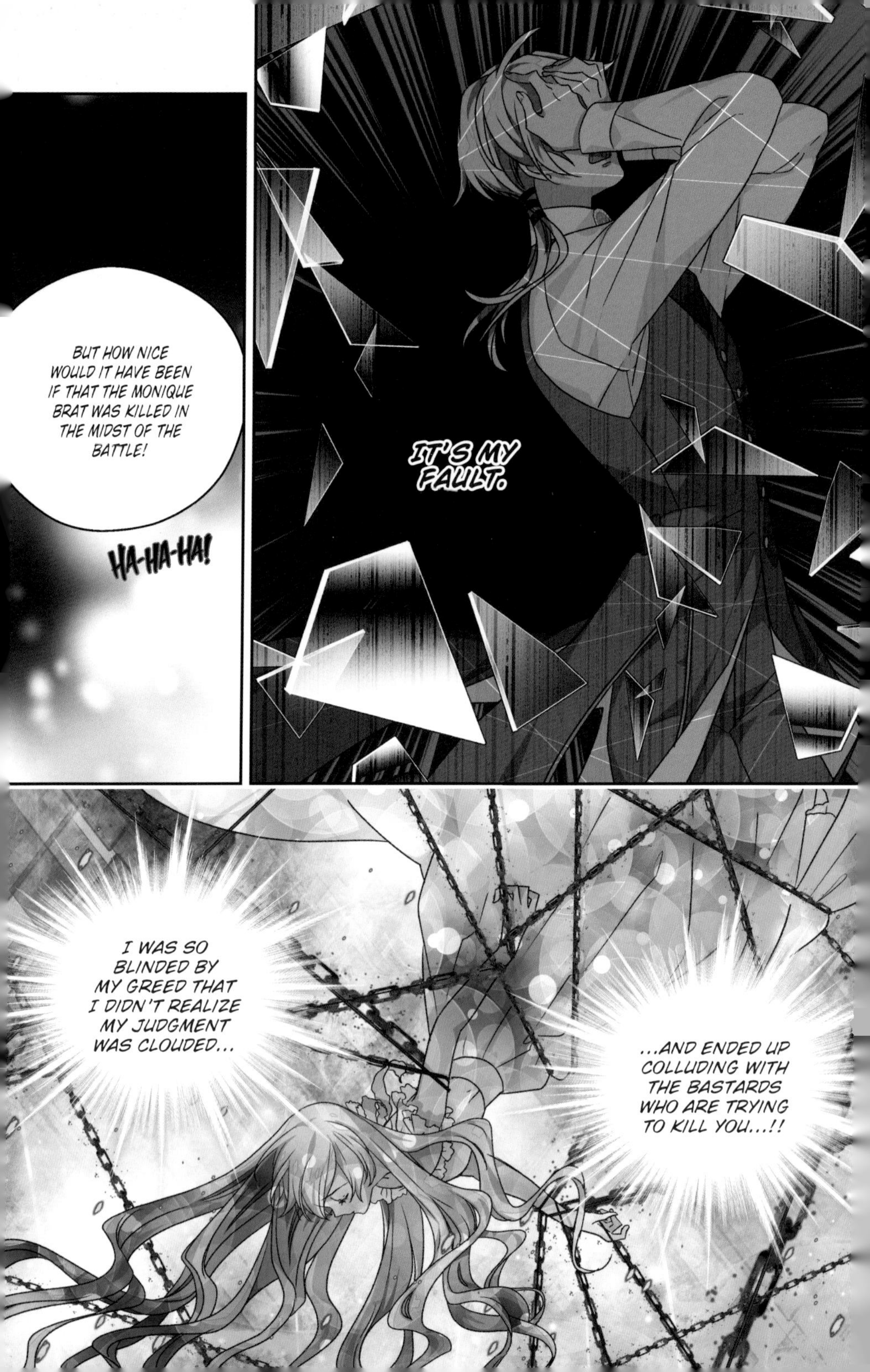
BUT HOW NICE WOULD IT HAVE BEEN IF THAT THE MONIQUE BRAT WAS KILLED IN THE MIDST OF THE BATTLE!
HA-HA-HA!
IT'S MY FAULT.
I WAS SO BLINDED BY MY GREED THAT I DIDN'T REALIZE MY JUDGMENT WAS CLOUDED...
...AND ENDED UP COLLUDING WITH THE BASTARDS WHO ARE TRYING TO KILL YOU...!!

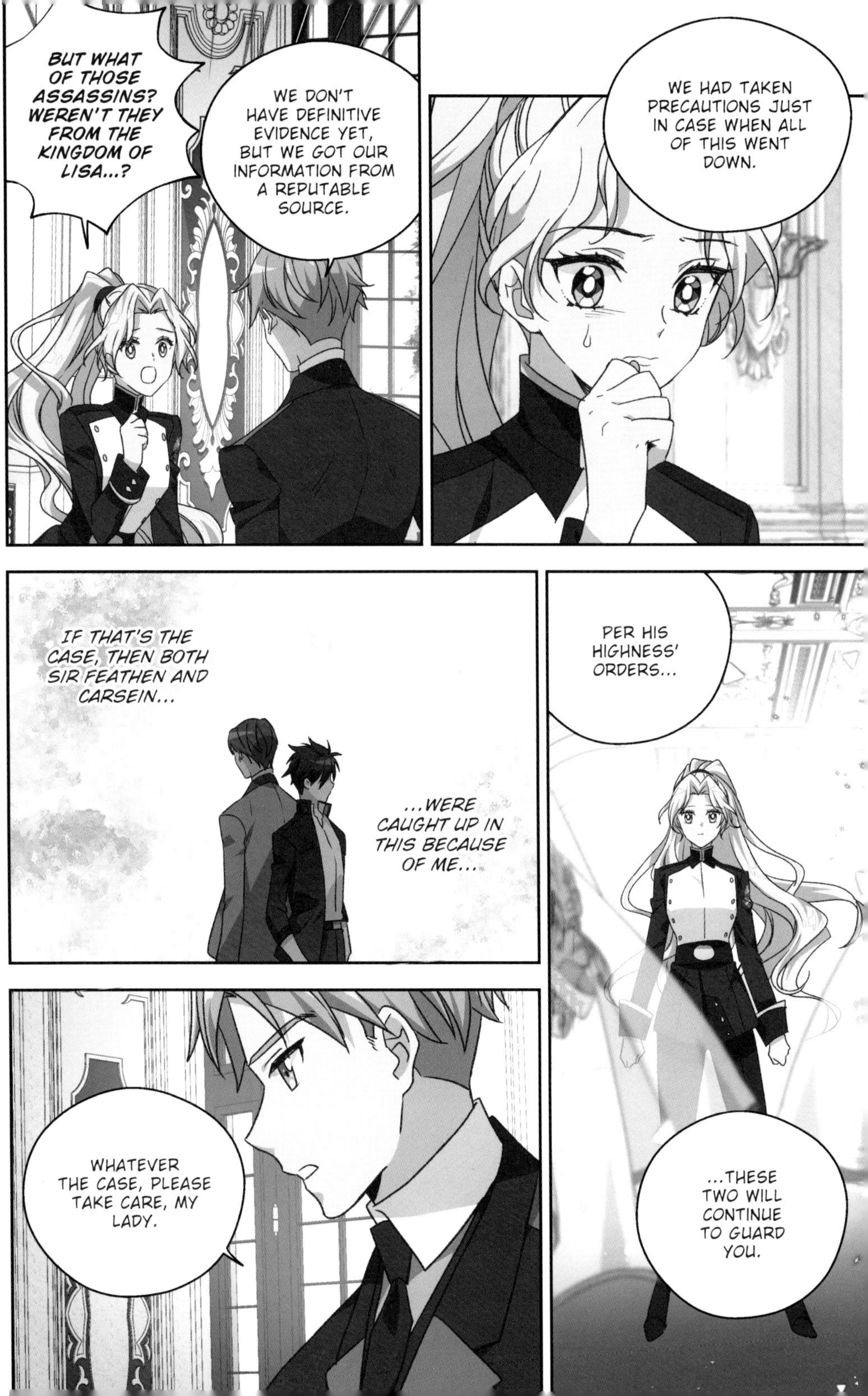

BUT WHAT OF THOSE ASSASSINS? WEREN'T THEY FROM THE KINGDOM OF LISA...?
WE DON'T HAVE DEFINITIVE EVIDENCE YET, BUT WE GOT OUR INFORMATION FROM A REPUTABLE SOURCE.
WE HAD TAKEN PRECAUTIONS JUST IN CASE WHEN ALL OF THIS WENT DOWN.
IF THAT'S THE CASE, THEN BOTH SIR FEATHEN AND CARSEIN...
...WERE CAUGHT UP IN THIS BECAUSE OF ME...
PER HIS HIGHNESS' ORDERS...
...THESE TWO WILL CONTINUE TO GUARD YOU.
WHATEVER THE CASE, PLEASE TAKE CARE, MY LADY.

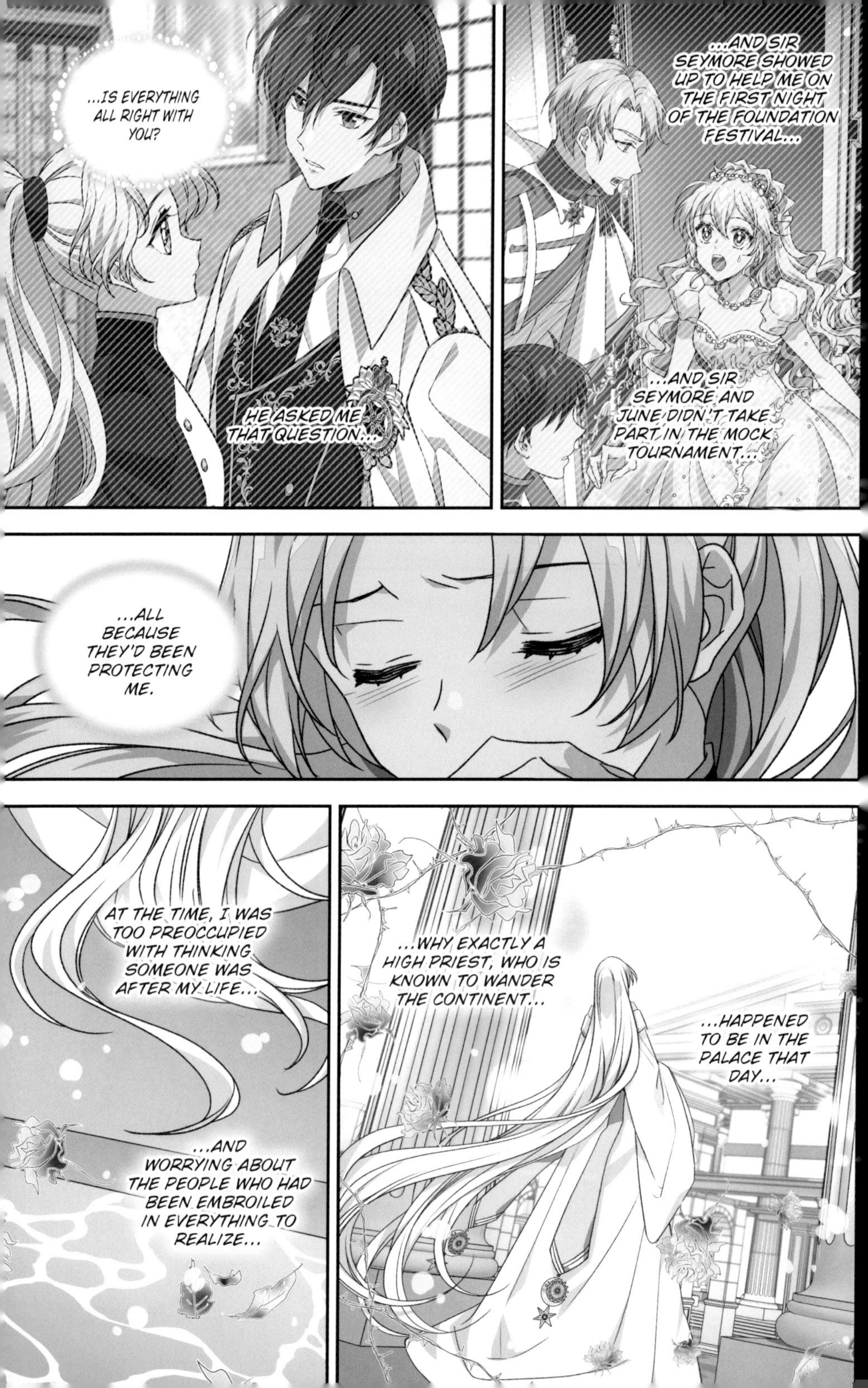
...IS EVERYTHING ALL RIGHT WITH YOU?
HE ASKED ME THAT QUESTION...
...AND SIR SEYMORE SHOWED UP TO HELP ME ON THE FIRST NIGHT OF THE FOUNDATION FESTIVAL...
...AND SIR SEYMORE AND JUNE DIDN'T TAKE PART IN THE MOCK TOURNAMENT...
...ALL BECAUSE THEY'D BEEN PROTECTING ME.
AT THE TIME, I WAS TOO PREOCCUPIED WITH THINKING SOMEONE WAS AFTER MY LIFE...
...AND WORRYING ABOUT THE PEOPLE WHO HAD BEEN EMBROILED IN EVERYTHING TO REALIZE...
...WHY EXACTLY A HIGH PRIEST, WHO IS KNOWN TO WANDER THE CONTINENT...
...HAPPENED TO BE IN THE PALACE THAT DAY...

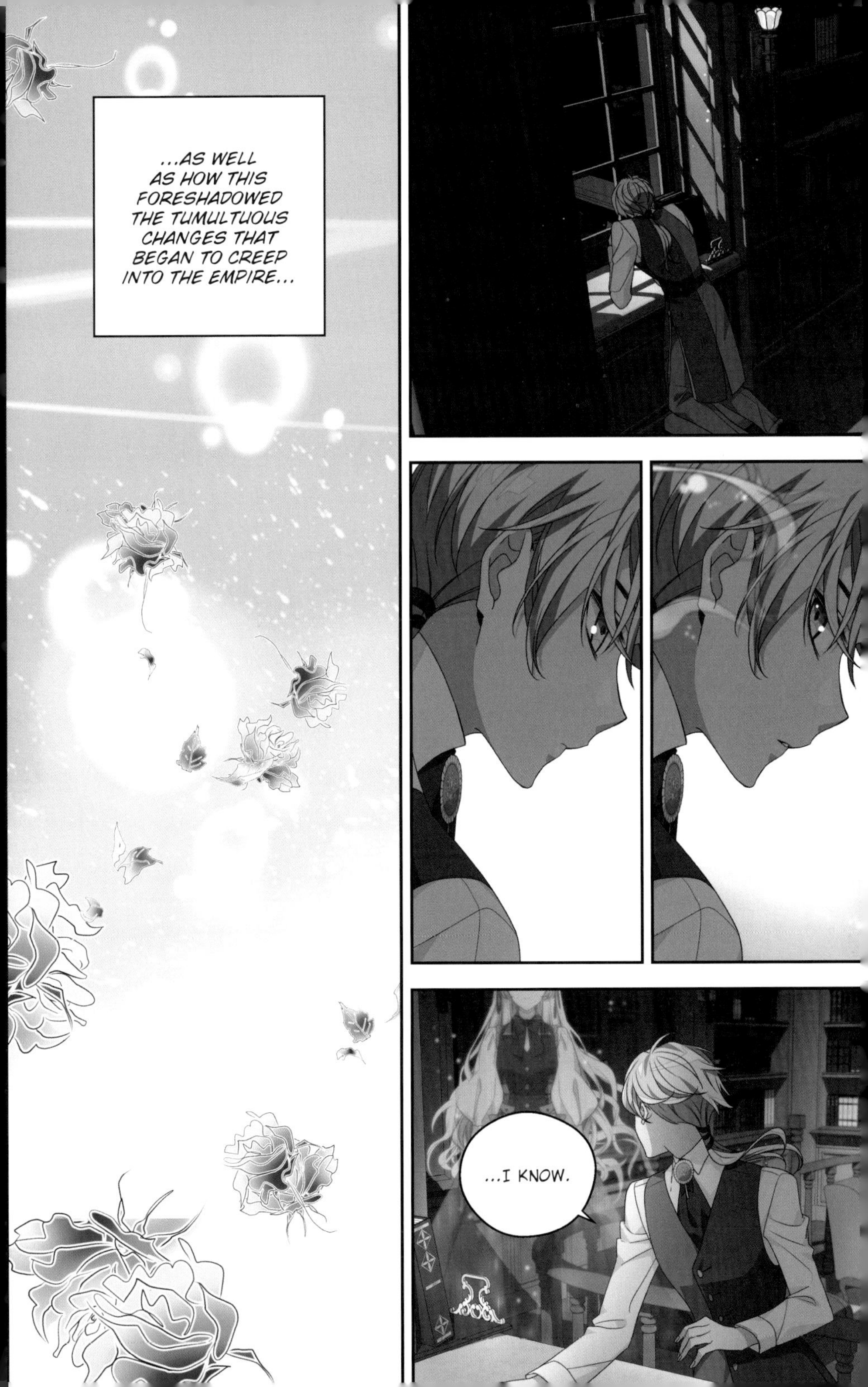
...AS WELL AS HOW THIS FORESHADOWED THE TUMULTUOUS CHANGES THAT BEGAN TO CREEP INTO THE EMPIRE...
...I KNOW.

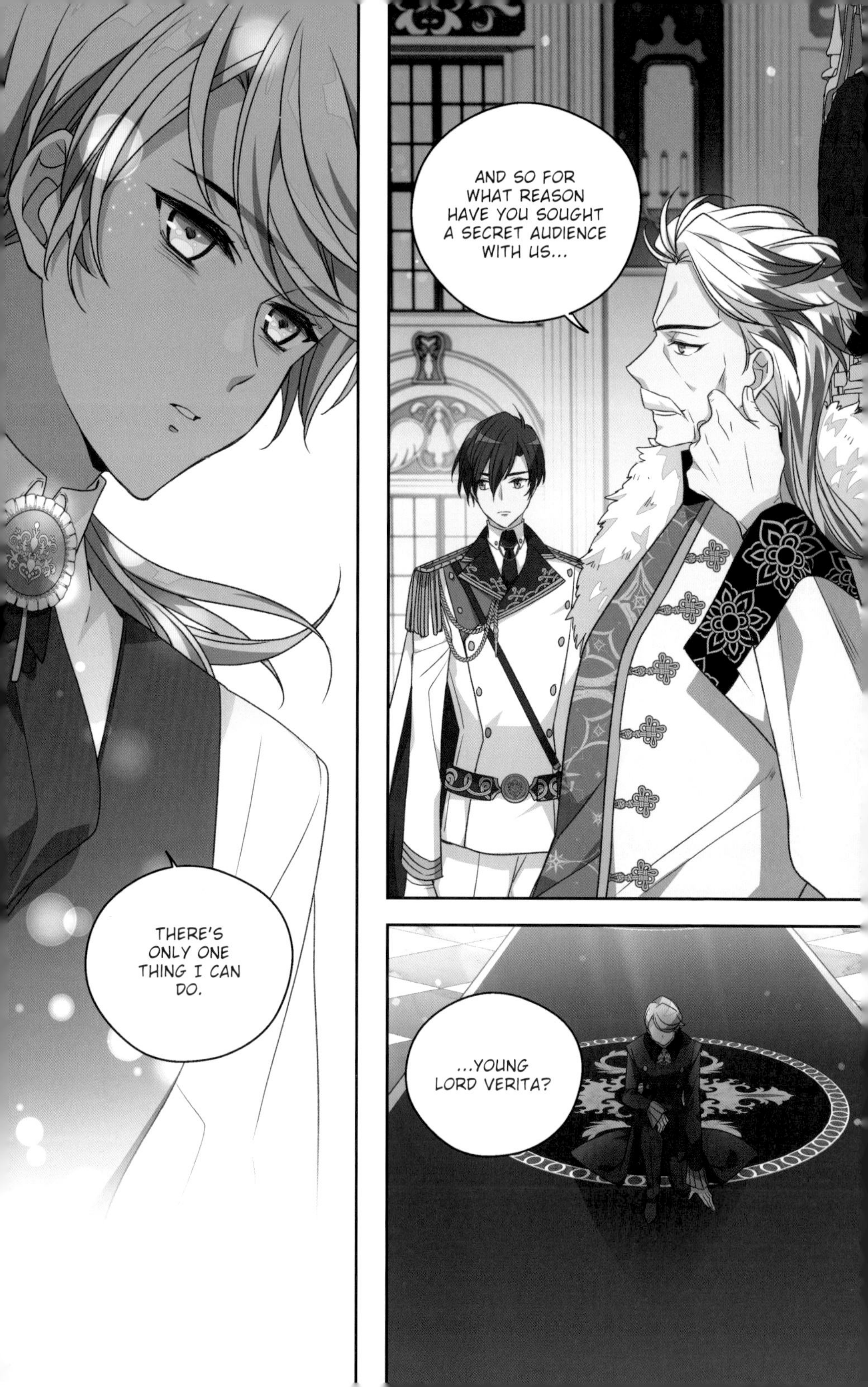
AND SO FOR WHAT REASON HAVE YOU SOUGHT A SECRET AUDIENCE WITH US...
...YOUNG LORD VERITA?
THERE'S ONLY ONE THING I CAN DO.

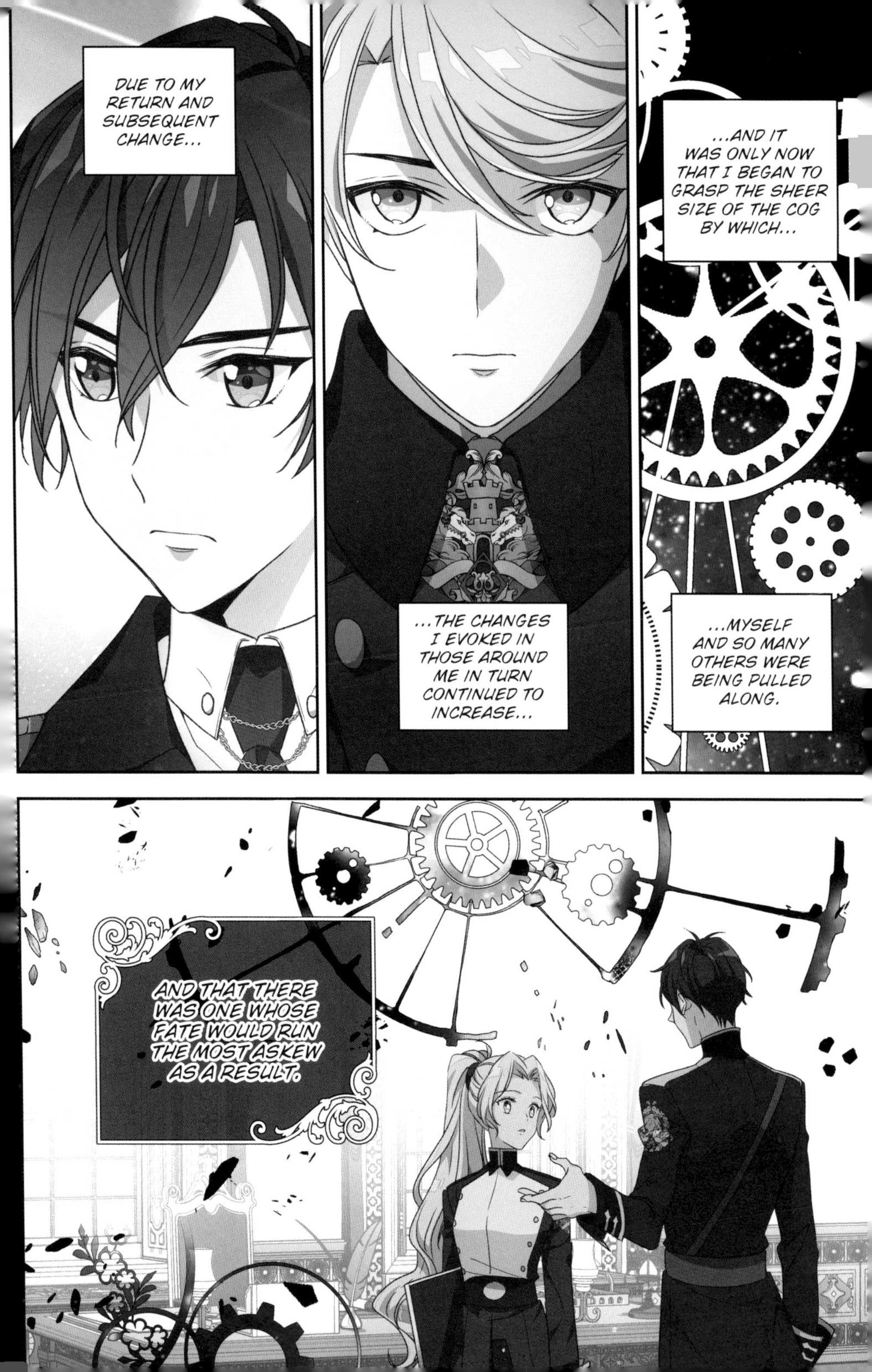
DUE TO MY RETURN AND SUBSEQUENT CHANGE...
...THE CHANGES I EVOKED IN THOSE AROUND ME IN TURN CONTINUED TO INCREASE...
...AND IT WAS ONLY NOW THAT I BEGAN TO GRASP THE SHEER SIZE OF THE COG BY WHICH...
...MYSELF AND SO MANY OTHERS WERE BEING PULLED ALONG.
AND THAT THERE WAS ONE WHOSE FATE WOULD RUN THE MOST ASKEW AS A RESULT.

The Abandoned Empress

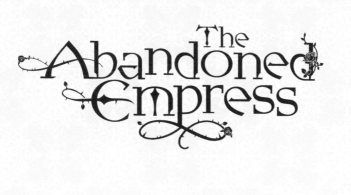

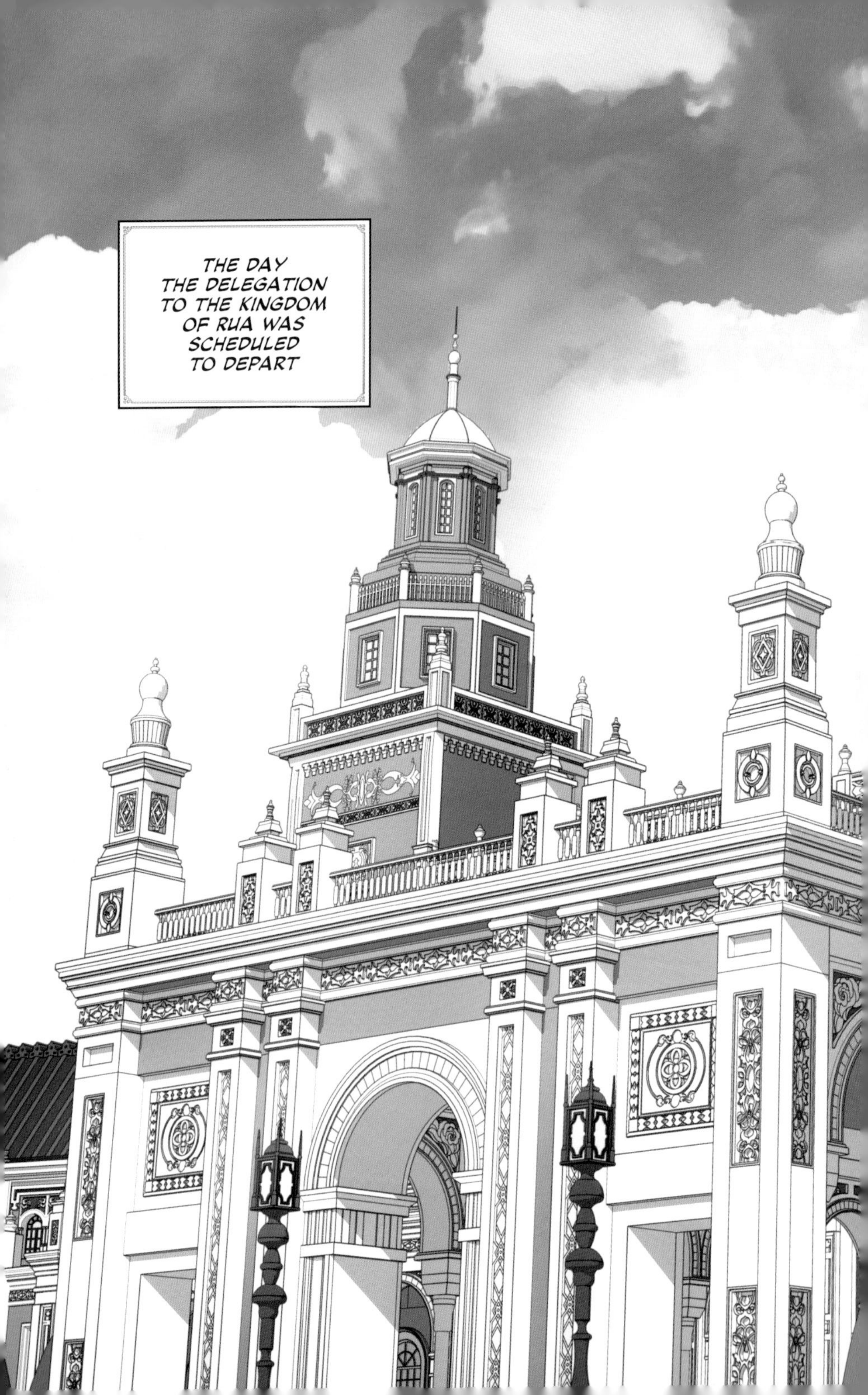
THE DAY THE DELEGATION TO THE KINGDOM OF RUA WAS SCHEDULED TO DEPART

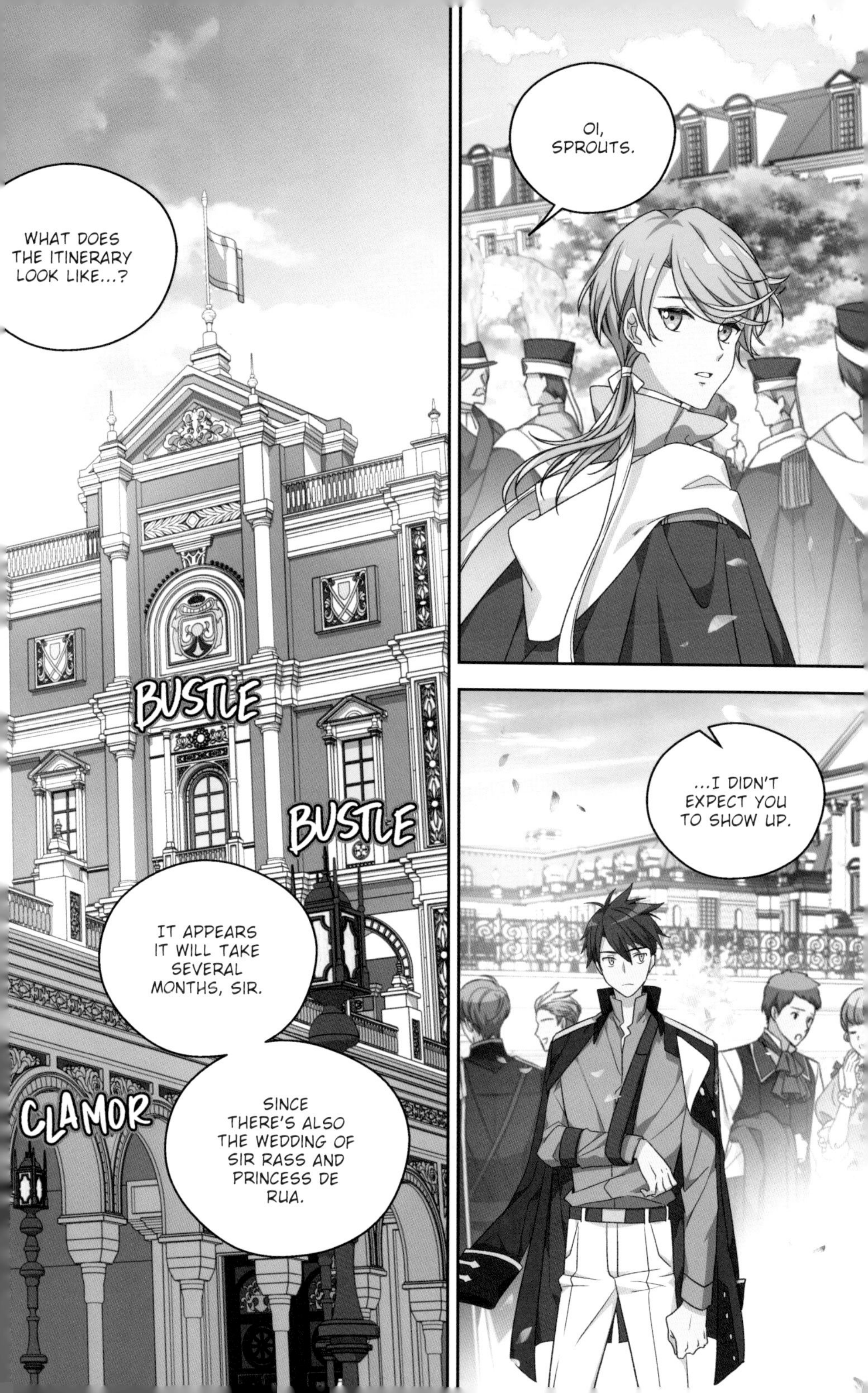
WHAT DOES THE ITINERARY LOOK LIKE...?
BUSTLE
BUSTLE
IT APPEARS IT WILL TAKE SEVERAL MONTHS, SIR.
CLAMOR
SINCE THERE'S ALSO THE WEDDING OF SIR RASS AND PRINCESS DE RUA.
OI, SPROUTS.
...I DIDN'T EXPECT YOU TO SHOW UP.

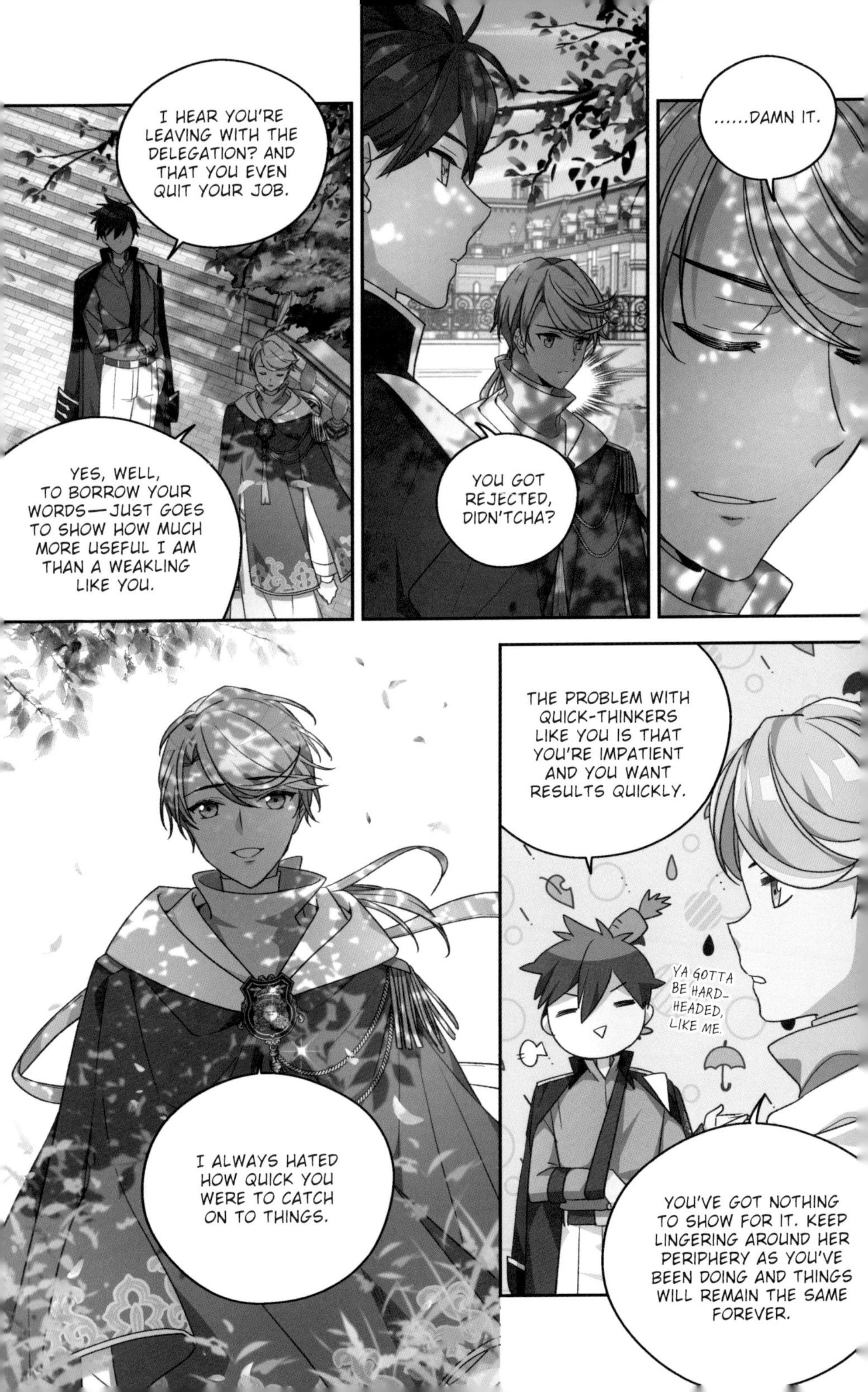
I HEAR YOU'RE LEAVING WITH THE DELEGATION? AND THAT YOU EVEN QUIT YOUR JOB.
YES, WELL, TO BORROW YOUR WORDS—JUST GOES TO SHOW HOW MUCH MORE USEFUL I AM THAN A WEAKLING LIKE YOU.
YOU GOT REJECTED, DIDN'TCHA?
......DAMN IT.
I ALWAYS HATED HOW QUICK YOU WERE TO CATCH ON TO THINGS.
THE PROBLEM WITH QUICK-THINKERS LIKE YOU IS THAT YOU'RE IMPATIENT AND YOU WANT RESULTS QUICKLY.
YA GOTTA BE HARD-HEADED, LIKE ME.
YOU'VE GOT NOTHING TO SHOW FOR IT. KEEP LINGERING AROUND HER PERIPHERY AS YOU'VE BEEN DOING AND THINGS WILL REMAIN THE SAME FOREVER.

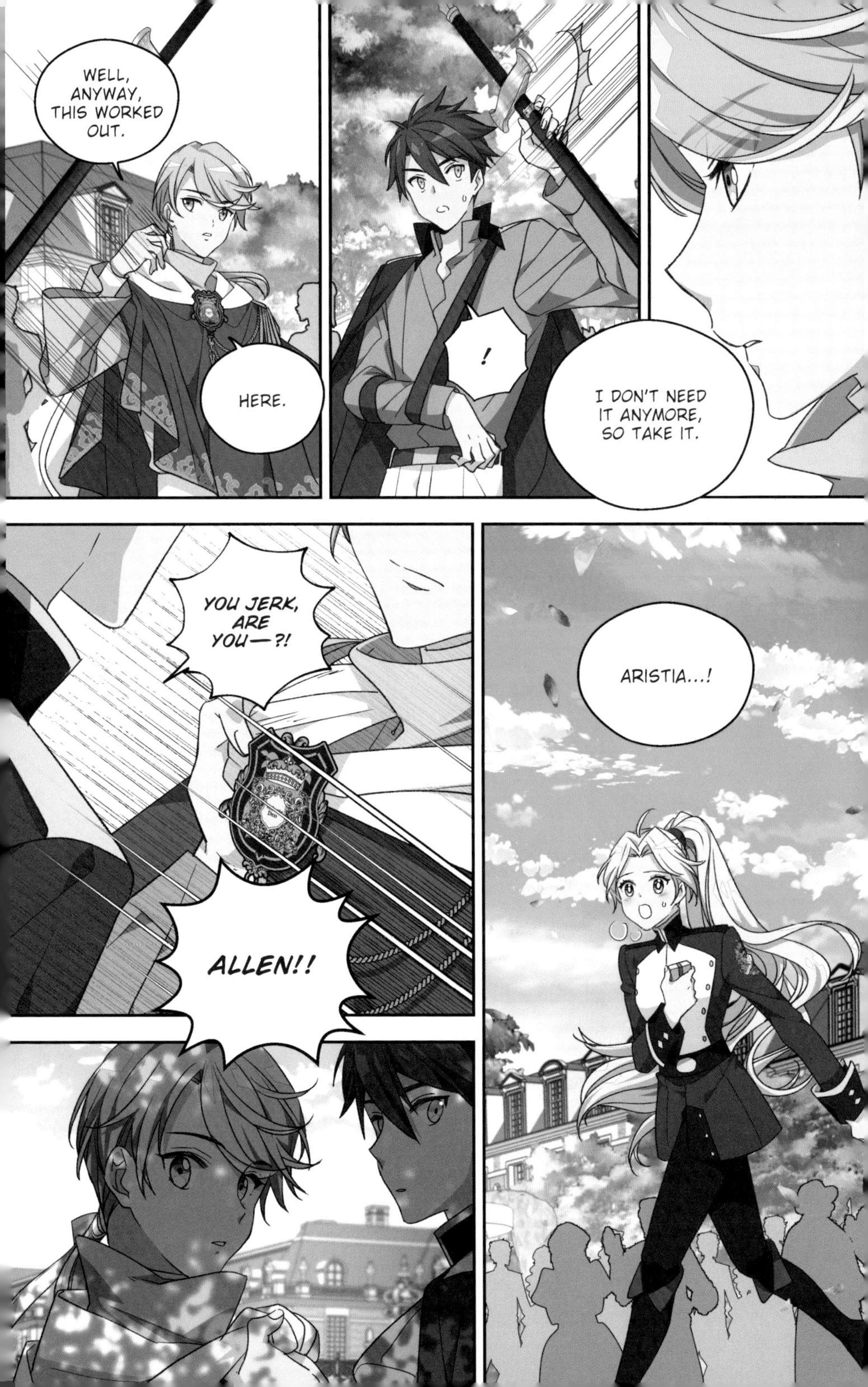
WELL, ANYWAY, THIS WORKED OUT.
HERE.
!
I DON'T NEED IT ANYMORE, SO TAKE IT.
YOU JERK, ARE YOU—?!
ALLEN!!
ARISTIA...!

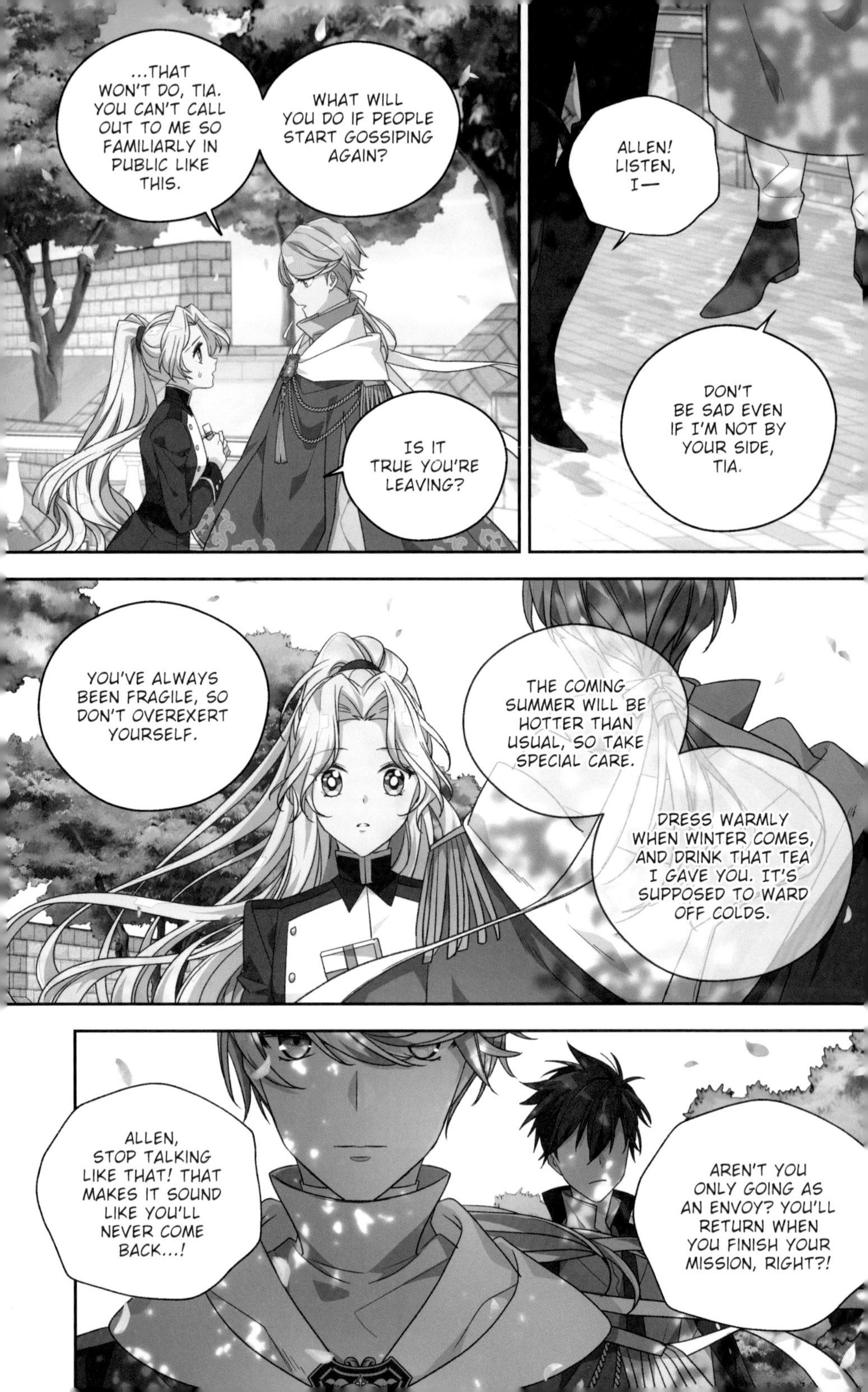
...THAT WON'T DO, TIA. YOU CAN'T CALL OUT TO ME SO FAMILIARLY IN PUBLIC LIKE THIS.
WHAT WILL YOU DO IF PEOPLE START GOSSIPING AGAIN?
IS IT TRUE YOU'RE LEAVING?
ALLEN! LISTEN, I—
DON'T BE SAD EVEN IF I'M NOT BY YOUR SIDE, TIA.
YOU'VE ALWAYS BEEN FRAGILE, SO DON'T OVEREXERT YOURSELF.
THE COMING SUMMER WILL BE HOTTER THAN USUAL, SO TAKE SPECIAL CARE.
DRESS WARMLY WHEN WINTER COMES, AND DRINK THAT TEA I GAVE YOU. IT'S SUPPOSED TO WARD OFF COLDS.
ALLEN, STOP TALKING LIKE THAT! THAT MAKES IT SOUND LIKE YOU'LL NEVER COME BACK...!
AREN'T YOU ONLY GOING AS AN ENVOY? YOU'LL RETURN WHEN YOU FINISH YOUR MISSION, RIGHT?!

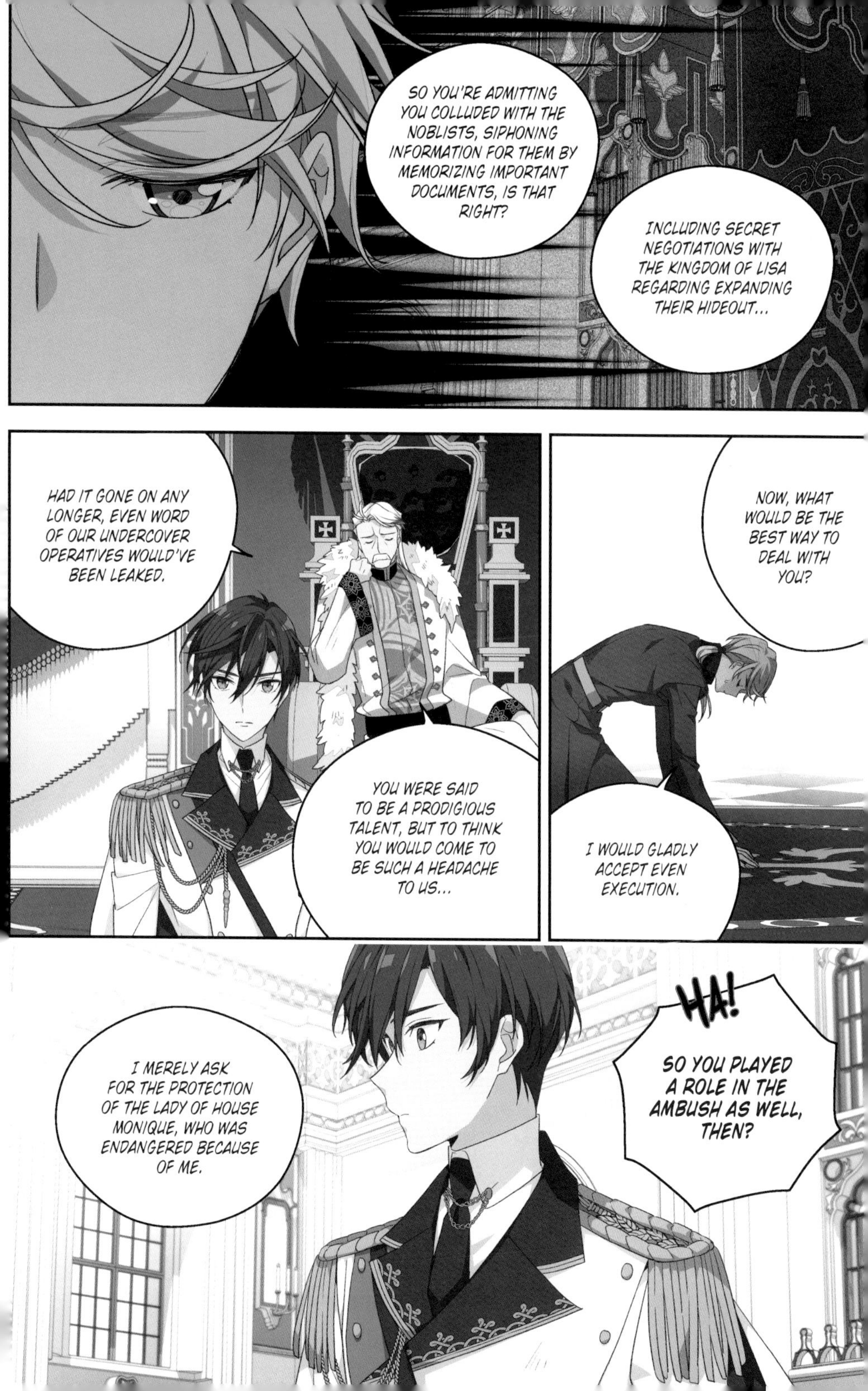
SO YOU'RE ADMITTING YOU COLLUDED WITH THE NOBLISTS, SIPHONING INFORMATION FOR THEM BY MEMORIZING IMPORTANT DOCUMENTS, IS THAT RIGHT?
INCLUDING SECRET NEGOTIATIONS WITH THE KINGDOM OF LISA REGARDING EXPANDING THEIR HIDEOUT...
HAD IT GONE ON ANY LONGER, EVEN WORD OF OUR UNDERCOVER OPERATIVES WOULD'VE BEEN LEAKED.
YOU WERE SAID TO BE A PRODIGIOUS TALENT, BUT TO THINK YOU WOULD COME TO BE SUCH A HEADACHE TO US...
NOW, WHAT WOULD BE THE BEST WAY TO DEAL WITH YOU?
I WOULD GLADLY ACCEPT EVEN EXECUTION.
I MERELY ASK FOR THE PROTECTION OF THE LADY OF HOUSE MONIQUE, WHO WAS ENDANGERED BECAUSE OF ME.
HA!
SO YOU PLAYED A ROLE IN THE AMBUSH AS WELL, THEN?

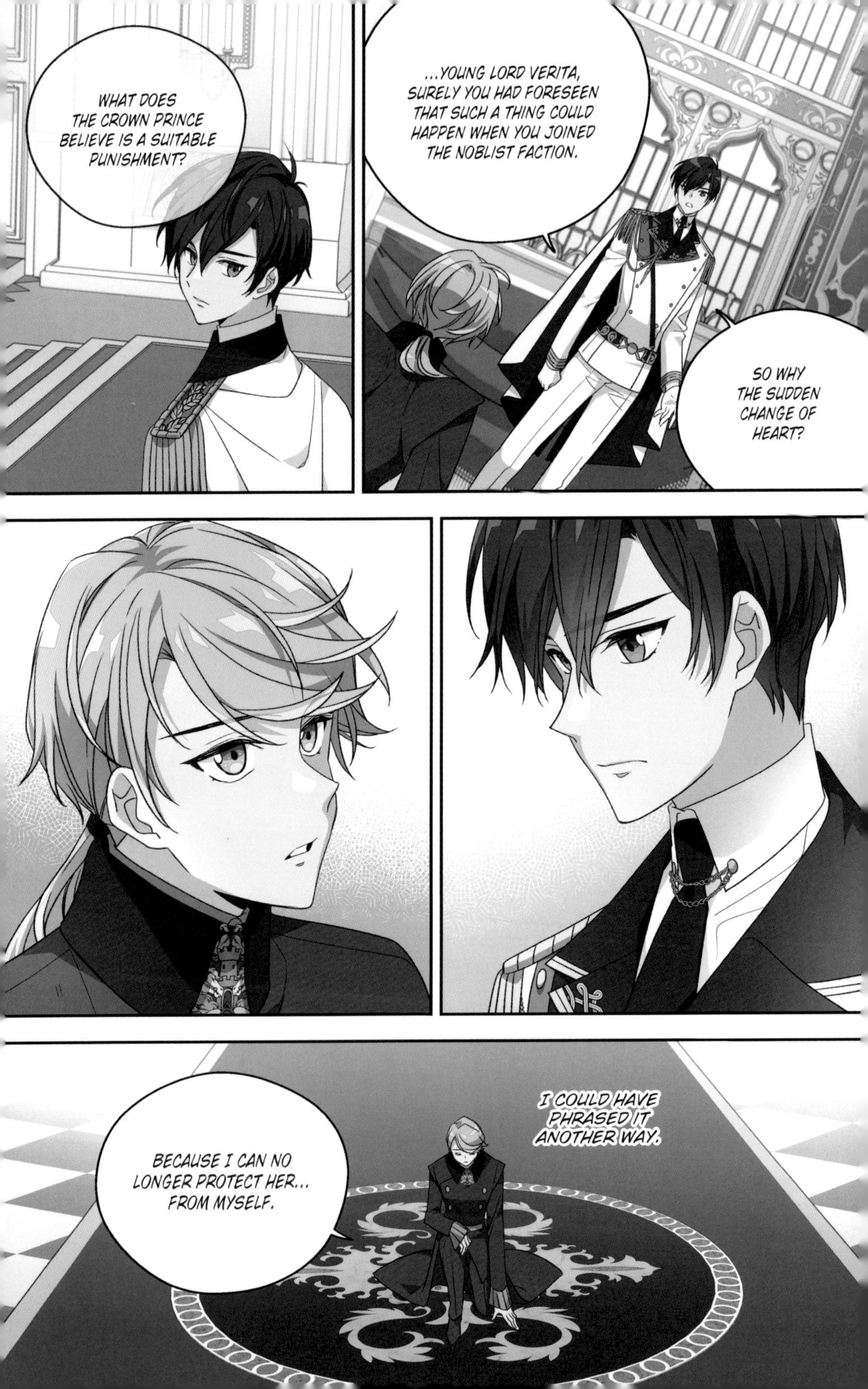
WHAT DOES THE CROWN PRINCE BELIEVE IS A SUITABLE PUNISHMENT?
...YOUNG LORD VERITA, SURELY YOU HAD FORESEEN THAT SUCH A THING COULD HAPPEN WHEN YOU JOINED THE NOBLIST FACTION.
SO WHY THE SUDDEN CHANGE OF HEART?
I COULD HAVE PHRASED IT ANOTHER WAY.
BECAUSE I CAN NO LONGER PROTECT HER... FROM MYSELF.

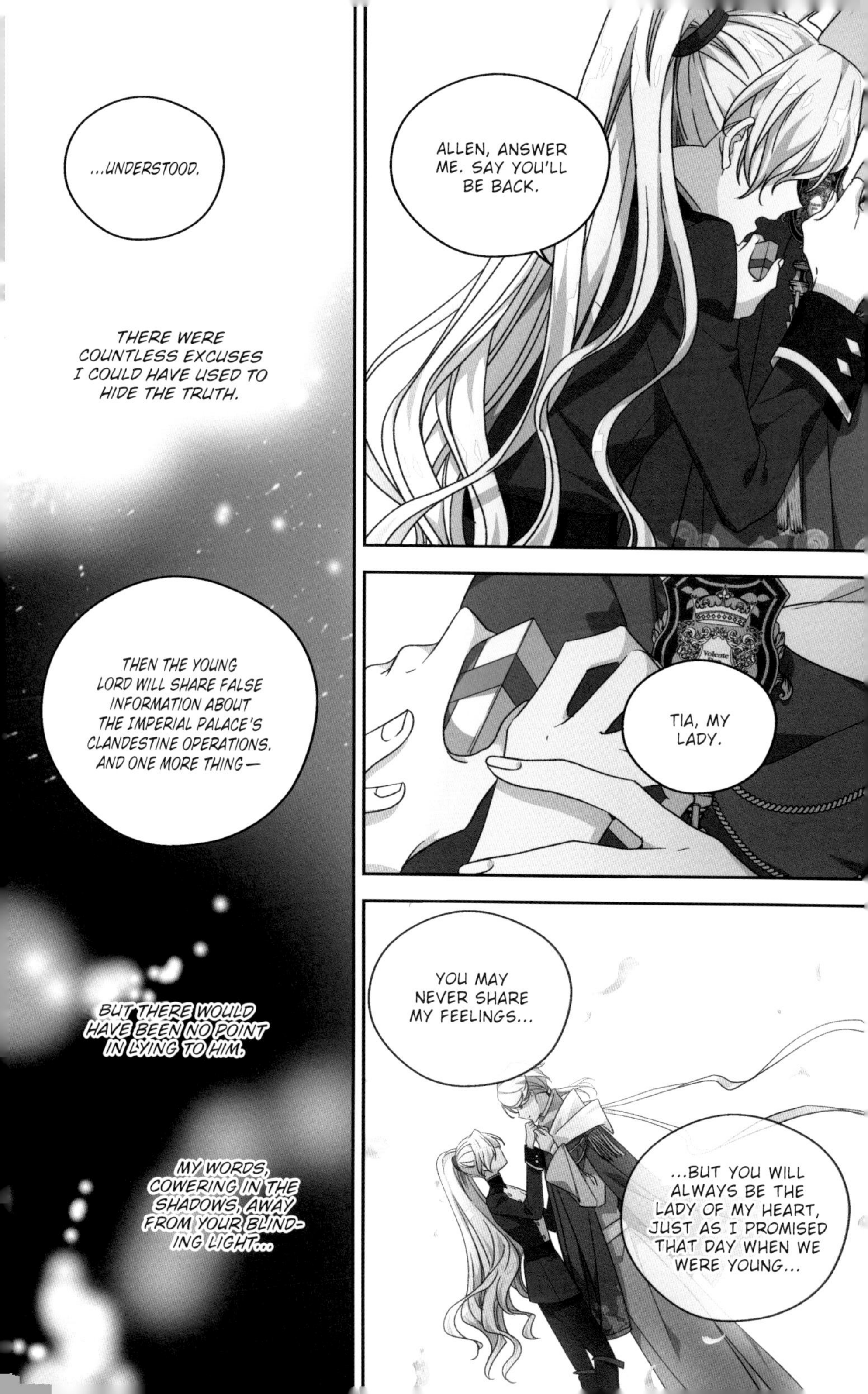
...UNDERSTOOD.
THERE WERE COUNTLESS EXCUSES I COULD HAVE USED TO HIDE THE TRUTH.
THEN THE YOUNG LORD WILL SHARE FALSE INFORMATION ABOUT THE IMPERIAL PALACE'S CLANDESTINE OPERATIONS. AND ONE MORE THING—
BUT THERE WOULD HAVE BEEN NO POINT IN LYING TO HIM.
MY WORDS, COWERING IN THE SHADOWS, AWAY FROM YOUR BLINDING LIGHT...
ALLEN, ANSWER ME. SAY YOU'LL BE BACK.
TIA, MY LADY.
YOU MAY NEVER SHARE MY FEELINGS...
...BUT YOU WILL ALWAYS BE THE LADY OF MY HEART, JUST AS I PROMISED THAT DAY WHEN WE WERE YOUNG...

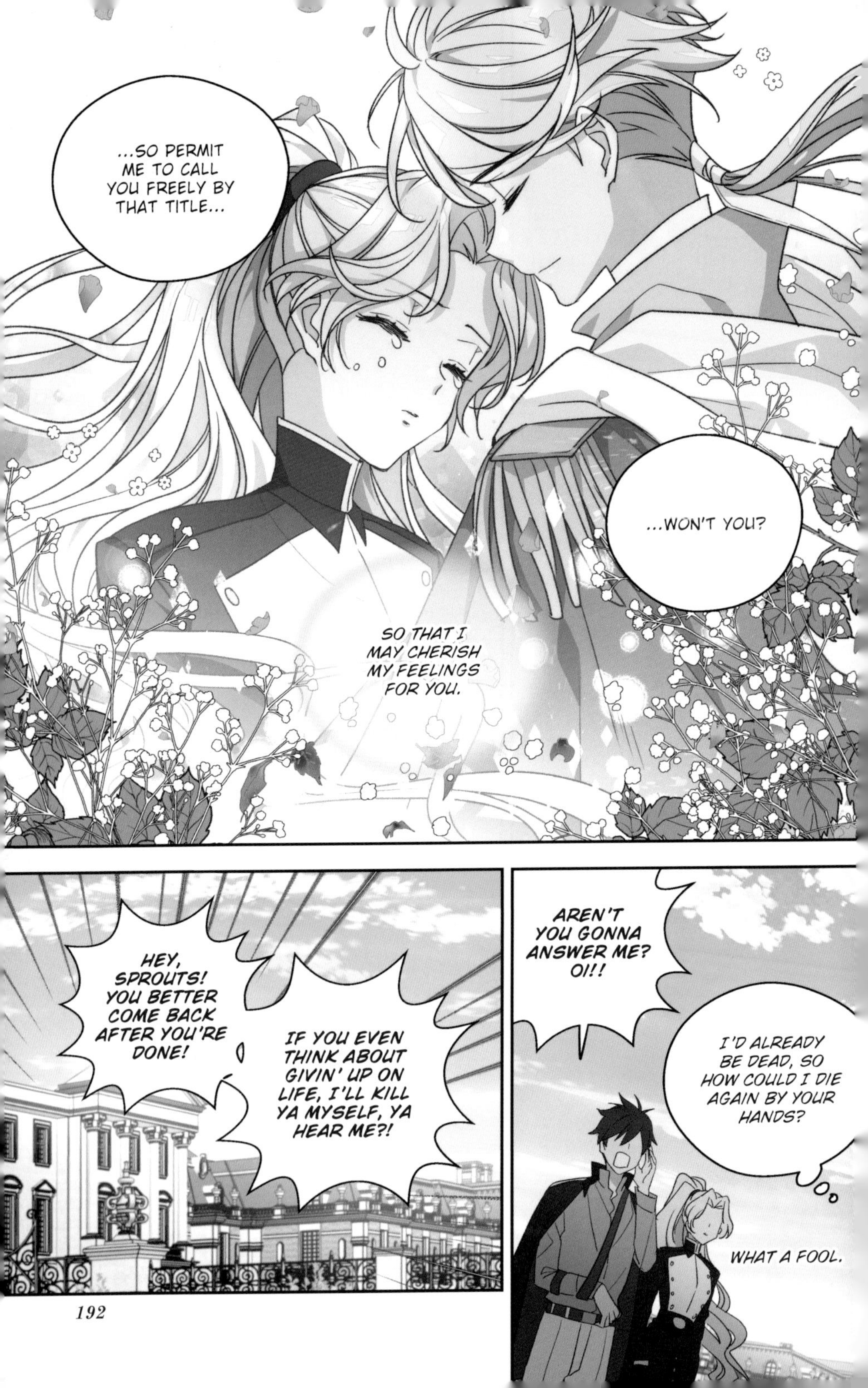
...SO PERMIT ME TO CALL YOU FREELY BY THAT TITLE...
SO THAT I MAY CHERISH MY FEELINGS FOR YOU.
...WON'T YOU?
HEY, SPROUTS! YOU BETTER COME BACK AFTER YOU'RE DONE!
IF YOU EVEN THINK ABOUT GIVIN' UP ON LIFE, I'LL KILL YA MYSELF, YA HEAR ME?!
AREN'T YOU GONNA ANSWER ME? OI!!
I'D ALREADY BE DEAD, SO HOW COULD I DIE AGAIN BY YOUR HANDS?
WHAT A FOOL.

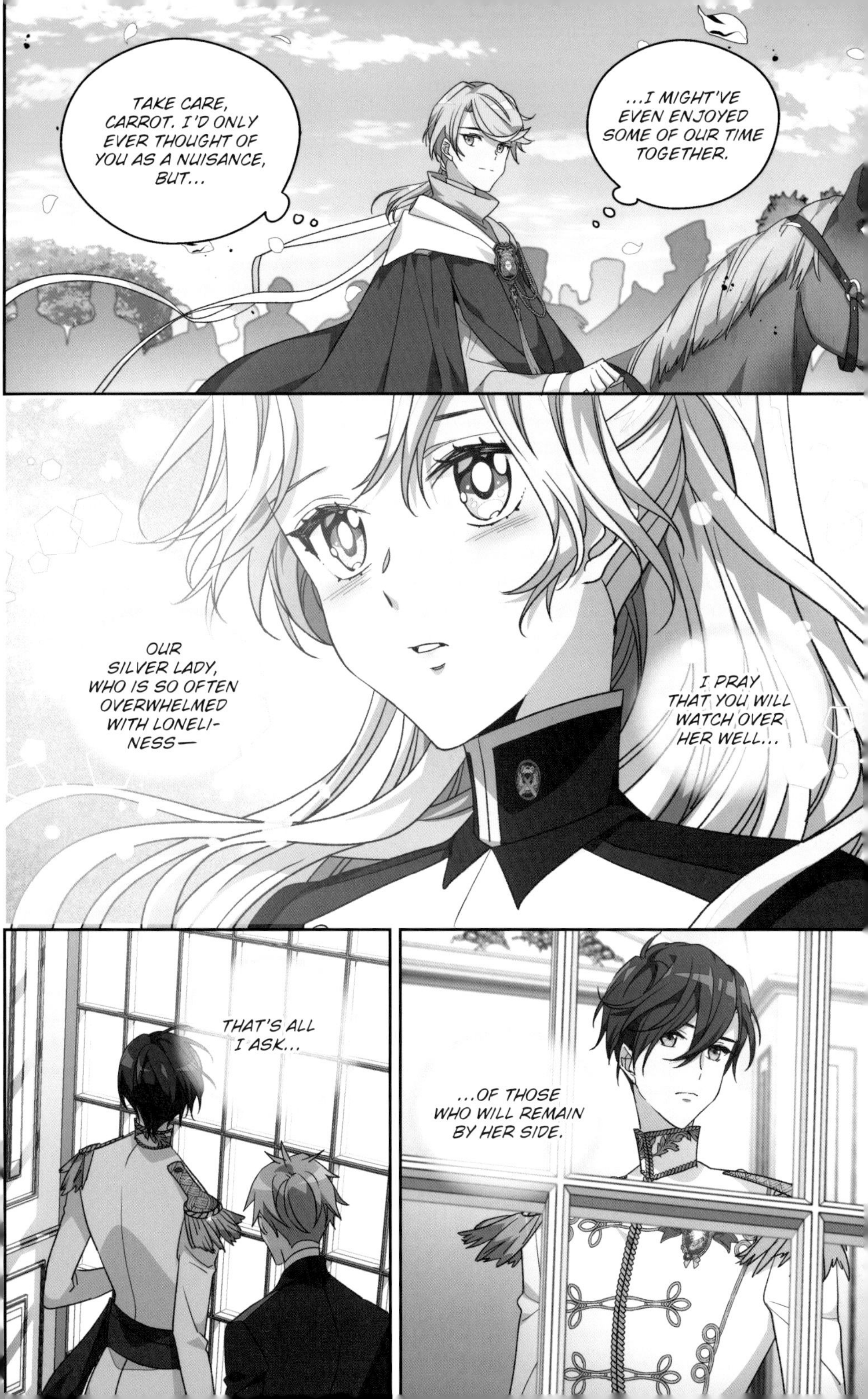
TAKE CARE, CARROT. I'D ONLY EVER THOUGHT OF YOU AS A NUISANCE, BUT...
...I MIGHT'VE EVEN ENJOYED SOME OF OUR TIME TOGETHER.
OUR SILVER LADY, WHO IS SO OFTEN OVERWHELMED WITH LONELI-NESS—
I PRAY THAT YOU WILL WATCH OVER HER WELL...
THAT'S ALL I ASK...
...OF THOSE WHO WILL REMAIN BY HER SIDE.

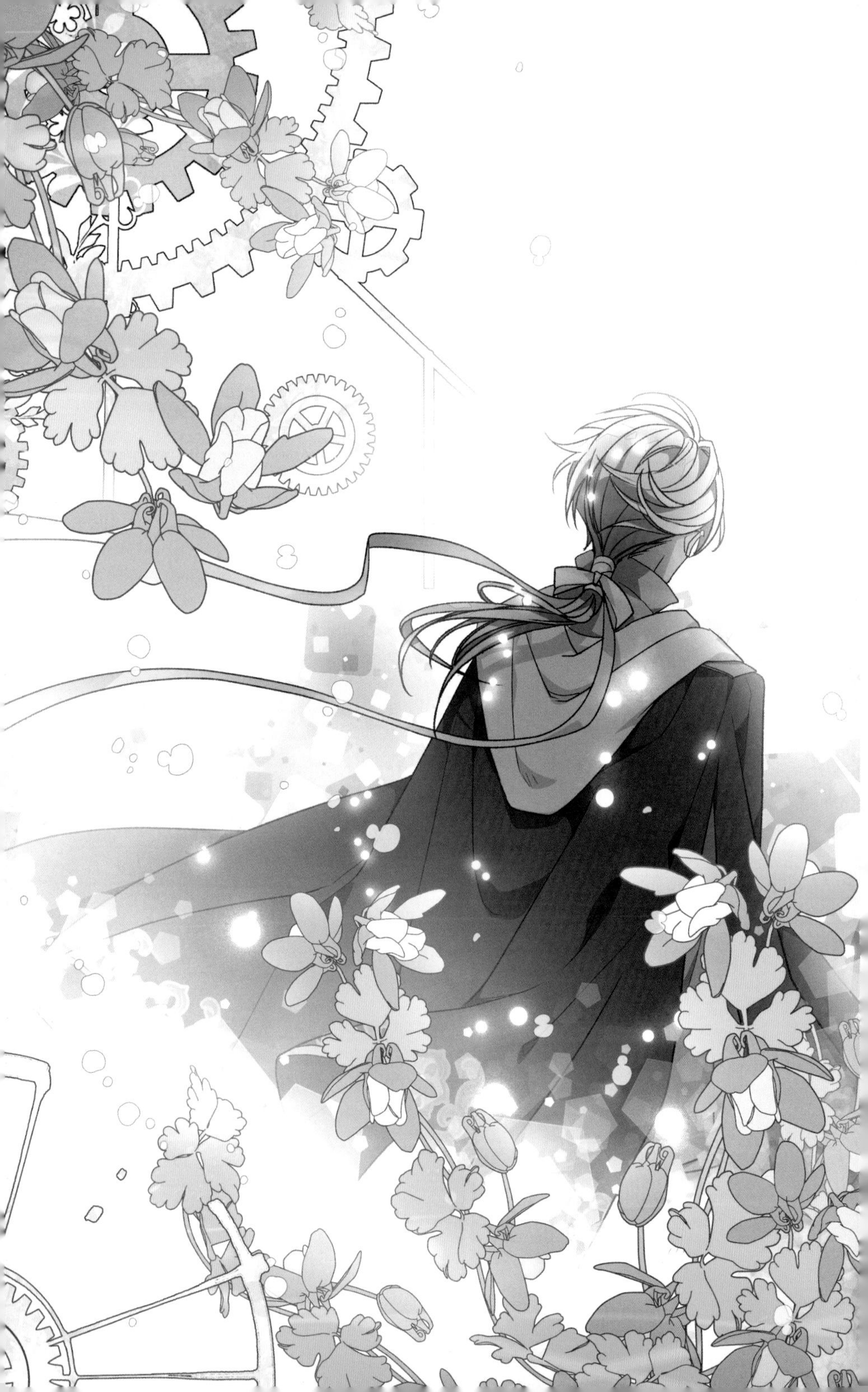

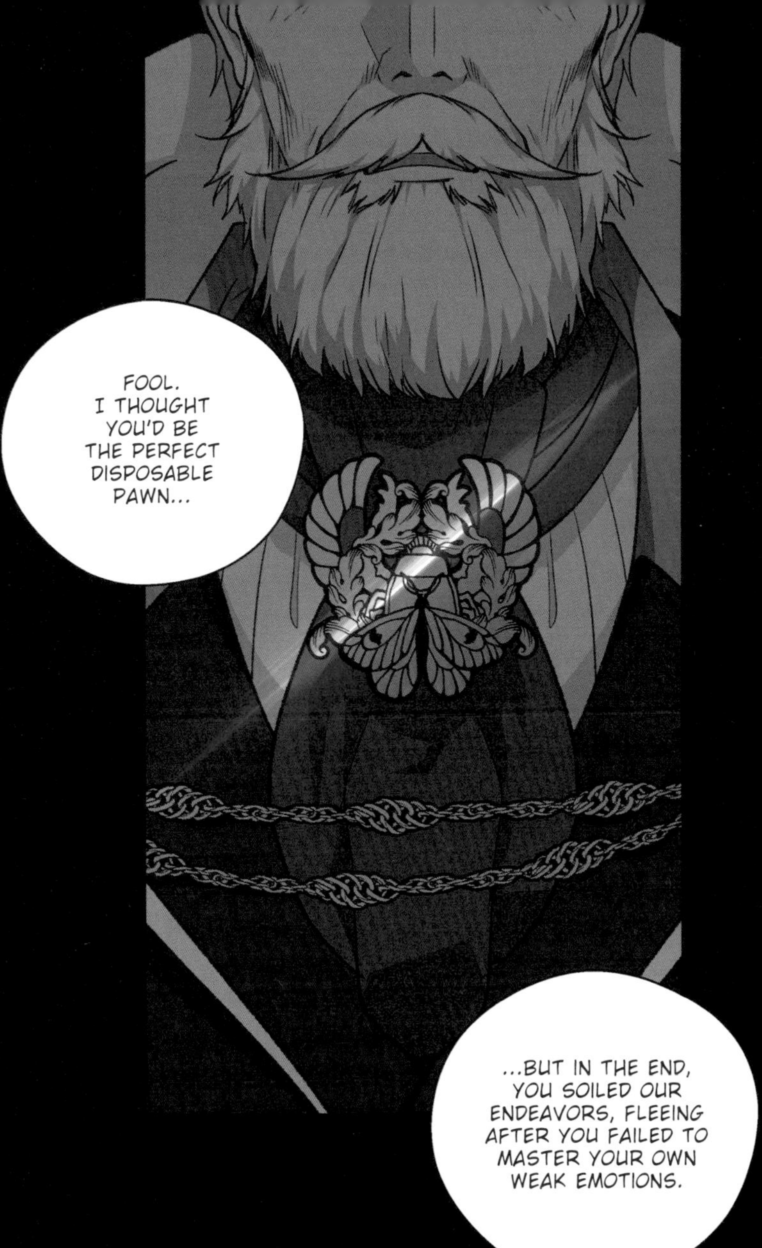
FOOL. I THOUGHT YOU'D BE THE PERFECT DISPOSABLE PAWN...
...BUT IN THE END, YOU SOILED OUR ENDEAVORS, FLEEING AFTER YOU FAILED TO MASTER YOUR OWN WEAK EMOTIONS.

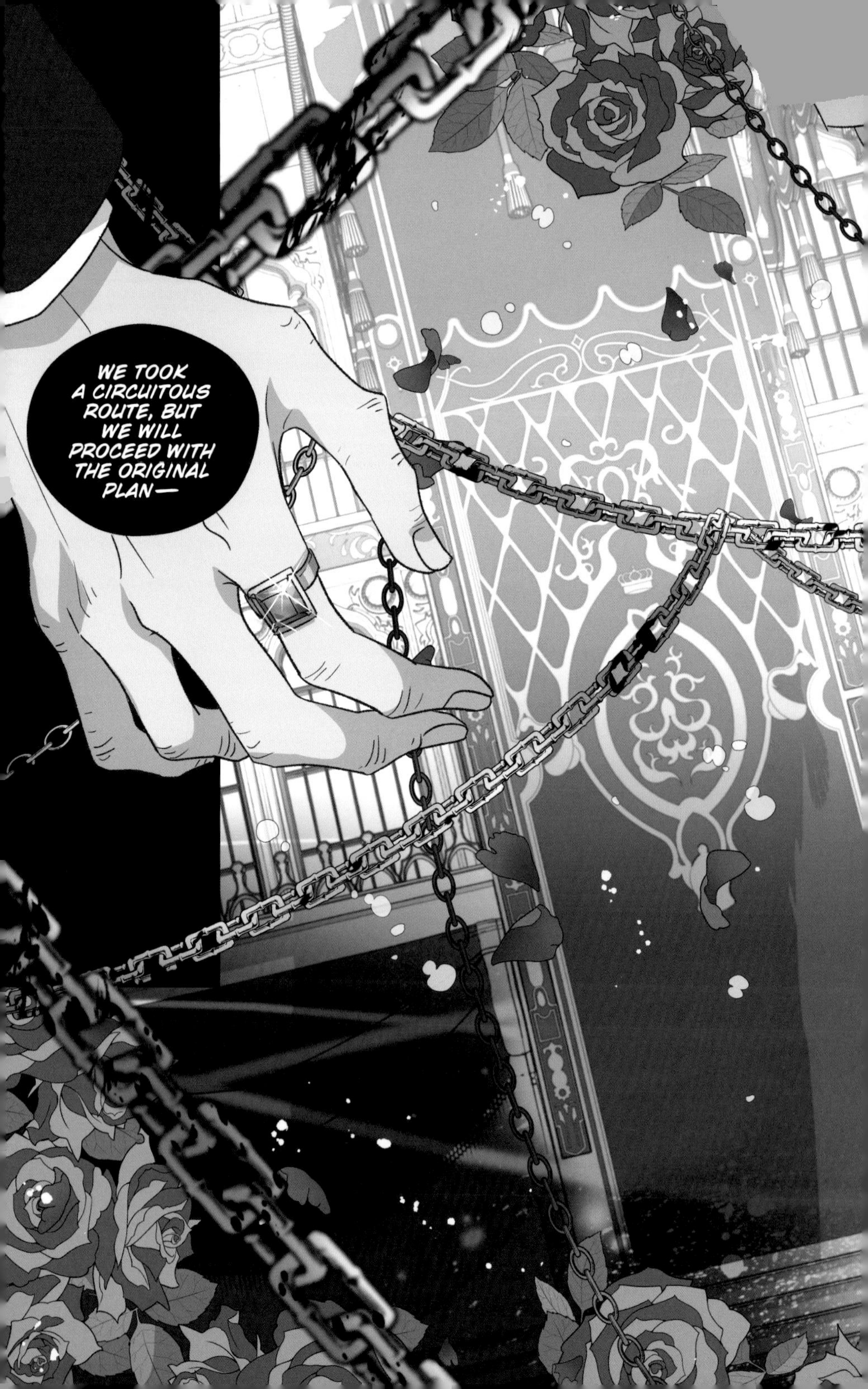
WE TOOK A CIRCUITOUS ROUTE, BUT WE WILL PROCEED WITH THE ORIGINAL PLAN—

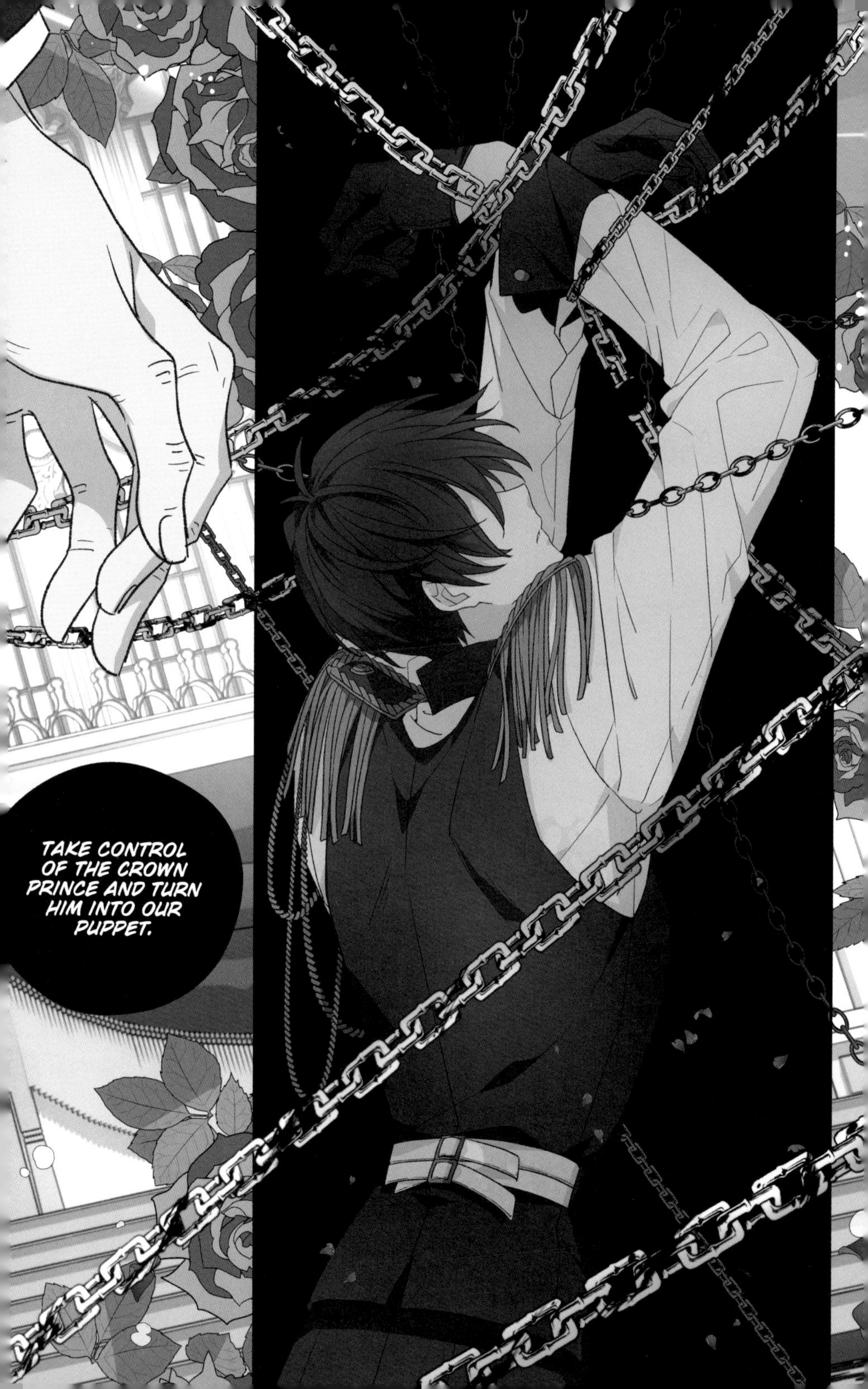
TAKE CONTROL OF THE CROWN PRINCE AND TURN HIM INTO OUR PUPPET.

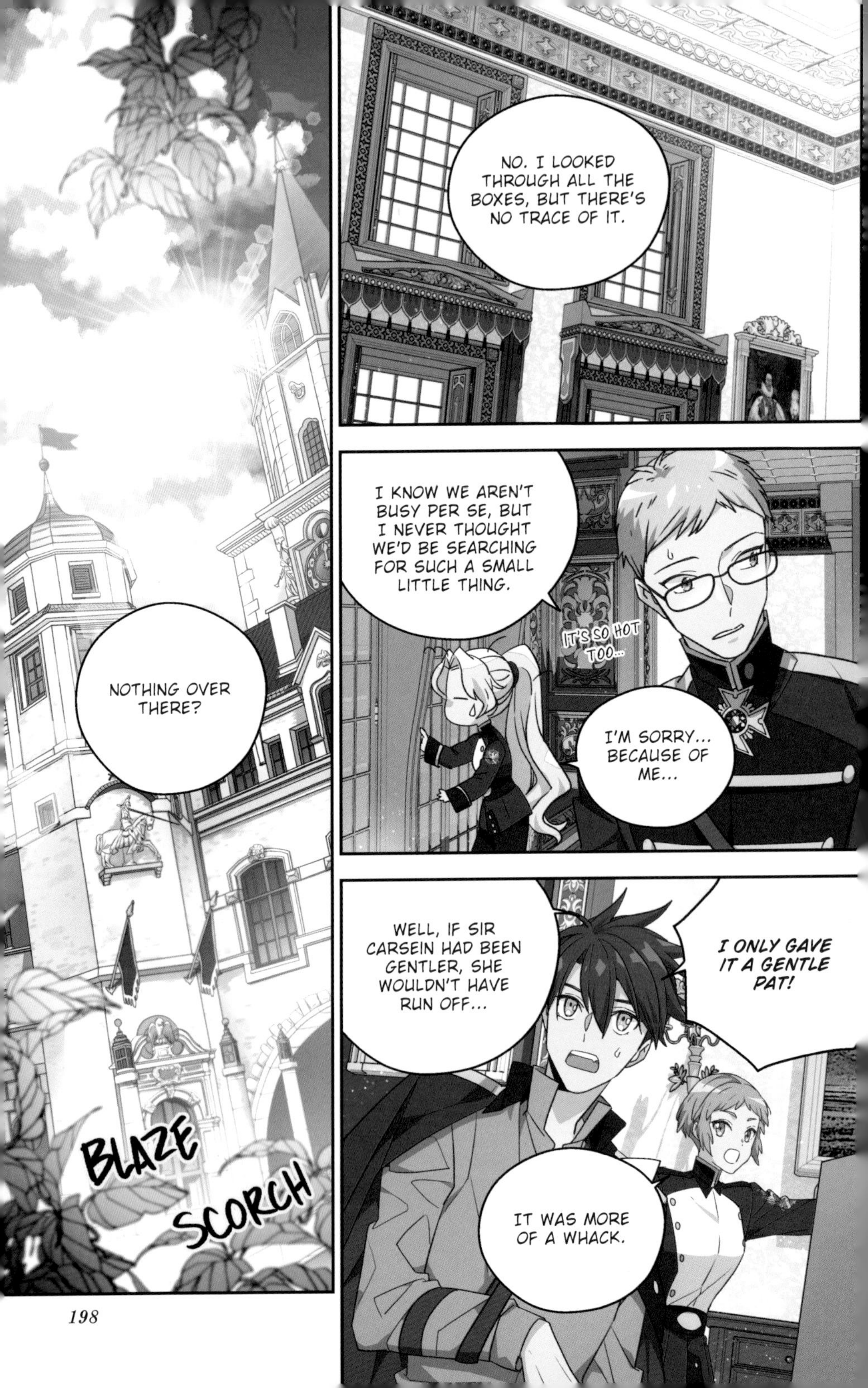
NOTHING OVER THERE?
BLAZE
SCORCH
NO. I LOOKED THROUGH ALL THE BOXES, BUT THERE'S NO TRACE OF IT.
I KNOW WE AREN'T BUSY PER SE, BUT I NEVER THOUGHT WE'D BE SEARCHING FOR SUCH A SMALL LITTLE THING.
IT'S SO HOT TOO...
I'M SORRY... BECAUSE OF ME...
WELL, IF SIR CARSEIN HAD BEEN GENTLER, SHE WOULDN'T HAVE RUN OFF...
I ONLY GAVE IT A GENTLE PAT!
IT WAS MORE OF A WHACK.

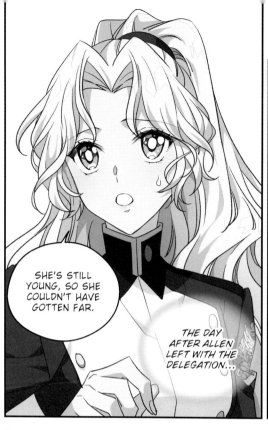

SHE'S STILL YOUNG, SO SHE COULDN'T HAVE GOTTEN FAR.

THE DAY AFTER ALLEN LEFT WITH THE DELEGATION...

...A SMALL BASKET ARRIVED WITH A LETTER SAYING...

"TAKE CARE OF THIS LITTLE ONE FOR ME."

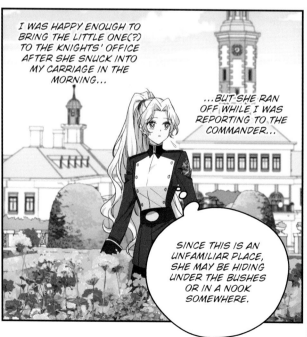

I WAS HAPPY ENOUGH TO BRING THE LITTLE ONE(?) TO THE KNIGHTS' OFFICE AFTER SHE SNUCK INTO MY CARRIAGE IN THE MORNING...

...BUT SHE RAN OFF WHILE I WAS REPORTING TO THE COMMANDER...

SINCE THIS IS AN UNFAMILIAR PLACE, SHE MAY BE HIDING UNDER THE BUSHES OR IN A NOOK SOMEWHERE.

WOULD SHE HAVE REALLY COME THIS FAR—

WHAT UTTER NONSENSE!

STARTLE

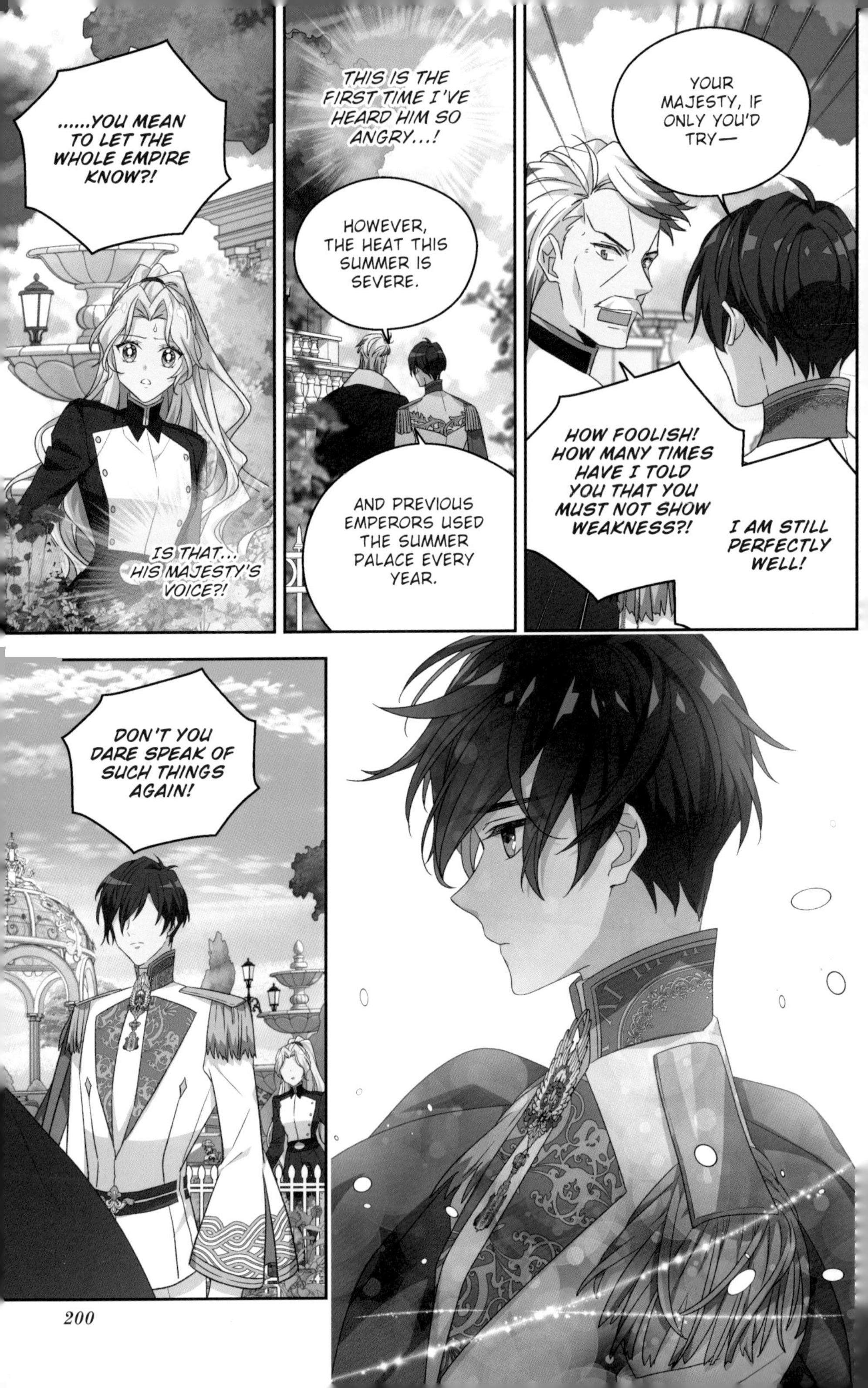
......YOU MEAN TO LET THE WHOLE EMPIRE KNOW?!
IS THAT... HIS MAJESTY'S VOICE?!
THIS IS THE FIRST TIME I'VE HEARD HIM SO ANGRY...!
HOWEVER, THE HEAT THIS SUMMER IS SEVERE.
AND PREVIOUS EMPERORS USED THE SUMMER PALACE EVERY YEAR.
YOUR MAJESTY, IF ONLY YOU'D TRY—
HOW FOOLISH! HOW MANY TIMES HAVE I TOLD YOU THAT YOU MUST NOT SHOW WEAKNESS?!
I AM STILL PERFECTLY WELL!
DON'T YOU DARE SPEAK OF SUCH THINGS AGAIN!

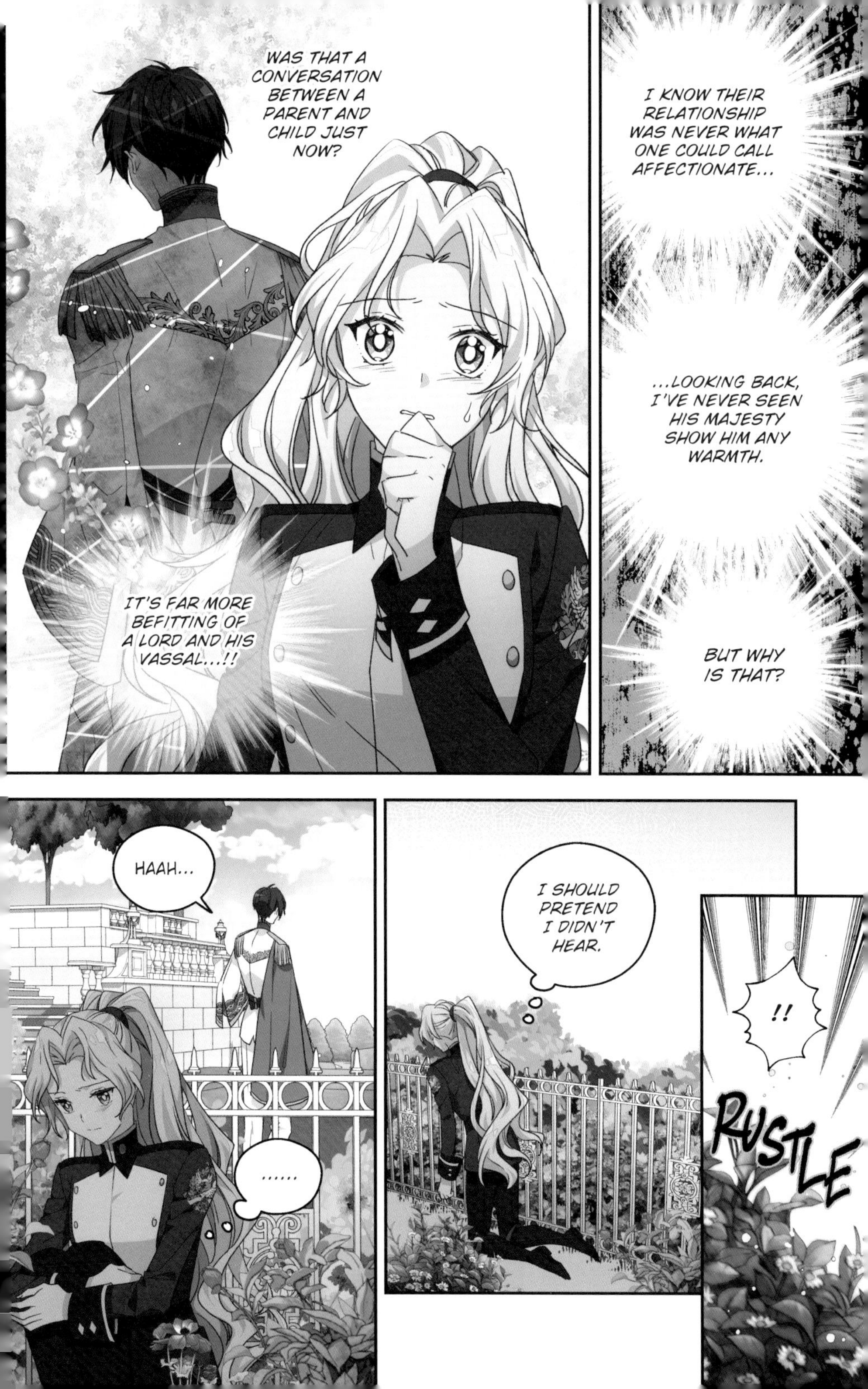

WAS THAT A CONVERSATION BETWEEN A PARENT AND CHILD JUST NOW?
IT'S FAR MORE BEFITTING OF A LORD AND HIS VASSAL...!!
I KNOW THEIR RELATIONSHIP WAS NEVER WHAT ONE COULD CALL AFFECTIONATE...
...LOOKING BACK, I'VE NEVER SEEN HIS MAJESTY SHOW HIM ANY WARMTH.
BUT WHY IS THAT?
HAAH...
......
I SHOULD PRETEND I DIDN'T HEAR.
!!
RUSTLE

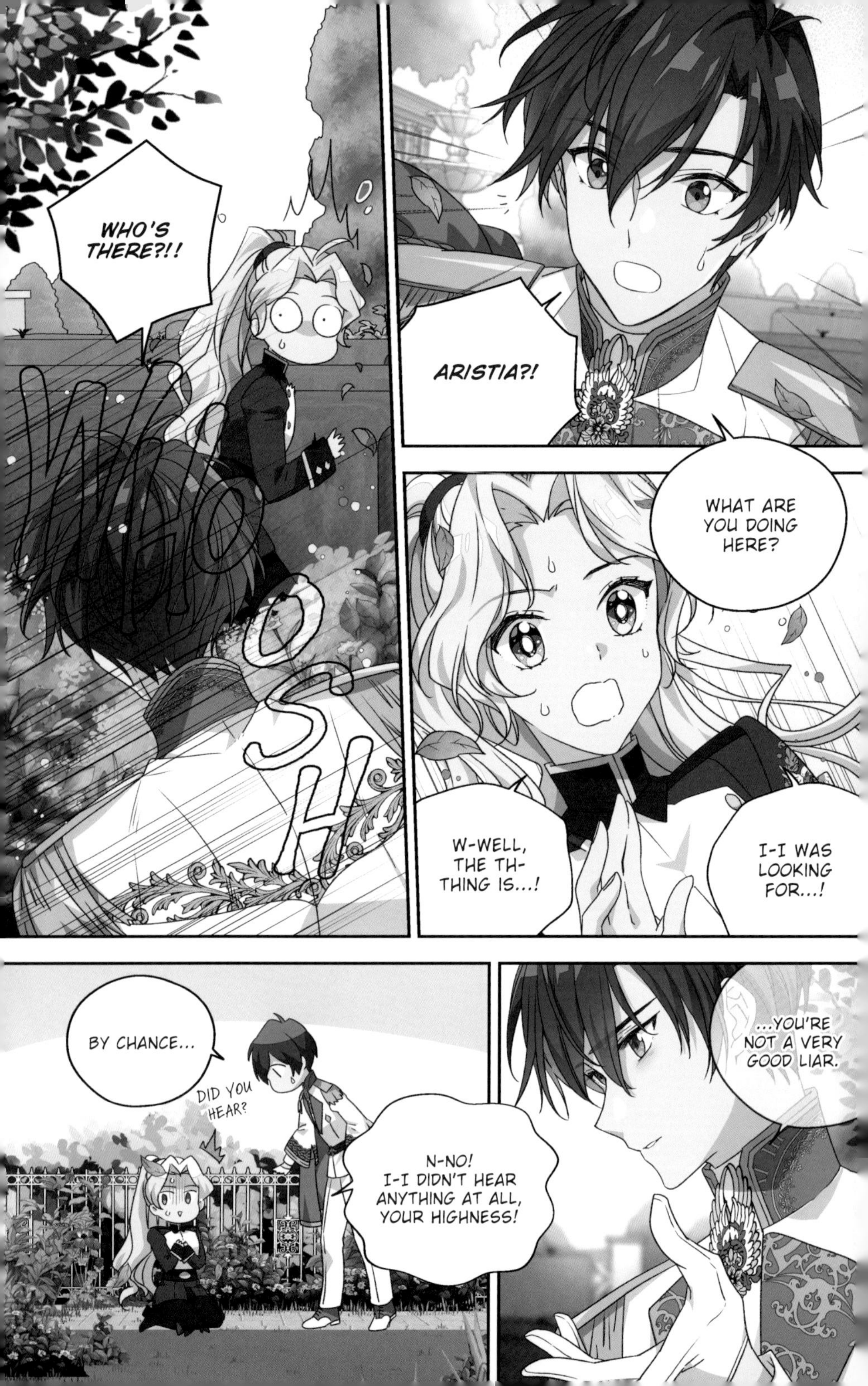
WHO'S THERE?!!
WHOOSH
ARISTIA?!
WHAT ARE YOU DOING HERE?
W-WELL, THE TH-THING IS...!
I-I WAS LOOKING FOR...!
BY CHANCE...
DID YOU HEAR?
N-NO! I-I DIDN'T HEAR ANYTHING AT ALL, YOUR HIGHNESS!
...YOU'RE NOT A VERY GOOD LIAR.

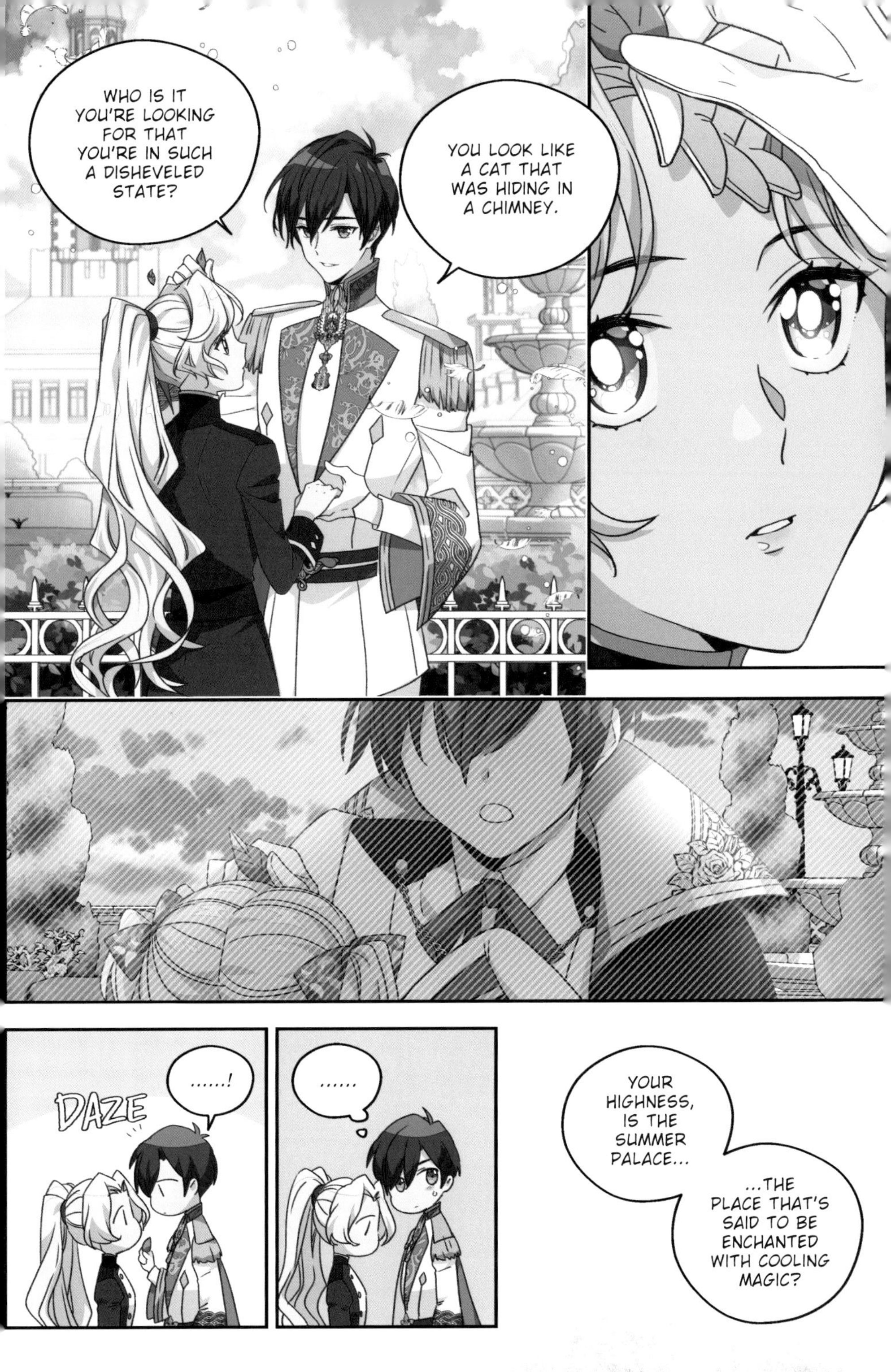
WHO IS IT YOU'RE LOOKING FOR THAT YOU'RE IN SUCH A DISHEVELED STATE?
YOU LOOK LIKE A CAT THAT WAS HIDING IN A CHIMNEY.
DAZE
......!
......
YOUR HIGHNESS, IS THE SUMMER PALACE...
...THE PLACE THAT'S SAID TO BE ENCHANTED WITH COOLING MAGIC?

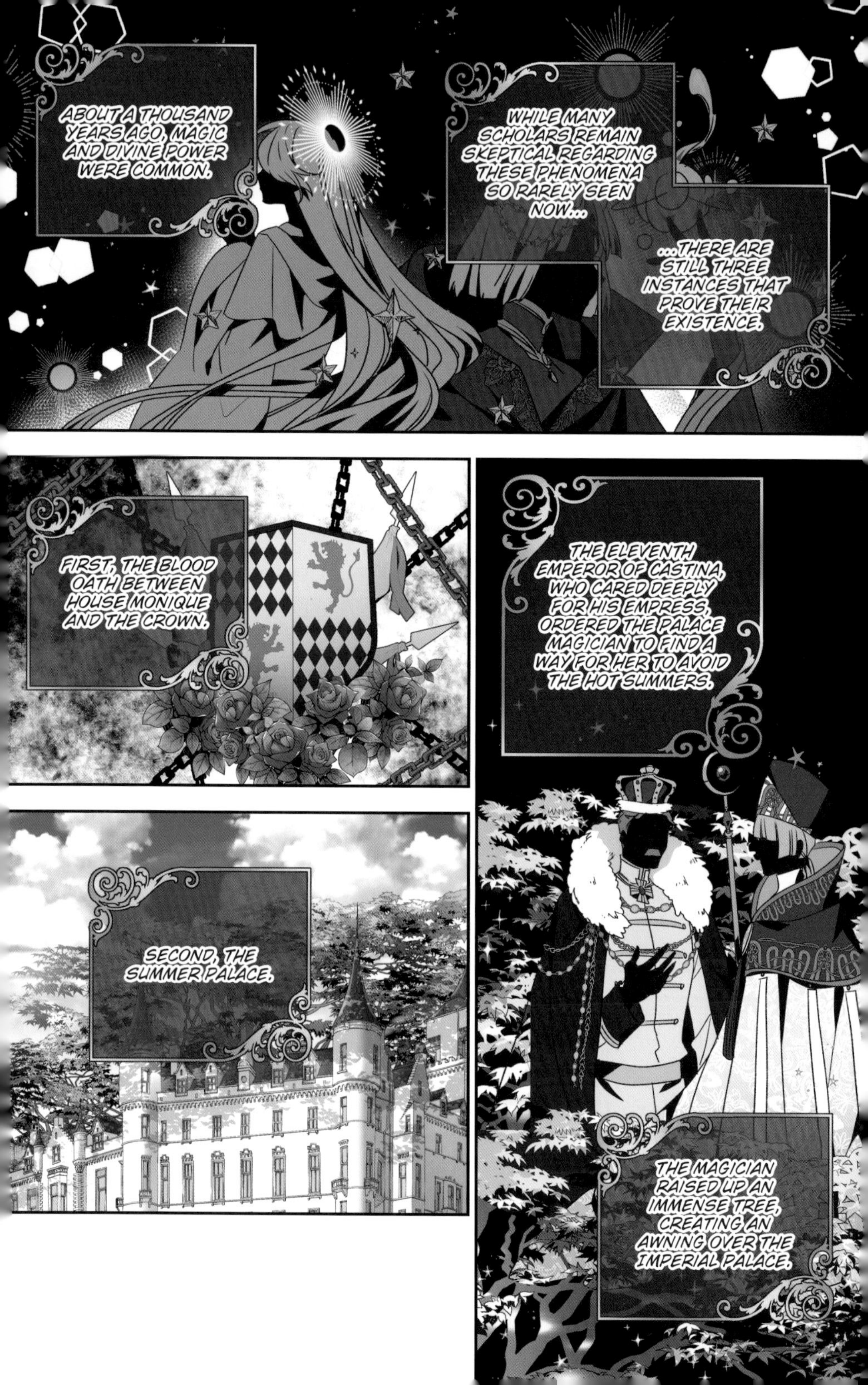
ABOUT A THOUSAND YEARS AGO, MAGIC AND DIVINE POWER WERE COMMON.
WHILE MANY SCHOLARS REMAIN SKEPTICAL REGARDING THESE PHENOMENA SO RARELY SEEN NOW...
...THERE ARE STILL THREE INSTANCES THAT PROVE THEIR EXISTENCE.
FIRST, THE BLOOD OATH BETWEEN HOUSE MONIQUE AND THE CROWN.
SECOND, THE SUMMER PALACE.
THE ELEVENTH EMPEROR OF CASTINA, WHO CARED DEEPLY FOR HIS EMPRESS, ORDERED THE PALACE MAGICIAN TO FIND A WAY FOR HER TO AVOID THE HOT SUMMERS.
THE MAGICIAN RAISED UP AN IMMENSE TREE, CREATING AN AWNING OVER THE IMPERIAL PALACE.

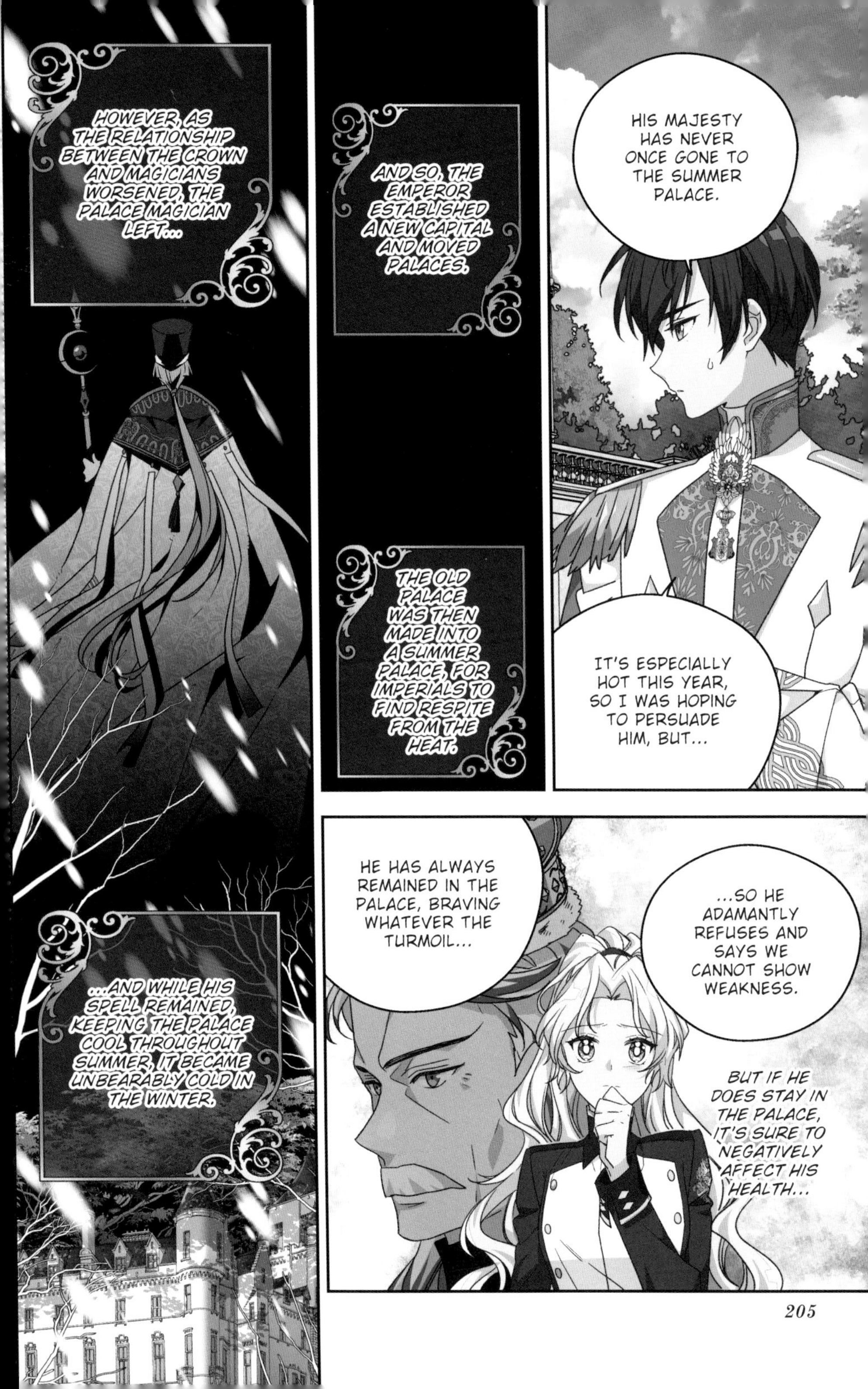
HOWEVER, AS THE RELATIONSHIP BETWEEN THE CROWN AND MAGICIANS WORSENED, THE PALACE MAGICIAN LEFT...
...AND WHILE HIS SPELL REMAINED, KEEPING THE PALACE COOL THROUGHOUT SUMMER, IT BECAME UNBEARABLY COLD IN THE WINTER.
AND SO, THE EMPEROR ESTABLISHED A NEW CAPITAL AND MOVED PALACES.
THE OLD PALACE WAS THEN MADE INTO A SUMMER PALACE, FOR IMPERIALS TO FIND RESPITE FROM THE HEAT.
HIS MAJESTY HAS NEVER ONCE GONE TO THE SUMMER PALACE.
IT'S ESPECIALLY HOT THIS YEAR, SO I WAS HOPING TO PERSUADE HIM, BUT...
HE HAS ALWAYS REMAINED IN THE PALACE, BRAVING WHATEVER THE TURMOIL...
...SO HE ADAMANTLY REFUSES AND SAYS WE CANNOT SHOW WEAKNESS.
BUT IF HE DOES STAY IN THE PALACE, IT'S SURE TO NEGATIVELY AFFECT HIS HEALTH...

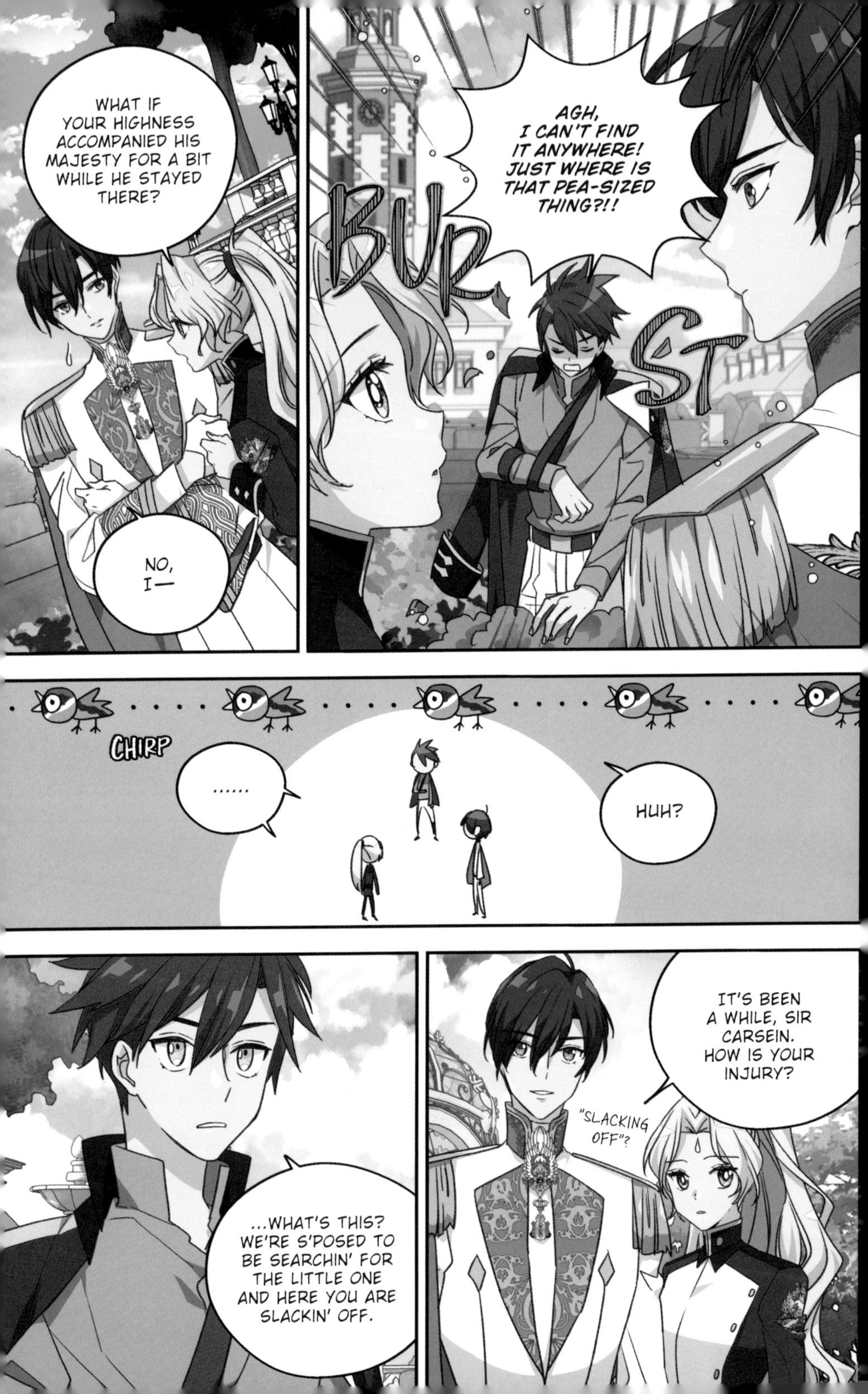
WHAT IF YOUR HIGHNESS ACCOMPANIED HIS MAJESTY FOR A BIT WHILE HE STAYED THERE?
NO, I—
AGH, I CAN'T FIND IT ANYWHERE! JUST WHERE IS THAT PEA-SIZED THING?!!
BURST
CHIRP
......
HUH?
...WHAT'S THIS? WE'RE S'POSED TO BE SEARCHIN' FOR THE LITTLE ONE AND HERE YOU ARE SLACKIN' OFF.
IT'S BEEN A WHILE, SIR CARSEIN. HOW IS YOUR INJURY?
"SLACKING OFF"?

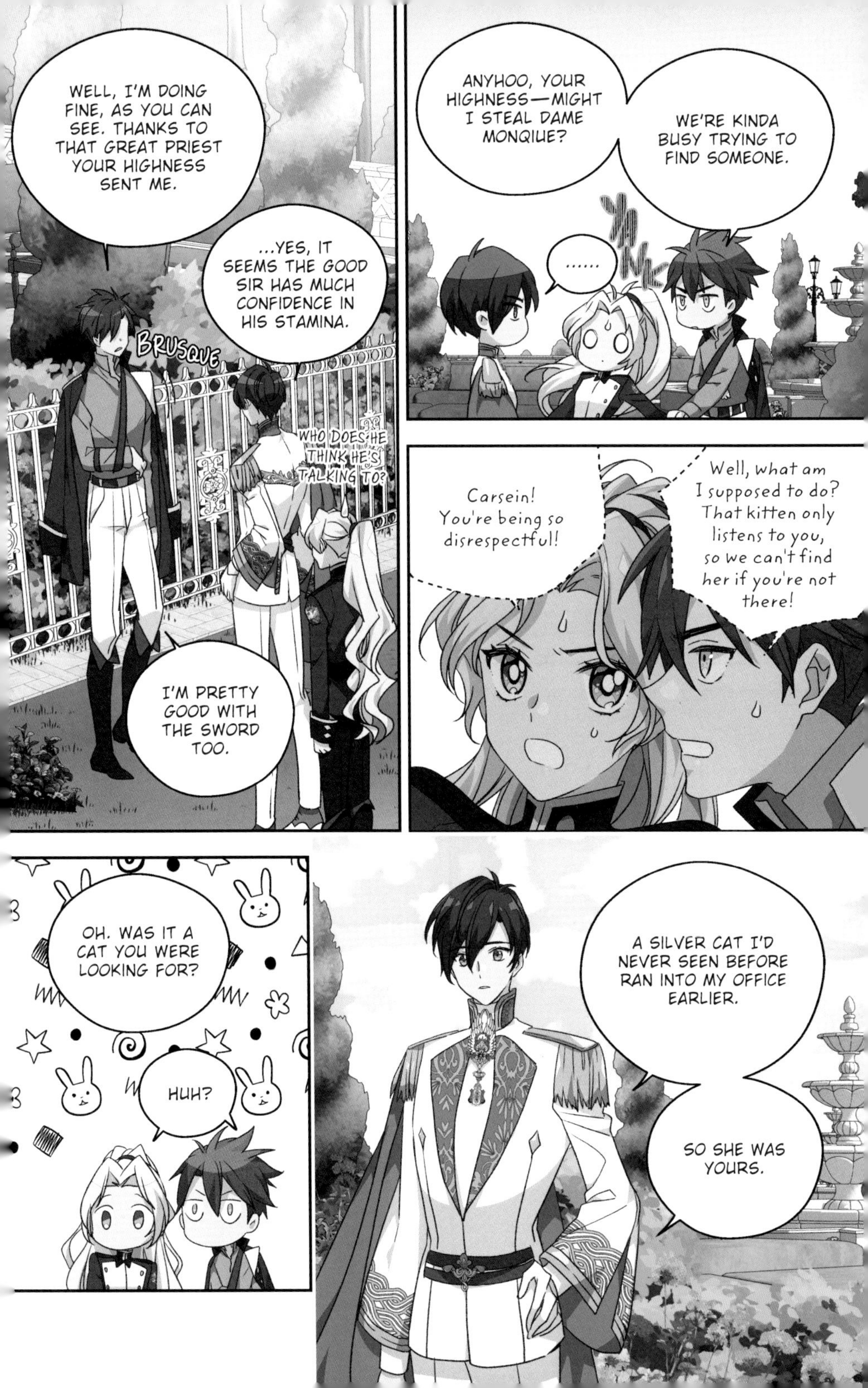
WELL, I'M DOING FINE, AS YOU CAN SEE. THANKS TO THAT GREAT PRIEST YOUR HIGHNESS SENT ME.
...YES, IT SEEMS THE GOOD SIR HAS MUCH CONFIDENCE IN HIS STAMINA.
BRUSQUE
WHO DOES HE THINK HE'S TALKING TO?
I'M PRETTY GOOD WITH THE SWORD TOO.
ANYHOO, YOUR HIGHNESS—MIGHT I STEAL DAME MONQIUE?
WE'RE KINDA BUSY TRYING TO FIND SOMEONE.
YANK
......
Carsein! You're being so disrespectful!
Well, what am I supposed to do? That kitten only listens to you, so we can't find her if you're not there!
OH. WAS IT A CAT YOU WERE LOOKING FOR?
HUH?
A SILVER CAT I'D NEVER SEEN BEFORE RAN INTO MY OFFICE EARLIER.
SO SHE WAS YOURS.

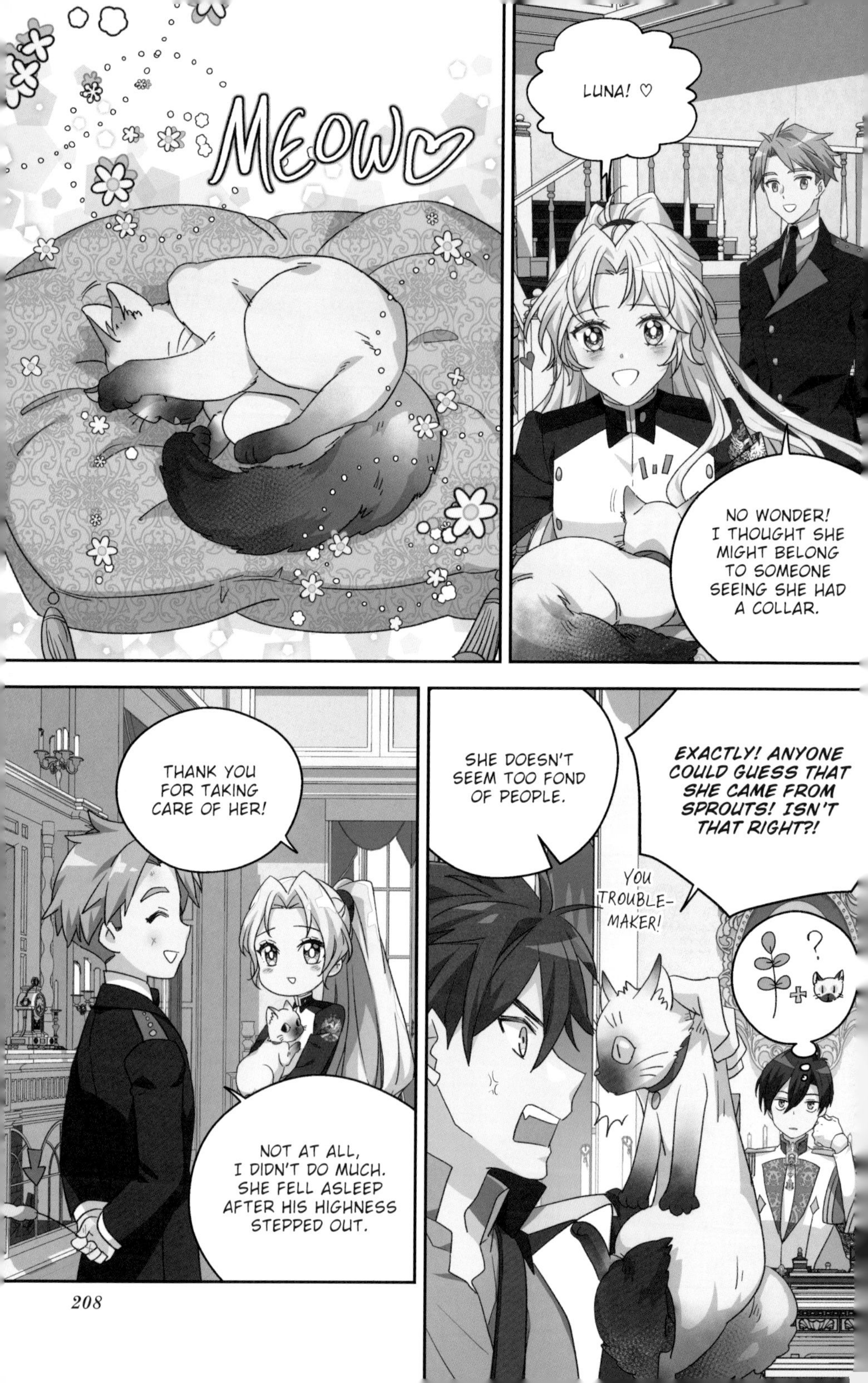
MEOW♡
LUNA! ♡
NO WONDER! I THOUGHT SHE MIGHT BELONG TO SOMEONE SEEING SHE HAD A COLLAR.
THANK YOU FOR TAKING CARE OF HER!
NOT AT ALL, I DIDN'T DO MUCH. SHE FELL ASLEEP AFTER HIS HIGHNESS STEPPED OUT.
SHE DOESN'T SEEM TOO FOND OF PEOPLE.
EXACTLY! ANYONE COULD GUESS THAT SHE CAME FROM SPROUTS! ISN'T THAT RIGHT?!
YOU TROUBLE-MAKER!
?

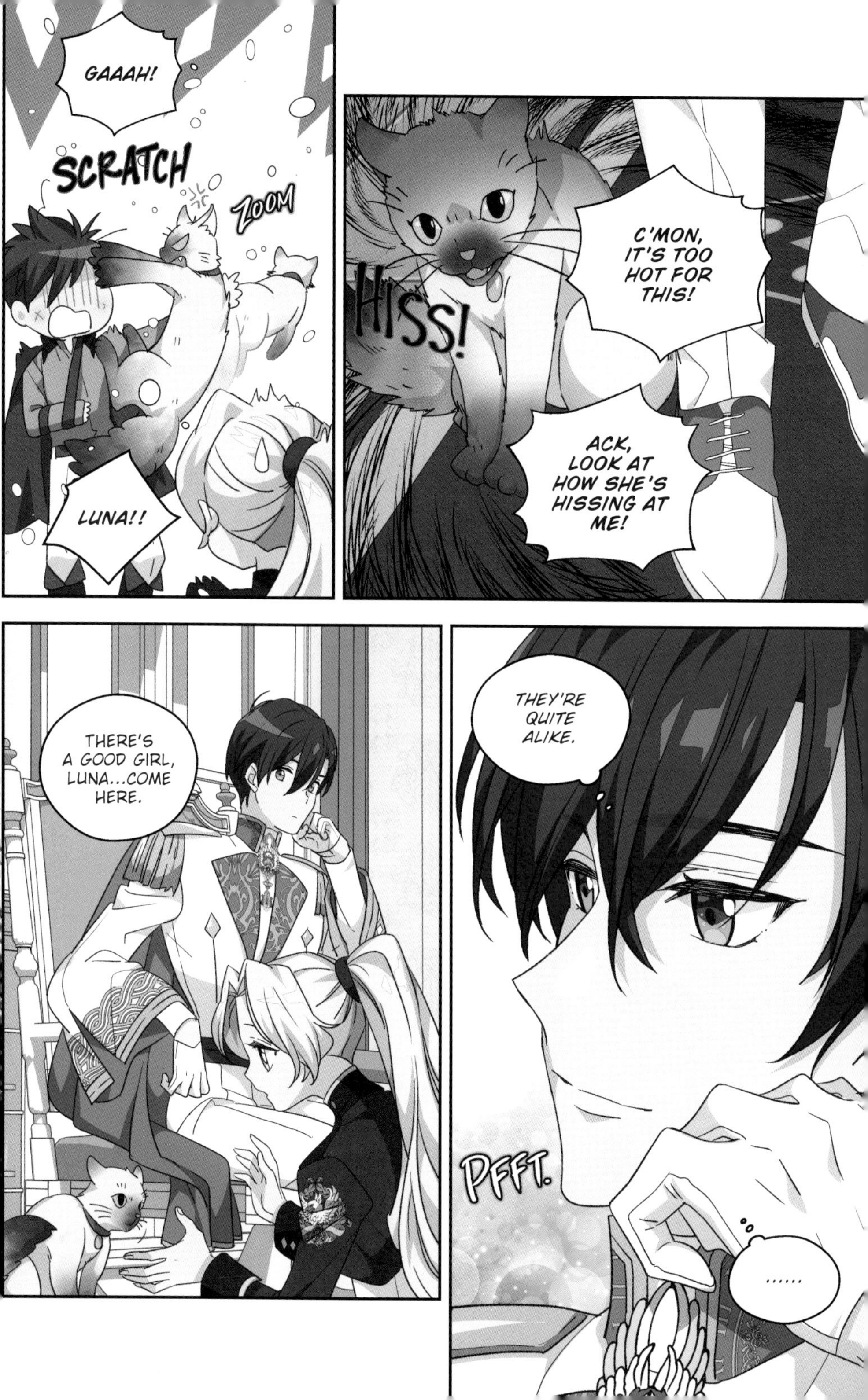
GAAAH!
SCRATCH
ZOOM
LUNA!!
HISS!
C'MON, IT'S TOO HOT FOR THIS!
ACK, LOOK AT HOW SHE'S HISSING AT ME!
THERE'S A GOOD GIRL, LUNA...COME HERE.
THEY'RE QUITE ALIKE.
PFFT.
......

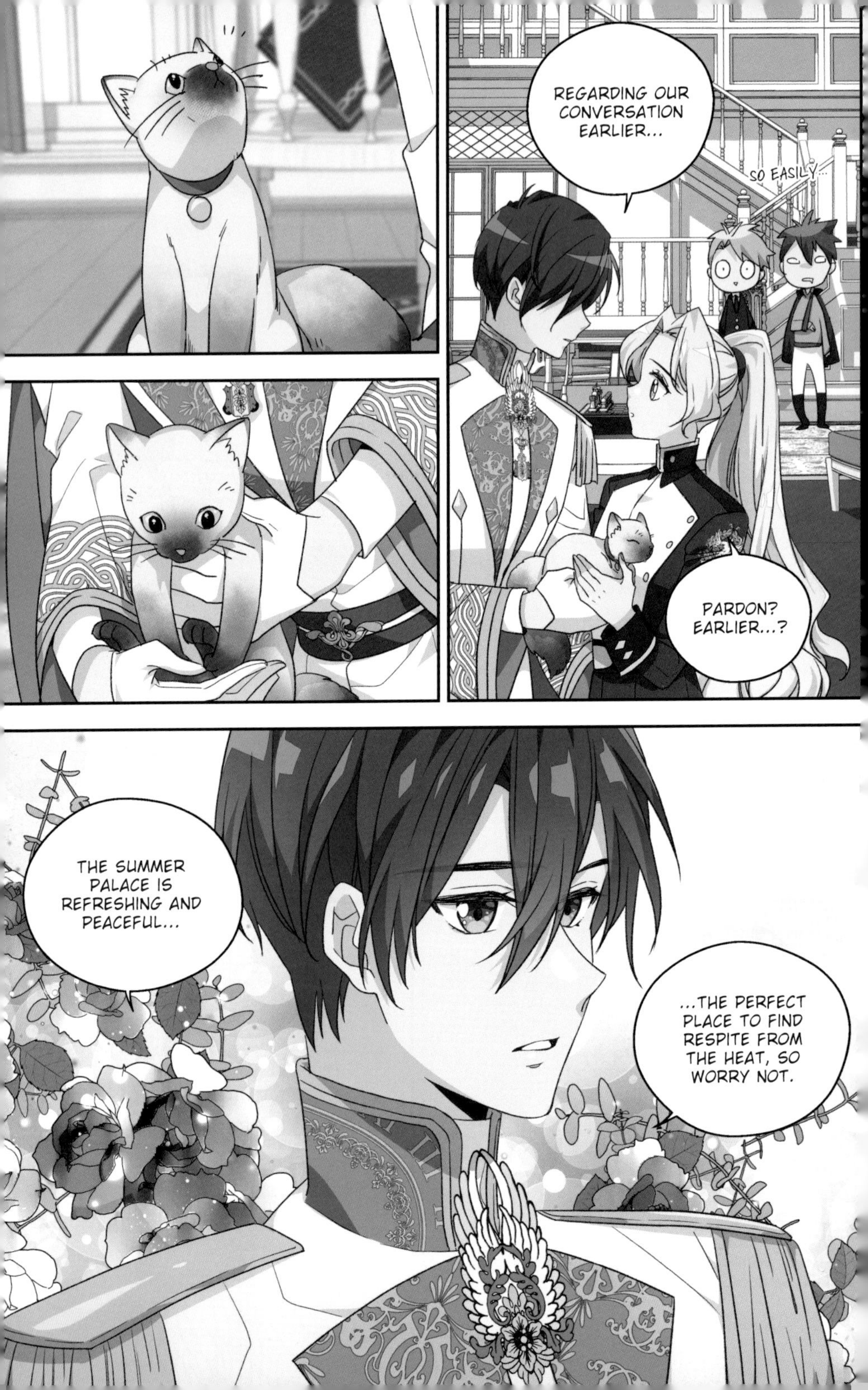
REGARDING OUR CONVERSATION EARLIER...
SO EASILY...
PARDON? EARLIER...?
THE SUMMER PALACE IS REFRESHING AND PEACEFUL...
...THE PERFECT PLACE TO FIND RESPITE FROM THE HEAT, SO WORRY NOT.

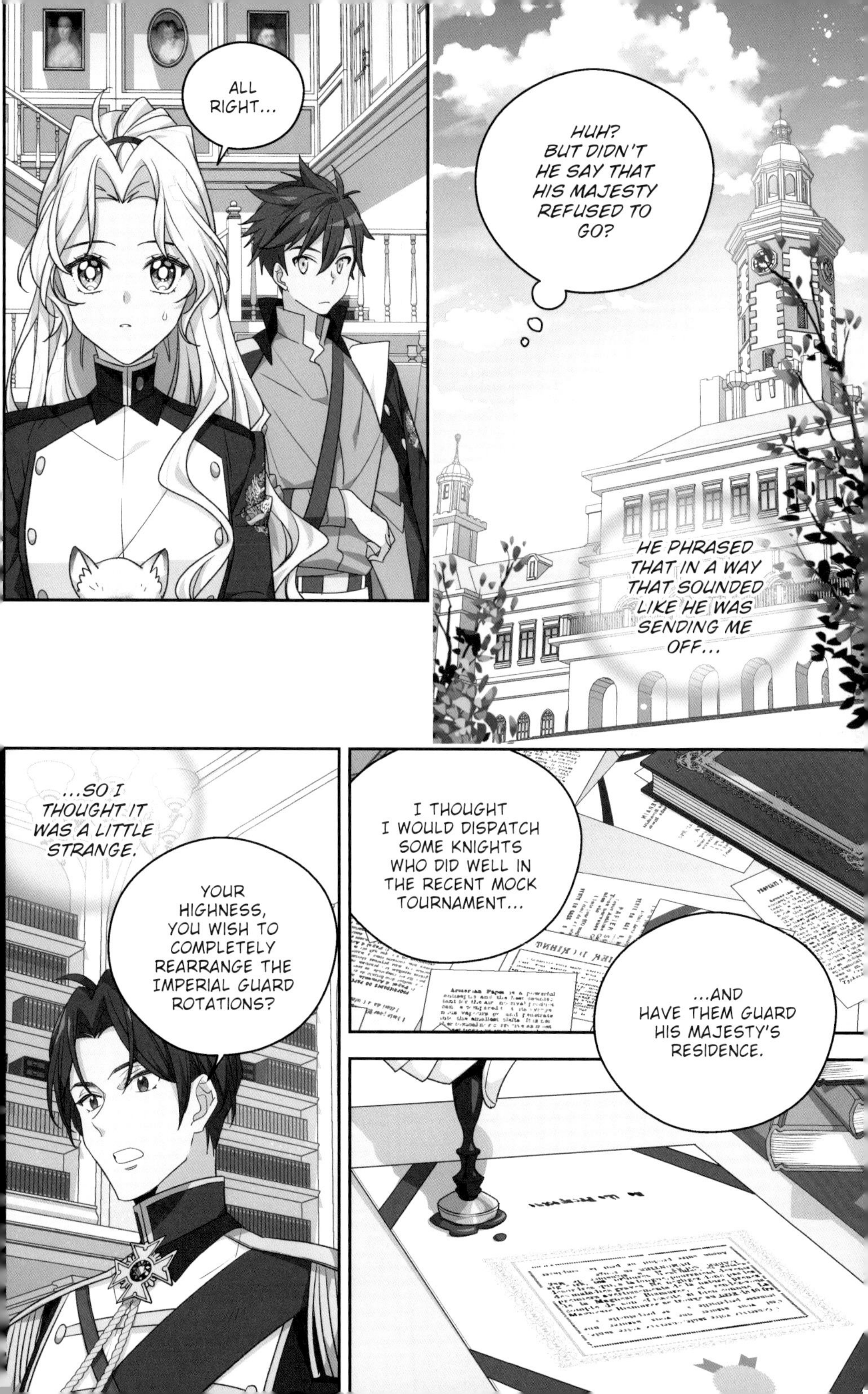
ALL RIGHT...
HUH? BUT DIDN'T HE SAY THAT HIS MAJESTY REFUSED TO GO?
HE PHRASED THAT IN A WAY THAT SOUNDED LIKE HE WAS SENDING ME OFF...
...SO I THOUGHT IT WAS A LITTLE STRANGE.
YOUR HIGHNESS, YOU WISH TO COMPLETELY REARRANGE THE IMPERIAL GUARD ROTATIONS?
I THOUGHT I WOULD DISPATCH SOME KNIGHTS WHO DID WELL IN THE RECENT MOCK TOURNAMENT...
...AND HAVE THEM GUARD HIS MAJESTY'S RESIDENCE.

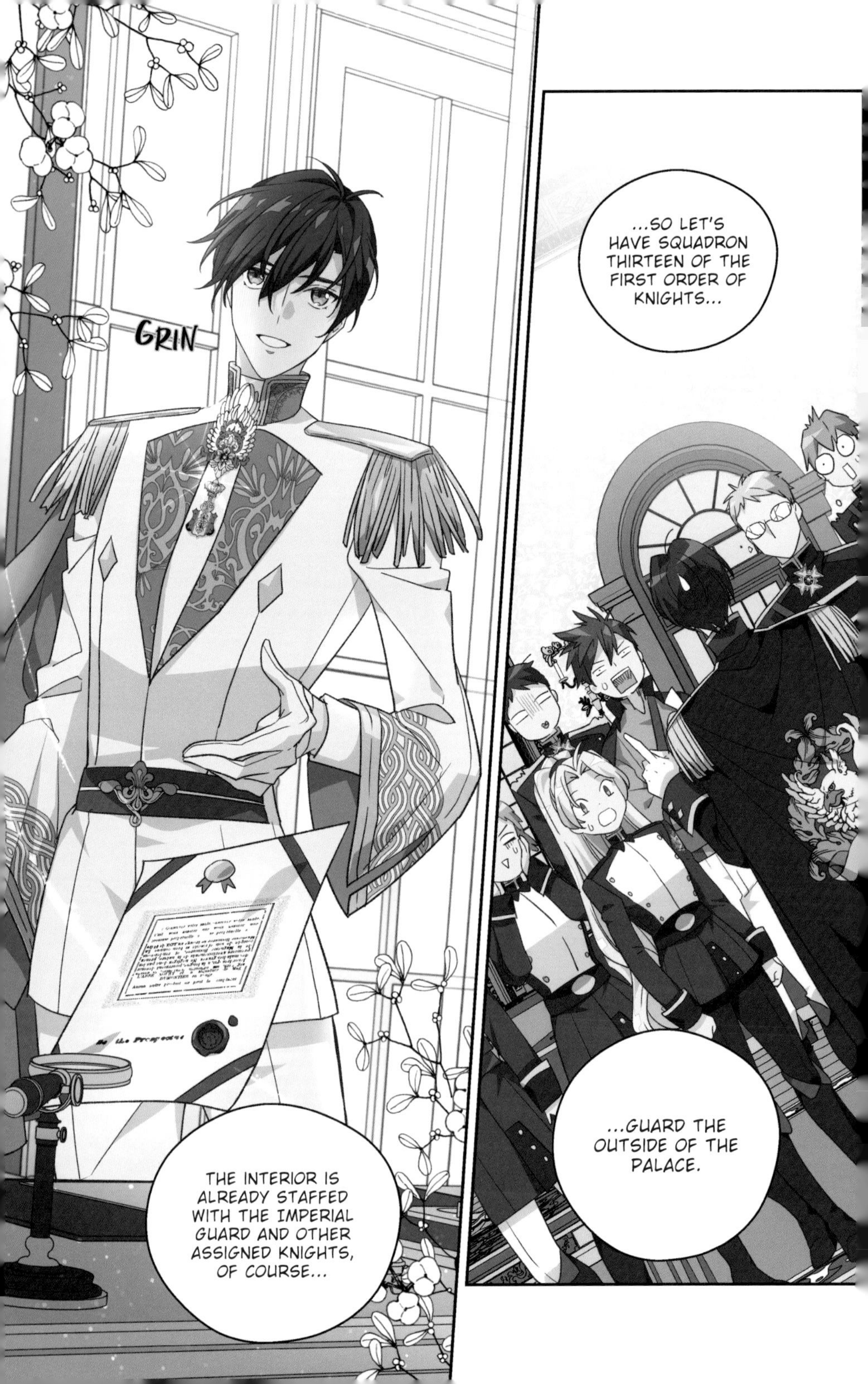
GRIN
THE INTERIOR IS ALREADY STAFFED WITH THE IMPERIAL GUARD AND OTHER ASSIGNED KNIGHTS, OF COURSE...
...SO LET'S HAVE SQUADRON THIRTEEN OF THE FIRST ORDER OF KNIGHTS...
...GUARD THE OUTSIDE OF THE PALACE.

The Abandoned Empress

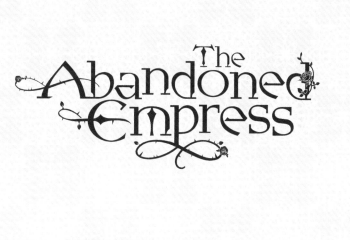

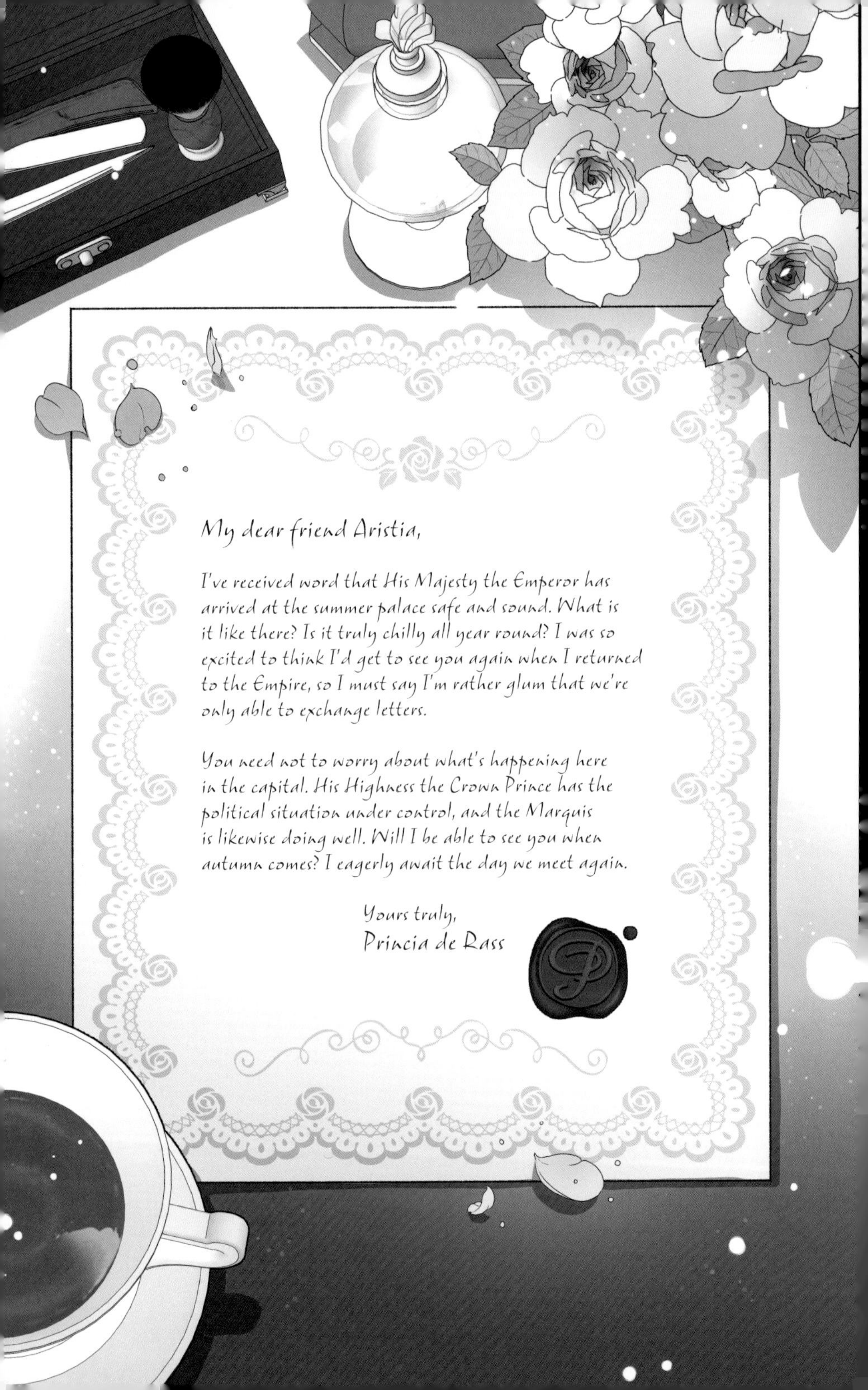

My dear friend Aristia,

I've received word that His Majesty the Emperor has arrived at the summer palace safe and sound. What is it like there? Is it truly chilly all year round? I was so excited to think I'd get to see you again when I returned to the Empire, so I must say I'm rather glum that we're only able to exchange letters.

You need not to worry about what's happening here in the capital. His Highness the Crown Prince has the political situation under control, and the Marquis is likewise doing well. Will I be able to see you when autumn comes? I eagerly await the day we meet again.

Yours truly,
Princia de Rass

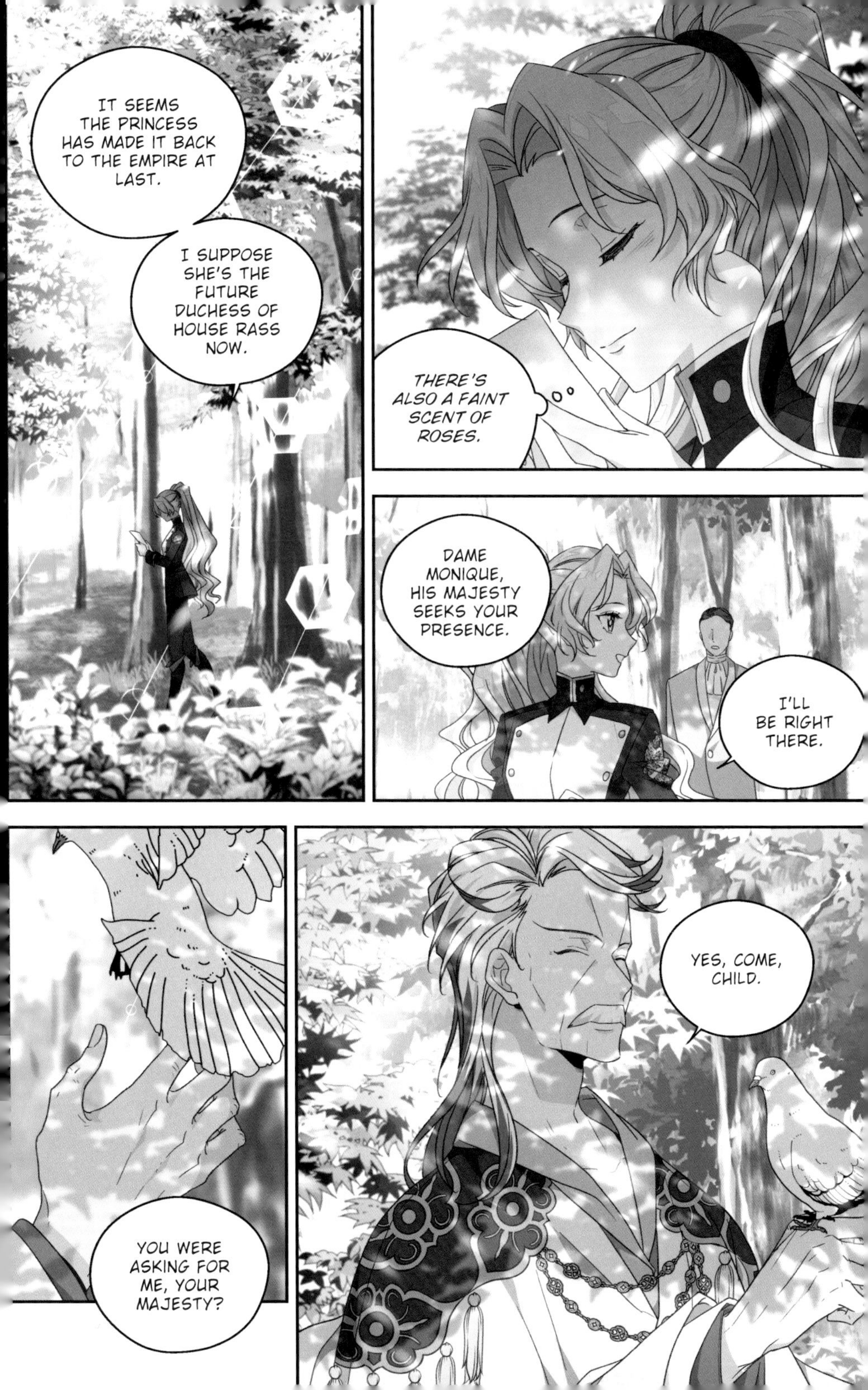
IT SEEMS THE PRINCESS HAS MADE IT BACK TO THE EMPIRE AT LAST.
I SUPPOSE SHE'S THE FUTURE DUCHESS OF HOUSE RASS NOW.
THERE'S ALSO A FAINT SCENT OF ROSES.
DAME MONIQUE, HIS MAJESTY SEEKS YOUR PRESENCE.
I'LL BE RIGHT THERE.
YOU WERE ASKING FOR ME, YOUR MAJESTY?
YES, COME, CHILD.

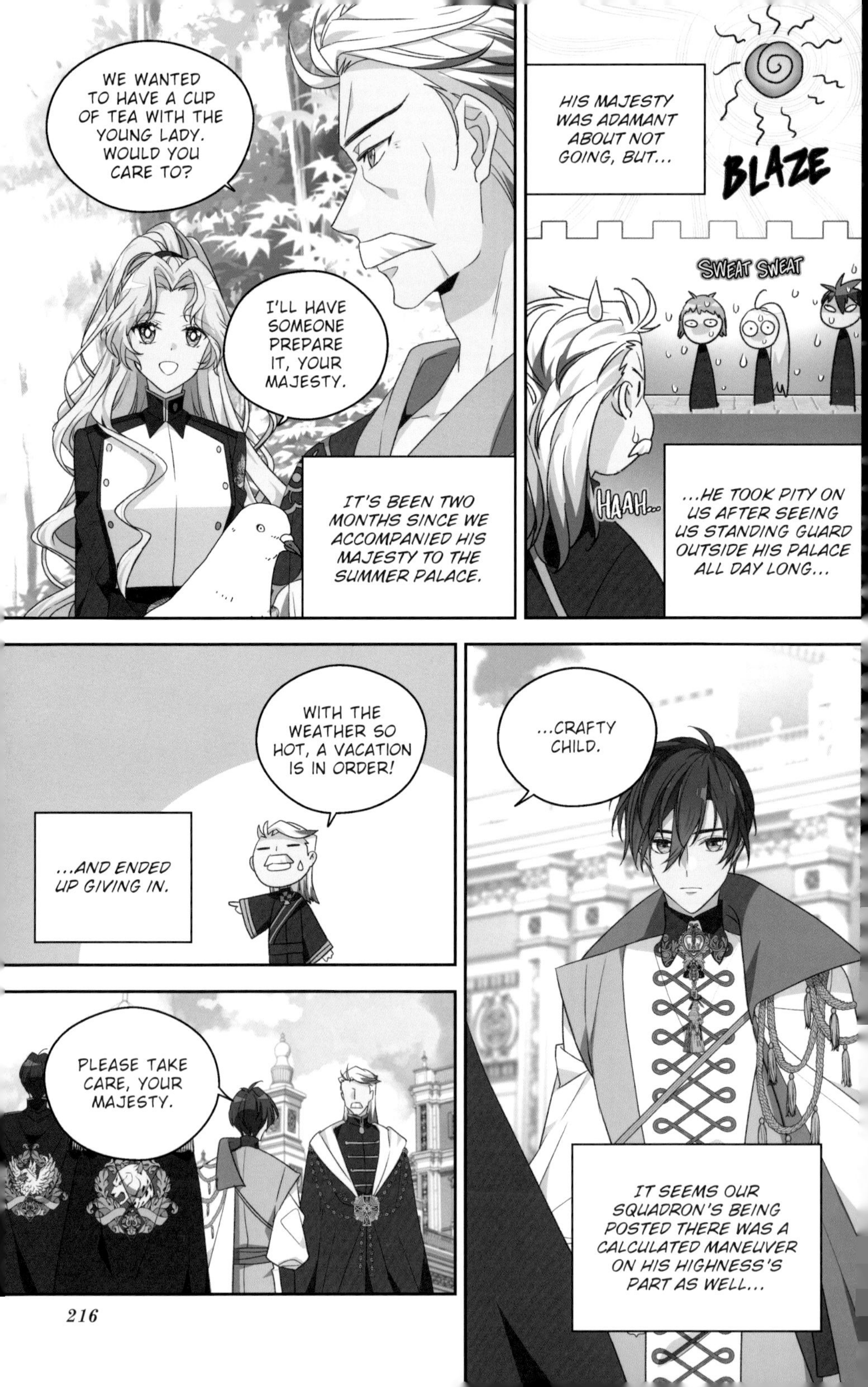

WE WANTED TO HAVE A CUP OF TEA WITH THE YOUNG LADY. WOULD YOU CARE TO?
I'LL HAVE SOMEONE PREPARE IT, YOUR MAJESTY.
IT'S BEEN TWO MONTHS SINCE WE ACCOMPANIED HIS MAJESTY TO THE SUMMER PALACE.
HIS MAJESTY WAS ADAMANT ABOUT NOT GOING, BUT...
BLAZE
SWEAT SWEAT
HAAH...
...HE TOOK PITY ON US AFTER SEEING US STANDING GUARD OUTSIDE HIS PALACE ALL DAY LONG...
WITH THE WEATHER SO HOT, A VACATION IS IN ORDER!
...AND ENDED UP GIVING IN.
...CRAFTY CHILD.
PLEASE TAKE CARE, YOUR MAJESTY.
IT SEEMS OUR SQUADRON'S BEING POSTED THERE WAS A CALCULATED MANEUVER ON HIS HIGHNESS'S PART AS WELL...

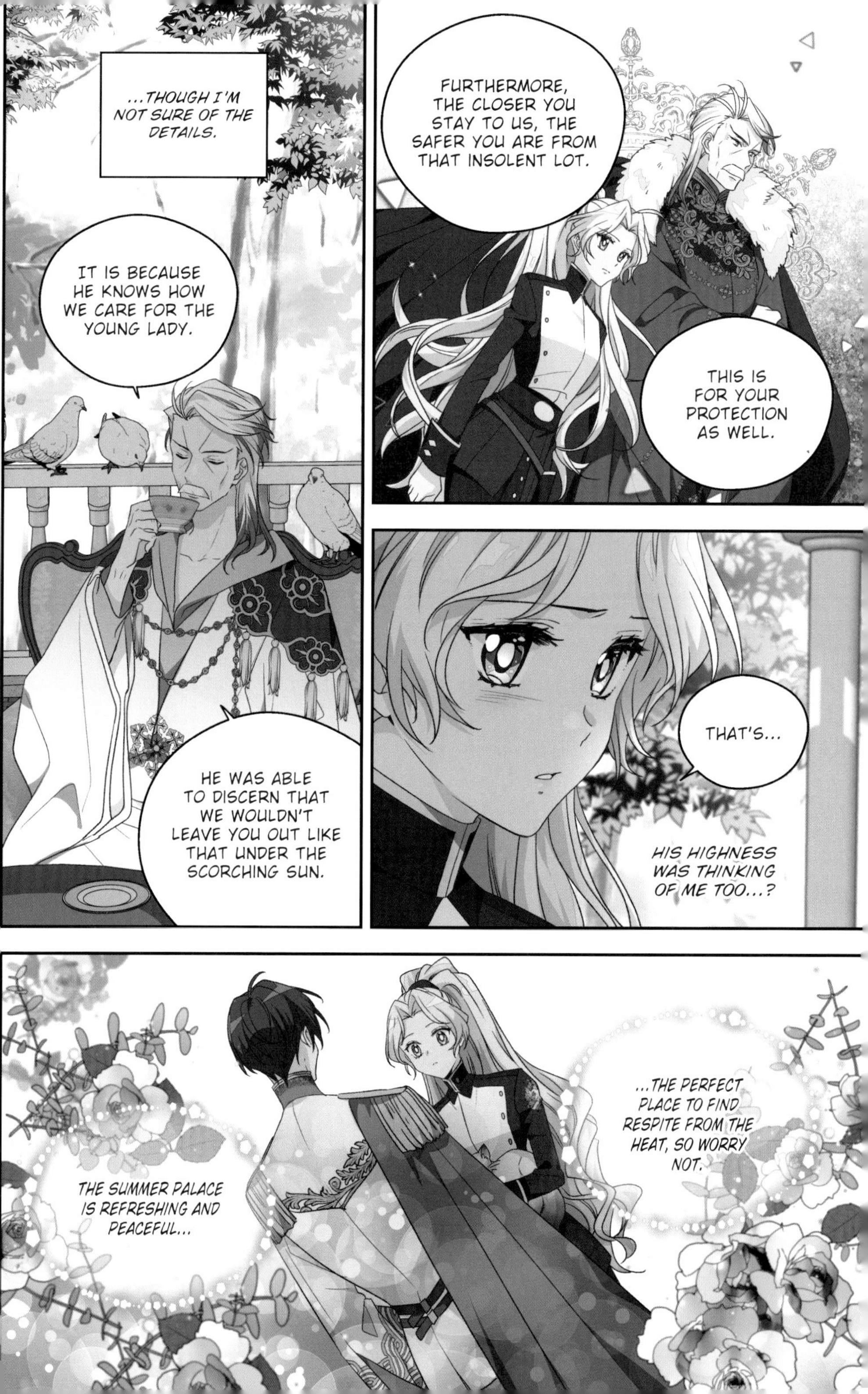
...THOUGH I'M NOT SURE OF THE DETAILS.
IT IS BECAUSE HE KNOWS HOW WE CARE FOR THE YOUNG LADY.
HE WAS ABLE TO DISCERN THAT WE WOULDN'T LEAVE YOU OUT LIKE THAT UNDER THE SCORCHING SUN.
FURTHERMORE, THE CLOSER YOU STAY TO US, THE SAFER YOU ARE FROM THAT INSOLENT LOT.
THIS IS FOR YOUR PROTECTION AS WELL.
THAT'S...
HIS HIGHNESS WAS THINKING OF ME TOO...?
THE SUMMER PALACE IS REFRESHING AND PEACEFUL...
...THE PERFECT PLACE TO FIND RESPITE FROM THE HEAT, SO WORRY NOT.

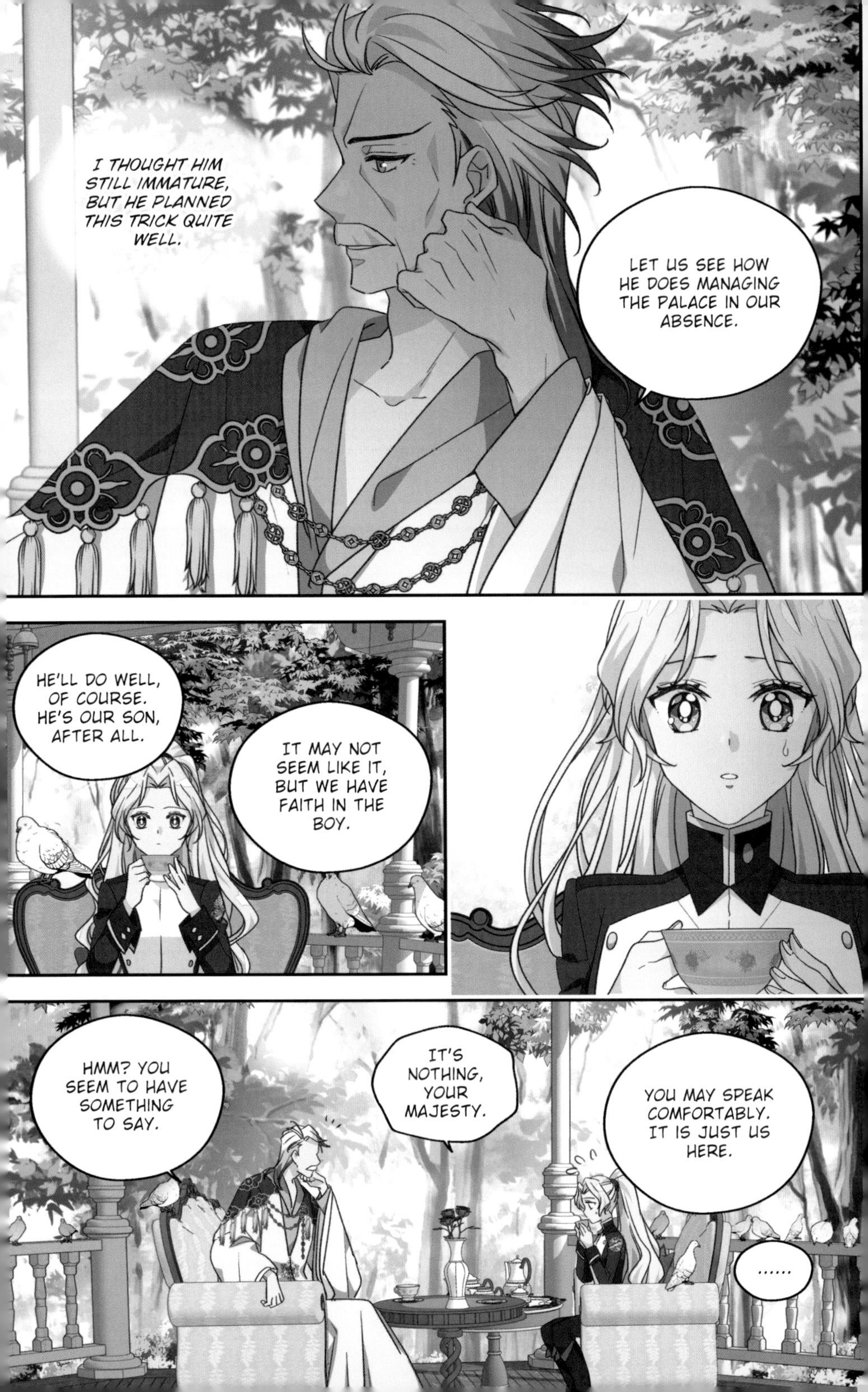
I THOUGHT HIM STILL IMMATURE, BUT HE PLANNED THIS TRICK QUITE WELL.
LET US SEE HOW HE DOES MANAGING THE PALACE IN OUR ABSENCE.
HE'LL DO WELL, OF COURSE. HE'S OUR SON, AFTER ALL.
IT MAY NOT SEEM LIKE IT, BUT WE HAVE FAITH IN THE BOY.
HMM? YOU SEEM TO HAVE SOMETHING TO SAY.
IT'S NOTHING, YOUR MAJESTY.
YOU MAY SPEAK COMFORTABLY. IT IS JUST US HERE.
......

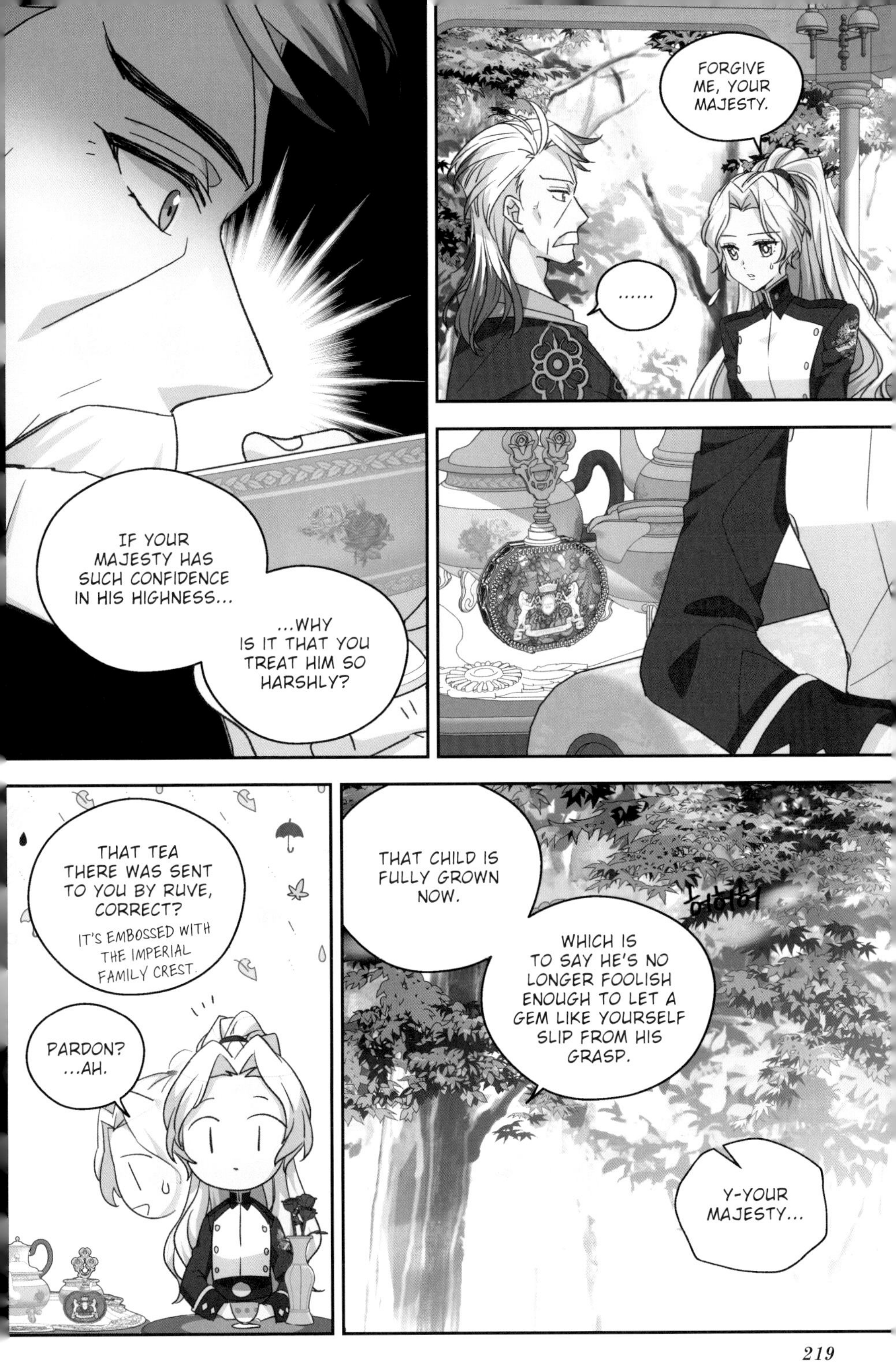
IF YOUR MAJESTY HAS SUCH CONFIDENCE IN HIS HIGHNESS...
...WHY IS IT THAT YOU TREAT HIM SO HARSHLY?
FORGIVE ME, YOUR MAJESTY.
......
THAT TEA THERE WAS SENT TO YOU BY RUVE, CORRECT?
IT'S EMBOSSED WITH THE IMPERIAL FAMILY CREST.
PARDON? ...AH.
THAT CHILD IS FULLY GROWN NOW.
WHICH IS TO SAY HE'S NO LONGER FOOLISH ENOUGH TO LET A GEM LIKE YOURSELF SLIP FROM HIS GRASP.
Y-YOUR MAJESTY...

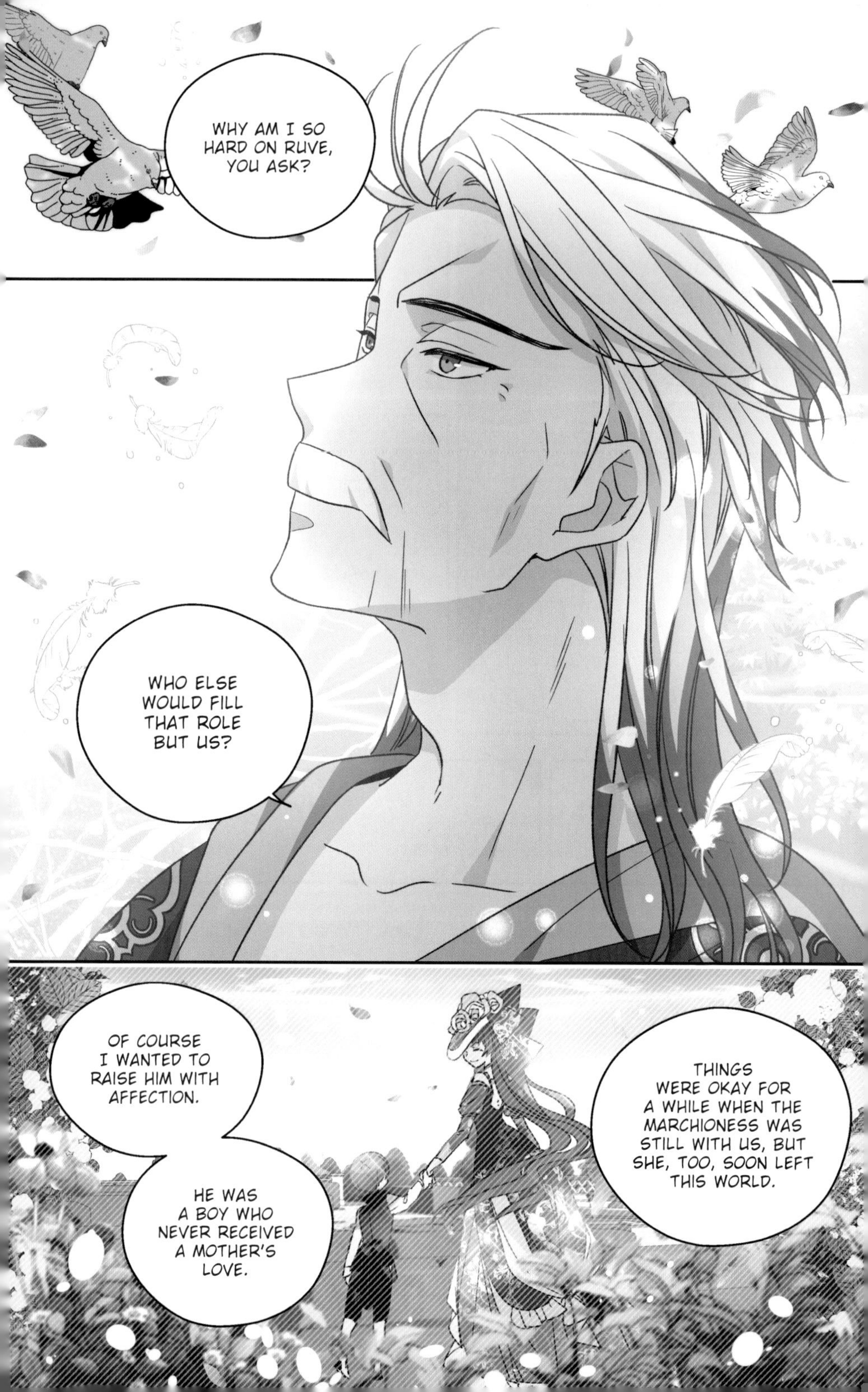
WHY AM I SO HARD ON RUVE, YOU ASK?
WHO ELSE WOULD FILL THAT ROLE BUT US?
OF COURSE I WANTED TO RAISE HIM WITH AFFECTION.
HE WAS A BOY WHO NEVER RECEIVED A MOTHER'S LOVE.
THINGS WERE OKAY FOR A WHILE WHEN THE MARCHIONESS WAS STILL WITH US, BUT SHE, TOO, SOON LEFT THIS WORLD.

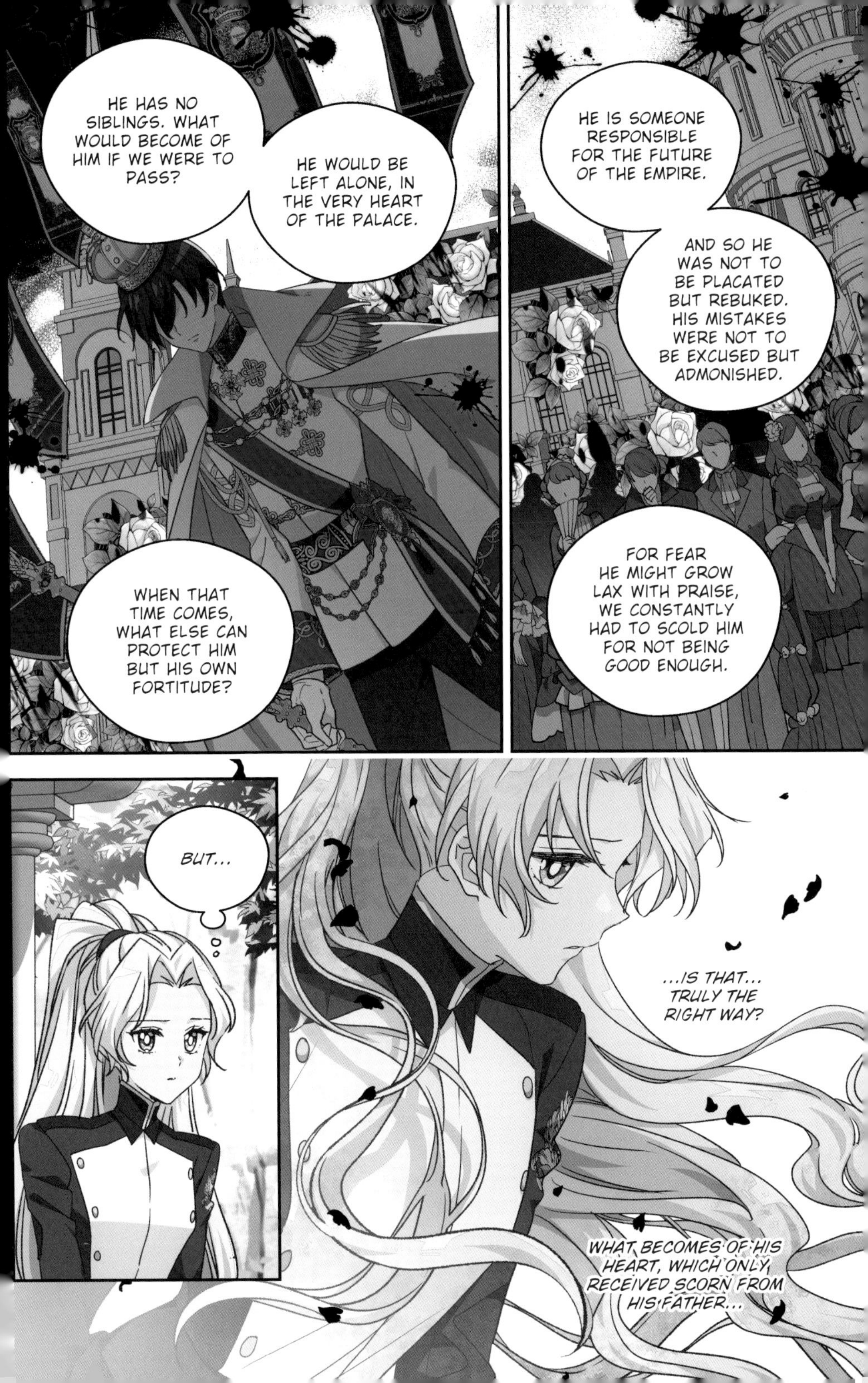
HE HAS NO SIBLINGS. WHAT WOULD BECOME OF HIM IF WE WERE TO PASS?
HE WOULD BE LEFT ALONE, IN THE VERY HEART OF THE PALACE.
WHEN THAT TIME COMES, WHAT ELSE CAN PROTECT HIM BUT HIS OWN FORTITUDE?
HE IS SOMEONE RESPONSIBLE FOR THE FUTURE OF THE EMPIRE.
AND SO HE WAS NOT TO BE PLACATED BUT REBUKED. HIS MISTAKES WERE NOT TO BE EXCUSED BUT ADMONISHED.
FOR FEAR HE MIGHT GROW LAX WITH PRAISE, WE CONSTANTLY HAD TO SCOLD HIM FOR NOT BEING GOOD ENOUGH.
BUT...
...IS THAT... TRULY THE RIGHT WAY?
WHAT BECOMES OF HIS HEART, WHICH ONLY RECEIVED SCORN FROM HIS FATHER...

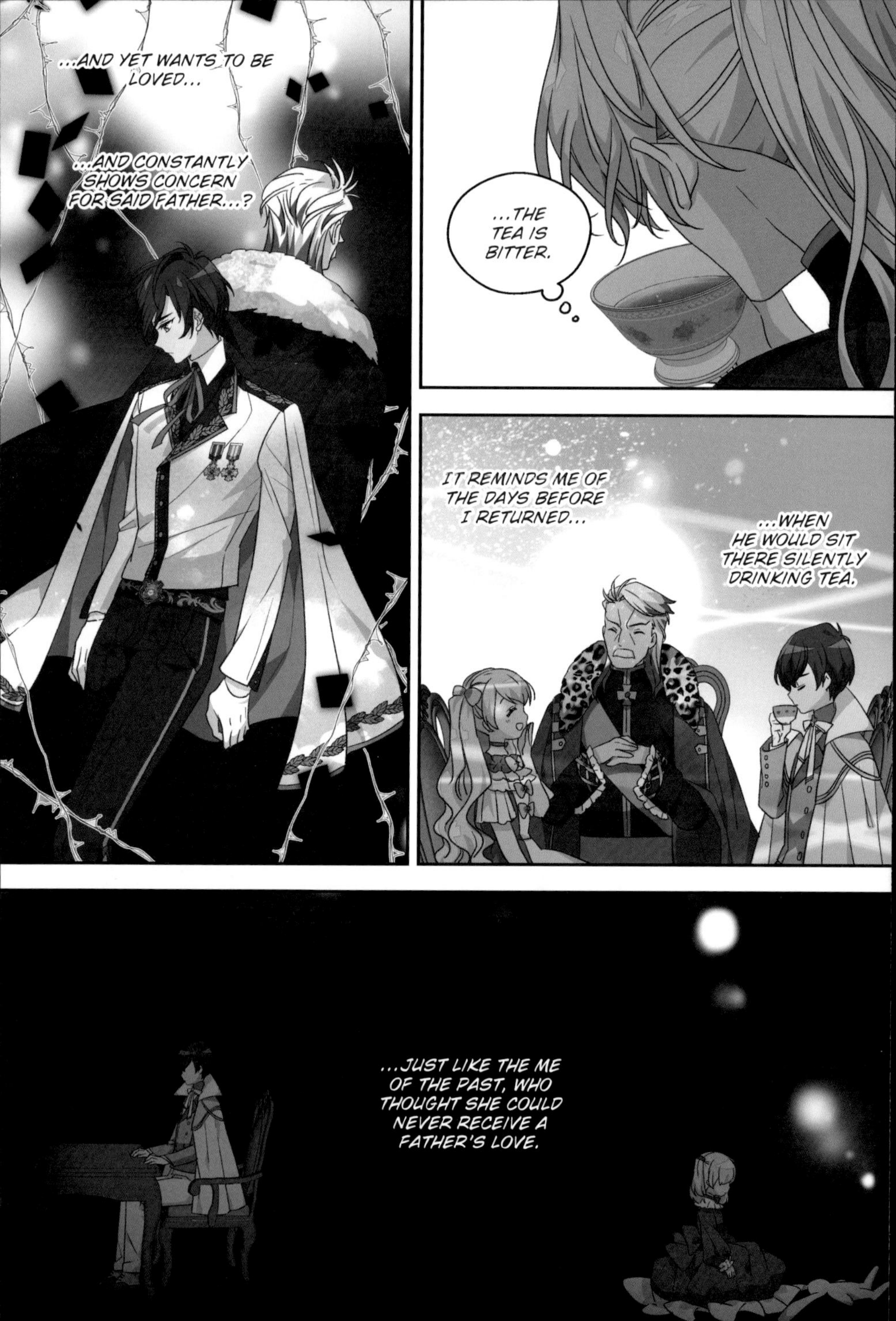
...AND YET WANTS TO BE LOVED...
...AND CONSTANTLY SHOWS CONCERN FOR SAID FATHER...?
...THE TEA IS BITTER.
IT REMINDS ME OF THE DAYS BEFORE I RETURNED...
...WHEN HE WOULD SIT THERE SILENTLY DRINKING TEA.
...JUST LIKE THE ME OF THE PAST, WHO THOUGHT SHE COULD NEVER RECEIVE A FATHER'S LOVE.

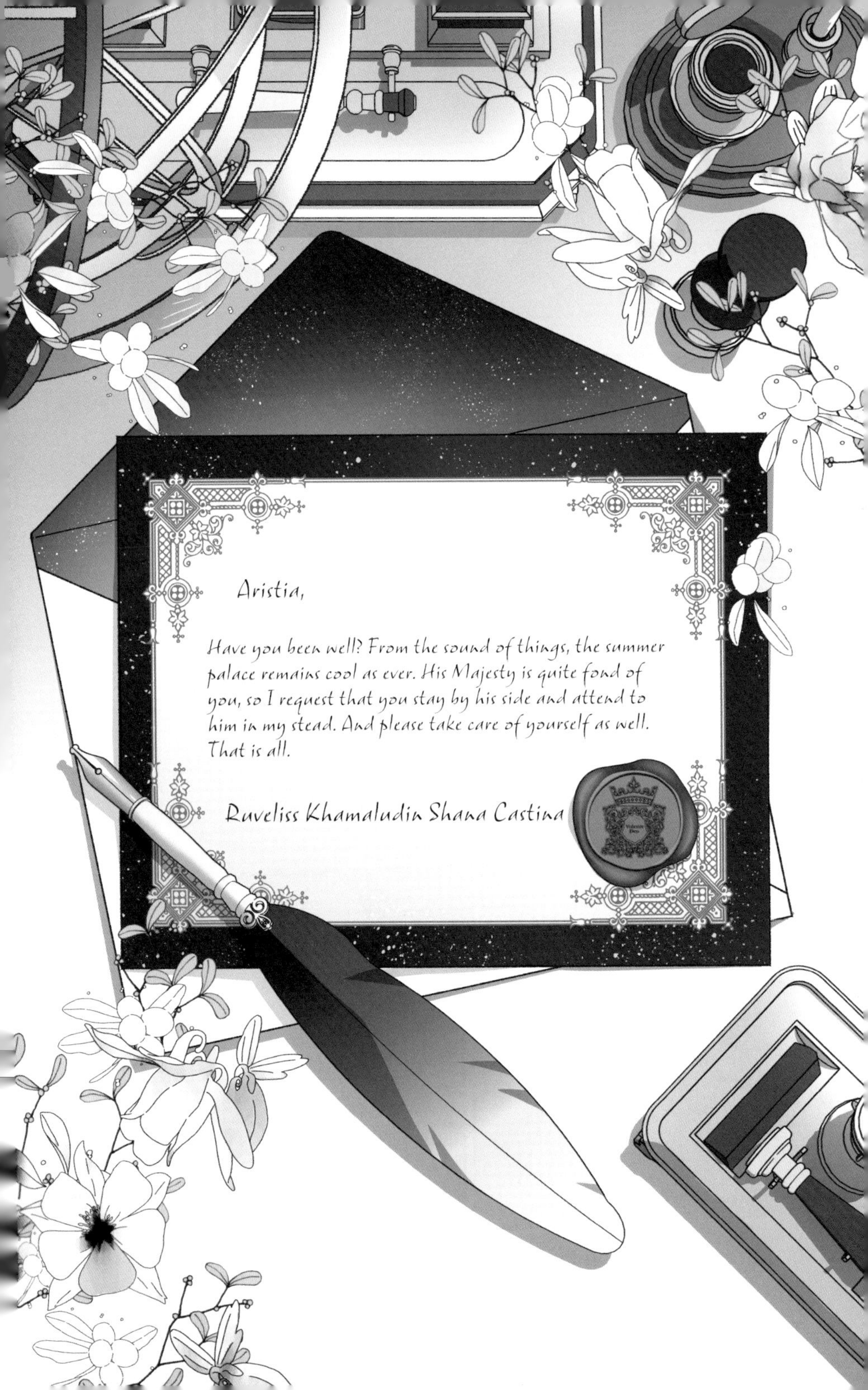
Aristia,
Have you been well? From the sound of things, the summer palace remains cool as ever. His Majesty is quite fond of you, so I request that you stay by his side and attend to him in my stead. And please take care of yourself as well. That is all.
Ruveliss Khamaludin Shana Castina

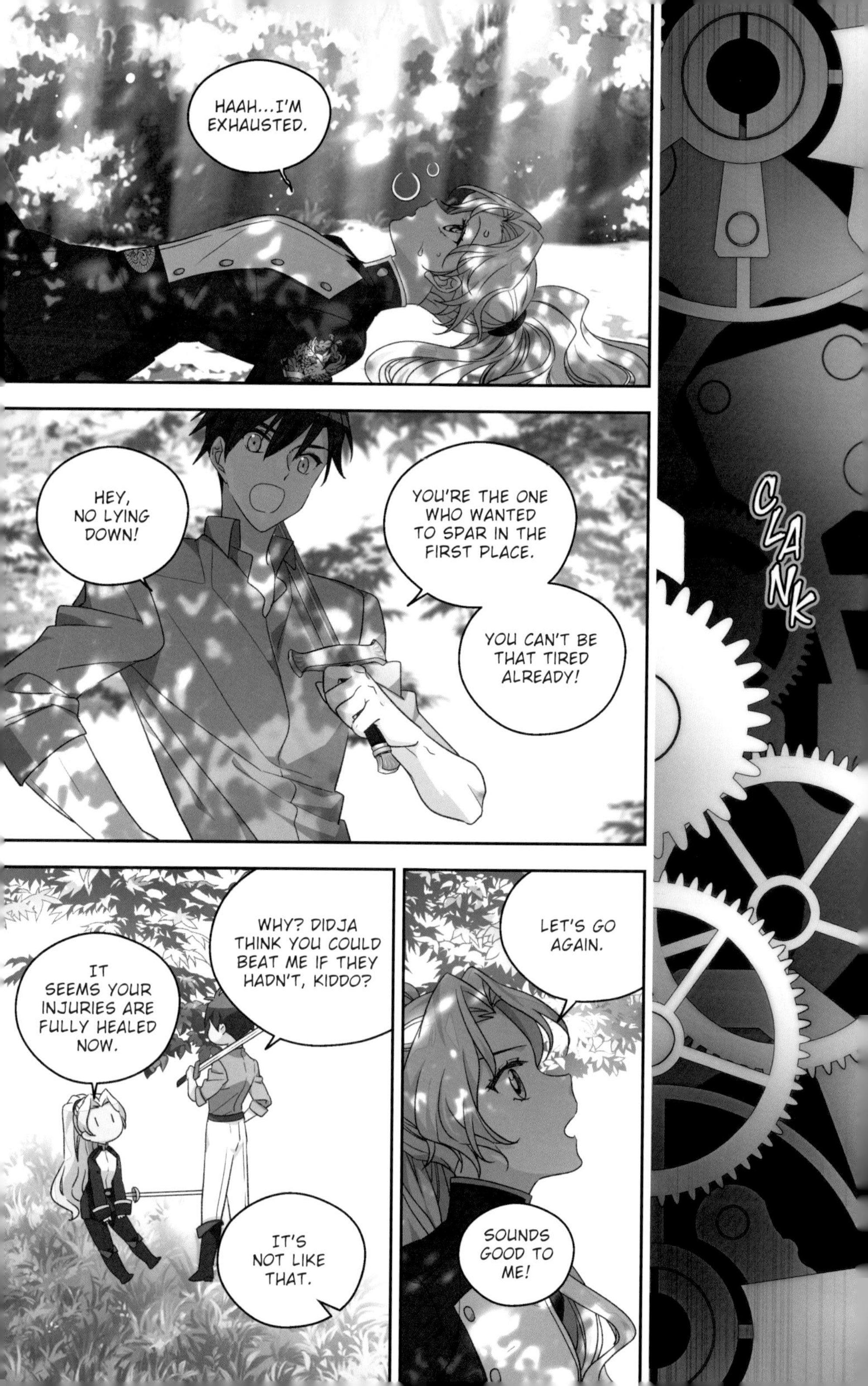
HAAH...I'M EXHAUSTED.
HEY, NO LYING DOWN!
YOU'RE THE ONE WHO WANTED TO SPAR IN THE FIRST PLACE.
YOU CAN'T BE THAT TIRED ALREADY!
CLANK
IT SEEMS YOUR INJURIES ARE FULLY HEALED NOW.
WHY? DIDJA THINK YOU COULD BEAT ME IF THEY HADN'T, KIDDO?
IT'S NOT LIKE THAT.
LET'S GO AGAIN.
SOUNDS GOOD TO ME!

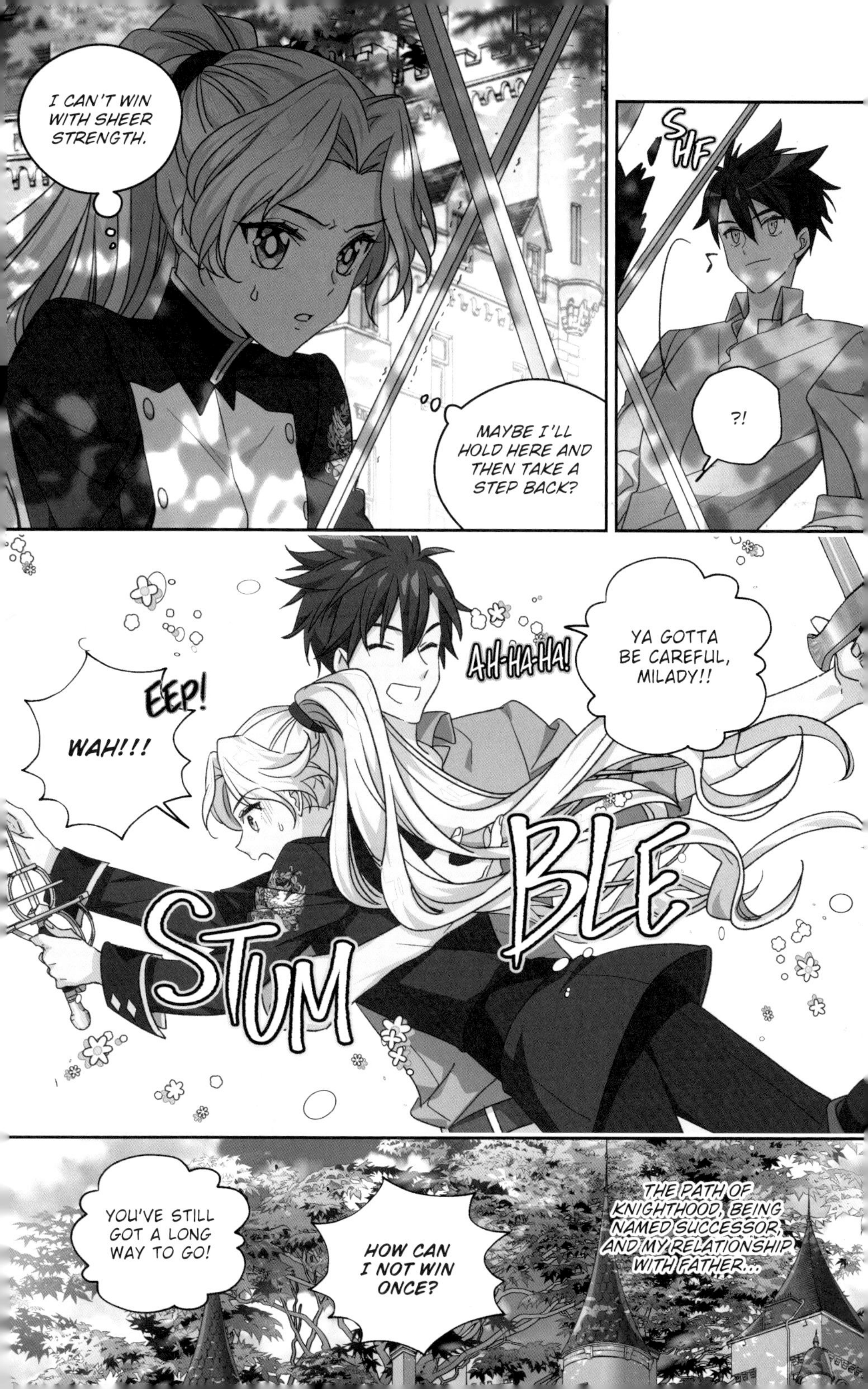
I CAN'T WIN WITH SHEER STRENGTH.
MAYBE I'LL HOLD HERE AND THEN TAKE A STEP BACK?
SHF
?!
EEP!
WAH!!!
STUMBLE
AH-HA-HA!
YA GOTTA BE CAREFUL, MILADY!!
YOU'VE STILL GOT A LONG WAY TO GO!
HOW CAN I NOT WIN ONCE?
THE PATH OF KNIGHTHOOD, BEING NAMED SUCCESSOR, AND MY RELATIONSHIP WITH FATHER...

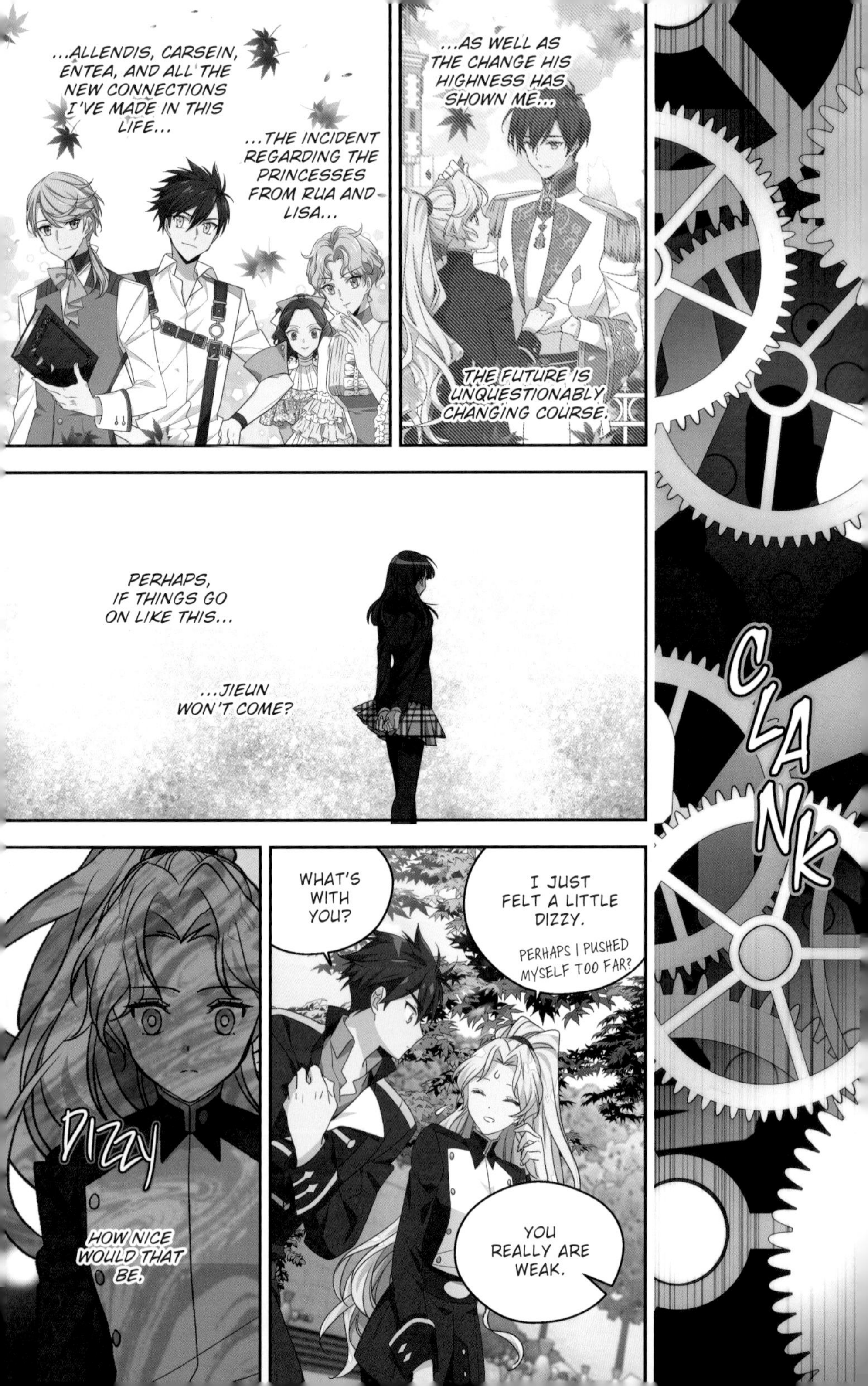

...ALLENDIS, CARSEIN, ENTEA, AND ALL THE NEW CONNECTIONS I'VE MADE IN THIS LIFE...
...THE INCIDENT REGARDING THE PRINCESSES FROM RUA AND LISA...
...AS WELL AS THE CHANGE HIS HIGHNESS HAS SHOWN ME...
THE FUTURE IS UNQUESTIONABLY CHANGING COURSE.
CLANK
PERHAPS, IF THINGS GO ON LIKE THIS...
...JIEUN WON'T COME?
HOW NICE WOULD THAT BE.
DIZZY
WHAT'S WITH YOU?
I JUST FELT A LITTLE DIZZY.
PERHAPS I PUSHED MYSELF TOO FAR?
YOU REALLY ARE WEAK.

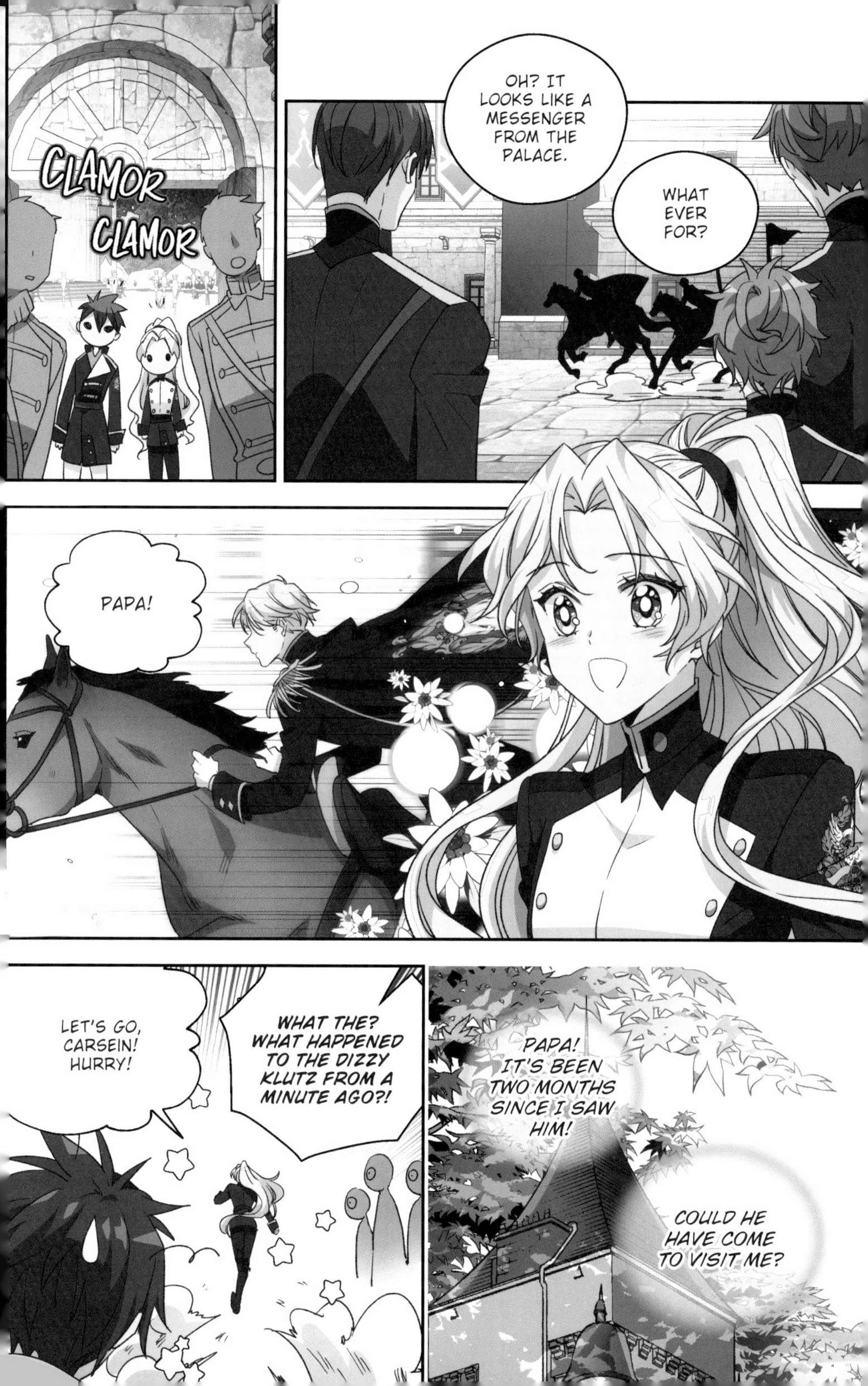
CLAMOR
CLAMOR
OH? IT LOOKS LIKE A MESSENGER FROM THE PALACE.
WHAT EVER FOR?
PAPA!
LET'S GO, CARSEIN! HURRY!
WHAT THE? WHAT HAPPENED TO THE DIZZY KLUTZ FROM A MINUTE AGO?!
PAPA! IT'S BEEN TWO MONTHS SINCE I SAW HIM!
COULD HE HAVE COME TO VISIT ME?

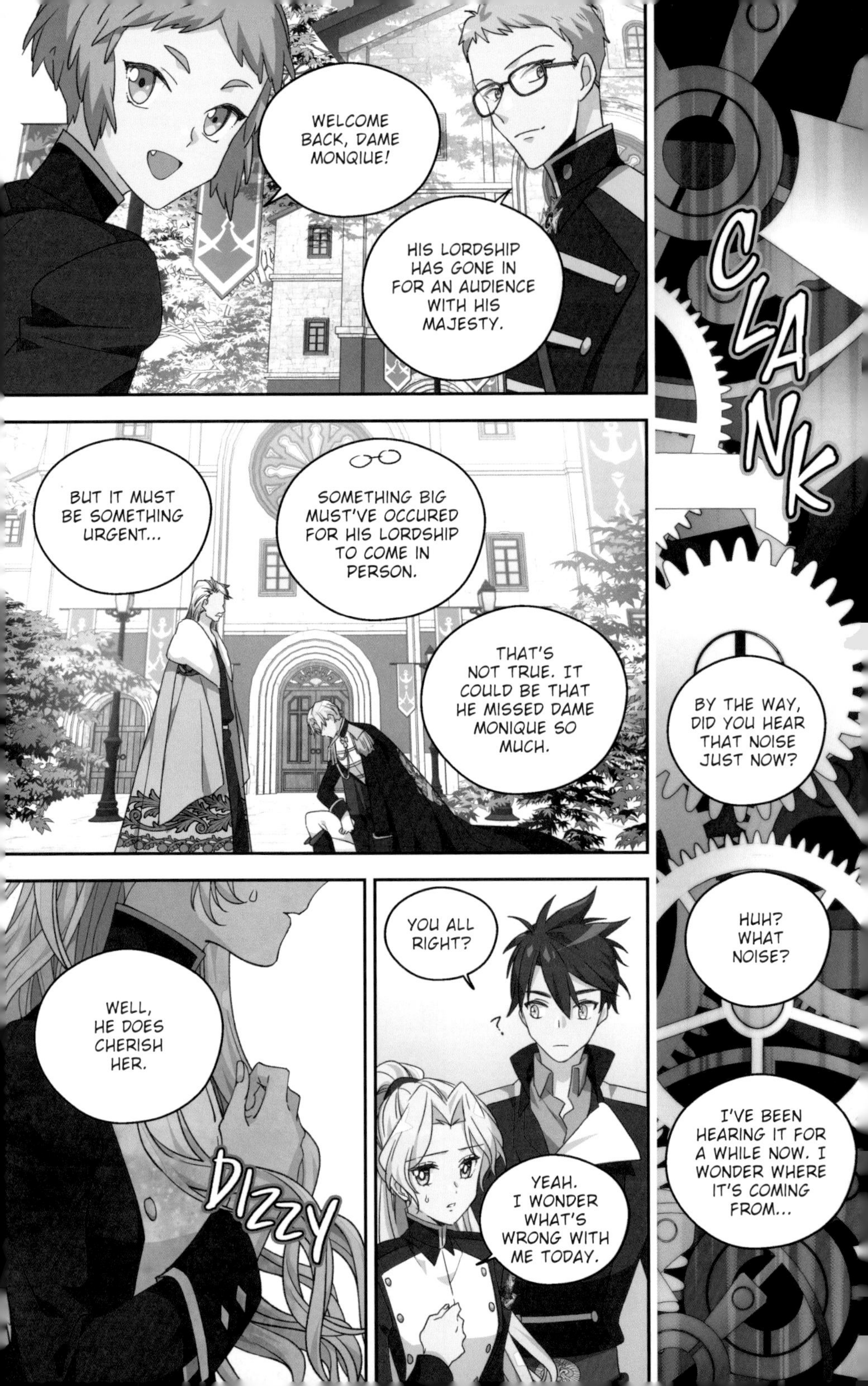
WELCOME BACK, DAME MONQIUE!
HIS LORDSHIP HAS GONE IN FOR AN AUDIENCE WITH HIS MAJESTY.
CLANK
BUT IT MUST BE SOMETHING URGENT...
SOMETHING BIG MUST'VE OCCURED FOR HIS LORDSHIP TO COME IN PERSON.
THAT'S NOT TRUE. IT COULD BE THAT HE MISSED DAME MONIQUE SO MUCH.
BY THE WAY, DID YOU HEAR THAT NOISE JUST NOW?
WELL, HE DOES CHERISH HER.
DIZZY
YOU ALL RIGHT?
YEAH. I WONDER WHAT'S WRONG WITH ME TODAY.
HUH? WHAT NOISE?
I'VE BEEN HEARING IT FOR A WHILE NOW. I WONDER WHERE IT'S COMING FROM...

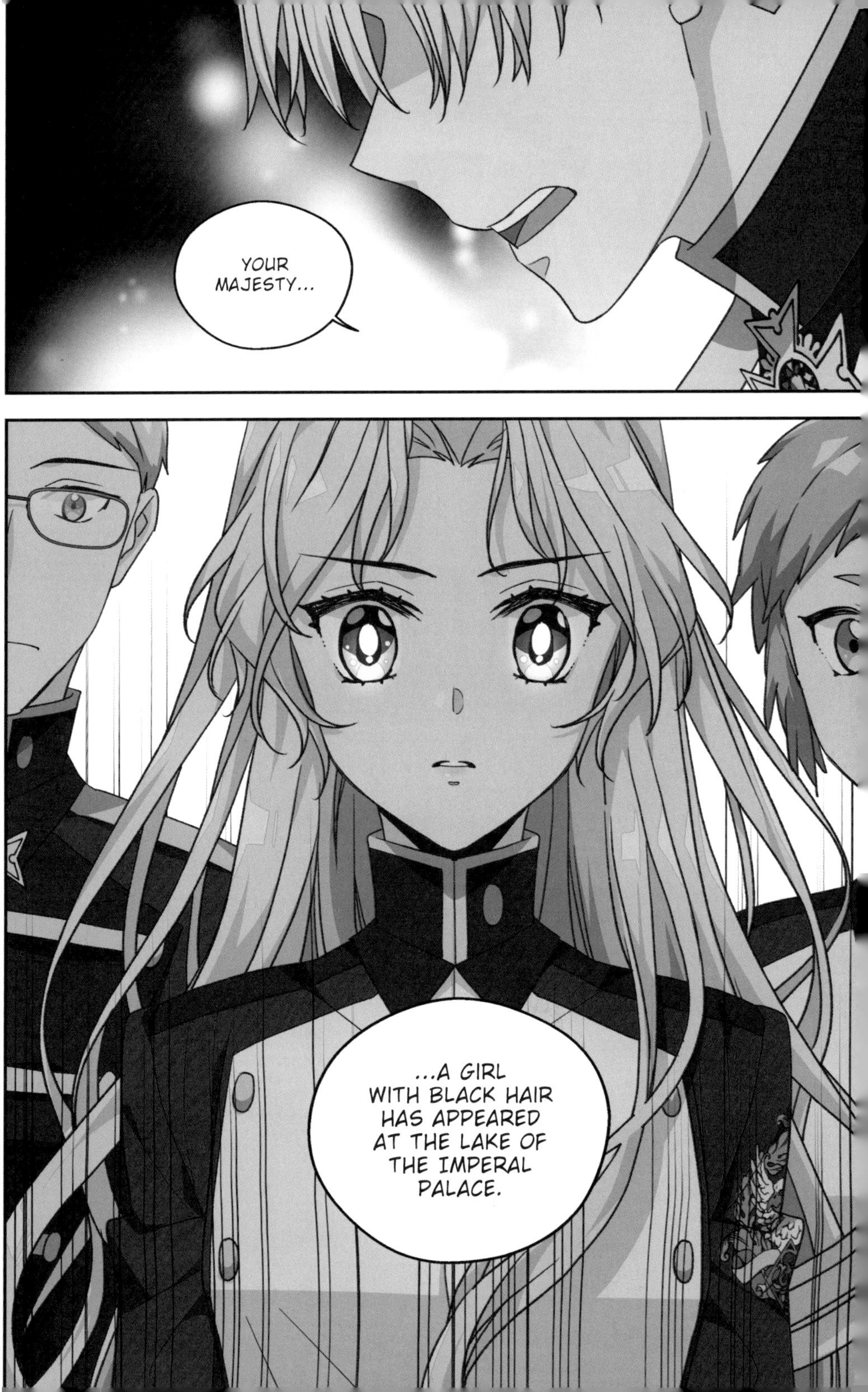
YOUR MAJESTY...
...A GIRL WITH BLACK HAIR HAS APPEARED AT THE LAKE OF THE IMPERAL PALACE.

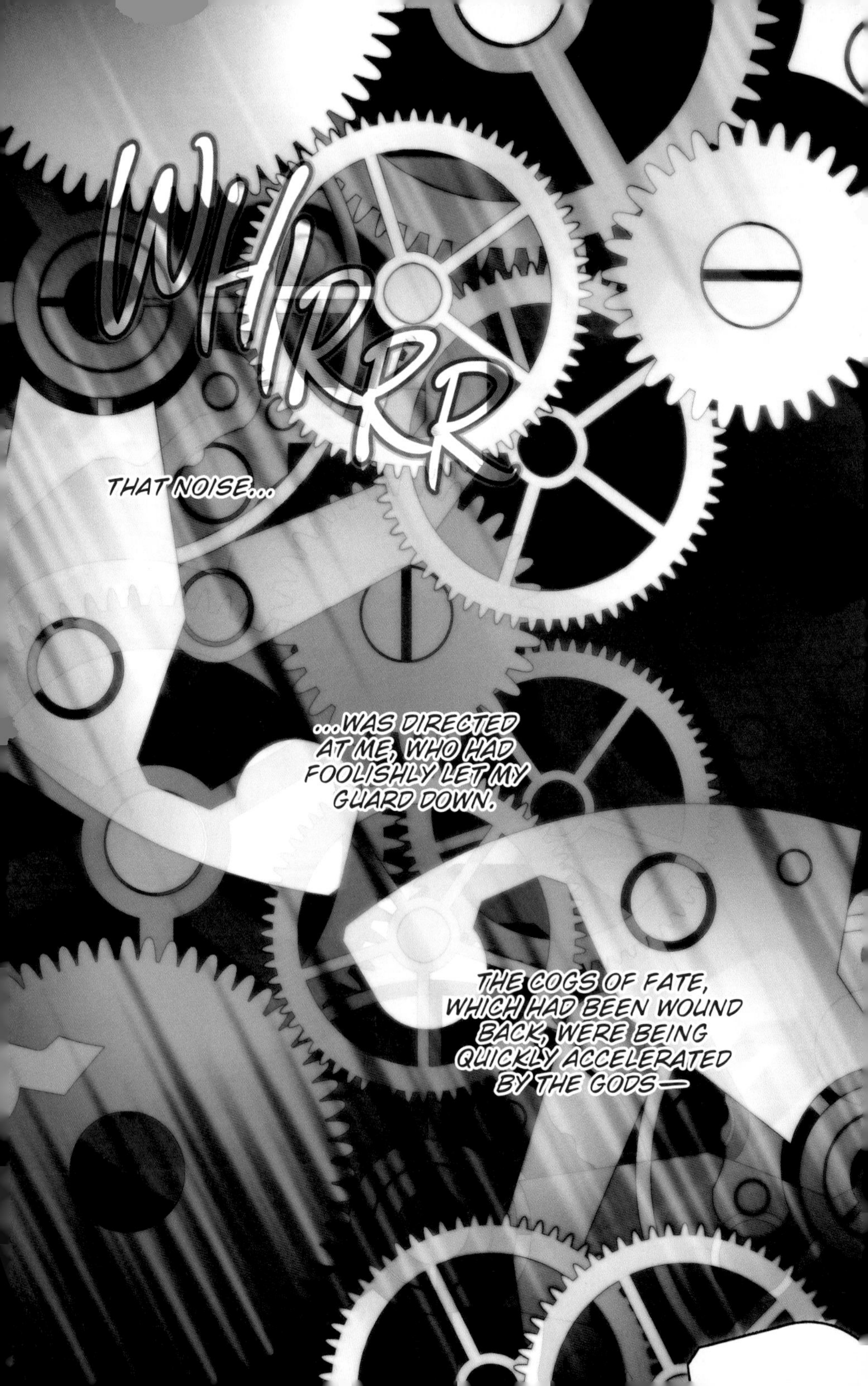
WHIRRR
THAT NOISE...
...WAS DIRECTED AT ME, WHO HAD FOOLISHLY LET MY GUARD DOWN.
THE COGS OF FATE, WHICH HAD BEEN WOUND BACK, WERE BEING QUICKLY ACCELERATED BY THE GODS—

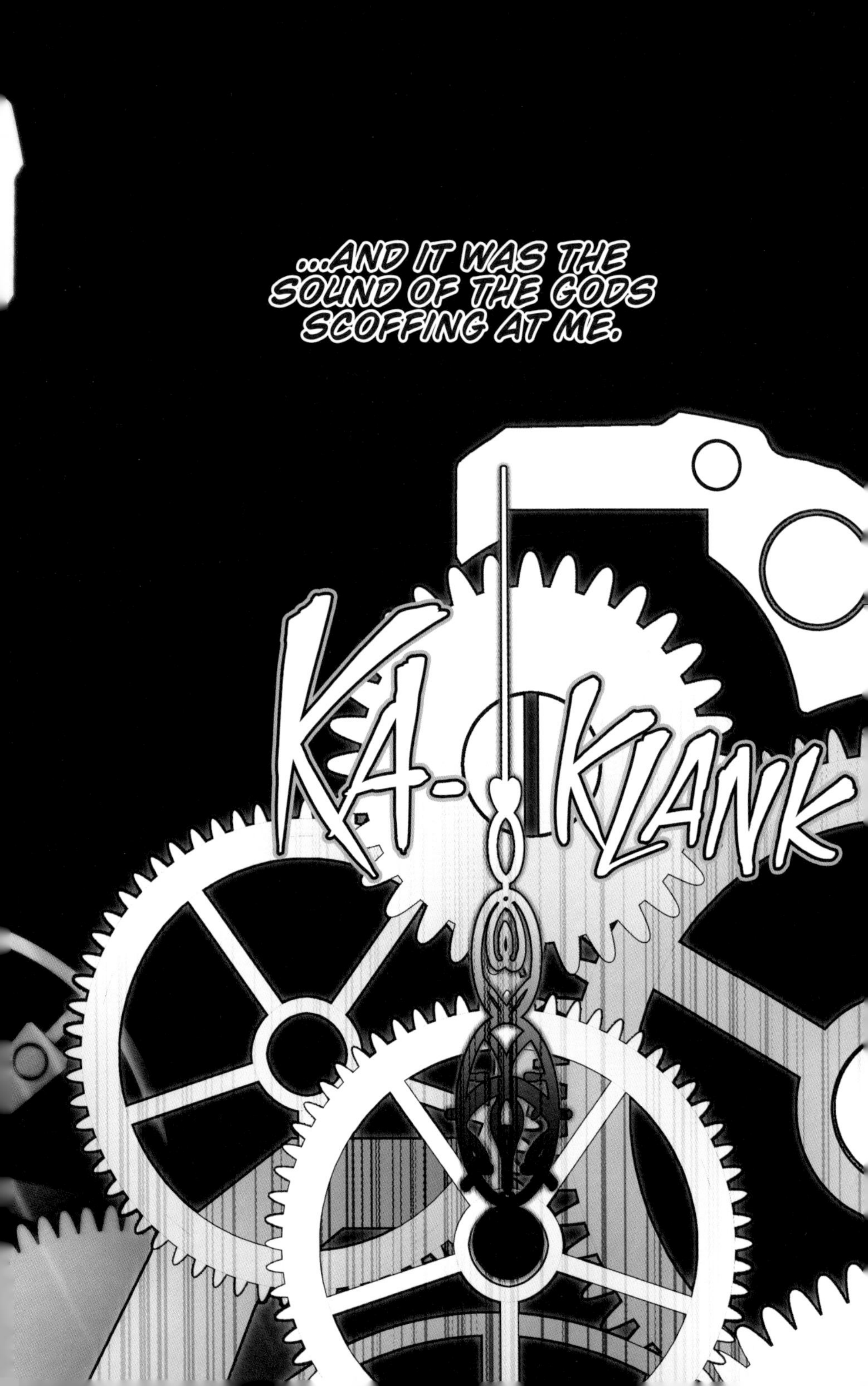
...AND IT WAS THE SOUND OF THE GODS SCOFFING AT ME.
KA-KLANK

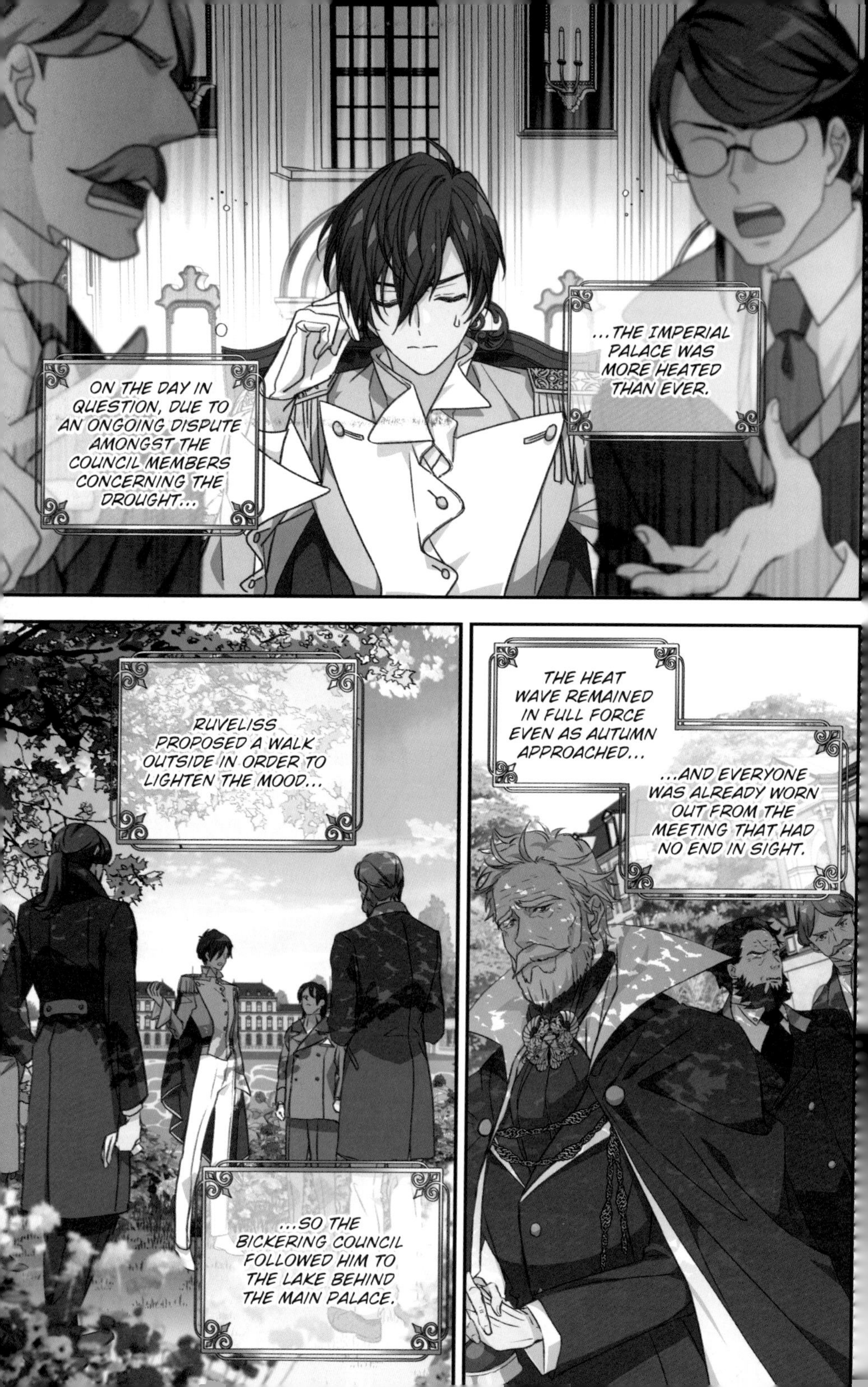

ON THE DAY IN QUESTION, DUE TO AN ONGOING DISPUTE AMONGST THE COUNCIL MEMBERS CONCERNING THE DROUGHT...
...THE IMPERIAL PALACE WAS MORE HEATED THAN EVER.
THE HEAT WAVE REMAINED IN FULL FORCE EVEN AS AUTUMN APPROACHED...
...AND EVERYONE WAS ALREADY WORN OUT FROM THE MEETING THAT HAD NO END IN SIGHT.
RUVELISS PROPOSED A WALK OUTSIDE IN ORDER TO LIGHTEN THE MOOD...
...SO THE BICKERING COUNCIL FOLLOWED HIM TO THE LAKE BEHIND THE MAIN PALACE.

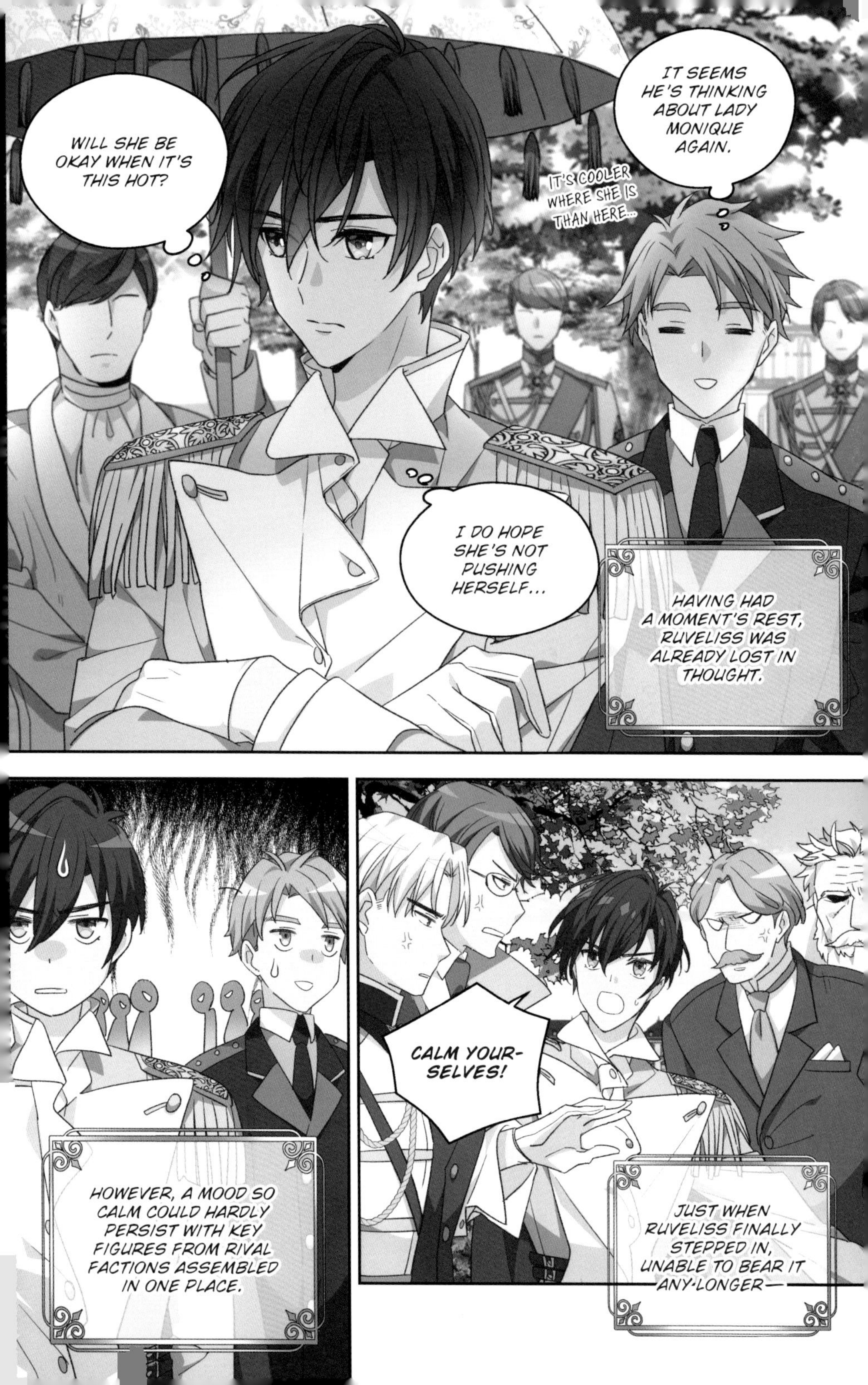
IT SEEMS HE'S THINKING ABOUT LADY MONIQUE AGAIN.
IT'S COOLER WHERE SHE IS THAN HERE...
WILL SHE BE OKAY WHEN IT'S THIS HOT?
I DO HOPE SHE'S NOT PUSHING HERSELF...
HAVING HAD A MOMENT'S REST, RUVELISS WAS ALREADY LOST IN THOUGHT.
HOWEVER, A MOOD SO CALM COULD HARDLY PERSIST WITH KEY FIGURES FROM RIVAL FACTIONS ASSEMBLED IN ONE PLACE.
CALM YOURSELVES!
JUST WHEN RUVELISS FINALLY STEPPED IN, UNABLE TO BEAR IT ANY LONGER—

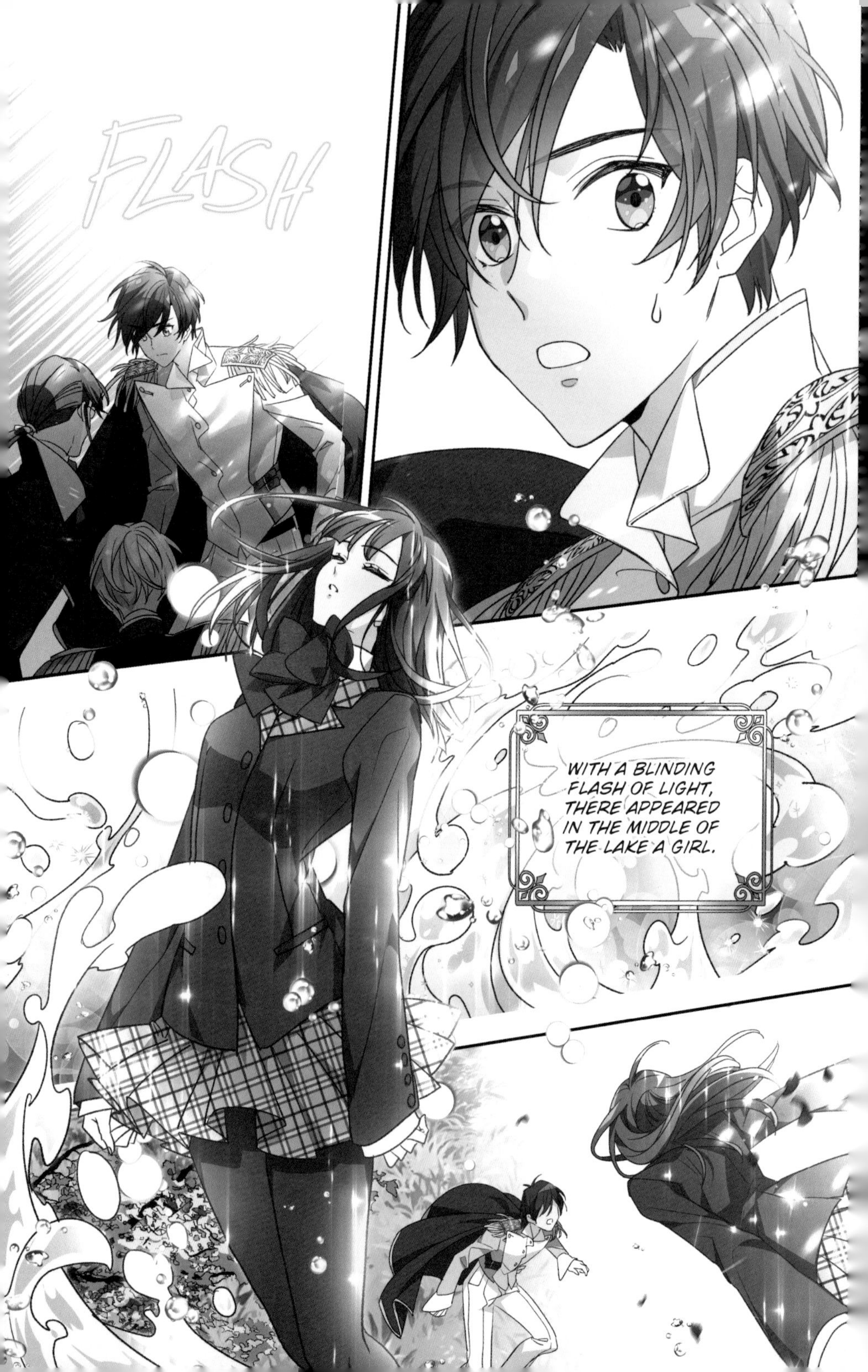
FLASH
WITH A BLINDING FLASH OF LIGHT, THERE APPEARED IN THE MIDDLE OF THE LAKE A GIRL.

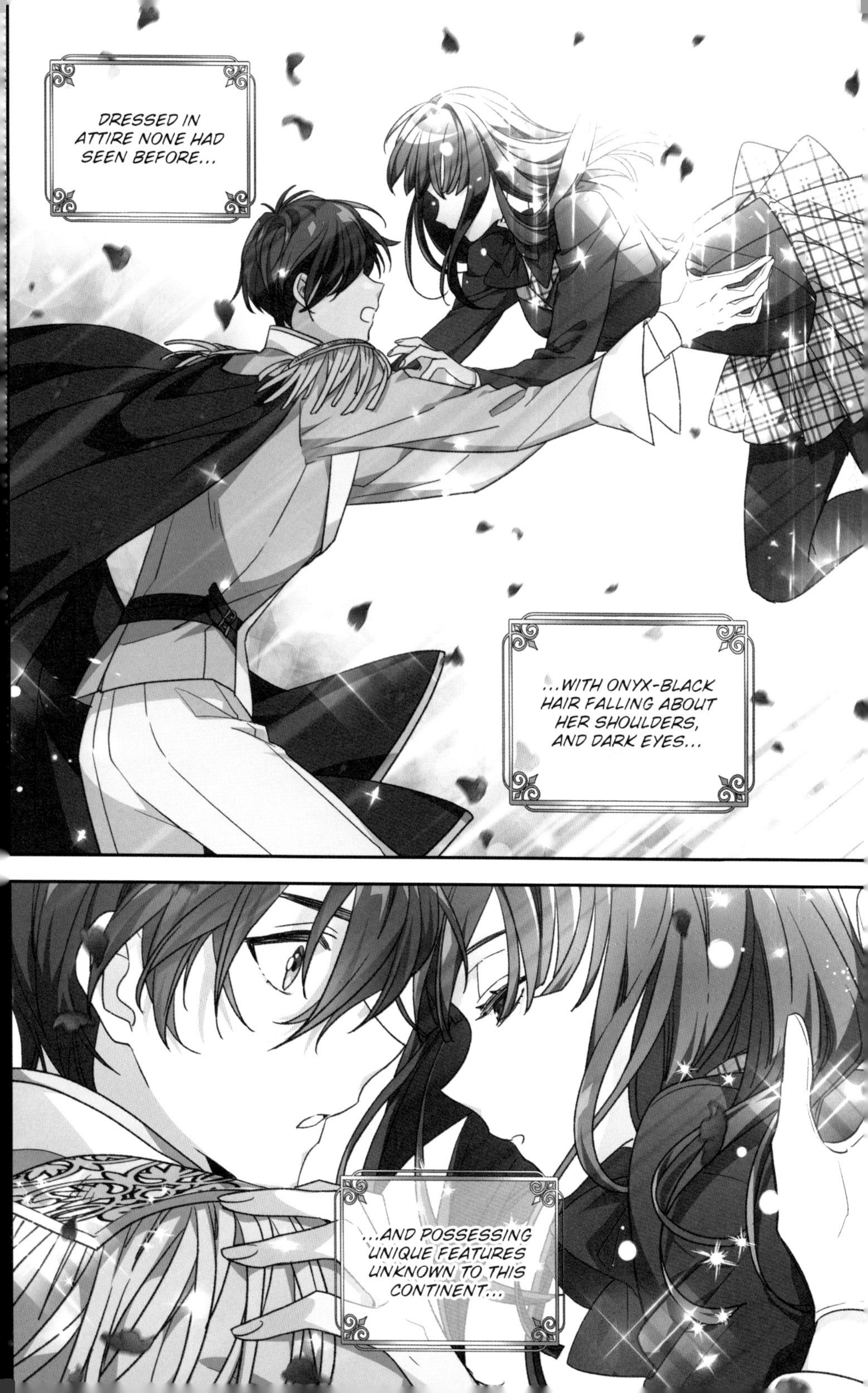
DRESSED IN ATTIRE NONE HAD SEEN BEFORE...
...WITH ONYX-BLACK HAIR FALLING ABOUT HER SHOULDERS, AND DARK EYES...
...AND POSSESSING UNIQUE FEATURES UNKNOWN TO THIS CONTINENT...

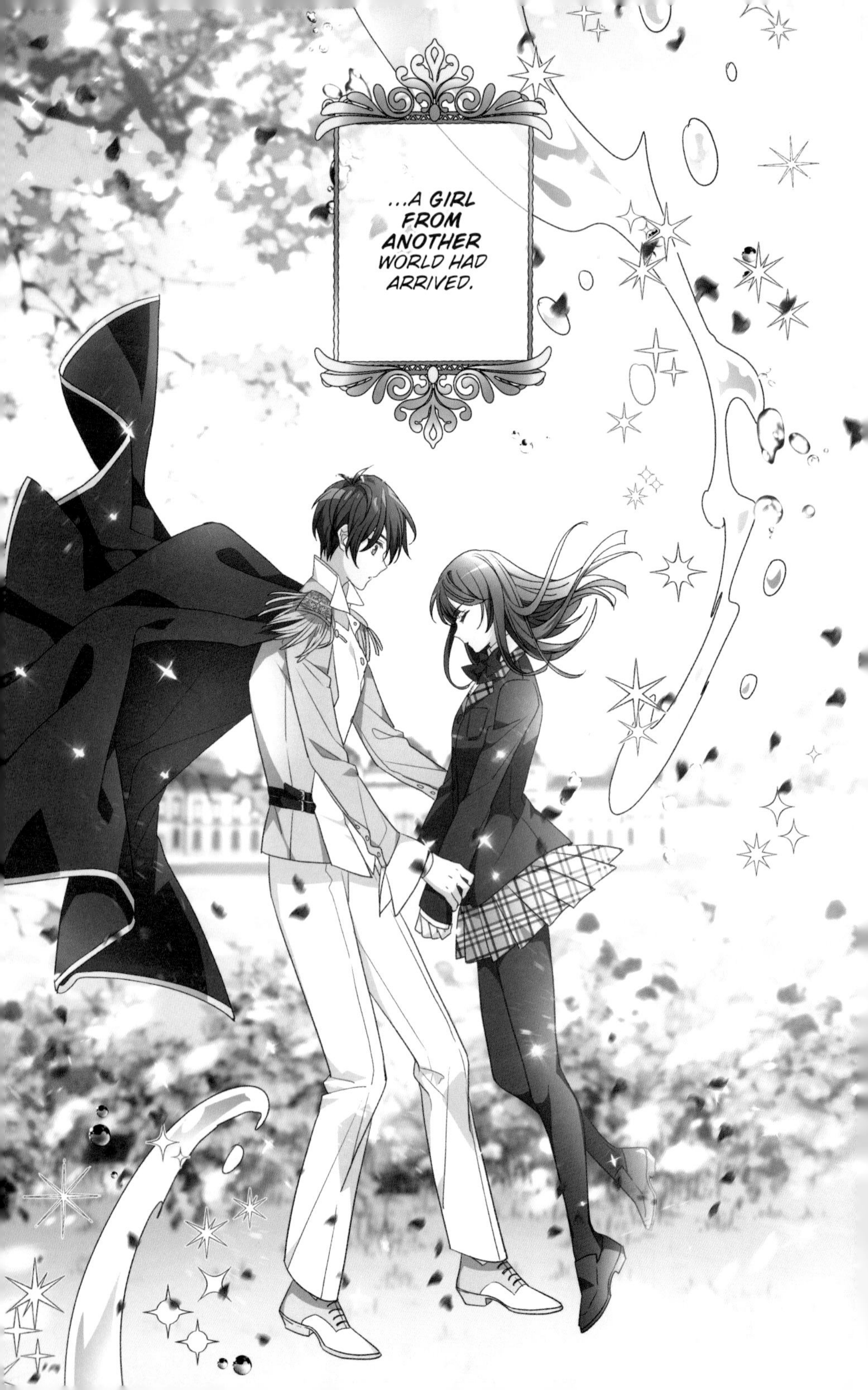
...A GIRL FROM ANOTHER WORLD HAD ARRIVED.

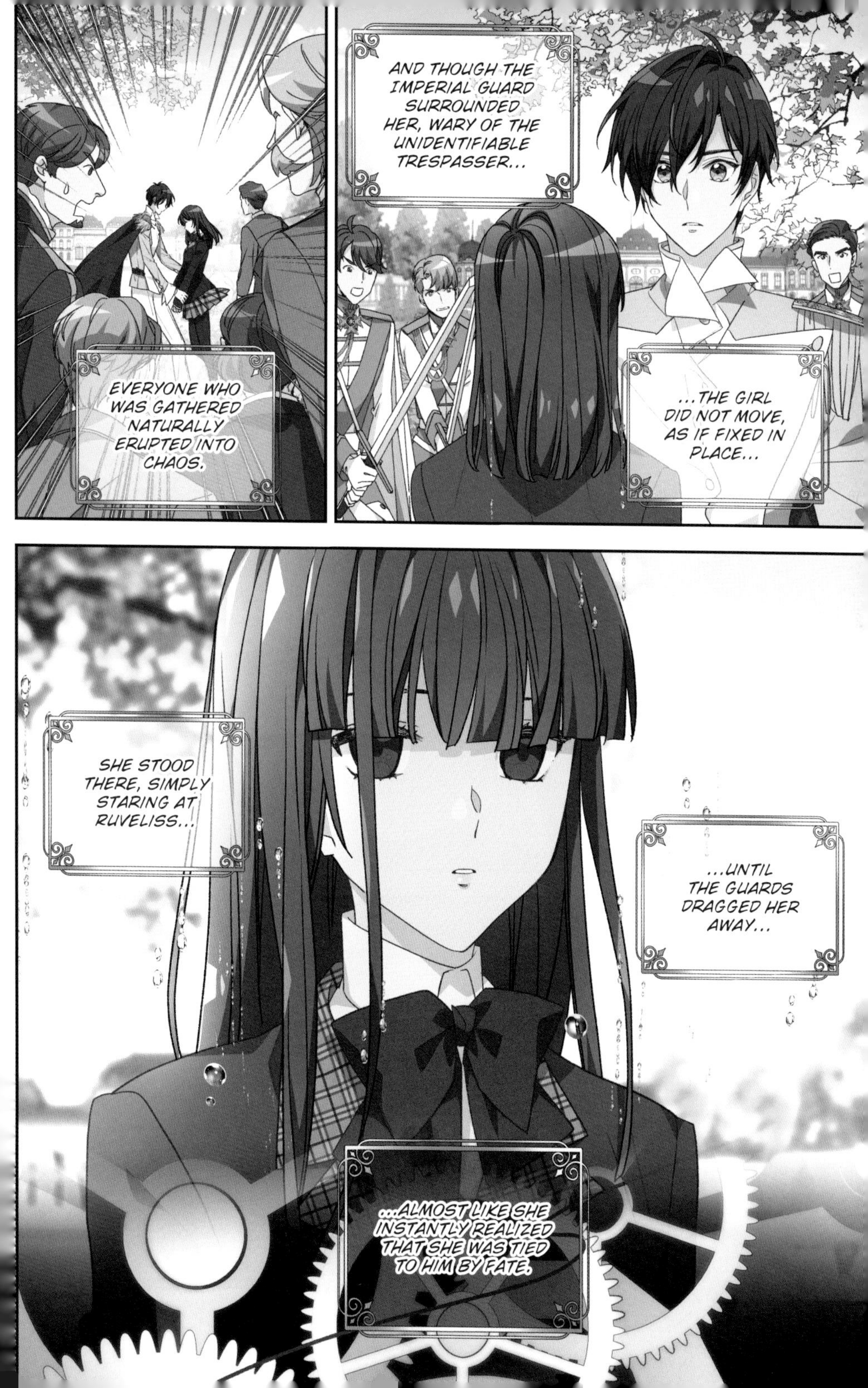
EVERYONE WHO WAS GATHERED NATURALLY ERUPTED INTO CHAOS.
AND THOUGH THE IMPERIAL GUARD SURROUNDED HER, WARY OF THE UNIDENTIFIABLE TRESPASSER...
...THE GIRL DID NOT MOVE, AS IF FIXED IN PLACE...
SHE STOOD THERE, SIMPLY STARING AT RUVELISS...
...UNTIL THE GUARDS DRAGGED HER AWAY...
...ALMOST LIKE SHE INSTANTLY REALIZED THAT SHE WAS TIED TO HIM BY FATE.

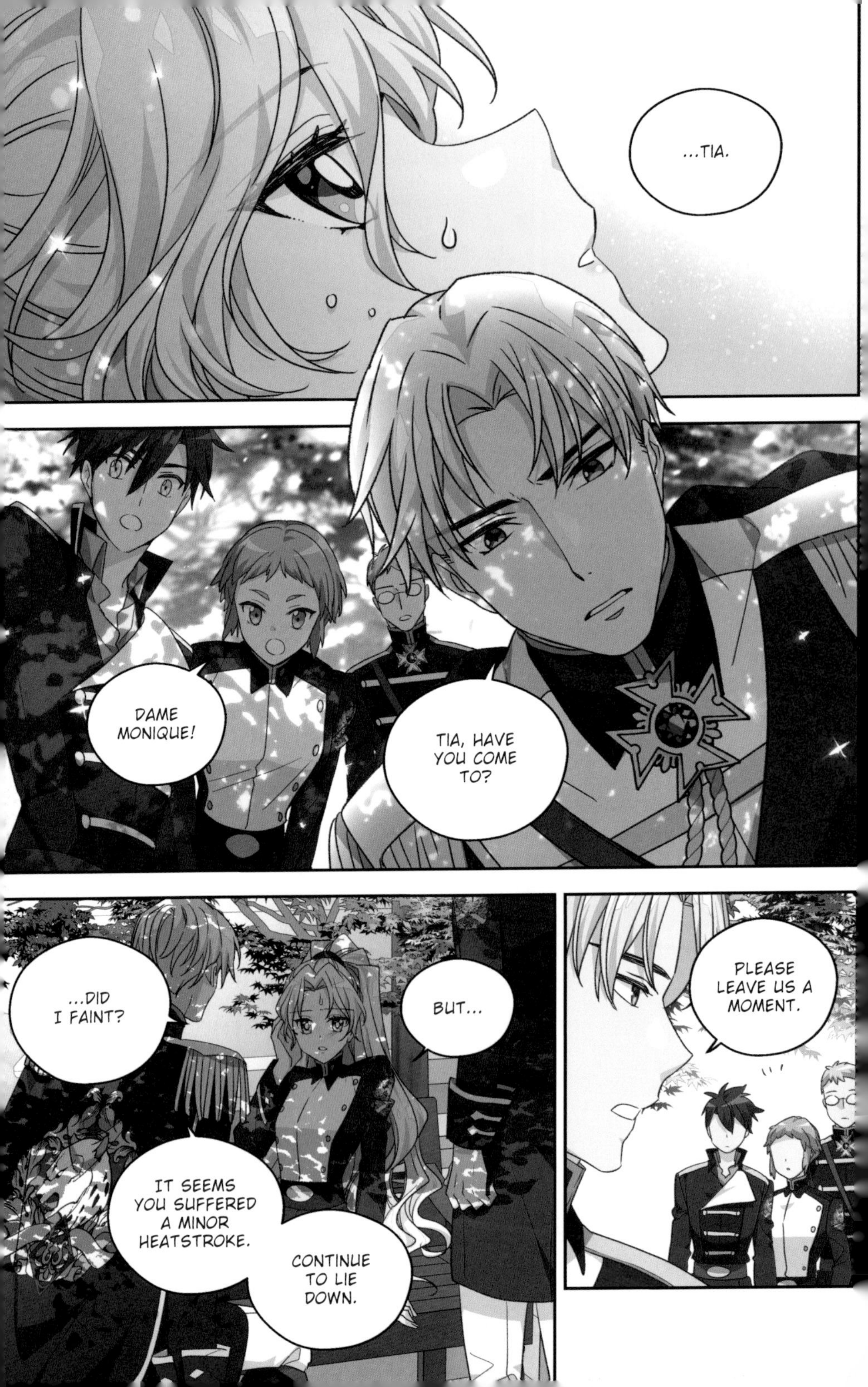
...TIA.
TIA, HAVE YOU COME TO?
DAME MONIQUE!
...DID I FAINT?
BUT...
IT SEEMS YOU SUFFERED A MINOR HEATSTROKE.
CONTINUE TO LIE DOWN.
PLEASE LEAVE US A MOMENT.

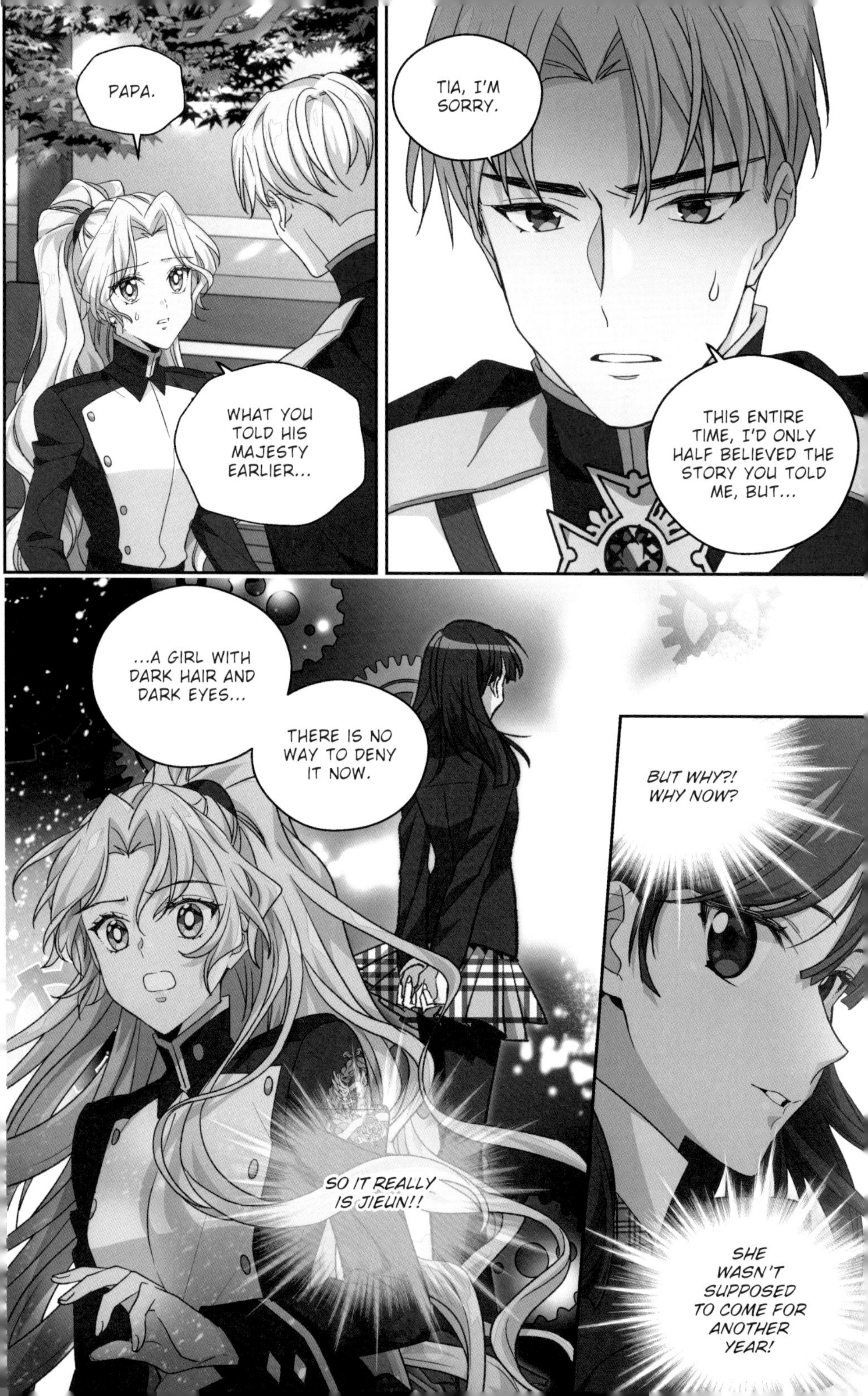
PAPA.
WHAT YOU TOLD HIS MAJESTY EARLIER...
TIA, I'M SORRY.
THIS ENTIRE TIME, I'D ONLY HALF BELIEVED THE STORY YOU TOLD ME, BUT...
...A GIRL WITH DARK HAIR AND DARK EYES...
THERE IS NO WAY TO DENY IT NOW.
SO IT REALLY IS JIEUN!!
BUT WHY?! WHY NOW?
SHE WASN'T SUPPOSED TO COME FOR ANOTHER YEAR!

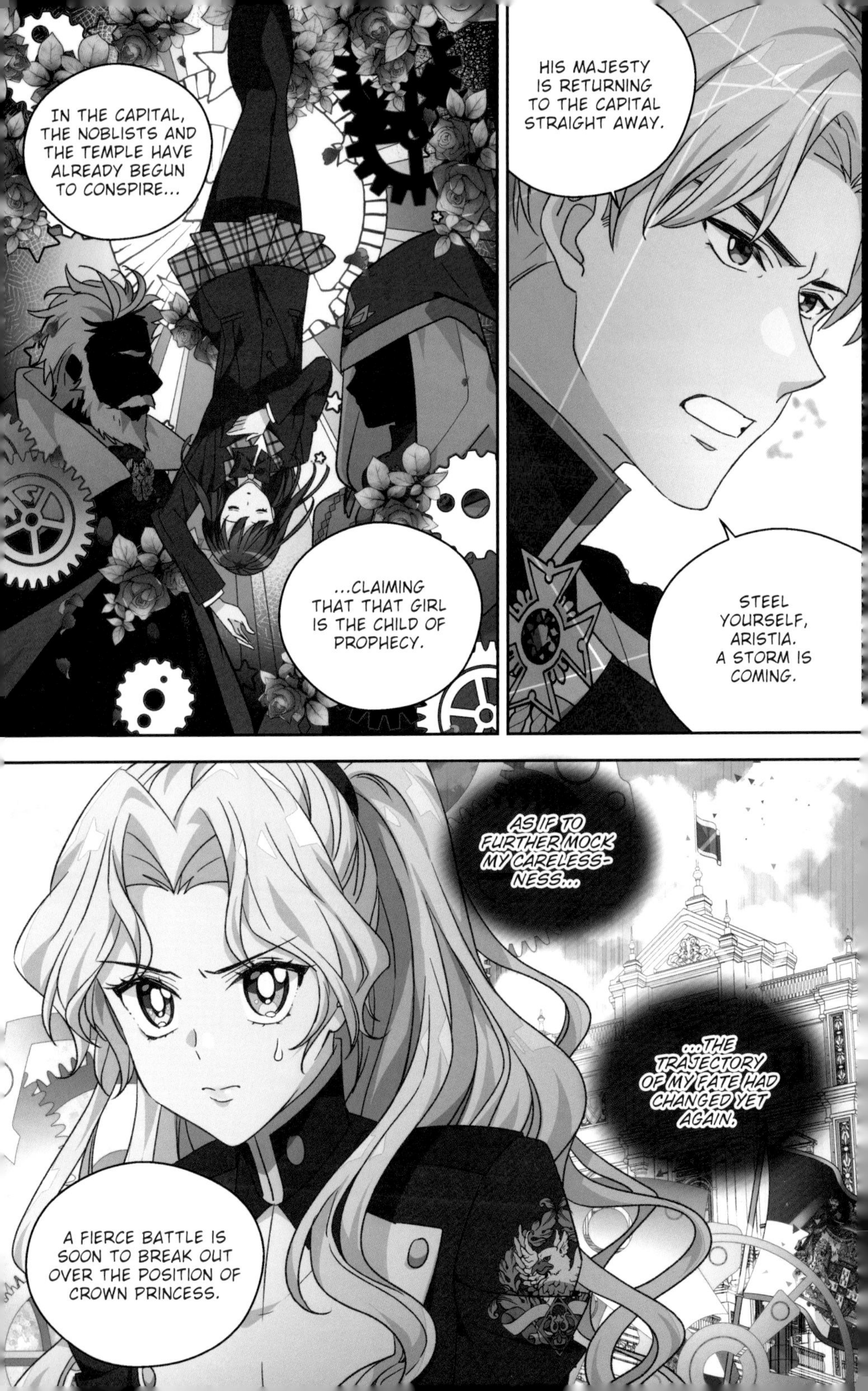
IN THE CAPITAL, THE NOBLISTS AND THE TEMPLE HAVE ALREADY BEGUN TO CONSPIRE...
...CLAIMING THAT THAT GIRL IS THE CHILD OF PROPHECY.
HIS MAJESTY IS RETURNING TO THE CAPITAL STRAIGHT AWAY.
STEEL YOURSELF, ARISTIA. A STORM IS COMING.
AS IF TO FURTHER MOCK MY CARELESS-NESS...
...THE TRAJECTORY OF MY FATE HAD CHANGED YET AGAIN.
A FIERCE BATTLE IS SOON TO BREAK OUT OVER THE POSITION OF CROWN PRINCESS.

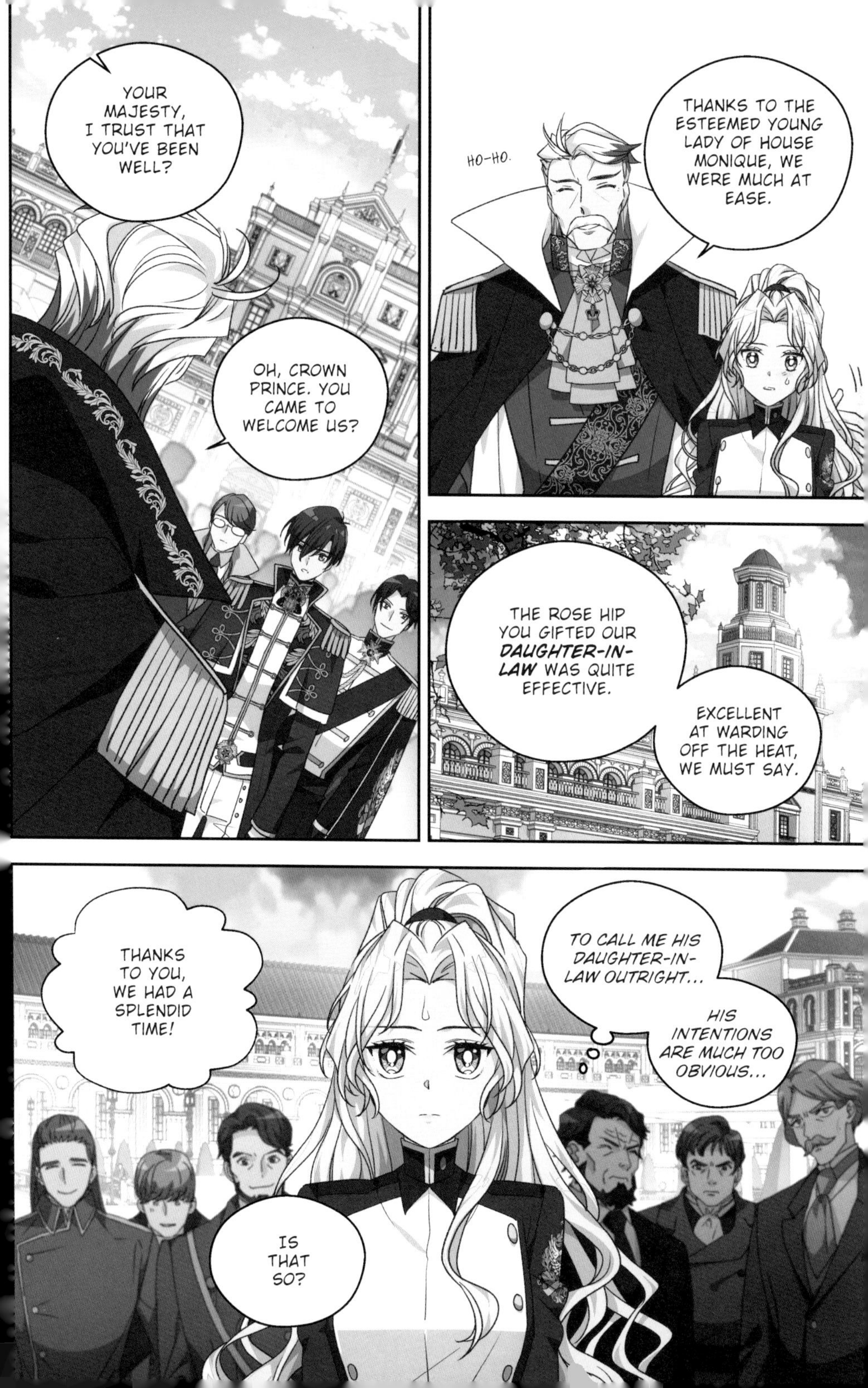
YOUR MAJESTY, I TRUST THAT YOU'VE BEEN WELL?
HO-HO.
THANKS TO THE ESTEEMED YOUNG LADY OF HOUSE MONIQUE, WE WERE MUCH AT EASE.
OH, CROWN PRINCE. YOU CAME TO WELCOME US?
THE ROSE HIP YOU GIFTED OUR *DAUGHTER-IN-LAW* WAS QUITE EFFECTIVE.
EXCELLENT AT WARDING OFF THE HEAT, WE MUST SAY.
THANKS TO YOU, WE HAD A SPLENDID TIME!
TO CALL ME HIS DAUGHTER-IN-LAW OUTRIGHT...
HIS INTENTIONS ARE MUCH TOO OBVIOUS...
IS THAT SO?

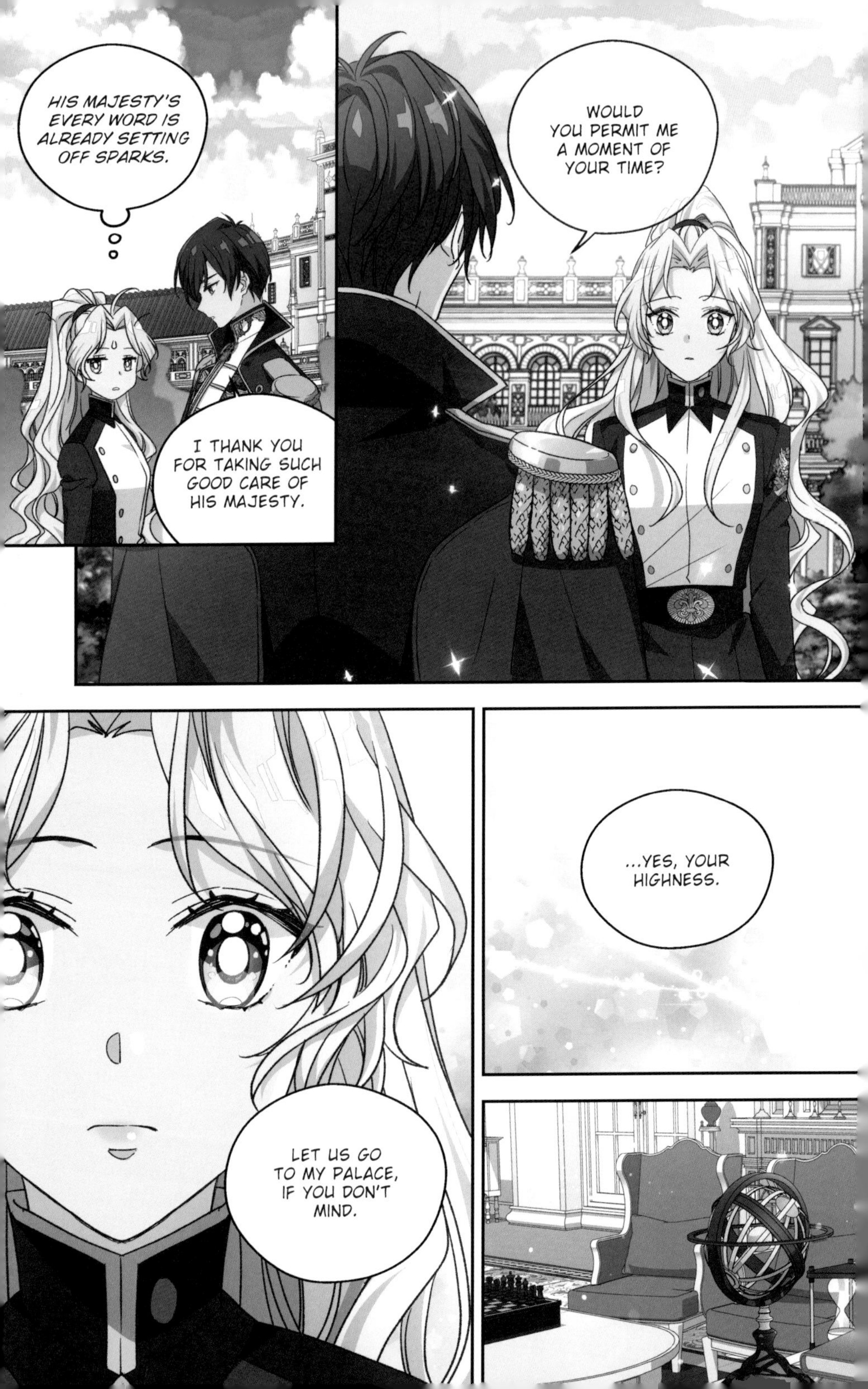
HIS MAJESTY'S EVERY WORD IS ALREADY SETTING OFF SPARKS.
I THANK YOU FOR TAKING SUCH GOOD CARE OF HIS MAJESTY.
WOULD YOU PERMIT ME A MOMENT OF YOUR TIME?
LET US GO TO MY PALACE, IF YOU DON'T MIND.
...YES, YOUR HIGHNESS.

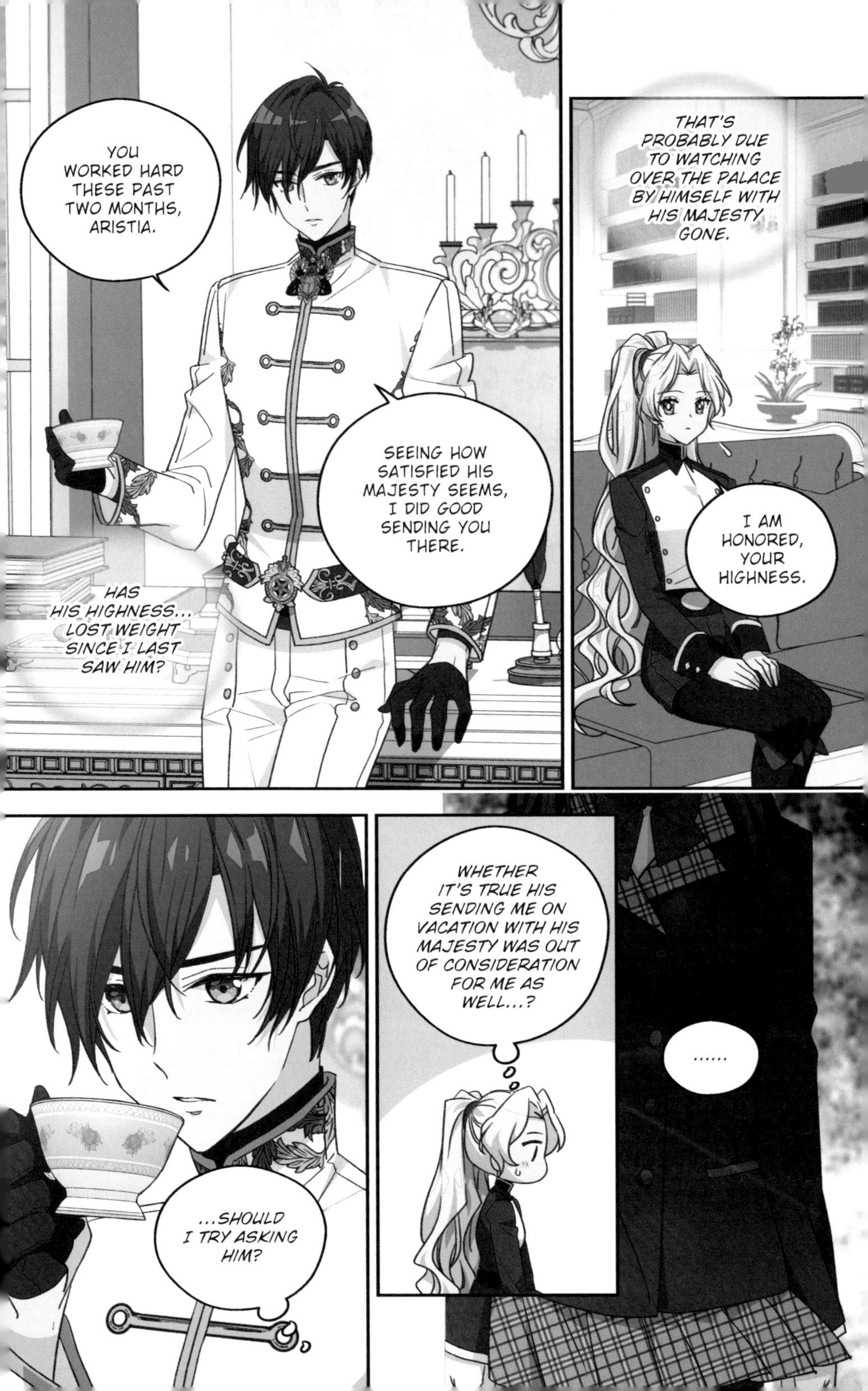
YOU WORKED HARD THESE PAST TWO MONTHS, ARISTIA.
SEEING HOW SATISFIED HIS MAJESTY SEEMS, I DID GOOD SENDING YOU THERE.
HAS HIS HIGHNESS... LOST WEIGHT SINCE I LAST SAW HIM?
THAT'S PROBABLY DUE TO WATCHING OVER THE PALACE BY HIMSELF WITH HIS MAJESTY GONE.
I AM HONORED, YOUR HIGHNESS.
WHETHER IT'S TRUE HIS SENDING ME ON VACATION WITH HIS MAJESTY WAS OUT OF CONSIDERATION FOR ME AS WELL...?
......
...SHOULD I TRY ASKING HIM?

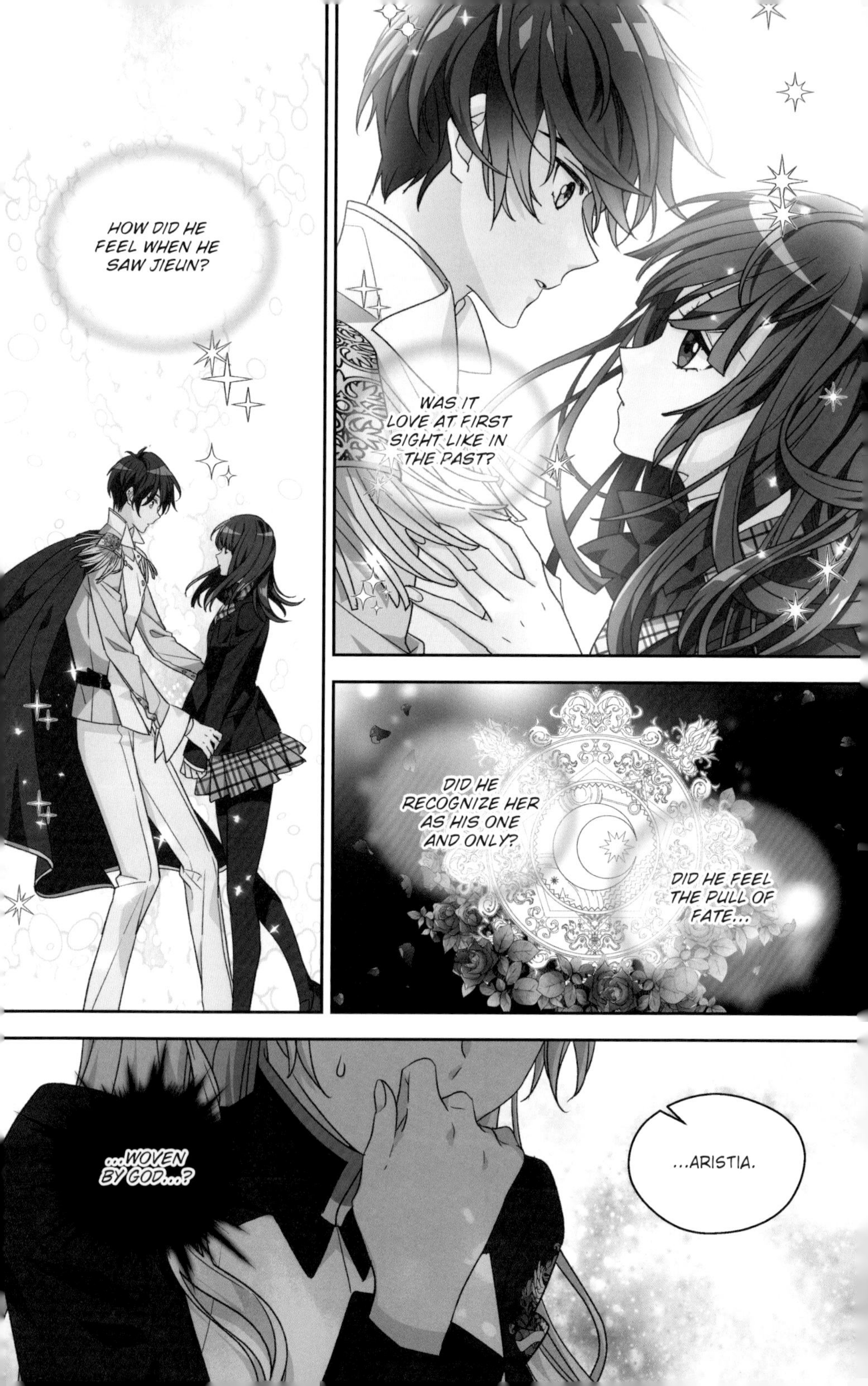
HOW DID HE FEEL WHEN HE SAW JIEUN?
WAS IT LOVE AT FIRST SIGHT LIKE IN THE PAST?
DID HE RECOGNIZE HER AS HIS ONE AND ONLY?
DID HE FEEL THE PULL OF FATE...
...WOVEN BY GOD...?
...ARISTIA.

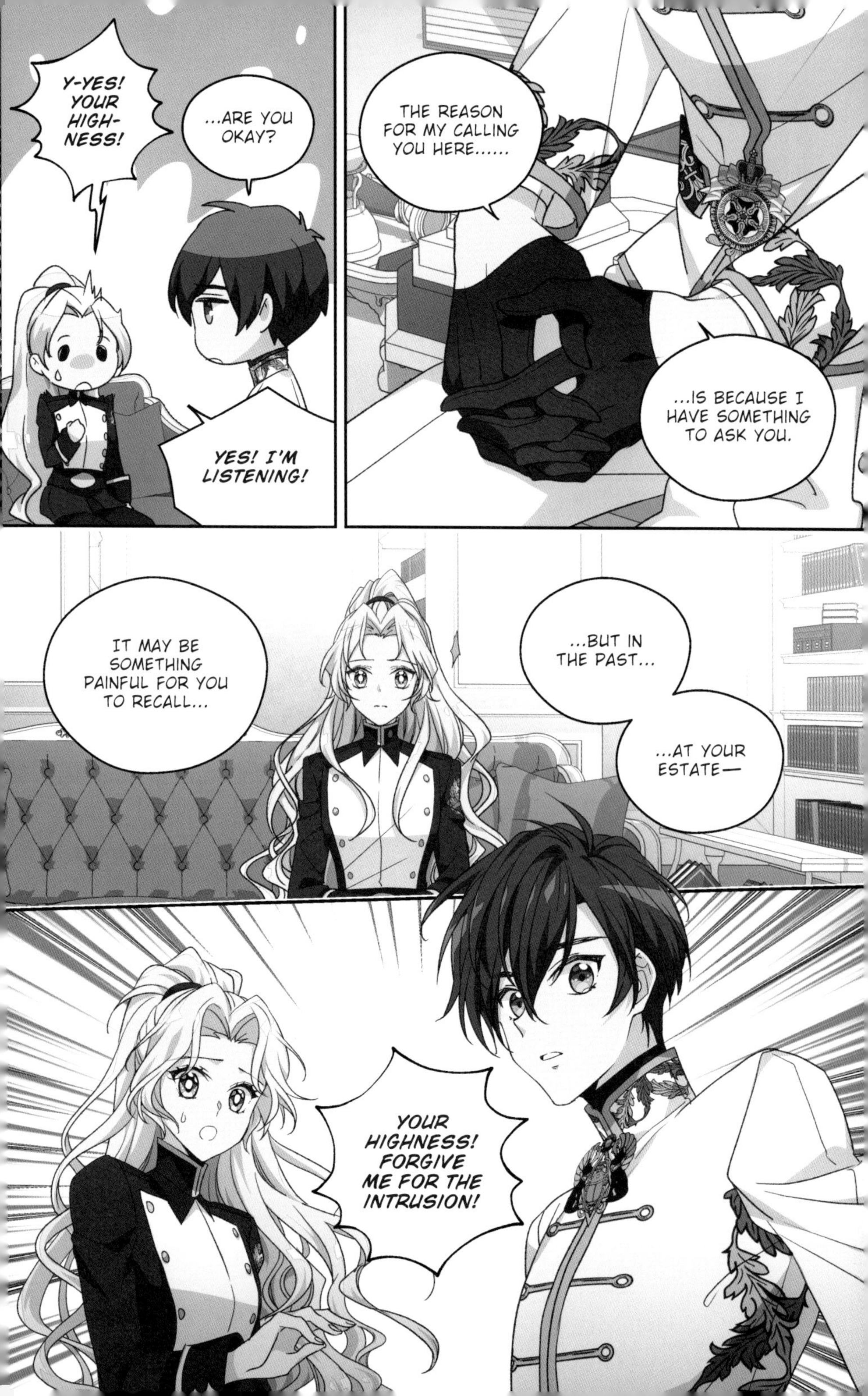
Y-YES! YOUR HIGH-NESS!
...ARE YOU OKAY?
YES! I'M LISTENING!
THE REASON FOR MY CALLING YOU HERE......
...IS BECAUSE I HAVE SOMETHING TO ASK YOU.
IT MAY BE SOMETHING PAINFUL FOR YOU TO RECALL...
...BUT IN THE PAST...
...AT YOUR ESTATE—
YOUR HIGHNESS! FORGIVE ME FOR THE INTRUSION!

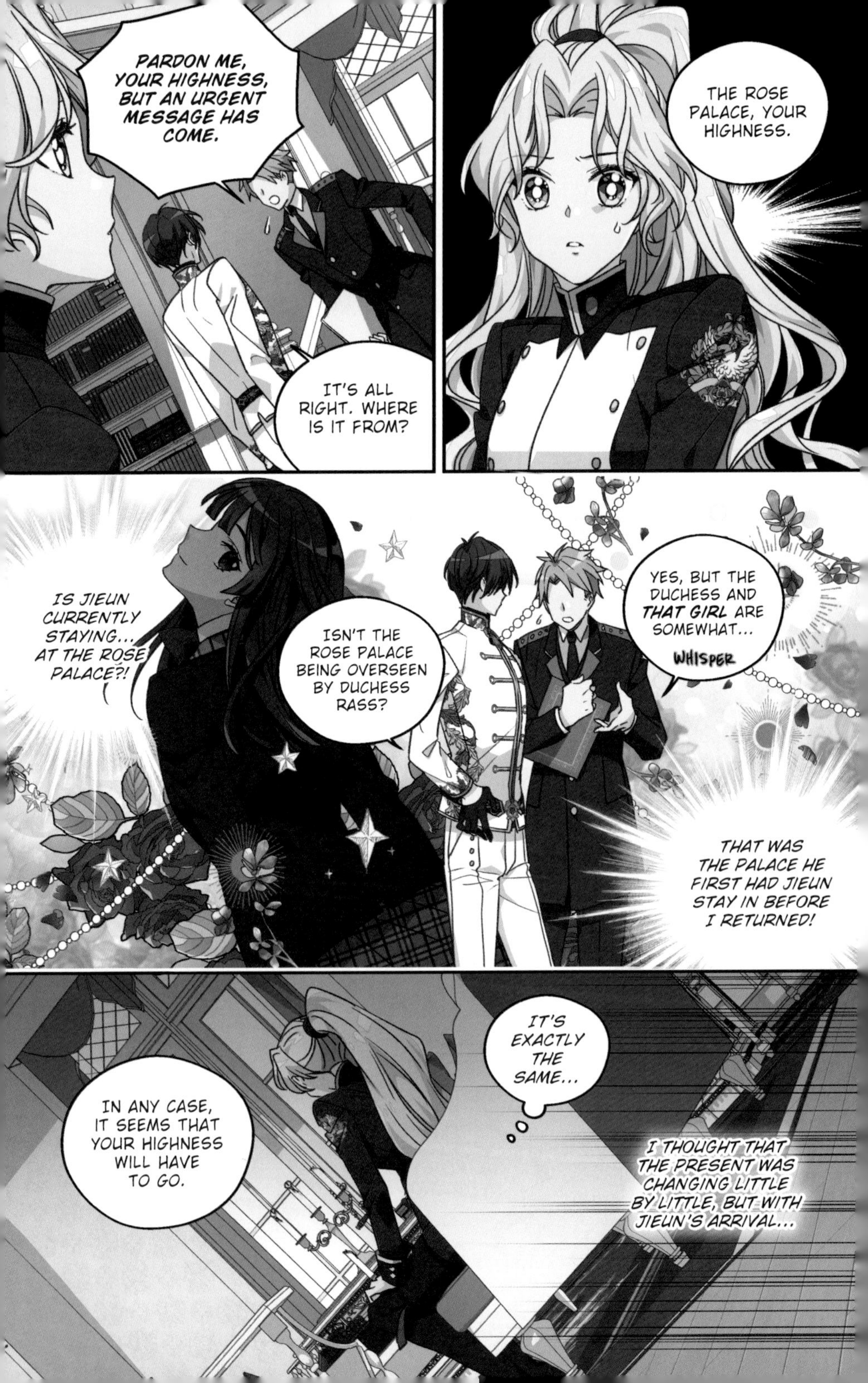
PARDON ME, YOUR HIGHNESS, BUT AN URGENT MESSAGE HAS COME.
IT'S ALL RIGHT. WHERE IS IT FROM?
THE ROSE PALACE, YOUR HIGHNESS.
IS JIEUN CURRENTLY STAYING... AT THE ROSE PALACE?!
ISN'T THE ROSE PALACE BEING OVERSEEN BY DUCHESS RASS?
YES, BUT THE DUCHESS AND THAT GIRL ARE SOMEWHAT...
WHISPER
THAT WAS THE PALACE HE FIRST HAD JIEUN STAY IN BEFORE I RETURNED!
IT'S EXACTLY THE SAME...
IN ANY CASE, IT SEEMS THAT YOUR HIGHNESS WILL HAVE TO GO.
I THOUGHT THAT THE PRESENT WAS CHANGING LITTLE BY LITTLE, BUT WITH JIEUN'S ARRIVAL...

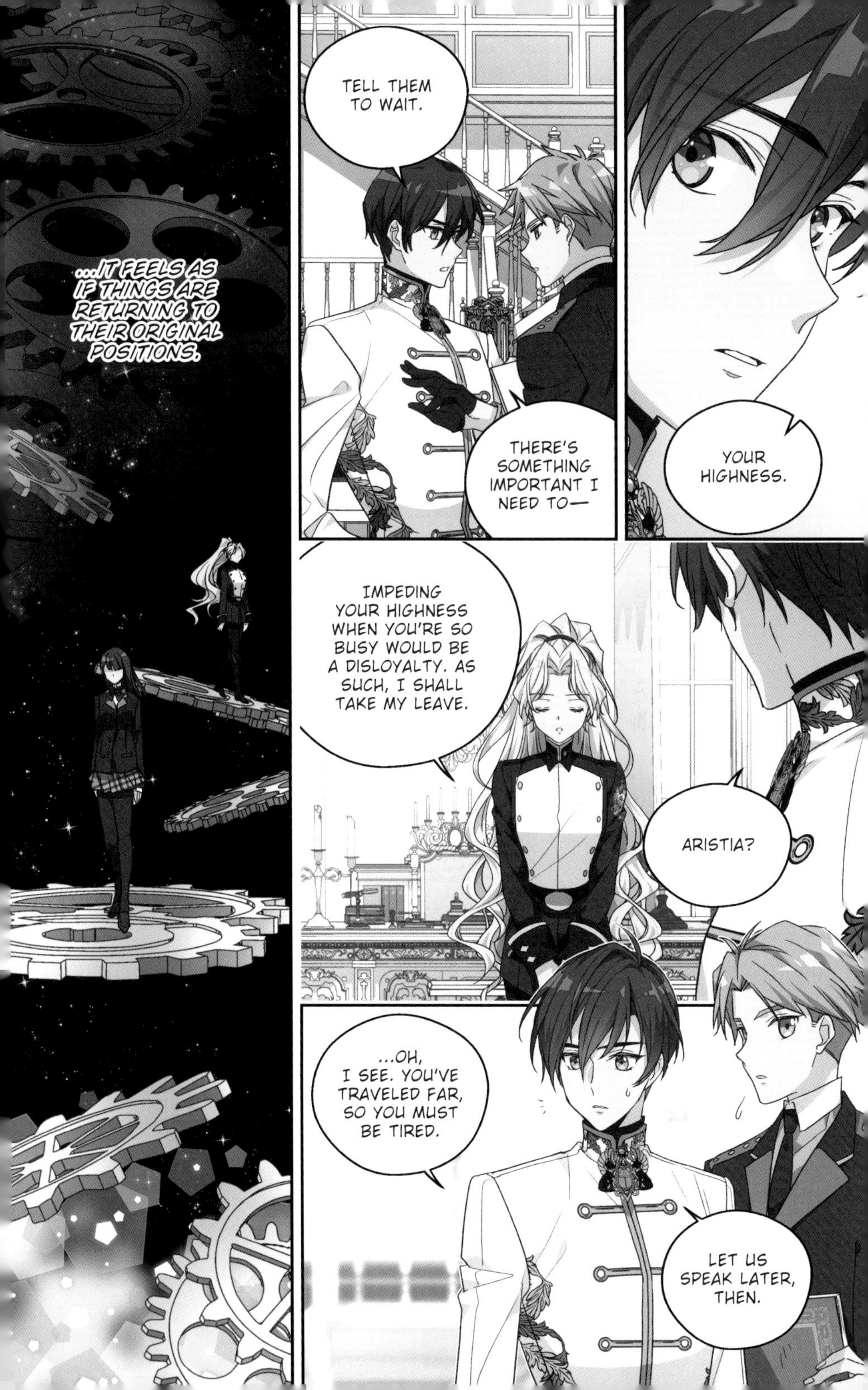
...IT FEELS AS IF THINGS ARE RETURNING TO THEIR ORIGINAL POSITIONS.
TELL THEM TO WAIT.
THERE'S SOMETHING IMPORTANT I NEED TO—
YOUR HIGHNESS.
IMPEDING YOUR HIGHNESS WHEN YOU'RE SO BUSY WOULD BE A DISLOYALTY. AS SUCH, I SHALL TAKE MY LEAVE.
ARISTIA?
...OH, I SEE. YOU'VE TRAVELED FAR, SO YOU MUST BE TIRED.
LET US SPEAK LATER, THEN.

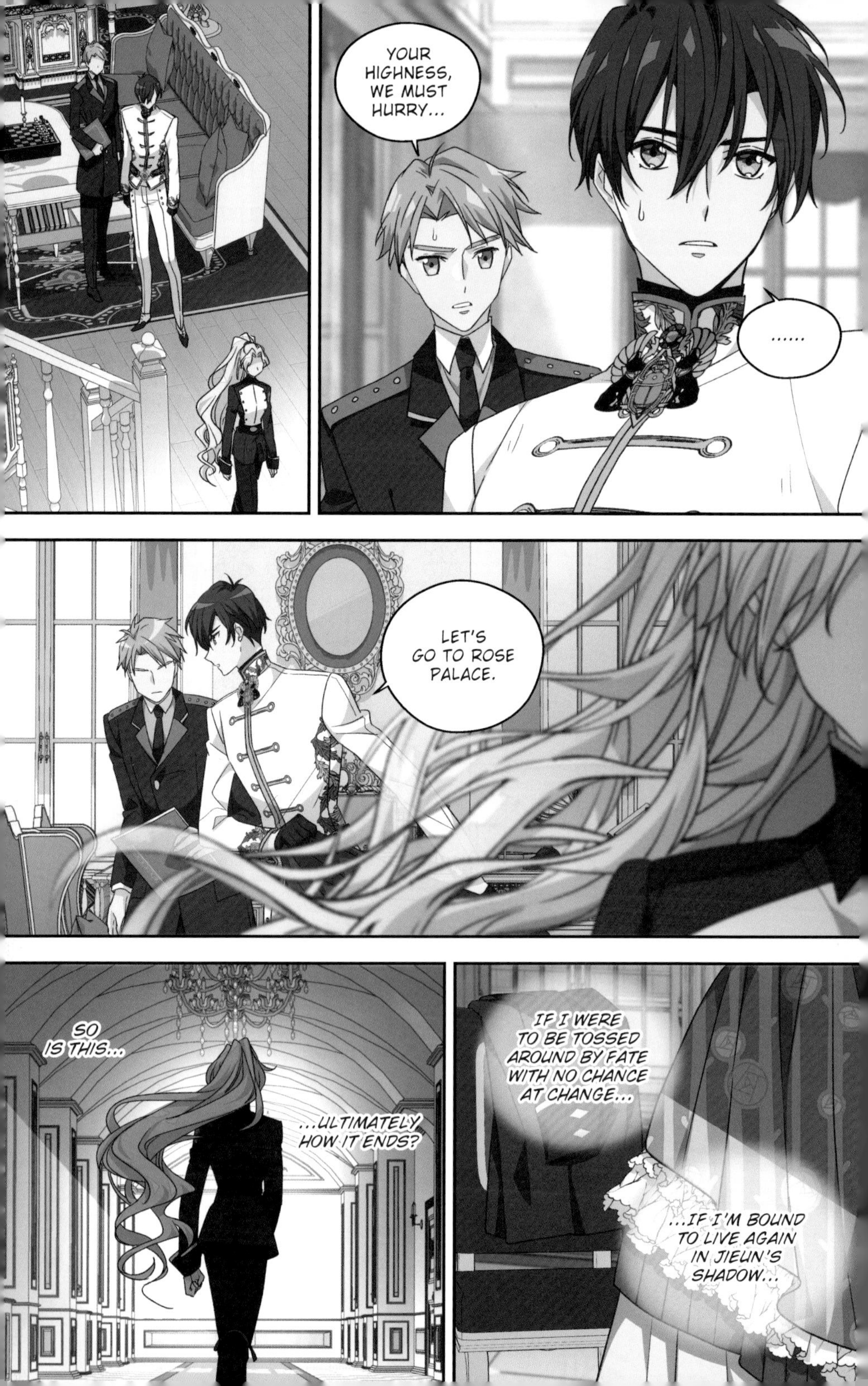
YOUR HIGHNESS, WE MUST HURRY...
......
LET'S GO TO ROSE PALACE.
SO IS THIS...
...ULTIMATELY HOW IT ENDS?
IF I WERE TO BE TOSSED AROUND BY FATE WITH NO CHANCE AT CHANGE...
...IF I'M BOUND TO LIVE AGAIN IN JIEUN'S SHADOW...

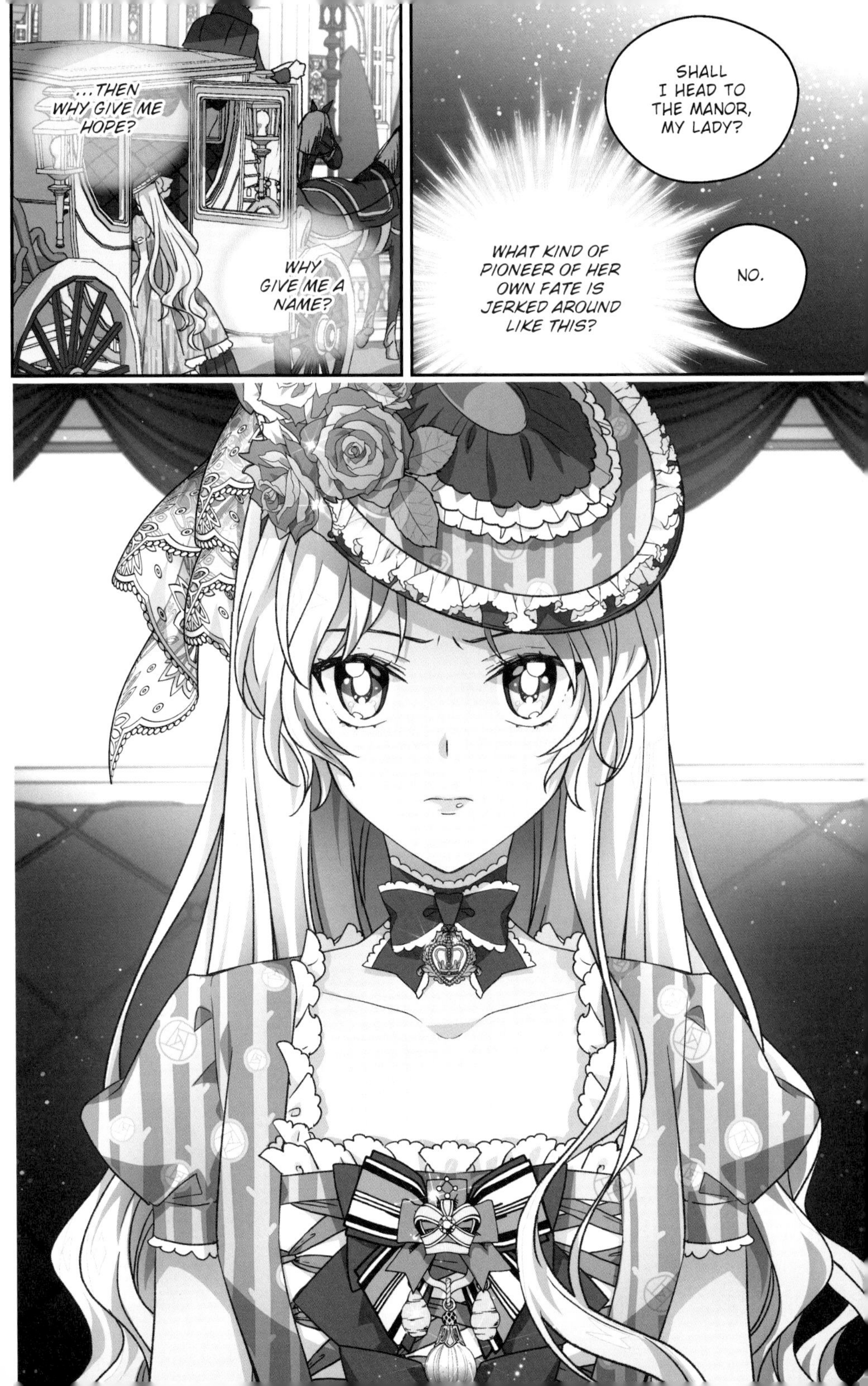

...THEN WHY GIVE ME HOPE?
WHY GIVE ME A NAME?
SHALL I HEAD TO THE MANOR, MY LADY?
WHAT KIND OF PIONEER OF HER OWN FATE IS JERKED AROUND LIKE THIS?
NO.

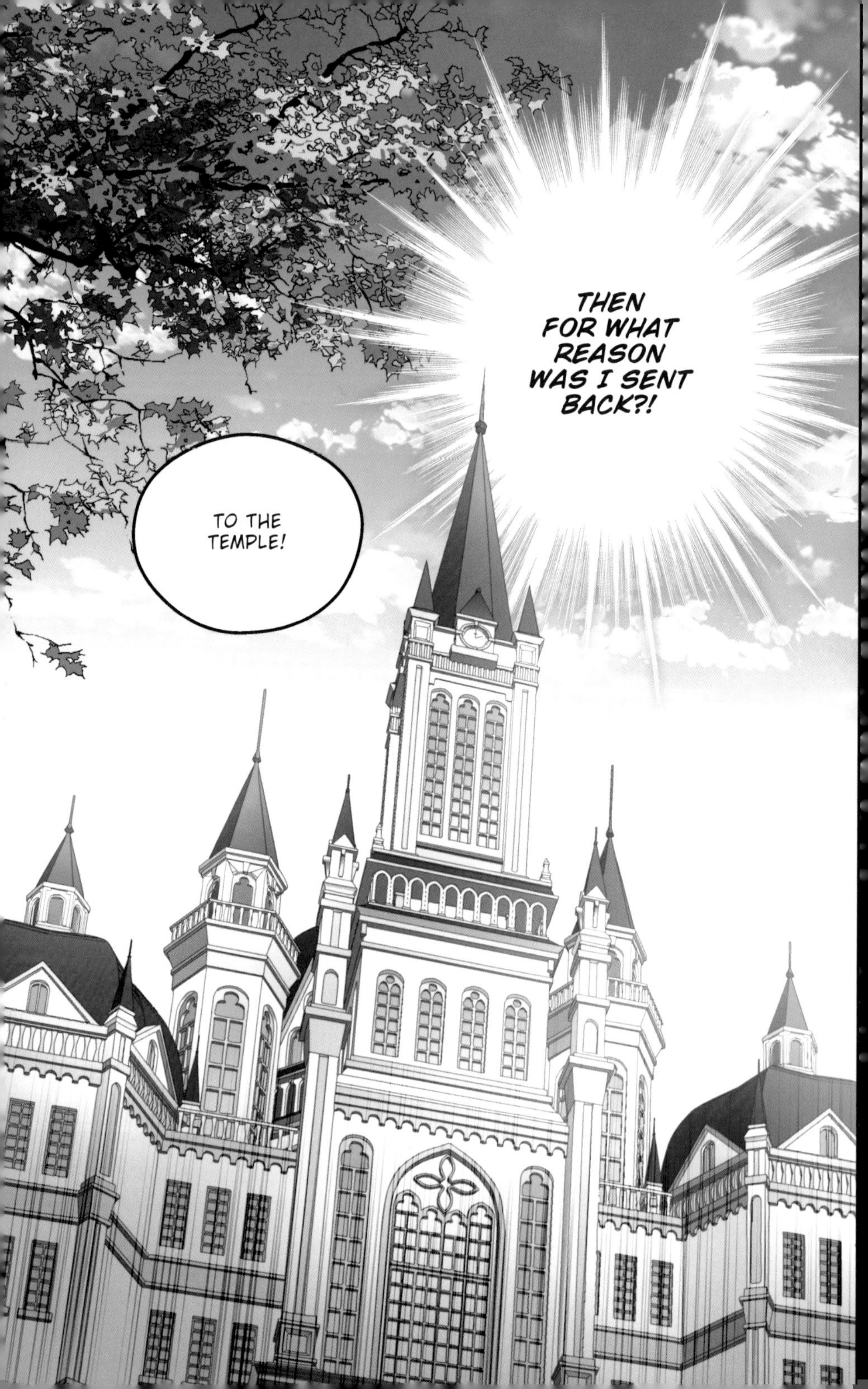
THEN FOR WHAT REASON WAS I SENT BACK?!
TO THE TEMPLE!

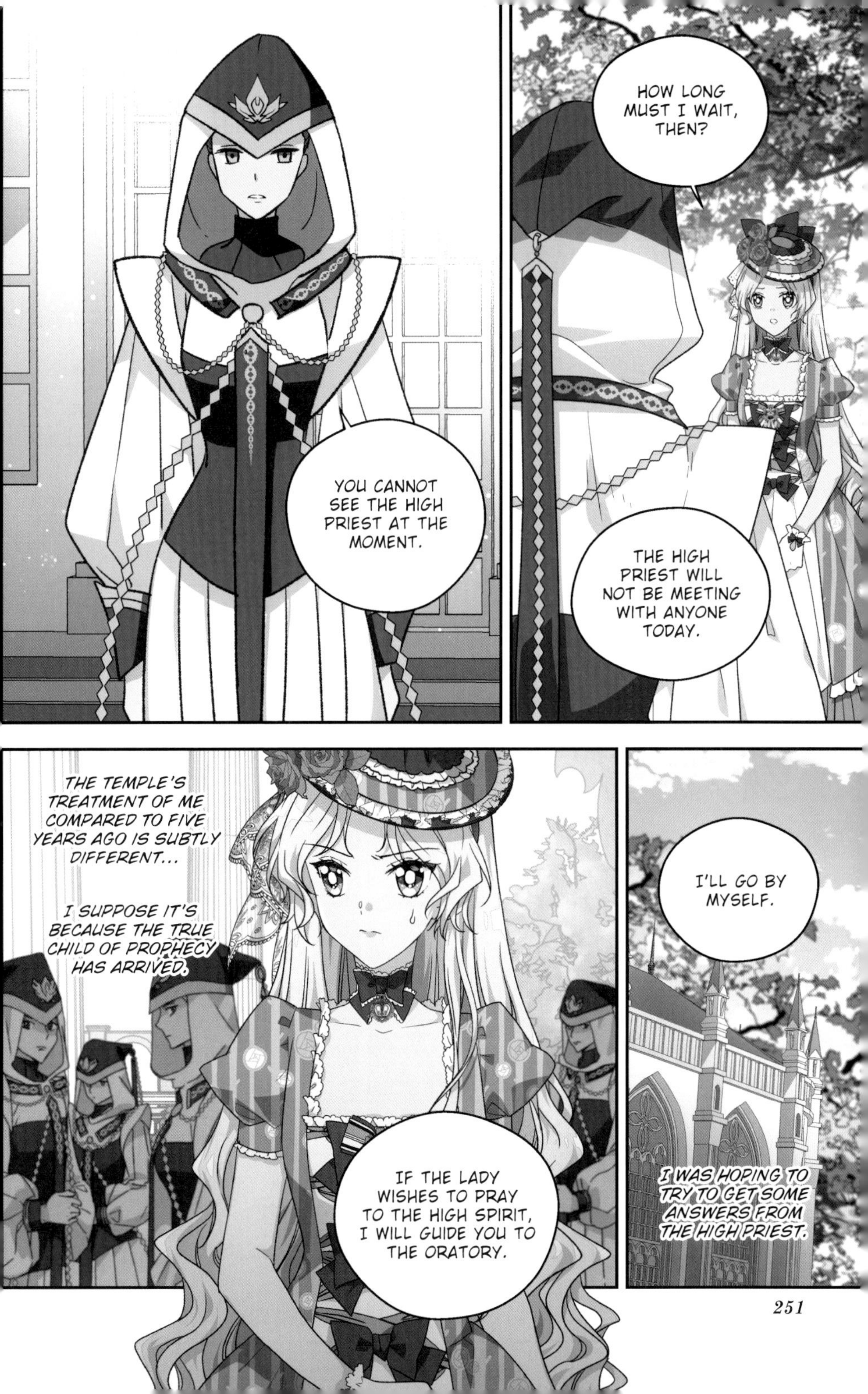
YOU CANNOT SEE THE HIGH PRIEST AT THE MOMENT.
HOW LONG MUST I WAIT, THEN?
THE HIGH PRIEST WILL NOT BE MEETING WITH ANYONE TODAY.
THE TEMPLE'S TREATMENT OF ME COMPARED TO FIVE YEARS AGO IS SUBTLY DIFFERENT...
I SUPPOSE IT'S BECAUSE THE TRUE CHILD OF PROPHECY HAS ARRIVED.
IF THE LADY WISHES TO PRAY TO THE HIGH SPIRIT, I WILL GUIDE YOU TO THE ORATORY.
I'LL GO BY MYSELF.
I WAS HOPING TO TRY TO GET SOME ANSWERS FROM THE HIGH PRIEST.

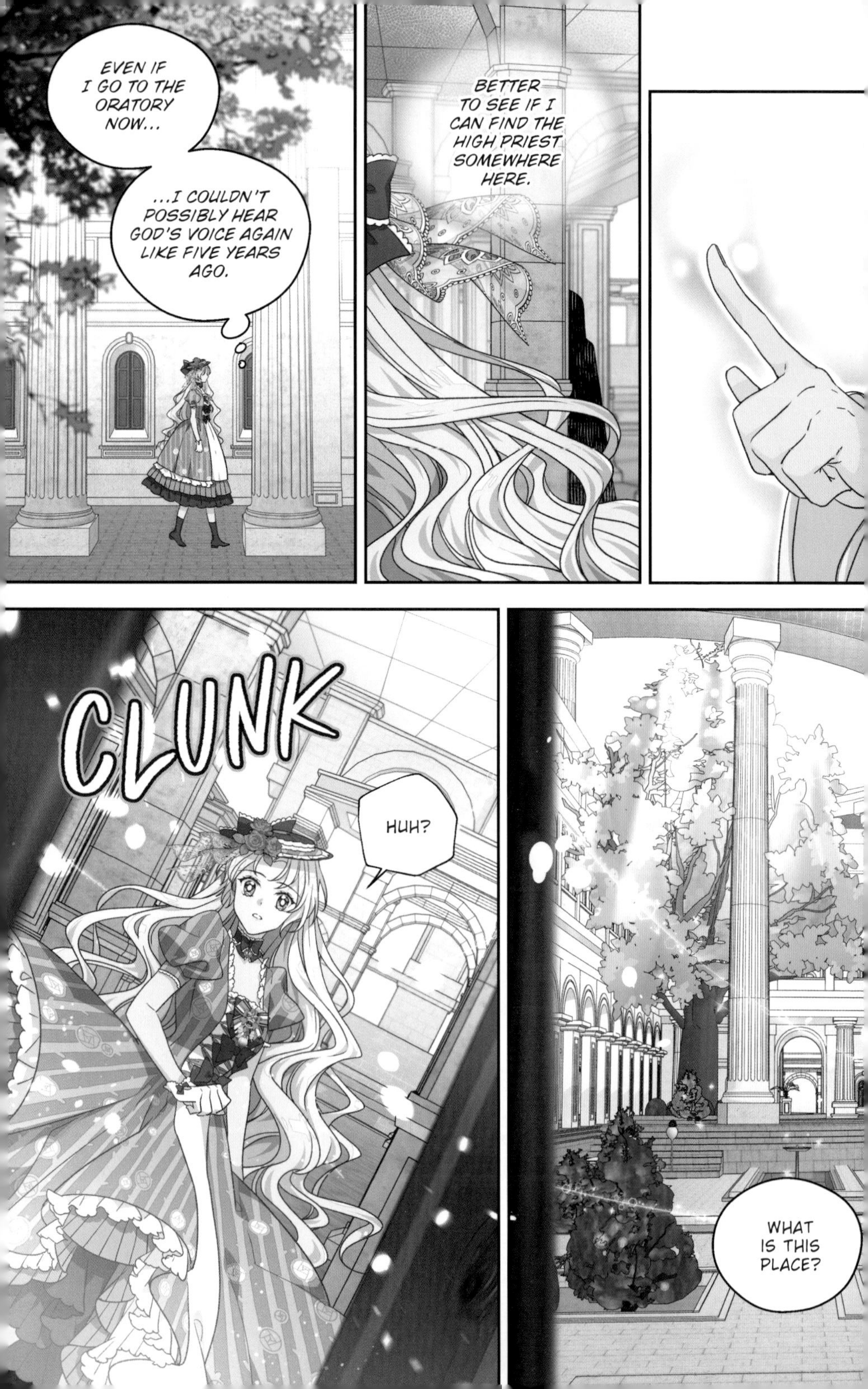
EVEN IF I GO TO THE ORATORY NOW...
...I COULDN'T POSSIBLY HEAR GOD'S VOICE AGAIN LIKE FIVE YEARS AGO.
BETTER TO SEE IF I CAN FIND THE HIGH PRIEST SOMEWHERE HERE.
CLUNK
HUH?
WHAT IS THIS PLACE?

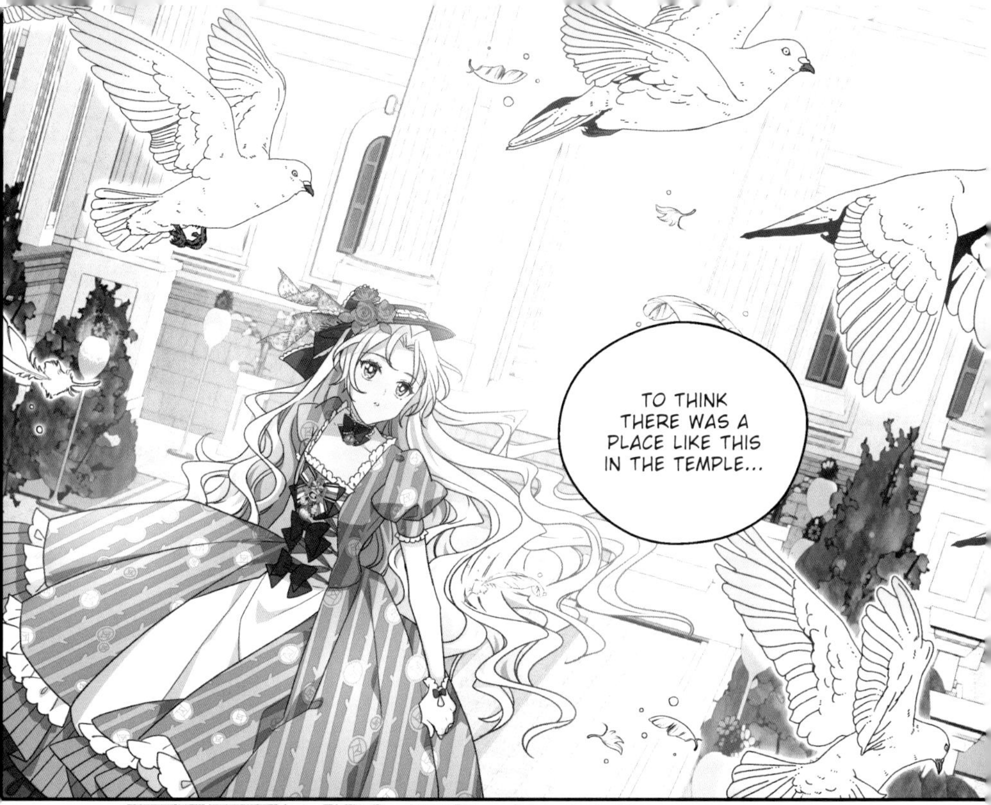
TO THINK THERE WAS A PLACE LIKE THIS IN THE TEMPLE...

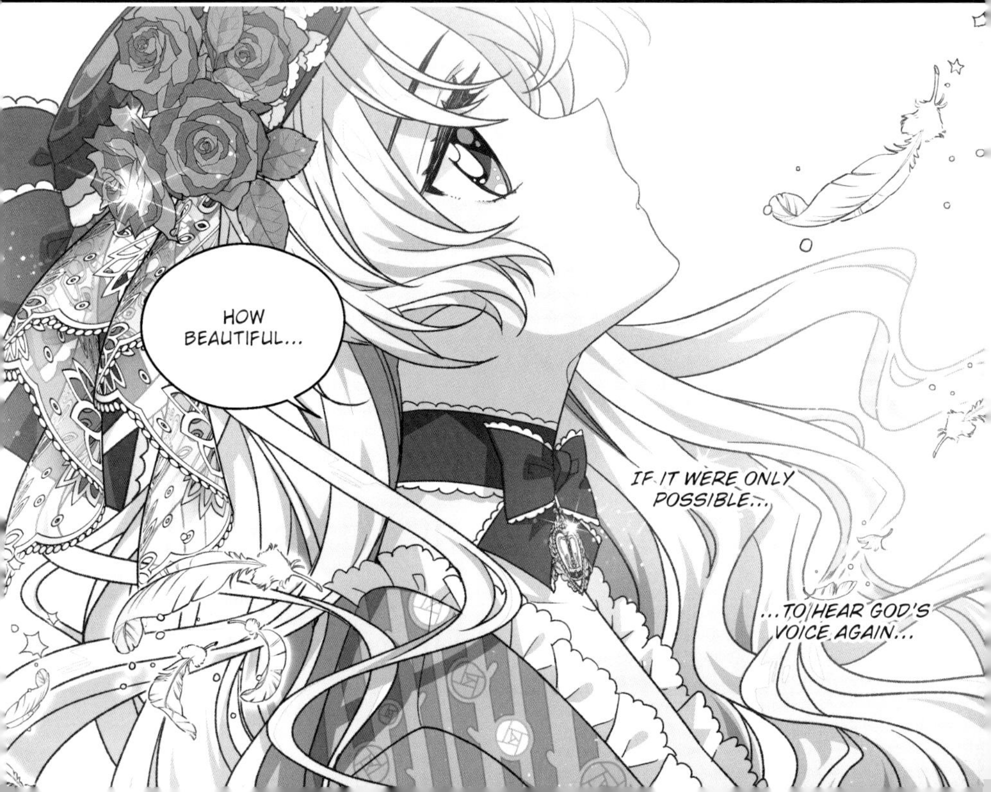
HOW BEAUTIFUL...
IF IT WERE ONLY POSSIBLE...
...TO HEAR GOD'S VOICE AGAIN...

THOU ART MY BELOVED CHILD. A CHILD WHO DWELLS AT PEACE WITH FATE.

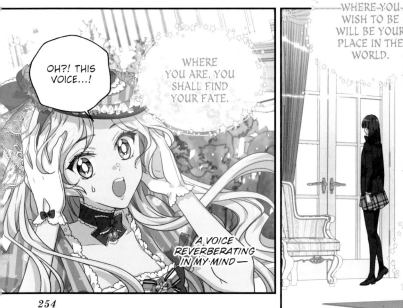

OH?! THIS VOICE...!

WHERE YOU ARE, YOU SHALL FIND YOUR FATE.

A VOICE REVERBERATING IN MY MIND—

WHERE YOU WISH TO BE WILL BE YOUR PLACE IN THE WORLD.

A VOICE I'VE HEARD ONCE BEFORE...!

...THAT LEAVES SUCH A STRONG PRESENCE AS IT ECHOES OUT.

YOUR NAME SHALL BE "THE ONE WHO HOLDS HER OWN FATE."

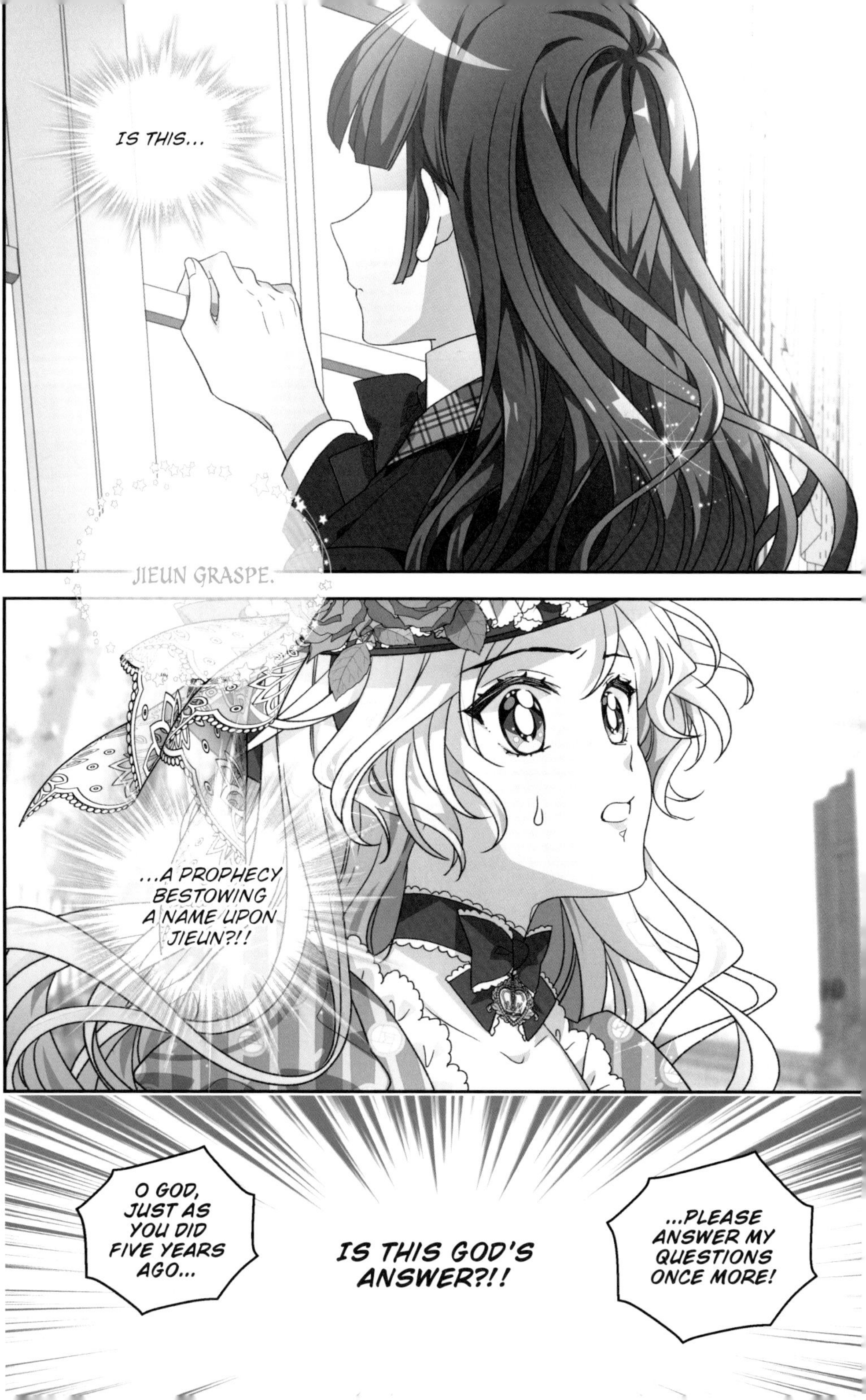
IS THIS...
JIEUN GRASPE.
...A PROPHECY BESTOWING A NAME UPON JIEUN?!!
O GOD, JUST AS YOU DID FIVE YEARS AGO...
IS THIS GOD'S ANSWER?!!
...PLEASE ANSWER MY QUESTIONS ONCE MORE!

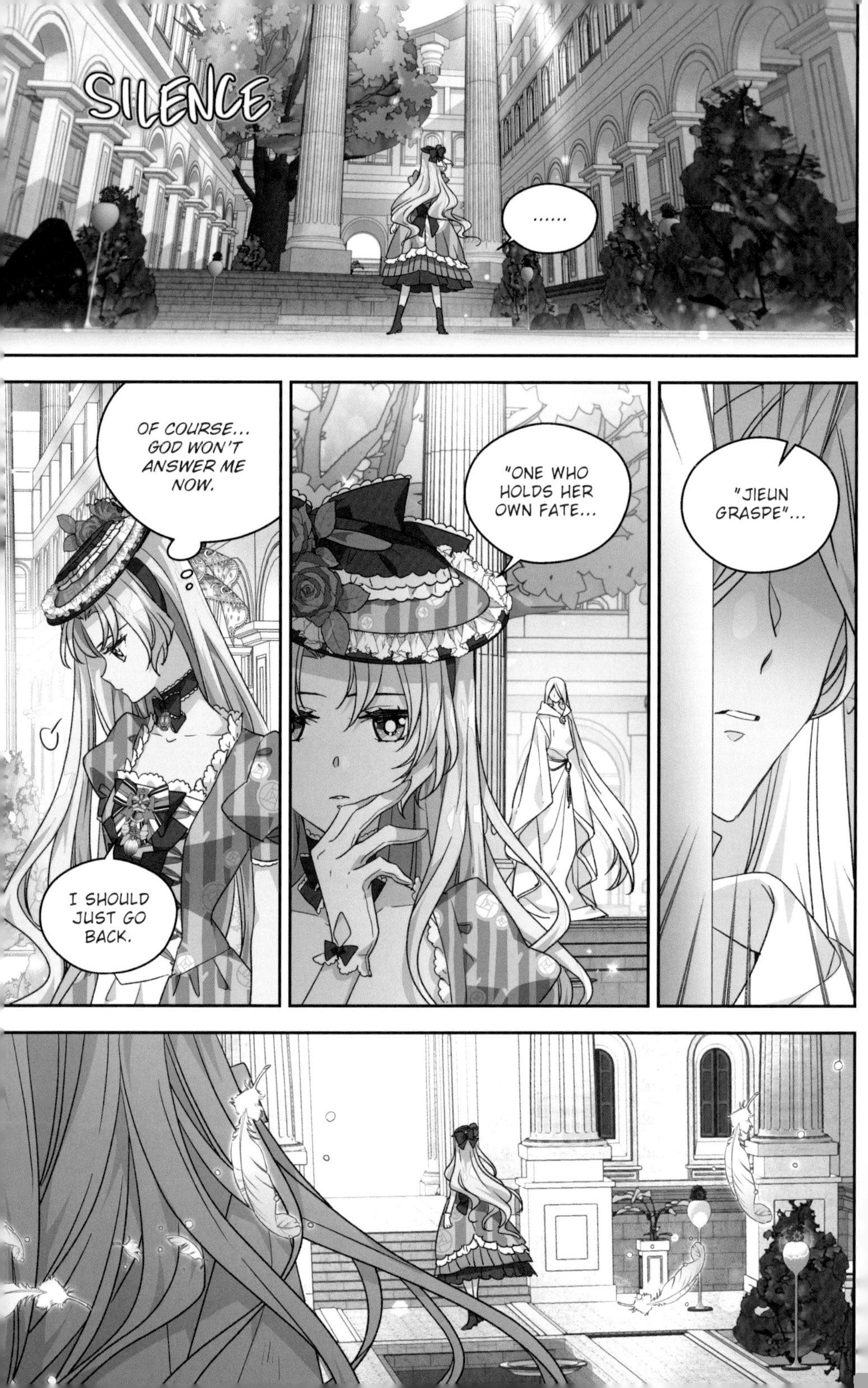
SILENCE
......
OF COURSE... GOD WON'T ANSWER ME NOW.
I SHOULD JUST GO BACK.
"ONE WHO HOLDS HER OWN FATE...
"JIEUN GRASPE"...

The Abandoned Empress

♦ Bonus Comics ♦

♦ The Path the Princess Walks

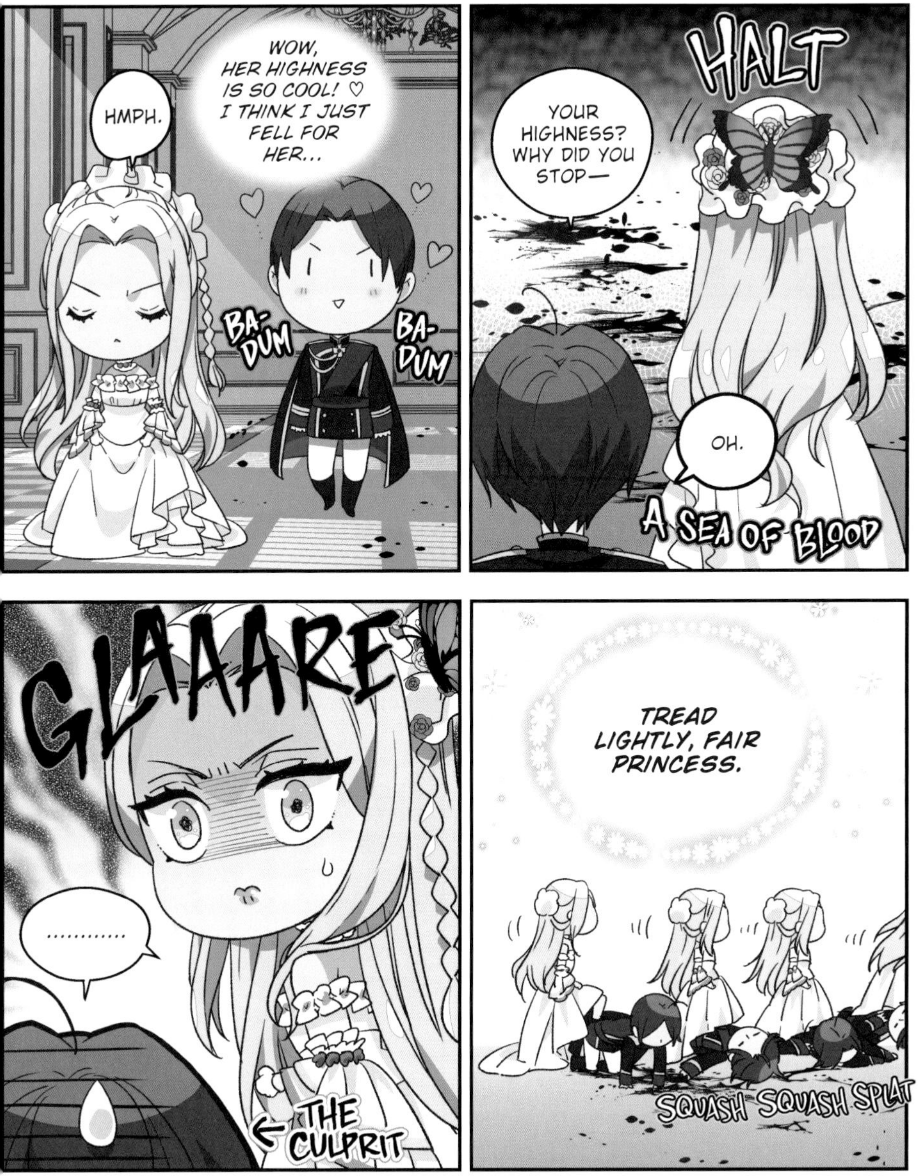
HMPH.
WOW, HER HIGHNESS IS SO COOL! ♡ I THINK I JUST FELL FOR HER...
BA-DUM
BA-DUM
HALT
YOUR HIGHNESS? WHY DID YOU STOP—
OH.
A SEA OF BLOOD
GLAAARE
....
← THE CULPRIT
TREAD LIGHTLY, FAIR PRINCESS.
SQUASH SQUASH SPLAT

LOVE CAN BRING A KNIGHT TO HIS KNEES.

♦ A Tale That May Or May Not Be True

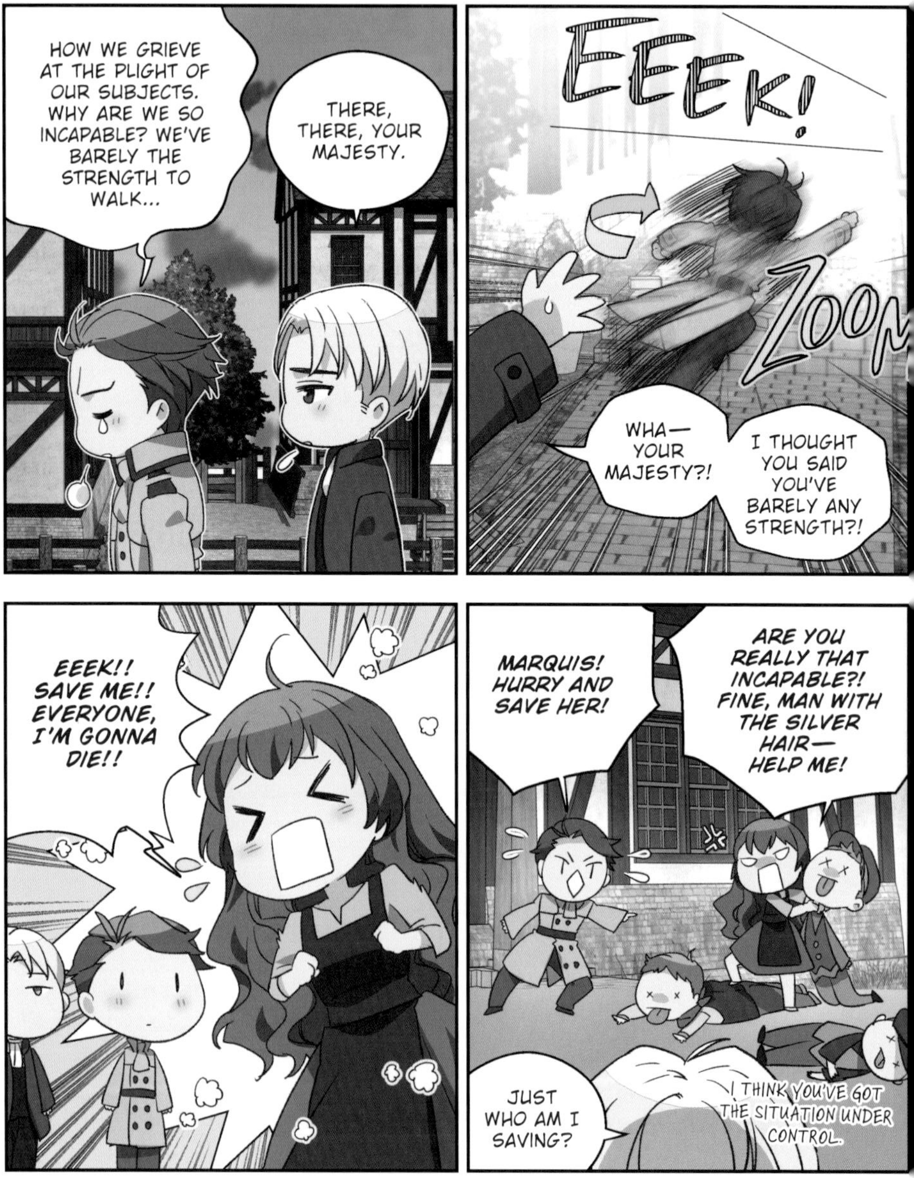

HOW WE GRIEVE AT THE PLIGHT OF OUR SUBJECTS. WHY ARE WE SO INCAPABLE? WE'VE BARELY THE STRENGTH TO WALK...
THERE, THERE, YOUR MAJESTY.
EEEK!
ZOOM
WHA— YOUR MAJESTY?!
I THOUGHT YOU SAID YOU'VE BARELY ANY STRENGTH?!
EEEK!! SAVE ME!! EVERYONE, I'M GONNA DIE!!
MARQUIS! HURRY AND SAVE HER!
ARE YOU REALLY THAT INCAPABLE?! FINE, MAN WITH THE SILVER HAIR— HELP ME!
JUST WHO AM I SAVING?
I THINK YOU'VE GOT THE SITUATION UNDER CONTROL.

THIS IS A JOKE.

♦ Character Is Destiny

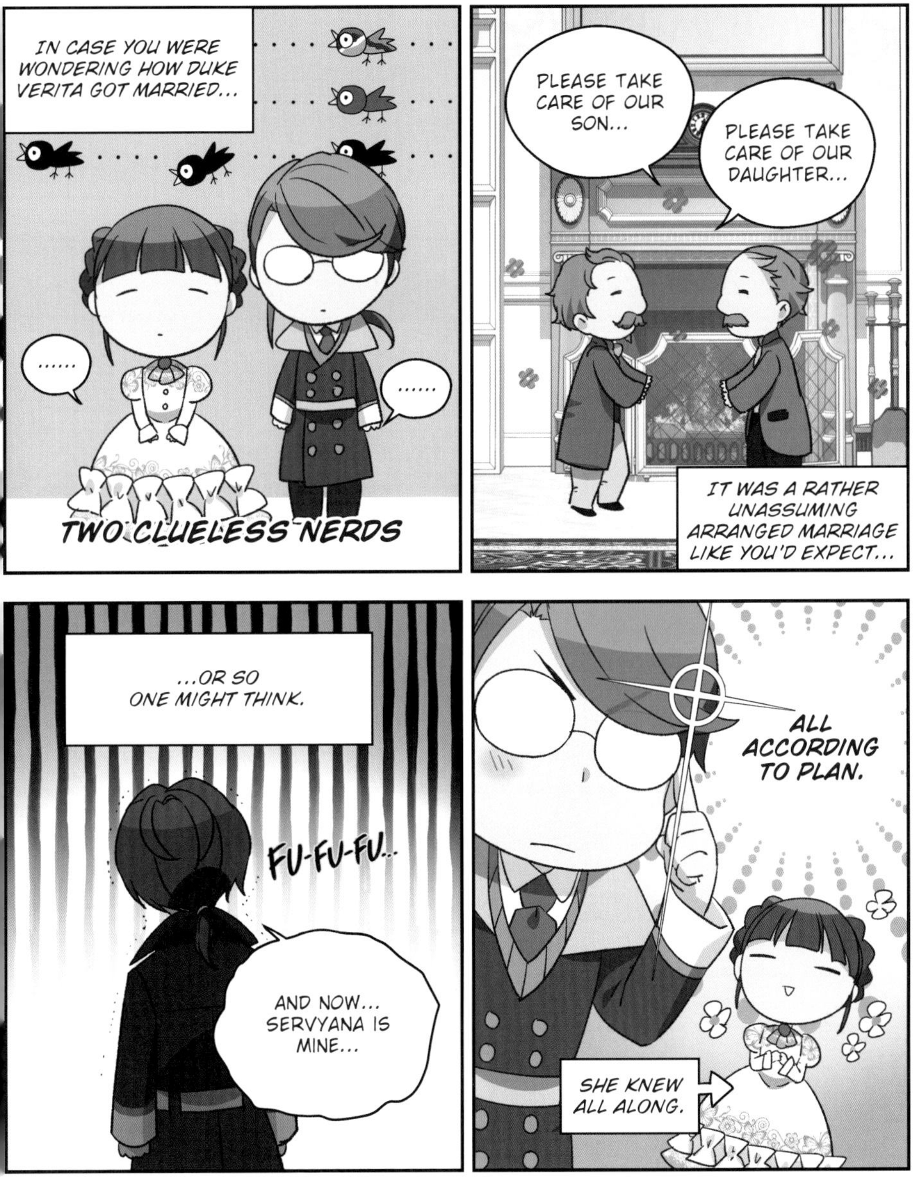
IN CASE YOU WERE WONDERING HOW DUKE VERITA GOT MARRIED...
......
......
TWO CLUELESS NERDS
PLEASE TAKE CARE OF OUR SON...
PLEASE TAKE CARE OF OUR DAUGHTER...
IT WAS A RATHER UNASSUMING ARRANGED MARRIAGE LIKE YOU'D EXPECT...
...OR SO ONE MIGHT THINK.
FU-FU-FU...
AND NOW... SERVYANA IS MINE...
ALL ACCORDING TO PLAN.
SHE KNEW ALL ALONG.

THIS IS NOT A JOKE.

I SHALL GO TO THE DUICAL HOUSE OF JENA.

THIS IS RATHER SURPRISING, YOUNG LADY JENA.

Jieun seems very different from in her past life.

THE EYES OF THE MARCHIONESS WHO CHASTISED ME THAT DAY WERE FULL OF LOVE.

Ruve shares a memory of Jeremia.

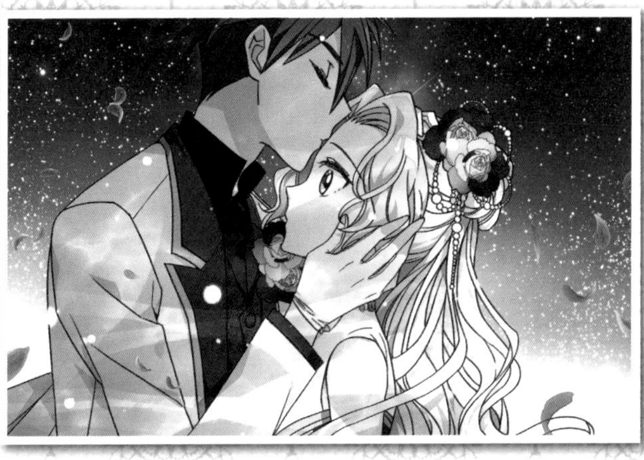

Carsein slowly reveals his true feelings.

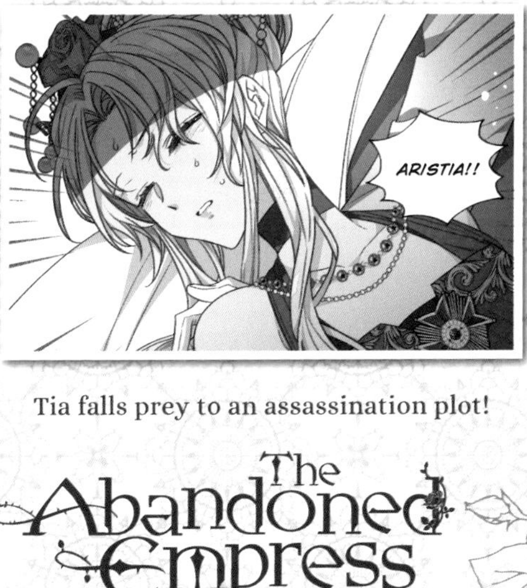
ARISTIA!!

Tia falls prey to an assassination plot!

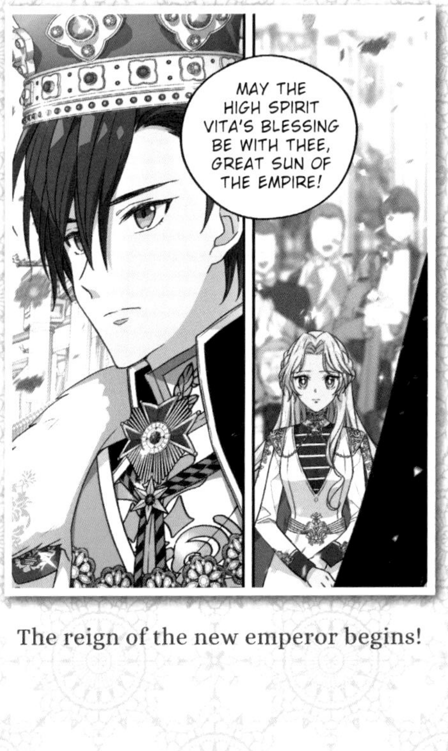
MAY THE HIGH SPIRIT VITA'S BLESSING BE WITH THEE, GREAT SUN OF THE EMPIRE!

The reign of the new emperor begins!

The Abandoned Empress

Volume 8 Out 2024!

The Abandoned Empress

INA
Original Story by **Yuna**

Translation: DAVID ODELL   Lettering: LYS BLAKESLEE

THE ABANDONED EMPRESS Volume 7
© INA, Yuna 2017 / D&C Media
All rights reserved.
First published in Korea in 2017 by D&C Media Co., Ltd.

English translation © 2023 by Yen Press, LLC

Yen Press
150 West 30th Street, 19th Floor
New York, NY 10001

Visit us at yenpress.com
facebook.com/yenpress
twitter.com/yenpress
yenpress.tumblr.com
instagram.com/yenpress

First Yen Press Edition: March 2024
Edited by Yen Press Editorial: Ellie Lee, Won Young Seo
Designed by Yen Press Design: Lilliana Checo, Wendy Chan

Yen Press is an imprint of Yen Press, LLC.
The Yen Press name and logo are trademarks of Yen Press, LLC.

The publisher is not responsible for websites (or their content) that are
not owned by the publisher.

Library of Congress Control Number: 2021943164

ISBNs: 978-1-9753-7359-7 (paperback)
978-1-9753-7360-3 (ebook)

1 3 5 7 9 10 8 6 4 2

TPA

Printed in South Korea